Matthew T. Riddling, MA

Matthew T. Riddling, MA

EXPERIMENTAL PSYCHOLOGY

Methods of Research
Sixth Edition

F. J. McGUIGAN

United States International University

PRENTICE HALL
Englewood Cliffs, NJ 07632

Library of Congress Cataloging-in-Publication Data

McGuigan, F. J. (Frank J.) [date]
   Experimental psychology : methods of research / F. J. McGuigan.—
6th ed.
     p. cm.
   Includes bibliographical references and index.
   ISBN 0-13-291014-4
    1. Psychology, Experimental. 2. Psychology—Research.
3. Experimental design. I. Title.
   BF181.M39 1993
   150′.724—dc20   92-33356
                                   CIP

Acquisitions editor: Julie Berrisford
Production supervision: Inkwell Publishing Services
Prepress buyer: Kelly Behr
Manufacturing buyer: Mary Ann Gloriande

©1993, 1990, 1983, 1978, 1968, 1960 by Prentice-Hall, Inc.
A Paramount Communications Company
Englewood Cliffs, New Jersey 07632

Printed in the United States of America

10 9 8 7 6 5 4 3

ISBN 0-13-291014-4

Prentice-Hall International (UK) Limited, *London*
Prentice-Hall of Australia Pty. Limited, *Sydney*
Prentice-Hall Canada Inc., *Toronto*
Prentice-Hall Hispanoamericana, S.A., *Mexico*
Prentice-Hall of India Private Limited, *New Delhi*
Prentice-Hall of Japan, Inc., *Tokyo*
Prentice-Hall of Southeast Asia Pte. Ltd., *Singapore*
Editora Prentice-Hall do Brasil, Ltda., *Rio de Janeiro*

To two charming ladies,
Constance and Joan

CONTENTS

Chapter 2

The Problem, *16*

Chapter 5

The Research Plan, *77*

Chapter 6

Experimental Design: The Case of Two Independent Groups, *99*

Chapter 7

Experimental Design: The Case of More Than Two Independent Groups, *130*

Chapter 10

Experimental Design: Single-Subject (*N* = 1) Research, 216

Appendix A

Statistical Tables, *291*

Appendix B

Writing Up Your Experiment, *299*

Appendix C

The Use of Computers in Research, *319*

PREFACE TO THE
FIRST EDITION

Experimental psychology was born with the study of sensory processes; it grew as additional topics, such as perception, reaction time, attention, emotion, learning, and thinking, were added. Accordingly, the traditional course in experimental psychology was a course the content of which was accidentally defined by those lines of investigation followed by early experimenters in those fields. But times change, and so does experimental psychology. The present trend is to define experimental psychology not in terms of specific content areas, but rather as a study of scientific methodology generally and of the methods of experimentation in particular. There is considerable evidence that this trend is gaining ground rapidly.

This book has been written to meet this trend. Their methods no longer confined to but a few areas, experimental psychologists conduct research in almost the whole of psychology—clinical, industrial, social, military,

and so on. To emphasize this point, we have throughout the book used examples of experiments from many fields, illustrative of many methodological points.

In short, then, the point of departure for this book is the relatively new conception of experimental psychology in terms of methodology, a conception which represents the bringing together of three somewhat distinct aspects of science: experimental methodology, statistics, and philosophy of science. We have attempted to perform a job analysis of experimental psychology, presenting the important techniques that the experimental psychologist uses every day. Experimental methods are the basis of experimental psychology, of course; the omnipresence of statistical presentations in journals attests the importance of this aspect of experimentation. An understanding of the philosophy of science is important to an understanding of what science is, how the scientific method is used, and particularly of where experimentation fits into the more general framework of scientific methodology. With an understanding of the goals and functions of scientific methodology, the experimental psychologist is prepared to function efficiently, avoiding scientifically unsound procedures and fruitless problems.

Designed as it is to be practical in the sense of presenting information on those techniques actually used by the working experimental psychologist, it is hoped for this book that it will help maximize transference of performance from a course in experimental psychology to the type of behavior manifested by the professional experimental psychologist.

My great appreciation to my students who have furnished both valuable criticisms of ideas and exposition and the reinforcement required for the completion of this project. I am also particularly indebted to Drs. Allen Calvin, Victor Denenberg, David Duncan, Paul Meehl, Michael Scriven, Kenneth Spence, and Lowell Wine.

PREFACE TO THE SIXTH EDITION

Thanks to suggestions of colleagues and students, I have effected a fair amount of reorganization for this edition. The effort was intended to hasten the student along in order to increase comprehension and study efficiency. One major reorganization was to integrate into one chapter the topics of correlational research and experimental designs involving correlations. Consequently, the three chapters that were previously devoted to correlational research, the two-matched-groups design, and repeated treatments for groups designs were shortened and combined into Chapter 9. There are now 12 chapters instead of 14. The section on the use of apparatus in Chapter 5 was also considerably consolidated.

The important topic of error variance and how to reduce it was brought forward into Chapter 6 so that students can relate it to research involving all the experimental designs.

Several topics have been placed in appendices to chapters so that the instructor may either assign them or skip them if emphasis on those topics is not desired. In particular, the sections on multibaseline group designs and statistical analysis of time-series designs were removed from the main body of Chapter 10. Similarly, the three possible effects of a treatment in time-series designs was appended to Chapter 11. Consequently, the instructor who considers these topics quite important may still assign them to students, or interested students may study them for themselves. As a result of some inefficient prose that developed through revisions over the previous five editions, I have now carefully processed each sentence throughout the entire text. This effort has "tightened up" the text and increased accuracy throughout.

To guide the student through the book more effectively I have added numerous section headings and printed major terms in bold print to highlight important topics.

The growing applications of computers in psychology are emphasized throughout the book, but particularly in the separate Appendix C on p. 319. Although computer statistical analysis is applicable to each design, the student must still understand what the computer is doing. Otherwise, blind use of computers results in numerous errors, and students compile statistics that are inapplicable, erroneous, inaccurate, and incomprehensible. By merely pushing certain buttons and selecting items from well-filled menus, students often end up with massive printouts that are not only unnecessary, but lead to violations of statistical assumptions and stated probability levels.

In this edition I continue to emphasize the mutual facilitation of pure and applied research and the wise application of effective research methods to benefit society. Strategies for the solution of societal problems are especially developed in Chapters 10 and 11. Psychology is going through changes and is in danger of losing the methodological sophistication that has propelled it to the forefront of social and biological sciences. Psychologists are leaders in business, industry, government, politics, and academia, and their research findings on topics important for the public are cited daily in the media. However, that preeminence may erode as many psychologists neglect the study and use of sound research methodology. This book has always attempted to develop a broad perspective about where sound psychological research fits within areas of public interest as well as more generally within science.

The previous editions of this book have been widely used in undergraduate courses. However, they have also found places in graduate courses on research methodology as well as in guiding researchers in the conduct of their own work.

Finally, I want to express my great appreciation to all the colleagues who have contributed to this and previous editions of the book. In particular, reviewers for this edition were Margaret Gittis, Rick Wesp, Paula Goolkasian, and Bernardo J. Carducci. Among the reviewers of the fifth edition whose names I have now been able to retrieve I express my great appreciation to Frank Etscorn, Ronald L. Webster, and Randall Flory. Those whose names I have not been able to retrieve are still thanked for their contributions. Special thanks are offered to Jackie Fisher, Kit Ching, Deanna Khan and Michelle Mullane for their excellent help with the preparation of this manuscript.

FJM

chapter 1

AN OVERVIEW OF EXPERIMENTATION

Major purpose:
To understand the basic nature of science and its application to psychological research.

What you are going to find:
1. Essential characteristics of science discussed as steps in the scientific method.
2. The salient aspects of psychological experimentation.
3. Definitions of critical terms.

What you should acquire:
A framework for incorporating the specific phases of psychological research to be detailed in the remaining chapters.

THE NATURE OF SCIENCE

The questions that concern psychologists are singularly challenging—the great complexity of the human mind means that it will probably be the last frontier of scientific understanding. The study of psychological problems, therefore, requires the most effective research methods available. Accumulation of experience over many centuries clearly indicates that scientific methods have yielded the soundest knowledge.

Definitions of Science

People define **"science"** in various ways, but generally they use either **content** or **process** definitions. A typical content definition is that "science is an accumulation of integrated knowledge," whereas a process definition is that "science is an activity of discovering important variables in nature, of relating those variables, and of explaining those relationships (laws)." A classical definition that incorporates content *and* processes is "science is an interconnected series of concepts and conceptual schemes that have developed as a result of experimentation and observations" (Conant, 1951, p. 25). A similar definition is that science is "a systematically organized body of knowledge about the universe, obtained by the scientific method."

Scientific and Nonscientific Disciplines

Sciences Use the Scientific Method. To understand some of the basic characteristics of science, we will first consider the various sciences as a group; we can then abstract the salient characteristics that distinguish those sciences from other disciplines. Figure 1-1 is a schematic representation of the disciplines we study, crudely categorized into three

groups (excluding the formal disciplines of mathematics and logic). The sciences are represented within the inner circle. The next circle embraces disciplines not usually regarded as sciences, such as the arts and the humanities. Outside that circle are yet other disciplines which, for lack of a better term, are designated as metaphysical disciplines.

The sciences in the inner circle certainly differ among themselves in a number of ways. But in what important ways are they similar to each other? Likewise, what are the similarities among the disciplines in the outer circle? What do the metaphysical disciplines outside the circle have in common? Furthermore, in what important ways do each of these three groups differ from each other? Answers to these questions should enable us to arrive at an approximation of a general definition of science.

One common characteristic of the sciences is that they all use the same general approach in solving problems—a systematic serial process called the *scientific method*. Neither of the other two groups explicitly uses this method.

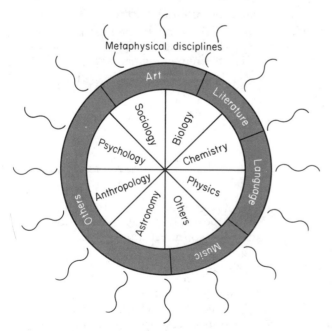

FIGURE 1-1 Three groups of disciplines that we study. Within the inner circle are the sciences. The second circle contains the arts and the humanities: metaphysical disciplines fall outside the circles.

Solvable and Unsolvable Problems. The disciplines within the two circles differ from the metaphysical disciplines with regard to the type of problem studied. Individuals who study the subject matter areas within the two circles attempt to consider only problems that can be solved; those whose work falls outside the circle generally study unsolvable problems. Briefly, a **solvable problem** is one that poses a question that can be answered with the use of our normal capacities. An **unsolvable problem** raises a question that is essentially unanswerable. Unsolvable problems often concern supernatural phenomena or questions about ultimate causes. For example, the problem of what caused the universe is unsolvable and is typical of studies in religion and classical philosophy.[1] Ascertaining what is and what is not a solvable problem is an extremely important topic and will be taken up in detail in Chapter 2.

Science is Empirical. It is important to emphasize that "solvable" and "unsolvable" are technical terms so that certain vernacular meanings should not be read into them. The classification is not meant, for instance, to establish a hierarchy of values among the various disciplines by classifying them according to the type of problem studied. We are not necessarily saying, for example, that the problems of science are "better" or more important than are the problems of religion. The distinction is that solvable problems may be *empirically* attacked. By **empirical** we mean relying upon observations of natural events, such as the behavior of other people. The person who attempts to solve problems through mysticism would not be using an empirical approach. Thus, *solvable problems are susceptible to empirical solution by studying observable events.* Unsolvable problems cannot be studied with the methods of empiricism. Individuals whose work falls within the two circles (particularly within the inner one) simply believe they must limit their study to problems that they are capable of solving. Of course, some scientists also devote part of their lives to the consideration of supernatural phenomena. But it is important to realize that when they do, they have "left the circle" and are, for that time, no longer behaving as scientists.

The distinction between scientific methods that solve problems through empiricism and nonscientific methods that seek to answer questions using nonempirical approaches is important. Some, for instance, use the method of authority to answer questions ("on this issue, St. Aquinas said . . ."). Others hold that revelation reveals truth through visions. While such nonscientific methods provide easier answers, diligent slaving over (empirical) data, tedious and demanding as it may be, has been well established as our only reliable source of knowledge in the long run.

Science Defined. First, sciences apply the scientific method to solvable problems. Second, the disciplines in the outer circle do not use the scientific method, but their problems are typically solvable. Third, the disciplines outside the circles neither use the scientific method nor pose solvable problems. Consequently we define **science** as *the application of the scientific method to solvable problems.* This definition incorporates both the process (method) and the content definitions of science in that the study of solvable problems results in systematic knowledge. Generally, neither of the other two groups of disciplines has *both* these features.

Psychology as a Science

Psychology is Materialistic, Objective and Deterministic. The consequences of this very general definition are enormous and lead us to specify several important scientific

---

[1]Crude categorizations are dangerous. In pointing out general differences among the three classes of disciplines, exceptions are ignored. For example, some theological problems, such as the effects of prayer on the human condition *are* solvable e.g., studies have been conducted to determine whether praying beneficially affects patients suffering from various diseases. Although it is possible to develop at least a limited science of religion, most theologians employ methods of authority and revelation, not being interested in answering their questions empirically.

concepts. The classical behaviorists, led by John B. Watson in the early part of the century, were instrumental in developing psychology as a science. Watson's program for a transition from a nonscience to a science was as follows: "If psychology is ever to become a science, it must follow the example of the physical sciences; it must become materialistic, mechanistic, deterministic, objective" (Heidbreder, 1933, p. 235). Watson's demand that we be **materialistic** states what is now obvious: namely, that we must study only physical events[2] such as observable responses, rather than ghostly "ideas" or a "consciousness" of a nonmaterial mind (see "materialism" in the glossary). Materialism is interrelated with objectivity, for it is impossible to be objective when attempting to study "unobservable phenomena" (whatever that might mean). We are **objective** in science-when we apply the **principle of intersubjective reliability**. We all have subjective experiences when we observe an event. *Intersubjective* means that two or more people may share the same experience. When they verbally report the same subjective experience, we conclude that the event really (reliably) occurred (was not a hallucination). In short, the data of science are public in that they are gathered objectively—scientifically observed events are reliably reported through the subjective perceptions of a number of observers, not just one. Watson's request that we be *deterministic* was not new in psychology but is critical for us. **"Determinism"** *is the assumption that there is lawfulness in nature.* If there is lawfulness, we are able to ascertain causes for the events that we seek to study. To the extent to which nature is nondeterministic, it is chaotic, with events occurring spontaneously (without

causes). We therefore cannot discover laws for any nondeterministic phenomena, if there be such. We have, incidentally, no assurance that all events are determined. However, we must assume that those that we study are lawful if we ever hope to discover laws for them (just as assuming that there are fish in the stream when you go fishing is a necessary condition for catching any).[3]

Behavior—the Most Complex Subject Matter. With these considerations and our general definition of science in hand, let us consider the scientific method as it is applied in psychology. The more abstruse and enigmatic a subject is, the more rigidly we must adhere to the scientific method and the more diligently we must control variables. Chemists work with a relatively limited set of variables, whereas psychologists must study considerably more complex phenomena. We cannot afford to be sloppy in our thinking or research. Since experimentation is the most powerful application of the scientific method, we shall focus on how we conduct experiments.

Experimentation—the Most Powerful Research Method. Using experiments as the ideal, we can better understand the shortcomings of the other research methods that we will also study later. The following brief discussion will provide an overview of the rest of the book. As an orientation to experimentation it will illustrate how the research psychologist proceeds. Because this overview is so brief, however, complex matters will necessarily be oversimplified. Possible distortions resulting from this oversimplification will be corrected in later chapters.

---

[2]Our everyday language sometimes leads us to unfortunate habits, such as the redundant term "physical events," which implies that there may be nonphysical events, a concept that staggers the imagination. References to nonphysical phenomena are precisely what Watson and his colleagues tried to eliminate from early psychology. The commonly used "empirical data" is another such redundancy.

[3]Watson's mechanism refers to the assumption that we behave in accordance with mechanical principles (those of physics and chemistry). But, since the issue of mechanisms versus vitalism in biology was settled many decades ago in favor of mechanism, the issue is now of historic interest only, and we shall not dwell on it here.

PSYCHOLOGICAL EXPERIMENTATION: AN APPLICATION OF THE SCIENTIFIC METHOD[4]

Stating the Problem

A psychological experiment starts with the formulation of a **problem**, which is usually best stated in the form of a question. The only requirement that the problem must meet is that it be solvable—the question that it raises must be answerable with the tools that are available to the psychologist. Beyond this, the problem may be concerned with any aspect of behavior, whether it is judged to be important or trivial. One lesson of history is that we must not be hasty in judging the importance of the problem on which a scientist works, for many times what was momentarily discarded as trivial or irrelevant contributed sizably to later scientific advances.

Formulating a Hypothesis

The experimenter formulates a tentative solution to the problem. This tentative solution is called a **hypothesis**; it may be a reasoned potential solution or only a vague guess, but in either case it is an empirical hypothesis in that it refers to observable phenomena i.e., behavior. Following the statement of the hypothesis, the experimenter *tests* it to determine whether the hypothesis is (probably) true or (probably) false. If true, it solves the problem the psychologist has formulated. To test the hypothesis, we must collect *data*, for a set of data is our only criterion. Various techniques are available for data collection, but experimentation is the most powerful.

---

[4]Some hold that we do not formally go through the following steps of the scientific method in conducting our research. However, a close analysis of our actual work suggests that we at least informally approximate the following pattern and, regardless, these steps are pedagogically valuable.

Selecting Participants

One of the first steps in collecting data is to select participants whose behavior is to be observed. The type of participant studied will be determined by the nature of the problem. If the concern is with psychotherapy, one may select a group of neurotics. A problem concerned with the function of parts of the brain would entail the use of animals (few humans volunteer to serve as participants for brain operations). Learning problems may be investigated with the use of college sophomores, chimpanzees, or rats. Whatever the type of participant, the experimenter typically assigns them to groups. We shall consider here the basic type of experiment, namely, one that involves only two groups.

Incidentally, those who collaborate in an experiment for the purpose of allowing their behavior to be studied may be referred to either as **participants** or by the traditional term **subjects**.

"Participants" is preferable and recommended in the American Psychological Associations Publications Manual, 1983. While "subjects" is acceptable, the term suggests, that people are being "used" or that there is a status difference between the experimenter and the subject (as a king and his subjects). Whether an animal should be referred to as a subject or a participant probably depends on an individual's philosophy of life. But, regardless, it is important that those who are studied in an experiment be well respected (see Appendix D on ethics). Experimental participants should have a prestigious status, for they are critical in the advancement of our science. Other terms (e.g., "children," "students," "animals") are alternatives.

Assigning Participants to Groups and Treatments (Conditions)

Participants should be assigned to groups in such a way that the groups will be approximately equivalent at the start of the experiment; this is accomplished through

FIGURE 1-2   Representation of a continuous variable that can vary by any amount.

randomization, a term to be used extensively throughout the book. The experimenter next administers an experimental treatment to one of the groups. The experimental treatment is that which one wishes to evaluate, and it is administered to the **experimental group**. The other group, called the **control group**, usually receives a normal or standard treatment. It is important to understand clearly just what the terms *experimental* and *control* mean.

Stimulus-Response Laws

In the study of behavior, the psychologist generally seeks to establish empirical relationships between **stimuli** aspects of the **environment** (the surroundings in which we live) and **responses** (aspects of behavior). These stimulus-response (S-R) relationships, known as laws, essentially state that if a certain environmental characteristic is changed, behavior of a certain type also changes.[5]

Independent and Dependent Variables. The stimulus event that is experimentally studied is an **independent variable**; the measure of any change in behavior is a **dependent variable**. Roughly, a variable is anything that can change in value or amount. The amount of a **variable** often differs in magnitude or strength. Thus, a variable generally is anything that may assume

---

[5] By saying that the psychologist seeks to establish relationships between environmental characteristics and aspects of behavior, we are being unduly narrow. Actually we are also concerned with processes that are not directly observed (variously called *logical constructs, intervening variables, hypothetical constructs,* and so forth). Since, however, it is unlikely that work of the student will involve hypotheses of such an abstract nature, they will not be elaborated here.

different numerical values. As the prominent psychologist E.L. Thorndike asserted, "anything that exists, exists in quantity," so that anything that exists is a variable. The brightness of light and the amount of pay a worker receives for performing a given task are independent variables that can be changed in value. The speed with which a football player runs the length of the football field, the number of trials required to learn a poem, and the number of words a patient says in a psychotherapeutic interview are examples of dependent variables.

Figure 1-2 represents speed of running a football field. This variable can obviously take on any of a large number of time values. In fact, it may assume any of an infinite number of such values, the least being, theoretically, zero seconds, and the greatest being an infinitely large amount of time. In actual situations, however, we would expect the variable to exhibit a value of a number of seconds. The point is that such a variable may assume any value, in terms of any number of seconds or fraction of a seconds, e.g., a player may run the field in 11.5, 12.7, or 18.6 seconds.

Continuous and Discontinuous Variables. Since this variable may assume any fraction of a value (it may be represented by any point along the line in Figure 1-2), it is called a **continuous variable**. A continuous variable is one that is capable of changing by any amount, even an infinitesimally small one. A variable that is not continuous is called a **discontinuous or discrete variable**. A discrete variable can assume only numerical values that differ by clearly defined steps with no intermittent values possible. For example, the number of people in a theater would be a discrete variable, for, barring an unusually messy affair, one would not expect to find a part of a person in such surroundings. Thus, one might find 1, 15, 299, or 302 people in a theater, but not 1.6 or 14.8 people. Similarly, gender (male or female) and eye color (brown, blue) are frequently cited as examples of discrete variables.[6]

Determining the Influence of an Independent Variable

To discover S-R laws the psychologist seeks to find relationships between independent and dependent variables. There are an infinite (or at least indefinitely large) number of independent variables available in nature for the psychologist to examine. But we are interested in discovering those relatively few that affect a given kind of behavior. In short, we may say that an **independent variable** is any variable that is investigated for the purpose of determining whether it influences behavior. Some independent variables that have been scientifically investigated are amount of stress, age, hereditary factors, endocrine secretions, brain lesions, drugs, loudness of sounds, and home environments.

Now with the understanding that an experimenter seeks to determine whether an independent variable affects a dependent variable (either of which may be continuous or discrete), let us relate the discussion to the concepts of experimental and control groups. To determine whether a given independent variable affects behavior, the experimenter administers one value of it to the experimental group and a second value of it to the control group. The value administered to the experimental group is the "ex-

perimental treatment," whereas the control group is usually given a "normal treatment." Thus, the essential difference between "experimental" and "normal" treatments is the specific value of the independent variable that is assigned to each group. For example, the independent variable may be the intensity of a shock (a continuous variable); the experimenter may subject the experimental group to a high intensity and the control group to a lower intensity or zero intensity.

Consider another example of how an independent variable might be used in an experiment. Visualize a continuum similar to Figure 1-2, composed of an infinite number of possible values that the independent variable may assume. If, for example, we are interested in determining how well a skill is retained as a result of the number of times it is practiced, our continuum would start with zero trials and continue with one, two, three, and so on, trials (this is a discrete variable).

Let us suppose that in a certain industry, workers are trained by performing an assembly line task 10 times before being put to work. After a while, however, it is found that the workers are not assembling the product adequately, and it is judged that they have not learned their task sufficiently well. Some corrective action is indicated, and the supervisor suggests that the workers would learn the task better if they were able to practice it 15 times instead of 10. Here we have the makings of an experiment of the simplest sort.

The independent variable is the number of times that the task is performed in training and we will assign it two of the possibly infinite number of values that it may assume—10 trials and 15 trials (see Figure 1-3). Of course, we could have selected any number of other values—1 trial, 5 trials, or 5,000 trials—but because of the nature of the problem with which we are concerned, 10 and 15 seem like reasonable values to study. We will have the experimental group practice the task 15 times, the control group 10 times. Thus, the control group receives the normal treatment (10 trials), and the ex-

---

[6]Some scientists question whether there actually are any discrete variables in nature. They suggest that we simply "force" nature into "artificial" categories. Color, for example, may more properly be conceived of as a continuous variable—there are many gradations of brown, blue, and so on. Nevertheless, scientists find it useful to categorize variables into classes as discrete variables and to view such categorization as an approximation.

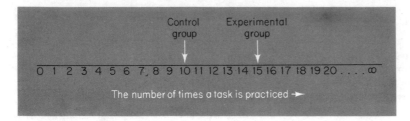

FIGURE 1-3 Representation of a discrete independent variable. The values assigned to the control and the experimental groups are 10 and 15 trials, respectively.

perimental group is assigned the experimental or novel treatment (15 trials). In another instance a group that is administered a zero value of the independent variable is called the control group and the group that is given some positive amount of that variable is the experimental group. Finally, if both treatments are novel ones, it is impossible to label the groups in this manner so they might simply be called "group 1" and "group 2."

The *dependent* variable is usually some well-defined aspect of behavior (a response) that the experimenter measures. It may be the number of times a person says a certain word or the rapidity of learning a task. In our example it is the number of items a worker on a production line can produce in an hour. The value obtained for the dependent variable is the criterion of whether the independent variable is effective, and that value is expected to be *dependent* on the value assigned to the independent variable. (The dependent variable is also dependent on some of the extraneous variables, discussed shortly, that are always present in an experiment.) Thus, an experimenter varies the independent variable and notes whether the dependent variable systematically changes. If it does change in value as the independent variable is manipulated, then it may be asserted that there probably is a relationship between the two. (The psychologist has discovered an empirical S-R law.) If the dependent variable does not change, however, it may be asserted that the independent and dependent variables are not related. For example, assume that a light of high intensity

is flashed into the eyes of each member of the experimental group, whereas those of the control group are subjected to a low-intensity light. The dependent variable might be the amount of contraction of the iris diaphragm (the pupil of the eye), which is an aspect of behavior, a response. If we find that the average contraction of the pupil is greater for the experimental than for the control group, we may conclude that intensity of light is an effective independent variable. We can then tentatively assert the following relationship: The greater the intensity of a light that is flashed into a person's eyes, the greater the contraction of the pupil will be. No difference between the two groups in the average amount of pupillary contraction would mean a lack of relationship between the independent and the dependent variables.

Controlling Extraneous Variables

Perhaps the most important principle of experimentation, stated in an ideal form, is that the experimenter must hold constant all the variables that may affect the dependent variable, except the independent variable(s) whose effect(s) is being evaluated. (In Chapter 4 we will enlarge on this brief statement.) Obviously there are a number of variables that may affect the dependent variable, but the experimenter is not immediately interested in these. For the moment the interest is in only one thing—the relationship, or lack of it, between the independent and the dependent variables. If the experimenter allows a number of other **extraneous vari-**

ables to operate freely in the experimental situation, the experiment might be contaminated. For this reason one seeks to *control* the extraneous variables in an experiment.

As a simple illustration of how an extraneous variable might contaminate an experiment, and thus make the findings unacceptable, reconsider the foregoing example. Suppose that, unknown to the experimenter, members of the experimental group had that morning received a routine vaccination with a serum that affected the pupil of the eye. In this event, measures of the dependent variable collected by the experimenter would have little value. For example, if the serum caused the pupil not to contract, the experimental and control groups might show about the same lack of contraction. It would thus be concluded that the independent variable did not affect the response being studied. The findings would falsely assert that the variables of light intensity and pupillary contraction are not related, when in fact they are. The dependent variable was affected by an extraneous variable (the serum), and the effects of this extraneous variable obscured the influence of the independent variable. This topic of controlling extraneous variables that might invalidate an experiment is of sufficiently great importance that an entire chapter will be devoted to it. In Chapter 4 we will study various techniques for dealing with unwanted variables in an experiment.

Conducting Statistical Tests

Returning to our general discussion of the scientific method as applied to experimentation, we have said that a scientist starts an investigation with the statement of a problem and that a hypothesis is advanced as a tentative solution. An experiment is then conducted to collect data—data that should indicate the probability that the hypothesis is "true" or "false." The scientist may find it advantageous or necessary to use certain types of apparatus and equipment in the experiment. The particular type of apparatus used will naturally depend on the nature of the problem. Apparatus is used for four reasons: (1) to administer the experimental treatment, (2) to collect data (3) to reduce experimenter influences, and (4) to analyze the data statistically, as with a computer.

The hypothesis that is being tested can be used to predict the way the data should point. The hypothesis may state that the experimental group will perform better than the control group. By confronting the hypothesis with the dependent variable values of the two groups, the experimenter can determine whether the hypothesis accurately predicted the results. But it is difficult to tell, simply by looking at unorganized data, whether the (dependent variable) values for one group are higher or lower than the values for the second group. Therefore, the data must be organized numerically to yield numbers that will provide an answer—for this reason we resort to statistics.

For example, we may compute average (mean) scores and find that the experimental group has a higher mean (say, 100) than the control group (say, 99). Although there is a difference between the groups, it is very small, and we must ask whether it is "real" or only a **chance** difference. What are the odds that if we conduct the experiment again, we would obtain similar results? If it is a "real," **reliable** difference, the experimental group should obtain a higher mean score than does the control group almost every time the experiment is repeated. If there is no reliable difference between the two groups, we would expect to find each group receiving the higher score half of the time. To tell whether the difference between the two groups in a single experiment is reliable, rather than simply due to random fluctuations (chance), the experimenter resorts to a **statistical test** (of which there is a variety). The particular statistical test(s) used will be determined by the type of data obtained and the general design of the experiment. On the basis of such tests, it can be determined whether the difference between the two groups is likely to be "real" (statistically reliable) or merely "accidental" (due only to chance). If the difference between the dependent variable values of the groups is statistically reliable, the difference is very probably not due to random fluctuation; it is therefore concluded that the independent variable probably is effective in influencing the dependent variable (providing that the extraneous variables have been properly controlled).

When you read psychological journals, you will note that "significant" is usually used to mean "reliable." However, to say that you have a **significant difference** between groups may suggest that your reliable difference is an important one, which of course it might not be at all. It is indeed confusing when psychologists try to communicate to a newspaper reporter, for instance, that a significant statistical test was not an important finding. As Porter (1973) pointed out,

. . . the technical jargon of statistics itself has a word and concept that fits the situation: *reliable*. A reliable outcome is one that can be expected to reappear on reexamination. A reliable difference will be found again if the experiment is repeated. An *F*, a *z*, or whatever is significant in that it signifies the reliability of whatever observation is under test. An extremely reliable difference can be every bit as trivial as its most untrustworthy counterpart; there is no need to mislead one's audience nor to delude oneself with *highly significant*. (pp. 188–189)

Thus, just as we synonymously use "subjects" and "participants" in psychological writings, "significant" and "reliable" are also synonymous, though "reliable" is preferable for reasons just cited.

By starting with two equivalent groups; administering the experimental treatment to one, but not to the other; and collecting and statistically analyzing the dependent variable data thus obtained, we may find a reliable difference between the two groups. We may legitimately assume that they differed because of the experimental treatment. Since this is the result that was predicted by our hypothesis, the hypothesis is supported, or confirmed. When a hypothesis is supported by experimental data, the

probability is increased that the hypothesis is true. On the other hand, if the control group is found to be equal or superior to the experimental group, the hypothesis is typically not supported by the data, and we may conclude that it is probably false. This step of the scientific method in which the hypothesis is tested will be considered more thoroughly in Chapter 6.

Generalizing the Hypothesis

Closely allied with testing of the hypothesis is an additional step of the scientific method—**generalization**. After completing the phases outlined previously, the experimenter may confidently believe that the hypothesis is true for the specific conditions under which it was tested. We must underline *specific* conditions, however, and not lose sight of just how specific they are in any given experiment. But the scientist qua scientist is not concerned with truth under a highly restricted set of conditions. Rather, we usually want to make as *general* a statement as we possibly can about nature. Herein lies much of our joy and grief, for the more we generalize our findings, the greater are the chances for error. Suppose that one has used college students as the participants in an experiment. This selection does not mean that the researcher is interested *only* in the behavior of college students. Rather, the interest is probably in the behavior of *all* human beings and perhaps even of *all* organisms. Because the hypothesis is probably true for a particular group of people, is it therefore probably true for all humans? Or must we restrict the conclusion to college students? *Or* must the focus be narrowed even further, limiting it to those attending the college at which the experiment was conducted? This, essentially, is the question of generalization—how widely can the experimenter generalize the results obtained? We want to generalize as widely as possible, yet not *so* widely that the hypothesis breaks down. The question of how widely we may safely generalize a hypothesis will be discussed in Chapter 12. The broad principle to remember now is that we should state that a hypothesis is applicable to as wide a set of conditions (e.g., to as many classes of people) as is warranted.

Making Predictions

The next step in the scientific method, closely related to generalization, concerns making **predictions** on the basis of the hypothesis. By this we mean that a hypothesis may be used to predict certain events in new situations—to predict, for example, that a different group of people will act in the same way as a group studied in an earlier experiment. Prediction is closely connected with another step of the scientific method—**replication**. By *replication* we mean that an additional experiment is conducted in which the *method* of the first experiment is precisely repeated. A confirmed hypothesis is thus a basis for predicting that a new sample of participants will behave as did the original sample. If this prediction holds in the new situation, the probability that the previously confirmed hypothesis is true is tremendously increased. The distinction between replicating a previous experiment and supporting the conclusion of a previous experiment should be emphasized. In a replication, the methods of an experiment have been repeated, but the results may or may not be the same as for the previous experiment. Sometimes researchers erroneously state that they have "replicated an experiment" when what they mean is that they have confirmed the findings of that experiment (using different methods).

Explanation

The relationship between the independent and the dependent variables may be formulated as an empirical law, particularly if the relationship has been confirmed in a replication of the experiment (in accordance with the experimenter's prediction). The final step in the scientific method is that of **explanation**. We seek to explain an empirical law by means of some appropriate theory. For instance, Galileo's experiments on falling bodies resulted in his familiar law of $S = \frac{1}{2}gt^2$, which was later explained by the theories of Newton (see Chapter 12).

Dissemination of Findings

It is, of course, crucial that the results of scientific research be communicated to interested others. The main vehicle for communication is publication in scientific journals. The tremendous value of dissemination of information is apparent when we view in retrospect the great advances in science that followed the invention of the printing press and the improvement in the modes of transportation.

OVERVIEW OF THE SCIENTIFIC METHOD

In summary let us set down the various steps in the scientific method, emphasizing, however, that there are no rigid rules to follow in doing this. In any process in which one seeks to classify into a number of arbitrary categories, some distortion is inevitable. Another author might offer a different classification, whereas still another one might refuse, even to attempt such an endeavor.

1. The scientist selects an area of research and states a problem for study.
2. A hypothesis is formulated as a tentative solution to the problem.
3. Data relevant to the hypothesis are collected.
4. A test is made of the hypothesis by confronting it with the data—we organize the data through statistical methods, and make appropriate inferences to determine whether the data support or refute the hypothesis.
5. Assuming that the hypothesis is supported, we may generalize to all things with which the hypothesis is legitimately concerned, in which case we should explicitly state the generality with which we wish to advance the hypothesis.
6. We may wish to make a prediction to new situations, to events not studied in the original experiment. In making a prediction we may test the hypothesis anew in the novel situation; that is, we might replicate (conduct the experi-

ment with a new sample of participants) to determine whether the estimate of the probability of the hypothesis can legitmately be increased.

7. We should attempt to explain our findings by means of a more general theory.

AN EXAMPLE OF A PSYCHOLOGICAL EXPERIMENT

To make the discussion more concrete by illustrating the application of the preceding principles, consider how an experiment might be conducted from its inception to its conclusion. This example is taken from the area of clinical psychology in which, like any applied area, it is methodologically difficult to conduct sound research. Let us assume that a clinician has some serious questions about the value of traditional psychotherapy for actually helping people. Traditional psychotherapy has been conducted primarily at the verbal level in which the client (or patient) and therapist discuss the client's problems. Psychoanalysis emphasized the value of "verbal outpouring" from the patient for the purpose of catharsis, originally referred to by Freud and Breuer as "chimney sweeping." In our example the therapist is not sure whether strict verbal interchange is effective or whether dealing directly with the client's behavior (as in clinical progressive relaxation or behavior modification) may be more effective. The problem may be stated as follows: Should a clinical psychologist engage in verbal psychotherapy and talk with clients about their problems, or should the psychologist attempt to modify behavior concerned with the problem, minimizing interaction at a strictly verbal level? Assume that the therapist believes the latter to be preferable. We simply note the hypothesis: If selected responses of a client undergoing therapy are systematically manipulated in accordance with principles of behavior theory, then recovery will be more efficient than if the therapist engages in strictly verbal discourse about the difficulties. We might identify the independent variable as "the amount of systematic manipulation of behavior" and as-

sign two values to it: (1) a maximal amount of systematic manipulation and (2) a zero amount of systematic manipulation of behavior (in which clients are left to do whatever they wish). In this zero amount of the experimental treatment, clients will presumably wish to talk about their problems, in which case the therapist would merely serve as a "sounding board" as in Carl Rogers's nondirective counseling procedures.

Suppose that the clinical psychologist has 10 clients and that they are randomly assigned to two groups of five each. A large amount of systematic manipulation of behavior will then be given to one of the groups, and a zero (or minimum) amount will be administered to a second group. The group that receives the lesser amount of systematic manipulation will be the control group, and the one that receives the maximum amount will be the experimental group.[7]

Throughout the course of therapy, then, the therapist administers the two different treatments to the experimental and the control groups. During this time it is important to prevent extraneous variables from acting differently on the two groups. For example, the clients from both groups would undergo therapy in the same office so that the progress of the two groups does not differ merely because of the immediate surroundings in which the therapy takes place.

The dependent variable here may be specified as the progress toward recovery. Such a variable is obviously rather difficult to measure, but for illustrative purposes we might use a time measure. Thus we might assume that the earlier the client is discharged by the therapist, the greater is the progress toward recovery. The time of discharge might be determined when the client's complaints are eliminated. Assuming

---

[7]Since it is not possible to avoid guiding the behavior of the clients completely, this example well illustrates that frequently it is not appropriate to say that a zero amount of the independent variable can be administered to a control group. Try as you might, the therapist cannot totally eliminate suggestion.

that the extraneous variables have been adequately controlled, the progress toward recovery (the dependent variable) depends on the particular values of the independent variable used, and on nothing else.

As therapy progresses, the psychologist collects data—specifically, the amount of time each client spends in therapy before being discharged. After all the clients are discharged, the therapist compares the times for the experimental group against those for the control group. Let us assume that the mean amount of time in therapy of the experimental group is lower than that of the control group and, further, that a statistical test indicates that the difference is reliable; that is, the group that received a minimum amount of systematic behavioral manipulation had a significantly longer time in therapy (the dependent variable) than did the group that received a large amount. This is precisely what the therapist's hypothesis predicted. Since the results of the experiment are in accord with the hypothesis, we may conclude that the hypothesis is confirmed.

Now the psychotherapist is happy, since the problem has been solved and the better method of psychotherapy has been determined. But has "truth" been found only for the psychologist, or are the results appliable to other situations—can other therapists also benefit by these results? Can the findings be extended, or generalized, to all therapeutic situations of the nature that were studied? How can the findings be explained in terms of a broader principle (a more general theory)? After serious consideration of these matters, the psychologist formulates an answer and publishes the findings in a psychological journal. Publication, incidentally, is important, for if research results are not communicated, they are of little value for the world. (See Appendix B, "Writing Up Your Experiment.")

Inherent in the process of generalization is that of prediction. In effect, what the therapist does by generalizing is to predict that similar results would be obtained if the experiment were repeated in a new situation.

In this simple case the therapist would essentially say that for other clients systematic manipulation of behavior will result in more rapid recovery than will mere verbal psychotherapy. To test this prediction, another therapist might conduct a similar experiment (the experiment is replicated). If the new findings are the same, the hypothesis is again supported by the data. With this independent confirmation of the hypothesis as an added factor, it may be concluded that the probability of the hypothesis is increased—that is, our confidence that the hypothesis is true is considerably greater than before.[8]

With this overview before us, let us now turn to a detailed consideration of the phases of the scientific method as it applies to psychology. The first matter on which we should enlarge is "the problem."

CHAPTER SUMMARY

I. The nature of science
  A. Definitions of science.
    1. Content definitions, for example, "an accumulation of integrated knowledge."
    2. Process definitions, for example, "formulating and explaining empirical laws."
    3. Combinations of content *and* process definitions, for example, "the application of the scientific method to solvable problems."
  B. Scientific and nonscientific disciplines.
    1. Science empirically applies the scientific method to solvable problems.
    2. The humanities and the arts use nonscientific methods to study solvable problems (typically).

---

[8]The oversimplification of several topics in this chapter is especially apparent in this fictitious experiment. First, adequate control would have to be exercised over the important extraneous variable of the therapist's own confidence in, and preference for, one method of therapy. Second, if would have to be demonstrated that the clients used in this study are typical of those elsewhere before a legitimate generalization of the findings could be asserted. Such matters will be handled in due time.

3. Metaphysical disciplines neither employ the scientific method nor pose solvable problems.

C. Some basic assumptions of science.

1. Materialism assumes that there are only physicalistic events in the universe, those that can be sensed with the limited receptor systems of humans (if there are nonphysical events, we have no way of ever finding that out).

2. Objectivity assumes that two or more people may share the same experience and reliably agree in their report of it (the principle of intersubjective reliability).

3. Determinism assumes that events are lawful, which is a necessary condition for formulating scientific laws. A nondeterministic world would be chaotic and random, precluding any scientific successes.

4. Mechanism assumes that organisms behave in accordance with the laws of physics.

D. Phases of the scientific method.

1. Formulate a solvable problem, one that is answerable with available tools.

2. Advance a hypothesis as a tentative solution to the problem.

3. Test the hypothesis by collecting data, and organizing them with statistical methods, and conclude whether the data support or refute the hypothesis.

4. Generalize the hypothesis (if it is confirmed).

5. Explain the findings by appropriately relating them to a more general hypothesis or theory.

6. Predict a new situation on the basis of the generalized hypothesis.

II. Experimentation—an application of the scientific method

A. State a Problem and Hypothesis

B. Test the Hypothesis

1. Select a sample of participants.

2. Randomly assign them to groups.

3. Randomly assign groups to conditions (treatments).

   a. The experimental group serves under a novel condition.

   b. The control group serves under a normal or standard condition.

4. Define the independent variable (an aspect of the environment that is systematically varied such that the normal value is assigned to the control group and the novel value to the experimental group).

5. Define the dependent variable (a well-defined aspect of behavior that is the criterion of whether the independent variable is effective).

6. Control relevant extraneous variables, those variables that may operate freely to influence the dependent variable; if they are not controlled, may not accurately assess the effect of the independent variable (remember the ideal principle that the effects all of the variables that may influence the dependent variable should be controlled.)

7. Conduct statistical tests to determine whether the two groups reliably differ on measures of the dependent variable so that you confirm or disconfirm the hypothesis.

8. Generalize and explain the hypothesis (but only if confirmed).

9. Predict to new situations, perhaps through replication (conducting the experiment with the same method.)

CRITICAL REVIEW FOR THE STUDENT

In studying this book, as with most of your studies, you should use the whole (rather than the part) method of learning. To apply the whole method here you would first read through the table of contents and thumb through the entire book, attempting to get a general picture of the task at hand. Then you would employ the naturally developed units of learning presented in the form of chapters. Chapter 1 is thus a whole unit which you would practice for several trials—first, quickly breeze through the chapter noting the important topics. Then read through the chapter hastily, adding somewhat more to your understanding of each topic. Then at some later time, when you *really* get down to business for the next "trial," read for great detail, perhaps even outlining or writing down critical concepts and principles. Finally, perhaps when an examination is imminent, review your outline or notes of this chapter along with those from other chapters of the book. To help you start off now, review the Glossary on p.000 for highlighted terms. You might also ask yourself questions such as the following:

1. What is the major difference between scientific and metaphysical endeavors?
2. Do you understand what Watson meant by, "If psychology is ever to become a science, it must follow the example of the physical sciences; it must become materialistic, mechanistic, deterministic, objective"?
3. Can you define "materialism," "determinism," and "objectivity"?
4. What is meant by "empiricism" and empirical S-R laws?
5. Are there firm, well-established steps in the scientific method that are accepted by all scientists? Why or why not?
6. List the steps of the scientific method as presented in this book.
7. Why do you think that the problems of psychology are held to be the most challenging and complex that we face? Maybe you disagree with this.
8. Can you define and identify examples of the following terms that are critical as you proceed on through the remaining chapters of the book?
   randomization
   experimental group
   control group
   a variable
   independent variable
   dependent variable
   continuous versus discrete variables
   extraneous variables
   control of extraneous variables
   statistical significance and statistical reliability
   replication
9. Edward L. Thorndike's complete statement, referred to on page 6, was that "If a thing exists, it exists in some amount. If it exists in some amount, it can be measured." Do you accept this?
10. You might look over the oversimplified example of an experiment in clinical psychology and think of a psychological problem that especially interests you. For instance, you might be concerned about developing a more effective penal system, controlling drug abuse, or ascertaining the systematic effect of amount of reinforcement on a pigeon's behavior. How would you design an experiment to solve your problem?
11. Finally, don't forget that your library is full of sources that you can use to elaborate on items covered in each chapter. For instance, you might wish to read further on the exciting history of the development of the concept of materialism. By getting a good start on your study of this first chapter, your learning of the rest of the book should be materially enhanced (no pun intended).

chapter 2

THE PROBLEM

Major purpose:

To understand the essential characteristics of scientific problems.

What you are going to find:

1. How we become aware of problems.
2. Principles for distinguishing between solvable and unsolvable problems.
3. Specific ways of formulating solvable problems, especially with operational definitions.

What you should acquire:

The ability to formulate precisely a researchable problem for yourself.

WHAT IS A PROBLEM?

A scientific inquiry starts when we have already collected some knowledge, and that knowledge indicates that there is something we don't know. It may be that we simply do not have enough information to answer a question, or it may be that the knowledge that we have is in such a state of disorder that it cannot adequately be related to the question. In either case we have a problem. The formulation of a problem is especially important, for it guides us in the remainder of our inquiry. Great creativity is required here if our research is to be valuable for society. A certain amount of genius is required to formulate an important problem with far-reaching consequences. Some people address only trivial problems or those with immediate payoff. The story is told of

Isaac Newton's request for research support from the king, phrased for illustrative purposes in terms of gravitational pull on apples to the earth. The king's grant committee rejected Newton's proposed research on gravitational theory, but they encouraged him to solve the problem of preventing the king's apples from bruising when they fell to the ground. Such limited perspective could have retarded the magnificent development of the science of physics. Let us now see, in a more specific way, how we become aware of a problem—it is hoped, of an important one.

WAYS IN WHICH A PROBLEM IS MANIFESTED

First, studying past research obviously helps you to become aware of problems so that you can formulate those that especially interest you. To study past research we are fortunate to have a number of important psychological journals available in our libraries (or professors' offices for reliable borrowers). These journals cover a wide variety of researchable topics so that you can select those concerned with problems of social psychology, clinical psychology, learning, or whatever interests you. To get an overall view of the entire field of psychology, and even of research in related fields, you might survey the numerous condensations that periodically appear in the journal entitled *Psychological Abstracts*. By studying our journals, we can note that the lack of sufficient knowledge that bears on a problem is manifested in at least three, to some extent overlapping, ways: (1) *when there is a noticeable gap in the results of investigations*, (2) when *the results of several inquiries disagree*, and (3) *when a "fact" exists in the form of unexplained information*. As you think through these ways in which we become aware of a problem, you might start to plan the introductory section of your first written experimental report. In the introduction you introduce your reader to the problem that you seek to solve and explain why the problem is important. Let us now focus on three ways of becoming aware of a problem.

A Gap in Our Knowledge

The most apparent way in which a problem is manifested is probably when there is a straightforward absence of information; we know what we know, and there is simply something that we do not know. If a community group plans to establish a clinic to provide psychotherapeutic services, a natural question for them to ask is: "What kind of therapy is the most effective?" Now the question is extremely important, but there are few scientifically acceptable studies that provide an answer. Here is an apparent gap in our knowledge. Collection of data with a view toward filling this gap is thus indicated.

Students most often conduct experiments in their classes to solve problems of this type. They become curious about why a given kind of behavior occurs, about whether a certain kind of behavior can be produced by a given stimulus, about whether one kind of behavior is related to another kind of behavior, and so forth. Frequently some casual observation serves as the basis for their curiosity and leads to the formulation of this kind of problem. For example, one student had developed the habit of lowering her head below her knees when she came to a taxing question on an examination. She thought that doing so facilitated her problem-solving ability, because she thereby got more blood into her brain. Queer as such behavior might strike you, or queer as it struck her professor (who developed his own problem of trying to find where she hid the crib notes that she was studying), such a phenomenon is possible. And there were apparently no relevant data available. Consequently, the sympathetic students in the class conducted a rather straightforward, if somewhat unusual, experiment: They auditorily presented problems as their participants' bodily positions were systematically maneuvered through space.

Similar problems that have been developed by students are as follows: What is the effect of consuming a slight amount of alcohol on motor performance (such as playing Ping-Pong) and on problem-solving ability?

Can the color of the clothes worn by a roommate be controlled through the subtle administration of verbal reinforcements? Do students who major in psychology have a higher amount of situational anxiety than those whose major is a "less dynamic" subject? Such problems as these are often studied early in a course in research methods, and they are quite valuable, at least in helping the student to learn appropriate methodology. As students read about previous experiments related to their problem, however, their storehouse of scientific knowledge grows, and their problems become more sophisticated in that they fall into the categories of contradictory results and attempts to explain isolated facts. One cannot help being impressed by the high quality of research conducted by undergraduate students toward the completion of a course in experimental methodology. Fired by their enthusiasm for conducting their own original research, they not uncommonly attempt to solve problems made manifest by *contradictory* results or by the existence of phenomena for which there is *no satisfactory explanation*.

Contradictory Results

To understand how the results of different attempts to solve the same problem may differ, consider three separate experiments that have been published in psychological journals. The common problem was: "When a person is learning a task, are rest pauses more beneficial if concentrated during the first part of the total practice session or if concentrated during the last part?" For instance, if a person is to spend 10 trials in practicing a given task, would learning be more efficient if rest pauses were concentrated between the first 5 trials (early in learning) or between the last 5 (late in learning)? In each experiment one group practiced a task with rest pauses concentrated early in the session. A second group practiced the task with rest pauses concentrated late in learning.

The results of the first experiment indicated that concentrating rest periods late in learning is superior; the second experiment showed that concentrating rest periods early led to superior learning; while the third experiment indicated that both groups learned about the same. Why do these three studies provide us with conflicting results?

One possible reason is that one or more of the experiments was poorly conducted—certain principles of sound experimentation may have been violated. Failure to control important extraneous variables is a common error that may produce conflicting results, e.g., extraneous variables in two individual experiments on the same problem assumed two different values so that they caused different dependent variable results.

The publication of two independent experiments with conflicting conclusions thus presents the psychological world with a problem. The solution is to identify the extraneous variable(s) so that it (they) can become an explicitly defined and manipulated independent variable to be systematically varied in replications of the two experiments. Let us illustrate with some experiments by Professor Ronald Webster and his students concerning language suppression. In the first, two pronouns were selected and repeatedly exposed in a variety of sentences to students in an experimental group. Control students were exposed to the same sentences except that other pronouns were substituted for the special two. The experimenter who presented the verbal materials sat outside the view of the students. Then, from a larger list of pronouns (that contained those two of special interest), both groups of students selected a pronoun to use in a sentence. More specifically, they were told to compose sentences using any of the pronouns from the list. It was found that the experimental group tended to avoid one of those pronouns to which they had previously been exposed, relative to the frequency of their selection by the control group. It was concluded that prior verbal stimulation produces a satiation effect so that there is a suppression of pronoun choice. This is a valuable conclusion, so the experiment was repeated, though, in contrast to the first experiment, the experimenter happened to sit in view of the students; quite possibly they could thus receive additional cues, such as cues when the experimenter recorded response information. The results of this repetition, needless to say, did not show a suppression effect of the two pronouns by the experimental group. Not to be discouraged, however, the original experiment was again repeated except this time it was made certain that the students could not see the experimenter. This time the results confirmed the original findings.

Apparently, the extraneous variable of experimenter location was sufficiently powerful to influence the dependent variable values. The fact that it was different in the second experiment led to results that conflicted with those of the first experiment, thus creating a problem. The problem was solved by controlling this extraneous variable, thus establishing the reason for the conflicting results. Incidentally, the effects of an extraneous variable may be studied in a simple factorial design. In this case, the first two experiments could be simultaneuosly repeated, systematically varying experimenter location. Thus, we would use the original control and experimental conditions in which participants could see or not see the experimenter, as in Table 2-1. We can observe that a simple factorial design is essentially one in which the experimenter conducts two two-group experiments simultaneously using two independent variables. (More about factorial designs can be found in Chapter 8.)

TABLE 2-1 Combining two simple two-group experiments into a factorial design to study an extraneous variable

Extraneous Variable Condition	Independent Variable Condition	
	Experimental	*Control*
Cannot see the experimenter	(These two groups comprise the first experiment.)	
Can see the experimenter	(These two groups comprise the second experiment.)	

Explaining a Fact

We become aware of a problem when we ask why a "fact" is so? A fact, existing in isolation from the rest of our knowledge, demands **explanation**. A science consists, not only of knowledge, but of *systematized* knowledge. The greater the systematization, the greater is the scientist's understanding of nature. Thus, when a new fact is acquired, the scientist seeks to relate it to the already existing body of knowledge. If the fact does not fit in with existing knowledge, a problem is made apparent. The collection of new information is necessary in order to relate the new fact to existing knowledge in such a manner that it will be explained. Some efforts to explain new facts have resulted in major discoveries. To learn how the discovery of a new fact created a problem, the solution of which had important consequences, consider the following example.

One day the Frenchman Henri Becquerel could not understand why a certain photographic film had been fogged. In thinking about it, he remembered a piece of uranium near the film before the fogging. Existing theory did not relate the uranium and the fogged film, but Becquerel suggested that the two events were connected. To relate the two events specifically, he postulated that the uranium gave off some unique kind of energy. He eventually determined that the metal emitted radioactive energy to cause the fogging, for which finding he received the Nobel Prize. This specification and explanation of an isolated fact led to a whole series of developments that have resulted in present-day theories of radioactivity, with monumental technological applications.

Examples of new portions of knowledge that have had revolutionary significance are rare in psychology, perhaps in part because it is such a young science. One such case in psychology may be Max Wertheimer's discovery of the *phi* phenomenon in the early part of this century and his classic attempt to explain it. The story is told that Wertheimer observed telephone poles while riding a train. But instead of seeing mere stationary telephone poles, first one and then another, he perceived movement from one pole to the next. With Wolfgang Köhler and Kurt Koffka (who were to become equally famous psychologists) as his subjects, he conducted systematic studies of the *phi* phenomenon (the perception of a particular kind of movement between stimuli that are actually stationary). Wertheimer, Köhler, and Koffka held that the existing theories of perception could not explain the *phi* phenomenon, and they therefore advanced a new set of theories. The essence of their reasoning was that the *phi* phenomenon could not be understood by analyzing the situation into its parts, but could be understood only by studying the whole complex without analysis. They concluded that one must study the *Gestalt* (a German word meaning configuration, the entire situation), a position that led to the birth and development of Gestalt psychology. Other more recent examples of discoveries that have had considerable influence in psychology are James Old's discovery of the pleasure center in the brain and B. F. Skinner's use of the dependent variable of rate of responding (see Chapter 10).

When a new theory explains a fact, it also applies to other phenomena; that is, theories are sufficiently general that they can explain many facts. Hence, the development of a theory that accounts for one fact may be a fertile source of additional problems in the sense that one may ask: "What other phenomena can it explain?" One of the most engaging aspects of the scientific enterprise is to tease out the implications of a general theory and to subject those implications to additional empirical tests. In this way the growth of knowledge progresses as we acquire a bit of information, as we advance tentative explanations of that information, and as we explore the consequences of those explanations. In terms of number of problems, science is a mushrooming affair. As Homer Dubs correctly noted as early as 1930, every increase in our knowledge results in a greater increase in the number of our problems. We can therefore judge a science's maturity by the number of problems

that it has; the more problems that a given science faces, the more advanced it is.

We will conclude this section with a special thought for the undergraduate student who might be worrying about how to find a problem on which to experiment. This difficulty is not unique for the undergraduate, for we often see Ph.D. students in a panic to select a problem, fearing that they will choose a topic inappropriate for the Nobel Prize. Both the undergraduate and the graduate student should relax on this point—just do the best that you can in selecting a problem, then don't worry about its worth. Most important, regardless of the problem you have selected, *make as sure as you can that you study it with sound research methodology.* You should not expect more than this from yourself. With increasing research practice, your research insight can grow to equal your aspirations. The thing to do is to get started.

DEFINING A SOLVABLE PROBLEM

A hypothesis is the tentative solution for a problem. However, in order actually to solve the problem the hypothesis must be testable, relevant to the problem, and empirically established as true.

The Proposed Solution Is Testable

Not all questions that people ask can be answered by science. As noted in Chapter 1, a problem can qualify for scientific study only if it is solvable. But how do we determine whether a problem is solvable or unsolvable? Briefly, a problem is solvable if it can be empirically answered in a yes or no fashion. More precisely, a solvable problem is one for which a *testable* hypothesis can be advanced as a tentative solution. *A problem is solvable if, and only if, one can empirically test its tentative solution (which is offered in the form of a hypothesis).* We must thus inquire into the nature of relevant, testable hypotheses. Before we start, however, please recognize that this question is exceedingly complex, with a stormy philosophical history that we need not analyze here. Since as empiricists we must get along with our research, we shall consider the nature of relevancy and of testability only insofar as they affect the everyday work of the research psychologist.

The Proposed Solution Is Relevant to the Problem

A hypothesis that is relevant to a problem is one that can solve the problem if it is true. Becquerel's hypothesis was relevant because it explained that the photographic film was fogged because of the radiation emitted by the uranium. This point may seem obvious, but many times the right answer has been given to the wrong problem. An irrelevant (but probably true) hypothesis for the problem of "Why do people smoke marijuana?" would be: "If a person smokes opium, then that person will experience hallucinations."

What Is a Testable Hypothesis? *A hypothesis is testable if, and only if, it is possible to determine that it is either true or false.*[1] Hypotheses take the form of propositions (or, equally, statements or sentences). If it is possible to determine that a hypothesis, stated as a proposition, is true or false, then the hypothesis is testable. If it is not possible to determine that the proposition is either true or false, then the hypothesis is *not* testable and should be discarded as being worthless to science. Thus, a problem (stated as a question) is solvable if it is possible to state a relevant hypothesis as a potential answer to the problem, and it must also be possible to determine that the hypothesis is either true or false. In short, a solvable problem is one for which a testable hypothesis can be stated.

Knowledge Is Expressed in the Form of Propositions. It follows from the preceding that knowledge is expressed in the form of propositions. The following statements are examples of what we call knowledge: "That table is brown." "Intermittent reforcement schedules during acquisition result in increased resistance to extinction." "$E = mc^2$." Events, observations, objects, or phenomena per se are thus not knowledge, and it is irrelevant here whether events are private or external to a person. For example, external phenomena such as the relative location of certain stars, a bird soaring through the air, or a painting are not knowledge; such things are neither true nor false, nor are our perceptions of them true or false for they are not propositions. Similarly a feeling of pain in your stomach or your aesthetic experience when looking at a painting are not in themselves instances of knowledge. *Statements* about events and objects, however, are candidates for knowledge. For example, the statements "He has a stomach pain" and "I have a stomach pain" may be statements of knowledge, depending on whether they are true. In short, the requirement that knowledge can occur only in the form of a statement is critical for the process of testability. If we determine that the statement of a hypothesis is true, then that statement is an instance of what we define as knowledge.

DEGREE OF PROBABILITY INSTEAD OF TRUE AND FALSE

We use the words "true" and "false" as approximations, for it is impossible to determine beyond all doubt that a hypothesis (or any other empirical proposition) is absolutely true or false. The kind of world that we have been given for study is simply not one of 100 percent truths or falsities. The best that we can do is to say that a certain proposition has a determinable degree of probability. Thus we cannot say in a strict sense that a certain proposition is true— rather, it is probable or very probable. Similarly another proposition is highly improbable; thus instead of false we substitute the term "degree of probability" for "true" and "false"; otherwise no empirical propositions would ever be testable since no empirical

---

[1] As we shall shortly see, we use the words "true" and "false" in the sense of approximations. More precisely, then it must be possible to determine that a hypothesis has a specifiable degree of probability attached to it. "True" then means that the hypothesis is extremely probable, while "false" means that it is extremely improbable.

proposition can ever be (absolutely) true or false. The main principle with which we shall be concerned, therefore, is that a *hypothesis is testable if, and only if, it is possible to determine a degree of probability for it*. By **"degree of probability"** we mean that the hypothesis has a probability value somewhere between 0.0 (absolutely false) and 1.0 (absolutely true). What is known as the *frequency definition of probability* would hold that a hypothesis that has a probability of $P = 0.99$ would be confirmed in 99 out of 100 unbiased experiments. In a sense, we could think of that hypothesis as "probably true." One that has a degree of probability of $P = 0.50$ would be "just as likely to be true as false," and one with a probability of $P = 0.09$ is "probably false."

In Summary. A problem is solvable if (1) a relevant hypothesis can be advanced as a tentative solution for it and (2) it is possible to test that hypothesis by determining a degree of probability for it.

KINDS OF POSSIBILITIES

Let us now focus on the word *possible* in the preceding statement. Does "possible" mean that we can test the hypothesis *now*, or at some time in the future? Consider the question, "Is it possible for us to fly to Uranus?" If by "possible" we mean that one can step into a rocket ship today and set out on a successful journey, then clearly such a venture is not possible. But if we mean that such a trip is likely to be possible sometime in the future, then the answer is yes. Consider then, two interpretations of "possible." The first interpretation we shall call **presently attainable** and the second **potentially attainable**.

Presently Attainable

This interpretation of "possible" states that the possibility is within our power at the present time. If a certain task can be accomplished with the equipment and other means that are immediately available, accomplishing the task is presently attainable. If the task cannot be accomplished with tools that are presently available, the solution to the implied problem is not presently attainable. For example, building a bridge over the Suwannee River (or even a tunnel under the English Channel) is presently attainable, but living successfully on Venus is not presently attainable.

Potentially Attainable

This interpretation concerns those possibilities that *may* come within the powers of people at some future time, but which are not possessed at the present. Whether they will actually be possessed in the future may be difficult to decide now. If technological advances are sufficiently successful that we actually come to possess the powers, then the potentially attainable becomes presently attainable. For example, a trip to Uranus is not presently attainable, but we fully expect such a trip to be technologically feasible in the future. Successful accomplishment of such a venture is proof that the task should be shifted into the presently attainable category. Less stringently, when we can specify the procedures for solving a problem, and when it has been demonstrated that those procedures can actually be used, then we may shift the problem from the potentially to the presently attainable category.

CLASSES OF TESTABILITY

These two interpretations of "possible" lead us to two corresponding classes of testability.

Presently Testable

If the determination of a degree of probability for a hypothesis is presently attainable, then the proposition is **presently testable**. This statement allows considerable latitude, which we must have to justify work on problems that have a low probability of being satisfactorily solved, as well as on straightforward, cut-and-dried problems. If one can conduct an experiment in which the probability of a hypothesis can be ascertained with the tools that are presently at hand, then clearly the hypothesis is presently testable. If we cannot now conduct such an experiment, the hypothesis is not presently testable.

Potentially Testable

A hypothesis is **potentially testable** if it may be possible to determine a degree of probability for it at some time in the future, if the degree of probability is potentially attainable. Although such a hypothesis is not presently testable, improvement in our techniques and the invention of new ones may make it possible to test it later. Within this category we also want to allow wide latitude. There may be statements for which we know with a high degree of certainty how we will eventually test them, although we simply cannot do it now. At the other extreme are statements for which we have a good deal of trouble imagining the procedures by which they will eventually be tested, but we are not ready to say that someone will not some day design the appropriate tools.

A WORKING PRINCIPLE FOR THE EXPERIMENTER

On the basis of the preceding considerations, we may now formulate our principles of action for hypotheses. First, since psychologists conducting experiments must work only on problems that have a possibility of being solved with the tools that are immediately available, we must apply the criterion of present testability in our everyday work. Therefore, only if it is clear that a hypothesis is presently testable should it be considered now for experimentation. The psychologist's problems that are not presently, but are potentially, testable should be set aside in a "wait-and-see" category. When sufficient advances have been made so that the prob-

lem can be investigated with the tools of science, it becomes presently testable and can be solved. If sufficient technological advances are not made, then the problem is maintained in the category of potential testability. On the other hand, if advances show that the problem that is set aside proves not to be potentially testable, it should be discarded as soon as this becomes evident, for no matter how much science advances, no solution will be forthcoming.

Applying the Criterion of Testability. In our everyday research we apply the preceding principles essentially as follows. First, we formulate a problem that we seek to solve, and then a hypothesis that is a potential solution of the problem. As we will note in the next chapter, the hypothesis is typically a statement that is general in scope in that it refers to a wide variety of events with which the problem is concerned. We then observe a sample of those events to collect data. Next we confront the hypothesis with those observations. In testing the hypothesis we conclude that the hypothesis is confirmed (supported) by the data or disconfirmed (not supported). More particularly, if the observations are in accord with our hypothesis, we conclude that the hypothesis is confirmed (it has a high degree of probability, e.g., $P = .80$); otherwise it is disconfirmed (its probability is low, e.g., $P = .15$). This extremely complex process of testing hypotheses will be elaborated on throughout the book, but for now it is important to note that there are two specific criteria for a hypothesis to be tested (and thus to be confirmed or disconfirmed):

criterion 1. Do all the variables contained in the hypothesis actually refer to (empirically) observable events?

criterion 2. Is the hypothesis formulated in such a way that it is possible to relate its components to empirically observable events and render a decision on its degree of probability?

If all the events referred to in the hypothesis are publicly observable (they satisfy the principle of intersubjective reliability), then the first criterion is satisfied. Ghosts, for instance, are not typically considered to be reliably observable by people in general, so that problems formulated about ghosts are unsolvable and corresponding hypotheses about them are untestable. If a hypothesis is well formed in accordance with our rules of language and if we can unambiguously relate its terms to empirically observable events, then our second criterion is satisfied. We should thus be able to render a confirmed-disconfirmed decision.

The components of a hypothesis might refer to events and objects that are readily observable, such as "dogs," "smell," "things," and thus satisfy the first criterion. However, the words might not be put together in accordance with the rules of language. For instance, one might put the words together to form such meaningless sentences as "smell do dogs," "dogs smell do things," and so on. Stated in such extreme forms, you might think that sensible scientists would never formulate unsolvable problems or corresponding untestable hypotheses. Unfortunately, however, we *are* frequently victimized by precisely these errors, although in more subtle forms. It is, in fact, often difficult to sift out statements that are testable from those that are untestable, even with the preceding criteria of testability. Those statements that merely pretend to be hypotheses are called **pseudostatements** or **pseudohypotheses**. Pseudostatements (such as "ghosts can solve problems") are meaningless (the corresponding problem, "Can ghosts solve problems?" is unsolvable) because it is not possible to determine a degree of probability for them. The task of identifying some pseudohypotheses in our science is easy, whereas identifying some others is difficult and exacting. Since the proper formulation of, and solution to, a problem is basic to the conduct of an experiment, it is essential that the experimenter be agile in formulating solvable problems and testable relevant hypotheses.

UNSOLVABLE PROBLEMS

The Unstructured Problem

The student just learning how to develop, design, and conduct experimental studies usually has difficulty in isolating pseudoproblems from solvable problems. This discussion about unsolvable problems, therefore, is to enhance your perspective so that you can become more proficient at recognizing and stating solvable problems. Your psychology instructor with years of experience, however, must accept that the vague, inadequately formulated problem will be asked by introductory students for many generations to come. How, for instance, can one answer such questions as: "What's the matter with his (her, my, your) mind?" "How does the mind work?" or "Is it possible to change human nature?" These problems are unsolvable because the intent is unclear and the domain to which they refer is so amorphous that it is impossible to specify what the relevant observations would be, much less to relate observations to such vague formulations. After lengthy discussion with the asker, however, it *might* be possible to determine what the person is *trying* to ask and thereby to reformulate the question so that it *does* become answerable. Perhaps, for example, suitable dissection of the question "What's the matter with my mind?" might lead to a reformulation such as "Why am I compelled to count the number of door knobs in every room that I enter?" Such a question is still difficult to answer, but at least the chances of success are increased because the question is now more precisely stated and refers to events that are more readily observable. Whether the game is worth the candle is another matter. For the personal education of the student, it probably is. Reformulations of this type of question, however, are not very likely to advance science.

Inadequately Defined Terms and the Operational Definition

Some Examples. Vaguely stated problems such as the preceding typically contain terms that are inadequately defined, which contributes to their vagueness. However, there may be problems that are solvable if we but knew what was meant by one of the terms contained in their statement. Consider, for example, the topical question "Can machines think?" This is a contemporary analog of the question that Thorndike took up in great detail early in the century: "Do cats reason?" Whether or not these problems are solvable depends on how "think" and "reason" are defined. Unfortunately, much energy has been expended in arguing such questions in the absence of clear specifications of what is meant by the crucial terms. Historically, the disagreements between the disciples Jung and Adler and the teacher Freud are a prime example. Just what *is* the basic driving force for humans? Is it the libido, with a primary emphasis on sexual needs? Is it Jung's more generalized concept of the libido as "any psychic energy?" Or is it, as Adler held, a compensatory energy, a "will to power"? This problem, it is safe to say, will continue to go unsolved until these hypothesized concepts are adequately defined, if in fact they ever are.

A question that is receiving an increasing amount of attention from many points of view is "How do children learn language?" In their step-by-step accounts of the process, linguists and psychologists frequently include a phase in language development that may be summarized as "Children learn to imitate the language production of adults around them." The matter may be left there with the belief that our understanding of this highly complex process is advanced. A closer analysis of "Do children learn language by imitation?" however, leads us to be not so hasty. Because we don't know what the theorist means by *imitation*—its sense may vary from a highly mystical interpretation to a concrete, objectively observably behavioral process—the question is unsolvable at this stage of its formulation.

One of the main reasons that many problems are unsolvable is that their terms have been imported from everyday language. Our common language is replete with ambi-guities, as well as with multiple definitions for some words. If we do not give cognizance to this point, we can expend our argumentative (and research) energies in vain. Everyone can recall, no doubt, at least several lengthy and perhaps heated arguments that, on more sober reflection, were found to have resulted from a lack of agreement on the definition of certain terms that were basic to the discussion. To illustrate, suppose a group of people carry on a discussion about happiness. The discussion would no doubt take many turns, produce many disagreements, and probably result in considerable unhappiness on the part of the disputants. It would probably accomplish little, unless at some early stage the people involved were able to agree on an unambiguous definition of happiness. Although it is impossible to guarantee the success of a discussion in which the terms are adequately defined, without such agreement there would be no chance of success whatsoever.

Solution Through Operational Definitions. The importance of adequate definitions in science cannot be too strongly emphasized. The main functions of good definitions are: (1) to clarify the phenomenon under investigation, and (2) to allow us to communicate with each other in an unambiguous manner. These functions are accomplished by the **operational definition** of the empirical terms with which the scientist deals.

When we face the problem of how to define a term operationally, we, in large part, address ourselves to the question of whether our problem is solvable. That is, with reference to the two criteria on p. 23 for ascertaining whether a problem is solvable, we made the point that the events referred to in the statement of the problem should all be publicly observable. If the terms contained in the statement of the problem can be operationally defined, then they are empirically observable by a number of people, and the scientist has moved a long way toward rendering the problem solvable.

Essentially, an *operational definition is one that indicates that a certain phenomenon exists, and does so by specifying precisely how (and preferably in what units) the phenomenon is measured.* That is, an operational definition of a concept consists of a statement of the operations necessary to produce the phenomenon. Once the method of recording and measuring a phenomenon is specified, that phenomenon is operationally defined. The precise specification of the defining operations obviously accomplishes the intent of the scientist—by performing those operations, a phenomenon is produced and a number of observers can agree on the existence and characteristics of the phenomenon. Hence, a phenomenon that is operationally defined is reproducible by other people, which is critical in science. Because we operationally define a concept, the definition of the concept consists of the objectively stated procedures performed in producing it. Others can then reproduce the phenomenon by repeating these operations. For example, when we define air temperature, we mean that the column of mercury in a thermometer rests at a certain point on the scale of degrees. Consider the psychological concept of hunger drive. One way of operationally defining this concept is in terms of the amount of time that an organism is deprived of food. Thus, one operational definition of *hunger drive* would be a statement about the number of hours of food deprivation. Accordingly, we might say that an organism that has not eaten for 12 hours is more hungry than is one that has not eaten for 2 hours.

A considerable amount of work has been done in psychology on steadiness. There are a number of different ways of measuring steadiness and, accordingly, there are a number of different operational definitions of the concept. Consider, for example, an apparatus that consists of a series of holes, varying from large to small in size, and a stylus (it's called the *Whipple Steadiness Test*). The participant holds the stylus as steadily as possible in each hole, one at a time, trying not to touch the sides. The number of contacts made is automatically recorded, and the steadier the person is, the fewer contacts

are made. This operational definition of steadiness is the number of contacts made by an individual when taking the Whipple Steadiness Test. But if we measured steadiness by using other types of apparatus, we would have additional operational definitions of steadiness. The several definitions of steadiness may or may not be related, so that a person may be steady by one measure but unsteady by another. Disagreements about steadiness could be reduced by agreements as to which definition is being used. The myriad definitions of anxiety have engendered many controversies for just this reason.

We can now see that the first step in approaching a problem is to define critical empirical terms operationally. Basically, what we are requiring is a specification of the laboratory methods and techniques for producing stimulus events and for recording and measuring response phenomena. We must be able to refer to ("point" to) some event in the environment that corresponds to each empirical term in the statement of problems (and of hypotheses). If no such operation is possible for *all* these terms, we must conclude that the problem is unsolvable and that the hypothesis is untestable. In short, by subjecting the problem to the criterion of operational definition of its terms, we render a solvable-unsolvable decision, on the basis of which we either continue or abandon our research on that question.

Operationism. Operational definitions derived from a movement known as **operationism**, which was initiated in 1927 by the physicist P. W. Bridgeman, a Nobel laureate who published some 750 titles. The prime assumption of operationism is that adequate definitions of the variables with which a science deals are a prerequisite to advancement. However, the term *operational definition* was not actually Bridgeman's. Rather, it was adapted by psychologists from Bridgeman's work. Since then, writings on operationism have involved many arguments. For instance, operationism has been criticized because the operational definitions are often specific to a particular empirical investigation. Variables specified in the statement of problems may be operationally defined in different ways by different experimenters, even though they are identified by the same word—the different definitions of anxiety being a case in point. *Anxiety* may be operationally defined by one experimenter through the use of the Taylor Scale of Manifest Anxiety, whereas a different researcher may define it in terms of the Palmar Perspiration Index. Unfortunately, different measures of anxiety may not correlate with each other. While the problem of different operational definitions of the same term is irritating, it is not at all insurmountable. We simply have a number of different definitions of anxiety which we might label, anxiety$_1$ anxiety$_2$, . . . , anxiety$_N$. As we advance in our studies, we might arrive at a **fundamental definition** of anxiety that would encompass all the specific definitions, so that there would be one general definition that would fit all experimental usages. As we seek a fundamental definition, which is a general definition of a concept that includes a number of more specific definitions, those specific operational definitions yield cues by which the fundamental definition can be established.

Operationism has also been criticized because it demands that all the phenomena with which we deal must be strictly observable, operationally definable. This requirement, if adhered to rigidly, would lead us to exclude prematurely certain phenomena from scientific investigation. Images, for instance, were forbidden in the vocabulary of many psychologists some years ago on the basis that it was not possible to define them operationally. Still it is important from a broad perspective that we maintain some concepts, as we did images, even though we are not presently able to specify how we would operationally define them. Eventually such phenomena might be subjected to fruitful scientific study, once advances in techniques for measuring them are made. Such concepts can thus be maintained in our "potentially solvable" category of problems.

Within recent years the topic of imagery and images has reentered psychology in a most impressive manner so that we are now objectively studying images in a number of different ways. A similar example in physics was when, in 1931, Pauli developed the notion of a neutrino, solely to preserve the laws of conservation. He knew he could not test the neutrino hypothesis—the proposed new particle was presumably not real and therefore could not be observed because it had zero charge and zero rest mass. However, 45 years later experimenters successfully detected the neutrino. This example illustrates how we can maintain an operational approach and still keep some concepts in our science that are not immediately susceptible to operational definition, for eventually those concepts may turn out to be of considerable importance.

In Conclusion. It is critical that we continue to use operational definitions in experimentation, for at least they communicate clearly just what the researcher did in measuring and recording the events studied in the research being reported. A more advanced discussion of operational definitions leads into matters far beyond what is required here.

Impossibility of Collecting Relevant Data

Problems that Are Unsolvable Because of Lack of Data. Sometimes we have a problem that is sufficiently precise and whose terms are operationally definable, but we are at a loss to specify how we would collect the necessary data. As an illustration, consider the possible effect of psychotherapy on the intelligence of a clinical patient who cannot speak. Note that we can adequately define the crucial terms such as "intelligence" and "therapy." The patient, we observe, scores low on an intelligence test. After considerable clinical work the patient's speech is improved; on a later intelligence test the patient registers a significantly higher score. Did the intelligence of the patient actually increase as a result of the clinical work? Alternatives are possible: Was the first intelligence score invalid because of the difficulties of administering the test to the nonverbal patient? Did the higher score result merely from "paying attention" to the patient? Was the patient going through some sort of transition period such that the mere passage of time (with various experiences) provided the opportunity for the increased score? Clearly it is impossible to decide among these possibilities, and the problem is not solvable as stated.

"If you attach the optic nerve to the auditory areas of the brain, will you sense visions auditorily?" Students will probably continue arguing this question until neurophysiological technology progresses to the point that we can change this potentially solvable problem to the presently solvable category. A similar candidate for dismissal from the presently solvable category is a particular attempt to explain reminiscence. To illustrate reminiscence, say that a person practices a task such as memorizing a list of words, although the learning is not perfect. The person is tested immediately after a certain number of practice trails. After a time during which there is no further practice, the person is tested on the list of words again. On this second test it is found that the individual recalls more of the words than on the first test. This is reminiscence. Reminiscence occurs when the recall of an incompletely learned task is greater after a period of time than it is immediately after learning the task. The problem is how to explain this phenomenon.

One possible explanation of reminiscence is that, although there are no formal practice trials following the initial learning period, the participant covertly practices the task; that is, the individual "rehearses" the task following the initial practice period and before the second test. This informal rehearsal could well lead to a higher score on the second test. Our purpose is not to take issue with this attempt to explain reminiscence but to examine a line of reasoning that led one psychologist to reject "rehearsal" as an explanation of the phenomenon.

The suggestion was that rehearsal cannot account for reminiscence because rats show reminiscence in maze learning, and it is not easy to imagine rats rehearsing their paths through a maze between trials. Such a statement cannot seriously be considered as bearing on the problem of reminiscence—there is simply no way at present to determine whether rats do or do not rehearse, assuming the common definition of "rehearse." Hence, the hypothesis that rats show reminiscence but do not rehearse is not presently testable. If we ever are successful in developing an effective "thought-reading machine" (as designed for humans by McGuigan, 1978), then we still would face the problem of applying it to the subhuman level. All of this does not mean, of course, that the rehearsal hypothesis or other explanations of reminiscence are untestable.

As another example of an unsolvable problem, consider testing two theories of forgetting: the disuse theory, which says that forgetting occurs strictly because of the passage of time; and the interference theory, which says that forgetting is the result of competition from other learned material. Which theory is more probably true? A classic experiment by Jenkins and Dallenbach (1924) is frequently cited as evidence in favor of the interference theory, and this is scientifically acceptable evidence. This experiment showed that there is less forgetting during sleep (when there is presumably little interference) than during waking hours. However, their data indicate considerable forgetting during sleep, which is usually accounted for by saying that even during sleep there is some interference (from dreaming, and so forth). To determine whether this is so, to test the theory of disuse strictly, we must have a condition in which a person has zero interference. Technically, there would seem to be only one condition that might satisfy this requirement—death. Thus the Jenkins-Dallenbach experiment does not provide a completely general test of the theory of disuse. Therefore, we must consider the problem of whether, during a condition of zero interference, there is no forgetting as a presently unsolvable problem, although it is potentially solvable (perhaps by advances in cryogenics wherein we can freeze, but still test, people).

The interested student should list a number of other problems and decide whether they are solvable. To start with: "Do people behave the same regardless of whether they are aware that they are participating in an experiment?" Can we answer the question of whether the person performs differently just because apparatus or a questionnaire or a test is used? Indeed, whether the observation of a phenomenon interferes with the phenomenon itself is a very general question in science. It is especially relevant in psychology.

Vicious Circularity

Vicious Circularity Renders Problems Unsolvable. Before concluding this section, consider a kind of reasoning that, when it occurs, is outrightly disastrous for the scientific enterprise. This fallacious reasoning, called **vicious circularity** occurs when an answer is based on a question and the question on the answer, with no appeal to other information outside this vicious circle. The issue is relevant to criterion number 2 on p. 23 for the proper formulation of a solvable problem. A historical illustration is the development and demise of the instinct doctrine. In the early part of our century "instinct naming" was a very popular game, and it resulted in quite a lengthy list of such instincts as gregariousness, pugnacity, and so on. The goal was to explain the occurrence of a certain kind of behavior, call it *X*, by postulating the existence of an instinct, say instinct *Y*. Only eventually did it become apparent that this endeavor led exactly nowhere, at which time it was discontinued. The game, to reconstruct its vicious circularity, went thus—Question: "Why do organisms exhibit behavior *X*?" Answer: "Because they have instinct *Y*." But the second question: "How do we know that organisms have instinct *Y*?" Answer: "Because they exhibit behavior *X*." The reasoning goes from *X* to *Y* and from *Y* to *X*, thus explaining nothing.

Problems that are approached in this manner constitute a unique class of unsolvable ones, and we must be careful to avoid the invention of new games such as drive or motive naming. To illustrate the danger from a more contemporary point of view, consider the question of why a given response did not occur. One possible answer is that an inhibitory neural impulse prevented the excitatory impulse from producing a response. That is, recent neurophysiological research has indicated the existence of efferent neural impulses that descend from the central nervous system, and they may inhibit responses. Behaviorists who rely on this concept may fall into a trap similar to that of the instinct doctrinists. That is, to the question "Why did response *X* fail to occur?" one could answer "Because there was an inhibitory neural impulse." Whereupon we must ask the second question again: "But how do you know that there was an inhibitory neural impulse?" If the answer is, in effect, "Because the response failed to occur," we can immediately see that the process of vicious circularity has been invoked. To avoid this fallacious reasoning, the psychologist must rely on outside information. In this instance, one should *independently* record the inhibitory neural impulse, so that there is a sound, rather than a circular, basis for asserting that it occurred. Hence the reasoning could legitimately go as follows: "Why did response *X* fail to occur?" "Because there was a neural impulse that inhibited it." "How do we know that there actually was such an impulse?" "Because we recorded it by a set of separate instruments," as did Hernández-Péon, Scherrer, and Jouvet (1956).

The lesson from these considerations of vicious circularity is that there must be documentation of the existence of phenomena that is independent of the statement of the problem and its proposed solution. Otherwise the problem is unsolvable—there is no alternative to the hypothesis than that it be true. The famous psychologist Edwin Guthrie's classical principle of learning states that when a response is once made to a stimulus pattern, the next time the stimulus pattern is presented, the organism will make the same response. To test his principle, suppose that we record a certain response to a stimulus. We later present the stimulus again and find that a different response occurs. The scientist who falls victim to the vicious circularity line of reasoning might say that, although the second presentation of the stimulus appeared to be the same as the first, it must not have been. Because the response changed, the stimulus must also have changed in some way that was not readily apparent. If the response did not change it is inferred that the stimulus did not change, but if the response changed, it is inferred that the stimulus must have changed as well. The response is thus the sole criterion for judging whether the stimulus changed (at least in this instance). A scientist who reasons thus would *never* be able to falsify the principle; hence the principle becomes untestable. To render the principle testable, there must be a specification of whether the stimulus pattern changed from the first to the second test—a specification that is independent of the response finding.

SOME ADDITIONAL CONSIDERATIONS OF PROBLEMS

A Problem Should Have Value

Even after we have determined that a problem is presently solvable, there are other criteria to be satisfied before considerable effort is expended in conducting an experiment. One desirable characteristic is that the problem be sufficiently important. Numerous problems arise for which the psychologist will furnish no answers immediately or even in the future, although they are in fact solvable. Some problems are just not important enough to justify research—they are either too trivial or too expensive (in terms of time, effort, and money) to answer. The problem of whether rats prefer Swiss or American cheese is likely to go unanswered for centuries; similarly, "why nations fight" is also likely to go unanswered—not because it is unimportant, but

because its answer would require much more effort than society seems willing to expend on it.

Some aspects of this discussion may strike you as representing a dangerous point of view. One might ask how we can ever know that a particular problem is really unimportant. Perhaps the results of an experiment on a problem that some regard as unimportant might turn out to be very important—if not today, perhaps in the future. Unfortunately there is no answer to such a position. Such a situation is, indeed, conceivable, and suggesting that a problem should be important might choke off some valuable research. However, if an experimenter can foresee that a study will have some significance for a theory or an applied practice, the results are probably going to be more valuable than if such consequences cannot be foreseen. There are some psychologists who would never conduct an experiment unless it were specifically influential on a given theoretical position. This might be too rigid a position, but it does have merit.

It is not easy to distinguish between an important problem and an unimportant one, but it can be fairly clearly established that some problems are more likely to contribute to the advancement of psychology than are others. It is a good idea for the experimenter to try to choose what is considered an important problem rather than a relatively unimportant problem. Within these rather general limits, no further restrictions are suggested. In any event, science is the epitome of the democratic process, and any scientist is free to work on any problem whatever. What some scientists would judge to be "ridiculous problems" may well turn out to have revolutionary significance. Some psychologists have wished for a professional journal with a title like *The Journal of Crazy Ideas* to encourage wild and speculative research.

Avoid the Impasse Problem

Sometimes the psychologist is aware of a problem that is solvable, adequately phrased, and important, but an accumulation of experiments on the problem shows contradictory results. And often there seems to be no reason for such discrepancies. That is what might be called **the impasse problem**. When faced with this situation, it would not seem worthwhile to conduct "just another experiment" on the problem, for little is likely to be gained, regardless of how the experiment turns out. The impasse problem exists when there are numerous contradictory experiments so that little is to be gained by adding more data to either side. Unless an experimenter can be imaginative and develop a new approach that has some chance of systematizing the knowledge in the area, it is probably best to stay out of that area and use one's limited energy to perform research on a problem that has a greater chance of contributing some new knowledge.

Psychological Reactions to Problems

Unfortunately, the existence of problems that lead to scientific advances can be a source of anxiety for some people. When there is a new discovery, people tend to react in one of two ways. The curious, creative person will adventurously attempt to explain it. The incurious and unimaginative person, on the other hand, may attempt to ignore the problem, hoping it will go away. A good example of the latter type of reaction occurred around the fifteenth century when mathematicians produced a "new" number they called zero. The thought that zero could be a number was disturbing, and some city legislative bodies even passed laws forbidding its use. The creation of imaginary numbers led to similar reactions; in some cases the entire arabic system of numerals was outlawed.

Negative reactions to scientific discoveries have not been confined to the lay person and in fact have been emotionally pronounced on the part of scientists. The open-mindedness of scientists is not universal. For example, it took astronomer-scientists an excessively long time to accept the Copernican theory of planetary motion, partly be-cause it seemed "simply absurd" to think that the earth moves. Mendel's great achievement—the development of this theory of genetic inheritance—failed to be accepted because among other reasons it was "too mathematical." Similarly, because English astronomers of 1845 distrusted mathematics, Adams's discovery of a new planet (Neptune) was not published.

One major error that has been committed by scientists throughout history is judging the quality of scientific research by the status of the researcher, as with the most interesting problems that Mendel faced. Mendel, it seems, wrote deferentially to one of the distinguished botanists of the time, Carl von Nägeli of Munich. Mendel, an unimportant monk from Brüun, was obviously a mere amateur expressing fantastic notions that ran, incidentally, counter to those of the master. Nevertheless, von Nägeli honored Mendel by answering him and by advising him to change from experiments on peas to ones on hawkweed. It is iroinic that Mendel took the advice of the "great man" and thus labored in a blind alley for the rest of his scientific life on a plant not at all suitable for the study of inheritance of separate characteristics.

Society in general, and scientists in particular, it is hoped, will eventually learn to assess advances in knowledge on the basis of a truth criterion alone, and the numerous sources of resistance to discoveries will be reduced and eliminated.

CHAPTER SUMMARY

I. Stating a problem
   A. A problem exists when we know enough to know that there is something we don't know. Three ways in which a problem is manifested are
      1. There is a gap in our knowledge.
      2. Results of different experiments arc inconsistent.
      3. An isolated fact exists which should be explained.
II. Science addresses only solvable problems.
   A. A problem is solvable if it is possible to advance a suitable hypothesis as a tentative solution for it.

B. A suitable hypothesis is one that is relevant to the problem and is empirically testable.
   1. With a relevant hypothesis, one can make an inference from the hypothesis to the problem such that if the hypothesis is true, the problem is solved.
   2. By "testable," we mean that it is possible to determine whether the hypothesis is true or false.

III. Replacing "true" and "false" with "degree of probability."
   A. A hypothesis is testable if, and only if, it is possible to determine a degree of probability for it.
   B. Degree of probability means that the hypothesis has a likelihood between 0.0 (it is false) and 1.0 (it is true).

IV. The kinds of possibilities
   A. Presently attainable.
   B. Potentially attainable.

V. Classes of testability
   A. Presently testable—we can test the hypothesis now with contemporary human capacities.
   B. The hypothesis is potentially testable, that is, we cannot test the hypothesis now, nor can we be sure that it can ever be tested so that it remains in a "wait-and-see" category. If technological advances are sufficient, then some day the potentially testable hypothesis is moved to the presently testable category.

VI. Applying the probability criterion of testability
   A. Do the phenomena referred to by the hypothesis concern empirically observable events?
   B. Is the hypothesis properly formulated so that it can be tested?

VII. Unsolvable problems
   A. The unstructured problem.
   B. Inadequately defined terms and the operational definition.
   C. Impossibility of collecting relevant data.
   D. Vicious circularity renders problems unsolvable.

VIII. Some additional considerations
   A. Problems should be technologically or theoretically important.

B. Problems of the impasse variety should be avoided.
C. Psychological reactions to problems—we should emphasize a truth criterion.

CRITICAL REVIEW FOR THE STUDENT

At the end of Chapter 1 we suggested some general methods that might enhance your effectiveness of studying. Perhaps at the end of each chapter you might review those suggestions and see how you can apply them to the new study unit. Remember, always try to study the *whole unit*. The ultimate whole study unit defined by this book is research methods, so that you really ought to breeze through the entire book to get a general picture and enhanced perspective of the field. When preparing for your final examination you will be able to review the entire field, forming a whole unit of research methods from your entire course. For now, however, some questions from this chapter for your "whole unit" of the problem are

1. Distinguish between a ("true") problem and a pseudoproblem—this leads you into the question of the distinction between solvable and unsolvable problems.
2. Can you make up some examples of problems that are unsolvable? Perhaps you might observe and ponder events about you and use them as stimuli, such as "What is that bird thinking about?"
3. Why is it necessary in science that a problem be solvable, at least in principle?
4. What is an operational definition? Do *all* terms used in psychology need to be operationally defined? (This question should also be considered throughout your more advanced study of scientific methodology.)
5. Finally you might start the formulation of your answer to the question that is the focus of all academic endeavors—"What is knowledge?"

chapter 3

THE HYPOTHESIS

Major purpose:

To understand the essential characteristics of scientific hypotheses.

What you are going to find:

1. That hypotheses are proposed relationships between variables and are tentative solutions to problems.
2. That their basic format is that of a general implication wherein one variable implies another.
3. That testable hypotheses always have a determinable degree of probability (they can never be absolutely true or false).

What you should acquire:

The capacity to state a hypothesis within the context of previous research, one that you can test in your own experiment.

THE NATURE OF A HYPOTHESIS

A scientific investigation must start with a solvable problem. A tentative solution is then offered in the form of a relevant hypothesis is that is empirically testable—it must be pos-sible to determine whether the hypothesis is probably true or probably false. If, after suitable experimentation, the relevant hypothesis is confirmed, it solves the problem. But if it is probably false, it obviously does not solve the problem.

Consider the question "Who makes a good bridge player?" Our hypothesis might be that "People who are intelligent and who show a strong interest make good bridge players." If the collection and interpretation of sufficient data confirm the hypothesis, the problem is solved because we can answer the question.[1] On the other hand, if we find that these qualities do not make for a good bridge player, we fail to confirm our hypothesis and we have not solved the problem.

Explanatory Power of Hypotheses. Frequently, a confirmed hypothesis that solves a problem can be said to explain issues with which the problem is concerned. Assume that a problem exists because we possess an isolated fact that requires an explanation. If we can appropriately relate that fact to some other fact, we might explain the first one. To understand this point note that a hypothesis is the tool by which we seek to accomplish such an explanation; that is, we use a hypothesis to state a possible relationship between one fact and other. If we find that the two facts are actually related in the manner stated by the hypothesis, then we have accomplished our immediate purpose—we have explained the first fact. (A more complete discussion of explanation is offered in Chapter 12.)

To illustrate, reconsider the problem in Chapter 2 about the photographic film that was fogged. This fact demanded an explanation, and Becquerel also noted a second fact: that a piece of uranium was lying near the film. His hypothesis was that some characteristic of uranium produced the fogging. His test of this hypothesis proved successful. By relating the fogging of the film to a characteristic of the uranium, the fact was thus explained.

---

[1] But the problem is not *completely* solved because further research is required to enlarge our solution, such as finding other factors that make good bridge players. A more extensive hypothesis might include the factor of self-discipline and thus have a higher probability than the earlier one since it contains more relevant variables, is more general, and offers a more complete solution.

What is a fact? *Fact* is a commonsense word, and as such its meaning is rather vague. We understand something by it, such as a fact is "an event of actual occurrence." It is something that we are quite sure has happened (Becquerel was quite sure that the film was fogged). Such commonsense words should be replaced, however, with more precise terms. For instance, instead of using the word *fact*, suppose that we conceive of the fogging of the film as a *variable*; that is, the film may be fogged in varying degrees, from a zero amount to total exposure. Similarly, the amount of radioactive energy given off by a piece of uranium is a variable that may range from zero to a large amount. Therefore, instead of saying that two *facts* are related, we may make the more productive statement that two *variables* are related. The advantages of this precision are sizable for we may now hypothesize a *quantitative* relationship—the greater the amount of radioactive energy given off by the uranium, the greater is the fogging of the film. Hence, instead of making the rather crude distinction between fogged and unfogged film, we may now talk about the *amount* of fogging. Similarly, the uranium is not simply giving off radioactive energy; it is emitting an amount of energy. We are now in a position to make statements of great precision and wide generality. Before, we could say only that if the uranium gave off energy, film would be fogged. Now we can say that if the uranium gives off little energy, the film will be fogged a small amount; if the uranium gives off a lot of energy, the film will be greatly fogged; **and so on**. With numbers we can make many more statements about the relationship between these two variables. Later we will discuss quantitative statements of hypotheses. But for now we may define a hypothesis as a testable statement of a potential relationship between variables that can explain "facts."

Other terms such as "theories," "laws," "principles," and "generalizations" state relationships between variables, just as do *hypotheses*. Distinctions among these relationships will be made later, but our discussion here and for the next several chapters will be applicable to any statement involving empirical relationships between variables, without distinguishing among them. The point to focus on is that an experiment is conducted to test an empirical relationship and, for convenience, we will usually refer to the statement of that relationship as a *hypothesis*. That a hypothesis is *empirical* means that it directly refers to data that we can obtain from our observation of nature. The variables contained in an empirical hypothesis are operationally definable and thus refer to events that can be directly measured.

ANALYTIC, CONTRADICTORY, AND SYNTHETIC STATEMENTS

To emphasize the importance of the empirical nature of a hypothesis, note that all possible statements (sentences; propositions) fall into one of three categories: **analytic, contradictory**, or **synthetic**. These three kinds of statements differ on the basis of their possible truth values. By **truth value** we mean whether a statement is true or false. Thus we may say that a given statement has the truth value of *true* (such a statement is "true") or that it has the truth value of *false* (this one is "false"). Because of the nature of their construction (the way in which they are formed), however, some statements can take on only certain truth values. Some statements, for instance, can take on the truth value of *true* only. Such statements are called analytic statements (other names for them are "logically true statements," or *tautologies*). Thus an *analytic statement is a statement that is always true—it cannot be false*. The statement "If you have a brother, then either you are older than your brother or you are not older than your brother" is an example of an analytic statement. Such a statement exhausts the possibilities, and, since one of the possibilities must be true, the statement itself must be true. On the other hand, a *contradictory statement* (sometimes also called a "self-contradiction" or a "logically false statement") *is one that always assumes a truth value*

of false; that is, because of the way in which it is constructed, it is necessary that the statement be false. A negation of an analytic statement is obviously a contradictory statement. For example, the statement "It is false that you are older than your brother or you are not older than your brother" (or the logically equivalent statement "If you have a brother, then you are older than your brother and you are not older than your brother") is a contradictory statement. Such a statement includes all the logical possibilities but says that all these logical possibilities are false.

Hypotheses Are Synthetic Statements. The third type of statement, the synthetic statement, is neither analytic nor contradictory. A *synthetic statement may be either true or false*; for example, the statement "You are older than your brother" may be either true or false. The important point for us is that a *hypothesis must be a synthetic statement*. Thus, any hypothesis must be capable of being established as (probably) true or false.

Another example of an analytic statement is "I am in Chicago or I am not in Chicago." This statement is necessarily true because no other possibilities exist. The contradictory proposition is "I am in Chicago and I am not in Chicago." Clearly such a statement is absolutely false, barring such unhappy possibilities as being in a severed condition. Finally, the corresponding synthetic statement is "I am in Chicago," a statement that may be *either* true or false, or, since no empirical statement may be strictly true or false, we use these terms in a sense of approximation so that they are "probably true" or "probably false."

Why should we state hypotheses in the form of synthetic statements? Why not use analytic statements, in which case it would be guaranteed that our hypotheses are true? The answer is to be found in an understanding of the function of the various kinds of statements. The reason that a synthetic statement may be true or false is that it refers to the empirical world; that is, it is an attempt to tell us something about nature. As we previously saw, every statement that refers to natural events might be in error. An analytic statement, however, is empty. Although absolutely true, it tells us nothing about the empirical world. This characteristic results because an analytic statement includes all of the logical possibilities, but it does not inform us which is the true one. This is the price that one must pay for absolute truth. If one wishes to state information about nature, one must use a synthetic statement, in which case the statement always runs the risk of being false. Thus, if someone asks me if you are older than your brother, I might give my best judgment and say, "You are older than your brother," which is a synthetic statement. I may be wrong, but at least I am trying to tell the person something about the empirical world. Such is the case with our scientific hypotheses; they may be false in spite of our efforts to assert true ones, but they are potentially informative in that they are our efforts to say something about nature.

The Value of Analytic and Contradictory Statements. If analytic statements are empty and tell us nothing about nature, why bother with them in the first place? The answer to this question could be quite detailed. Suffice it to say here that analytic statements are valuable for facilitating deductive reasoning (logical inferences) which are necessary in testing hypotheses, as we shall discuss in Chapter 12. Statements in mathematics and logic are analytic and contradictory statements and are valuable for science because they allow us to transform synthetic statements without adding additional knowledge. The point is that science uses all three types in different ways, emphasizing that the synthetic proposition is for stating hypotheses—they are our attempts to say something informative about the natural world.

THE MANNER OF STATING HYPOTHESES

Granting, then, that a hypothesis is a statement of a potential empirical relationship between two or more variables, and also that it is possible to determine a degree of probability for it, we might well ask what form that statement (proposition) should take, that is, precisely how should we state hypotheses in scientific work?

Hypotheses Are "If . . . , Then . . ." Relationships

One of the greatest philosophers of all time, Lord Bertrand Russell, answered this question by proposing that the logical form of the **general implication** be used for expressing hypotheses. Using the English language, the general implication may be expressed as: "*If . . . , then . . . .*"; that is, *if* certain conditions hold, *then* certain other conditions should also hold. To better understand the "if . . . , then . . ." relationship, let *a* stand for the first set of conditions and *b* for the second. In this case the general implication would be "If *a*, then *b*." But to communicate the conditions indicated by *a* and *b*, we must state two propositions—the symbols *a* and *b* stand for propositions that express these two sets of conditions. If we join these two simple propositions, as we do when we use the general implication, then we end up with a single compound proposition. This compound proposition is our hypothesis.

The proposition *a* is the antecedent condition of the hypothesis (it comes first), and *b* is the consequent condition of the hypothesis (it follows the antecedent condition). A hypothesis, we said, is a statement that relates two variables, which are the antecedent and consequent conditions. The symbols *a* and *b* are called *propositional variables*. A hypothesis thus proposes a relationship between two (propositional) variables by means of the general implication as follows: "If *a* is true, then *b* is true." The general implication is simply a proposition that says that if such and such is the case (*a*), then such and such else is implied (*b*). The general implication is a standard logical proposition relating two variables, *a* and *b*, which may stand for whatever we wish. If we suspect that two particular variables are related, we might hypothesize a relationship between them. For example, we might think that industrial work groups that are in great inner conflict have decreased production levels. Here the two variables are: (1) the amount of inner conflict in an industrial work group, and (2) the amount of production that work groups turn out. We can formulate two propositions: (1) "An industrial work group is in great inner conflict," and (2) "That work group will have a decreased production level." If we let *a* stand for the first proposition and *b* for the second, our hypothesis would read: "*If* an industrial work group is in great inner conflict, *then* that work group will have a decreased production level."

With this understanding of the general implication for stating hypotheses, it is well to inquire about the frequency with which Russell's proposal is used in psychology. The answer is clear: The explicit use of the general implication is almost nonexistent. Two samples of hypotheses, essentially as they were stated in professional journals, should illustrate the point:

1. The purpose of the present investigation is to study the effects of a teacher's verbal reinforcement on pupils' classroom demeanor.
2. Giving students an opportunity to serve on university academic committees results in lower grades in their classes.

Clearly these hypotheses, or implied hypotheses, fail to conform to the form specified by the general implication. Is this bad? Are we committing serious errors by not precisely heeding Russell's advice? Not really—it is always possible to restate such hypotheses as general implications as follows. Within the first hypothesis are the two variables of amount of verbal reinforcement and amount of acceptable classroom behavior for which the corresponding propositions are: (1) a teacher verbally reinforces a student for desirable classroom performance, and (2) the student's demeanor improves. The hypothesis relating these two propositional variables is "*If* a teacher verbally reinforces a student for acceptable classroom behavior, *then* the student's classroom behavior will improve."

Similarly, for the second hypothesis, the propositions containing the relevant variables are: (1) students are given the opportunity to serve on university academic committees, and (2) those students achieve lower grades in their classes. The hypothesis: "*If* students are given the opportunity to serve on university academic committees, *then* those students will achieve lower grades in their classes."

It is apparent that these two hypotheses fit the "If *a*, then *b*" form, although it was necessary to modify somewhat the original statements. Even so, these modifications did not change their meaning.

What we have said to this point, then, is that we implicitly use the general implication to state hypotheses, even though they appear to be expressed in a variety of other ways. We thus can restate such hypotheses explicitly as general implications. Using the form of the general implication to state hypotheses is important because we determine whether hypotheses are confirmed by making certain inferences to them from experimental findings. The rules of logic tell us what kind of inferences are legitimate, or *valid*. To determine whether the inferences are valid, the statements involved in the inferences (e.g., the hypotheses) can be stated as general implications. Hence, to understand experimental inferences, we must use standard logical forms, as will be explained when we discuss experimental inferences in Chapter 12.

Another reason for stating a hypothesis as a general implication is that doing so may help to clarify the reason for conducting the experiment. That is, by succinctly and logically writing down the purpose of the experiment as a test of a general implication, the experimenter is forced to come to grips with the precise nature of the relevant variables. Any remaining vagueness in the hypothesis can then be removed when operational definitions of the variables are stated.

Mathematical Statements of Hypotheses

Yet another form for stating hypotheses involves mathematical statements essentially as follows: $Y = f(X)$. That is, a hypothesis stated in this way proposes that some variable Y is related to some variable X or, alternatively, that Y is a function of X. Such a mathematically stated hypothesis fits our general definition of a hypothesis as a statement that two variables are related. Although the variables are quantitative (their values can be measured with numbers), they may still refer to whatever we wish. In psychology, the classical paradigm for the statement of our laws has been in the form of R as a function of S; that is, $R = f(S)$. In this instance we identify a response variable (R) that systematically changes as the stimulus (S) is varied. For the hypothesis about the students on committees, we could assign numbers to the independent variable which would be X in the equation $Y = f(X)$. Thus the extent to which students serve on committees might be quantified with a scale such that 0.0 would indicate no service, 1.0 a little service, 2.0 a medium amount of service, and so on. Course grades, the dependent variable Y, are similarly quantified such that an A is 4.0, a B is 3.0, and so on. The hypothesis could then be tested for all possible numerical values of the independent and the dependent variables.

Thus, even though a hypothesis is stated in a mathematical form, that form is basically of the "If a, then b" relation. Instead of saying "If a, then b," we merely say "If (and only if) X is this value, then Y is that value." For example, if X is 3 (medium committee service), then Y is 2.0 (an average grade).

The General Implication is an Approximation to a Probability Statement

All hypotheses have a probability character in that none of them can be absolutely true or false. Yet the preceding hypotheses in the logical form of "If a, then b" or the mathematical form of $R = f(S)$ are absolute in that we do not attach a probability value to them. The statement "If a, then b" strictly speaking can only be true or false. Consequently, remember that these forms of statements are used in a sense of approximation

and implicitly include the qualifier that they are probable or improbable.[2]

Causal Connections Between Antecedent and Consequent Conditions

One final matter about the logical character of scientific laws is that our laws must express a stronger connection between the antecedent and consequent conditions than mere accidental connection. Consider that "all tennis balls in Harry's tennis bag are yellow." It is apparent that there is no necessary, causal connection between the antecedent condition of the balls being in Harry's tennis bag and the consequent condition that those balls are yellow. No one is likely to maintain, for instance, that if a particular white ball were placed into Harry's tennis bag, that the ball would become yellow. Harry just couldn't have that kind of mystical power!

Our laws should have some element of necessity between the antecedent and consequent conditions, as in the statement "Copper always expands on heating." Rephrasing this sentence as a general implication, "If copper is heated, then it will expand," indicates that heating the copper (the antecedent condition) physically necessitates expansion (the consequent condition). In contrast, merely placing a white ball into Harry's tennis bag does not necessitate it becoming a yellow tennis ball. This matter is important when we contrast experimental with correlational research. The laws that derive from experimental research *do* have an element of necessity between the antecedent and consequent conditions: when derived from a sound experiment, we arrive at a *casual* law; that is, the independent variable, as stated in the antecedent condition, *causes* the value of the dependent variable (as stated in the consequent condition). But this element of

---

[2]To be more precise, formal statement of our hypotheses should actually be within the calculus of probability (probability logic) so that a hypothesis would be stated $A \underset{p}{\supset} B$ where p states the degree of probability for the relationship (see McGuigan, 1956).

causal necessity cannot be asserted when we merely find a correlation between two variables. However, more of this will be discussed later.

TYPES OF HYPOTHESES

The general implication, being a good form for stating hypotheses, must also allow us conveniently to generalize our laws. Consider the previous example in which we said that if an industrial work group has a specific characteristic, certain consequences follow. We did not specify what industrial work group, although it was understood that the hypothesis concerns at least *some* such group. But might it hold for all industrial work groups? The answer to this question is unclear, and there are two possible courses: (1) we could say that the particular work group is unspecified from all possible work groups, thus leaving the matter up in the air, or (2) we could assert a universal hypothesis with the implicit understanding that we are talking about *all* industrial work groups in conflict. In this instance, if you take *any* industrial group in conflict, the consequences specified by the hypothesis should follow. To advance knowledge, we choose the latter interpretation, for if the former interpretation is followed, no definite commitment is made, and if nothing is risked, nothing is gained. If in later research it is found that the hypothesis is *not* universal in scope (it is not applicable to *all* industrial work groups), it must be limited. This is a definite step forward because, although of restricted generality, it is at least true for the subdomain of work groups to which it is addressed.

Universal and Existential Hypotheses

Although the goal of the scientist is to assert hypotheses in as universal a fashion as possible, we should explicitly state the degree of generality with which we are asserting them. Let us, therefore, investigate the possible types of hypotheses that are at the disposal of the scientist.

The first type is the **universal hypothesis**, which asserts that the relationship in question holds for all values of all variables that are specified, for all time, and at all places. An example of the universal hypothesis would be "For all college students, if they are rewarded for showing up on time to serve as participants in psychology experiments, then they will be prompt." However, because there are so many exceptions in behavior, universal hypotheses in psychology typically have to be restricted in scope. We must exclude from our universal statements those exceptions when we discover them.

The **existential hypothesis** asserts that the relationship stated in the hypothesis holds for at least one particular case ("existential" implies that one exists); for instance, "There is at least one college student who, if he or she is rewarded for showing up on time, will be prompt." Examples of the existential hypothesis abound, e.g., one of Clark Hull's classical empirical generalizations says in effect that *at least some* drive conditions activate habits that have been acquired under different drive conditions. Because of its frequent use in psychology, it may be concluded that the existential hypothesis is useful in psychological research. This is because many times a psychologist can soundly assert that a given phenomenon exists but doesn't know how often it occurs. One famous example is the pioneering research of Hermann Ebbinghaus, who used himself as a subject. At a time in the last century when it was generally considered impossible to study the higher mental processes, Ebbinghaus proceeded to measure his own memory and forgetting. Fortunately for us he had not been trained as a psychologist, so he did not know that what he was attempting to accomplish was "impossible." By thus demonstrating how memory can be experimentally attacked in at least one person, he opened up an entire new field which also contributed sizably to the quantitative measurement of other mental processes. One positive finding such as that of Ebbinghaus is sufficient to establish the existence of a phenomenon, the next step being to determine the generality of the law. The increased frequency with which one participant is studied, as in single case methodology (the "$N = 1$ design" as in Chapter 10), provides other illustrations of existential hypotheses.

From Existential to Limited Universal Hypotheses. After confirming an existential hypothesis that establishes the existence of a phenomenon, how might we approach the question of the phenomenon's generality? Typically, phenomena specified in existential hypotheses are difficult to observe, and one cannot easily leap from this type of highly specialized hypothesis to an unlimited, universal one. Rather, the scientist seeks to establish the conditions under which the phenomenon does and does not occur so that we can eventually assert a universal hypothesis with necessary qualifying conditions. In one test of an existential hypothesis, the notion was that auditory hallucinations in paranoid schizophrenics were the product of the patient covertly speaking in a slight whisper. The existential hypothesis was that "There is at least one paranoid schizophrenic such that if there are auditory hallucinations experienced, then there are covert speech responses." The research confirmed this hypothesis by ascertaining that slight speech responses coincided with the patient's report of hearing voices. Presumably the auditory hallucinations were produced by the patient covertly talking to himself. Once the phenomenon was established, the credibility of some sort of universal hypothesis increased; the question is just how a universal hypothesis should be advanced and suitably qualified. To answer this question, one would attempt to record covert speech responses during the hallucinations of other patients. No doubt failure should sometimes be expected, and the phenomenon might be observable, for instance, only for paranoid schizophrenics who have auditory hallucinations and not for those who have visual or olfactory hallucinations. Furthermore, success might occur only for "new" patients and not for chronic psychotics. But whatever the specific conditions under which the phe-

nomenon occurs, research should eventually lead to a universal hypothesis that includes a statement that limits its domain of application. For instance, such a qualified universal hypothesis might say that "For all paranoid schizophrenics who will admit to auditory hallucinations and who have been institutionalized for less than a year, if they auditorially hallucinate, then they emit covert speech responses."

We can thus see how research progresses in a piecemeal, step-by-step fashion. Our goal is to formulate propositions of a general nature, but this is accomplished by studying one specific case after another, one experimental condition after another, and only gradually arriving at statements of increasing generality.

One reason to establish universal statements is that the more general statement has the greater predictive power. Put the other way, a specific statement has limited predictive power. Consider the question, for example, of whether purple elephants exist. Certainly no one would care to assert that all elephants are purple, but it would be quite interesting if one such phenomenon were observed; the appropriate hypothesis, therefore, is of the existential type. Should it be established that the existential hypothesis was confirmed, the delimiting of conditions might lead to the universal hypothesis that "For all elephants, if they are in a certain location, are 106 years old, and answer to the name 'Tony,' then they are purple." It is clear that such a highly specific hypothesis would not be very useful for predicting future occurrences—an elephant that showed up in that location at some time in the distant future would be unlikely to have the characteristics specified.

ARRIVING AT A HYPOTHESIS

In spite of considerable research on creativity, thinking, imagination, concept formation, and the like, it still is difficult to specify the process by which we arrive at a hypothesis. Some possible general sources of hypotheses follow.

Abstracting Similarities

In such creative phases, the scientist may survey various data, abstract certain characteristics of those data, perceive some similarities in the abstractions, and relate those similarities to formulate a hypothesis. For instance, the psychologist largely observes stimulus and response events. It is noted that some stimuli are similar to other stimuli and that some responses are similar to other responses. Those stimuli that are perceived as similar according to a certain characteristic belong to the same class, and similarly for the responses. Consider a Skinner box in which a rat presses a lever and receives a pellet of food. A click is sounded just before the rat presses the lever. After a number of associations between the click, pressing the lever, and eating the pellet, the rat learns to press the lever when a click is sounded.

The experimenter judges that the separate instances of the lever-pressing response are sufficiently similar to classify them together. In like manner the clicks are similar enough to form a general class. The psychologist thus uses classifications to distribute a number of data into a smaller number of categories that can be handled efficiently. Then, by assigning symbols to the classes, the psychologist attempts to formulate relationships among the classes. A hypothesis is thus formulated such as, "If a click stimulus is presented a number of times to a rat in an operant box, and if pressing a lever and eating a pellet frequently follow, then the rat will press the lever in response to the click on future occasions." Although some scientists seem to go through such steps systematically and others do so more haphazardly, all seem to approximate them to some extent.

Forming Analogies

Abstracting characteristics from one set of data and attempting to apply them to another phenomenon seems to be a form of reasoning through analogy. One classical philosopher wrote in this regard: "It is a well known fact that most hypotheses are derived from analogy. . . . Indeed, careful investiga-

tions will very likely show that all philosophic theories are developed analogues" (Dubs, 1930, p. 131). In support he pointed out that John Locke's conception of simple and complex ideas was probably suggested by the theory of chemical atoms and compounds that was becoming prominent in his day. Assuming that hypotheses *are* developed by analogy, how does one formulate *good* hypotheses? The answer probably is that we learn this skill in the same manner that we learn everything else—by practice.

Some hypotheses are obviously more difficult to formulate than others. Perhaps the more general a hypothesis is, the more difficult it is to conceive. The important general hypotheses must await the genius to proclaim them, at which time science makes a sizable spurt forward, as happened in the case of Newton and Einstein. To formulate useful and valuable hypotheses, a scientist needs, first, sufficient experience in the area and, second, the quality of "genius." One main problem in formulating hypotheses in complex and disorderly areas is the difficulty of establishing a new "set"—the ability to create a new solution that runs counter to, or on a different plane from, the existing knowledge. This is where scientific genius is required. As has been said, every great idea started with a minority of one.

Extrapolating from Previous Research

The hypotheses that we formulate are almost always dependent on the results of previous scientific inquiries. The findings from one experiment serve as stimuli to formulate new hypotheses; although results from one experiment are used to test the hypothesis, they can also suggest additional hypotheses. For example, if the results indicate that the hypothesis is false, they can possibly be used to form a new hypothesis that *is* in accord with the experimental findings. In this case the new hypothesis must be tested in a new experiment.

But what happens to a hypothesis that is disconfirmed? If there is a new (potentially better) hypothesis to take its place, it can be readily discarded. But if there is no new hypothesis, then we are likely to maintain the false hypothesis, at least temporarily, for no hypothesis ever seems to be finally discarded in science unless it is replaced by a new one.

CRITERIA OF HYPOTHESES

Once we have formulated a hypothesis, how do we know whether it is a "good" one? Of course, we will eventually test it, and certainly a confirmed hypothesis is better than a disconfirmed one in that it solves a problem and thus provides some additional knowledge. But even so, some confirmed hypotheses are better than other confirmed hypotheses. We must now ask what we mean by "good" and by "better." The following are criteria by which to judge hypotheses. Each criterion should be read with the understanding that the one that best satisfies it is the preferred hypothesis, assuming that the hypothesis satisfies the other criteria equally well. It should also be understood that these are flexible criteria, offered tentatively. As the information in this important area increases, they will no doubt be modified. The hypothesis

1. *Must be testable.* The hypothesis that is presently testable is superior to one that is only potentially testable.
2. *Should be in general harmony with other hypotheses in the field of investigation.* Although this is not essential, the disharmonious hypothesis usually has the lower degree of probability. For example, the hypothesis that eye color is related to intelligence is at an immediate disadvantage because it conflicts with the existing body of knowledge. Considerable other knowledge (such as that hair color is not related to intelligence) suggests that the "eye color" hypothesis is not true—it is not in harmony with what we already know.
3. *Should be parsimonious.* If two different hypotheses are advanced to solve a given problem, the more **parsimonious** one is to be preferred. For example, if we have evidence that a person has correctly guessed the symbols (hearts, clubs, diamonds, spades) on a number of cards

more often than by chance, several hypotheses could account for this fact. One might postulate extrasensory perception (ESP), whereas another might say that the subject "peeked" in some manner. The "peek" hypothesis would be more parsimonious because it does not require that we hypothesize very complex mental processes.

The principle of parsimony has been expressed in various forms. For instance, William of Occam's rule (called *Occam's razor*) held that entities should not be multiplied without necessity, a rule similar to W. G. Leibniz' principle of the identity of indiscernibles. Lloyd Morgan's canon is a famous application of the principle of parsimony to psychology: "In no case is an animal activity to be interpreted in terms of higher psychological processes, if it can be fairly interpreted in terms of processes which stand lower in the scale of psychological evolution and development" (Morgan, 1906, p. 59). These three principles have the same general purpose, that of seeking the most parsimonious explanation of a problem. Thus we should prefer a simple over a complex hypothesis if both have equal explanatory power; we should use a simple versus a complex concept if the simpler one will serve as well (e.g., peeking at the cards versus ESP). We should not ascribe higher capacities to organisms if the postulation of lower ones can equally well account for the behavior to be explained.

4. *Should have logical simplicity.* By this we mean logical unity and comprehensiveness, not ease of comprehension. Thus, if one hypothesis can account for a problem by itself and another hypothesis can also account for the problem but requires a number of supporting hypotheses or ad hoc assumptions, the former is to be preferred because of its greater logical simplicity. (The close relationship of this criterion to that of parsimony should be noted.)
5. *Should answer (be relevant to) the particular problem addressed,* and not some other one. It would seem unnecessary to state this criterion, except that, as we have noted, examples can be found in the history of science in which the right answer was given to the wrong question. It is often important to make the obvious explicit.
6. *Should be expressed in a quantified form, or be susceptible to convenient quantification.* The hypothesis that is more highly quantified is to be preferred. The advantage of a quantified over a nonquantified hypothesis was illustrated ear-

lier in the example from the work of Becquerel.

7. *Should have a large number of consequences and should be general in scope.* The hypothesis that yields a large number of deductions (consequences) will explain more facts that are already established and will allow more predictions about events that are as yet unstudied or unestablished (some of which may be unexpected and novel). In general the hypothesis that leads to the larger number of important deductions will be the more fruitful hypothesis.

THE GUIDANCE FUNCTION OF HYPOTHESES

We have already discussed ways in which hypotheses allow us to establish "truth," but how do we know where to start our search? The answer is that hypotheses direct us. An inquiry cannot proceed until there is a suggested solution to a problem in the form of some kind of hypothesis, even if it is but lightly held as an initial working hypothesis.

In the seventeenth century Francis Bacon proposed that the task of the scientist is to classify the entire universe. Unfortunately, the number of data in the universe is indefinitely large, if not infinite. In such a complex world we must have some kind of guide for our observations. Otherwise, we would have little reason for not sitting down where we are and describing a handful of pebbles or whatever else happens to be near us. We must set some priority on the kind of data that we study, and this is accomplished by hypotheses. They guide us to make observations pertinent to our problem; they tell us which observations are to be made and which observations are to be omitted. If we are interested in why a person taps every third telephone pole, a hypothesis would probably guide us to understand compulsions better. It would take a long time if we started out in a random direction to solve this problem by counting the number of blades of grass in a field, for example.

Suppose you were interested in why people have headaches. You might recall that

you had headaches when you were upset. What, you ask yourself, happens in your body at such times to produce headaches? One thing that you notice is that you were uptight, that your muscles were excessively tensed. This observation leads you to formulate the hypothesis that "If one's muscles are excessively tense, then the frequency of headaches increases." This hypothesis then guides you to make observations about the degree of muscular tension in people and the frequency of headaches. It further guides you to a therapeutic intervention. For example, you can teach people to relax their muscles and observe whether the frequency of their headaches decreases. The hypothesis could guide you to make yet other observations, such as whether you can prevent headaches in children who have not yet developed them.

ON ACCIDENT, SERENDIPITY, AND HYPOTHESES

One reason for the great difficulty of understanding that part of nature called the *behavior of organisms* is the expanse of the behavioral realm: the number of response events that we could conceivably study staggers the imagination. A "dust-bowl empiricist" guided by Francis Bacon's philosophy probably wouldn't get beyond classifying types of doorknob responses. Consequently we need to assign priorities to the kinds of behavioral phenomena on which we experiment. Hypotheses, we have said, serve this function—they help to tell us which of an indefinitely large number of responses are more likely to justify our attention. During the conduct of an experiment to test a certain hypothesis, however, one need not be blind to other events. Experimenters should be alert to all manner of happenings other than that to which they are *primarily* directing their attention. Some chance observation unrelated to the hypothesis being tested may lead to the formulation of an even more important hypothesis. We have mentioned several examples of accidental observations in science, which are sufficiently important that a unique term **serendipity** has been coined for it. "Serendipity" was borrowed from Walpole's "Three Princes of Serendip" by the world-famous physiologist Walter Cannon (1945). Walpole's story concerned the futile search for something, but the finding of many valuable things that were not sought. So it is in science—one may vainly seek "truth" by being guided by one hypothesis but in the search may accidentally observe an event that leads to a more fruitful hypothesis. The researcher Fisher, trying to set off drives (such as hunger and thirst) by direct chemical stimulation of specific brain cells, was the beneficiary of serendipity. He knew that the injection of a salt solution into the hypothalamus of goats increased the thirst drive, thus resulting in their drinking large quantities of water. Analogously, Fisher sought to inject the male sex hormone into a rat's brain to trigger male sexual behavior. As he told the story of "The Case of the Mixed-up Rat":

By one of those ironic twists that are so typical of scientific research, the behavioral change produced in my first successful subject was a completely unexpected one. Within seconds after the male hormone was injected into his brain he began to show signs of extreme restlessness. I then put in his cage a female rat that was not in the sexually receptive state. According to the script I had in mind, the brain injection of male hormone should have driven the male to make sexual advances, although normally he would not do so with a nonreceptive female. The rat, however, followed a script of his own. He grasped the female by the tail with his teeth and dragged her across the cage to a corner. She scurried away as soon as he let go, whereupon he dragged her back again. After several such experiences the male picked her up by the loose skin on her back, carried her to the corner and dropped her there.

I was utterly perplexed and so, no doubt, was the female rat. I finally guessed that the male was carrying on a bizarre form of maternal behavior. To test this surmise I deposited some newborn rat pups and strips of paper in the middle of the cage. The male promptly used the paper to build a nest in a corner and then carried the pups to the nest. I picked up the paper and pups and scattered them around the cage; the male responded by rebuilding the nest and retrieving the young.

After about 30 minutes the rat stopped behaving like a new mother; apparently the effect of the injected hormone had worn off. Given a new injection, he immediately returned to his adopted family. With successive lapses and reinjections, his behavior became disorganized; he engaged in all the same maternal activities, but in a haphazard, meaningless order. After an overnight rest, however, a new injection the next day elicited the well-patterned motherly behavior.

The case of the mixed-up male rat was a most auspicious one. Although the rat had not followed the experimenter's script, the result of this first experiment was highly exciting. It was an encouraging indication that the control of behavior by specific neural systems in the brain could indeed be investigated by chemical means. We proceeded next to a long series of experiments to verify that the behavior in each case was actually attributable to a specific chemical implanted at a specific site in the brain rather than to some more general factor such as mechanical stimulation, general excitation of the brain cells, or changes in acidity or osmotic pressure. (Fisher, 1964, pp. 2–4)

Fisher's experience of serendipity well illustrates the flexibility that is characteristic of the successful scientist. While testing one hypothesis we should continue to be alert to accidental occurrences that will stimulate other research. The experimenter who patiently and flexibly observes behavior in an experiment can get many hints for the development of new hypotheses. The position has been taken, though, that scientists should not, or do not explicitly, test hypotheses. This may seem to be an extreme position, but the advocacy of it has been quite explicit. For example, "People don't usually do research the way people who write books about research say that people do research" (Bachrach, 1965, p. ix). The argument is that, while testing a hypothesis, one may thereby be blinded to other potentially important events through "*hypothesis myopia,* a common disease among researchers holding certain preconceived ideas that might get in the way of discovery" (Bachrach, 1965, p. 22).

The fault with this argument is that it erroneously places the blame on the hypothesis, not where the blame properly belongs. A *hypothesis* does not blind an experimenter, though experimenters may blind themselves. All manner of biases, as we have seen (p. 31), may operate against scientific discovery so that a hypothesis is not the only possible "set of preconceived ideas that might get in the way of scientific discovery." The term *hypothesis myopia* should be replaced with *experimenter myopia*.

To exorcise the hypothesis from scientific research is to throw the baby out with the bath water. Experimentation best proceeds by explicitly formulating and testing hypotheses, yet keeping alert for accidental occurrences that may lead to even more valuable hypotheses. On the other hand, overemphasis of the role of accident in scientific discovery is dangerous, as one cannot enter the laboratory with the happy confidence that "serendipity will save the day." The hard facts of everyday experimentation are that most accidental occurrences have little significance—the investigation of each odd little rise in an extended performance curve, the inquiry into every consequence of equipment malfunction on a subject's behavior, the quest for the "why" of every unscheduled response can consume all of an experimenter's energy. We must keep our eyes on the doughnut and not on the hole.[3]

_____
[3] A satire on methodological errors illustrates absurd reliance on serendipity with the researcher who seized the opportunity to collect data when he was stalled on a darkened subway train with the following:

Basic unprinciple: The investigator makes maximum use of the unusual, timely, or newsworthy situation with whatever is at hand.

Example. A random sample of subway riders was tested during a prolonged service blackout to identify those personality characteristics associated with panic during enforced isolation. Analysis of handwriting samples and of figure drawings indicates that uneven line pressure and poorly articulated limbs are associated with verbal and motoric indices of panic. These results are interpreted somewhat guardedly because illumination was inadequate during part of the experiment" (White & Duker, 1971, p. 398).

Amount of light certainly was an important extraneous variable!

To Review. We started with a consideration of a problem that a psychologist seeks to solve. The psychologist initially states the problem very clearly and then proposes a solution to the problem in the form of a hypothesis. The psychologist should formulate both the problem and the hypothesis clearly and succinctly. These formulations can also be used in the later write-up of the experiment. As we shall see in Appendix B, the psychologist will formulate the problem with such phrases as "The statement of the problem is . . ." or "It was the purpose of this experiment to . . ." The hypothesis is then expressed in such ways as "It was expected that . . ." or "It was hypothesized that . . ." We defined the hypothesis, the tentative solution to the problem, as a testable statement of a potential relationship between two or more variables. Hypotheses are synthetic statements in that they are not empty but are attempts to say something about nature. Nor are they absolutely true or false—rather, they have a determinable degree of probability. The most prominent type of hypothesis is the universal one, and it is, at least ideally, stated in the form of a general implication. Existential hypotheses, those that state that there is at least one phenomenon that has a given characteristic, are useful in science too.

CHAPTER SUMMARY

I. The nature of a hypothesis
   A. It is a tentative solution to the problem addressed.
   B. It is empirical, meaning that it refers to data that we can obtain by observation of natural phenomena.
   C. It is a testable statement (proposition).
   D. The variables in an empirical hypothesis are operationally definable.
   E. Ideally, it is a quantitative relationship between two variables.
II. Classifications of all statements
   A. Analytic statements—necessarily true but empirically empty.
   B. Contradictory statements—necessarily false and empirically empty.

C. Synthetic statements—may be true or false and potentially carry information. Hypotheses are synthetic statements.

III. Characteristics of hypotheses
   A. Hypotheses are basically stated as general implications, in the form "If a is true, then b is true." In this case a is the antecedent condition, and b is the consequent condition.
   B. A hypothesis stated in probability logic might read. $A \underset{b}{\ni} B$.
   C. A mathematical statement of a hypothesis would be $R = f(S)$.
   D. Hypotheses are never absolutely true or false, but have a determinable degree of probability.
   E. In an experiment, confirmed hypotheses also express a necessary (causal) connection between the antecedent and the consequent condition. The element of necessity does not occur in statements based on correlational research.

IV. Types of hypotheses
   A. Universal hypotheses—assert that the relationship holds for all values of the variables contained in it for all time and at all places.
   B. Existential hypotheses—assert that the relationship holds for at least one case.

V. Arriving at a hypothesis
   A. Abstract similarities to form and relate a stimulus class and a response class.
   B. Reason, perhaps by analogy, and *practice* creating hypotheses.
   C. Rely heavily on findings from previous experiments to extrapolate potential answers to new problems.

VI. Criteria of hypotheses
   A. Are Testable.
   B. Are Harmonious (compatible) with other hypotheses.
   C. Are Parsimonious, as in Occam's razor or Morgan's canon (principles of parsimony).
   D. Answer the problem addressed.
   E. Have logical simplicity.
   F. Are Quantifiable.
   G. Are Fruitful, yielding numerous consequences.

VII. Use hypotheses to guide research to economize research efforts.
   A. Be aware of serendipity, for it may lead to something of importance that was not expected in the research.
   B. But avoid experimenter myopia.

VIII. On accident, serendipity, hypotheses

CRITICAL REVIEW FOR THE STUDENT

1. A hypotheses is posed as a potential solution to a problem. In formulating the problem the experimenter has to isolate potentially relevant variables for study. How do you define the hypothesis conceived in this way, and in what sense might it be a solution to the problem?

2. The term *empirical* is central to our study. What do we mean when we refer to an *empirical* hypothesis? If you cannot do so now, in your later study you might consider the question of what some *nonempirical* hypotheses are.

3. Discuss the statement of hypotheses as non-quantified and as quantified statements. What is the advantage of stating hypotheses as quantified relationships?

4. Can an empirical hypothesis be strictly true or false, or must it always have a probability value attached to it that is less than certainty?

5. Distinguish between existential and universal hypotheses. In anticipation of the chapter on single participant research, you might carry on the question for yourself of the relationship between existential hypotheses and hypotheses concerned with $N = 1$ research.

6. How do we determine the value of a hypothesis? Are there a limited number of criteria for this purpose?

7. Could science proceed as efficiently without hypotheses and theories as with them?

chapter 4

THE EXPERIMENTAL VARIABLES AND HOW TO CONTROL THEM

Major purpose:

To analyze an experiment into its component variables and consider the potential relationships among them.

What you are going to find:

1. Independent variables subclassified as stimulus and organismic variables.
2. Ways of measuring and evaluating dependent variables.
3. Empirical laws formulated as independent-dependent variable relationships.
4. Methods of controlling extraneous variables so as to arrive at those laws unambiguously.

What you should acquire:

The ability to specify and control independent, dependent, and extraneous variables and to formulate them into empirical laws.

An experimental hypothesis is an assertion that systematic variation of (1) an **independent variable** produces lawful changes in (2) a **dependent variable**. If the findings of a suitably conducted experiment are in accord with the hypothesis, we increase our belief in that causal assertion. A critical characteristic of a sound experiment is that (3) the **extraneous variables** are controlled. The independent, dependent, and extraneous variables are, in an experiment, the three salient classes[1] of variables that require special attention. Effective control of the extraneous variables will allow us to reach a sound conclusion as to whether the independent variable does in fact causally affect the dependent variables.

THE INDEPENDENT VARIABLE

Stimulus Variables

In experimentation the independent variable is a stimulus, where the word *stimulus* broadly refers to any aspect of the environment (physical, social, and so on) that excites the receptors. Examples of stimulus variables that might affect a particular kind of behavior are the effects of different sizes of type on reading speed, the effects of different styles of type on reading speed, the effects of intensity of light on the rate of conditioning, the effects of number of people present at dinner on the amount of food eaten, the effects of social atmosphere on problem-solving ability. The administration of drugs in psychopharmacological research could also qualify as a stimulus variable, with the qualification that one then manipulates the internal environment, that under the skin.

When we use the term "stimulus," though, we actually mean a certain *stimulus class*. A stimulus class is a number of similar instances of environmental events that are classified together. For instance, if the letter *P* is the stimulus in an information processing experiment, each presentation of *P* would be a *stimulus instance* of the stimulus class that consists of all possible letter Ps. The same principle holds for responses so that we speak of *response instances of a response class*.

Organismic Variables

The possible relationships between organismic variables and behavior are studied using the method of systematic observation rather than experimentation. An *organismic variable* is any relatively stable physical characteristic of the organism such as sex, eye color, height, weight, and body build, as well as such psychological characteristics as intelligence, educational level, neuroticism, and prejudice. The reason that we cannot study the effects of organismic variables in an experiment, at least with humans, is that we do not have the power to produce specific values of them, a point that we shall enlarge on shortly.

THE DEPENDENT VARIABLE

Response Measures

Since in psychology we study behavior, and since the components of behavior are responses, our dependent variables are response measures. "Response measures" is also an extremely broad class that includes such diverse phenomena as number of drops of saliva a dog secretes, number of errors a rat makes in a maze, time it takes a person to solve a problem, amplitude of electromyograms (electrical signals given off by muscles when they contract), number of words spoken in a given period of time, accuracy of throwing a baseball, and judgments of people about certain traits. But whatever the response, it is best to measure it as precisely as possible. In some experiments great precision can be achieved, and in others the characteristics of the events dictate cruder measures. Here are some standard ways of measuring responses.

---

[1] By so classifying these variables we can more clearly recognize them and deal with them in experiments, and can thereby better form relationships among them. However, as with any system of classification, there are always disadvantages. Sometimes, for instance, it is difficult to force variables into categories, which means that some classificatory decisions are quite arbitrary. The criterion of any classificatory system is whether it works; that is, is it fruitful for formulating laws? To emphasize this arbitrary nature, other systems in psychology are (1) stimulus, organic, response, and hypothetical state variables; (2) environmental, task, instructional, and subject variables; and (3) stimulus, organismic, response, and antecedent variables.

Accuracy. One way to measure response accuracy would be with a metrical system such as when we fire a rifle at a target. Thus, a hit in the bull's-eye might be scored a five, in the next outer circle a three, and in the next circle a one. Frequency of successes or errors is another response measure of accuracy, for example, the number of baskets that one makes from the free-throw line on a basketball court or the number of errors one makes when taking a test.

Latency. This is the time that it takes from the onset of a stimulus to the start of a response, as in reaction time studies. The experimenter may provide a signal to which the participant must respond. Then the time interval between the onset of the stimulus and the onset of the response is measured. The time interval between shooting a starting pistol and when a runner's feet leave the starting blocks in the 100-meter dash would be the response **latency**.

Duration (Speed). This is a measure of how long it takes to complete a response, once it has started. For pressing a telegraph key, the time measure would be quite short. But for solving a difficult problem, the time measure would be long. The duration of a person running a dash would be the time between leaving the starting blocks until the tape is reached. To emphasize the distinction between latency and duration measures: *latency is the time between the onset of the stimulus and the onset of the response*, and *speed or duration is the time between the onset and termination of the response.*

Frequency and Rate. Frequency is the number of times a response occurs, as in how many responses an organism makes before extinction of a conditional response. The frequency of responding for a given period of time is the **rate of responding**. If a response is made 10 times in 1 minute, the rate of responding is 10 responses per minute. The rate gives an indication of the probability of the response—the higher the rate, the greater the probability that it will occur in the situation at some future time. Response rate is often used in experiments in operant

conditioning. For example, an organism is placed in a Skinner box, and each depression of a lever is automatically recorded on a moving strip of paper. Professor B.F. Skinner once said that his greatest accomplishment was in his use of response rate as a measure of behavior.

Additional Response Measures. Other examples are level of ability that a person can manifest (e.g., how many problems of increasing difficulty one solves with an *unlimited* amount of time) or the intensity of a response (e.g., the amplitude of the galvanic skin response in a conditioning study). Sometimes it is difficult to measure the dependent variable adequately with any of the aforementioned techniques. In this event one might devise a rating scale. A rating scale for anxiety might have five gradations: 5 meaning "extremely anxious;" 4, "moderately anxious"; and so on. Competent judges would then mark the appropriate position on the scale for each participant, or the participants could even rate themselves.

Objective tests can serve as dependent variable measures. For example, you might wish to know whether psychotherapy decreases a person's neurotic tendencies, in which case you might administer a standard test. If a suitable standard test is not available, you might construct your own, as one student did in developing a "Happiness Scale."

These are some of the more commonly used measures of dependent variables. Some of these ideas, combined with your own ingenuity, could provide an appropriate dependent-variable measure for the independent variable that you wish to study.

Selecting a Dependent Variable

Behavior is exceedingly complex, and at any given time an organism makes a fantastically large number of responses. Just how does an experimenter determine which dependent variable to record and measure? Take Pavlov's simple conditioning experiment with dogs. Although his dependent variable was amount of salivation, the dog was also breathing at a certain rate, wagging its tail, moving its legs, pricking up its ears, and so on. Out of this mass of behavior, Pavlov successfully selected a response measure that was an excellent criterion for his independent variables. Had he picked some other response measure, our understanding of conditioning could have been retarded.

Every stimulus evokes responses. The problem of selecting a dependent variable, then, would seem simply to be to find all the responses that are influenced by a given stimulus. However, it is not quite that simple because it is impossible to discover and record every such response. Luck, as in the process of serendipity, often plays a role. For example, the discovery of the following schizophrenic-like dependent variable was a most serendipitous event.

The discovery that serotonin is present in the brain was perhaps the most curious turn of the wheel of fate. . . . Several years ago Albert Hofman, a Swiss chemist, had an alarming experience. He had synthesized a new substance, and one afternoon he snuffed some of it up his nose. Thereupon he was assailed with increasingly bizarre feelings and finally with hallucinations. It was six hours before these sensations disappeared. As a reward for thus putting his nose into things, Hofman is credited with the discovery of lysergic acid diethylamide (LSD), which has proved a boon to psychiatrists because with it they can induce schizophrenic-like states at will. (Page, 1957, p. 55)

On the other hand if you have a precise hypothesis, it indicates the dependent variable in which you are interested; it specifies that a certain independent variable will influence a certain dependent variable. You merely select a measure of that dependent variable and test your hypothesis with it. Pavlov's astute observations led him to formulate a specific hypothesis for which salivation was the dependent variable.

Validity of the Dependent Variable

You must be sure that the data you record actually measure the dependent variable specified by your hypothesis. Suppose that Pavlov had measured change of color of his dog's hair? This is a grotesque example, but more subtle errors of the same type occur. To study emotionality as a dependent variable, one might have several judges rate the participants on this behavior. Whatever the results, one should ask whether the judges actually rated emotionality, or did they unknowingly rate some other characteristic such as "general disposition to life," "intelligence," or "personal attractiveness"? This brings us to the first requirement for a dependent variable—it must be *valid*. By **validity** we mean that the data reported are actual measures of the dependent variable as it is operationally defined; that is, *the question of validity is whether the operationally defined dependent variable truly measures that which is specified in the consequent condition of the hypothesis.*

Definitions Are Arbitrary. "Now," you might say, recalling our discussion on operational definitions, "if the experimenter defined emotionality as what the judges reported, then that is by definition emotionality—you can't quarrel with that." And so we can't, at least on the grounds that you offered. We recognize that anyone can define anything any way that they want. You can, if you wish, define the four-legged object with a flat surface from which we eat as "a chair" if you like. Nobody would say that you can't. However, we must ask you to consider a social criterion: Is that the name usually used by other people? If you insist on calling tables "chairs," nobody should call you wrong, for definitions are neither true nor false, only arbitrary. The only criterion of a definition is whether it facilitates communication, and you would be at a distinct disadvantage there. When you invite your dinner guests to be seated on a table and to eat their food from a chair, you will get some quizzical responses, to say the least.

Use of Commonly Accepted Dependent Variables. So the lesson is this: Although you may define your dependent variable as you wish, it is wise to define it as it is customarily used. If there is a certain widely accepted definition for your dependent variable, you should use it (or one that correlates highly with it). A standardized psychometric test could constitute a good operationally defined dependent variable that has demonstrated validity. For instance, the Manifest Anxiety Scale (Taylor, 1953) could be a valid, operationally defined measure of anxiety as a dependent variable. We may only add that other operational definitions of anxiety could lead to different experimental conclusions.

Invalid Dependent Variables. Consider some other examples. Suppose you define your dependent variable as the number of problems of a certain kind solved within a given period of time. If the test has a large number of problems that vary in difficulty, then it may well be valid. But if all the problems are easy, you probably would be measuring reading speed rather than problem-solving ability. That is, regardless of the fact that "problems" are contained in the test, those who read fast would get a high score and those who read slowly would get a low score. This would *not* be a valid measurement of problem-solving ability (unless, of course, problem-solving ability and reading speed are reliably correlated). Or to make the matter even simpler, if you construct a very short test composed of extremely easy problems, all the participants would get a perfect score, unless you are working with retarded individuals. This test is not a valid measure of the dependent variable either.

Say you are interested in whether infants could learn to pull a white versus a black cord in their cribs if you always feed them after they pull the white one. The test is to give them a number of trials with the two choices of a black and a white cord, but the white cord is always on the right. Assume that the preponderance of choices we record are with the white cord. We might conclude that the pulling response was successfully reinforced because the infants chose the color for which they were previously fed. But are we really measuring the extent to which they chose the *white* cord? Infants, like adults,

may be right handed, left handed, or ambidextrous. If we have studied a group of infants who are all right handed, they probably pulled whatever was on the right, here the white cord, regardless of its color. Thus, our measure may simply have been of handedness rather than of the dependent variable in which we are interested. Hence we would have measured frequency of using the preferred hand rather than frequency of choosing the white cord.

Problems of validation of the dependent variable can be tricky, and pitfalls await unwary experimenters. As a minimum, you are now aware of the existence of the problem and potential errors. After considerable reflection and study of previous research in your problem area, you can increase your chances of selecting a valid dependent-variable measure.

Our study of extraneous variables will facilitate your understanding of selection of valid measures. In the foregoing example, the extraneous variable of position of the white and black cords caused an invalid dependent-variable measure.

Reliability of the Dependent Variable

Reliability Defined. The second requirement is that a dependent variable should be reliable. **Reliability** *means the degree to which participants receive about the same scores when repeated measurements of them are taken.* For example, an intelligence test is sufficiently reliable if people make approximately the same score every time they take the test, such as an IQ of 105 the first time, 109 the second, and 102 the third. However, if a typical individual scored 109, 183, and 82, the test could not be considered reliable, for the repeated measurements vary too much.

Determining Reliability of a Dependent Variable. An experimenter could first obtain measures on the dependent variable, preferably from individuals not involved in the experiment; then the same participants would be retested after a period of time and the correlation between the two sets of measures computed. If the correlation is high, the dependent-variable measure is reliable; otherwise, it is not. Another approach would be to compute a split-half reliability coefficient if the dependent variable is a measure that could be divided in half. For instance, if it consists of 20 problems, the experimenter could therefore obtain a total score for the odd-numbered and for the even-numbered problems. A correlation coefficient between these two resulting scores for all the participants would indicate the degree of reliability.

Experimenters frequently study people's behavioral characteristics that change with the passage of time, such as a learning process or the growth of state anxiety. In such a case the correlation of successive scores would be high, providing that the participants maintain about the same rank order of scores on each testing. For example, if three people made scores of 10, 9, and 6 on the first testing and 15, 12, and 10, respectively, on the second testing, the correlation (and therefore reliability) would be high since they maintained the same relative ranks. If, however, their rank order changed, the reliability would be lower. Regardless of whether the measures of the dependent variable change with time, a correlation coefficient can be computed to determine the extent to which the dependent variable is reliable.

Difficulties Encountered. Unfortunately experimenters seldom consider the reliability of their dependent variables; otherwise, we would know a lot more about this important topic. At the same time it is often unrealistic to try to determine reliability. In some situations the dependent variable is more reliable than a computed correlation coefficient would indicate. Sometimes the people studied are too homogeneous to allow the computed correlation value to approach the true value. For instance, if all participants in a learning study had precisely the same ability to learn the task presented them, then (ideally) they would all receive exactly the same dependent-variable scores on successive testings; the computed correla-

tion would not be indicative of the true reliability of the dependent variable. Another reason for a different computed correlation than the true one is that the scale used to measure the dependent variable may have insufficient range. To illustrate again by taking an extreme case, suppose that only one value of the dependent variable were possible. In this event all participants would receive that score, say, 5.0, and the computed correlation would again not be the true one. More realistically, an experimenter might use a five-point scale as a measure of a dependent variable, but the only difference between this one and our absurd example is one of degree. The five-point scale might still be too restrictive in that it does not sufficiently differentiate among true scores; two individuals, for instance, might have true scores of 3.6 and 3.9, but on a scale of five values they would both receive scores of 4.0. Finally, dependent-variable measures sometimes cannot be administered more than once because novelty is one of their critical features, as in studies of problem solving.

The Prevalent Procedure. Recognizing that the determination of reliability is desirable but often not feasible, what do the experimenters do? They plan experiments and collect data. If group means differ reliably, the difference may suggest some tentative conclusions about reliability.

In particular, group means that differ reliably (i.e., more than can be expected by random fluctuations) indicate a sufficiently reliable dependent variable, for lack of reliability makes for only random variation in values. On the other hand, if two groups do not differ reliably, the dependent-variable values are probably due to random (chance) variation. The typical conclusion would then be that variation of the independent variable does not affect the dependent variable. But other reasons are also possible. It may be that the dependent variable is unreliable. So this approach to determining reliability is a one-way affair: *If there are statistically reliable differences among groups, the dependent variable is probably reliable; if there are no significant differences, then no conclusion about its reliability is possible* (at least on this information only). If replications of the experiment yield consistent results repeatedly, certainly the dependent variable is reliable.

In Conclusion. The concepts of validity and reliability have been extensively used by test constructors, yet have been almost totally ignored by experimenters although they are of great importance in experimentation. If you have a totally unreliable dependent variable, then, regardless of experimental conditions, values would vary at random. With all dependent variable values varying in a chaotic manner, it is impossible to determine the effectiveness of the independent variables. If the dependent variable is reliable but not valid, an erroneous conclusion may be reached, e.g., if one performs a learning experiment and the dependent variable actually measures motivation, then obviously any conclusions with regard to learning are baseless. Without a valid and reliable dependent variable, an experiment is worthless.

Multiple Dependent-Variable Measures

Any independent variable may affect several aspects of behavior, and in many experiments a number of measures actually are recorded. For example, measures of the behavior of the infants in the cord-pulling study might include the time that it takes them to pull the cord once the cords are presented to them (response latency), the time that it takes them to complete the pulling response once the response started (response duration), the number of trials required to learn to pull the correct cord during the learning phase, and the number of errors made during the learning and during the test phases. Such an experiment could be regarded as one with four dependent-variable measures, in which case the experimenter might conduct four separate statistical tests to see whether the groups differ on *any* of the four dependent variables. Should this procedure be used, it would be valuable to compute correlations among the several dependent variables. You might find that two of them correlate quite highly, in which case they are measuring largely the same thing. Consequently, there is little point in recording both measures in future experimentation; you could select the easiest with which to work. However, the correlations between your dependent variables should be *quite* high before you eliminate any of them. I once conducted an experiment using three dependent variables and found their correlations to be .70, .60, and .80.[2] Yet there was a reliable difference between groups on only one of the three measures.

Ideally you should measure every dependent variable that might reasonably be affected by your independent variable, although this is obviously not feasible. At least you can try to measure several, which not only would increase your understanding of the behavior you are studying, but would also increase your chances of finding a statistically reliable difference between your groups. In practical research there is a special danger in using only one dependent variable measure. For instance, if you are testing the effectiveness of a method of learning for school children, all important ramifications of the method should be considered. If you measured only amount of time to acquire a skill, other, perhaps more important, considerations might be neglected—for example, effectiveness of a method might become clear only after passage of time.

Multiple Dependent Variable Measures and Fundamental Definitions. If only one dependent variable is measured in an experiment, that operationally defined measure is

---

[2]See Chapter 9 for a discussion of correlation and an interpretation of these numbers. Incidentally, such a correlation should be computed separately for each group in the experiment; that is, one should not combine all participants from all groups and compute a general correlation coefficient (e.g., for two groups, one would compute two correlation coefficients). In your future study be alert to the differences between intra- and interclass correlations.

specific to the particular investigation. Indeed, precise definitions of dependent variables are frequently unique to any given experiment. For example, operational definitions of "response strength" and "anxiety" differ widely in different studies. Furthermore, different measures of them typically correlate poorly with each other. Such specificity no doubt impedes our progress. The use of multiple dependent-variable measures in a single study could help correct this matter. In a single study, for instance, the use of a number of measures of anxiety could help us understand the extent to which each definition of anxiety overlaps with other definitions and to what extent each is independent of others. As a consequence, we could make progress toward establishing general, fundamental definitions. **Fundamental definitions** are general in two senses: They are universally accepted, and they encompass a variety of specific concepts. A fundamental definition of anxiety would encompass several specific definitions, with each specific definition weighted according to how much of the fundamental definition it accounts for.[3] For instance, each definition of anxiety may be an indicator of a generalized, fundamental concept:

fundamental concept of anxiety = $f(\text{anxiety}_1, \text{anxiety}_2, \ldots, \text{anxiety}_N)$

Thus in any experiment, by simultaneously measuring several indicators of a concept by several different dependent variables, their interrelationships can be studied in order to advance toward the development of the fundamental concept. Eventually, it could be possible to then form a direct measure of the fundamental concept itself as a single dependent variable measure. The problem of which measure of anxiety, or whatever, would then be solved and the criticism of the specificity of operational definitions could be eliminated.

Growth Measures

In psychology, experimenters often measure variables that change with time, as in learning studies. For example, we may be interested in how a skill grows with repeated practice with two different methods. Frequently a statistical test is conducted on terminal data, that is, data obtained on only the last trial during learning. However, the learning curves of the two groups could provide considerable information about how the two methods led to their terminal points; participants using one method might have been "slower starters" but gained more rapidly at the end. Such growth measures of behavior can be more extensively studied with a statistical technique known as *trend analysis*. Trend analysis allows you to compare learning curves, for instance, at specific points or even in their entirety. In your future studies you may want to be alert to trend analysis, which is also related to experimental designs in which there are repeated measures on the same participants (Chapter 9).

Delayed Measures

Another important question concerns the retention of experimental effects. For example, one method might lead to better learning than does a second, but is that advantage maintained over a period of time? Suppose you use one method to train mechanics for a highly technical job following which another researcher trains them on a different job. Since the mechanics will not use your training for awhile, you would be interested not only in whether the first method is the more efficient for learning but also in whether that method leads to the best retention. In an experiment you might have the trainees return to you for another test just before they started their on-job duty. Such a delayed test would indicate which of the two methods is superior in the long run.

Delayed measures are especially im-

---

[3]The amount of the fundamental definition accounted for by a specific one is determined in turn by the amount of extraneous variation from which it is free and by its independence from other components or indicators.

portant in the evaluation of educational curricula. Evaluations of instructors also often change and might be improved if taken some years after graduation. Unfortunately researchers seldom take delayed measures of their experimental effects, even when such a practice would be quite easy for them.

TYPES OF EMPIRICAL RELATIONSHIPS IN PSYCHOLOGY

Having specified two subclasses of independent variables—stimulus and organismic—and having elaborated on the nature of dependent variable measures, we now turn to relationships among these classes of variables. There are two principal classes of empirical laws involving independent variables: (1) stimulus-response relationships which result from the use of the experimental method and (2) organismic-response laws which are derived from the use of the method of systematic observation.

Stimulus-Response Laws

This type of law states that a certain response class is a function of a certain stimulus class and may be symbolized as $R = f(S)$. To establish an S-R law, a given stimulus is systematically varied as the independent variable to determine whether a given response (the dependent variable) also changes in a lawful manner. In a study, for instance, we might vary lighting conditions on a given object to see if a person's verbal report of its size changes (the response measure).

Organismic-Behavioral Laws

This type of relationship asserts that a response class is a function of a class of organismic variables, which is symbolized $R = f(O)$. Research seeking to establish this kind of law aims to determine whether certain characteristics of an organism are associated with certain types of responses. We might wonder, for instance, if people who are short

and stout behave differently than do people who are tall and thin. Using the method of systematic observation, we could collect two such groups of people and compare them on degree of happiness, general emotionality, or amount of verbosity.

The Mathematical Statement of Laws

The form $R = f(S)$ follows directly from our statement of hypothesized relationships between independent and dependent variables. As shown in Chapter 3, this mathematical statement is a special case of the more general "if a, then b" relationship. We should add that more complex relationships than these may also be sought, as for instance, those that would occur if you investigated the relationship among two stimuli and a given response [$R = f(S_1S_2)$], or among a stimulus, response, and organismic variable [$R = f(O, S)$].

A Note Of Caution. Our efforts to formulate powerful stimulus-response laws can be successful, however, only if we adequately control the extraneous variables that are always present in any psychological investigation. We shall note that our formulation of organismic-behavioral laws will always be tainted because of the impossibility of controlling all extraneous variables in formulating them. Similarly, extraneous variables are never controlled in correlational research, so that we never know which causal factors are influential in correlational relationships.

THE NATURE OF EXPERIMENTAL CONTROL

The strength of civilization is based, at rock bottom, on the amount and kinds of reliable knowledge that have been accumulated. But the progress has been slow and painfully achieved, often retarded by great wars and other disasters. Within this perspective we should be proud of our achievements—of the stories of the acquisition of knowledge and of the development of sound methods for acquiring that knowledge. Among the most striking advances in methodology was the recognition of the necessity for "normal" control conditions against which to evaluate experimental treatments.

To reach this relatively advanced stage, methodologists probably engaged in considerable trial and error wherein there were a number of improperly controlled investigations. Even these "semiexperiments" should be admired, for they were imaginative indeed. One example is ". . . Herodotus' quaint account of the experiment in linguistics made by Psammetichos, King of Egypt (*Historiae* II, 2). To determine which language was the oldest, Psammetichos arranged to have two infants brought up without hearing human speech and to have their first utterances recorded. When a clear record of the children's speech had been obtained, ambassadors were sent around the world to find out where this language was spoken (specifically, where the word for "bread" was *bekos*). As a result of his experiment, Psammetichos pronounced Phrygian to be the oldest language, though he had assumed it was Egyptian before making the test" (Jones, 1964, p. 419).

A more sophisticated, but still ancient, investigation *did* include a control condition: "Athenaeus, in his *Feasting Philosophers* (*Deiphosophistae*, III, 84–85), describes how it was discovered that citron was an antidote for poison. It seems that a magistrate in Egypt had sentenced a group of convicted criminals to be executed by exposing them to poisonous snakes in the theater. It was reported back to him that, though the sentence had been duly carried out and all the criminals were bitten, none of them had died. The magistrate at once commenced an inquiry. He learned that when the criminals were being conducted into the theater, a market woman out of pity had given them some citron to eat. The next day, on the hypothesis that it was the citron that had saved them, the magistrate had the group divided into pairs and ordered citron fed to one of a pair but not to the other. When the two were exposed to the snakes a second time, the one that had eaten the citron suffered no harm,

the other died instantly. The experiment was repeated many times and in this way (says Anthenaeus) the efficacy of citron as an antidote for poison was firmly established" (Jones, 1964, p. 419). In such ways the logic of experimental control developed, slowly leading to our present level of methodological sophistication.

The problem of controlling variables, a critical phase in the planning and conduct of experiments, requires particular vigilance. To start, the word "control" implies that the experimenter has a certain power over the conditions of an experiment; that power is to manipulate variables systematically in an effort to arrive at a sound empirical conclusion. Let us illustrate by using the previous pharmacological example.

Independent-Variable Control

First, the magistrate exercised control over his independent variable by producing the event that he wished to study. This, the first sense of the word "control," is *when the independent variable is varied in a known and specified manner*. Here the independent variable was the amount of citron administered, and it was *purposively* varied in two ways: zero and some positive amount.

Extraneous-Variable Control

The second sense of *control* was when the magistrate sought to determine whether variation of amount of citron administered to the poisoned men would affect their impending state of inanimation (certainly a clear-cut dependent-variable measure, if ever there was one). To find out whether these two variables were related, however, one should ask about other (extraneous) variables that also might have affected the men's degree of viability. If there were such, the relationship that the magistrate sought might have been hidden from him. Some substance in the men's breakfast, for instance, might have been an antidote; the men might have been members of a snake cult and thereby developed an immunity;

and so forth. In the absence of knowledge of such extraneous variables, it was necessary to assume that they might have affected the dependent variable. Hence their possible effects were controlled; that is, the magistrate formed two equivalent groups and administered citron to only one. In this way the two groups presumably were equated with regard to all extraneous variables so that their only difference was that one received the hypothesized antidote. The fact that only members of the group that received citron survived ruled out further consideration of the extraneous variables. With this control effected, the magistrate obtained the relationship that he sought, and our second sense of "control" is illustrated: *Extraneous variable control* is *the regulation of extraneous variables.*

An extraneous variable is one that operates in the experimental situation in addition to the independent variable. Since it might affect the dependent variable, and since we are not immediately interested in ascertaining whether it does affect the dependent variable, it must be regulated so that it will not mask the possible effect of the independent variable.

Prevent Confounding of Variables. Failing to control adequately extraneous variables results in a **confounded** experiment, a disastrous consequence for the experimenter; that is, if an extraneous variable is allowed to operate systematically in an uncontrolled manner, it and the independent variable are confounded. Consequently, the dependent variable is not free from irrelevant influences. Suppose, for example, that those who received citron had been served a different breakfast than had the control participants. In this case the magistrate would not know whether it was citron or something in the breakfast of the experimental group that was the antidote—type of breakfast would thus have been an extraneous variable that was confounded with the independent variable. Confounding occurs where there is an extraneous variable that is systematically related to the independent variable, and it *may*

act on the dependent variable; hence the extraneous variable may affect the dependent-variable scores of one group, but not the other. If confounding is present, then the reason that any change occurs in the dependent variable cannot be ascribed to the independent variable.

In Summary. *Confounding occurs when an extraneous variable is systematically related to the independent variable, and it might differentially affect the dependent-variable values of the two or more groups in the investigation.* This is an important definition, and you should commit it to memory. Especially note the word *differentially.* If variation of the independent variable is systematically accompanied by variation of an extraneous variable, and if the dependent variable values for the groups differ, the dependent variable is differentially affected; consequently that extraneous variable is confounded with the independent variable.

A Psychological Example. To illustrate further these two senses of "control," and also to get closer to home, consider the question of whether vitamin A affects visual abilities. The independent variable is the amount of vitamin A administered, and the dependent variable is the number of letters that can be seen on a chart. To exercise control of the independent variable, assume that one group receives three units of vitamin A, a second group five units, while a control group receives a placebo but no vitamin A. To illustrate extraneous variable control, note that lighting conditions for the test are relevant to the number of letters that the participants can correctly report. Suppose, for example, that the test is taken in a room in which the amount of light varies throughout the day and further that group 1 is run mainly in the morning, group 2 around noon, and group 3 in the afternoon. In this case some participants would take the test when there is good light; others, when it is poor. The test scores might then primarily reflect the lighting conditions rather than the amount of vitamin A administered; in that case the possible effects of vitamin A would be masked. Put another way, the amount of lighting and amount of vitamin A would be confounded. Lack of control over this extraneous variable would leave us in a situation in which we do not know which variable or combination of variables is responsible for influencing our dependent variable.

Just to develop this point briefly, consider some of the possibilities when light is the only uncontrolled extraneous variable. Assume that the value of the dependent variable increases as the amount of vitamin A increases—that is, the group receiving the five-unit dose has the highest dependent-variable score, the three-unit group is next, and the zero-unit group has the lowest test score. What may we conclude about the effect of vitamin A on the dependent variable? Since light is uncontrolled, it may actually be the factor that influences the dependent-variable scores. Or perhaps uncontrolled lighting has a detrimental effect such that, if it were held constant, the effects of vitamin A would be even more pronounced—for example, if the five-unit group received a score of 10, it might have received a score of 20 if light had been controlled. Another possibility is that the light has no effect, in which case our results could be accepted as valid. But since we do not know this, we cannot reach such a conclusion. When an independent variable is confounded with an extraneous variable, there is necessarily ambiguity in interpreting its effects. However, when there is more than one confounded extraneous variable, the situation is nearer total chaos.

In Summary. Experimental control is the direct, intentional regulation of experimental variables, of which there are two classes: independent and extraneous. (The dependent variable is another class which we seek to control indirectly by exercising independent variable control.) Through extraneous-variable control, one regulates the extraneous variables—other variables that may influence the behavior of the participants—to prevent confounding. If extraneous-vari-

able control is adequate, an unambiguous statement on the causal relationship between the independent and dependent variables can be made. If extraneous-variable control is inadequate, however, the conclusion must be tempered. The extent to which it must be tempered depends on a number of factors, but, frequently inadequate extraneous-variable control leads to no conclusion whatsoever concerning a causal relationship.

Two Kinds of Control of the Independent Variable

We have said that control of the independent variable occurs when the researcher varies the independent variable in a known and specified manner. There are essentially two ways in which an investigator may exercise control of the independent variable: (1) *purposive variation (manipulation) of the variable*, and (2) *selection of the desired values of the variable from a number of values that already exist.* When purposive manipulation is used, an *experiment* is being conducted, but selection is used, in **the method of systematic observation**. If you are interested in whether the intensity of a stimulus affects the rate of conditioning, you might vary intensity in two ways—high and low. If the stimulus is a light, such values as 2 and 20 candle power might be chosen. You would, then, at random: (1) assign the sample of participants to two groups, and (2) randomly determine which group would receive the low-intensity stimulus, which one the high. In this case you are *purposely varying (manipulating* the independent variable (this is an experiment). The decision as to what values of the independent variable to study and, more important, which group receives which value is *entirely up to you.* Perhaps equally important, you also "create" the values of the independent variable.

To illustrate *control of the independent variable by selection of values* as they already exist (the method of systematic observation), consider the effect of intelligence on problem solving. Assume that the researcher is not interested in studying the effects of minor differences of intelligence but wants to study widely differing values of this variable, such as an IQ of 135, a second of 100, and a third of 65. Up to this point the procedures for the two types of control of the independent variables are the same; the investigator determines what values of the variables are to be studied.

However, in this case, the investigator must find certain groups that have the desired values of intelligence. To do this one might administer intelligence tests at three different institutions. First, one might study bright college students to obtain a group with an average IQ of 135. Second, one might choose a rather nonselective group such as high school students or army personnel for an average value of 100. Third, one might find a special institution that would yield a group with an average IQ of 65. With these three groups constructed, a test of problem-solving ability would be administered and the appropriate conclusion reached. Observe that the values of the independent variable have been selected from a large population. *The IQs of the people tested determined who would be the participants. The researcher has not, as in the experimental example, determined which participants would receive which value of the independent variable.* In selection it is thus the other way around: *the value of the independent variable determines which participants will be used.* It is apparent that in independent variable control by selection of values as they already exist in participants, *the participants are not randomly assigned to groups*—this is a critical shortcoming of the method of systematic observation.

Furthermore it is not really practical to predetermine precise IQ values, as in our example. What the researcher is more likely to do is to say, "I want a very high intelligence group, a medium group, and a very low intelligence group," then settle for whatever IQs are obtained—in this case the averages might be 127, 109, and 72, which would probably still accomplish this particular purpose.

In Summary. **Purposive manipulation** of an independent variable occurs when the investigator determines the values of the independent variable, "creates" those values, and determines which group will receive which value. Independent variable control through selection occurs when the investigator chooses participants who already possess the desired values of the independent variable.

Confounding in the Method of Systematic Observation. The distinction between both ways of controlling the independent variable is important. To emphasize this, consider what would be the investigator's appropriate conclusion in the intelligence problem-solving example. Consider the *confounding* in this investigation. We have three groups who differ in intelligence. But in what other respects might they differ? The possibilities are so numerous that we shall list only three: socioeconomic status, the degree of stimulation of their environments, and motivation to solve problems. Hence, whatever the results on the problem-solving tests, there is atrocious confounding of our independent variable with extraneous variables. We would not know to which variable, or combination of variables, to attribute possible differences in dependent-variable scores. This is not so with an experiment like our light-conditioning example. In that experiment, whatever the extraneous variables might be, their effects would be randomized out—distributed equally—over all groups.

When a stimulus variable is the independent variable, purposive manipulation is used. If the independent variable is an organismic variable, however, selection is the independent-variable control procedure. For example, with intelligence (or number of years of schooling, or chronic anxiety, and so on) as the independent variable, we have no practical alternative but to select participants with the desired values. It might be possible to manipulate purposively some of these variables, but the idea is impractical. It is admittedly difficult, say, to raise a person in such a way (manipulating the environment or administering various drugs) that the person will have an IQ of the desired value; we doubt that you would try to do this.

A number of studies have been conducted to determine whether cigarette smoking is related to lung cancer. The paradigm, essentially, has been to compare people who do not smoke with those who do. The independent variable is thus the degree of smoking. Measures of the dependent variable are then taken—frequency of occurrence of lung cancer. The results have been generally decisive in that smokers more frequently acquire lung cancer than do nonsmokers. Nobody can argue with this statement. However, the additional statement is frequently made: Therefore, we may conclude that smoking causes lung cancer. On the basis of the evidence presented, such a statement is unfounded, for the type of control of the independent variable that has been used is that of selection of values.[4] Additional variables may be confounded with the independent variable. In fact quite serious researchers have held that people who are predisposed to have lung cancer more frequently acquire the smoking habit, thus reversing the casual relationship.

The only behavioral approach to determine the cause-effect relationship is to exercise control through purposive manipulation, that is, to select at random a group who have never been exposed to the smoking habit (e.g., children or isolated cultural groups), randomly divide them into two groups, and randomly determine which group will be smokers and which the abstainers. Of course, the experimenter must make sure that they adhere to these instructions over a long period. As members of the two groups acquire lung cancer, the accumulation of this evidence would decide the question. While this experiment will probably never be conducted, the main point of this discussion is emphasized: Confounding oc-

curs when selection of independent-variable values is used (the method of systematic observation) but can be prevented when purposive manipulation through experimentation is properly employed. To highlight this difference we refer to "normal" groups of participants as *control* groups in an experiment, but in the method of systematic observation they are **comparison groups**.

The use of "control groups" immediately tells you that an experiment was conducted. Reference to "comparison groups" indicates that the method of systematic observation was used.

EXTRANEOUS VARIABLES

At any given moment a fantastically large number of stimuli impinge on an organism, all of which affect behavior, if only in some subtle way. But in any given experiment we are usually only interested in whether one stimulus class affects one class of responses. Hence, for this immediate purpose, we would like to eliminate from consideration all other variables. If this were possible, we could conclude that any change in our dependent variable is due only to the variation of our independent variable.

However, if these other (extraneous) variables are allowed to influence our dependent variable, any change in our dependent variable could not be ascribed to variation of our independent variable. *We would not know which of the numerous variables caused the change.* To control the experimental situation so that these other extraneous variables can be dismissed from further consideration, we must first identify them. Since it would be an endless task to list all the variables that *might* affect the behavior of an organism, we must limit our question: Of those variables, which are likely to affect our dependent variable? Although still a difficult question, we can immediately eliminate many possibilities. For example, if we are studying a learning process, we would not even consider such variables as color of the

---

[4]However, the relevant research does not deny a causal relationship. In fact one is quite likely, so the wise person, considering the mathematical expectancy, would want to bet that smoking does cause cancer.

chair in which the participant sits or brand of pencil used. Our list of extraneous variables to be considered could start with our literature survey. We can thus study previous experiments to find out which variables have influenced our dependent variable and note which extraneous variables previous experimenters have controlled. Discussion sections of earlier articles may include variables recommended for future consideration. In these ways, and after considerable reflection concerning other variables, we can list extraneous variables that should be considered.

Specifying Extraneous Variables to Be Controlled

Of these potentially relevant extraneous variables, we must next decide which should be controlled, that is, variables that probably will affect our dependent variable. These are the variables to which the techniques of control soon to be discussed need to be applied. It is sufficient for now to state the end result—the changes in the dependent variable will be ascribed to the independent variable rather than to the controlled extraneous variables. After considering this and the following steps, we shall illustrate all steps with an example.

Specifying Extraneous Variables That Cannot Reasonably Be Controlled

A simple answer to the question of which of the specified extraneous variables should be controlled is that we should control all of them. Although that *might* be possible, it would be too expensive in terms of time, effort, and money. For example, suppose that the variation in temperature during experimental sessions is two degrees. Although possible to control, it probably would not affect your dependent variable. The game is probably "not worth the candle," particularly when you consider the large number of other variables in the same category. With the limited amount of energy and resources available, the experimenter should seek to control only those major variables that are potentially relevant.

The Effectiveness of Randomization. But what if these minor variables might accumulate to have a rather major effect on the dependent variable, thus invalidating the experiment? Even if its effect is not great, should even a minor extraneous variable be allowed to influence the dependent variable? If the experimenter is not going to control some variables, what can be done about them? In thinking about these points, we must remember that there will always be a large number of variables in this category. The question is, will they affect one of our groups to a greater extent than another? If they do not *differentially* affect our groups, then our worries are lessened. We can assume that such variables will "randomize out," that, in the long run, they will affect our groups equally. If it is reasonable to make this assumption, then this type of variable should not delay us further. When we later discuss *randomization* as a technique of control, we will elaborate on this.

When to Abandon an Experiment

Up to this point we have been optimistic, assuming that we can control all the important relevant variables so that their effects are essentially equal on all groups. If this assumption is unreasonable, then the experimenter should consider the possibility of abandoning the experiment. Even if one is not sure on this point, perhaps it would be best *not* to conduct it. Sometime after assessing the various control problems, the experimenter must ascertain what will be gained by going ahead. In cases of inadequate extraneous variable control, the answer need not be that nothing will be gained; it may be that further insight or beneficial information will be acquired concerning the control problem. But one should realize that this *is* the situation and be realistic in understanding that it may be better to discontinue the project.

Techniques of Control

Although experimenters try to exercise adequate experimental control, sometimes a crucial, uncontrolled extraneous variable is discovered only after the data are compiled. Short-comings in control are found even in published experiments. Certainly, confounds that can elude the experimenter, the editor, and the journal consultants are quite subtle. Furthermore, errors of control are not the sole property of young experimenters; they may be found in the work of some of the most respected and established psychologists. How can we reduce them?

After giving much thought to potential errors, after checking and rechecking yourself, you might obtain critiques from colleagues. An "outsider" probably has a different mind set and might see something that you missed. This is an important point! A scientist calls on colleagues to check steps of an experiment from beginning to end, including reading drafts of the write-up. Early in their careers students should learn to help each other in such ways, too. It is amazing to note that some students don't even bother to read their papers over for corrections before "handing them in."

After an important extraneous variable is specified, how is it to be controlled? What techniques are available for regulating it so that the effects of the independent variable on the dependent variable can be clearly isolated? The following common techniques illustrate major principles that can be applied to a wide variety of specific control problems.

1. Elimination. The most desirable way to control extraneous variables is simply to eliminate them from the experimental situation. For example, some laboratories are sound deadened and opaque to eliminate extraneous noises and lights. In fact, architects and university administrators are often dismayed to find that psychologists design their laboratory buildings with no windows, making them "unusual" in appearance on campuses. Even so, most extraneous variables cannot be eliminated. In the previous example of the effect of vitamin A on ability to read letters, the extraneous variable was the amount of lighting. Obviously light is needed to read. Other extraneous variables that one would have a hard time eliminating are gender, age, and intelligence.

2. Constancy of Conditions. Extraneous variables that cannot be eliminated might be held constant throughout the experiment. The same value of it is thus present for all participants. Perhaps the time of day is an important variable in that people perform better on the dependent variable in the morning than in the afternoon. To hold time of day constant, all participants might be studied at about the same hour on successive days. Although amount of fatigue would not really be held constant for all participants on all days, this procedure would certainly help.

Another example of this technique would be to hold the lighting conditions constant in our vitamin A chart-reading experiment. Thus we might simply pull down the blinds in the experimental room and have the same light turned on for all participants.

One of the standard applications of the technique of holding conditions constant is to conduct experimental sessions in the same room. Thus, whatever might be the influence of the particular characteristics of the room (gaiety, odors, color of the walls and furniture, location), it would be the same for all participants. In like manner, to hold various organismic variables constant (educational level, sex, age), we would select participants with the characteristics that we want, for example, they all have completed the eighth grade and no more, all are male, or all are 50 years old.

Many aspects of the experimental procedure are held constant, such as instructions to participants. The experimenters thus read precisely the same set of instructions to all participants (except as modified for different experimental conditions). But even the same words might be read with different intonations and emphases, in spite of the experimenter's efforts at constancy. For more precise control, some experimenters present standardized instructions with a tape recorder.

Procedurally, all participants should go through the same steps in the same order. For instance, if the steps are to greet the participants, seat them, read instructions, attach blindfolds, start the task, and so on, then one would not want to blindfold some participants *before* the instructions were read and others *afterward*. The attitude of the experimenter should also be held as constant as possible for all participants. If one is jovial with one participant and gruff with another, confounding of experimenter attitude with the independent variable would occur. The experimenter can practice the experimental procedure until it becomes so routine that each participant can be treated in mechanical fashion. The same experimenter usually collects all of the data, but if different experimenters are used unsystematically, a serious error may result. In one experiment, for instance, an experimenter ran rats for 14 days but was absent on the fifteenth day. The rats' performance for that day was sufficiently atypical to warrant the conclusion that different methods of picking them up was responsible for the change, not the experimental treatment.

The apparatus for administering the experimental treatment and for recording the results should be the same for all participants. Suppose, for example, that two different carousel projectors are used to present stimuli, one for the experimental group and the other for the control group. If that for one group is faster or more noisy, or projects a sharper image, confounding would result. The technique of constancy of conditions dictates that all participants use the same carousel projector, recording apparatus or other equipment.

3. Balancing. When it is not feasible to hold constant conditions, the experimenter may balance out the effect of extraneous variables. **Balancing** may be used in two situations: (1) where one is unable to identify the extraneous variables, and (2) where they *can* be identified and one takes special steps to control them.

Balancing for Unspecified Extraneous Variables. Consider an experiment to determine whether a prolonged period of training in rifle firing increased the steadiness with which soldiers held their weapons. Previous research had indicated that the steadier a rifle was held, the more accurate was the shooting. Thus, if you could increase steadiness through rifle training, you *might* thereby increase rifle accuracy. Tests for rifle steadiness were given before and after rifle training in a pretest-posttest design. As we can see in Table 4-1, steadiness scores increased suggesting that training does increase steadiness.

However, another set of data from a control group that did not receive rifle training, changes the picture. From Table 4-2 we can see that, not only did the steadiness scores of the untrained group also increase, but that they increased more than those of the trained group. To conclude that rifle training is the variable responsible for the increase in scores, the experimental group had to show a significantly greater increase than did the control group. Thus, rifle training

TABLE 4-1 Mean Steadiness Scores of Soldiers before and after Rifle Training

Before Training		After Training
64.61	Training period	105.74

TABLE 4-2 Mean Steadiness Score of Trained and Untrained Groups

	Before Training		*After Training*
Trained (experimental) groups	64.61	Training period	105.74
Untrained (control) group	73.39	No training period	129.67

was *not* the reason for the increase in steadiness. Other variables must have operated to produce that change—variables that operated on both groups. The point is that *whatever the variables, they were controlled by the technique of balancing* (i.e., their effects on the trained group were balanced out—equalized by—the use of the control group). Relevant extraneous variables affected both groups equally. But we may speculate about these extraneous variables. For example, the rifle training was given during the first two weeks of the soldiers' army life. Perhaps the drop in scores merely reflected a general adjustment to initial emotional impacts. Or the soldiers could have learned enough about the steadiness test in the first session to improve their performance in the second (a practice effect). Whatever the extraneous variables, the effects were controlled (balanced) by the use of the control group.

The logic is that if the groups are treated in the same way except with regard to the independent variable, then any dependent-variable difference between them is ascribable to the independent variable (at least in the long run). Thus we need not specify all of the relevant extraneous variables. For instance, suppose that there are three unknown extraneous variables operating on the experimental group in addition to the independent variable. Their effects can be balanced out by allowing them to operate also on the control group. Therefore the independent variable is the only one that can differentially influence the two groups (Figure 4-1).

More Than One Control Group To Evaluate an Extraneous Variable. Several control groups can be used to evaluate the influence of extraneous variables, to analyze the total situation into its parts. Suppose that we are interested in the effect of extraneous variable 1 of Figure 4-1. To evaluate it we need only add an additional control group that receives a zero value of it, as illustrated in Figure 4-2. Extraneous variable 1 possibly influences the dependent variable for the experimental group and control group 1. Since this variable is not operating for control group 2, a comparison of the two *control* groups indicates the effect of extraneous variable 1. Consider one of the extraneous variables that was operating in the rifle

FIGURE 4-1 Representation of the use of the control group as a technique of balancing.

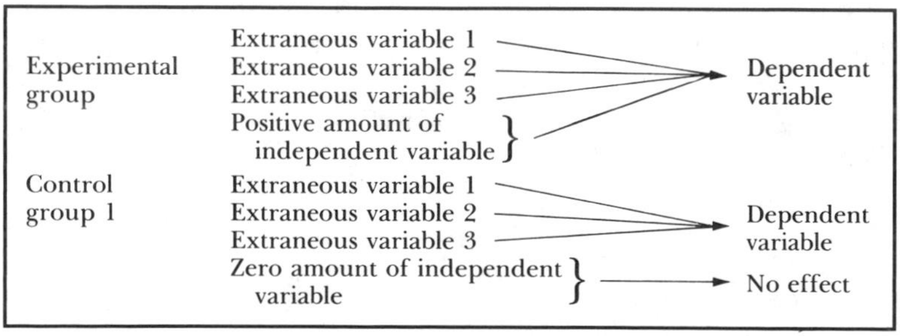

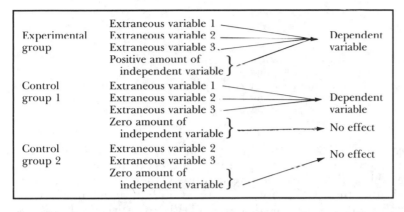

FIGURE 4-2 The use of a second control group to evaluate the effect of an extraneous variable.

steadiness experiment: practice in the test situation (acquaintance with testing procedure, learning how to hold the rifle, and so on).

For instance, to assess the effect of practice, we add a second control group that does not take the initial steadiness test. Thus, Table 4-3 illustrates the pretest-posttest design as in Table 4-2, except for the addition of the second control group. A comparison of the steadiness scores of the two untrained groups after training should indicate any effect of the initial test. If, for instance, control group 2 is less steady than control group 1 on the second test, the first test increases steadiness.

Balancing To Control a Known Extraneous Variable. Consider the need to control the sex (gender) variable. The simplest procedure, obviously, is to use only males or only females. However, if you study only one gender you cannot safely generalize your results to the other gender. If, then, you use

both genders, you need to balance the gender variable over the two groups. To balance out gender, you merely assign an equal number of each sex to each group. Thus, if gender is relevant to the dependent variable, its effects would be the same for each experimental condition. Similarly, one could control the age of the participants by assigning an equal number of each age classification to each group. The same holds true for an apparatus variable. Suppose that two experimental instruments are to be used to save time. They may or may not have slight differences, but to make sure that this variable is controlled, half of the participants in each group should use each instrument. Thus, whatever the differences in the instruments, their respective effects on the dependent variable would be the same for both groups. Similarly, if two experimenters collect data, the experimenter variable needs to be balanced across conditions. For this, each experimenter collects data from an equal number of participants in each group.

TABLE 4-3 Possible Experimental Design for Also Assessing the Effect of Practice on the First Steadiness Test

	Receive Test before Training?	*Receive Training?*	*Receive Test after Training?*
Trained (experimental) group	yes	yes	yes
Untrained (control) group 1	yes	no	yes
Untrained (control) group 2	no	no	yes

TABLE 4-4   A Design in Which Experimenters and Gender Are Simultaneously Balanced

Group I	Group II
15 males—experimenter 1	15 males—experimenter 1
15 males—experimenter 2	15 males—experimenter 2
15 females—experimenter 1	15 females—experimenter 1
15 females—experimenter 2	15 females—experimenter 2

Balancing Two Extraneous Variables Simultaneously. Suppose that you wish to control two extraneous variables through balancing. For instance, if you study two genders and have two experimenters collect data, the balancing arrangement could be that of Table 4-4. One group could then receive the experimental treatment while the other would be the control group.

As a final example, say that our purpose is to determine how well rats retain a black-white discrimination learned in a T maze. We have trained them always to run to a black goal box where they are fed, with no food in the white box. After a number of trials they run consistently to the black box, avoiding the white box. We then measure retention after three months' absence from the maze and find that they still run to the black box. Have they remembered well? Our conclusion should not be hasty. For we know that rats are nocturnal animals and prefer dark places over light ones. In particular they prefer black goal boxes over white ones *before any training*. Hence it is possible that they would go more frequently to the black box on the test trials *regardless of the previous training* and thus may not have "remembered" anything. For this reason we need to balance the colors of the reward boxes. To do this we train half our animals to run to the black box for food and half to run to the white box for food.[5] If, on the test trials, the animals trained to go to white show a preference for white, we would have more

confidence that they retained the discrimination, for regardless of the color to which they were trained, they retained the habit over the three-month period. The effect of color could not be the variable that influenced their behavior.

4. Counterbalancing. In some experiments each participant serves under two or more different experimental conditions; e.g., to determine whether a stop sign should be painted red or yellow, we might measure reaction times to them. Suppose that we present the red sign, then the yellow, and find that reaction time is less to the yellow one. Do we now recommend yellow stop signs to the traffic bureau? Since the participants were first exposed to the red sign their reaction time included learning to operate the experimental apparatus and adapting to the experimental situation. Then they were exposed to the yellow sign. Hence their lower reaction time to yellow might merely reflect practice and adaptation effects rather than effect of color—color of sign and amount of practice are confounded. To control the extraneous variable of amount of practice, we can use the method of **counterbalancing**. For this, half the participants react to the yellow sign first and the red sign second, whereas the other half would experience the red sign first and the yellow sign second (see Table 4-5).

The general principle of counterbalancing is that in repeated treatment experiments, *each condition* (e.g., color of sign) *must be presented to each participant an equal number of times, and each condition must occur an equal number of times at each practice session. Furthermore, each condition must precede and follow all other conditions an equal number of times.*

---

[5] Also, we randomly alternate the positions (right and left) of the white and black boxes to assure that the animals are not learning mere position habits, such as always turning right.

TABLE 4-5 Counterbalancing to Control an Extraneous Variable

Number of Participants	Experimental Session (Order Number)	
	First	Second
One-half of participants	Present yellow sign	Present red sign
One-half of participants	Present red sign	Present yellow sign

For instance, in Table 4-5 we can note that each color of sign was presented an equal number of times to each participant and that the yellow and red sign occurred an equal number of times in both practice sessions; furthermore the yellow sign preceded and followed the red sign and equal number of times just as the red sign preceded and followed the yellow sign and equal number of times.

Any Number of Experimental Conditions Can Be Counterbalanced. For instance, if we have three colors of signs (red, R; yellow, Y; and green, G), one-sixth of the participants would react to each order specified in Table 4-6. To see how the requirements for counterbalancing the effects of three variables are satisfied, note that each color of sign is presented twice at each session, that each participant receives each color once, and

TABLE 4-6 A Counterbalanced Design for Three Independent Variables

Number of Participants	Experimental Session (Order Number)		
	First	Second	Third
1. One-sixth of participants	R	Y	G
2. One-sixth of participants	R	G	Y
3. One-sixth of participants	Y	R	G
4. One-sixth of participants	Y	G	R
5. One-sixth of participants	G	R	Y
6. One-sixth of participants	G	Y	R

that each color precedes and follows each other color twice. Accordingly, a minimum of six participants are required, with any multiple of six sufficing (12, 18, and so on).

Controlling Order Effect. Counterbalancing is designed to meet a problem created when there is more than one experimental session—that is, when the participants' performance might improve due to practice—but there can also be a decrement in performance due to fatigue. The method of counterbalancing is designed to distribute these practice and fatigue effects equally over all conditions. Hence, whatever their effect, (called **order effects**), they influence behavior under each condition equally since each condition occurs equally often at each stage of practice.

The Problem of Differential Transference. However, in using counterbalancing one assumes that the effect of presenting one variable before a second is the same as presenting the second before the first—for example, that the practice effects of responding to the red sign first are the same as for responding to the yellow sign first. This might not be the case, so that seeing the red sign first might induce a greater practice (or fatigue) effect, possibly leading to erroneous conclusions. More generally, counterbalanced designs entail the assumption that there is no differential (asymmetrical) transfer between conditions. **Differential transfer** means that *the transfer from condition 1* (when it occurs first) *to condition 2 is different from the transfer from condition 2* (when it occurs first) *to condition 1.* If this assumption is not justified, there will be difficulties in the statistical analysis (in particular, there will be interactions among order and treatment variables, a concept that will be discussed later in the book). For example, in a study of the effects of air pressure on card-sorting behavior, one group of men first sorted cards when the pressure surrounding them was elevated. They then sorted cards at a normal pressure. A second group of men experienced the normal condition first, followed by the elevated condition. Many slow responses occurred for the first group of men under the elevated condition, as you might expect. But when they sorted cards under normal pressure, these men made almost as many slow responses as they did under the elevated condition. The second group, on the other hand, made a fewer number of slow responses under normal pressure and made almost the same number of slow responses when they shifted. In other words, card-sorting behavior (the dependent variable) was influenced by the *order* of presenting the experimental conditions. As a result, when the results for the first and second sessions were combined, the effect of variation of pressure was obscured, and the statistical test indicated (erroneously) that it was not a reliable effect. In general, *differential transfer reduces the recorded difference between two conditions*, but it may also exaggerate the difference. The lesson, then, is that if you use counterbalancing as a technique of control, you should examine your data for asymmetrical transfer effects.

To see how to do that, assume that those who received condition A first obtained a score of 5 on the dependent variable. Then, when subjected to the second condition B, they received a value of 7. Conversely, the other half of the participants received dependent variable values of 3 for condition B and 5 for A. We can see in the left of Table 4-7 that the difference for both groups was the same, namely. 2. In this case, transfer was symmetrical—there was no differential transfer. The effect of going from the first condition to the second was the same for both groups, regardless of whether A or B occurred first. On the other hand, suppose that the differences were 2 and 4 as shown

in the right side of Table 4-7. Now half the participants increased their scores by 4 instead of 2. Clearly, there was asymmetrical transfer in this second example.

In the first example where transfer was symmetrical, it would be legitimate to combine the values for A and compare them with the values for B. That is, you could sum 5 plus 5 and compare those values to 3 plus 7. However, where there was asymmetrical transfer, we would not combine the results for A and compare them with B. You would want to treat them separately with the qualification that the effect of having B occur first and A second was greater than the effect of going from A first to B second.

Balancing Is Not Counterbalancing. Students sometimes confuse *balancing* and *counterbalancing*, perhaps because they are both techniques of control with "balancing" in common for their names. A little reflection should eliminate such confusion: *Counterbalancing* is used when each participant receives more than one treatment (AB or BA) and the purpose is to distribute order effects (fatigue, practice) equally over all experimental conditions (as in Table 4-5). In *balancing* each participant receives only one experimental treatment—extraneous variables are balanced out by having them affect members of the experimental group equally with those of the control group. A participant thus serves only under an experimental *or* a control condition such that any extraneous variables (practice, fatigue) exert equal influences (are "balanced out") on the two groups. Balancing occurs in independent group research whereas counterbalancing occurs in repeated treatment research.

TABLE 4-7   Illustration of Symmetrical vs. Asymmetrical Transfer Between Conditions A and B

| Number of Participants | Transfer Is Symmetrical | | | Transfer Is Not Symmetrical | | |
	Condition (Order)		Difference	Condition (Order)		Difference
One-half of participants	A First	B Second		A First	B Second	
	5	7	2	5	7	2
One-half of participants	B First	A Second		B First	A Second	
	3	5	2	3	7	4

5. *Randomization.* **Randomization** is a procedure that assures that each member of a population or universe has an equal probability of being selected. If you flip an unbiased coin in an unbiased manner, the likelihood of a head or tail occurring is equal. If you select your participants in an unbiased manner from a population of 500 students, each of those students has an equal possibility of serving in your experiment. Using a table of random numbers from a statistics book can assure such random selection.

Randomization is used as a control technique because the experimenter takes certain steps to equalize effects of extraneous variables on the different groups. Randomization has two general applications: (1) where it is known that certain extraneous variables operate in the experimental situation, but it is not feasible to apply one of the preceding techniques of control, and (2) where we assume that some extraneous variables will operate, but cannot specify them and therefore cannot apply the other techniques. In either case we take precautions that enhance the likelihood of our assumption that the effects of extraneous variables will "randomize out," that is, that whatever their effects, they will influence both groups to approximately the same extent. Just how do we do this?

Consider the extraneous variable of lighting in the room which we previously discussed. If the experimental group is tested in the morning when there is subdued lighting and the control group tested in the afternoon when bright sun comes through the window, clearly there is a confound. That is, we would expect vision scores to be lower for the group tested under subdued lighting conditions than for the group tested under bright lighting conditions regardless of which was the experimental group—the better the lighting, the better the dependent variable values, regardless of any possible effect of the independent variable. But if each participant regardless of group, has an equal opportunity to serve in the morning or in the afternoon, then, on the average,

lighting will affect both groups equally. The great value of randomization is that it randomly distributes extraneous effects, whatever they may be, over the experimental and control conditions. This balancing out occurs whether you have identified certain extraneous variables or not because the effects of unknown and unspecified extraneous variables are equally distributed across conditions.

By randomly assigning participants to the groups, individual differences are generally equalized so that the groups are equivalent for values of all organismic variables. Note, however, that when using the method of systematic observation, we do *not* randomly assign participants to groups, which is another illustration of why we can expect confounds when using nonexperimental methods. But more on this point soon.

To expand, notice how extensive the differences are among any group of participants—they differ in previous learning experiences, level of motivation, amount of food eaten on the experimental day, romantic relationships, and money problems—any of which may affect our dependent variable. Of course, such variables cannot be controlled by any of the previous techniques. But if participants are randomly assigned to experimental and control groups, we may assume that the effects of such variables are about the same on the behavior of both groups. The two groups should thus differ on these and other variables only within the limits of random sampling. Whatever those differences between groups (small, we expect), they are taken into account by our statistical tests. Statistical tests are designed precisely to tell us whether the groups differ on a basis other than that of random fluctuations (chance).

One of the most incredible examples of confounding that I have ever encountered occurred because the experimenter failed to assign his participants randomly to groups. It would not have been incredible, perhaps, had it been committed by a high school student, but it was done by a knowledgeable graduate student. The student's dependent variable, speed of running a maze, called for the experimental group of rats to have the greater speed. The experiment never got off the ground because, in assigning rats to groups, the experimenter merely reached into the cages and assigned the first rats that came into his hands to the experimental group and the remainder to the control group. The more active animals no doubt popped their heads out of the cage to be grasped by the experimenter, while the less active ones cowered in the rear of the cage. Despite the training administered to the groups, the experimental group had the speedier rats. Experimental treatments and initial (native) running ability were thus confounded. The experimenter who does not take specific steps to assure randomization (such as randomly assigning participants to groups) can become the victim of a confounded experiment.

The potential extraneous variables that might appear in the experimental situation are considerable, such as the ringing of campus bells, the clanging of radiator pipes, peculiar momentary behavior of the experimenter (such as a tic, sneezing, or scratching), an outsider intruding, odors from the chemistry laboratory, or the dripping of water from leaky pipes. Controlling these variables is difficult. Signs placed on the door of the laboratory to head off intrusions are not always read. A sound-deadened room may help but may not be available. It is simply impossible to control all extraneous variables intentionally by the first four techniques listed here. Accordingly, the next best option is to take explicit steps to assure that the effects of extraneous variables will randomize out so that they will not differentially affect our groups. One such step is to alternate the order in which we run our participants. Thus, if we randomly assign the first individual to the experimental group, the next would be in the control group, the third would be randomly assigned to either the control or experimental group, whereupon the fourth would be in the alternative group, and so forth. In this way we could expect, for example, that if a building construction operation is going on that is particularly bothersome, it will affect several participants in each group and both groups approximately equally.

An Example of Exercising Extraneous-Variable Control

To illustrate some of our major points and to try to unify our thinking about con-

FIGURE 4-3   Flow chart of steps to be followed in controlling variables.

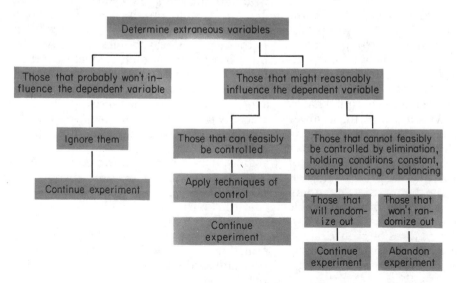

trol procedures, consider an experiment to determine whether the amount of stress on students influences the amount of hostility they will verbally express toward their parents during group discussions. We form two groups and vary the independent variable (amount of stress) with a heightened amount exerted on the experimental group and a normal amount of the control group. The dependent variable—amount of hostility verbally expressed toward the parents—is quantified from tape recordings of discussions. Referring to Figure 4-3, our first step in control is to determine the extraneous variables that are present. Through the procedures previously specified we might arrive at the following list: gender and age of participants, whether their parents are living or dead, place of the experiment, time of day, characteristics of experimenter, lighting conditions, environmental noises, number of the discussion groups, family background and ethnic origin of participants, their educational level, recent experiences with parents, general aggressive tendencies, frustrations, previous feelings toward parents, and eye color.

The next step is to determine those extraneous variables that might reasonably influence the dependent variable. One that probably wouldn't influence the dependent variable and thus can be ignored is eye color. However, even though there are variables that we can ignore, remember that they are, in actuality, controlled through the techniques of balancing and randomization.

To deal with the others, we can control the following by holding conditions constant: place of experiment—by holding sessions for both groups in the same room; time of day—by holding sessions at the same hour for both groups (on different days); lighting conditions—by having the same lights on for both groups with no external light allowed; group size—by having the same number in each group; and experimenter characteristics—by having the same experimenter appear before both groups with a consistent experimenter attitude.

The variables of gender, age, educational level, and parents living or dead could be controlled by balancing. We could assign an equal number of each gender to each group, make sure that the average age of each group is about the same, distribute educational level equally between both groups, and assign an equal number of participants whose parents are living to each group. However, simultaneous balancing of *all* these variables would be difficult (if not impossible) with a small number of participants. In fact, two variables would probably be a maximum. We might select gender and parents living or dead as the most important and balance them out. If we use college students, educational level and age would be about the same, so that they can be included with the following as variables that we do not consider it feasible to control by our first four techniques: noises, family background, ethnic origin, recent experiences with parents, general aggressive tendencies, extent of frustration, and previous feelings toward parents. Some of these might be considered important, and it would certainly be desirable to control them. Most of them are difficult to measure, however, and thus are hard to control explicitly. Is it reasonable to assume that they will randomly affect both groups to approximately the same extent? It is if participants are randomly assigned to groups (except insofar as we have restricted the random process through balancing). But we can always check the validity of this assumption by comparing the groups on any given variable. Since this assumption seems reasonable to make in the present example, we shall conclude that the conduct of the experiment is feasible as far as control problems are concerned; we have not been able to specify any confounding effects that would suggest that the experiment should be abandoned.

The Experimenter as an Extraneous Variable

Several times we have mentioned the need to control experimenter influences on the dependent variable, but the topic is sufficiently important that we shall briefly emphasize it here. In the experimental report techniques of controlling the experimenter variable and the *number* of data collectors should be specified. The most apparent violation of sound control procedures occurs when one experimenter collects data for a while, then is relieved by another—with no plan for assigning an equal number of participants in each group to each experimenter; however, far more subtle effects are also possible, as when the experimenter's expectations as to how the participants should behave influences how the participants do, in fact, behave.

The experimenter's race has been shown sometimes to affect the participant's responses, as have differences in such characteristics as gender, age, ethnic identity, prestige, anxiety, friendliness, dominance, and warmth. The experimenter has also been shown to affect scores on such tasks as intelligence tests, projective tests, verbal conditioning tasks, and various physiological and educational measures (Barber, 1976). We shall enlarge on experimenter effects in Chapter 12 when we consider the possible limitations of these variables on generalizations from the data.

Experimenter Bias. Sometimes the experimenter may pay more attention to the experimental group than to the control group, which also unintentionally influences the results. The expectation that the participants would have when differentially attended to could quite sizably influence their behaviors.

One way to study such possible experimenter biases would be to balance the number of participants across several experimenters as illustrated in Table 4-4 on page 66. You could then analyze the data separately for each experimenter. If the results differed depending on who collected the data, you certainly have a problem as we will develop later in Chapter 12. In some cases, it might be possible not to inform the data collector of the nature of the hypothesis or in which experimental condition the participant is serving. Using this highly desirable method of control,

which defines **double-blind experiments**, it is highly unlikely that experimenter effects would be confounded with your independent variable. The technique of elimination could also be used, by instructing participants entirely by means of automated equipment such as tape recorders. A more extreme example of automated control in this day of widely used microcomputers is the total computerization of laboratories. In such laboratories, no experimenter intervention is used at all. Thus the participants merely show up for their appointment and check in with the computer, which programs them through the entire experiment. As we shall discuss in Appendix C, however, there are definite pitfalls in overreliance on the computer in research.

Experimenter Influences on Animal Behavior. The subtle effects that the experimenter can have on the participants need not be limited to humans, for the experimenter can also influence the behavior of animals. Consider the classic case of the exceptional horse, Clever Hans. Early in the nineteenth century, Clever Hans toured Germany with his trainer, apparently demonstrating remarkable cognitive feats. By stomping the correct number of times, Clever Hans indicated the correct answer to problems of addition, subtraction, multiplication, division, and all the factors of a number—he even added fractions. His stomping indicated the day of the week on which a certain date would fall. He indicated perfect pitch and could identify chords played on a musical instrument. If a chord was not pleasing, he indicated which notes should be removed. He could "read" German by choosing one of several cards that contained the desired word and by tapping his hoof to indicate rows and columns of a specially prepared table of the alphabet. He would nod if he understood a question, shake his head if he did not, and move his head in various directions to answer yes or no.

There was much skepticism about Hans's abilities, so a panel was assembled that included two zoologists, a psychologist, a horse trainer, and a circus manager. To study

Hans's ability, they had strangers, in addition to the trainer, ask Hans questions, which he successfully answered. For example, when asked the square root of 16, Hans tapped four times. The panel's report confirmed Hans's amazing cognitive abilities.

However, the psychologist Oskar Pfungst varied the methodology by also having someone who didn't know the correct answer ask the questions. His results showed that Hans was successful in solving 9 out of 10 problems if the interrogator knew the answers, but his score was only one out of 10 if the interrogator did not know the answers. By careful study of the interrogator, Pfungst observed that when Hans had stomped the correct number of times, such as four times for the square root of 16, the interrogator unintentionally and almost imperceptibly yielded cues. Thus, instead of using higher mental processes, Hans had learned to observe such subtle cues as those of slight change in the posture, breathing, or facial cues of the interrogator. When those cues were observed, Hans stopped stomping. Consequently, the number of times that he had stomped indicated the correct answer. Such unintentional, subtle cues like facial expressions and variations in the voice given off by experimenters in psychological research can communicate even to animal participants just what the experimenter expects of their behavior, thereby unnaturally influencing it. Nevertheless, one must admit that Hans was indeed clever. But, evoking Morgan's canon of parsimony, we need not attribute Hans's cleverness to higher mental processes.

Problems of Experimenter Effects on Human Research. To summarize and extend our discussion, consider the following points made by Barber (1976).

1. *The investigator paradigm effect.* This pitfall is caused by the investigator's general beliefs and methods. For instance, one can fail to see events that are present and see nonexistent events, as when nearly 100 papers on N-rays were printed in a single year (1904). After the discovery of X-rays, many scientists were deluded into "seeing" N-rays. Eventually, it was shown that all the effects attributed to N-rays were due to wishful thinking and to the difficulty of studying by eye the brightness of faint objects.

2. *The investigator experimental design effect.* Different conclusions may be obtained depending upon the type of design used. For instance, in Chapter 9 we show that different conclusions may result depending on whether one uses a between-groups or a within-groups design.

3. *The investigator loose procedure effect.* As we have emphasized, if detailed procedures in a study are not adhered to, varied results may be obtained. The experimental procedure must be precise, spelled out, followed in detail, and the same for all participants under each condition.

4. *The investigator data analysis effect.* As we emphasize continuously, the appropriate statistical analysis must be conducted, and it must be accurate. There are several specific instances that Barber lists:
   - If a large number of data have been collected and the statistical analysis has not been preplanned, the investigator may select those data that confirm his or her hypothesis and ignore any conflicting data. An analogy is with the use of a projective technique such as the Rorschach—the investigator can project onto the data his or her own expectancies and pull out whatever findings he or she may wish.
   - Investigators may fail to report data that disconfirm their hypotheses. It is said that many experimenters have file cabinets full of unpublished experiments that "didn't turn out right."
   - Incidental data may be collected that are not directly related to the hypothesis being tested. If reliable findings are not found for the hypothesis, then data on these other variables may be used so that there is at least something positive to report.
   - Post hoc analyses may be made without correcting for the disturbed probability level (see Chapter 7).
   - If you conduct a large number of statistical tests, 5 percent of them will be erroneously reliable by chance at the .05 level (Chapter 6). The experimenter may select only those positive results to report, ignoring 95 percent of the statistical tests that are negative.
   - The experimenter may misrecord data.

5. *The investigator fudging effect.* The effect may not be outright fraud, but merely pushing the data by letting desires and biases influence the way the data are analyzed and reported. One may select or throw out certain data to reach a probability level of .05. There are famous cases of fudging, as well as of outright fraud.

6. *The experimenter personal attributes effect* (as discussed in this chapter).

7. *The experimenter-failure-to-follow-the-procedure effect* (see effect 3).

8. *The experimenter unintentional expectancy effect.* Here, unintentionally cues may be given to influence the subject's behavior, such as changes in the experimenter's facial expression. Such cues may influence a participant's response so as to please the experimenter.

CHAPTER SUMMARY

I. Two classes of independent variables that can be studied to see if they affect a given dependent variable are
   A. Stimulus variables, which are quantifiable changes in energy (such as light or sound) that can affect behavior.
   B. Organismic variables, which are characteristics of humans and animals (such as intelligence) that can be systematically studied to see if they are related to certain behaviors.

II. The dependent variable is the behavioral criterion of whether an independent variable is effective.
   A. Response measures of the dependent variable include
      1. Accuracy.
      2. Latency.
      3. Speed (duration).
      4. Frequency (and, therefore, rate).
   B. When selecting a dependent variable you should consider
      1. Its validity. It should measure that which is specified in the consequent condition of the hypothesis.
      2. Its reliability. It should yield about the same values when repeated measures of it are taken.
      3. Multiple dependent measures. You should take more than one measure if you reasonably can.

4. Growth measures to study your dependent variable as it might change over time.

5. Delayed measures. In an effort to see if the effect of the independent variable is lasting, you can take "follow-up" measures.

III. Empirical relationships: If confirmed, independent-dependent variable relationships typically are of two kinds:
   A. Stimulus-response laws—these result from experiments.
   B. Organismic-response laws—these result from the method of systematic observation.

IV. The nature of experimental control
   A. Control of the independent variable is exercised by purposively varying it in a systematic way.
   B. With extraneous variable control you regulate extraneous variables to prevent confounding. Confounding occurs when an extraneous variable is systematically related to the independent variable, and it might differentially affect the dependent variable values of the two (or more) groups in the investigation.
   C. Kinds of control of the independent variable:
      1. It may be purposively varied in an experiment.
      2. Independent variable control may be exercised by selection of organismic characteristics (the method of systematic observation).
   D. Techniques for controlling the extraneous variables:
      1. Eliminate them, if possible, as in sound deadening to shield out noises.
      2. Hold conditions constant so that they are the same for all participants.
      3. Balance conditions so that they affect both (all) groups equally.
      4. Counterbalance conditions so that each condition is presented to each participant an equal number of times, and each condition occurs an equal number of times at each practice session. Furthermore, each condition must precede and follow all other conditions an equal number of times.
      5. Randomize the possible effects of extraneous variables so that, on the av-

erage, they affect both (all) groups equally.

E. The experimenter variable is an especially important variable to be controlled. Experimenter characteristics and experimenter bias deserve special attention.

CRITICAL REVIEW FOR THE STUDENT— SOME CONTROL PROBLEMS

In the following investigations you should specify the control problems and the techniques that would solve them. Or perhaps you might decide that the experiments should not have been conducted, in which case you should justify that conclusion.

To set the tone, consider an experiment in which the control, if such existed, was outlandish. One day a general called to tell me that he was repeating an experiment that I had conducted on rifle marksmanship and to invite me to visit him. I made the trip, and we immediately drove to the rifle range to observe the progress of the experimental group. However, it was more enjoyable watching the general than the new army trainees. While they were shooting, the general would walk along the line, kicking some into the proper position, lying down beside others to help them fire, and so on. Eventually the general suggested that we leave. That was fine, except that I wanted to observe the control group, whereupon the general suggested that I (not us) walk over the adjacent hill to study it. On my way I privately communicated to the sergeant on how enthusiastic the experimental participants were. The sergeant explained that that was what the general wanted—that the general *expected* the experimental group to fire better than the control group and they "darn" well knew that was what had better happen. When I got to the other side of the hill, I was amazed at the contrast. Those participants constituted the most morose, depressed, laconic control group I had ever seen. The sergeant in charge of *this* group knew that

they should not perform as well as the experimental group. Clearly nobody wanted the general to be disappointed (their motivations are too numerous to cite here). Needless to say, when the general reported the results of the experiment, they strongly favored the experimental group. More than just the placebo effect was present here.

In another interesting experience, this one with the placebo effect, I was periodically bringing a paranoid schizophrenic from the hospital to my laboratory purely to measure his covert speech behavior during his auditory hallucinations. After about the fourth trip, he volunteered to me that he was getting much better, so much so in fact that he had been granted a weekend leave to go home. While I was doing nothing but making electromyographic measures of his speech musculature, he profusely thanked me, "Doctor," for everything that I had done for him.

Let us now see if you can spot any similar errors in the following:

1. The problem of whether children should be taught to read by the word method or by the phonics method has been a point of controversy for many years. Briefly, the word method teaches the child to perceive a word as a whole unit, whereas the phonics method requires the child to break the word into parts. To attempt to decide this issue, an experimenter plans to teach reading to two groups, one by each method. The local school system teaches only the word method. "This is fine for one group," the experimenter says. "Now I must find a school system that used the phonics method." Accordingly, a visit is made to another town that uses the phonics method, where a sample of children are tested to see how well they can read. After administering an extensive battery of reading tests, it is found that the children who used the phonics method are reliably superior to those who learned by the word method. It is then concluded that the phonics method is superior to the word method. Do you accept or reject this conclusion? Why?

2. A military psychologist is interested in whether training to fire a machine gun from

a tank facilitates accuracy in firing the main tank gun. A company of soldiers with no previous firing experience is randomly divided into two groups. One group receives machine gun training; the other does not. Both groups are then tested on their ability to fire the larger tank gun. There are two tanks that can fire on targets in a field. The machine-gun-trained group is assigned one tank and a corresponding set of targets, whereas the control group fires on another set of targets from the second tank. The tests show that the group previously trained on the machine gun is reliably more accurate than is the control group. The conclusion is that machine gun training facilitates accuracy on the main tank gun.

3. A psychologist tests the hypothesis that early toilet training leads to a personality of excessive compulsiveness about cleanliness, and, conversely, that late toilet training leads to sloppiness. Previous studies have shown that middle-class children receive their toilet training earlier than do lower-class children so that one group is formed of middle-class children and another of lower-class children. Both groups are provided with a finger painting task, and such data are recorded as the extent to which children smear their hands and arms with paints, whether they clean up after the session, and how many times they wash the paints from their hands. Comparisons of the two groups on these criteria indicate that the middle-class children are reliably more concerned about cleanliness than are those of the lower class. It is thus concluded that early toilet training leads to compulsive cleanliness, whereas later toilet training results in less concern about personal cleanliness.

4. In studying the function of the hypothalamus within the brain, a physiological psychologist randomly assigns some cats to two groups. The hypothalamus is removed from the cats in one group, and the second (control) group is not operated on. On a certain behavior test it is found that the group operated on is reliably deficient, compared with the control group. The psychologist concludes that the hypothalamus is responsible for the type of behavior

that is "missing" in the group that was operated on.

5. A hypothesis is that emotionally loaded words like *sex* and *prostitute* must be exposed for a longer time to be perceived than neutral words. To test this hypothesis, various words are exposed to participants for extremely short intervals. In fact, the initial exposure time is so short that no participant can report *any* of the words. The length of exposure is then gradually increased until each word is correctly reported. The length of exposure necessary for each word to be reported is recorded. It is found that the length of time necessary to report the emotionally loaded words is longer than that for the neutral word. It is concluded that the hypothesis is confirmed.

6. A physician conducted an experiment to study the effect of acupuncture on pain. Half the participants were treated for painful shoulders through acupuncture, whereas the other half received no special treatment. The participants who received acupuncture treatment reported a reliable improvement in shoulder discomfort to a "blind" evaluator after treatment. However, no statistically reliable improvement was reported by the control group. The physician concluded that acupuncture is an effective treatment for chronic shoulder pain.

7. Two educational psychology classes were used to study the effects of grades as rewards or punishments. The same instructor taught both classes. In one class students were given A, B, C, D, or F grades, whereas the other class either passed or failed. Tests indicated that there were no reliable differences between the two classes in terms of achievement, attitudes, or values. The conclusion was that students learn just as well without the reward or punishment of grades. The researcher also observed a difference in classroom atmosphere in which the pass-fail class was more relaxed and free of grade-oriented tensions with better rapport between the instructor and students.

chapter 5

THE RESEARCH PLAN

Major purposes:

To specify in detail each step in the conduct of a research project.

What you are going to find:

1. Distinctions between experimental and non-experimental methods.

2. A guide for planning and conducting a research project from its inception to its conclusion.

What you should acquire:

The ability to develop a detailed research plan for a project of your own.

THE EVIDENCE REPORT

A scientific inquiry starts with a solvable problem that may be stated as a question (Chapter 2). A hypothesis is then advanced as a possible solution (Chapter 3). To test the hypothesis, empirical results from a study are summarized in the form of an **evidence report**, a sentence that concisely states what was found in the inquiry. Once the evidence report has been formed, it is related to the hypothesis. By comparing the hypothesis (the prediction of how the results of the experiment will turn out) with the evidence report (the statement of how the results *did* turn out), it is possible to determine whether the hypothesis is probably true or false. We now need to inquire into the various methods in psychology of obtaining data that may be used to arrive at an evidence report.

METHODS OF OBTAINING AN EVIDENCE REPORT

The methods to be discussed have the common characteristic of facilitating the systematic collection of data that can be used to formulate an evidence report.

Nonexperimental Methods

We emphasize experimental methods because they yield the soundest conclusions. We judge the effectiveness of nonexperimental methods relative to experimental methods. Nonexperimental methods are valuable too, and we develop them in Chapters 9 and 11. The manner of classifying the nonexperimental methods is somewhat arbitrary and varies with the classifying authority. Methods that can be contrasted with the experimental method are the *clinical method* (sometimes called the case history method or the life history method), *naturalistic observational methods, survey research, archival research, correlational research*, and *quasi-experiments*.

The Classical Clinical Method. Traditionally, the psychologist used **the clinical method** in an attempt to help a client solve personal problems, be they emotional, vocational, or whatever. In a common form of the clinical method, the psychologist collects relevant information about the person from birth on. Some of the techniques for collecting this information are the intensive interview, perusing records, administering psychological tests, questioning other people about the individual, studying written works of the person, or obtaining biographical questionnaires. On the basis of the resulting information, the psychologist tries to determine the factors that led to the person's problem. This leads to the formulation of an informal hypothesis as to the cause of the person's problem; the collection of further data will help to confirm or disconfirm the hypothesis. Once the problem and the factors that led to its development are laid bare for the person, the psychologist can try to help the individual achieve a better adjustment to the circumstances. It should be noted that the clinical method is generally used in an applied, as opposed to a basic, sense, since its usual aim is to solve a practical problem, not to advance science. However, observation of behavior through this method can be a source of more general hypotheses that can be subjected to stringent testing. Furthermore, the research-oriented clinician can systematically collect data based on progress of a number of clients in an effort to validate whatever therapeutic method is used (see Chapters 10 and 11).

Naturalistic Observation Methods. In **naturalistic observation**, the researcher records ongoing behavior as it naturally occurs. No effort is made to produce or control behavior as is done in experimentation. Often, systematic data are gathered on behavior in naturally existing groups such as families, preschoolers, and school classes. The observations are preferably made in unobtrusive ways so that natural patterns of behavior are preserved. Unfortunately behavioral research has often lacked unobtrusive naturalistic observation methodology—one possible solution being in the use of radio telemetry in which voice or other data may be detected from the participants and "radioed" through transmitters to the receiver of the researcher. A sizable amount of naturalistic observation research is conducted in educational, developmental, clinical, and social areas, together with discussion of lively methodological issues. These procedures have their own distinct problems of design and analysis.

As an example of the use of this method, children at free play on a variety of play equipment could be studied to determine what kinds of skills children of a certain age possess. Their behaviors could be observed, recorded, and categorized. Another example of the use of naturalistic observation was the classic, still famous study of panic caused by Orson Welles's radio dramatization of H. G. Wells's *War of the Worlds*. Psychologists interviewed people who participated in it to try to determine why the panic occurred. Ethologists also use this method in their study of animals in their natural environment. The famous studies by the ethologist Konrad Lorenz resulted in a classification of 20 different specific behaviors of ducks.

In one application of this method, sometimes referred to as "participant-observer research," the researcher actually joins a group to surreptitiously record behavior. As one example, Geller, Russ, and Altomari (1986) studied beer drinking among a sample of 243 Caucasian college students. They were unobtrusively observed drinking beer in five public drinking establishments and at their university student center. The results are presented in Figure 5-1, where we can study the number of ounces of beer consumed by each student (left vertical axis) as functions of gender and kind of beer container. It was concluded that females drank less beer than did males. It was also determined that males consumed beer at the rate of .92 ounces per minute. On the right vertical axis we can study how long the students stayed in the bar and can note, interestingly, that the female students stayed for a longer period of time than did the males. Further-

more, students drank significantly more beer when drinking in groups and when purchasing beer in pitchers versus cups or bottles. The authors interpreted the results as meaning that male college students were more at risk for driving while intoxicated than were females. Their reasoning was that males drank more beer at a faster rate, were quicker to leave a particular bar, and, when they purchased beer in pitchers and drank in groups, were more likely to consume an excessive amount of beer in amounts that often resulted in intoxication. The authors suggested that there might be server intervention programs developed to prevent student driving while intoxicated.

This example serves to illustrate well that while causal relationships can be established in experimental research, they cannot be so firmly established in nonexperimental research; only correlational relations result in all of these nonexperimental methods. In this instance, while it is plausible that the evidence report implies that male college students are more at risk for driving while intoxicated than are females, other conclusions are also possible. For one, the research by no means established that anybody was intoxicated. While I would not want to de-

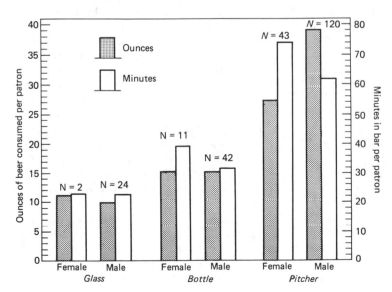

FIGURE 5-1 Ounces of beer consumed and minutes spent in bar per patron as functions of gender and type of beer container. [Geller, Russ, and Altomari (1986)].

fend the possibility against a radical feminist group, it could be that males really were no more at risk than females when both had been drinking beer.

Survey Research. Surveys are conducted to assess people's verbal reports of their attitudes, beliefs, and feelings about specific issues. The technique of survey research has been highly developed so that, when proper sampling was taken, extremely accurate results have been obtained; for example, the outcome of a presidential election often can be successfully predicted within minutes after polls close in the eastern part of the United States.

However, in assessing one's attitudes, beliefs, etc., it is clear that questionnaires indicate only what people say they believe, which can be quite different from what they really believe. The results of surveys must therefore be qualified in that respect.

Archival Research. In this method, the researchers do not actually collect data themselves, but they obtain data from public records, archives, and so on. The researcher merely analyzes the data and attempts to draw certain conclusions from them. The method can be valuable in many respects. For instance, there is no other way to collect data on suicides and homicides. Unfortunately, though, archival data are subject to all kinds of pitfalls, as we shall develop in Chapter 11.

Establishing Coefficients. The aim here is to seek relationships between variables by calculating correlation coefficients, as we shall see in Chapter 9. Again, it is not possible to infer causal relationships using this method since there is no independent variable that is purposively manipulated.

Quasi-experimental Methods. The defining characteristic of this approach is that there is no attempt to randomly assign participants to groups. Rather, already formed groups are studied in efforts to infer causal relationships. The major methods of quasi-experimentation, such as the method of sys-

tematic observation, will be elaborated in Chapter 11.

Experimental Methods

Although the evidence reports obtained by nonexperimental methods can be used for testing hypotheses, such reports do have important limitations that will be discussed after a consideration of the experimental method. The conclusions reached with them are always lower in probability than when sound experimental methods are used. While they can furnish valuable information, it is important to recognize their limitations when we do use them.

In the early stages of the development of a science, nonexperimental methods tend to be more prominent. In some sciences—sociology, for example—there is little hope that anything but nonexperimental methods can be generally used. This is primarily because sociology is largely concerned with the effect of the prevailing culture and social institutions on behavior, and it is difficult to manipulate these two factors as independent variables in an experiment. In those fields that are ultimately susceptible to experimentation, however, a change in methodology eventually occurs as knowledge accumulates. Scientific investigations become more searching because the "spontaneous" happenings in nature are not adequate to permit the necessary observations. This leads to the setting up of special conditions to bring about the desired events under circumstances favorable for scientific observations, and experiments originate.

In an experiment the researcher takes an active part in producing the event. By creating the event to be studied, it can be made to occur at a specific time so that the experimenter is fully prepared to record and measure it accurately. The precise conditions under which the event occurred can be recorded so that the experimenter, as well as other experimenters, can replicate the experiment. By actively producing the event, the experimental and control conditions can be systematically varied so that it can be determined whether the dependent-variable measures thereby also vary systematically.

CONTRASTING EXPERIMENTAL AND NONEXPERIMENTAL METHODS

Purposive Manipulation Versus Selection of Values of the Independent Variable. The one characteristic that all nonexperimental methods have in common is that the variables being evaluated are not purposively manipulated by the researcher. Since psychology is the study of the behavior of organisms, in using nonexperimental methods the psychologist typically must wait until the behavior of interest occurs naturally. Not having control over the variable to be studied, the researcher can observe the event only in its natural state.

To emphasize this critical distinction between nonexperimental and experimental methods, consider the way that learning speed changes with age. We have two different age groups—one of 20-year-olds and the second of 60-year-olds—learn the same task. At first glance this might appear to be an "experiment," but it is not because the independent variable (age of the participant) was not purposively manipulated. Rather, we *selected* our participants because they differed in age. "Age of participants" simply is not a variable over which a researcher has control. We cannot say to one person, "You will be 20 years old," and to another, "You will be 60 years old." Participants in an experiment are randomly assigned to the experimental and control groups, but in the method of systematic observation, they are not. Although two groups are used in each case, the "normal" one is called a **control group** in an experiment, whereas when using nonexperimental methods the normal group is called a **comparison group**. In a comparison group the participants are already formed together and *selected* for study because of some common characteristic—

thus they are not randomly assigned to the "normal" or "standard" condition.

This critical difference in design is a major reason why, in the experimental method, the conclusion is more highly regarded than if it is tested by a nonexperimental method. Put another way, an evidence report obtained through experimentation is more reliable than when obtained through the use of a nonexperimental method. This is true because the interpretation of the effect an independent variable is clearer in an experiment. Ambiguous interpretation of results is typical in nonexperimental methods primarily because of a lack of control over extraneous variables. It is difficult, or frequently impossible, in a systematic observation study to be sure that the findings, with respect to the dependent variable, are due to the independent variable.—They may result from some uncontrolled extraneous variable that happened to be present in the study. In nonexperimental methods it is also usually more difficult to define the variables studied than in the case where they are actually produced, as in an experiment.

There Is Less Error Variance in Experimental Research. Another reason that experimentation is to be preferred is that there is more "noise" in nonexperimental research. As we shall develop in Chapter 6 it is important to reduce the error variance (the "noise") in research. The more noise there is, the harder it is to hear something. Analogously, the greater the error variance there is in research, the harder it is to discover a law about behavior. One major contributor to error variance is the number of uncontrolled extraneous variables. As a result of the increased noise due to poor control, the possibility of establishing lawful relationships about behavior is markedly reduced.

All of this does not mean, however, that the experimental method is a perfect method for answering questions. Certainly it can lead to errors, and, in the hands of poor experimenters, the errors can be great.

Relatively speaking, however, the experimental method is preferred *where it can be appropriately used.* But if it cannot be used, then we must do the next best thing and use a nonexperimental method. Thus, when it is not reasonable to produce the events that we wish to study, as in the example of a panic, we must rely on nonexperimental methods. But we must not forget that when events are *selected* for study, rather than *produced* and *controlled,* caution must be exercised in reaching a conclusion.

A Criticism of the Experimental Method. When an event is brought into the laboratory for study (as it usually is), the nature of the event is thereby changed. For one thing, the event does not naturally occur in isolation, as it is made to occur in the laboratory, for in natural life there are always many other variables that influence it. Criticism of experiments on such grounds is based on a misunderstanding of experimental methodology. The essence of studying an event in the laboratory is that we really want to know what the event is like when it *is* uninfluenced by other events. It is then possible to transfer the event back to its natural situation, at which time we know more about how it is produced. The fact that any event may appear to be different in the natural situation, as compared with the laboratory, simply means that it is also being influenced by other variables, *which in their turn* need to be brought into the laboratory for investigation. Once all the relevant variables that exist under natural conditions have been studied in isolation in the laboratory and it has been determined in what way they all influence the dependent variable and each other, then a thorough understanding of the natural event will have been accomplished. Such a piecemeal analysis of events in the laboratory is necessary for an adequate understanding of them.

Certain characteristics of behavior are simply too complex to understand through the casual observation of everyday life—it may not be possible to find the relevant variables that determine a certain kind of behavior through naturalistic observation. Sensitive recording devices of the laboratory used under controlled conditions may be required to ascertain which variables are responsible for an event. These findings can then be used for better understanding the complex world at large. For instance, casual observation over the centuries had ingrained in people the notion that a response can be eliminated by punishing the perpetrator. However, it was not possible to understand adequately the true effects of punishment until the phenomenon was dissected in the laboratory. Although people may think that punishment causes a response to disappear immediately, experimentation has demonstrated that the punished response is only temporarily suppressed and can reappear once the threat of further punishment is removed. A more effective technique for eliminating a response is the process of extinction, discovery of which required laboratory investigation.

In spite of these strong statements in favor of the laboratory analysis of events, the possibility exists that an event actually is changed or even "destroyed." This occurs when the experimenter has not been successful in transferring the event into the laboratory. A different event from that which was desired is thus produced. Perhaps a person behaves differently in an experiment than in "real life." Merely being aware of participating in an experiment may cause one to behave in an unusual manner. This is certainly possible and poses a methodological problem that often must be handled astutely. On the other hand, events may not be adequately studied unless thay *are* brought into the laboratory where suitable control can be employed. Consequently even if an event is distorted by observation, it is studied with this effect held constant.

TYPES OF EXPERIMENTS

Exploratory Versus Confirmatory Experiments

A number of terms refer to different types of experiments, although the same general experimental method is used for all. For instance, whether an experimenter conducts an exploratory or a confirmatory experiment depends on the amount of knowledge relevant to the problem being studied. If there is insufficient knowledge to formulate a possible solution, an **exploratory experiment** would be performed. In an exploratory experiment there is no basis to predict the effect of the independent variable on the dependent variable. Exploratory experiments are thus conducted in the preliminary stages of investigating a problem area. As more information is accumulated, we become more capable of formulating hypotheses that allow us to predict how an experiment can turn out. At this more advanced stage we can conduct **confirmatory experiments** to test explicit hypotheses. Put another way, the exploratory experiment is used primarily to discover if new independent variables are influential in affecting a given dependent variable. In the confirmatory experiment we also determine the extent and precise way in which one variable influences the other (i.e., the functional, quantitative relationship between the independent and the dependent variable). A common descriptive term for the exploratory experiment is "I wonder what would happen if I did this?" whereas the confirmatory experiment analogously is "I'll bet this would happen if I did this." In either case, however, the purpose is to arrive at an evidence report. If the experiment is exploratory, the evidence report can be the basis for formulating a specific, precise hypothesis. In a confirmatory experiment the evidence report is used to test the hypothesis; if the hypothesis is not in accord with the evidence report, it can be modified to fit the data better, then tested in a new experiment. If the hypothesis is supported by the evidence report, then its probability of being true is increased. Different experimental designs are usually used in each case, one type being more efficient for the exploratory experiment and another for the confirmatory experiment, as we will discuss later.

Crucial Experiments

Sometimes you may run across the term "crucial experiment" (*experimentum crucis*), which is an experiment that purports to test all possible hypotheses simultaneously. For instance, if the results of an experiment come out one way, one hypothesis is confirmed and a second hypothesis is disconfirmed, but if the results point another way, the first hypothesis is disconfirmed and the second is confirmed. Ideally a crucial experiment is one whose results support one hypothesis and disconfirm all possible alternatives. However, we can probably never be sure that we have succeeded in stating all possible alternative hypotheses, so that we can probably never have a true crucial experiment. The concept is important for us as an ideal so that we should direct our experimentation toward this ideal, even though we may have to settle for approximations to it.

Pilot Studies

The term *pilot study* or *pilot experiment* has nothing to do with the behavior of aircraft operators, as one student thought, but refers to a preliminary experiment, one conducted prior to the major experiment. It is used, usually with only a small number of subjects, to suggest what specific values should be assigned to the variables being studied; to try out certain procedures to see how well they work; and, more generally, to find out what mistakes might be made in conducting the actual experiment so that the experimenter can be ready for them. It is a dress rehearsal of the main performance.

In conducting research, of course, there are numerous problems that are difficult to anticipate. Some of these problems can be specified by means of a pilot study. When you design your research, you develop the best plan that you can at the time. In conducting the pilot study, you collect information that will help you assess the effectiveness of your plan. Perhaps the pilot study will encourage you to continue with the procedure and design that you tentatively developed, perhaps it will give you important suggestions for modifying the plan, or it might suggest to you that you should abandon that plan and develop a different strategy altogether.

Field Studies

In field research, efforts are made to discover relationships in the real social structures of everyday life. Field studies may be true experiments or they may take the form of some kind of nonexperimental method such as a quasi-experimental design, which we will discuss in Chapter 11. Since field studies occur in an everyday life setting, control is markedly reduced relative to laboratory research. As a result, the error variance (noise) is usually considerably increased in field studies relative to laboratory research.

PLANNING AN EXPERIMENT

The Antecedent Conditions of the Hypothesis Must Be Satisfied. In designing an experiment, the researcher seeks to obtain data that are relevant to a hypothesis that can solve a problem. This involves questions about experimental technique, such as: What apparatus will best allow manipulation and observation of the phenomenon of interest? What extraneous variables may contaminate the phenomenon of primary interest and are therefore in need of control? Which events should be observed and which should be ignored? How can the behavioral data best be observed, recorded, and quantified? By considering these and similar problems, an attempt is made to rule out the possibility of collecting irrelevant evidence. For instance, if the antecedent conditions of the hypothesis are not satisfied, the evidence report will be irrelevant to the hypothesis and further progress in the inquiry is prohibited. Put another way, the hypothesis says that *if* such and such happens (the antecedent conditions of the hypothesis), *then* such and such should occur (the conse-

quent conditions of the hypothesis). The hypothesis amounts to a contract that the experimenter has signed—the experimenter has agreed to assure that the antecedent conditions are fulfilled. If the experimenter fails to fulfill that agreement, then whatever results are collected will have nothing to do with the hypothesis; they will be irrelevant and thus cannot be used to test the hypothesis. This points up the importance of adequately planning the experiment. If the experiment is improperly designed, then either no inferences can be made from the results, or it may only be possible to make inferences to answer questions that the experimenter has not asked; this is another instance of giving the right answer to the wrong question, particularly by neophyte experimenters. If the only result of an experiment is that the experimenter learns that these same errors should not be made in the future, this is very expensive education indeed.

The experimenter should draft a thorough plan before the experiment is conducted. Once the complete plan of the experiment is set down on paper, it is desirable to obtain as much criticism of it as possible. The experimenter often overlooks many important points or looks at them with a wrong, preconceived set; the critical review of others may bring potential errors to the surface. No scientist is beyond criticism, and it is far better to accept criticism before an experiment is conducted than to make errors that might invalidate the experiment. We shall now suggest a series of steps that the researcher can follow in planning a study. Note that sizable portions of the experimental plan can later be used for the write-up (as specified in Appendix B).

Outline for an Experimental Plan

1. Label the Experiment. The title should be clearly specified, as well as the time and location of the experiment. As time passes and the experimenter accumulates a number of experiments in the same problem area, this information can be referred to without much chance of confusing one experiment with another.

2. Survey the Literature. Previous work that is relevant to the experiment should be studied. This is a particularly important phase in the experimental plan for a number of reasons. First, it helps in the formulation of the problem. The experimenter's vague notion of a problem is frequently made more concrete by consulting other studies. Or the experimenter thus may be led to modify the original problem in such a way that the experiment becomes more valuable. Another reason for this survey of pertinent knowledge is that it may reveal whether the experiment even needs to be conducted. If essentially the same experiment has previously been conducted by somebody else, there is certainly no point in repeating the operation, unless it is specifically designed to confirm previous findings. Other studies in the same area are also the source of suggestions about extraneous variables that need to be controlled and hints on how to control them.

The importance of the literature survey cannot be overemphasized. Experimenters who slight it usually pay a penalty in the form of errors in the design or some other complication. The knowledge in psychology is growing all the time, making it more difficult for one person to comprehend the findings in any given problem area. Therefore this step requires particularly close attention. Also, since relevant studies should be summarized and referred to in the write-up of the experiment, this might just as well be done before the experiment is conducted, thus combining two steps in one.

We are very fortunate in psychology to have the *Psychological Abstracts*, which make any such survey relatively easy.[1] Every stu-

dent of psychology should attempt to develop a facility in using the *Abstracts*. You can also look for previously published articles on your research problem in such other sources as the *Science Citation Index, Social Science Index*, and various computer search facilities that are available in university libraries. The largest and most in-depth computer search available in the field of psychology is the Psych Lit, otherwise known as the Silver Platter.

3. State the Problem. The research is being conducted because there is a lack of knowledge about something. The statement of the problem expresses the lack of knowledge. The problem should be developed in some detail through a series of logical steps citing previous research. However, the problem should be stated concisely and unambiguously in a single sentence, preferably as a question. The statement of the problem question should be answered unambiguously, either positively or negatively. If the question cannot be so answered, *in general* we can say that the experiment should not be conducted. Every worthwhile experiment involves a gamble. If the problem cannot be definitely answered either positively or negatively, the experimenter has not risked anything and therefore cannot hope to gain new knowledge.

4. State the Hypothesis. The variables specified in the statement of the problem are explicitly stated in the hypothesis. Natural languages (e.g., English) are usually employed for this purpose, but other languages (e.g., mathematical or logical ones) can also be used and, in fact, are preferable.

While the "if . . . , then . . ." relationship was suggested as the basic form for stating the hypothesis, the actual sentence need not be given explicitly as an "if . . . , then . . ." sentence. What is important is that the hypothesis can be restated in that logical fashion.

5. Define the Variables. The independent and dependent variables have been specified in the statement of the problem and of the

---

[1] *Psychological Abstracts* is a professional journal published by the American Psychological Association. It summarizes the large majority of psychological research and classifies it according to topics (and authors) so that it is fairly easy to determine what has previously been done on any given problem. The last issue of each volume specifies all the research for that volume.

hypothesis. They must now be *operationally defined* so that they are clear and unambiguous. This phase is critical for if all the experimental variables cannot be operationally defined, the hypothesis is untestable.

6. Apparatus. Every experiment involves two things: (1) an independent variable must be manipulated, and (2) the resulting value of the dependent variable must be recorded. Perhaps the most frequently occurring type of independent variable in psychology is the presentation of certain values of a stimulus, and in every experiment a response is recorded. Both these functions may be performed manually by the experimenter. However, it is frequently desirable, and in fact sometimes necessary, to resort to mechanical, electrical, or electronic assistance. Computers may be valuable here (see Appendix C). Two general functions of apparatus in psychological experimentation are: (1) to facilitate the administration of the experimental treatment, and (2) to aid in recording the resulting behavior. Let us consider how these two functions might be accomplished.

A major research question in psychology, psycholinguistics, neuroscience, and linguistics concerns how humans process and understand language. There is good evidence that we subvocalize what we read as an aid to comprehension. When we subvocalize, our speech muscles are active; that is, they contract in very complex patterns just as when we speak out loud. Some research has sought to determine the latency of the speech muscle responses to words that were presented. For this purpose, apparatus was required to present words for extremely short durations. Such apparatus is called a tachistoscope, which can be a modification of a typical Kodak carousel projector as illustrated in Figure 5-2.

To detect the latencies of speech muscle responses to the linguistic stimuli, electromyographic records of the speech muscles are taken ("electro" refers to electric, "myo" to muscle, and "graphic" to writing so that "electromyographic" means "writing electrical signals from muscles"). When muscles contract, they generate very slight electrical signals (called muscle action potentials) that can be amplified, recorded, and measured (as in Figure 5-2). They need to be amplified considerably, perhaps 50,000 times, because the muscle contractions are often so small that any movement cannot be seen by the naked eye. Through electromyography (Figure 5-3), it has been determined that these small, covert responses (subvocalizations) in the speech muscles occur when we process linguistic stimuli. The question is, how rapidly do these responses occur?

Davis measured latencies of covert speech responses to words of approximately 44 milliseconds from the lips and 85 milliseconds measured from the tongue (1 millisecond is 1/1000 of a second); these latencies are less than the time that it takes to perceive a word, namely about 200 milliseconds. Thus the onset of the covert speech response is rapid enough in the period between the presentation of the word and the perception of the stimulus for the speech muscles to be part of the process of perception. That is, information that comes in through the eyes is responded to by the speech muscles so that, in effect, what we see we silently say to ourselves. Then we hear the silent speech that we say to ourselves whereupon we comprehend what we read. These data thus support a neuromuscular model of perception whereby comprehension of language occurs as reverberating circuits carry information between the brain and the muscles (McGuigan, 1978, 1993).

The main point here, however, is to illustrate the function of apparatus. First, apparatus was used to present word stimuli tachistocopically at various lengths of exposure. In this case, slides were first projected for such a short period of time that the words could not be perceived. Then, the apparatus allowed increased exposure duration so that eventually the participants could identify the words being presented. The second function of apparatus in research—recording the values of the dependent variable—was fulfilled by the electromyographic equipment. It allowed electrical

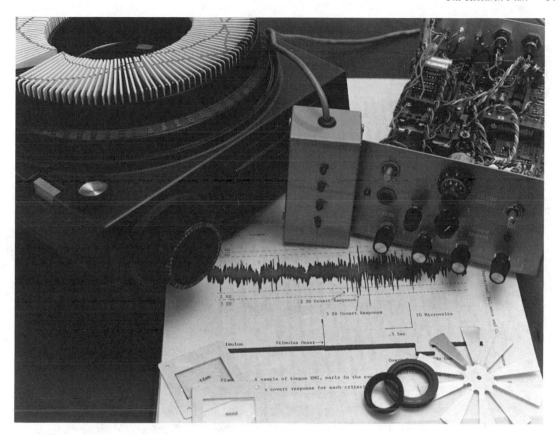

FIGURE 5-2   A carousel projector modified to become a tachistoscope so that words can be visually presented for extremely brief exposure periods. The apparatus to the right (upside down to show its interior) controlled the exposure period. A special shutter and lens are shown in the lower right, while sample slides are at the lower left. A sample electromyographic tracing from the tongue is shown to define covert responses to the words (Davis, 1983).

measurement of covert speech muscle responses so that they could be observed and measured.

The types of apparatus used in behavioral experimentation are so numerous that we cannot attempt a systematic coverage of them here. For further information you might refer to the psychological journal entitled *Behavior Research Methods, Instruments, & Computers*, which is probably in your library. In addition to specific apparatus applications, you can also find references to recent textbooks on the subject. We shall now briefly illustrate further the value of apparatus, as well as offer some cautions.

7. Control the Variables. In this phase of planning the experiment the scientist must consider all of the variables that might contaminate the experiment; one should attempt to evaluate any and all extraneous variables that might affect the dependent variable. It may be decided that some of these variables might act in such a way that they will invalidate the experiment or at least leave the conclusion of the experiment open to question. Such vari-

FIGURE 5-3   Apparatus for electromyographically measuring small-scale, covert behavior. The electrical activity generated when covert speech muscles responded were electromyographically recorded, as illustrated in Figure 5-2. The experimenter monitors the stimulus on the computer and the covert behaviors on the oscilloscope while the subject tries to read the projected words. You can note taped electrodes on the subject's lips and at the eyes.

ables need to be controlled. The techniques for achieving control demand much attention, as emphasized in Chapter 4. To be brief here, we must make sure that no extraneous variable might *differentially* affect the behavior of our groups—that is, that no such variable might affect one group differently than another as far as values of the dependent variable are concerned.

In the course of examining variables that may influence a dependent variable, preferably on the basis of information afforded by previous research, if you decide that a cer-

tain variable is not likely to be influential, it may be reasonable to ignore it. Other variables, however, might be considered to be relevant, but there are difficulties in controlling them. Perhaps it is reasonable to assume that such variables will exert equal effects, at random, on all conditions. If this assumption seems tenable, the experimenter might choose to proceed. But if the assumption of adequate control of extraneous variables is tenuous, then the difficulty may well be of such serious proportions that it would be wiser to abandon the experiment.

8. Select a Design. So far we have concentrated on the two-groups design in which the results for an experimental group are compared to those for a control group. We shall consider later a number of other designs from among which the experimenter may choose the one most appropriate to the problem at hand. For example, it may be more advantageous to use several groups, instead of just two, in which case a **multigroups design** would be adopted (Chapter 7). Another type of design, which in many cases is the most efficient and which is increasingly being used in psychology, is the **factorial design** (Chapter 8.) Here, however, we will continue illustrating principles of experimentation by means of the basic two-groups design—that of randomly assigning participants to an experimental or a control group. These principles will be extended when we illustrate more complex designs, such as those in which there are more than two experimental and control conditions in which case there are more than two independent groups of participants.

9. Select and Assign Participants to Groups. The experimenter conducts an experiment in order to conclude something about behavior. To do this, of course, one must select certain participants to study. But from what collection of people (or animals, and so on) should the participants be selected? This is an important question because we want to generalize findings from the participants that we study to the larger collection of participants from which they were chosen (see step 14, p. 96).

Defining a Population and Sample. The larger collection of participants is the **population** (or **universe**) under study; those who participate in an experiment constitute a **sample**. The *population* of participants is defined as all possible individuals that might be selected for study. The population might be all possible college students in the United States, and the sample might be those that you selected for study from a psychology class in your university. More generally, *population* means the total number of possible items of a class that might be studied—it is the entire class or collection of items from which a sample can be taken. Thus, a population need not refer only to people, but to any type of organism: amoebae, rats, jellyfish. Furthermore, the definition is worded so that it can and does refer to inanimate objects. For example, we may have a population of types of therapy (directive, nondirective, relaxation, behavioral, and so forth) or of learning tasks (hitting a baseball, learning a maze, etc.). Or an experimenter may be interested in sampling a population of stimulus conditions (high, medium, and low meaningfulness of words) or a population of experiments (three separate experiments that test the same hypothesis). In engineering a person may be interested in studying a population of the bridges of the world; an industrial psychologist may be concerned with a population of whiskey products.

Specify the Population with Great Precision. For the moment let us merely concern ourselves with participant populations and leave other populations until later (see Chapter 12). In specifying a population we must note particularly relevant characteristics, for example, if we are concerned with a population of people, we might specify the age, sex (gender), education, socioeconomic status, and race. If we are working with animals, we might wish to specify the species, gender, age, strain, experience, and habituation procedures.

Given a well-defined population to study, then, we have the problem of how actually to study it. If it is a small population, it may be possible to observe all individuals. Adequately studying an entire population is preferable to studying a sample of it. We once conducted some consumer research studies in which we were supposed to obtain a sample of 18 people in a small town in the High Sierras. After considerable difficulty we were able to locate the "town" and after further difficulty were eventually able to find an eighteenth person. In this study the entire population of the town was exhausted (as was the author), and more reliable results were obtained than if a smaller sample of the town were selected. (As it turned out, however, not a single person planned on purchasing TV sets, dishwashers, or similar electrical appliances during the next year, largely because the town did not have electricity.) However, the population to be studied is seldom so small that it can be exhausted by the researcher. More likely the population is too large to be studied in its entirety, and the researcher must resort to studying a sample. In that case, the experimenter must select a number of participants and study them. One technique for selecting a sample is that of **randomization**. In random selection of a sample of participants from a population, each member of the population has an equal chance of being chosen. For instance, if we wish to draw a random sample from a college of 600 students, we might write the names of all the students on separate pieces of paper. We would then place the 600 slips of paper in a (large) hat, mix thoroughly, and, without looking, draw our sample. If our sample is to consist of 60 students, we would select 60 pieces of paper. Of course, there are simpler techniques to achieve a random sample, such as taking an already published list of all 600 students and selecting every tenth one to form our sample. To select the first name, we would randomly select 1 of the first 10 participants, and then count successive tens from there.

The Sample Should be Representative. Once the experimenter randomly selects a sample, it is then assumed that the sample is typical of the entire population—that a **representative sample** has been drawn. Drawing samples at random is usually sufficient to assure that a sample is representative, but the researcher may check on this if it is desired. For instance, if values are available for the population, they can then be compared with the sample values. If one is studying the population of people in the United States, a large amount of census information is readily available on educational levels, age, sex, and so on. We can compute certain of these statistics for a sample and

compare these figures with those for the general population. If the values are close, we can assume that the random sample *is* representative. Assuring that a sample is similar to the population in a number of known characteristics implies that it is also similar with respect to characteristics for which no data are available. This could be a dangerous assumption, but it is certainly better than if there were no check on representativeness.

Assigning Participants to Groups. Once the population has been specified, a sample drawn from it, and a type of experimental design determined, the sample should be randomly assigned to groups. By using randomization we assure ourselves that each participant has an equal opportunity to be assigned to each group. Some procedure such as coin flipping can be used for this purpose. For example, suppose that we have a sample of 20 participants and that we have two groups. If the first coin flip comes up "heads," the first participant would be placed in group 1. But if it is "tails," that participant would be placed in group 2. We would then do likewise for the second participant, and so on until we have 10 participants in one group. The remaining ones would then be assigned to the other group.

Assigning Groups to Experimental Conditions. We randomly determine which group is to be the experimental group and which is to be the control group. For instance, we might make a rule that if a "head" comes up, group 1 is the experimental group and group 2 the control group, or visa versa.

The Many Uses of Randomization. By now you no doubt have acquired a "feel" for the importance of randomization in experimental research—the random selection of a sample of participants from a population, the random assignment of participants to groups, and the random determination of which of the two groups will be the experimental group and which will be the control group. It is by the process of randomization that we attempt to eliminate biases (errors) in our experiment. When we want to make statements about our population of participants, we generally study a sample that is representative of that population. If our sample is not representative, then what is true of our sample may not be true of our population, and we might make an error in generalizing the results obtained from our sample to the population. Random assignment of our sample to two groups is important because we want to start our experiment with groups that are essentially equal. If we do not randomly assign participants to two groups, we may well end with two groups that are unequal in some important respect. If we assign participants to groups in a nonrandom manner, perhaps just looking at each participant and saying, "I'll put you in the control group," we may have one group being more intelligent than the other; consciously or unconsciously, we may have elected the more intelligent participants for the experimental group.

Limitations in Randomization. Having thus emphasized the importance of these procedures, we must hasten to add that the use of randomization does not guarantee that our sample is representative of the population from whence it came or that the groups in an experiment are equal before the administration of the experimental treatment. For, by an unfortunate quirk of fate, randomization may produce two unequal groups—one group may, for example, turn out to be significantly more intelligent than the other. However, randomization is typically the best procedure that we can use, and we can be sure that, at least in the long run, its use is justified. For any given sample or in any given experiment, randomization may well result in errors, but here, as everywhere else in life, we must play the probabilities. If a very unlikely event occurs (e.g., if the procedure of randomization leads to two unequal groups), we will end up with an erroneous conclusion. Eventually, however, due to the self-checking nature of science, the error can be discovered.

Determining the Number of Groups. The actual number of groups to be used in an experiment is determined by the number of independent variables, by the number of values of them that are selected for study, and by the nature of the extraneous variables to be controlled. If we have a single independent variable that we vary in two ways, we would have two groups—an experimental and a control group. If we select three values of the independent variable for study, then we would assign our sample of participants to three groups. For example, say you are interested in whether the amount of student competition in a class increases cheating behavior on examination. The independent variable of amount of competition might be varied in three ways so that participants would be randomly assigned to three groups who experience little, average, and excessive amounts of competition. (In a free moment you might ponder how you would operationally define the dependent variable of amount of cheating.)

Usually an equal number of participants are assigned to each group. Thus, if we have 80 participants in our sample and if we vary the independent variable in four ways, we would have four groups in the experiment, with probably 20 participants in each group. It is not necessary, however, to have the same number of participants in each group, and the experimenter may determine the size of each group in accordance with criteria that we shall take up later.

10. Specify the Experimental Procedure. The procedure for conducting the data collection phase of the experiment should be outlined in great detail. The experimenter should precisely formulate how the values of the independent variable are to be administered and how the values of the dependent variable are to be recorded, and should carefully plan how the participants will be treated, how the stimuli will be administered, and how the response will be observed and recorded. Instructions to the participants (if humans are used) should be written out. The experimenter might start an outline right from greeting the participant and carrying through each step, to saying "goodbye."

In the initial stage of giving instructions to the participant, the investigator explains all aspects of the research that might reasonably be expected to influence willingness to participate; the researcher should also ask if the participant has any questions and answer those questions to the maximum extent possible. Use a practice session too to make sure that the participant can follow the instructions. Having obtained the willing cooperation of the participant, the participant should then sign a statement of **informed consent**. You may think that the signed statement of informed consent is not really necessary in minimal-risk research, such as you will probably be conducting. However, for your own protection it is still a good idea to have a written agreement on record stating that the participant engaged in the research willingly and with knowledge about what was to happen. For elaboration of these and other aspects of ethics in research, see Appendix D on ethical principles.

Don't forget too that it is also advisable to conduct a pilot study with a few participants to see how the procedure works. Often such "dress rehearsals" will suggest new points to be covered and modification of procedures already set down.

11. *Evaluate the Data.* The data of the experiment are usually subjected to statistical analysis to ascertain the reliability of the results. Suppose that in a two-group design the sample mean for the experimental group is 14.0 units (on some response measure) and that for the control group is 12.1 units. However, this sample mean difference may not be reliable—it may be a chance difference and not a "real" one. If the difference is not reliable, the outcome may be reversed the next time the experiment is conducted. A statistical technique can be used to determine whether a sample difference between the mean dependent variable scores of two groups is reliable. The statistical analysis can tell you, in effect, the odds

that the difference between the groups might have occurred by chance. If the probability is small that this difference is due to random fluctuations, then we may conclude that the difference *is* reliable, that the experimental group *is* reliably superior to the control group.

The main point here is that the data are evaluated by a statistical test, a number of which are available. However, some tests are appropriate to one kind of data or experimental design and some are not, but they all require that certain assumptions be met. These will be discussed later, but for now let us emphasize that one should plan the complete procedure for statistical analysis *prior* to conducting the experiment. Sometimes experimenters do not do this and find that there are serious problems in the statistical analysis that could have been prevented by better planning. Lack of rigor in the use of statistics can invalidate the experiment.[2]

12. *Form the Evidence Report.* We have said that the evidence report is a summary statement of the findings of the experiment, but it tells us something more. It tells us whether the antecedent conditions of the hypothesis held (were actually present) in the experiment. More completely, then, the evidence report is a statement of whether the antecedent conditions of the hypothesis obtained and the consequent conditions specified by the hypothesis were found to occur. If the consequent conditions were found to occur, the evidence report is positive; if not, the evidence report is negative. To illustrate, consider the hypothesis: "If a teacher praises a student for good reading performance, then the student's reading competence will increase." An experiment to test this hypothesis might have the participants in an experimental group receive praise each time they exhibit good reading performance. No praise would be given to the members of the control group when they read well. Let us assume that the experimental group exhibits

---

[2] A "nonstatistical," though rigorous, approach will be presented in Chapter 10.

a reliably greater increase in reading competence than does the control group. Referring to the hypothesis, the antecedent condition *was* satisfied, and the consequent condition was found to be the case. We may thus formulate our evidence report: "Students were praised by a teacher when they exhibited good reading performance, and they exhibited an increase in reading competence (as compared with the control group)." In short, the evidence report is a sentence that asserts that the antecedent conditions held *and* that the consequent conditions either did or did not hold—it is of the form "*a* and *b*," in which *a* stands for the antecedent conditions and *b* for the consequent conditions of the hypothesis.

13. Make Inferences from the Evidence Report to the Hypothesis. In this phase the evidence report is related to the hypothesis to determine whether the hypothesis is probably true or false. For this, an inference from the evidence report to the hypothesis is essentially as follows: If the evidence report is positive, the hypothesis is confirmed (the evidence report and the hypothesis coincide—what was predicted to happen by the hypothesis actually happened, as stated by the evidence report). If, however, the evidence report is negative, the hypothesis is not confirmed.

14. Generalize the Findings. The extent to which the results can be generalized depends on the extent to which the populations with which the experiment is concerned have been specified and the extent to which those populations have been represented in the experiment by random sampling. Consider, for example, that the experimenter specified this population as all the students at Ivy College. If a random sample of students[3] was drawn from that population, the experimental results may be

generalized to that population; it may then be asserted that what was true for this sample is probably true for the whole population. Of course, if the population was not adequately defined or the sample was not randomly drawn, no such generalization is justifiable; strictly speaking, the results would apply only to the sample studied.

A SUMMARY AND PREVIEW

We have covered the major phases of experimentation, and you should now have a good idea of the individual steps and how they fall into a logical pattern. Our first effort to present the whole picture was in Chapter 1. In Chapters 2 and 3 and in this section we have attempted to enlarge on some of the steps. Thus, in Chapter 2 we considered the nature of the problem, and in Chapter 3 we discussed the hypothesis. These two initial phases of planning the experiment were summarized in the preceding steps 3 and 4. Next we said that the variables specified by the hypothesis should be operationally defined (step 5). The use of apparatus for presenting stimuli and for recording responses was discussed as step 6. The important topic of control was considered (step 7) but was enlarged on in Chapter 4. Following this we pointed out that several designs are possible in addition to the two-groups design on which we have largely concentrated (step 8). The ways in which several different research designs may be used is the subject of Chapters 6–11. Next we took up the selection of participants and assignments of them to groups (step 9). Step 10 consisted of a brief discussion of experimental procedure, and in step 11 we offered a preview of statistical analysis that will be more thoroughly covered in connection with the different experimental designs. The formation of the evidence report and the way in which it is used to test the hypothesis were covered in steps 12 and 13. Finally, we briefly considered the problem of generalization (step 14). As we continue through the book, each of these points will continue to appear in a vari-

---

[3] To illustrate the importance of operationally defining terms such as "student," consider the university president's reply to the question of how many students there were at his university. After some thought he said, "About 10 percent."

ety of places, even though separate chapters may not be devoted to them. As a summary of this section, as well as to facilitate your planning of experiments, we offer the following checklist.

1. Label the experiment.
2. Summarize previous relevant research.
3. State your problem, preferably as a question.
4. State your hypothesis.
5. Define your variables.
6. Specify your apparatus.
7. State the extraneous variables that need to be controlled and the ways in which you will control them.
8. Select the design most appropriate for your problem.
9. Indicate the manner of selecting your participants, the way in which they will be assigned to groups, and the number to be in each group.
10. List the steps of your experimental procedure, including ethical principles to be followed.
11. Specify the type of statistical analysis to be used.
12. State the possible evidence reports. Will the results tell you something about your hypothesis no matter how they come out?
13. Determine whether you can make unambiguous inferences from the evidence report to the hypothesis.
14. Determine to what extent you will be able to generalize your findings.

Now, after presenting the steps of experimentation in an orderly and logical manner, let us conclude this section with a tempering comment. An advertisement for an employment agency could well state that "there is always a future in apparatus maintenance." A widely held belief is that each experimentalist has a personal poltergeist who capriciously intervenes in the laboratory at just the right time. Many common "laws of experimentation" reflect the consequences: "Anything that can go wrong will"; "Everything goes wrong at one time"; "Things take more time to repair than they do"; "If several things can go wrong, the one that will

go wrong is that which will do the most harm"; "If your lab seems to be going well, you have overlooked something"; and the like.

After faithfully following the prescriptions offered in this chapter, students typically experience difficulties in the conduct of an experiment that they summarize by such phrases as "everything's a mess." By this they apparently mean such things as the equipment stopped working in the middle of an experimental session, some participants were uncooperative, a fatal error in control of variables was detected after the data were collected, and so forth. If such difficulties occur, they are not the sole possession of students; sophisticated researchers also experience such grief, but they have learned to be more agile and are better able to recover when troubles appear. Adjustments nearly always are required; for example, if the data for one student must be disregarded because of procedural errors, they can be replaced by substituting another student under the same conditions. The 14 steps offered here may help you plan your experiment carefully to anticipate problems and help reduce the number of experimental errors. Experienced psychologists themselves profit to the extent to which they formulate and adhere to a precise experimental plan.

CONDUCTING AN EXPERIMENT: AN EXAMPLE

One of the values of conducting a study early in your research methods course is that it affords you the opportunity to make errors that you can learn to avoid. Commence work on a problem early, regardless of the simplicity of the experiment or of whether it will contribute new knowledge. Too many students think that their first study has to be an important one. Certainly we want to encourage the conduct of important research, but the best way to reach that point is to practice. One possibility to facilitate practice is simply to repeat a classic study such as the following one based on research by E.L. Thorndike.

The fact that this is a simple, straightforward experiment using minimal equipment allows us better to illustrate the points that we have previously covered.

The Problem and Hypothesis. One class decided to study the effect of knowledge of results on performance. The question was whether informing a person of how well a task is performed facilitates the learning of that task. The title was "The Effect of Knowledge of Results on Performance."

The problem was then stated: "What is the effect of knowledge of results on performance?" and the students conducted a rather thorough literature survey on that topic. The hypothesis was "If knowledge of results is furnished to a person, then that person's performance will be facilitated." (Note that the statement of the problem and the hypothesis has implicitly determined the variables; they next need to be made explicit.) The task for the participants was to draw, while blindfolded, a 5-inch line. The independent variable, amount of knowledge of results, was varied from zero (no information) to a large amount, operationally defined as telling the participants whether the line drawn was "too long," "too short," or "right." "Too long," in turn, was defined as any line 5¼ inches or longer, "too short" as any line 4¾ inches or shorter, and "right" as any line between 5¼ inches and 4¾ inches. The dependent variable value was determined by actual length of 50 lines drawn by each person. More precisely, each person's total performance was the sum total of all deviations of 5-inch lines on all 50 trials.

The Apparatus. This consisted of a drawing board on which was affixed ruled paper, a blindfold, and a pencil. The paper was easily movable for each trial and was ruled in such a manner that the experimenter could tell immediately within which of the three intervals (long, short, or right) the participants' lines fell.

Participants. Since there were two values of the independent variable (a positive and a zero amount), two groups were required—an experimental group received knowledge of results, whereas a control group did not. The participant population was defined as all the students in the college. From a list of the student body, 60 individuals were randomly assigned for study and randomly divided into two groups.[4] It was then randomly determined which was the experimental group and which was the control.

Control of Extraneous Variables. Next it was determined which extraneous variables might influence the dependent variable and therefore needed to be controlled. Our general principle of control is that both groups should be treated alike in all respects, except for different values of the independent variable (in this case different amounts of knowledge of results). Hence, essentially the same instructions were read to both groups, a constant "experimental attitude" was maintained in the presence of both groups (the experimenter did not frown at some of the subjects while being jovial with others). Incidental cues were eliminated insofar as possible (the experiment would have been invalidated, for example, if experimenters held their breath just when the participant's pencil reached the 5-inch mark). Such incidental cues, not only would have furnished some knowledge of results to an alert control participant, but also would have increased the amount of knowledge of results for the experimental participants.

Is the amount of time between trials an important variable? From the literature survey, previous research suggested that it was. Generally, the longer the time between trials, the better the performance. The intertrial interval was therefore controlled by holding it constant for all participants. After each response, precisely 10 seconds elapsed

---

[4] It was correctly assumed that all 60 participants would cooperate. However, the widespread practice among experimenters of using students in introductory psychology classes as volunteers does not result in a random sample and thus leads to the question of whether the sample is representative of some population, such as that of all the students in the college.

before the participant's hand was returned to the starting point for the next trial. What other extraneous variables might be considered? Perhaps the time of day at which the experiment is conducted is important; a person might perform better in the morning than in the afternoon or evening. If the experimental group was run in the morning and the control group in the afternoon, then no clear-cut conclusion about the effectiveness of knowledge of results could be drawn. One control measure might be to run all participants between 2 P.M. and 4 P.M. But even this might produce differences, since people might perform better at 2 P.M. than at 3 P.M. Furthermore it was not possible to run the experiment with all the participants within this one hour on the same day, so the experiment had to be conducted over a period of two weeks. Does it make a difference whether students participate on the first day or the last day for the two weeks? It may be that examinations are being given concurrent with the first part of the experiment, causing nervousness. Then again it may be that people tested on Monday perform differently than if they are tested on Friday.

The problem of how to control this time variable was rather complex. The following procedure was chosen (see Chapter 4 for an elaboration): All participants were run between 2 P.M. and 4 P.M. When the first participant reported to the laboratory, a coin flip determined assignment to either the experimental or control group. If that person was placed in the control group, the next participant was assigned to the experimental group. The third participant was similarly assigned to one group and the fourth participant to the other, and so on for the remainder of the participants for as many days as the experiment was conducted. This procedure rather safely assures that whatever the effects of time differences on the participants' performance, they were balanced— that they affected both groups equally. This is so because, in the long run, we can assume that an equal number of individuals from both groups participated during any given

time interval of the day and on any particular day of the experiment.

Another control problem concerns the individual characteristics of the experimenter, a topic that we shall explore later. In this experiment all students in the experimental psychology class ran participants. However, each student-experimenter ran an equal number of participants and also an equal number of participants in each group. If one student-experimenter ran more participants than another or if the students did not run an equal number of experimental and control participants, experimenter characteristics might have differentially affected the dependent-variable measures of the two groups. The experimenter variable was thus adequately controlled.

These illustrations should be sufficient to illustrate the control problems involved, although you should think of some additional variables that the class also considered. For example, do distracting influences exist, such as noise from air conditioners and people talking? These could be controlled to some extent, but not completely. In the case of those that could not be reasonably controlled, it was assumed that they affected both groups equally—that they "randomized out." For instance, there is no reason to think that various distracting influences should affect one group more than the other. After surveying the possibilities the class concluded that there were no extraneous variables that would differentially affect the dependent-variable scores of the two groups. In other words, all extraneous variables were either intentionally controlled or would randomly affect both groups equally.

Procedure. The plan for this phase was as follows: After the participant enters the room and is greeted, the person is seated at a table, briefly told what the experiment is about and asked to complete an informed consent form. For information about informed consent and about research ethics more generally, you should study Appendix D. Then the participant is given the following instructions: "I want you to draw some straight lines that are 5 inches long, while you are blindfolded. You are to draw them horizontally like this (experimenter demonstrates by drawing a horizontal line). When you have completed your line, leave your pencil at the point where you stopped. I shall return your hand to the starting point. Also, please keep your arm and hand off the table while drawing your line. You are to have only the point of the pencil touching the paper. Are there any questions?" The experimenter answers any questions by repeating the pertinent parts of the instructions and then blindfolds the participant. "Now I am going to blindfold you." The experimenter then uncovers the apparatus and places the pencil in the participant's hand. The individual's hand is guided to the starting point, and the instruction is given: "Ready? Start." The appropriate knowledge of results is given to the individual immediately after the pencil stops. No information is given to the control participants. When a trial is completed, there is a 10-second wait, after which the hand is returned to the starting point. Then the person is told: "Now draw another line 5 inches long. Ready? Start." The experimenter must move the paper before each trial so that the participant's next response can be recorded. This same procedure is followed until the participant has drawn 50 lines. The experimenter then removes the blindfold, thanks the participant, and requests that the experiment not be discussed (with other students). Finally, the experimenter explains the nature of the experiment and answers all questions (this is referred to as "debriefing").

Following this, the students collect their data. It was reassuring, although hardly startling, to find that knowledge of results did, in fact, facilitate performance.

Illustration of the final steps of the planning and conduct of an experiment (statistical treatment of the data, forming the evidence report, confronting the hypothesis with the evidence report, and generalization of the findings) will be offered when these topics are emphasized later. In due course, we will consider how the findings of an experiment may contribute to the formulation of empirical laws and how they might fit into some theoretical framework.

CHAPTER SUMMARY

In this chapter we presented the major aspects of experimentation as an organized unit. The intent is to help you to start with the development and formulation of a problem and to work through the important phases that allow you to arrive at a sound empirical conclusion. The formulation of your experimental plan (which can also help in the later write-up of your research) assists you to think through each important step of your research. At selected points in your study, especially as you are planning and writing up your own research, you should find that these outlines provide valuable guidance. With your later study (of this book and in subsequent courses), you should be able to add to the skeleton presented in this chapter.

I. An evidence report, a statement of the results of a scientific investigation may be obtained with

A. Nonexperimental methods such as the clinical method, naturalistic observational research, survey research, archival research, correlation research, and quasi-experiments. One prominent quasi-experimental method is the method of systematic observation wherein participants are studied in preformed groups, rather than being randomly assigned to treatment conditions.

B. The experimental method. A distinguishing characteristic of this method is that the event to be studied is intentionally produced; consequently, the experimenter is prepared to study it accurately. Participants are also randomly assigned to conditions and the selection of which group receives which treatment is randomly made.

II. Types of experiments include exploratory versus confirmatory experiments, crucial experiments, pilot studies, and field studies.

III. A research plan should include the following steps (which may serve as a checklist):
   A. Label the experiment.
   B. Summarize previous relevant research.
   C. State your problem, preferably as a question.
   D. State your hypothesis.
   E. Define your variables.
   F. Specify your apparatus.
   G. State the extraneous variables that need to be controlled and the ways in which you will control them.
   H. Select the design most appropriate for your problem.
   I. Indicate the manner of selecting your participants, the way in which they will be assigned to groups, and the number to be in each group.
   J. List the steps of your experimental procedure, including ethical considerations.
   K. Specify the statistical analysis to be used.
   L. State the possible evidence reports. Will the results tell you something about your hypothesis no matter how they come out?
   M. Can you make unambiguous inferences from the evidence report to the hypothesis?
   N. To what extent will you be able to generalize your findings?

IV. Finally, don't get discouraged if your research does not come off in a completely orderly fashion—it seldom does!

SOME REVIEW QUESTIONS FOR THE STUDENT

1. What is the major contrasting feature between experimental and nonexperimental methods?
2. Review (and perhaps outline) the relevant steps in planning an experiment. You might make notes about important topics mentioned but not yet covered (such as statistical analysis).
3. In preparation for the first study to be conducted in your class, you could select a problem for yourself and develop an outline of an experimental plan. This would be especially useful to you in bringing out some questions that may not yet have occurred to you.
4. Select some psychological journals from your library and study how the various components covered there were handled by other authors.
5. How do you adequately "debrief" human participants in a research study? Do you recognize any difficulty in carrying out other items referred to in Appendix D on research ethics?

chapter 6

EXPERIMENTAL DESIGN: THE CASE OF TWO INDEPENDENT GROUPS

Major purpose:

To test an empirical hypothesis through statistical analysis of dependent-variable values for two groups.

What you are going to find:

1. Computational equations for the mean, standard deviation, and variance.

2. How these values form the basis for conducting a *t*-test, which is a statistical method for determining whether the dependent-variable means of two groups reliably differ.

3. Detailed instructions on how to conduct and interpret a *t*-test.

What you should acquire:

The ability to analyze and interpret statistically the data from a two-group investigation by means of the *t*-test.

You have now acquired a general understanding of how to conduct experiments. In Chapters 1 and 5 we covered the major phases of experimentation, but in presenting an overall picture it was necessary to cover some phases hastily. In the remaining chapters we will concentrate on these rela-tively neglected areas while continuing to show how the phases fit into the general research picture. Our first focus is on the selection of a design.

Although there are a number of experimental designs, we have thus far concentrated on one that involves **two independent**

groups. Since this design is basic, this chapter will provide a foundation from which we can move to more complex (although not necessarily more difficult to comprehend) designs.

A GENERAL ORIENTATION

Recall that when we study two independent groups, we may use an experimental design, or we may use the method of systematic observation. In conducting an experiment, we randomly assign participants to the two independent groups forming a **two-randomized-groups design**. In using the method of systematic observation, however, we select two groups with differing characteristics that are already formed. The *t*-test is appropriate statistically to analyze the data from either design. We shall concentrate on the experimental design because, as we have detailed, it is the more powerful.

To summarize briefly what has been said about the two-randomized-group design, recall that the experimenter operationally defines an independent variable to be varied in two ways. The two values assigned to the independent variable may be referred to as two *conditions, treatments*, or *methods*. The question is then whether these two conditions differentially affect the dependent variable. To answer, we define a population about which we wish to make a statement and randomly select a sample of participants for study; what is observed for the sample is inferred to be true for the population. However, to be realistic, researchers seldom define their populations with precision. Rather, as in the study of humans, their populations are usually assumed to be those humans living today. Sometimes the population can be more precisely defined, as in the case of industrial workers who are performing a given assembly task. Or, in the case of testing methods of learning, it could be defined as pupils in the sixth grade throughout the United States. Research commonly conducted on problems within the fields of information processing, linguis-

tic perception, or language learning assume that the population is *Homo Sapiens*. It is common practice for the sample to consist of volunteers from an introductory psychology class. The question of generalization from that nonrandomly selected sample to the population is taken up in Chapter 1. For now, we conform to the typical procedure of assuming that we can reasonably generalize from that sample. Assuming that we have 60 students who will cooperate, we next divide them into two groups. Any method that would assure that the participants are randomly assigned to the two groups would suffice, e.g., the name of the first participant drawn from a hat would be assigned to group 1, the second to group 2, and so on until we have two groups of 30 participants each. A simple flip of a coin would then tell us which is to be the experimental group and which the control group. The reason that this is called the *two-randomized-groups design* is now quite apparent: Participants are randomly assigned to two groups and their treatments are randomly determined too.

ESTABLISHING "EQUALITY" OF GROUPS THROUGH RANDOMIZATION

A basic and important presupposition made in any type of design is that the means (averages) of the groups on the dependent variable do not differ reliably at the start of the experiment. In a two-groups design the two values of the independent variable are then respectively administered to the two groups. For example, a positive amount is administered to the experimental group and a zero amount to the control group. The dependent-variable scores for all participants are then recorded and statistically analyzed. If the statistical test indicates that the two groups are reliably different, it may be concluded that this difference is due to the variation of the independent variable: Assuming that the proper experimental controls have been in effect, it may be concluded that the two different values of the independent variable are effective in producing the differences in the dependent variable.

If the 60 participants are randomly assigned to two groups, it is reasonable to assume that the two groups are essentially equal, but approximately equivalent with respect to what? The answer might be that the groups are equivalent in many respects. And such an answer is easy to defend, assuming that the randomization has been properly carried out. In any given experiment, however, we want the two groups to be equal only on those factors that might affect our dependent variable. If the dependent variable is rate of learning a visual task, we would want the two groups to be equivalent at least with respect to intelligence and visual ability; for example, we would want the means of intelligence and visual acuity scores to be essentially the same, for these two factors probably influence scores on our dependent variable.

"Unequal" Groups Are Unlikely

Sometimes students criticize the randomized-groups design by pointing out that "by chance" (i.e., due to random fluctuations) we could end up with unequal groups. It is possible that one group would be more intelligent, on the average, than the other group. Even though it is possible that one group would have a higher mean intelligence score, it is unlikely, particularly if a large number of participants is used in both groups. For it can be demonstrated that the larger the number of people randomly assigned to the two groups, the closer their means will approach each other. Hence, although with a small number of participants it is unlikely that the means of the two groups will differ to any great extent, a difference is more likely than if the number were large. The lesson should be clear: If you wish to reduce the difference in the means of the two groups, use a large number of participants.[1]

---

[1] In making this point we are ignoring the distributions of the scores. Hence, the matter is not quite this simple, but the main point is sound.

"Unequal" Groups Are Possible

Even with a comparatively large number of participants it is still possible, although unlikely, that the means of the groups will differ considerably due to random fluctuations. Suppose, for example, that we measured intelligence, and obtained a mean intelligence quotient of 100 for one group and mean of 116 for the second. By using appropriate statistical techniques we can determine that such an event should occur by chance less than about 5 times out of 100. If we ran the experiment 100 times and assigned participants to two groups at random in each experiment, a difference between the groups of 16 IQ points (e.g., $116 - 100$) or more should occur by chance in only about 5 of the experiments. Differences between the two groups of less than 16 IQ points should occur more frequently, and differences between the two groups of 24 points or more should occur less than one time in 100 experiments, on the average. Most frequently, then, there should be only a small difference between the two groups.

"But," the skeptical student continues, "suppose that in the particular experiment that I am conducting (I don't care about the other 95 or 99 experiments) I *do* by chance assign my participants to two groups of widely differing ability. I would think that the group with the mean IQ of 116 would have a higher mean score on the dependent variable than does the other group, *regardless of the effect of the independent variable*. I (the experimenter) would then conclude that the independent variable is effective, when, in fact, it isn't."

Compare Group Means on Relevant Variables

One cannot help but be impressed by such a convincing attack, but retreat at this point would be premature, for there are still several weapons that can be brought into the battle. First, if one has doubts as to the equivalence of the two groups, their scores on certain variables can be computed to see how their means actually compare. Thus, in the example, we would measure the participants' IQs and visual acuity, compute the means for both groups, and compare the scores to see if there is much difference. If there is little difference, we know that our random assignment has been at least fairly successful. This laborious and generally unnecessary precaution actually has been taken in a number of experiments.[2]

Analysis of Covariance

"But," the student continues tenaciously, "suppose I find that there is a sizable difference and that I find this out only after all the data have been collected. My experiment would be invalidated." Yet there is hope. In this case we could use a statistical technique that allows us to equate the two groups with respect to intelligence; that is, we could statistically "correct" for the difference between the two groups and determine whether they differ on the dependent variable for a reason other than intelligence. Put another way, we could statistically equate the two groups on intelligence so that differences on this extraneous variable would not differentially affect the dependent-variable scores. This statistical technique is known as the *analysis of covariance*, and is presented in many books on statistics.

Science Is Self-Correcting

"Excellent," the student persists, "but suppose the two groups differ in some respect for which we have no measure and that this difference will sizably influence scores on the dependent variable. I now understand that we can probably correct for the difference between the two groups on factors such as intelligence and visual acuity, because these are easily measurable variables. But what if the

---

[2] In the experiment on rifle marksmanship discussed in Chapter 4, for instance, it was determined that four groups did not reliably differ on the following extraneous variables: previous firing experience, left-or-right-handedness, visual acuity, intelligence, or educational level.

groups differ on some factor that we do not think to measure? In this case we would be totally unaware of the difference and draw illegitimate conclusions from our data."

"You," we say to the student, secretly admiring the demanding perseverance, "have now put us in such an unlikely position that we need not worry about its occurrence. Nevertheless, it *is* possible, just as it is possible that you will be hit by a car today while crossing the street. And, if there is some factor for which we cannot make a correction, the experiment might well result in erroneous conclusions." The only point we can refer to here is one of the general features of the scientific enterprise: Science is self-correcting! Thus, if any given experiment leads to a false conclusion, and if the conclusion has any importance at all, an inconsistency between the results of the invalid experiment and data from a later experiment will become apparent. The existence of this problem will then lead to a solution, which, in this case, will be a matter of discarding the incorrect conclusion.

STATISTICAL ANALYSIS OF THE TWO-INDEPENDENT-GROUPS DESIGN

In Chapter 1 we posed the following problem: After the experimenter has collected data on the dependent variable, the wish is to determine whether one group is superior to the other. The hypothesis may predict a higher mean for the experimental group than for the control group. The first step in testing the hypothesis is to compute the mean scores on the dependent variable for the two groups. It might be found that the experimental group has a mean score of 40, whereas the control group has one of 35. Can we conclude that this 5-point difference is reliable, or is it merely the result of random fluctuations, of experimental error? Let us now consider a statistical test, known as the "*t*-test" (note that this is a lowercase *t*, not a capital *T*, which has another denotation in statistics), which is frequently used to answer this question.

It is common to enter experimental data into a computer that is programmed to conduct a statistical analysis such as giving you the value of *t*. As we develop in Appendix C, the modern uses of the computer are wonderful, but the computer cannot be used blindly. It is critical to understand what the computer is doing and to be able to check the program to confirm that it is indeed accurate. Many errors can be made if the experimenter does not know how to manually compute the *t*-test or more complex statistical analysis. Thus, while the use of computers for statistical analysis is encouraged the user should have a thorough understanding of what the computer is doing. For these reasons we will proceed with manual computations of our statistical analyses.

Computing a Mean

The first step in computing a *t*-test value is to compute the means of the dependent-variable scores of the two groups concerned. The equation for computing a mean (symbolized $\overline{X}$) is

(6-1) $$\overline{X} = \frac{\Sigma X}{n}$$

Σ is the symbol for summation and may be interepreted as "sum of." It simply instructs you to add whatever is to the right of it.[3] In this case, the letter X is to the right of Σ so we must now find out what values X stands for and add them. Here X merely indicates the score that we obtained for each participant. Suppose, for instance, that we give a test to a class of five students, with these resulting scores:

	X
Joan	100
Constance	100
Richard	80
Betty	70
Joe	60

To compute ΣX we merely add the X scores: $\Sigma X = 100 + 100 + 80 + 70 + 60 = 410$. The n in Equation 6-1 stands for the number of people in the group. In this example, then, $n = 5$. Thus to compute X we simply substitute 410 for ΣX, 5 for n in Equation 6-1, and then divide n into ΣX. Thus the mean score of the group of 5 students is:

$$\overline{X} = \frac{410}{5} = 82.00$$

Incidentally, let us emphasize the great importance of distinguishing between capital letters and lowercase letters in conducting statistical analyses. We mentioned that you should not use a capital T when referring to the *t*-test. Similarly, do not use a lowercase x for a capital X, for those two mean completely different things. Another example is the difference between capital N and lowercase n, as we shall develop shortly. Precision in such matters can be of considerable importance, a topic that you can reflect on when you are looking at the wing of the airplane on which you are riding—you hope that the engineer who designed the wing paid attention to the symbols.

Testing the Difference Between Means

We shall use the *t*-test for this purpose. The equation for computing *t* is:

(6-2) $$t = \frac{\overline{X}_1 - \overline{X}_2}{\sqrt{\frac{SS_1 + SS_2}{(n_1 - 1) + (n_2 - 1)}\left(\frac{1}{n_1} + \frac{1}{n_2}\right)}}$$

Although this equation may look forbidding to the statistically naive, such an impression should be short-lived for *t* is actually rather simple to compute. To illustrate, consider a fascinating experiment on RNA (ribonucleic acid) in the brain during memory storage.[4] First, a group of 7 rats were trained to approach the food cup in a Skinner box every

---

[3] More precisely, Σ instructs you to add all the values for the symbols that are to its right, values that were obtained from your sample.

[4] Conducted by Babich, Jacobson, Bubash, and Jacobson (1965).

time a click was sounded. The animals rarely or never approached the food cup when the click was absent. On the day after this training was completed, the animals were sacrificed, their brains were removed, and RNA was extracted from a selected portion. RNA was also extracted from the brains of 89 untrained rats. Approximately eight hours after extraction, the RNA from each of the rats, trained and untrained, was injected into live, untrained rats. Hence 15 live rats were injected with RNA: Seven (the experimental group) received RNA from trained rats and 8 (the control group) from untrained rats. Both groups were then tested in a Skinner box by presenting 25 separate clicks, and the number of times they approached the food cup was counted. The hypothesis, amazing as it might sound, was to the effect that memory storage could be passed on by means of injections of RNA or associated substances. It was therefore predicted that the experimental group would approach the food cup more often during the test trials than would the control group. The number of times that each rat approached the food cup during the 25 test trials is presented in Table 6-1.

To obtain an evidence report that will tell us whether the hypothesis is probably true or false, we first compute group means. Note that subscripts have been used in Equation 6-2 to indicate which group the various values are for. In this case, $\overline{X}_1$ stands for the mean of group 1 (the experimental group), and $\overline{X}_2$ for the mean group 2 (the control group). In like manner SS_1 and SS_2 stand for what is called the **sum of squares** for groups 1 and 2, respectively, and n_1 and n_2 are the respective numbers in the two groups (lowercase n's, not capital Ns). We can now determine that $\Sigma X_1 = 48$, while $\Sigma X_2 = 8$. Since the number of animals in group 1 is 7, $n_1 = 7$. The mean for group 1 (i.e., $\overline{X}_1$) may now be determined by substitution in Equation 6-1:[5]

TABLE 6-1 Number of Food Cup Approaches per Animal During 25 Test Trials

	Group 1		Group 2
Animal Number	Experimental Rats X_1	Animal Number	Control Rats X_2
1	1	8	0
2	3	9	0
3	7	10	0
4	8	11	1
5	9	12	1
6	10	13	1
7	10	14	2
	$\Sigma X_1 = 48$	15	3
			$\Sigma X_2 = 8$

$$\overline{X}_1 = \frac{48}{7} = 6.86$$

Similarly, for group 2 ($n_2 = 8$),

$$\overline{X}_2 = \frac{8}{8} = 1.00$$

We now need to compute the sum of squares (a value that will be used extensively in later chapters) for each group. The equation for the sum of squares (SS) is

(6-3)
$$SS = \Sigma X^2 - \frac{(\Sigma X)^2}{n}$$

Equation 6-3 contains two terms with which we are already familiar, namely n and ΣX. The other term, ΣX^2, instructs us to add the squares of all the values for a given group. Thus, to compute ΣX^2 for group 1 we should square the value for the first animal, add it to the square of the score for the second, add both of these values to the square of the score for the third, and so on.

---

[5] In your computations you would be wise to pay attention to the significant figures, an indication of the accuracy of your measurements and computations. To determine the accuracy of a measurement, you count the number of digits, for example, 21 is correct to two significant figures, 1.2 to two significant figures, .012 to two significant figures, and 1.456 to four significant figures. The final value of statistics, like a mean or standard deviation, should be rounded off to one more significant figure than for the raw data. Intermediate calculations for the t-test can be safely performed by carrying three more digits than are carried by the data.

By thus squaring the scores for the animals in both groups of Table 6-1 and summing them, we obtain

	Group 1			Group 2	
Animal Number	*Experimental Rats* X_1	X_1^2	*Animal Number*	*Control Rats* X_2	X_2^2
1	1	1	8	0	0
2	3	9	9	0	0
3	7	49	10	0	0
4	8	64	11	1	1
5	9	81	12	1	1
6	10	100	13	1	1
7	10	100	14	2	4
		$\Sigma X_1^2 = 404$	15	3	9
					$\Sigma X_2^2 = 16$

To avoid a common error, be aware that ΣX^2 is *not* the square of ΣX. That is, $(\Sigma X)^2$ is not equal to ΣX^2. For instance, the $\Sigma X_1 = 48$. The square of this value is $(\Sigma X_1)^2 = 2,304$, whereas $\Sigma X_1^2 = 404$.

Now we substitute the appropriate values into Equation 6-3 and compute the sum of squares for each group. We know that for group 1 $\Sigma X_1 = 48$, $\Sigma X_1^2 = 404$, and $n_1 = 7$. Hence,

$$SS_1 = 404 - \frac{(48)^2}{7} = 404 - \frac{(48 \cdot 48)}{7}$$

$$= 404 - \frac{(2,304)}{7} = 404.000 - 329.143$$

$$= 74.857$$

Similarly, the values to compute the sum of squares for group 2 are $\Sigma X_2 = 8$, $\Sigma X_2^2 = 16$, and $n_2 = 8$.

Therefore,

$$SS_2 = 16 - \frac{(8)^2}{8} = 16 - \frac{64}{8} = 8.000$$

To summarize for Equation 6-2 the values required to compute *t* for this experiment,

Group 1	Group 2
$\bar{X}_1 = 6.86$	$\bar{X}_2 = 1.00$
$n_1 = 7$	$n_2 = 8$
$SS_1 = 74.857$	$SS_2 = 8.000$

Substituting these values in Equation 6-2, we obtain

$$t = \frac{6.86 - 1.00}{\sqrt{\left[\frac{74.857 + 8.000}{(7 - 1) + (8 - 1)}\right]\left(\frac{1}{7} + \frac{1}{8}\right)}}$$

We now need to go through the following steps in computing *t*:

1. Obtain the difference between the means: $6.86 - 1.00 = 5.86$
2. Add $SS_1 + SS_2$: $74.857 + 8.000 = 82.857$.
3. Compute $n_1 - 1$: $7 - 1 = 6$.
4. Compute $n_2 - 1$: $8 - 1 = 7$.
5. Add $\frac{1}{n_1} + \frac{1}{n_2} = \frac{1}{7} + \frac{1}{8} = \frac{8}{56} + \frac{7}{56} = \frac{15}{56}$.

The results of these computations are

$$t = \frac{5.86}{\sqrt{\left(\frac{82.857}{6 + 7}\right)\left(\frac{15}{56}\right)}}$$

In the next stage divide the two denominators (13 and 56) into their respective numerators (82.857 and 15):

$$t = \frac{5.86}{\sqrt{(6.374)(.2679)}}$$

Then multiply the values in the denominator:

$$t = \frac{5.86}{\sqrt{1.708}}$$

The next step is to find the square root of 1.708, which is 1.307. Dividing as indicated, we find *t* to be

$$t = \frac{5.86}{1.307} = 4.48$$

Although the computation of *t* is straightforward, the beginning student is likely to make an error in its computation. The error is generally not one of failing to follow the procedure, but one of a computational nature (dividing incorrectly, failing to square terms properly, making mistakes in addition).

Great care must be taken in statistical work; *each step of the computation must be checked*! To learn to compute t, you should work on all the exercises at the end of the chapter until your answers are correct. (We might also note that the value under the square root sign is always positive. If it is negative in your computation, go through your work to find the error.)

One point in need of expansion concerns the numerator statement that $\overline{X}_2$ should be subtracted from $\overline{X}_1$. But we are conducting a *two-sided test*, as against a *one-sided test*. Consequently, we are interested only in the absolute difference between the means; hence, the smaller mean should be subtracted from the larger. For example, if in your experiment you find that $\overline{X}_2$ is greater than $\overline{X}_1$ ($\overline{X}_2 > \overline{X}_1$), then you merely subtract $\overline{X}_1$ from $\overline{X}_2$; that is, Equation 6-2 would have as its numerator $\overline{X}_2 - \overline{X}_1$.

A one-sided test is conducted if there is a very good reason to predict that one mean will be higher than the other. For instance, you might test a theory that precisely predicts that $\overline{X}_1$ is greater than $\overline{X}_2$. In that case, you are not interested in whether $\overline{X}_2$ is greater than $\overline{X}_1$. The difference between a one-and a two-sided test is important, as we shall shortly develop.

The Null Hypothesis

The reason we want to obtain a value of t, we said, is to determine whether the difference between the means of two groups is the result of random fluctuations or whether it is a reliable difference. To approach an answer we must consider a **null hypothesis**, a concept that it is vital to understand.[6] The null

hypothesis that is generally used in a two-independent-group design states that *there is no difference between the population means on the dependent variable of the two groups*. Note that we wish to contrast the two population *means*, because some students misstate the null hypothesis by saying that "there is no difference between two groups." There always are *many* differences between any two groups, but we are interested only in the means of the dependent variable.

Also note that the null hypothesis concerns *population* means—we want to know whether the *true* means of our groups differ where the population mean is the true mean. Because we can seldom study a population in its entirety, the way to determine whether the true (population) means differ is to compare the two sample means. We thus subtract the mean for one sample group from the other, as specified in the numerator of Equation 6-2. If the difference between our sample means is quite small, we would be inclined to conclude that the difference is due to chance. If the difference is quite large, it is probably not due to random fluctuations.

The null hypothesis is a hypothesis that we attempt to disprove (reject). The null hypothesis asserts that the difference between the population means is zero. We seek to determine that it is false, that there is such a difference. Hence, if the null hypothesis is rejected, we can conclude that there (probably) is a true difference between our groups. Furthermore, if it was a properly conducted experiment, this difference is due to varia-

---

[6] The term *null hypothesis* was first used by Sir Ronald A. Fisher (personal communication). He chose the term *null hypothesis* without "particular regard for its etymological justification but by analogy with a usage, formerly and perhaps still current among physicists, of speaking of a null experiment, or a null method of measurement, to refer to a case in which a proposed value is inserted experimentally in the apparatus and the value is corrected, adjusted, and finally verified, when the correct value has been found; because the set-

up is such, as in the Wheatstone Bridge, that a very sensitive galvanometer shows no deflection when exactly the right value has been inserted.

"The governing consideration physically is that an instrument made for direct measurement is usually much less sensitive than one which can be made to kick one way or the other according to whether too large or too small a value has been inserted.

"Without reference to the history of this usage in physics. . . . One may put it by saying that if the hypothesis is exactly true no amount of experimentation will easily give a significant discrepancy, or, that the discrepancy is null apart from the errors of random sampling."

tion of the independent variable. That is, if we can reject the null hypothesis, we can conclude that the dependent-variable differences between our groups was caused by the difference in the values in the independent variable. In this case, we will conclude that our hypothesis was probably true.

On the other hand, if we cannot reject the null hypothesis, then we cannot assert that there is a difference between the two groups; variation of our independent variable is thus probably not effective and the empirical hypothesis is probably false.

The Distinction Between Populations and Samples. This distinction is of great importance, as we shall develop in the last chapter when we discuss the mechanics of generalization. In science we seek to make statements about populations, about all humans, about all dogs, about all airplanes, and so on. The characteristics of populations are called **parameters**, whereas the characteristics of samples are **statistics**. A **parameter** is a measure ascertained from all possible observations of a population, whereas a *statistic* is a value computed only from a sample. The distinction between parameters and statistics is highlighted by using Greek letters as symbols for parameters. Thus μ (the lowercase Greek letter mu) stands for the population mean in contrast to $\overline{X}$, which is the sample mean. The usual null hypothesis that we test when using the two-independent-groups design is $\mu_1 - \mu_2 = 0$, or, equally $\mu_1 = \mu_2$. If the difference between the sample means $(\overline{X}_1 - \overline{X}_2)$ is small, then we are likely to infer that there is no difference between the population means, and, thus, that $\mu_1 - \mu_2 = 0$. (The null hypothesis is true.) On the other hand, if $\overline{X}_1 - \overline{X}_2$ is large, then the null hypothesis that $\mu_1 - \mu_2 = 0$ is probably not true. Note, however, that this is a null hypothesis only for the two-independent-groups design. When we discuss other designs, other null hypotheses will be tested.

To elaborate briefly on the nature of parameters, we note that the parameter (the population symbol) for correlation is ρ (the lowercase Greek letter rho) versus the sample symbol of r and that the Greek letter σ (the lowercase Greek letter sigma) indicates the population's standard deviation versus the sample value s.

In Summary. We seek to falsify the null hypothesis. The null hypothesis states that the difference between our two groups is zero ($\mu_1 - \mu_2 = 0$). If the difference between our sample means ($\overline{X}_1 - \overline{X}_2$) is large, then the null hypothesis is probably false and we reject it. However, if the difference between the sample means is small, we fail to reject the null hypothesis—thus, $\mu_1 - \mu_2 = 0$. When we fail to reject the null hypothesis, we conclude that any difference between our sample means is due to chance (random fluctuations).

How Large Is "Large"?

Tabled Probability Values The question now is how large the difference must be between $\overline{X}_1$ and $\overline{X}_2$ to assert that it is *not* due to random fluctuations alone. This question can be answered by the value of t; if t is sufficiently large, the difference is too large to be attributed solely to random fluctuations. To determine how large "sufficiently large" is, we may consult the table of t. But, before doing this, there is one additional value that we must compute—the *degrees of freedom (df)*—to ascertain the appropriate tabled probability value.

Degrees of Freedom. The degrees of freedom available for the t-test are a function of the number of participants in the experiment. More specifically, $df = N - 2$,[7] where N is the number of subjects in one group (n_1) plus the number of subjects in the other group (n_2). Hence, in our example we have

$$N = n_1 + n_2 \quad \text{that is,} \quad N = 7 + 8 = 15;$$

therefore

$$df = 15 - 2 = 13$$

---

[7]This equation for computing *df* is only for the application of the *t*-test to two independent groups. We shall use other equations for *df* when considering additional statistical tests.

The concept of degrees of freedom and its meaning is discussed in the appendix to this chapter so that we can get along with our calculation of the value of *t*.

The t Table To determine the probability associated with *t*, let us now turn to a table of *t* (Table A-1 in Appendix A) armed with two values: *t* = 4.48 and *df* = 13. The table of *t* is organized around two values: a column labeled *df* and a row labeled *P* (for probability). The *df* column is on the extreme left and the *P* row runs across the top of the table. Values of *t* are the numbers that complete the table. Our purpose is to determine the value of *P* that is associated with a specific value of *t* and *df*. For this, we run down the *df* column until we arrive at the specific value of *df*; in this case, 13 *df*. We then read across the row marked 13 *df*, which contains several values for *t*: 0.128, 0.259, 0.394, and so on. We read across this row until we come to a value close to ours—in this case, 4.48. The largest value of *t* in this row, 4.221, is the closest match we can make to 4.48, so we read up the column that contains 4.221 to determine what value of *P* is associated with it—in this case 0.001.

Let us make a general observation: The larger the *t*, the smaller the *P*. For example, with 13 *df*, a *t* of 0.128 has a *P* of 0.9 associated with it, whereas with the same *df*, a *t* of 1.771 has a *P* of 0.1. From this observation and our study of the tabled values of *t* and *P*, we can conclude that if a *t* of 4.221 has a *P* of 0.001, any *t* larger than 4.221 must have a smaller *P* than 0.001. It is sufficient for our purposes simply to note this fact without attempting to make it any more precise.

Testing the Null Hypothesis

When we report a computed *t* we write an equation that indicates the number of *df* (here 13) within parentheses, for example, *t* (13) = 4.48. Next, we interpret the fact that a *t* of 4.48 has a *P* of less than 0.001 ($P < 0.001$) associated with it. (The symbol < indicates that the value to the right is greater than the value to the left.) This finding indicates that a mean difference between groups of the size obtained (5.86) has a probability of less than 0.01; that is, a difference of this size between the means may be expected less than one time in 100 by chance (0.01 = 1/100). Put another way, if the experiment had been conducted 100 times, by chance we would expect a difference of this size to occur about once, provided the null hypothesis is true. This, we must all agree, is a most unlikely occurrence. It is so unreasonable, in fact, to think that such a large difference could have occurred by chance on the very first of the hypothetical 100 experiments that we prefer to reject "chance" as the explanation. We therefore choose to reject the null hypothesis that $\mu_1 - \mu_2 = 0$; that is, we refuse to regard it as reasonable that the true difference between the means of the two groups is zero when we have obtained such a large difference in sample means, as indicated by the respective values of 6.86 and 1.00. But if a difference of this size is not attributed to chance alone, what reason can we give for it? If all the proper safeguards of experimentation have been observed, it seems reasonable to assert that the two groups differed because they received different values of the independent variable. Hence, the independent variable probably influenced the dependent variable, which was precisely the purpose of the experiment.

Specifying the Criterion for the Test

Setting P is Arbitrary. There are still some questions about this procedure that we need to answer. One question concerns the value of *P* required to reject the null hypothesis. We said that the *P* of less than .01 associated with our *t* was sufficiently small that the null ("chance") hypothesis was rejected. But just how large may *P* be for us to reject the notion that our mean difference was due to chance; that is, how small must *P* be before we reject the null hypothesis? For example, with 13 *df*, if we had obtained a value of 1.80 for *t*, we find in Table A-1 in Appendix A that the value of *P* is less than 0.10. A corresponding difference between two group means could be expected by chance about 10 times out of 100. Is this sufficiently unlikely that we can reject the null hypothesis? The question is this: How small must P be for us to reject the null hypothesis? The answer is that this is an arbitrary decision that the experimenter makes prior to collecting data. Thus one may say, "If the value of t that I obtain has a P of less than 0.05, I will reject my null hypothesis." Similarly, you may set P at 0.01, or even 0.90 if you wish, providing you do it *before* you conduct your experiment. For example, it would be inappropriate to run a t-test, determine P to be 0.06, and then decide that if P is 0.06 you will reject the null hypothesis. Such an experimenter might always reject the null hypothesis, for the criterion (the value of P) for rejecting it would be determined by whatever P was actually obtained. An extreme case would be obtaining a P of 0.90, and then setting 0.90 as the criterion. The sterility of such a decision is apparent, for the corresponding mean difference would occur by chance 90 times out of 100. It is unreasonable to reject a null hypothesis with such a large P, for it is an error to falsely reject a null hypothesis.

The Seriousness of the Decision Sets the Value of P. Although the actual decision of what value of P to set is arbitrary, there are some guidelines. One criterion is how important it is to believe in the conclusion— that is to avoid the error of rejecting the null hypothesis when it is in fact true. If you are conducting an experiment on a new vaccine that could affect the lives of millions of people, you would want to be quite conservative, perhaps setting $P = 0.01$ so that only one time in a hundred would you expect your results to have occurred by chance. Serious events, like designing airplane wings or conducting brain operations might suggest being more conservative such as setting a value of 0.001. Even 0.0001 would not be unrealistic under certain extreme conditions. Conversely, if it is an industrial experiment testing an improved gizmo that could provide the company with a financial return, a liberal criterion might be established such as $P = 0.10$. For psychological experimentation $P = 0.05$ is typically the standard. Unless otherwise specified, it is generally understood that the experimenter has set a $P = 0.05$ prior to conducting the experiment. In short, a value of P is established prior to the collection of the data that serve as the criterion for testing the null hypothesis. If the tabled value of P associated with the computed value of t is less than that criterion, then you reject your null hypothesis; otherwise, you fail to reject it.

Testing the Empirical Hypothesis. Let us now apply these considerations to our example. The hypothesis held that the experimental animals should approach the food cup more frequently than the controls should. The mean scores were 6.86 and 1.00 respectively. The t-test yielded a value of 4.48, which, with 13 df, had a P of less than 0.01. Since 0.01 is less than 0.05, we reject the null hypothesis and assert that there is a true difference between our two groups (that the null hypothesis is not tenable). Furthermore, the direction of the difference is that specified by the empirical hypothesis; that is, the evidence report asserts that the values for the experimental rats were reliably higher than those for the controls. We conclude that the hypothesis is confirmed.

The following rule may now be stated: *If the empirical hypothesis specifies a directional difference between the means of two groups, and if the null hypothesis is rejected with a difference between the two groups in the direction specified, then the empirical hypothesis is confirmed.* Thus there are two cases in which the empirical hypothesis would not be confirmed: first, if the null hypothesis was not rejected; and, second, if it were rejected, but the difference between the two groups was in the opposite direction specified by the empirical hypothesis. To illustrate this latter possibility, let us assume a t of 2.40 ($P < 0.05$). With the mean score for the controls higher than that for the experimental rats, we fail to confirm the empirical hypothesis even though we reject the null hypothesis.

One- Versus Two-Tailed Tests

We have used a **two-tailed test** in this example, i.e., we didn't care which sample mean was larger. With 13 *df* and a criterion of *P* = 0.05, a value of *t* required for rejecting the null hypothesis would be at least 2.160. However, if you used a **one-tailed test** you would have required only a value of *t* = 1.771, as can be noted in the table of *t* in Table A-1. When you know enough to predict confidently the direction of the mean differences, remember that you can use a one-tailed test. (You specify that one sample mean is to be greater than the other.) In this case, as you can observe from a careful study of the table of *t*, it is easier to reject your null hypothesis. That is, a lower value of *t* is required to reject the null hypothesis when using a one-tailed test.

The word "tail" refers to a tail of the distribution of *t*. As you can see in Figure 6-1, in a one-tailed test you are only interested in whether your value of *t* falls in the upper tail, which region is twice as large as that for a two-tailed test. With the critical region for rejecting your null hypothesis being twice as

large for the one-tailed test, it is obviously more likely to reject a null hypothesis than when using a two-tailed test.

STEPS IN TESTING AN EMPIRICAL HYPOTHESIS

Let us now summarize each major step that we have gone through in testing an empirical hypothesis. For this purpose you might design a study to compare the amount of anxiety experienced by majors in different college departments.

1. State the problem. For example, Is there a difference in anxiety among college departmental majors?
2. State the hypothesis. For example, "If the anxiety scores of English and psychology students are measured, the psychology students will have the higher scores."
3. The experiment is designed according to the procedures outlined in Chapter 4, for example, "anxiety" is operationally defined (such as scores on the Manifest Anxiety Scale, Taylor, 1953), samples from each population are drawn, and so on.

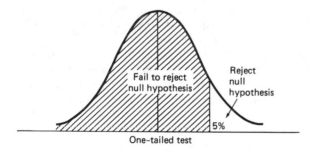

One-tailed test

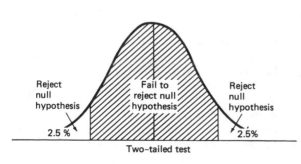

Two-tailed test

FIGURE 6-1 The critical region in one tail of a distribution of *t* for rejecting a null hypothesis is twice as large for a one-tailed test (upper figure) as it is for a two-tailed test (lower figure). In either case, if the value of your computed *t* falls anywhere within the critical regions, you reject your null hypothesis. Otherwise, you *fail* to reject the null hypothesis. Note that you can never accept a null hypothesis, you merely fail to reject it.

4. The null hypothesis is stated: $\mu_1 - \mu_2 = 0$; "There is no difference in the population means of the two groups."

5. A probability value for determining whether to reject the null hypothesis is established, for example, if $P < 0.05$, then the null hypothesis will be rejected; if $P > 0.05$, the null hypothesis will not be rejected. Unless otherwise stated, it is assumed that you are conducting a two-tailed test, which is more conservative.

6. Collect the data and statistically analyze them. Compute the value of t and ascertain the corresponding P.

7. If the means are in the direction specified by the hypothesis (if the psychology students have a higher mean score than do the English students) and if the null hypothesis is rejected, it may be concluded that the hypothesis is confirmed. If the null hypothesis is not rejected, it may be concluded that the hypothesis is not confirmed. Or, if the null hypothesis is rejected, but the means differ in the direction opposite to that predicted by the hypothesis, then the hypothesis is not confirmed.

"BORDERLINE" RELIABILITY

An experimenter who sets a conventional criterion and obtains a P of 0.30 obviously fails to reject the null hypothesis. But suppose that P is 0.06. One might argue, "Well, this isn't quite 0.05, but it is so close that I'm going to reject the null hypothesis anyway. This seems reasonable because the mean difference that I obtained can be expected only 6 times out of 100 by chance when the null hypothesis is true. Surely this is not much different than a probability of 5 times out of 100." To this there is only one answer: The t-test is decisive—a P of 0.06 is not a P of 0.05 and there is no alternative but to fail to reject the null hypothesis. If the experimenter had set the criterion as a P of 0.06 before the experiment was conducted, then we would have no quarrel—the experimenter could, in this event, reject the null hypothesis. But since a criterion of a P of 0.05 was established, one cannot modify it *after* the data are collected. A gambling analogy might be pursued: If one bets at the horse races, the bet must be placed prior to the start of the race, for the selection of a horse that "almost won" will evoke little sympathy from the cashier's window—if you know a racetrack where you can make a bet after the race is over, or where an argument that your horse lost only by a nose (borderline reliability) would be financially rewarded, I hope that you will not just write me a postcard, but that you will call me collect immediately.

On the other hand, we must agree that a P of 0.06 *is* an unlikely event by chance. Our advice is: "Yes. It looks like you *might* have something. It's a good time for further experimentation. Conduct a new experiment and see what happens. If, in this replication, you come out with a reliable difference, you are quite safe in rejecting the null hypothesis. But if the value of t obtained is quite far from a computed value of 0.05 in this new, independent test, then you have saved yourself from making an error."

*A P Cannot Be **Very Reliable***. There is a reverse error that is also far too frequently made in psychology. This error also concerns changing your criterion for rejecting the null hypothesis after your statistical analysis is conducted, but it is changed in the other direction. Assume that you have set a criterion of $P = 0.05$ but your computed value of t would have been reliable beyond the 0.01 level. In this case you might be tempted to report the value of your t as less than 0.01 and say "it was *very* reliable," even though you set your criterion as 0.05 before you conducted your study. However, the probability values upon which the table of t were computed were not based on how far into the critical region your value of t might be. As illustrated in Figure 6-2, the *only* question is whether the value of your computed t fell within the critical region, or whether it did not. It makes absolutely no difference *where* in the critical region the value of your computed t might have fallen. Thus, to say that the value of your computed t was very reliable, rather than merely saying that it

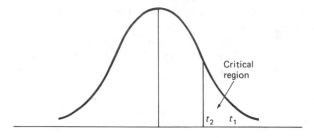

FIGURE 6-2 Once the criterion for testing a null hypothesis is set, it should not be changed. The computed probability associated with the t-test merely tells you whether or not the value falls within the critical region. It is irrelevant *where* in the critical region the value might fall, so that t_1 would be no more or no less probable than t_2.

was or was not reliable, is like saying that a woman who is pregnant is very pregnant. There are no degrees of pregnancy!

THE STANDARD DEVIATION AND VARIANCE

To understand the character of the statistical assumptions underlying the t-test to be discussed in the next section, as well as to employ the concepts of **standard deviation** and **variance** in a number of other contexts, it is advisable that we present them here. Suppose someone asks us about the intelligence of the students at a college of 1,000 students. One thousand scores is a very cumbersome number! If we start reading them, our inquirer undoubtedly would withdraw the question well before we reach the thousandth score. A more reasonable procedure for telling one about the intelligence scores of the college students would be to resort to certain summary statements. We could, for instance, tell our inquirer that the *mean* intelligence of the student body is 125, or whatever. Although this would be informative, it would not be adequate, for there is more to the story than that. Whenever we describe a group of data, we need to offer *two* kinds of statistics—**a measure of central tendency** and a **measure of variability**. Measures of central tendency tell us something about the central-point value of a group of data. They are kinds of *averages* that tell us about the *typical* score in a distribution of data. The most common measure of central tendency is the **mean**. Other measures of central tendency are the **mode** *(the most frequently occurring value in the distribution)* and the **median** *(that value above which are 50 percent*

of the scores and below which are 50 percent of the scores). You should pay close attention to these definitions, as confusion about these averages is not uncommon. I recall, for instance, the military training officer who told me that we had to "work harder to get more of the trainees *above* the median."

Measures of variability tell us how the scores are spread out—they indicate something about the nature of the *distribution* of scores. In addition to telling us this, they also tell us about the range of scores in the group. The most frequently used measure of variability, probably because it is usually the most reliable of the measures (in the sense that it varies least from sample to sample), is the *standard deviation*. The standard deviation is symbolized by s.

To illustrate the importance of measures of variability we might imagine that our inquirer says to us: "Fine. You have told me the mean intelligence of your student body, but how *homogeneous* are your students? Do their scores tend to concentrate around the mean, or are there many that are considerably below the mean?" To answer this we might resort to the computation of the standard deviation. *The larger the standard deviation, the more variable are our scores.* To illustrate, let us assume that we have collected the intelligence scores of students at two different colleges. Plotting the number of people who obtained each score at each college, we might obtain the distributions shown in Figure 6-3.

By computing the standard deviation[8] for

---

[8] Note again that we are primarily concerned with values for samples. From a sample value, a population value (σ) may be inferred.

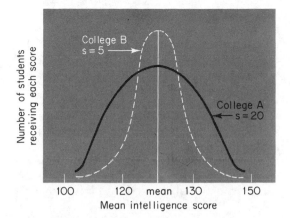

Number of students receiving each score

College B
s = 5

College A
s = 20

100 120 mean 130 150
Mean intelligence score

FIGURE 6-3 Distributions of intelligence scores at two colleges.

the two groups, we might find their values to be 20 for college A and 5 for college B. Comparing the distributions for the two colleges, we note that there is considerably more variability in college A than in college B; that is, the scores for college A are more spread out than for college B. The standard deviation tells us that the larger value for the standard deviation indicates the greater variability of the distribution of scores. The standard deviation (for a normal distribution) also gives us the more precise bit of information that about two-thirds of the scores fall within the interval that is one standard deviation above and one standard deviation below the mean. To illustrate, let us first note that the mean intelligence of the students of the two colleges is the same, 125. If we subtract one standard deviation (i.e., 20) from the mean for college A and add one standard deviation to that mean, we obtain two values: 105 (125 − 20 = 105) and 145 (125 + 20 = 145). Therefore about two-thirds of the students in college A have an intelligence score between 105 and 145. Similarly, about two-thirds of the students at college B have scores between 120 (125 − 5) and 130 (125 + 5). Hence we have a further illustration that the scores at college A are more spread out than are those at college B. Put another way, the scores of college B students are the more *homogeneous* (meaning that they are more similar), whereas the scores of college A are more *heterogeneous* (less homogeneous). We might for a moment

speculate that College A is rather lenient in its selection of students, as might be the case in some state universities. College B is more selective, having a rather homogeneous student body, as would be a private institution with high tuition costs.

The symbol s^2 is known as the *variance* of a set of values. It has essentially the same characteristics as the standard deviation and is merely the square of the standard deviation. Hence if $s = 5$, then $s^2 = 25$. To illustrate these statistics further, consider the dependent-variable scores in Table 6-1. The easiest computational equation for the standard deviation is

$$(6\text{-}4) \qquad s = \sqrt{\frac{n\Sigma X^2 - (\Sigma X)^2}{n(n - 1)}}$$

You can note that earlier in this chapter we computed the components for this equation. They are

Experimental Rats	*Control Rats*
$\Sigma X_E = 48$	$\Sigma X_C = 8$
$\Sigma X_E^2 = 404$	$\Sigma X_C^2 = 16$
$n = 7$	$n = 8$

Substituting these values into Equation 6-4 we obtain s_E for the experimental group

$$s_E = \sqrt{\frac{7(404) - (48)^2}{7(7 - 1)}}$$

$$= \sqrt{\frac{2{,}838 - 2{,}304}{7(6)}}$$

$$= \sqrt{\frac{524}{42}}$$

$$= \sqrt{12.4762}$$

$$= 3.53$$

Hence

$$s_E^2 = (3.53)(3.53) = 12.48$$

For the control group, s_C is:

$$s_C = \sqrt{\frac{8(16) - (8)^2}{8(8 - 1)}}$$

$$= \sqrt{\frac{128 - 4}{8(7)}}$$

$$= \sqrt{\frac{64}{56}}$$

$$= \sqrt{1.1459}$$

$$= 1.07$$

Hence

$$s_C^2 = (1.07)(1.07) = 1.14$$

We can thus see that the variability of the experimental group is considerably larger than that for the control group, a fact that is readily ascertainable by a glance at the data in Table 6-1. There we may observe that the values for the experimental group range from one to ten. (The **range** another common measure of variability, is $10 - 1 = 9$.) On the other hand, the range of scores for the control group is from zero to three (hence, the range = 3). Obviously, the range of a distribution of scores equals the highest value minus the lowest value. Clearly the values for the experimental group are more variable (more heterogeneous), whereas those for the control group are less variable (more homogeneous). One significance of this difference in homogeneity of variances is that there is a violation of a statistical as-

sumption for the *t*-test, as we shall see in the next section. Incidentally, we might note that if all the values for one group are the same, for example, 7, both the standard deviation and the variance would be zero, for there would be 0 variability among the values.

Finally we may note that if the sum of squares (*SS*) has been already computed for a distribution using Equation 6-3, most of the calculations for *s* have been completed as well. Therefore the computed value of *SS* can merely be substituted into Equation 6-5.

$$(6\text{-}5) \qquad s = \sqrt{\frac{SS}{(n - 1)}}$$

Thus, since $SS = 74.857$ for the experimental group,

$$s = \sqrt{\frac{74.857}{6}}$$

$$= 3.53$$

ASSUMPTIONS UNDERLYING THE USE OF STATISTICAL TESTS

We make certain assumptions when we apply statistical tests to the experimental designs presented in this book. In general these are that: (1) the population distribution is normal; (2) the variances of the groups are homogeneous ("equal"); (3) the treatment effects and the error effects are additive; and (4) the dependent-variable values are independent. Very approximately, assumption 1—that of normality—means that the distribution is bell-shaped, or Gaussian, in form (as in Figure 6-1). Assumption 2 holds that the way in which the distributions are spread out is about the same for the different groups in the experiment; a bit more precisely, it means that the standard deviations of each group's dependent-variable scores multiplied by themselves (that is, their "variances") are about the same (homogeneous). To help you visualize the character of assumption 3, assume that any given dependent variable is a function of two classes of variables—your independent variable and the various extraneous variables. Now we may assume that the dependent-variable values due to these two sources of variation can be expressed as an algebraic sum of the effect of one and the effect of the other; that is, if R is the response measure used as the dependent variable, if I is the effect of the independent variable, and if E is the combined effect of all of the extraneous variables, then the additivity assumption says that $R = I + E$.

Various tests are available in books on statistics to determine whether your particular data allow you to regard the assumptions of homogeneity of variance, of normality, and of additivity as tenable. It does not seem feasible at the present level, however, to elaborate these assumptions or the nature of the tests for them. In addition it is often difficult to determine whether the assumptions *are* sufficiently satisfied; that is, these tests are rather insensitive. The consensus is that rather sizable departures from assumptions 1, 2, and 3 can be tolerated and still yield valid statistical analyses. Our statistical tests are quite robust in that they lead to proper conclusions often with deviations from these assumptions. For instance, in the experiment in this chapter on RNA, the variances of the groups are *not* homogeneous; that is, the variance of the experimental group is 12.48 and that for the control group is 1.14. One alternative to a *t*-test is what is known as a *nonparametric test*, also known as a distribution-free test. Non-parametric tests do not make assumptions about distributions such as normality and homogeneity. Parametric tests, like the *t*-test, do make these assumptions about the parameters of the distributions. That parametric tests are remarkably robust because major deviations from their basic assumptions can be tolerated is illustrated here because the same conclusions follow from the *t*-test and from the Mann-Whitney U Test, a nonparametric test. We may add that the assumptions of normality and homogeneity may be violated with increasing security as the number of participants per group increases. For further

information on assumptions, you should consult any of the easily available statistics books.

The fourth assumption, however, is essential, since each dependent-variable value must be independent of every other dependent-variable value. For example, if one value is 15, the determination that a second value is, say, 10 must in no way be influenced by, or related to, the fact that the first value is 15. If participants have been selected at random, and if one and only one value of each dependent variable is used for each participant, then the assumption of independence should be satisfied.

However, in some research, several dependent-variable values may be collected for each participant, perhaps as in a learning experiment. Consider, for instance, an experiment (Table 6-2) in which there are three participants under each of two conditions (A and B) with five repeated dependent-variable scores for each participant. If you separately enter *all* the data of Table 6-2 directly in the computation of the value of *t*, you would commit an independence error. For instance, for participant 1, a student might add 3, 2, 3, 5, and 6 and also sum their squares, and similarly employ five (instead of one) dependent-variable values for the other participants. Then all 30 dependent-variable values might erroneously be employed to compute $N = 30$, so that $df = 30 - 2 = 28$. This is a grossly inflated value for the degrees of freedom (recall that the larger the number of degrees of freedom in Table A-1 in Appendix A, the smaller the value of *t* required for the rejection of the null

TABLE 6-2 Illustration of the Use of Repeated Dependent-Variable Values for Each of the Participants

Condition A		Condition B	
Participant Number	*Trial* 1 2 3 4 5	*Participant Number*	*Trial* 1 2 3 4 5
1	3 2 3 5 6	*1*	9 4 6 7 8
2	4 1 1 4 4	*2*	8 9 3 7 9
3	6 9 4 9 9	*3*	7 8 2 8 6

hypothesis). The correct *df* here is $df = N - 2 = 6 - 2 = 4$.

We prevent this error by *employing one and only one dependent-variable value for each participant*. If this is a learning experiment, you could use the last dependent-variable value so that *t* would be computed using the values on trial 5—that is 6, 4, and 9, versus 8, 9, and 6. Another common method of avoiding the error of inflated degrees of freedom is to compute a representative value for each participant, for example, to compute a mean for each row of dependent-variable values, as in Table 6-3. In this instance the *t* between the two groups would be based on the mean values for condition A (3.8, 2.8, 7.4) versus those for condition B (7.0, 7.2, 6.2). Did condition A differ reliably from condition B?

YOUR DATA ANALYSIS MUST BE ACCURATE

In one sense this section should be placed at the beginning of the book, in the boldest type possible. For no matter how much care you give to the other aspects of experimentation, if you are not accurate in your records and statistical analysis, the experiment is worthless. Unfortunately there are no set rules that anybody can give you to guarantee accuracy. The best that we can do is to offer you some suggestions which, if followed, will reduce the number of errors and, if you are sufficiently vigilant, eliminate them completely.

The first important point concerns "attitude." Sometimes students think that they can record their data and conduct their statistical analysis only once, and in so doing, they have amazing confidence in the accuracy of their results. Checking is not for them! Although it is very nice to believe in one's own perfection, I have observed enough students *and* scientists over a sufficiently long period of time to know that this is just not reasonable. We all make mistakes.

The best attitude for you, as a scientist to take is not that you *might* make a mistake, but that you *will* make a mistake; the only problem is where to find it. Accept this suggestion or not, as you like. But remember this: At least the first few times that you conduct an analysis, the odds are about 99 to 1 that you will make an error. As you become more experienced, the odds might drop to about 10 to 1. For instance, studies of *articles already published in professional journals* have yielded several different kinds of errors, including miscalculation of statistical tests. I once had occasion to decide a matter with one of our most outstanding statisticians, George Snedecor, for which we ran a simple statistical test. Our answer was obviously absurd, so we tried to discover the error. After several checks, however, the fault remained obscure. Finally, a third person, who could look at the problem from a fresh point of view, checked our computations and found the error. This world-famous statistician admitted that he was never very good in arithmetic, and he frequently made errors in addition and substraction, so checking his arithmetic was very important for him. If *he* had to check carefully himself, certainly we do too.

The first place that an error can be made occurs when you start to obtain your data.

TABLE 6-3   Employing the Mean of the Trial Values for Each Participant of Table 6-2

| | Condition A | | | Condition B | |
Participant Number	Trial 1 2 3 4 5	$\overline{X}$	Participant Number	Trial 1 2 3 4 5	$\overline{X}$
1	3 2 3 5 6	3.8	1	9 4 6 8 8	7.0
2	4 1 1 4 4	2.8	2	8 9 3 7 9	7.2
3	6 9 4 9 9	7.4	3	7 8 2 8 6	6.2

Usually the experimenter observes behavior and records data by writing them down or entering them directly into a computer. Sometimes, however, data are recorded automatically by a computer, as discussed in Appendix C; in that case special precautions must be observed in order to guarantee the accuracy of the recording system.

Suppose that you are studying students who are performing a card-sorting task and that you are recording: (1) latency of their decision as to whether a card should be placed in a container to their left or to their right, (2) duration of their performance time, and (3) whether they placed the card to the left or to the right. Your record must identify each student and have three columns for your three kinds of data. You then note the data for each student in the appropriate column. Once you indicate the time values and the direction, you move on to your next participant; the event is over and there is no possibility for further checking. Hence any error you make in recording your data is uncorrectable. You should therefore be exceptionally careful in recording the correct value. You might fix the value firmly in mind, asking yourself all the time whether you are transcribing the correct value. After it is written down or entered into your computer, check yourself again to make sure that it is correct. If the value that you have entered seems out of line, double-check it. After double-checking an unusual datum, make a note that it is correct, for later on you might return to it with doubt. For instance, if your students take about 2 seconds to perform the task, and you write down that one had a response duration value of 7 seconds, take an extra look at the timer to make sure that this reading is correct. If it is, make a little note beside "7 seconds," indicating that the value has been checked.

Experimenters may transcribe original written records of behavior into a computer or onto another sheet for their statistical analysis. Such a job is tedious and conducive to errors, so that considerable vigilance must be exercised. The finished job should be checked to make sure that no errors in transcription have been committed. It is also advisable to indicate when you have checked a number or operation. One way to accomplish this is to place a small dot above and to the right of the value (do not place it so low that the dot might be confused with a decimal point) or, if you use a computer you could enter an unusual symbol behind the number. One value of indicating a checked result is that at some later time you will know that the work has been checked.

In writing data on a sheet, legibility is of utmost importance, for the misreading of numbers is a frequent source of error. You may be surprised at the difficulty you might have in reading your own writing, particularly after a period of time. If you use a pencil, that pencil should be sharp and hard, to reduce smudging. If possible record your data in ink, and if you have to change a number, thoroughly erase it or eradicate it with ink eradicator if possible.

Whether you use a written record or directly enter your data into a computer, completely label all aspects of your data sheet, since you may later refer to those data. Label the experiment clearly, giving its title, the date, place of conduct, and so on. You should unambiguously label each source of data. Your three columns might be labeled "latency of response from the onset of the start light," "time in making the response," and "direction of placing the card (left or right)." Each statistical operation should be clearly labeled. If you run a *t*-test, for instance, the top of your record should state that it is a *t*-test between such and such conditions, using such and such a measure as the dependent variable. In short, label everything pertinent to the records and analysis so that you can return to your work years later and readily understand it.

The actual conduct of the statistical analysis is probably the greatest source of error. In computer analysis, the program may be in error or improperly used (see Appendix C). In manual analysis, you should check each step as you move along. For example, if you begin by computing the sums and sums of squares for your groups, check them before you substitute these values into your equation, for if they are in error, all your later work will have to be redone. Similarly, each multiplication, division, subtraction, and addition should be checked immediately, before you move on to the next operation that incorporates the result. After you have computed your statistical test, checking each step along the way, you should put it aside and do the entire analysis again, without looking at your previous work. Perhaps the best strategy is to conduct your analysis manually and then check it with your computer program. If your two independent computations agree, you probably have the correct end value.

NUMBER OF PARTICIPANTS PER GROUP

"How many people should I have in my groups?" is a question that students usually ask in a beginning course in research methodology. One traditional procedure is to study a number of participants, more or less arbitrarily determined, and see how the results turn out. If the groups differ reliably, the experimenter may be satisfied with that number, or additional participants may be studied to confirm the reliable findings. On the other hand, if the groups do not differ reliably but the differences are promising, more participants may be added in the hope that the additional data will produce reliability.[9]

---

[9] This latter procedure cannot be defended in other than a preliminary investigation because one who keeps adding participants until a reliable difference is obtained may capitalize on chance. For example, if one runs 10 participants per group and obtains a t value that approaches a probability level of 0.05, perhaps 10 more participants might be added to each group. Assume that the mean difference is now reliable. But the results of these additional participants might be due merely to chance. The experiment is stopped, and success proclaimed. If still more participants were studied, however, reliability would be lost, and the experimenter would never know this fact. If such an experiment is to be cross-validated (replicated), this procedure is, of course, legitimate.

Although we cannot adequately answer the student's question, we can offer some guiding considerations. First, the larger the number of participants run, the more reliably we can estimate any mean difference between groups. This is a true and sure statement, but it does not help very much. We can clearly say that 100 participants per group is better than 50. You may want to know if 20 participants per group is enough. That depends, first, on the size of the "true" (population) mean difference between your groups and, second, on the size of the variances of your groups. What we can say is that the larger the true difference between groups, the smaller will be the number of participants required for the experiment; and the smaller the group variances, the fewer participants will be required. Now if you have good estimates of the mean difference and variances, the number of participants required can also be estimated. Unfortunately, experimenters do not usually have this information. Possible sources of this information are experiments reported in the literature which are similar to the one you want to run and from which you can abstract the necessary information, or a pilot study conducted by yourself to yield estimates of the information that is needed. Regardless, given these two bits of information, the following is a procedure for determining the minimum number of participants required for possibly rejecting the null hypothesis.

Suppose that you conduct a two-randomized-groups experiment. You estimate (on the basis of previously collected data) that the mean score of condition A is 10 and that the mean of condition B is 15. The difference between these means is 5. You also estimate that the variances of your two groups are both 75. Say that you set your probability level at 0.05, in which case the value of t that you will need to reject the null hypothesis is *approximately* 2 (you may be more precise if you like). Assume that you want an equal number of participants in both groups. Now we have this information:

$$\overline{X}_1 - \overline{X}_2 = 5$$

$$S_1^2 \text{ and } S_2^2 \text{ both } = 75$$

$$t = 2$$

With a bit of diligence we can solve Equation 6-2 for n instead of for t. By algebraic manipulation[10] we find that, on the preceding assumptions, Equation 6-2 becomes

$$(6\text{-}6) \qquad n = \frac{2t^2 s^2}{(\overline{X}_1 - \overline{X}_2)^2}$$

Substituting these values in Equation 6-6 and solving for n, we find

$$n = \frac{2(2)^2(75)}{(15 - 10)^2} = \frac{600}{25} = 24$$

We can say, therefore, that with this true mean difference, and with these variances for our two groups, and using the 0.05 level of reliability, we need a minimum of 24 participants per group to reject the null hypothesis. We have only approximated the value of t necessary at the 0.05 level, however, and we have not allowed for any possible increase in the variance of our two groups. Therefore we should underline the word *minimum*. To be safe, then, we should probably run somewhat more than 24 participants per group; 30 would seem reasonable in this case—an approximate number that has traditionally been used in experimentation.[11]

The Main Point. You should have a sufficient number of participants per group to reject the null hypothesis if indeed it should be rejected. Consequently, there is no magic number aside from the aforementioned considerations. In fact, if the true mean differences are quite large and the variance is quite small, you may be able to reject your

---

[10] The algebraic manipulation may become clearer if you refer to yet another form of Equation 6-2, which is Equation 9-3 on page 191.

[11] This procedure is offered only as a rough guide, for we are neglecting power considerations of the statistical test. This procedure has a minimal power for rejecting the null hypothesis.

null hypothesis with only several participants per group. One student demonstrated that 10 participants per group were sufficient because she rejected her null hypothesis. Yet the dean did not want to sign her dissertation because he rigidly believed that each group should have 30 participants.

ERROR VARIANCE

A major research strategy is to increase the chance of rejecting the null hypothesis, *if in fact it should be rejected*. The point may be illustrated by taking two extremes. If you conduct a "sloppy" experiment (e.g., the controls are poor or you keep inaccurate records), you reduce your chances of rejecting a null hypothesis that really should be rejected. On the other hand, if you conduct a highly refined experiment (it is well controlled, you keep accurate records, and so on), you increase the probability of rejecting a null hypothesis that really should be rejected. In short, if there is a lot of "noise" in the experimental situation, the dependent-variable values are going to vary for reasons other than variation of the independent variable. Such "noise" obscures any systematic relationship between the independent and dependent variable. There are two general ways in which an experimenter can increase the chances of rejecting a null hypothesis that really should be rejected: (1) increase the difference between the dependent-variable means of the groups (e.g., the numerator of the t-ratio), and (2) decrease the variability in the experiment (e.g., the denominator of the t-ratio).

We know that the larger the value of t, the greater is the likelihood that we will be able to reject the null hypothesis. Hence our question is: How can we design an experiment such that the value of t can legitimately be increased? In other words, how can we increase the numerator of Equation 6-2 and decrease the denominator? The numerator can often be increased by exaggerating the difference in the two values of the independent variable. For instance, if you ask whether amount of practice affects amount learned, you are more likely to obtain a reliable difference between two groups if they practice 100 trials versus 10 trials than if they practice only 15 trials versus 10 trials. This is so because you would probably increase the difference between the means of the dependent variable of the two groups, and, as we said, the greater the mean difference, the larger will be the value of t. Let us now consider the denominator of Equation 6-2.

In every experiment there is a certain **error variance**, and in our statistical analysis we obtain an estimate of it. In the two-group designs the error variance is the *the denominator of the* t *ratio* (just as it is the denominator of the F ratio). Basically, *the error variance in an experiment is a measure of the extent to which participants treated alike exhibit variability of their dependent-variable values.* There are many reasons why we obtain different values for participants treated alike. For one, organisms are all "made" differently, and they all react somewhat differently to the same experimental treatment. For another, it simply is impossible to treat all participants in the same group precisely alike; we always have a number of randomly changing extraneous variables differentially influencing the behavior of our participants. And, finally, some of the error variance is due to imperfections in our measuring devices. No device can provide a completely "true" score, nor can we as humans make completely accurate and consistent readings of the measuring device.

In many ways it is unfortunate that dependent-variable values for participants treated alike show so much variability, but we must learn to live with this error variance. The best we can do is attempt to reduce it. To emphasize why we want to reduce error variance, say that the difference between the means of two groups is 5. Now consider two situations, one in which the error variance is large, and one in which it is small. For example, say that the error variance is 5 in the first case, but 2 in the second. For the first case, then, our computed t would be $t = 5/5 = 1.0$, and for the second it would be

$t = 5/2 = 2.5$. Clearly, in the first case we would *fail* to reject our null hypothesis, whereas in the second case we are likely to reject it. In short, if our error variance is excessively large, we probably will fail to reject the null hypothesis. But if the error variance is sufficiently small, we increase the chances of rejecting the null hypothesis.

Ways to Reduce Error Variance

Granting, then, that it is highly advisable to reduce the variances for our groups, how can we accomplish this? There are several possibilities.

Reduce Individual Differences. First, recall that our participants, when they enter the experimental situation, are all different, and that the larger such differences are, the greater will be the variances of our groups. Therefore one obvious way to reduce the variances of our groups, and hence the error variance, is to reduce the extent to which our participants are different. Psychologists frequently increase the homogeneity of their groups by selection. For example, we work with a number of different strains of rats. In any given experiment, however, all the rats are usually taken from a single strain—the Wistar strain, the Sprague-Dawley strain, or whatever. If a psychologist randomly assigns rats from several different strains to groups, variances are probably going to increase. Working with humans is more difficult, but even here the selection of participants who are similar is a frequent practice and should be considered. For example, using college students as participants undoubtedly results in smaller variances than if we selected participants at random from the general population. But you could even be selective in your college population; you might use only females, only students with IQs above 120, only those with low-anxiety scores, and so on.

However, one serious objection to selecting participants is that you thus restrict the extent to which you can generalize your results. Thus if you sample only high-IQ students, you will certainly be in danger if you try to generalize your findings to low-IQ students, or to any other population that you have not sampled. For this reason, selection of homogeneous participants for only two groups in an experiment (e.g., experimental versus control groups) should be seriously pondered before it is adopted. The greater the extent to which you select homogeneous participants, the less sound will be your basis for a broad generalization.

One solution to this problem, as we shall develop in Chapter 12, is to incorporate systematically an organismic variable (like intelligence) into a factorial design. By studying the effects of your independent variable as a function of several degrees (levels) of intelligence, you not only might reduce your error variance but also ascertain any limitations to your generalizations.

Use Precise Procedures. You can reduce your variances with your experimental procedure. The ideal is to treat all participants in the same group as precisely alike as possible. We cannot emphasize this too strongly. We have counseled the use of a tape recorder for administering instructions, in order that all participants would receive precisely the same words, with precisely the same intonations. If you rather casually tell them what to do, varying the way in which you say it with different people, you are probably increasing your variances. Similarly, the greater the number of extraneous variables that are operating in a random fashion, the greater your variances will be. If, for example, noises are present in varying degrees for some individuals but not present at all for others, your group variances are probably going to increase. Here again, however, you should recognize that when you eliminate extraneous variables, you might restrict the degree of generalizing to situations where they are present. For example, if all your participants are located in sound-deadened rooms, then you should not, strictly speaking, generalize to situations where noises are randomly present. But, since we usually are not trying to generalize,

at least not immediately, to such uncontrolled stimulus conditions, this general objection need not greatly disturb us.

Reduce Errors. To reduce your variances, reduce errors in reading your measuring instruments, in recording your data, and in your statistical analysis. The more errors that are present, the larger will be the variances, assuming that such errors are of a random nature. This point also relates to the matter of the reliability of your dependent variable, or perhaps more appropriately to how reliably you measured it. Hence the more reliable your measures of the dependent variable, the less will be your error variance. One way in which the reliability of the dependent-variable measure can be increased is to make more than one observation on each participant; if your experimental procedure allows this you would be wise to consider it.

Other Ways. These three techniques can reduce the error variance by reducing the variances of your groups. Another possible technique for reducing the error variance concerns the design that you select. The clearest example for the designs that we have considered would be to replace the two-randomized-groups design with the matched-groups design for two groups (see Chapter 9), providing that there is a substantial correlation between the independent variable and dependent variable. The factorial design can also be used to decrease your error variance. For example, you might incorporate an otherwise extraneous variable in your design and remove the variance attributable to that variable from your error variance.

Another technique that is frequently effective in reducing error variance is the "analysis of covariance." Briefly, this technique enables you to obtain a measure of what you think is a particularly relevant extraneous variable that you are not controlling. This usually involves some characteristic of your participants. For instance, if you are conducting a study of the effect of certain psychological variables on weight, you might use as your measure the weight of your participants before you administer your experimental treatments. Through analysis of covariance, you then can "statistically control" this variable; that is, you can remove the effect of initial weight from your dependent variable scores, thus decreasing your error variance. We might note that the degree of success in reducing error variance with the analysis of covariance depends on the size of the correlation between your extraneous variable and your dependent variable. The application of this statistical technique, however, is not always simple: It can be seriously misused, and one cannot be assured that it can "save" a shoddy experiment. Some researchers overuse this method, as in the instance of a person I once overheard asking of a researcher, "Where is your analysis of covariance?"—the understanding in his department was that it is *always* used in experimentation. In your future study of experimentation and statistics, you might learn how this technique is applied.

Referring back to Equation 6-2, we have seen that as the variances of our groups decrease, the error variance decreases, and the size of t increases. The other factor in the denominator is n. As the size of n increases, the error variance decreases. This occurs for two reasons: because we use n in the computation of variances and because n is also used otherwise. We might comment that increasing the number of participants per group is probably one of the easiest ways to decrease, usually very sharply, the error variance.

We have tried in this section to indicate the importance of the reduction of error variance in experimentation and to suggest some of the ways that it might be accomplished. Unfortunately it is not possible to provide an exhaustive coverage of the available techniques, because of both lack of space and complexities that would take us beyond our present level of discussion. Excellent treatments of this topic are available in books on experimental design, although they require a somewhat advanced knowledge of experimentation and statistics.

In Summary. The following are the more important points that have been made. First, the likelihood of rejecting the null hypothesis can be increased by increasing the difference between the values of the independent variable administered to the groups in the experiment and by decreasing the error variance. Specific ways that one is likely to decrease error variance are: (1) select homogeneous participants according to their scores on some relevant measure; (2) standardize, in a strict fashion, the experimental procedures used; (3) reduce errors in observing and recording the dependent variable values (and make more than one measurement on each participant if practicable); (4) select a relatively precise design; (5) increase the number of participants per group; and (6) as we shall see in the next section, replicate the experiment.

REPLICATION

In the history of science many, many astounding findings have been erroneously reported. Recently a major psychologist, who had attained such fame that he had been knighted by the queen, was reported to be scientifically dishonest in his research implicating heredity in intelligence—nobody had repeated his research and it was reported to be a hoax, although it had formed the basis for important social movements. We have emphasized the *self-correcting feature of science*—if a scientist errs, for whatever reason, the error will be discovered, at least if it had any importance. The basic criterion in science for evaluating the validity of our conclusions is that research is repeated. The technical term for repeating an experiment is *replication*. By replication, we mean that *the methods employed by a researcher are repeated in an effort to confirm or disconfirm the findings obtained*. We say that an experiment was replicated when the experimental procedures were repeated on a new sample of participants. The replication may be by the original researcher, or preferably by another in a different laboratory—the latter would result in a higher probability of the conclusions (if they conformed to the original ones) than the former because any bias would be reduced, independent apparatus would be used, and so on. Note an important distinction: *replication refers to repeating the experiment, not to confirming the original findings.* Hence the replication of an experiment may either confirm or disconfirm (be consonant with or contradictory to) the findings of the earlier experiment. Unfortunately there is a tendency for some to say that they "failed to replicate an experiment," which literally means that they failed to repeat the original methodology—what they mean to say is that they *did* replicate the experiment but failed to duplicate the findings. The distinction is an important one, analogous to the one that should be made between obtaining "no results" and obtaining "negative results."

Although it is at the heart of our science, replication is relatively rare. This is understandable but unfortunate. Priority for publishable space in our journals is given to original research. We thus probably retain many untruths that were the result of chance (the 5 times out of 100 that the null hypothesis was erroneously rejected). Several solutions are possible. One is to include an earlier experiment in a new one and extend it by including another independent variable, such as with a factorial design. Another is to encourage student research (masters' theses, and so on) as replications, perhaps with short sections of our journals devoted to such studies. The problem should be *very* seriously considered. But the point here is that, not only does replication correct errors, but it can also reduce error variance.

If you *do* replicate, how might you combine the results of replications? There are a number of procedures available in statistics books for this purpose (and also in previous editions of this one). For instance, suppose that the computed probability for your t-test is 0.08 and 0.10 in a replication. In neither experiment could you reject the null hypothesis, but by combining the results you would be able to reject it. More precisely, the compound probability for this example would be less than 0.05, and you could *reject* the null hypothesis.

SUMMARY OF THE COMPUTATION OF t FOR A TWO-INDEPENDENT-GROUPS DESIGN

We have emphasized the great value of computer analysis as well as the importance of understanding what the computer is doing. If you are able to follow the steps in this section, you will have achieved that understanding for this application of the *t*-test. For elaboration of the use of the computer in Psychology, refer to Appendix C. Assume that we have obtained the following dependent-variable values for the two groups and that we seek to test the null hypothesis that $\mu_1 = \mu_2$ (or equally, $\mu_1 - \mu_2 = 0$):

Group 1	Group 2
10	8
11	9
11	12
12	12
15	12
16	13
16	14
17	15
	16
	17

1. Start with Equation 6-2, the equation for computing *t*:

$$t = \frac{\overline{X}_1 - \overline{X}_2}{\sqrt{\left[\dfrac{SS_1 + SS_2}{(n_1 - 1) + (n_2 - 1)}\right]\left(\dfrac{1}{n_1} + \dfrac{1}{n_2}\right)}}$$

2. Compute the sum of X_1 (i.e., ΣX_1), the sum of X_2 (i.e., ΣX_2) and n for each group:

Group 1	Group 2
$\Sigma X_2 = 108$	$\Sigma X_2 = 128$
$\Sigma X_2 = 1,512$	$\Sigma X_2 = 1,712$
$n = 8$	$n = 10$

3. Using Equation 6-1, compute the means for each group:

$$\overline{X}_1 = \frac{108}{8} = 13.50 \qquad \overline{X}_2 = \frac{128}{10} = 12.80$$

4. Using Equation 6-3, compute the sums of squares for each group:

$$SS_1 = \Sigma X_1^2 - \frac{(\Sigma X_1)^2}{N_1} = 1,512 - \frac{108}{8}$$
$$= 54.000$$

$$SS_2 = 1,712 - \frac{(128)^2}{10} = 73.600$$

5. Substitute the preceding values in Equation 6-2:

$$t = \frac{13.50 - 12.80}{\sqrt{\left[\dfrac{54.000 + 73.600}{(8-1) + (10-1)}\right]\left(\dfrac{1}{8} + \dfrac{1}{10}\right)}}$$

6. Perform the operations as indicated and determine that the value of t is

$$t = \frac{0.70}{\sqrt{(7.975)(.2250)}} = \frac{0.70}{\sqrt{1.7944}}$$
$$= \frac{0.70}{1.3395} = .523$$

7. Determine the number of degrees of freedom associated with the preceding value of t:

$$df = N - 2 = 18 - 2 = 16$$

8. Enter the table of t, and determine the probability associated with this value of t. In this example $0.70 > P > 0.60$. Therefore, assuming a required reliability level of 0.05, the null hypothesis is not rejected and we reach the appropriate conclusion about our empirical hypothesis.

CHAPTER SUMMARY

I. The basic experiment is that in which a sample of participants is *randomly* assigned to two groups, typically an experimental and a control group. In the method of systematic observation participants are in preformed groups so they are not randomly assigned to conditions. With either method the t-test is an appropriate method of statistical analysis.

II. A null hypothesis is formulated that there is no difference between the population means of the two groups; for example, $\mu_1 = \mu_2$.

III. To test the null hypothesis, the difference between the sample mean values of the two groups on the dependent-variable measure is computed.

IV. The probability that the mean difference could have occurred by chance (i.e., as a result of random fluctuations) is assessed by conducting a t-test.

V. The t-test is a ratio between the mean difference between your groups and the error variance in the experiment; the error variance is a direct function of the variability of the dependent-variable scores. That variability may be measured by the variances or the standard deviations of the groups.

VI. Into the t table are entered the computed value of t and the appropriate number of degrees of freedom, where $df = n_1 + n_2 - 2$.

VII. If the computed value of t exceeds the tabled value for your predetermined criterion (e.g., 0.05), you may reject your null hypothesis; otherwise, you *fail* to reject it.

VIII. If you reject your null hypothesis, you confirm your empirical hypothesis, assuming that the mean difference is in the direction specified by the empirical hypothesis; otherwise, you fail to confirm (you disconfirm) the empirical hypothesis.

IX. However, all statistical tests are based on certain assumptions.
   A. For the t-test (and the F-test soon to be discussed) the assumptions are that
      1. The population distribution is normal.
      1. The variances of the groups are homogeneous.
      3. The treatment effects and the error effects are additive.
      4. The dependent variable values are independent.
   B. The first three assumptions may be violated to some extent but not the assumption of independence.
   C. We should add a fifth major assumption that is even more critical, namely, that the data recording and analyses are accurate!

X. Finally, we noted that the optimal number of participants in an experiment is that number that is sufficient to allow rejection of the null hypothesis if it should be rejected. That number is determined by the size of the population mean difference and the population variances. Traditionally, the optimal number is considered to be about 30 per group, though in class experimentation we would not expect students typically to have that large a number.

XI. In any experiment it is important to achieve a high degree of precision, which means that the error variance should be small. The error variance in an experiment is the measure of the extent to which participants treated alike exhibit variability in dependent variable values. In a two-independent-group experiment it is represented by the denominator of the t ratio. When using analysis of variance, error variance is represented by the denominator of the F ratio. Reducing error variance increases the probability of rejecting a null hypothesis that really should be rejected. Error variance may be reduced by

   A. Being accurate in all aspects of measurements, as in keeping accurate records.

   B. Achieving effective experimental control.

   C. Selecting a suitable experimental design, such as a matched-groups design; a function of the correlation between the matching and the dependent variable scores is thus removed from the error variance, as in the last term in the denominator of Equation 6-2.

   D. Selecting homogeneous participants, although this reduces the extent to which you can generalize your findings; that is, you can generalize to participants only to the extent that you have sampled their population.

   E. Having consistent experimental procedures, such as the same instructions for all people in a group.

   F. Taking more than one dependent variable measure on each participant and combining them, as in averaging those measures.

   G. Considering the use of analysis of covariance.

   H. Increasing the number of participants per group.

   I. Replicating your experiments.

   J. Being alert to other ways to reduce error variance, as discussed later in the book.

CRITICAL REVIEW FOR THE STUDENT

1. Important terms and concepts that you should concentrate on are
   Randomization
   Self-correction in science
   Mean
   Sum of squares
   The null hypothesis
   Tabled probability value
   Degrees of freedom
   Standard deviation and variance
   The statistical assumption of independence

2. Problems (answers in Appendix E.)

Before you start to work a problem, you should study this section. Here is an example of how a student's paper should look when answering a question involving statistical analysis. Note that each step was carefully specified, that each calculation was confirmed as indicated by the small dot above each number, that no steps were skipped, and that the student actually answered the empirical question (rather than merely saying "the null hypothesis was rejected" or some similar incomplete statement). We emphasize that statistics are tools for us and that they are useless if we do not end up with an answer to the question that was asked. If we are left dangling with just a statistical conclusion not related to the empirical hypothesis, we might as well have gone to the beach.

The question asked in this study was whether administration of a particular drug increased errors in a psychomotor task, the study being a well-conducted experiment, the details of which need not concern us here.

The null hypothesis was that $\mu_1 = \mu_2$, where conditions 1 and 2 were no drug and drug, respectively. The criterion for rejecting the null hypothesis was $P = 0.01$.

   A. An experimenter runs a well-designed experiment wherein $n_1 = 16$ and $n_2 = 12$. A t of 2.14 is obtained. With a criterion of $P = 0.05$, can the null hypothesis be rejected?

Conditions

1. No Drug	2. Drug
0	6
2	4
2	3
0	3
1	4

No Drug Condition		Drug Condition	
X_1	X_1^2	X_2	X_2^2
0	0	6	36
2	4	4	16
2	4	3	9
0	0	3	9
1	1	4	16

$n_1 = 5$ $\Sigma X_1 = 5$ $\Sigma X_1^2 = 9$ $\Sigma X_2 = 20$ $\Sigma X_2^2 = 86$ $n_2 = 5$

$$\overline{X}_1 = \frac{\Sigma X_1}{n} = \frac{5}{5} = 1.00$$

$$\overline{X}_2 = \frac{\Sigma X_2}{n} = \frac{20}{5} = 4.00$$

$$(6\text{-}2) \quad t = \frac{\overline{X}_1 - \overline{X}_2}{\sqrt{\left(\frac{SS_1 + SS_2}{(n_1 - 1) + (n_2 - 1)}\right)\left(\frac{1}{n_1} + \frac{1}{n_2}\right)}}$$

We need to find SS_1 and SS_2

$$SS_1 = \Sigma X_1^2 - \frac{(\Sigma X_1)^2}{n_1} = 9 - \frac{(5)^2}{5} = 9 - \frac{25}{5}$$

$$\underline{SS_1 = 9 - 5 = 4.00}$$

$$SS_2 = \Sigma X_2^2 - \frac{(\Sigma X_2)^2}{n_2} = 86 - \frac{(20)^2}{5} = 86 - \frac{400}{5}$$

$$\underline{SS_2 = 86 - 80 = 6.00}$$

substituting in equation (6-2):

$$t = \frac{4.00 - 1.00}{\sqrt{\left(\frac{4.00 + 6.00}{(5-1)+(5-1)}\right)\left(\frac{1}{5} + \frac{1}{5}\right)}} = \frac{3.00}{\sqrt{\left(\frac{10.00}{8}\right)\left(\frac{2}{5}\right)}}$$

$$t = \frac{3.00}{\sqrt{(1.25)(0.40)}} = \frac{3.00}{\sqrt{0.50}} = \frac{3.00}{0.7071}$$

$$t = 4.24$$

calculate the df = n-2

$$df = 5+5-2=8 \quad so \quad t\,(8)= 4.24$$

Look in t-table : $\quad P < 0.01 \,, \quad t_{.01} = 3.355$

∴ The Null hypothesis is rejected at the 0.01 level

Empirical Conclusion:

The administration of the drug increased errors in the psychomotor task.

B. An experimenter obtains a computed t of 2.20 with 30 df. The means of the two groups are in the direction indicated by the empirical hypothesis. Assuming that the experiment was well designed and that the experimenter has set a P of 0.05, did the independent variable influence the dependent variable?

C. It is advertised that a certain tranquilizer has a curative effect on psychotics. A clinical psychologist seeks to determine whether this is true. A well-designed experiment is conducted with the following results on a measure of psychotic tendencies. Assuming that the criterion for rejecting the null hypothesis is $P = 0.01$ and assuming that the lower the score, the greater the psychotic tendency, determine whether the tranquilizer has the advertised effect.

Values for the group
that received the tranquilizer

2, 3, 5, 7, 7, 8, 8, 8

Values for the group
that did not receive the tranquilizer

1, 1, 1, 2, 2, 3, 3

D. A psychologist hypothesizes that people who are of similar body build work better together. Accordingly, two groups are formed. Group 1 is composed of individuals who are of similar body build, and group 2 consists of individuals with different body builds. Both groups perform a task that requires a high degree of cooperation. The performance of each participant is measured (the higher the score, the better the performance on the task). The criterion for rejecting the null hypothesis is $P = 0.02$. Was the empirical hypothesis confirmed or disconfirmed?

Group 1

10, 12, 13, 13, 15, 15, 15, 17, 18
22, 24, 25, 25, 25, 27, 28, 30, 30

Group 2

8, 9, 11, 15, 16, 16, 16, 19, 20, 21
25, 25, 26, 28, 29, 30, 30, 32, 33, 33

E. On the basis of personal experience, a marriage counselor suspects that when one spouse is from the north and the other is from the south, the marriage has a likelihood of being unsuccessful. Two groups of participants are selected: Group 1 is composed of marriage partners, both of whom are from the same section of the country (either north or south), and group 2 consists of marriage partners of whom one is from the north and one is from the south. A criterion for rejecting the null hypothesis is not set, so that a $P = 0.05$ is assumed. Ratings of the success of the marriage (the higher the rating, the better the marriage) are obtained. Assume that adequate controls have been effected. Is the suspicion confirmed?

Group 1

1, 1, 1, 2, 2, 3, 3, 4, 4, 5, 6, 6, 7, 7

Group 2

1, 1, 2, 3, 4, 4, 5, 5, 6, 7

3. When you conduct your first research project, you might consider reviewing your data sheets together with your statistical analyses and relate those items to the discussion starting on page 121. Were you systematic in collecting and recording your data? Were your statistical analyses neatly and accurately carried out? Did you check yourself on each step or have a colleague double-check you? (If your work was not accurate, you probably could have saved yourself the time in even conducting your study.)

Appendix
The Meaning of Degrees of Freedom

Degrees of freedom is a concept that expresses how much freedom you have in determining values in an array of numbers. For instance, consider the following set of data:

$$
\begin{array}{r}
7 \\
6 \\
5 \\
8 \\
\underline{9} \\
35
\end{array}
$$

Once the sum of 35 has been determined, then only four of the other values may vary freely. That is, you are free to select any value that you want for any four of the numbers, but the fifth one is determined. For instance, instead of 7, 6, 5, and 8, you could select the values of 8, 7, 6, and 9. But in either case, to equal 35, the fifth value must be 5. You thus have four degrees of freedom for this array of five numbers. The combination of the sum and any other four values absolutely determines the value of the fifth numeral. The fifth number has no freedom to vary so you only have four degrees of freedom.

To elaborate, consider the following data:

a.		b.	
10		18	
6		8	
8		2	
7		3	
$\dfrac{x}{40}$		$\dfrac{x}{40}$	

In each case, x is equal to 9. The value of 9 is thus absolutely determined by the other four numbers and the sum. As long as the sum is 40 and there are five observations, then any four of the observations may assume any value. However, the fifth value may not vary once the other values have been determined. We have thus lost that one degree of freedom. The degrees of freedom that one has in working with a set of data are always less than the number of observations in the set of data.

If we were conducting a statistical analysis in which we compute one sum (on, equally, one mean), then we will have one less degree of freedom than we do observations. If we have two sums or, equally, two means in the statistical analysis, then the degrees of freedom are the number of observations less two. In the *t*-test for two independent groups, we calculate the mean for each group. Consequently our degrees of freedom are $N - 2$. In a different application of the t-test known as the matched or paired t-test, only one mean is calculated. Consequently, for the paired t-test, the degrees of freedom would be one less than the number of values entered into the equation for t; for example, $df = n - 1$. The same rationale defines the degrees of freedom for other statistics, such as for the Pearson coefficient of correlation and experimental designs requiring analysis of variance. We shall specify the equations for computing degrees of freedom for each of these statistical analyses, for they differ in each case.

Incidentally, the more degrees of freedom that are available, the smaller is the effect of the independent variable required to reject the null hypothesis, as in Table A-1 of t in Appendix A. That means that the more participants in your study, the more likely you are to reject your null hypothesis (if it should be rejected).

chapter 7

EXPERIMENTAL DESIGN: THE CASE OF MORE THAN TWO INDEPENDENT GROUPS

Major purpose:

To extend principles of research and statistical analysis from a two-group to a multigroup design.

What you are going to find:

1. A detailed discussion of the advantages of using more than two groups.

2. Three methods of statistical analysis that you can use, depending upon your purposes:

   a. For limited, planned pairwise comparisons, use the *t*-test.

   b. To make all possible pairwise ad hoc comparisons, use the *t*-test as adjusted with the Bonferroni test.

   c. For an overall test among all means, use analysis of variance with the *F*-test.

What you should acquire:

The ability to conduct a multigroup experiment and appropriately analyze it; especially, you should clearly understand the use of analysis of variance, as it is also critical for future chapters.

THE VALUE OF MORE THAN TWO GROUPS

A Three-Group Example. Designs in psychological research usually employ more than two groups. Suppose a psychologist has two methods of remedial reading available. They are both presumably helpful to students who have not adequately learned to read by the usual method, but which is superior? Furthermore, is either of these methods *actually* superior to the normal method? To answer these questions, one could design an experiment that involves several groups, e.g., assume that 60 students who show marked reading deficiencies are randomly assigned to three groups. The first group would be taught to read using method A and the second group by method B. A comparison of the results from these two groups would tell which, if either, is the superior method. To determine whether either method is superior to the normal method of teaching, the third group would train with the normal method as a control group. After a sufficient period of time, perhaps nine months, a standard reading test would be administered to compare reading proficiency of the three groups.

Disadvantages of a Series of Separate Two-Group Experiments. To answer these questions by means of two-group experiments we could conduct one experiment in which method A is compared with method B; a second in which method A is compared with the control condition, and a third experiment in which method B is compared with the control condition. Such a strategy is obviously less desirable, for not only would more work and participants be required, but the problem of controlling extraneous variables would be sizable. For example, to hold the experimenter variable constant, the same experimenter should conduct all three experiments. Even so, it is likely that the experimenter would behave differently in the first and last experiments, perhaps due to improvement in teaching proficiency or because of boredom or fatigue. Therefore the

design in which three groups are used simultaneously is superior in that less work is required, fewer participants are used, and experimental control can be more effective.

Rationale for a Multigroup Design. The independent-groups design for the case of more than two groups can be applied to a wide variety of problems, e.g., the influence of the amount of noise on information processing efficiency, the influence of method of relaxation on alleviating tension headaches, the influence of number of reinforcements upon conditioning, or the influence of various kinds of interpolated activities upon memory. The procedure for applying a multigroup design (i.e., a design with more than two groups) to any of these problems would be to select several values of the independent variable and randomly assign a group of participants to each value. For example, to study the influence of number of biofeedback training sessions on the degree to which headaches are alleviated, we might choose the following values of this independent variable: 0 sessions, 1 sessions, 5 sessions, 10 sessions, 15 sessions, and 20 sessions. Having selected six values of the independent variable, we would have six different groups of participants. To study the influence of amount of noise on information processing efficiency, we might select four values of the independent variable: 0, 5, 10, and 15 amounts. We would then randomly assign our participants to four groups and study one group under each condition.

These considerations now make apparent yet another advantage of a multigroup over a two-group design; that is, if you attack any of the preceding problems with a two-group design, you have to decide which two values of the independent variable to employ. In our example concerning biofeedback training we selected six values to study. Which two would you use in a two-group study design?

Suppose the six-group design yields the following values: no difference among the 0-, 1-, and 5-session conditions, but the remaining conditions are superior to the first three (Figure 7-1). The conclusion from this

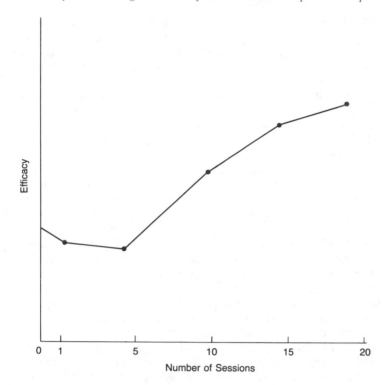

FIGURE 7-1   A two-group design using 0 and 5 biofeedback sessions would not have determined that the number of sessions was an effective independent variable.

six-group experiment would be that the variation of number of sessions from 0 to 5 sessions does not affect headaches; however, a larger number of sessions does increase biofeedback efficacy. If a two-group design had been used with only 0 and 5 sessions as valves of the independent variable, the results would suggest that variation of number of sessions does not affect headaches, a conclusion that would be in error. Thus, the more values of the independent variable sampled, the better is the evaluation of its influence on the given dependent variable.

Establishing Quantitative Relationships. Research in any given area usually progresses through two stages: First, we seek to determine which of the many possible independent variables influences a given dependent variable; second, when a certain independent variable has been identified as influential on a dependent variable, we attempt to establish the precise quantitative relationship between them. Even though a two-group design might accomplish the first

purpose, it cannot accomplish the second, for an adequate relationship cannot be specified with only two values of the independent variable (and therefore only two values of the dependent variable). To illustrate this point refer to Figure 7-2, where the values of an independent variable are indicated on the horizontal axis, and the dependent variable values are read on the vertical axis.[1] The two plotted points (obtained from a two-group design) indicate that, as the value of the independent variable increases, the mean value of the dependent variable also increases. However, this is a crude picture, for it tells us nothing about what happens between (or beyond) the two plotted points. See Figure 7-3 for a few of the infinite number of possibilities.

———————

[1] The range of the independent variable in the following discussions should be clear from the context: for example, from zero to infinity. We shall also assume that the data points are highly reliable and thus not the product of random variation.

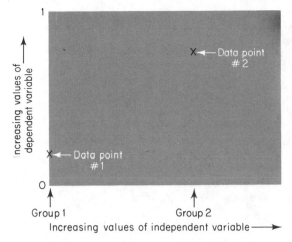

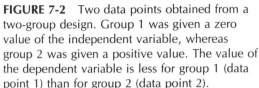

FIGURE 7-2 Two data points obtained from a two-group design. Group 1 was given a zero value of the independent variable, whereas group 2 was given a positive value. The value of the dependent variable is less for group 1 (data point 1) than for group 2 (data point 2).

By using a three-group design the relationship may be established more precisely. For this, we can add a third group that receives a value of the independent variable halfway between those of the other two groups of Figure 7-2. If the mean dependent-variable value for group 3 is that depicted in Figure 7-4, we would conclude that the relationship is probably a linear (straight-line) function. Of course, we might be wrong. That is, the relationship is not necessarily the straight line indicated in Figure 7-4, for another may be the "true" one, such as one of those shown in Figure 7-5. Nevertheless, with only three data points we prefer to bet that the straight line is the "true" relationship because it is the simplest

of the several possible relationships. Experience suggests that the simplest curve usually yields the best predictions; therefore, we would predict that if we obtain a data point for a new value of the independent variable (in addition to the three already indicated in Figure 7-4), the new data point would fall on the straight line. Different predictions would be made from the other curves of Figure 7-5.

To illustrate, suppose that we add a fourth group whose independent variable value is halfway between those of groups 1 and 3. On the basis of the four relationships depicted in Figure 7-5, we could make four different predictions about the dependent-variable value of this fourth group. First,

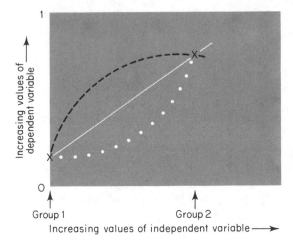

FIGURE 7-3 The actual relationship between the independent and the dependent variable is partially established by the two data points. However, the curves that may pass through the two points are infinite in number. Three possible relationships are shown.

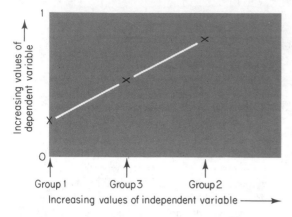

FIGURE 7-4   The addition of a third data point (group 3) suggests that the relationship is a linear function.

using the straight-line function, we would predict that the data points for the fourth group would be those indicated by X_1 in Figure 7-6, that is, if the straight line is the "true" relationship, the data point for the fourth group should fall on that line. The three curves of Figure 7-5, however, lead to three additional (and different) predictions.

Assume that the mean value for group 4 is actually that indicated by the X_1 of Figure 7-6. This increases our confidence in the straight-line function; it, rather than the other possible functions, is probably the "true" one. If these were actually the results, our procedure of preferring the simplest

curve as the "true" one (at least until contrary results are obtained) is justified. This procedure is called **inductive simplicity**—the safest induction is that the simplest relationship provides the best prediction of additional data points. In this case we select the simplest relationship that fits the data points, which is a straight line. With the randomized design for more than two groups you can establish as many data points as you wish.

Selecting   Independent-Variable   Values. One general principle of experimentation when using a two-group design is that it is advisable to choose rather extreme val-

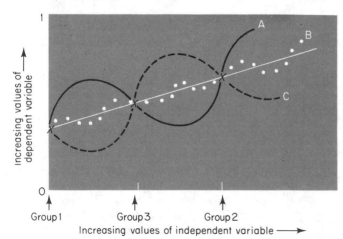

FIGURE 7-5   Other curves may possibly pass through the three data points.

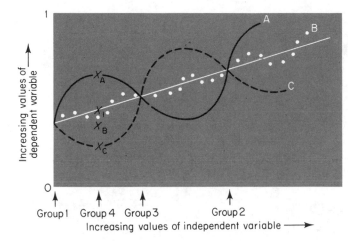

FIGURE 7-6 Four predictors of a data point for group 4. From the straight line of Figure 7-4, we would predict that the dependent variable value is that indicated by X_1. From the three curves of Figure 7-5 (curves A, B, and C), we would predict that the data point would be that indicated by the X_A, the X_B, and the X_C, respectively.

ues of the independent variable.[2] If we had followed this principle, we would not have erred in the example concerning the influence of the number of biofeedback sessions on alleviation of headaches. Instead of choosing 0- and 5 session conditions as we did, we should have selected 0 and 9 sessions. In this event the two-group design would have led to a conclusion more in line with that of the six-group design. However, it should still be apparent that the six-group design yielded considerably more information, allowing us to establish the relationship between the two variables with a high degree of confidence.

Even so, the selection of extreme values for two groups can lead to difficulties in addition to those already considered. To illustrate, assume that the two data points obtained are those indicated by the *X*s in Figure 7-7. The obvious conclusion is that manipulation of the independent variable does not influence the dependent variable, for the dependent variable values for the two groups are the same. The best inference is that there is a lack of relationship as indicated by the horizontal straight line fitted to the two points. Yet the actual relationship may be the curvilinear one of Figure 7-8 a relationship that could be uncovered with a three-group design. The corresponding principle with a three-group design is thus to *select two rather extreme values of the independent variable and also one value midway between them.* Of course, if the data point for group 3 had been the same value as for groups 1 and 2, the we would be more confident that the independent variable did not affect the dependent variable.

To summarize, psychologists seek to determine which of a number of independent variables influence a given dependent variable and also attempt to establish the quantitative relationship between them. With a two-group design one is never sufficiently sure that the appropriate values of the independent variable were selected in the attempt to determine whether that variable is effective. By using more than two groups, however, we increase our chances of: (1) accurately determining whether a given independent variable is effective, and (2) specifying the quantitative relationship between the independent and the dependent variable. For these reasons two-group designs

---

[2] Let us emphasize the word *rather*, for seldom would we want to select independent-variable values for two groups that are really extreme. This is so because it is likely that all generalizations in psychology break down when the independent variable values are unrealistically extreme. Weber's law, which you probably studied in introductory psychology, is a good example. Although Weber's law holds rather well for weights that you can conveniently hold in your hand, it would obviously be absurd to state that it is true for extreme values of weights such as those of atomic size or those of several tons.

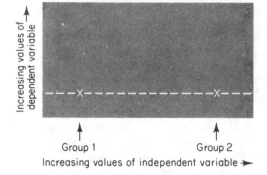

FIGURE 7-7   Two data points for extreme values of the independent variable using a two-groups design. These points suggest that the independent variable does not affect the dependent variable.

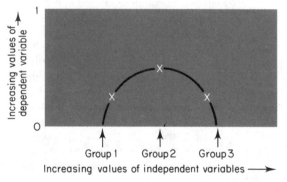

FIGURE 7-8   Postulated actual relationship for the data points of Figure 7-7. This relationship would be specified with a suitable three-group design.

are now less frequently used since multigroup designs are more effective.

LIMITATIONS OF A TWO-GROUP DESIGN

To illustrate concretely the pitfalls of a two-group design, we consider an experiment in which a rat is placed in a Skinner box. A light is presented to the animal, and, after the lapse of some specific amount of time, a pellet of food is delivered. Once the light and food are associated a number of times, the animal is allowed to press a bar. Each depression of the bar results in the onset of the light. The independent variable is the length of time that the light is on *prior* to the delivery of the pellet. The dependent variable is the number of bar-pressing responses that occur within a 10-minute period. Hence the greater the number of responses, the stronger the secondary reinforcing properties of the light have become.

Now place yourself in the position of the experimenter as you design this experiment. In the training phase you present a light to the rat, after which you deliver a pellet of food. If you use a two-group design, what two time values would you select to separate these two presentations? As a control condition you would want to use a zero value, presenting the light and food simultaneously with no time intervening. But what would be the value of your second condition? Suppose that, because you had to do something,[3] you decided to turn on the light one second before the delivery of the food.

If you actually conducted this experi-

---

[3] In research, as in many phases of life, one frequently faces problems for which no appropriate response is available. A principle that I have found useful was given by a college mathematics teacher (Dr. Bell) to be applied when confronted with an apparently unsolvable math problem: "If you can't do anything, do something." You will be delighted at the frequency with which this principle leads, if not directly, at least indirectly, to success.

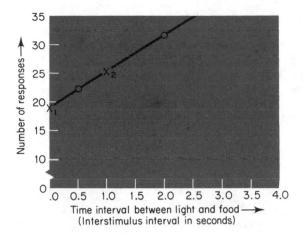

FIGURE 7-9 Two data points for a two-groups design. Data point 1 (indicated by X_1) resulted from a 0-second time interval during acquired reinforcement training, and data point 2 (X_2) resulted from a 1-second delay. The suggestion is that the longer the time interval, the larger will be the number of resulting responses. Hence the prediction for other time interval values, such as 0.5 and 2.0 seconds, are indicated by the circles (from Bersh, 1951).

ment, your results should resemble those in Figure 7-9; that is, the animals who had a 0.0-second delay between light onset and delivery of food would make 19 bar presses within the 10-minute test period, but approximately 25 responses would be made by the animals for whom light preceded food by 1.0 second during training. Hence the light acquires stronger secondary reinforcing properties when it precedes food by 1 second than when it occurs simultaneously with food. May we now conclude that the longer the time interval between presentation of light and food, the stronger the acquired reinforcing properties of the light? To study this question we have fitted a straight line to the data points in Figure 7-9.

But before we can have confidence in this conclusion, we must face gnawing questions such as what would have happened had there been a 0.5-second delay or a 2.0-second delay? Would dependent variable values for 0.5 and 2.0 seconds have fallen on the straightline, as suggested by the two circles in Figure 7-9? The answer, of course, is that we would never know unless there were an experiment involving such conditions. Fortunately, in this instance relevant data are available. In addition to the 0.0-second and the 1.0-second delay conditions, data points for delays of 0.5 seconds, 2.0 seconds, 4.0 seconds, and 10.0 seconds, and the complete curve are presented in Figure 7-10. By studying Figure 7-10 we can see how erroneous would be the conclusion

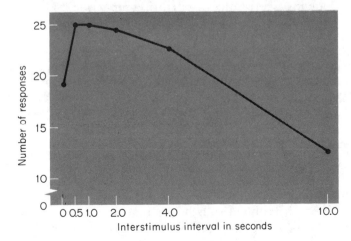

FIGURE 7-10 Number of bar presses as a function of the interstimulus interval during acquired reinforcement training (Bersh, 1951).

based on the two-groups experiment. Instead of a 0.5-second delay resulting in about 22 responses, as predicted with Figure 7-9, a 0.5-second delay led to results about the same as a 1.0-second delay, after which the curve, instead of continuing to rise, falls rather dramatically. In short, the conduct of a two-groups experiment on this problem would have resulted in an erroneous conclusion: The number of bar presses increases from a 0.0-to a 0.5-second delay which is about the same as for a 0.5-to a 1.0-second delay, after which the number decreases. This complex relationship could not possibly have been determined by means of a single two-group design. The more values of the independent variable sampled, the better will be our quantitative estimation of its influence on a given dependent variable. There are no hard and fast rules for selecting an independent variable as a possible influence on a dependent variable nor for determining the number of values of the independent variables studied. The general perspective that we considered in Chapter 2 is relevant here, i.e., once the problem has been selected, the hypothesis formed, and the independent and dependent variables specified, you then determine how many values of the independent variable you will test. For this you need to assess your resources (number of participants available, limitations of time and efforts, etc.), study similiar research in the literature, conduct a pilot study, etc. Many of these decisions depends on the importance of the research to you. For a preliminary project in a research methods class, you need to get along hastily with your project. However, when conducting a doctoral dissertation you can expect to spend much more time and energy.

STATISTICAL ANALYSIS OF A DESIGN WITH MORE THAN TWO INDEPENDENT GROUPS

As in previous designs we need to determine whether the dependent-variable values of our groups differ reliably. However, we now have more than two group means to compare. Unfortunately, for our present purposes there is much disagreement among statisticians and among psychologists as to what statistical procedure is most appropriate for this type of problem. The disagreements stem from testing different null hypotheses and from emphasizing different aspects of the empirical question. We will restrict ourselves, however, to statistical procedures that apply to your immediate research questions.

Planned (a priori) versus Post Hoc (a posteriori) Comparisons. As background for the discussion that follows, recall the topic of borderline reliability; you can relate that point to the present discussion; namely, conducting an experiment is like placing your bet before a race starts. You must specify a criterion for rejecting the null hypothesis prior to collecting your data and maintain it throughout. For instance, if you find that a computed t would have been reliable at the 0.07 level, if then you adopt $P = 0.07$, you do not have a true value of P.

For it to be a true value, you must *plan* your comparisons before you start your statistical analysis. **Planned comparisons** *are thus those that are specified while you are designing your experiment.* Furthermore, *they are explicit tests of your empirical hypothesis.* Since you must plan the comparisons before you look at your data, they are synonymously referred to as **a priori comparisons**. Planned pairwise comparisons are limited in number, as we shall develop further.

In contrast, **post hoc comparisons** *are those made after you have studied the data,* which is why they are also referred to as *a posteriori comparisons.* Post hoc comparisons are made in accordance with the serendipity principle; that is, after conducting your experiment you may find something interesting that you were not initially looking for. For instance, you might have planned a comparison between groups 1 versus 3 and 2 versus 3, but after looking at your data you discover that comparisons between groups 1 versus 2, or even group 1 versus the combined results of groups 2 versus 3 are valuable. Although you thereby disturb your stated criterion of $P = 0.05$, you may still make such post hoc comparisons because you should extract every reasonable bit of information from your experiment. However, you then must realize that you *have* disturbed your criterion of $P = 0.05$ (or whatever) and make appropriate adjustments. The ultimate in post hoc pairwise comparisons would be where you make all possible comparisons between your groups, taken two at a time and between the various combinations of groups. Even if you specify that you are going to make all possible pairwise comparisons prior to conducting your experiment, you still disturb your probability criterion. In either case you need to make some probability adjustments to $P = 0.05$. This point will be elaborated when we take up our second question.

Specifying Your Research Questions. There are three basic questions that you should consider.

First, do you want to make comparisons only between certain *pairs of groups?* For example, if you have three groups in your study, you could test group 1 against group 2 and then group 1 against group 3; these would be **limited pairwise comparisons**. In making limited pairwise comparisons, you do not make all possible pairwise comparisons. Neither are you interested in combining groups to test them against some other group(s), e.g., you would not combine the results from groups 1 and 2 to test those combined groups against group 3.

Second, do you want to make all possible comparisons between the separate groups taken two at a time? In this case, you would test group 1 against group 2, group 2 against group 3, and group 1 against group 3, *thus making* **all possible pairwise comparisons**.

Third, do you want to determine *whether there is a reliable difference between any pair of groups, without specifying which pair of groups differs?* For example, if there are five groups in your experiment, you could conduct a single statistical test to tell you whether any pair of those groups differs reliably but unfortu-

nately the test would not tell you which pair or pairs differ.

Before we answer these three questions, it is important to make a distinction between planned and post hoc comparisons. In answering question 1, we are making planned or a priori comparisons, while in answering question 2, we are making post hoc or a posteriori comparisons. In answering question 3, we are not making any specific (pairwise) comparisons between groups at all, so this distinction is not relevant for that question.

Limited Pairwise Comparisons

For the first question, you can proceed directly to the analysis of your multigroup study with the test that you have already employed—the *t*-test. However, you cannot legitimately conduct all possible *t*-tests; you must limit yourself to selected comparisons. To understand this point (remembering that *r* stands for number of groups), the equation for determining the *possible* number of pairwise comparisons (C_p) that can be made is

$$(7\text{-}1) \qquad C_p = \frac{r(r-1)}{2}$$

For instance, if you have three groups, $r = 3$, so that the number of possible pairwise comparisons is

$$C_p = \frac{3(3-1)}{2}$$
$$= \frac{3 \cdot 2}{2}$$
$$= 3$$

The three possible comparisons are between groups 1 and 2, between groups 2 and 3, and between groups 1 and 3. If you have four groups, you can readily determine that there are 6 possible pairwise comparisons; with five groups, there are 10. The number of *legitimate* pairwise comparisons (C_L) you can make is determined by the number of degrees of freedom for your groups, that is,

$r - 1$. For a three-group experiment, $df = 3 - 1 = 2$, so that you could, for instance, legitimately run *t*-tests between groups 1 versus 2 and 2 versus 3. For a four-group experiment, $df = 4 - 1 = 3$. You could thus use one degree of freedom for comparing group 1 versus 2, a second degree of freedom for group 3 versus group 4, and perhaps your third degree of freedom for group 2 versus group 3. The principle is that you should use all four means when conducting your statistical tests; we may note that the first two comparisons (1 versus 2, and 3 versus 4) are totally independent. However, the third comparison (2 versus 3) is correlated (not independent) with the other two comparisons since only groups 2 and 3 were used in those first two comparisons.

Why It Is Not Legitimate to Conduct All Possible *t*-tests.

Suppose that we conduct a two-group experiment and set our criterion for rejecting the null hypothesis at $P = 0.05$. This means that if we obtain a *t* that has a *P* of 0.05, the odds are 5 in 100 that a *t* of this size or larger could have occurred by chance. Since this would happen only rarely (5 percent of the time), we reason that the *t* was not the result of random fluctuations. Rather, we prefer to conclude that the two groups are "really" different as measured by the dependent variable. We thus reject our null hypothesis and conclude that variation of the independent variable was effective in producing the difference between our two groups. After completing that research, say that we conduct a new two-group experiment. Note that the two experiments are independent of each other. In the second experiment we also set our criterion at 0.05 and follow the same procedure as before. Again, this means that the odds are 5 in 100 that a *t* of the corresponding size could have occurred by chance.

But let us ask a question. Given a required level of $P = 0.05$ in each of the two experiments, what are the odds that by chance the *t* in one, the other, or both experiments will be statistically reliable? Before you reach a hasty conclusion, let us caution you that the probability is *not* 0.05. Rather, the joint probability could be shown to be 0.0975.[4] That is, the odds of obtaining a *t* that is reliable at the 0.05 level in either or both experiments are 975 out of 10,000. This is certainly different from 0.05, i.e., 500 out of 10,000. . . .[11]

To illustrate, consider an analogy: What is the probability of obtaining a head in two tosses of a coin? On the first toss it is one in two, and on the second toss it is one in two. But the probability of obtaining two heads on two successive tosses (before your first toss) is $\frac{1}{2} \times \frac{1}{2} = \frac{1}{4}$. To develop the analogy further, the probability of obtaining a head on the first toss or on the second toss or on both tosses (again, computed before *any* tosses) is $P = 0.75$.

Now let us return to our three-group experiment in which there are three possible *t*-tests. Assume that we set a required probability level of 0.05 as our criterion for *each t*. What are the odds of obtaining a reliable *t* when we consider all *t*-tests and their combinations? That is, what are the odds of obtaining a reliable *t* in at least one of the following situations?

First:	Between groups 1 and 2
or Second:	Between groups 1 and 3
or Third:	Between groups 2 and 3
or Fourth:	Between groups 1 and 2 and also between groups 1 and 3
or Fifth:	Between groups 1 and 2 and also between groups 2 and 3
or Sixth:	Between groups 1 and 3 and also between groups 2 and 3
or Seventh:	Between groups 1 and 2 and also between groups 2 and 3 and also between groups 1 and 3

The answer to this question is more complex than before, but we *can* say that it is not 0.05. Rather, it is noticeably greater than

---

[4]By the following equation: $P_j = 1 - (1 - a)^k$ where P_j is the joint probability, a is the reliability level, and k is the number of independent experiments. For instance in this case $a = .05$, $k = 2$. Therefore $P_j = 1 - (1 - 0.05)^2 = 0.0975$.

0.05. This is because by just conducting a number of *t*-tests, we increase the odds that we will obtain a reliable difference by chance. If we conduct 100 *t*-tests, 5 of those are expected to be reliable by chance alone. Furthermore, by conducting all possible *t*-tests in a multigroup experiment, some of those *t*-tests (as we noted before) are not independent, which also increases the chances of obtaining a reliable *t* by chance.[5] In short, increasing the number of *t*-tests that you conduct disturbs the probability criterion of 0.05 for rejecting the null hypothesis.[6] In these ways you capitalize on chance, increasing the odds of rejecting the null hypothesis at times when it should not be rejected. But by restricting yourself to the number of *legitimate* comparisons that can be made, as determined by the equation $df = r - 1$, the consensus among researchers and statisticians is that you thereby do not greatly disturb the criterion of $P = 0.05$.

In Summary. If you choose to make pairwise comparisons in a multigroup experiment with the *t*-test, you are on safe ground if you limit the number of comparisons to that specified by $C_L = r - 1$.[7] There is only one qualification—you should state precisely the comparisons you are going to make before you look at your data. This does not mean, however, that you cannot conduct other *t*-tests after studying your results; that is, you can make *a posteriori comparisons*, even making all possible pairwise comparisons.

All Possible Pairwise Comparisons

In comparing all possible group means making post hoc comparisons, you need to adjust your stated criteria for testing null hypotheses. All proposed solutions for this problem, and there are many, employ the same basic logic. That is, since the stated probability value (e.g., $P = 0.05$) is not the true value, efforts are made to modify P so that it is a more realistic value. These procedures then arrive at a "truer" value of P that decreases the odds that you will falsely reject the null hypothesis. That is, the adjustment protects you from concluding that there is a reliable mean difference between your groups, when in fact the true difference is zero. For instance, if you conduct 20 *t*-tests, by chance you can expect one of those values to indicate statistical reliability (5 percent of $20 = 1$). To protect yourself against this chance error, you could lower your stated criterion for rejecting the null hypothesis from 0.05 to 0.01; with this more conservative criterion, you would expect *no* reliable values for your *t*-tests by chance (1 percent of 20 is only .2 percent). A search of psychology journals by Holland and Copenhaver (1988) found ". . . numerous instances . . . of . . . erroneous rejection of [null] hypotheses . . ." for this reason (p. 149).

The simplest procedure for adjusting the criterion for rejecting the null hypothesis is the Bonferroni test.[8] To conduct a Bonferroni test, you merely divide your stated crite-

---

[5] When we say "reliable *t*" (or a "reliable *F*") this is just a shorthand way of stating that the *t* indicated that there is a reliable difference between the means of our two groups.

[6] There is yet another reason that you disturb the criterion of $P = 0.05$ when making all possible pairwise comparisons: The means are not independent. For example, in a four-group experiment you may compare groups 1 versus 2 and groups 3 versus 4, which are totally independent comparisons. However, the remaining comparisons of groups 1 versus 3 and 1 versus 4, and group 2 versus 3 and 4 are not independent of the first two comparisons or of each other. This excessive number of correlated comparisons further disturbs the stated probability of *P*.

[7] The procedure here is to apply Equation 6-2 to compute *t* using only the data for the two groups being compared. Thus if you are testing groups 1 versus 2, you would not use the values for group 3. In contrast you could use a pooled estimate of your error in the denominator of the *t* ratio which would be computed with values from all three groups. There are advantages and disadvantages to both procedures, as hopefully you will learn in your later study.

[8] The original reference is not available because we apparently do not know who Bonferroni was. There was a similar problem with the *t*-test. The *t*-test is referred to as Student's *t*, because it was originally published anonymously. It was merely signed "A Student," because the author worked for a Dublin brewery that would not allow him to disclose his name. Years later it was discovered to be William Sealy Gosset.

rion by the number of possible comparisons and employ the resulting probability value (level). For example, in a three-group experiment, the number of possible comparisons (C_p) is three. Hence, if your stated level would have been 0.05, that value divided by three equals approximately 0.017. You then merely replace 0.05 with 0.017 to test your null hypothesis. Referring to the t table (Table A-1) with a t of 0.017 and 10 df, for instance, for a three-group experiment in which we wish to make all possible comparisons, we find that the value of t at 0.02 level is 2.764 and at 0.01 level 3.169. Interpolating between the 0.02 and 0.01 values, we find that a value of $t = 2.886$ corresponds to our adjusted probability level of 0.017. Consequently, to reject the null hypothesis for each of the three pairwise comparisons, our computed value of t must be greater than 2.886. For instance, if we find that the value of t between groups 1 and 3 equals 2.900, we would conclude that those two groups differ reliably. But if the t between groups 2 and 3 equals 2.800, we would conclude that they do not differ reliably. Incidentally, note that the value of t corresponding to a P of 0.05 with 10 df is 2.228. Had we not corrected the criterion of $P = 0.05$, we would have made an error by concluding that groups 2 and 3 were reliable and different.

In a four-group experiment we saw that $C_p = 6$. Hence, to use the Bonferroni test to make all possible comparisons, our adjusted probability level would be $\frac{0.05}{6} = 0.008$. Consequently, to make these six comparisons, the computed value of t for each pairwise comparison would have to exceed $P = 0.008$. With 10 degrees of freedom the value of t required to reject the null hypothesis is 3.484.

More sophisticated statistical procedures for making all possible pairwise comparisons are known as *multiple comparison tests (procedures)* and are found in standard statistics books. Some of these tests can even be employed for making nonpairwise comparisons, too, such as combining means of groups and testing various combinations

thereof. One multiple comparison test, Duncan's New Multiple Range Test, was explained in detail in earlier editions of this book. However, there is much disagreement among statisticians and psychologists about how best to answer our second question when making more than the legitimate number of comparisons between and among groups. In part, these disagreements stem from different types of hypotheses that are being tested and different aspects of the question that are emphasized. The Bonferroni method should suffice for at least your elementary work, however.

Overall (Omnibus) *F*-Tests and the Analysis of Variance

Overall versus Partial NULL Hypothesis. To answer the third question, we can conduct a statistical analysis to determine whether there is a reliable difference between any *pair of means* in a multigroup design. For this purpose the null hypothesis is that all population means of the groups are equal. This is called an **overall (omnibus or complete) null hypothesis**. If there are three groups in the experiment, the overall null hypothesis would state that $\mu_1 = \mu_2 = \mu_3$.[9] The null hypotheses between pairs of groups, (e.g., group 1 versus 2) are called **partial null hypotheses**. Let us emphasize how an overall null hypothesis is different from a partial null stated for a pairwise comparison. The difference between these two null hypotheses is critical for understanding our answer to the third question. In particular, if we reject the overall null hypothesis we only know that there is at least one reliable difference between means of a pair of groups, but we don't know which group differs from which. If this overall null hypothesis is for a three-group design, rejection of it could mean that the mean for group 1

---

[9] An alternative statement is that $\mu_1 = \mu_2$, $\mu_1 = \mu_3$, and $\mu_2 = \mu_3$. Yet another form, somewhat more sophisticated, is that the population means of the group are themselves equal and that they equal the overall mean of all groups combined.

reliably differs from that for group 2, or that it reliably differs from that for group 3, or that the mean difference between groups 2 and 3 is reliable. Keeping this overall null hypothesis in mind, let us return to it after we discuss *analysis of variance*. Learning how to conduct an analysis of variance is not just important for this purpose, but it is critical for applications to other designs discussed in later chapters.

How to Conduct an Analysis of Variance. You are already acquainted with the term *variance*, which will facilitate the ensuing discussion. It would be helpful to review it now (page 116).

The simplest application of analysis of variance would be to test the mean difference between two independent groups. Equivalent results would be obtained by conducting the *t*-test on a two-group design. That is, we could analyze a two-group design by using either the *t*-test or analysis of variance (with the *F*-test, to be explained shortly) and obtain precisely the same conclusions. Let us say that the dependent-variable values that result from a two-group design are those plotted in Figure 7-11. That is, the frequency distribution to the left represents values for the participants in group 1, and that to the right is for group 2.

Total Sum of Squares = Between-Groups Sum of Squares + Within-Groups Sum of Squares. Now are the means of these groups reliably different? To answer this question by using analysis of variance, we first determine the **total sum of squares**. The total sum of squares is a value that results when we take all participants in the experiment into account as a whole. The total sum of squares is computed from the dependent-variable values of all the participants, ignoring that some were under one experimental condition while others were under another experimental condition. Once completed, the total sum of squares is partitioned (analyzed) into parts. In particular, there are two major components: the sum of squares **between groups** and the sum of squares **within groups**. Roughly, the sum of squares between groups may be thought of as determined by the extent to which the sample means of the two groups differ.

The Meaning of Within and Between Groups. In Figure 7-11 the size of the between-groups sum of squares is approximately indicated by the distance between the two means. More accurately we may say that the larger the difference between the means, the larger the between-groups sum of squares. The within-groups sum of squares,

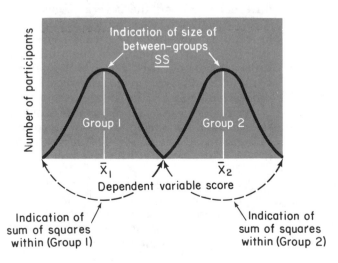

FIGURE 7-11 An approximate indication of the nature of within- and between-groups sums of squares using only two groups.

on the other hand, is determined by the extent to which the members of each group differ among themselves on the dependent-variable measure. If the participants in group 1 differ sizably among themselves, and/or if the same is true for members of group 2, the within-groups sum of squares is going to be large. And the larger the within-groups sum of squares, the larger will be the error variance in the experiment. By way of illustration, assume that all those in group 1 have been treated precisely alike. Hence if they were precisely alike when they went into the experiment, they should all receive the same value on the dependent variable. If this happened, the within-groups sum of squares (as far as group 1 is concerned) would be zero, for there would be no variation among their values. Of course, the within-groups sum of squares is unlikely ever to be zero, since all the participants are not the same before the experiment and the experimenter is never able to treat all precisely alike.

Let us now reason by analogy with the *t*-test

$$t = \frac{\overline{X}_1 - \overline{X}_2}{\sqrt{\frac{SS_1 + SS_2}{(n_1 - 1) + (n_2 - 1)}\left(\frac{1}{n_1}\right) + \left(\frac{1}{n_2}\right)}}$$

You will recall that the numerator of Equation 6-2 is a measure of the difference between the means of two groups. It is thus analogous to our between-groups sum of squares. The denominator of Equation 6-2 is a measure of the error variance in the experiment and is thus analogous to our within-groups sum of squares. This should be apparent when one notes that the denominator of Equation 6-2 is large if the variances of the groups are large, and small if the variances of the groups are small. Recall that the larger the numerator and the smaller the denominator of the *t* ratio, the greater is the likelihood that the two groups are reliably different. The same is true in our analogy: The larger the between-groups sum of squares and the smaller the within-

groups sum of squares, the more likely our groups are to be reliably different. Looking at Figure 7-11 we may say that the larger the distance between the two means and the smaller the within (internal) variances of the two groups, the more likely they are to be reliably different. For example, the difference between the means of the two groups of Figure 7-12 is more likely to be statistically reliable than the difference between the means of the two groups of Figure 7-11. This is so because the difference between the means in Figure 7-12 is represented as greater than that for Figure 7-11 and also because the within-groups sum of squares in Figure 7-12 is represented as less than that for Figure 7-11.

We have discussed the case of two groups. Precisely the same general reasoning applies when there are more than two groups: The total sum of squares in the experiment is analyzed into two parts, the within- and the among-groups sum of squares. (*Between* is used for two groups; *among* is the same concept applied to more than two. As you can see in your dictionary, it is incorrect to say "between several groups." "Between" rather than "among" is the correct term when only two things serve as objects. "Among" is applied to three or more when they are considered collectively.) If the differences among the several means are large, the among-groups sum of squares will be large. If the differences among the several means are small, the among-groups sum of squares will be small. If the participants who are treated alike differ sizably, then the within (internal) sum of squares of each group will be large. If the individual group variances are large, the within-groups sum of squares will be large. The larger the among-groups sums of squares and the smaller the within-groups sum of squares, the more likely it is that the means of the groups differ reliably.

Computational Equations. We have attempted to present, in a surface fashion, the major rationale underlying analysis of variance. As we now turn to the computation of the several sums of squares, we shall be more

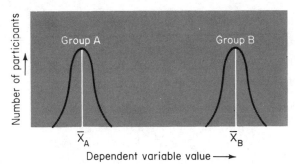

FIGURE 7-12 A more extreme mean difference between two groups than that shown in Figure 7-11. Here the between-groups sum of squares is greater but the within-groups sum of squares (variability) is less.

precise. The equations to be given are based on the following reasoning, and their computation automatically accomplishes what we are going to say. First, an overall mean is computed that is based on all the dependent-variable values in the experiment taken together (ignoring the fact that some participants were under one condition and others under another condition). Then the total sum of squares is computed as a measure of the deviation of all the values from this overall mean. The among-groups sum of squares is a measure of the deviation of the means of the several groups from the overall mean. The within-groups sum of squares is a pooled sum of squares based on the deviation of the scores in each group from the mean of that group. As we proceed, we will enlarge on these introductory statements.

To compute the total *SS* that will be analyzed into its parts, consider a generalized equation for computing the total *SS*

$$(7\text{-}2) \quad \text{total } SS = (\Sigma X_1^2 + \Sigma X_2^2$$
$$+ \ldots + \Sigma X_r^2)$$
$$- \frac{(\Sigma X_1 + \Sigma X_2 + \Sigma X_3 + \ldots + \Sigma X_r)^2}{N}$$

As before, the subscript *r* simply indicates that we continue adding the values indicated (the sum of *X*-squares and the sum of *X*s, respectively) for as many groups as we have in the study.

Our next step is to analyze the total *SS* into components—that among groups and that within groups. A generalized equation for computing the among-groups *SS* is

(7-3)
$$\text{among } SS = \frac{(\Sigma X_1)^2}{n_1} + \frac{(\Sigma X_2)^2}{n_2} + \frac{(\Sigma X_3)^2}{n_3}$$
$$+ \ldots + \frac{(\Sigma X_r)^2}{n_r}$$
$$- \frac{(\Sigma X_1 + \Sigma X_2 + \Sigma X_3 + \ldots + \Sigma X_r)^2}{N}$$

The within-groups component of the total *SS* may be computed by subtraction. That is,

$$(7\text{-}4) \quad \text{within-groups } SS = \text{total } SS$$
$$- \text{among-groups } SS$$

In a more-than-two-randomized-groups design, of course, there may be any number of groups. To compute the several *SS* we must compute the ΣX and ΣX^2 separately for each group. The subscripts, as before, indicate the different groups. Hence ΣX_1 is the sum of the dependent-variable values for group 1, ΣX_3^2 is the sum of the squares of the dependent-variable values for group 3, and so forth. *N* remains the *total* number of participants in the experiment and *n* the number in each group.

An Illustration of the Analysis of Variance Procedure. Consider an experiment (related to one previously analyzed on pages 103–105) on classical conditioning of planarians to a light.[10] More specifically, one

[10] From an experiment by Jacobson, Fried, & Horowitz, 1966.

group (group CC for "classical conditioned") received paired presentation of a light and a shock. The planarians normally contract when shocked, but after conditioning they also contracted to the conditional stimulus, the light. Group PC (for "pseudoconditioning") was treated in the same way as group CC, but the light and shock were not paired; that is, these planarians were shocked and received light on their trials, but the light and shock were not associated so that conditioning could not occur. The third group (NC for "nonconditioned") simply remained in their home containers and were not exposed to the experimental situation.

After this procedure was followed, untrained planarians were injected with ribonucleic acid (RNA, cf. page 106) from the three groups. More specifically, a new group of planarians received RNA that was extracted from group CC, a second naive group received injections of RNA from group PC, and a third received injections from group NC. These new groups were then tested to see how often they would emit the conditional response (contraction) to the conditional stimulus (light). The number of conditional responses made by each animal during 25 test trials is presented in Table 7-1.

To compute the total SS, we may write a specialized form of Equation 7-2 for three groups as follows:

(7-5) $\text{total } SS = (\Sigma X_1^2 + \Sigma X_3^2 + \Sigma X_3^2)$

$$- \frac{(\Sigma X_1 + \Sigma X_2 + \Sigma X_3)^2}{N}$$

We can see that the sum of X for group NC is 40, for group PC it is 46, and for group CC it is 205. Or, written in terms of Equation 7-5, we may say that $\Sigma X_1 = 40$, $\Sigma X_2 = 46$, and $\Sigma X_3 = 205$. Similarly, $\Sigma X_1^2 = 104$, $\Sigma X_2^2 = 154$, $\Sigma X_3^2 = 1,721$, and $N = 75$. Substituting these values in Equation 7-5, we find the total SS to be

$\text{total } SS = (104 + 154 + 1,721)$

$$- \frac{(40 + 46 + 205)^2}{75} = 849.92$$

TABLE 7-1 Number of Responses on the 25 Test Trials for Each Injected Planarian

Planarians Injected with RNA from:		
Group 1 (NC)	*Group 2 (PC)*	*Group 3 (CC)*
0	0	6
0	0	6
0	0	6
0	0	7
1	0	7
1	0	7
1	0	7
1	0	7
1	0	8
1	1	8
1	1	8
1	2	8
1	2	8
1	2	9
1	2	9
2	3	9
2	3	9
2	3	9
2	3	9
3	3	9
3	3	9
3	4	10
3	4	10
4	5	10
5	5	10
ΣX: 40	46	205
ΣX^2: 104	154	1721
n: 25	25	25
$\bar{X}$: 1.60	1.84	8.20

To compute the among-groups SS for the three groups, we substitute the appropriate values in Equation 7-6, the specialized form of Equation 7-3 for three groups. This requires that we merely substitute the value of ΣX for each group, square it, and divide by the number of participants in each group. Since the last term is the same as the last term in Equation 7-5, we need not compute it again, *providing* there was no error in its computation the first time. Making the appropriate substitutions from Table 7-1 and performing the indicated computations, we find that

(7-6) $\text{among-groups } SS = \dfrac{(\Sigma X_1)^2}{n_1} + \dfrac{(\Sigma X_2)^2}{n_2}$

$$+ \frac{(\Sigma X_3)^2}{n_3} - \frac{(\Sigma X_1 + \Sigma X_2 + \Sigma X_3)^2}{N}$$

$$= \frac{(40)^2}{25} + \frac{(46)^2}{25} + \frac{(205)^2}{25} - 1{,}129.08$$

$$= 700.56$$

Substituting in Equation 7-4,

$$\text{within-groups } SS = 849.92 - 700.56$$
$$= 149.36$$

In conducting this analysis of variance, you may have wondered, "Where are the variances?" They are referred to in our sample values, not as variances, but as *mean squares*. That is, we are computing sample values as estimates of population values. The mean squares (sample values) are estimates of the variances (population values). For example, the mean square within groups is an estimate of the within-groups variance. *The rule for computing mean squares is simple: Divide a given sum of squares by the appropriate degrees of freedom.*

Degrees of Freedom. In introducing the *equations for the three degrees of freedom* let us emphasize what we have done with regard to sums of squares. We have computed a total *SS* and partitioned it into two parts, the among *SS* and the within *SS*. The same procedure is followed for *df*. First, we determine that

(7-7)   total $df = N - 1$

Then, that

(7-8)   among $df = r - 1$

And that

(7-9)   within $df = N - r$

For our example, $N = 75$ and $r = 3$, so that

$$\text{total } df = 75 - 1 = 74$$

$$\text{among } df = 3 - 1 = 2$$
$$\text{within } df = 75 - 3 = 72$$

And we may note that the among *df* plus the within *df* equals the total *df*, i.e., $72 + 2 = 74$.

Mean Squares. We need to compute a mean square for the among-groups source of variation and one for the within-groups. For the former we divide the among-groups *SS* by the among-groups *df*, and similarly for the latter. For example, the within-groups mean square is 149.36 divided by 72. These values are then entered in a summary table (Table 7-2).

The F-Test. Now recall that if the among-groups mean square is sufficiently large, relative to the within-groups mean square, the dependent-variable values for the groups differ reliably (probably). But again we face the problem: Just how large is "sufficiently large," that is, how sizable must the among component be relative to the within component in order for us to conclude that a given independent variable *is* effective? To answer this we apply the *F*-test, developed by the outstanding statistician Sir Ronald Aymer Fisher (named in his honor by another outstanding statistician, George W. Snedecor). The *F* statistic for this design may be defined as follows.[11]

(7-10) $F = \dfrac{\text{mean square among groups}}{\text{mean square within groups}}$

This statistic is obviously easy to compute, and we may recall the similarity between it and the *t*-test. In both cases the numerator is an indication of the mean differences between or among groups (plus error variance), and the denominator is an indication of only the error variance. More particu-

---

[11] This is only one of a number of applications of the *F*-test. *F* is always a ratio of two variances, and the fact that variances other than those in Equation 7-10 are sometimes used should not be a source of confusion. Simply realize that *F* may also be used in ways different than the one discussed here.

TABLE 7-2   Summary Table for An Analysis of Variance for Planarian RNA Conditions

Source of Variation	Sum of Squares	df	Mean Square	F
Among groups	700.56	2	350.28	169.22
Within groups	149.36	72	2.07	
Total	849.92	74		

larly, in this simple application (of many) of the F-test, the numerator contains an estimate of the error variance plus an estimate of the "real" effect (if any) of the independent variable. The denominator is only an estimate of the error variance, that is:

(7-11) $$F = \frac{\text{Estimate of group mean difference} + \text{estimate of error variance}}{\text{estimate of error variance}}$$

Now you can see what happens when you divide the numerator by the denominator: The computed value of F reflects the effect that the independent variable had in producing a difference between means. For example, suppose the independent variable is totally ineffective in influencing the dependent variable. In this case we would expect (at least in the long run) that the numerator would not contain any contribution from the independent variable (there would be no "real" among-groups mean square). Hence the value for the numerator would be only an estimate of the error variance; a similar estimate of the error variance is in the denominator. Therefore in the long run (with a large number of df) if you divide a value for the error variance by a value for the error variance, you obtain an F of about 1.0.

Thus, *any time we obtain an F of approximately 1, we can be rather sure that variation of the independent variable did not produce a difference in the dependent-variable means of our groups*. If the numerator is somewhat larger than the denominator (the among-groups mean square is somewhat larger than the within-groups mean square), how much larger must it be before we can conclude that the means of the groups are really different? If the numerator is quite large (relative to

the denominator), the value of F will be large. This is the same question we asked concerning the t-test; that is, how large must t be before we can reject our null hypothesis? We shall answer this question for the F-test in a manner similar to that for the t-test. To compute F, we have divided the mean square within groups (2.07) into the mean square between groups (350.28) and inserted the resulting value (169.22) in Table 7-2.

The F Table. Just as with the t-test, we must next determine the value of P that is associated with our computed value of F. Assume that we have set a criterion of $P = 0.05$. If the value of F has a probability of less than 0.05, then we may reject the overall null hypothesis; we may assert that there is a statistically reliable difference among the means of the groups. If, however, the P associated with our F is greater than 0.05, then we fail to reject the null hypothesis. We then conclude that there is no reliable difference among the group means (or, more precisely, that not a single pair of means differ reliably).

To ascertain the value of P associated with our F, refer to Table A-2 in Appendix A, which fulfills the same function as the table of t, although it is a bit different to use. Let us initially note that: (1) "df associated with the numerator" is across the top, and (2) "df associated with the denominator" is down the left side. Therefore we need *two df* values to enter the table of F. In this example we have 2 df for among groups (the numerator of the F-test) and 72 df for within groups (the denominator for the F-test). Hence we find the *column* labeled "2" and read down to find a *row* labeled "72." There is none, but there are rows for 60 and 120 *df*; 72 falls between the two values found in rows for 60 and 120 *df*. In both rows for 60 and 120 *df* we find rows for a *P* of 0.01, for a *P* of 0.05, for a *P* of 0.10 and a *P* of 0.20. We are making a 0.05-level test, so we shall ignore the other values of *P*. With 2 and 72 *df*, we interpolate between 3.15 and 3.07 and find that we must have an *F* of 3.13 at 0.05 level. Since the computed *F* (169.22) exceeds this value,[12] the overall null hypothesis is rejected—we conclude that there is at least one reliable difference between the pairs of means. Assuming that there were proper experimental techniques, we conclude that variation of the independent variable reliably influenced the dependent variable. More specifically, injection of RNA caused the groups to differ reliably on the dependent-variable measure.

You should study the table of *F* to make sure that you understand it adequately. To provide a little practice, say that you have six groups in your experiment with 10 chimpanzees per group. You have five degrees of freedom for your among source of variation, and 54 *df* for the within. Assume a 0.01-level test. What is the value of *F* required to reject the overall null hypothesis? To answer this question, enter the column labeled "5" and read down until you find the row for 54 *df*. There is no row for 54 *df* so you must interpolate between the tabled values of 40 *df* and 60 *df*. If there were 40 *df* for you within groups, a computed *F* of 3.51 would be required to reject the null hypothesis; similarly, if you had had 60 *df*, you would have required an *F* of 3.34. By interpolating linearly we find that an *F* of 3.39 is required for the 0.01 level with 5 and 54 *df*. Try some additional problems for yourself.

Shortcomings of the Overall Null Hypothesis. If you had conducted the preceding experiment, you might feel quite happy with yourself; you would have succeeded in rejecting the overall null hypothesis. But wait a moment. Remember the null hypothesis

you tested? Your conclusion is thus that there is at least one mean difference between your groups. But where is it? Is it between groups 1 and 2, between groups 1 and 3, between groups 2 and 3, or are two, or all, of these mean differences reliable? The answer is that you simply do not know from your *F*-test. In short, if you were interested in the third question, you have now answered it! An overall analysis of variance and the corresponding *F*-test tells you whether there is one or more reliable difference between pairs of means in your groups.

Many years ago when we were first developing some degree of statistical sophistication, psychologists used a two-stage method of multiple comparisons as follows. They first conducted an overall *F*-test; if it was not reliable, they concluded that there was no reliable difference between any pairs of means (which, incidentally, need not be the case). But if the value of *F* allowed the null hypothesis to be rejected, they then conducted all possible *t*-tests to ascertain where the reliable difference(s) might be. By conducting all possible *t*-tests, you disturb your stated probability level, which is one reason that this approach is inappropriate.[13] Furthermore, in retrospect, it is apparent that a researcher who follows such a procedure has confused our second and third questions. One who makes all possible pairwise comparisons after a reliable *F*-test is really interested in the second question, which means that there is no reason to test an overall null hypothesis with the *F*-test. If you are inter-

---

[12] A bit of an understatement.

[13] As Ryan (1980) pointed out, the leading statistician Tukey disowned his multiple comparison procedure, known as *Tukey's gap test*, for this reason. Ryan states the problem as follows: "The partial null hypothesis is important: Suppose that we have 10 populations, of which 9 are equal and 1 has a mean much larger than the others. Then the preliminary omnibus test (*F* or any other) is likely to be significant, and we proceed to make individual tests on pairs. We now have 36 comparisons in which the null hypothesis is true. If we make these tests at the nominal [stated] .05 level of significance, it is almost certain that one or more specific comparisons will be falsely declared significant. This is true even if the pairwise test is properly designed for any heterogeneity of variance that may exist" (pp. 354–355).

ested in making all possible pairwise comparisons, there is no need to conduct an analysis of variance; you should go directly to making all possible pairwise comparisons with the *t*-test and adjust your stated probability levels with the Bonferroni test. To illustrate this procedure, let us run *t*-test using the data in Table 7-1. For your own practice you should compute those values, and you will find them to be

between groups 1 and 2: $t_{12} = $ .56
between groups 1 and 3: $t_{13} = 18.08$
between groups 2 and 3: $t_{23} = 14.90$

Adjusting our stated probability level with the Bonferroni test to 0.017 (as we previously did) we find by interpolation that the required value of *t* with 48 *df* in Table A-1 is 2.401. Consequently, the mean differences between groups 1 and 3 and between groups 2 and 3 are both reliable, but that between groups 1 and 2 is not. Group 3, which received the RNA from the planarians that were classically conditioned, thus made reliably more contractions to the light during the test trials than did the other two (control) groups. The "data would seem to suggest that a specific learned response was transferred by way of the injection of the RNA preparation" (Jacobson, Fried, & Horowitz, 1966, p. 5).

Limited Pairwise Comparisons. Finally, let us illustrate the application of the limited pairwise comparison approach with this experiment. In this case you are not interested in making all possible comparisons between your groups. Your empirical hypothesis suggests that group 3 should make more contractions than should groups 1 and 2, but the comparison between groups 1 and 2 is rather uninteresting; your hypothesis says nothing about this comparison—it is merely in the design for control purposes. In this event you go directly to your *t*-test analysis to make the two legitimate pairwise comparisons. Since the *t* values for these comparisons were, respectively, 18.85 and 18.17, you can reject the two null hypotheses and reach

the conclusion that group 3 made reliably more contractions (as did the original authors). There was no need or even any value in conducting an overall *F*-test. In terms of null hypotheses you should thus not test the overall null but go directly to your partial null hypotheses. Your time has not been wasted by learning analysis of variance here, however, because it is critical in the analysis of other designs, such as the factorial.

CHAPTER SUMMARY

I. A single multigroup design has several advantages over a series of two-group experiments.
  A. It is more efficient for the experimenter.
  B. Fewer participants are required.
  C. Experimental control can be more effective.
  D. You can study more values of an independent variable (this allows you to increase your chances of determining whether an independent variable does affect a dependent variable, and also increases your ability to specify the functional relationship between them).

II. There are several methods of statistical analysis, depending on your purpose.
  A. To make limited (planned) comparisons only between pairs of individual groups according to the equation $df = r - 1$, you test those pairwise null hypotheses directly with the *t*-test.
  B. To make all possible pairwise comparisons, as for post hoc comparisons, adjust your stated probability level to a more realistic one. For this you may use the Bonferroni test, in which case you divide your stated probability level (e.g., 0.05) by the number of possible comparisons (e.g., 3) and employ the resulting adjusted probability level (e.g., 0.017) to test your null hypotheses.
  C. To determine whether there is a reliable difference between *any* pair of means in a multigroup design, you would test an overall null hypothesis stating that there is no true difference among the means of the several groups. For this you could conduct an overall analysis of variance and an omnibus *F*-test as in the following summary of statistical analysis.

III. The strategy for an analysis of variance.
   A. Compute the total variance of the experiment.
   B. Analyze that variance into a between- (or among-) groups component and into a within-groups component. The among-groups variance is an indication of the extent to which the groups differ on the dependent-variable measure, and the within-groups variance is an indication of experimental error.
   C. If the former is reliably greater than the latter, as determined by division with the *F*-test, your independent variable was probably effective.

STATISTICAL SUMMARY

Limited Pairwise Comparisons

Here pairwise null hypotheses are tested by series of *t*-tests, e.g., in a three-group experiment the null hypotheses could be $\mu_1 = \mu_2$ and $\mu_2 = \mu_3$.

The number of legitimate, planned pairwise comparisons that you can make is determined by the number of degrees of freedom for groups, which is the number of groups $(r) - 1$. For example, with five groups in your experiment, $df = 5 - 1 = 4$, so that you could legitimately make four pairwise comparisons. You could, for example, conduct *t*-tests for groups 1 versus 2, 2 versus 3, 3 versus 4, and 4 versus 5.

All Possible Pairwise Comparisons

The null hypotheses in this approach also are pairwise so that with three groups they are $\mu_1 = \mu_2$, $\mu_1 = \mu_3$ and $\mu_2 = \mu_3$. If you conduct all possible pairwise comparisons, you can use the Bonferroni test to adjust the level of P.[14] For this you merely divide the stated probability level by the number of possible comparisons and employ the resulting adjusted level to test your values of *t*. For example, with three independent

___
[14]For more powerful, but more complex multiple tests see Holland and Copenhaver (1988).

groups in your experiment, the number of possible comparisons (C_p) is three, as determined by Equation 7-1:

$$C_p = \frac{r\,(r-1)}{2}$$

If your probability criterion is 0.05, that value divided by 3 equals approximately 0.017. You then replace 0.05 with 0.017 for testing your three null hypotheses with the *t*-test.

Summary of the Computation of Analysis of Variance and the F-Test for an Independent Groups Design with More Than Two Groups

This approach tests an overall null hypothesis, which for four groups is $\mu_1 = \mu_2 = \mu_3 = \mu_4$.

Assume that the following dependent-variable values have been obtained for the four groups of participants:

Group 1	Group 2	Group 3	Group 4
1	2	8	7
1	3	8	8
3	4	9	9
5	5	10	9
5	6	11	10
6	6	12	11
7	6	12	11

1. First we wish to compute ΣX, ΣX^2, and n, and it is always informative to compute the mean $(\overline{X})$ for each group, too:

Group	1	2	3	4
ΣX	28	32	70	65
ΣX^2	146	162	718	617
n	7	7	7	7
$\overline{X}$	4.00	4.57	10.0	9.29

2. To compute the total sums of squares we use Equation 7-2.

$$(7\text{-}2) \quad \text{total } SS = (\Sigma X_1^2 + \Sigma X_2^2 + \dots (\Sigma X_r^2)$$
$$- \frac{(\Sigma X_1 + \Sigma X_2 + \Sigma X_3 + \dots + \Sigma X_r)^2}{N}$$

Substituting these values into Equation 7-2, we obtain:

$$\text{total } SS = (146 + 162 + 718 + 617)$$
$$- \frac{(28 + 32 + 70 + 65)^2}{28}$$
$$= 1{,}643 - \frac{(195)^2}{28}$$
$$= 1{,}643 - \frac{38{,}025}{28}$$
$$= 1{,}643 - 1{,}358.04 = 284.96$$

Next we compute the among-groups SS as follows:

$$(7\text{-}3) \quad \text{among } SS = \frac{(\Sigma X_1)^2}{n_1} + \frac{(\Sigma X_2)^2}{n_2}$$
$$+ \frac{(\Sigma X_3)^2}{n_3} + \ldots + \frac{(\Sigma X_r)^2}{n_r}$$
$$- \frac{(\Sigma X_1 + \Sigma X_2 + \Sigma X_3 + \ldots + \Sigma X_r)^2}{N}$$

Substituting the appropriate values, we can determine that the among SS is

$$\text{among } SS = \frac{(28)^2}{7} + \frac{(32)^2}{7}$$
$$+ \frac{(70)^2}{7} + \frac{(65)^2}{7} - 1{,}358.04$$
$$= \frac{784}{7} + \frac{1{,}024}{7} + \frac{4{,}900}{7}$$
$$+ \frac{4{,}225}{7} - 1{,}358.04$$
$$= 112.00 + 146.29 + 700.00$$
$$+ 603.57 - 1{,}358.04$$
$$= 1{,}561.86 - 1{,}358.04$$
$$= 203.82$$

The within-groups source of variation may be computed by subtraction as follows:

$$(7\text{-}4) \quad \text{within } SS = \text{total } SS - \text{among } SS$$

Substituting as appropriate,
$$\text{within } SS = 284.96 - 203.82 = 81.14$$

We summarize these values for the sources of variation in Table 7-3, and compute the degrees of freedom as follows:

$$\text{among-groups } df = r - 1$$
$$= 4 - 1 = 3$$
$$\text{within-groups } df = N - r$$
$$= 28 - 4 = 24$$
$$\text{total } df = N - 1$$
$$= 28 - 1 = 27$$

The mean squares are computed by dividing each among-groups source of variation by the appropriate degrees of freedom, for example, $\frac{203.82}{3} = 67.94$. These values are entered into Table 7-3.

Finally, to compute the F-test, the within-groups mean square is divided into the among-groups mean square: $\frac{67.94}{3.38} = 20.10$. This is the last entry in Table 7-3.

TABLE 7-3   Summary Table of the Analysis of Variance

Source of Variation	Sum of Squares	df	Mean Square	F
Among groups	203.82	3	67.94	20.
Within groups	81.14	24	3.38	
Total	284.96	27		

Finally, we enter Table A-2 with 3 and 24 degrees of freedom. We find that a tabled value of 3.01 is required at the 0.05 level. Since our computed value of 20.10 exceeds this tabled value, we conclude that there is at least one pairwise comparison between the means of our four groups that reliably differs. Consequently, we reject the null hypothesis that there is no true difference among the means of our four groups. We conclude that at least one mean is reliably different from at least one other mean.

CRITICAL REVIEW FOR THE STUDENT

1. Make up a problem and a hypothesis that is of interest to you and design two experiments to test the hypothesis. The first design should employ two groups, the second, three groups. After you have completed this exercise, what

might you learn from the possible dependent variable scores about the advantages of the three-group design?

2. What are the three basic questions that you ask when analyzing a multigroup design? These concern: (a) limited pairwise comparisons, (b) all possible pairwise comparisons, and (c) testing an overall null hypothesis. Also state computational null hypotheses for these three questions.

3. Problems

   A. An experimenter was interested in assessing the relative sociability scores of different majors in a college. Random samples of students who were majoring in English, art, and chemistry were selected, and they were administered a standardized test of sociability. Assume a 0.05 criterion for testing the overall null hypothesis that there is no mean difference between any part of the three groups. (Note that you are not testing to determine which of the three pairwise comparisons might be reliably different.)

	Sociability Scores	
English Majors	*Art Majors*	*Chemistry Majors*
0, 1, 3, 5	3, 5, 6, 6	5, 7, 9, 9

   B. A physical education professor is interested in the effect of practice on the frequency of making goals in hockey. After consulting a psychologist, the following experiment was designed. Five groups were formed such that group 1 received the least practice, group 5 the most practice. Dependent-variable values represent the number of goals made by each participant over a season. You need to decide which amount of practice should be recommended. To help you reach this conclusion make the following planned comparisons: groups 1 versus 2, groups 2 versus 3, groups 3 versus 4, and groups 4 versus 5. After conducting *t*-tests for these compari-

sons, what is the reasonable recommendation?

		Group		
1	*2*	*3*	*4*	*5*
		Number of Training Trials		
0	*10*	*30*	*70*	*100*
	Number of Goals Made by Each Participant			
0	2	4	24	24
1	2	5	25	24
3	1	7	23	25
0	4	9	23	25
0	0	8	25	22
2	0	7	22	24
1	0	6	24	22
0	3	8	23	26
3	2	9	22	24
1	1	9	24	23

   C. An experiment is conducted to determine which of three methods of teaching Spanish is superior. Assuming that the experiment has been adequately conducted, that a criterion of $P = 0.05$ has been set for each partial null hypothesis, and that a higher test score indicates better performance after training on the three methods, which method is to be preferred? To answer this question, use the approach of making all possible pairwise comparisons.

Scores of Three Groups in an Experiment on Methods of Teaching Spanish

Method A		*Method B*		*Normal Method*	
15	16	22	12	17	2
17	12	25	19	6	8
12	11	23	24	9	9
13	19	17	26	11	14
10	19	29	29	4	7
19	14	26	30	3	8
17	15	25	26	8	6
21	17	24	27	9	5
14	13	27	21	12	16
15	12	31	23	6	9

chapter 8

EXPERIMENTAL DESIGN: THE FACTORIAL DESIGN

Major purpose:

To extend your research principles to the factorial design—in general, the most valuable experimental design in psychology.

What you are going to find:

1. A discussion of the relative advantages of the factorial design.
2. A detailed explanation of the critical concept of interaction.
3. Step-by-step procedures for statistical analysis with analysis of variance and the *F*-test.

What you should acquire:

The ability to conduct and analyze a factorial design and to interpret the results, especially those for an interaction.

OVERVIEW

Factorial Design Defined. The preceding designs are appropriate to the investigation of a single independent variable. If the independent variable is varied in only two ways, the two-group design is used. If the inde-

pendent variable is varied in more than two ways, the multigroup design is used. But to study more than one independent variable in a single experiment, the **factorial design** can be used. *A complete factorial design is one in which all possible combinations of the selected values of each of the independent variables are used.*

Illustration of a Factorial Design. Consider an experiment that was conducted on learning during hypnosis. The two independent variables are: (1) whether the participants are hypnotized, and (2) high or low susceptibility to being hypnotized. Variation of these two independent variables is diagrammed as in Figure 8-1. The factorial design, showing all possible combinations of the values of the independent variables, is represented in Table 8-1.

Table 8-1 shows that there are four possible combinations of the values of the independent variables. Each possible combination is represented by a box, a **cell**: (1) hypnotized and low susceptibility; (2) not hypnotized and low susceptibility; (3) hypnotized and high susceptibility; (4) not hypnotized and high susceptibility. With four experimental conditions there are four groups in the experiment.

The participants were first tested for hypnotic susceptibility and two classes were formed: those high and those low in susceptibility. Then those high in susceptibility were randomly assigned to either the hypnotic or the nonhypnotic conditions and similarly for those who tested low in susceptibility.

The experiment was then conducted essentially as follows. First, all participants, while in the waking state, were presented with a paired-associate learning task, and the number of errors that they required to learn the task were tabulated. A similar count was made on a comparable paired-associate list during the experimental conditions. The de-

TABLE 8-1   Diagram of a Factorial Design

Hypnotic Susceptibility	Degree of Hypnosis	
	Hypnotized	*Not Hypnotized*
Low	1	2
High	3	4

pendent-variable measure was the difference in number of errors made on the two occasions. Thus, the groups were treated as follows: Group 1 consisted of participants for whom the pretest showed a low susceptibility to hypnosis, and they learned the second list while hypnotized; group 2 was also made up of those low in susceptibility, but they learned the second list when in a normal awake state; group 3 consisted of participants who were quite susceptible to hypnosis, and they learned the second list while hypnotized; group 4 was composed of highly susceptible participants who learned the second list when not hypnotized. A statistical analysis of the dependent-variable scores should then provide information concerning the following questions:

1. Does being hypnotized influence learning?
2. Does susceptibility to hypnotism influence learning?
3. Is there an **interaction** between degree of hypnosis and susceptibility to being hypnotized?

The procedure for answering the first two questions is straightforward, but the third

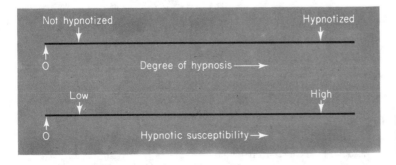

FIGURE 8-1   Variation of two independent variables, each in two ways.

will require a little more consideration. Let us examine the dependent-variable values actually obtained for each group (Table 8-2). Then we place the means for the four groups in their appropriate cells (Table 8-3).

ASSESSING THE TWO INDEPENDENT VARIABLES

Does Hypnosis Affect Learning? To answer the first question, we shall study the effect of being in a hypnotized state on learning scores. For this purpose we shall ignore the susceptibility variable. We have 8 highly susceptible individuals who were hypnotized and 8 with low susceptibility who were hypnotized. Ignoring that 8 were high and 8 were low in susceptibility, we have 16 people who learned while in a state of hypnosis. Similarly, we have 16 people who learned when they were not hypnotized. We therefore have two groups who, as a whole, were treated similarly except with regard to the hypnosis variable. *For the hypnosis-nonhypnosis comparison, it is irrelevant that half of each group were high in susceptibility and half were low in susceptibility*—the susceptibility variable is balanced out. To make our comparison we need merely compute the mean for the 16 hypnotized individuals and for the 16 nonhypnotized participants. To do this we have computed the mean of the means for the two groups who were hypnotized (Table 8-3). (This is possible because the *n*'s for each mean are equal.) The mean of − 14.25 and − 23.25 is − 18.75, and, similarly, the mean is 0.38 for the nonhypnotized participants. Since the two means (− 18.75 and − 0.38) are markedly different, we suspect that being hypnotized *did* influence the dependent variable. We shall, however, have to await the results of a statistical test to find out if this difference is reliable.

If you find it difficult to ignore the susceptibility variable when considering the hypnosis variable, look momentarily at the factorial design as if it were just one experiment in which only the degree of hypnosis is varied. In this case the susceptibility variable can be temporarily considered as an extraneous variable whose effect is balanced out. Thus the two-group design would look like that indicated in Table 8-4.

For question 2 we shall compare the high-

TABLE 8-2   Dependent Variable Values for the Four Groups That Compose the Factorial Design of Table 8-1*

		Group	
1 (*Hypnotized—* *low susceptibility*)	*2* (*Not hypnotized—* *low susceptibility*)	*3* (*Hypnotized—* *high susceptibility*)	*4* (*Not hypnotized—* *high susceptibility*)
0	9	− 16	− 4
− 8	1	0	8
1	− 5	− 20	− 10
− 20	− 14	− 41	9
− 17	− 2	− 32	− 10
− 43	− 3	− 6	− 23
− 4	14	− 42	29
− 23	9	− 29	− 14
n: 8	8	8	8
Σ*X*: − 114	9	− 186	− 15
Σ*X²*: 3,148	593	6,002	1,927
X̄: − 14.25	1.12	− 23.25	− 1.88

*With appreciation to W. F. Harley, Jr., and W. F. Harley, Sr., personal communication.

TABLE 8-3 Means for the Experimental Conditions Placed in Their Cells

	Degree of Hypnosis		
Susceptibility	*Hypnotized*	*Not Hypnotized*	*Means*
Low	− 14.25	1.12	− 6.57
High	− 23.25	− 1.88	− 12.57
Means:	− 18.75	− .38	− 9.57

versus low-susceptibility classification and ignore the hypnosis variable. In Table 8-3, the mean of the 16 participants who were low in susceptibility is − 6.57, and the mean of the 16 who were high in susceptibility is − 12.57. The difference between these means is not as great as before, suggesting that perhaps this variable did not greatly, if at all, influence the learning scores. Again, however, we must await the results of a statistical test for reliability before making a final judgment.

THE CONCEPT OF INTERACTION

Now that we have preliminary answers to the first questions, let us turn to the third: Is there an interaction between the two variables? **Interaction** is one of the most important concepts in research. If you adequately understand it, you will have ample opportunity to apply it in a wide variety of situations; it will shed light on a large number of problems and considerably increase your understanding of behavior.

First, let us approach the concept of interaction from an overly simplified point of view. Assume the problem is of the following sort: Is it more efficient (timewise) for a man who is dressing to put his shirt or his trousers on first? At first glance it might seem that a suitable empirical test would yield one of two answers: (1) shirt first, or (2) trousers first. However, in addition to these possibilities there is a third answer: (3) it depends. Now, "it depends" embodies the basic notion of interaction. Suppose a linear analysis of the data indicates what "it" depends on. We may find that it is more efficient for tall men to put their trousers on first but for short men to put their shirts on first. In this case we may say that our answer depends on the body build of the man who is dressing. Or, to put it in terms of an interaction, we may say that *there is an interaction between body build and putting trousers or shirt on first*. This is the basic notion of interaction. Let us take another example from everyday life before we consider the concept in a more precise manner.

I once had to obtain the support of a senior officer in the Army to conduct an experiment. To control certain variables (e.g., the effect of the company commander), I wanted to use only one company. There were four methods of learning to be studied, so it was planned to divide the company into four groups. Each group (formed into a platoon) would then learn by a different method. The officer, however, objected to

TABLE 8-4 Looking at One Independent Variable of the Factorial Design as a Single Two-Group Experiment

Value of independent variable	*Group 1 (hypnotized)*	*Group 2 (not hypnotized)*
n	16	16
Mean dependent-variable score	− 18.75	− .38

this design. He said, "We always train our men as a whole company. You are going to train the men in platoon sizes. Therefore, whatever results you obtain with regard to platoon-size training units may not be applicable to what we normally do with company-size units." I had to agree, and the point is quite a sophisticated one. It is possible that the results for platoons might be different from the results for companies—there may be an *interaction* between size of personnel training unit and the type of method used. In other words, one method might be superior if used with platoons, but another with companies. Actually, previous evidence suggested that such an interaction was highly unlikely in this situation, so I didn't worry about it, although the senior officer continued to be slightly distressed.

Interaction Defined. These simplistic examples allow us to state that an *interaction exists between two independent variables if the dependent-variable value that results from one independent variable is determined by the specific value assumed by the other independent variable.*

A Psychological Illustration. An interaction obtained in a psychological study comes from research conducted by Berry and McArthur (1986). These researchers predicted that information indicating *negligent criminal behavior* would be more believable when the defendant was baby-faced. On the other hand, they predicted that information indicating *intentional* criminal behavior would be more believable when the defendant was mature-faced. Here, then, is a study in which an interaction was explicitly predicted.

The participants in this experiment read copies of fictitious pretrial reports in which a young man was charged with some criminal offense. One set of reports described the crime as resulting only from *negligence*. For example, the report indicated that the defendant forgot to warn a customer about the potential hazards of a product he was selling. Another set of reports described the incident as being one of *intentional deception*, such as misleading a customer about such dangers in order to make a sale. Thus, the first independent variable was degree of criminal behavior which was varied two ways—from negligence to intentional. The second independent variable was the facial maturity of the defendant, and it was systematically manipulated by attaching a photograph to the report. One set of photographs was of faces of adult men who had been judged to be baby-faced, while another set of photographs was of adult men who had been judged to be mature in facial appearance.

The results are plotted in Figure 8-2, where the dependent variable, conviction rate, is plotted on the vertical axis. On the horizontal axis we indicate whether the offense was negligent or intentional. The highest data point is for baby-faced defendants who were recommended as being guilty of negligent offenses—the conviction rate recommended for them being 0.82. In contrast, the conviction rate for baby-faced defendants recommended as guilty of intentional offenses was only slightly above 0.50. Mature-faced defendants had a somewhat higher conviction rate, approximately 0.60 for intentional offenses, but they were recommended as being guilty of negligent offenses with a rate of only about 0.50.

The results thus indicate that the participants more often recommended the conviction of baby-faced men for crimes of negligence. The mature-faced men, on the other hand, were more frequently recommended for conviction as guilty of intentional crimes. In short, there is an interaction between the independent variables of facial maturity and perceived type of criminal behavior. That is, whether adult men were perceived as being more frequently guilty of negligence versus intentional criminal offenses depended upon whether they were mature-faced or baby-faced. Or, synonymously, whether maturity of the face was related to recommended conviction rate depended upon whether the crime was one of being guilty of negligence or of an intentional offense.

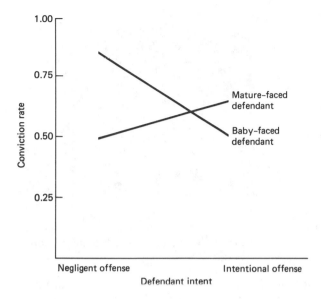

FIGURE 8-2 Proportion of participants recommending conviction as a function of negligent vs. intentional criminal behavior and the apparent maturity of the defendants' faces. An interaction exists between the independent variables of criminal behavior and the maturity of the defendant's face. From Berry & McArthur (1986).

Answering the Third Question. To return now to our hypnosis experiment and to illustrate a possible interaction, momentarily assume that there is an interaction between the two variables of degree of hypnosis (hypnotized and nonhypnotized) and susceptibility to being hypnotized (high and low). The in teraction would mean that the results (learning scores) for degree of hypnosis would depend upon the degree of susceptibility of the participant. Or, more precisely, one might state such an interaction as follows: *whether being hypnotized affects amount learned depends on the degree of susceptibility of the participants.*

Illustrating a Lack of Interaction. To enlarge on our understanding of this critical concept, temporarily assume the fictitious sample (not population) values in Figure 8-3 that indicate a *lack* of an interaction. On the horizontal axis we have shown the two values of the susceptibility variable. The data points represent fictitious means of the four conditions: point $\overline{X}_1$ is the mean for the low-susceptibility hypnotized group; $\overline{X}_2$ is for the low-susceptibility nonhypnotized group; $\overline{X}_3$, the high-susceptibility hypnotized group; and $\overline{X}_4$, the high-susceptibility nonhypno-

tized group. The line that connects points 1 and 3 represents the performance of the hypnotized participants, half of whom were low and half high in susceptibility. The line through points 2 and 4 represents the performance of the nonhypnotized participants. If these were real data, what would be the effects of the independent variables? First, variation of the degree of susceptibility would be said not to affect learning, for both lines are essentially horizontal. Second, the nonhypnotized performed better than did the hypnotized participants because the "nonhypnotized" line is higher than the "hypnotized" line. Third, the difference between the low-susceptibility hypnotized group and the low-susceptibility nonhypnotized group (difference A) is about the same as the difference between the high-susceptibility hypnotized and the high-susceptibility nonhypnotized groups (difference B). *The performance of participants who were and were not hypnotized is thus essentially independent of their degree of susceptibility. No interaction exists between these two variables.* Put another way: If the lines drawn in Figure 8-3 are approximately parallel (i.e., if difference A is approximately the same as difference B), it is likely that no interaction exists between the variables.[1] However, if the lines based on these sample means are clearly not parallel [i.e., if difference A is distinctly (reliably) different from difference B], an interaction is present.

Another way of illustrating the same point is to compute the differences between the means of the groups. The means plotted in Figure 8-3 are specified in the cells of Table 8-5. We have computed the necessary differences so that it can be seen that the difference between the participants with low susceptibility who were hypnotized and those who were not hypnotized is -10.00 and that, for the high-susceptibility participants, it is -8.75. Since these are similar differences, there is probably no interaction present. The same conclusion would be reached by comparing differences in the

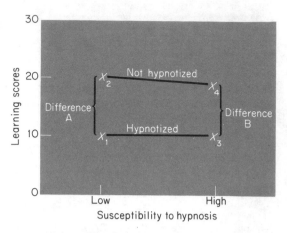

FIGURE 8-3 Illustration of a lack of interaction with fictitious sample means.

in Table 8-6. In this case our lines would like those in Figure 8-4.

Now we note that the lines are not parallel; in fact they cross each other. Hence, if these were real data, we would make the following statements: The performance of low-susceptibility participants who are not hypnotized is superior to that of low-susceptibility participants who are hypnotized, but high-susceptibility participants who are hypnotized perform better than high-susceptibility participants who are not hypnotized. Or, the logically equivalent statement is: The effect of being hypnotized depresses performance for low-susceptibility participants but facilitates performance for high-susceptibility participants. Put in yet other words: The difference between being hypnotized and not being hypnotized depends on the susceptibility of the participants, or, equally, the

TABLE 8-5 Illustration of a Lack of an Interaction with Fictitious Means

| Susceptibility | Degree of Hypnosis | | Difference |
	Hypnotized	Not Hypnotized	
Low	10	20	-10.00
High	10	18.75	-8.75
Difference	0.00	1.25	1.25

other direction; that is, since 0.00 and 1.25 are approximately the same, no interaction exists. Incidentally, the -10.00 is difference A of Figure 8-3, and -8.75 is difference B. Clearly, if these differences are about the same, the lines will be approximately parallel.

At this point you may be disappointed that we did not illustrate an interaction. This can easily be arranged by assuming for the moment that the data came out as indicated

[1] Let us emphasize that these are *sample* values and not *population* values. Thus, although this statement is true for sample values, it is true for population (true) values. If the lines for the population values are even *slightly* nonparallel, there is an interaction.

TABLE 8-6 New Fictitious Means Designed to Show an Interaction

| Susceptibility | Degree of Hypnosis | | Means |
	Hypnotized	Not Hypnotized	
Low	69.1	90.0	79.55
High	91.7	80.0	85.85
Means:	80.40	85.00	82.70

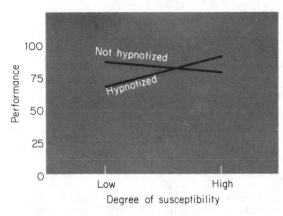

FIGURE 8-4 Illustration of a possible interaction with fictitious sample means.

difference between degree of susceptibility depends on whether the participants are hypnotized.

This discussion should clarify the meaning of *interaction*. This is a rather difficult concept, however, and the examples in the remainder of the chapter should help to illuminate it further. Note for now, though, that reliably nonparallel lines indicate an interaction, *but the lines do not need to intersect each other*.

To summarize. When selected values of two (or more) *independent variables are studied in all possible combinations, a factorial design is used.* We have illustrated the factorial design by using two independent variables with two values of each. In this case, participants are assigned to the four experimental conditions. *Analysis of the dependent variable data yields information on: (1) the influence of each independent variable on the dependent variable, and (2) the interaction between the two independent variables.*

STATISTICAL ANALYSIS OF FACTORIAL DESIGNS

We have compared the means for each of the experimental conditions in the hypnosis experiment and studied the concept of an interaction, but this has provided only tenta-

tive answers; firmer answers await the application of statistical tests to the data. For example, to find out whether the apparently sizable difference in means between those who were and were not hypnotized is reliable, we must conduct a statistical analysis. For this purpose we shall conduct an *analysis of variance*, the rudiments of which were presented in Chapter 7.

Analysis of Variance for a 2 × 2 Factorial Design

To repeat what we said about computer analysis, a good researcher must understand what a statistical program is actually doing. To reach that understanding, the researcher should know how to compute the statistical analysis in a step-by-step fashion. Furthermore, the researcher must be able to select the specific statistical analysis program appropriate for the particular problem at hand. For example, there are a number of applications of analysis of variance such as different ones for different estimates of error variance. Finally, it is not terribly uncommon to find computer programs that will give you erroneous answers. For these reasons we proceed with our step-by-step analysis for the factorial design.

The first step in conducting an analysis of variance for the factorial design closely follows that for a multigroup design. We wish to compute the total sum of squares (*SS*) and partition it into two major components, the among-*SS* and the within-*SS*. Let us return to the data in Table 8-2, which are summarized in Table 8-7.

Computing Sums of Squares To compute the total *SS*, we substitute the appropriate values from Table 8-7 in Equation 8-1, which for four groups (always the case for the 2 × 2 design) is

(8-1) $\quad$ total SS
$$= (\Sigma X_1^2 + \Sigma X_2^2 + \Sigma X_3^2 + \Sigma X_4^2)$$
$$- \frac{(\Sigma X_1 + \Sigma X_2 + \Sigma X_3 + \Sigma X_4)^2}{N}$$

TABLE 8-7   A Summary of the Components for Analysis of Variance (from Table 8-2)

	Group		
1 *(Hypnotized—* *low susceptibility)*	*2* *(Not hypnotized—* *low susceptibility)*	*3* *(Hypnotized—* *high susceptibility)*	*4* *(Not hypnotized—* *high susceptibility)*
n: 8	8	8	8
ΣX: -114	9	-186	-15
ΣX^2: 3,148	593	6,002	1,927
$\bar{X}$: -14.25	1.12	-23.25	-1.88

$$= (3{,}148 + 593 + 6{,}002 + 1{,}927)$$
$$- \frac{(-114 + 9 - 186 - 15)^2}{32}$$
$$= 8{,}743.88$$

Next, to compute the among-groups *SS*, we substitute the appropriate values in Equation 8-2, which for four groups is

(8-2)   among-groups *SS*

$$= \frac{(\Sigma X_1)^2}{n_1} + \frac{(\Sigma X_2)^2}{n_2} + \frac{(\Sigma X_3)^2}{n_3} + \frac{(\Sigma X_4)^2}{n_4}$$
$$- \frac{(\Sigma X_1 + \Sigma X_2 + \Sigma X_3 + \Sigma X_4)^2}{N}$$

among-groups *SS*

$$= \frac{(-114)^2}{8} + \frac{(9)^2}{8}$$
$$+ \frac{(-186)^2}{8} + \frac{(-15)^2}{8} - 2{,}926.12$$
$$= 3{,}061.12$$

And, as before, the within-groups *SS* may be obtained by subtraction, as in Equation 8-3.

(8-3)   within-groups *SS*
        = total *SS* − among-groups *SS*
        = 8,743.88 − 3,061.12 = 5,682.76

This completes the initial stage of the analysis of variance for a 2 × 2 factorial design, for we have now illustrated the com-putation of the total *SS* and the within *SS*. As you can see, this initial stage is the same as that for a design using any number of designs. But we now proceed further.

The among-groups *SS* tells us something about how all groups differ. However, we do not make simultaneous comparisons of all four groups, but only seek to answer our three questions: That is, we are interested in whether variation of each independent variable affects the dependent variable and whether there is a significant interaction. The first step is to compute the *SS* between groups for each independent variable. Using Table 8-1 as a guide, we may write our equations for computing the between-groups *SS* for the specific comparisons.

The groups are as labeled in the cells. Thus, to determine whether there is a significant difference between the two values of the first variable (hypnosis), we need to compute the *SS* between these two values as follows:

(8-4)   *SS* between amounts of first
        independent variable

$$= \frac{(\Sigma X_1 + \Sigma X_3)^2}{n_1 + n_3} + \frac{(\Sigma X_2 + \Sigma X_4)^2}{n_2 + n_4}$$
$$- \frac{(\Sigma X_1 + \Sigma X_2 + \Sigma X_3 + \Sigma X_4)^2}{N}$$

Then we compute the *SS* between the conditions of the second independent variable:

(8-5) SS between amounts of second
independent variable

$$= \frac{(\Sigma X_1 + \Sigma X_2)^2}{n_1 + n_2} + \frac{(\Sigma X_3 + \Sigma X_4)^2}{n_3 + n_4}$$
$$- \frac{(\Sigma X_1 + \Sigma X_2 + \Sigma X_3 + \Sigma X_4)^2}{N}$$

In Summary. We conduct statistical tests to determine whether degree of hypnosis (our first independent variable) influences the dependent variable, whether hypnotic susceptibility (our second independent variable) influences the dependent variable, and whether there is a significant interaction.

To determine the effect of being hypnotized we need to test the difference between the hypnotized and the nonhypnotized conditions. To make this test we ignore the susceptibility variable in the design.

Making the appropriate substitutions in Equation 8-4 we can compute the

SS between the hypnosis conditions

$$= \frac{(-114 - 186)^2}{8 + 8} + \frac{(9 - 15)^2}{8 + 8} - 2,926.12$$
$$= \frac{(90,000)}{16} + \frac{(36)}{16} - 2,926.12 = 2,701.13$$

This value will be used to answer the first question. However, we shall answer all questions at once, rather than piecemeal, so let us hold it until we complete this stage of the inquiry. We have computed a sum of squares among all four groups (i.e., 3,061.12), and it can be separated into parts. We have computed the first part, the sum of squares between the hypnosis conditions (2,701.13). There are two other parts: the sum of squares between the susceptibility condition and for the interaction. To compute the SS for susceptibility we use Equation 8-5.

Substituting the required values in Equation 8-5 we determine that

SS between susceptibility conditions

$$= \frac{(-114 + 9)^2}{8 + 8} + \frac{(-186 - 15)^2}{8 + 8}$$
$$- 2,926.12 = 288.00$$

The among SS has three parts. We have directly computed the first two parts. Hence the difference between the sum of the first two parts and the among SS provides the third part, that for the interaction

(8-6) interaction SS = among SS
           − between SS for first variable
              (hypnosis)
           − between SS for second variable
              (susceptibility)

Recalling that the among SS was 3,061.12, the between SS for the hypnosis conditions was 2,701.13, and the between SS for the susceptibility conditions was 288.00, we find that the SS for the interaction is

interaction SS = 3,061.12 − 2,701.13
             − 288.00 = 71.99

This completes the computation of the sums of squares. These values should all be positive. If your computations yield a negative SS, check your work until you discover the error.

Constructing a Summary Table. There are only several minor matters to discuss before the analysis is completed. Before we continue, however, let us summarize our findings to this point in Table 8-8.

Determining Degrees of Freedom. To determine the *df* for this application of the analysis-of-variance procedure, we repeat the equations in Chapter 7:

(8-7) total $df = N - 1$

(8-8) among (or between) $df = r - 1$

(8-9) within $df = N - r$

TABLE 8-8 Sums of Squares for the 2 × 2 Factorial Design

Source of Variation	Sum of Squares
Among groups	(3,061.12)
Between hypnosis (H)	2,701.13
Between susceptibility (S)	288.00
Interaction: hypnosis × susceptibility (H × S)	71.99
Within groups	5,682.76
Total	8,743.88

In our example, $N = 32$ and r (number of groups) = 4. Hence the total df is $32 - 1 = 31$, the among df is $4 - 1 = 3$, and the within df is $32 - 4 = 28$.

The similarity between the manner in which we partition the total SS and the total df may also be continued for the among SS and the among df. The among df is 3. Since we analyzed the among SS into three parts, we may do the same for the among df, one df for each part (one df for each part is only true for a 2 × 2 factorial design). Take the hypnosis conditions first. Since we are temporarily ignoring the susceptibility variable, we have only two conditions of hypnosis to consider or, if you will, two groups. Hence the df for the between-hypnosis conditions is based on $r = 2$. Substituting this value in Equation 8-8, we see that the between-hypnosis df is $2 - 1 = 1$. The same holds true for the susceptibility variable; there are two values; hence, $r = 2$ and the df for this source of variations is $2 - 1 = 1$.

Now for the interaction df. Note in Table 8-9 that the interaction is written as hypnosis × susceptibility. We abbreviate the notation by using H × S. This is read "the interaction between hypnosis and susceptibility." The × sign may be used as a mnemonic device for remembering how to compute the interaction df: Multiply the number of degrees of freedom for the first variable by that for the second. Since both variables have one df, the interaction df is also one; that is, $1 \times 1 = 1$. This accounts for all three df that are associ-

ated with the among SS.[2] These findings, added to Table 8-8, form Table 8-9.

Computing Mean Squares. In the 2 × 2 factorial design there are four **mean squares** in which we are interested. In this experiment they are: (1) between hypnosis conditions, (2) between susceptibility conditions, (3) the interaction, and (4) within groups. To compute the mean squares for the between-hypnosis and between-susceptibility sources of variation, we divide those sums of squares by their corresponding df:

$$\text{mean square between-hypnosis conditions} = \frac{2,701.13}{1} = 2,701.13$$

$$\text{means square between-susceptibility conditions} = \frac{288.0}{1} = 288.0$$

Similarly, the within-groups mean square is computed:

$$\frac{5,682.76}{28} = 202.95$$

These values are then added to our summary table of the analysis of variance, as we shall show shortly.

Computing F-Tests. This completes the analysis of variance for the 2 × 2 design, at least in the usual form. We have analyzed the total sum of squares into its components. In particular, we have three "between" sums of squares to study and a term that represents the experimental error (the within-group mean square). The "between" components indicate the extent to which the various experimental conditions differ. For instance, a sizable "between" component, such as that for the hypnosis conditions, in-

---

[2] If this is not clear, then you might merely remember that the df for the between SS in a 2 × 2 design is always the same, as shown in Table 8-9; that is, the df and the SS between each independent variable condition is 1, and for the interaction, 1.

TABLE 8-9 Sums of Squares and *df* for the 2 × 2 Factorial Design

Sources of Variation	Sums of Squares	df
Among groups	(3,061.12)	(3)
Between hypnosis (H)	2,701.13	1
Between susceptibility (S)	288.00	1
Interaction: hypnosis × susceptibility (H × S)	71.99	1
Within groups	5,682.76	28
Total	8,743.88	31

dicates that hypnosis influences the dependent variable. Hence we need merely conduct the appropriate *F*-tests to determine whether the various "between" components are reliably larger than would be expected by chance. The first *F* to compute is that between the two conditions of hypnosis.[3] To do this we merely substitute the appropriate values in Equation 7-10. Since the mean square between the hypnosis conditions is 2,701.13 and the mean square within groups is 202.95, we divide the former by the latter:

$$F = \frac{2,701.13}{202.95} = 13.30$$

The *F* between the hypnosis susceptibility conditions is

$$F = \frac{288.00}{202.95} = 1.41$$

The *F* for the interaction is

$$F = \frac{71.99}{202.95} = 0.35$$

---

[3] The factorial design offers us a good example of a point we made in Chapter 7 about planned comparisons: that is, if we have specific questions, then there is no need to conduct an *F*-test for the among-groups source of variation. With this design we are exclusively interested in whether our two independent variables are effective and whether there is an interaction. Hence we proceed directly to these questions without running an overall *F*-test among all four groups, although such may be easily conducted.

These values have been entered in Table 8-10, which is the final summary of our statistical analysis. This is the table that you can present in the results section of an experimental write-up.

The summary values in this table can be quite useful for a variety of purposes, such as indicating the variances for your conditions under the mean square, MS column; however, the standard practice of journals has been to abbreviate the findings, excessively I believe. Nevertheless, the form for presenting a reliable *F* is:

$$F (1/28) = 13.30, \quad P < 0.05$$

Thus the degrees of freedom are presented within the parentheses and whether or not the *F* was significant is indicated by the attached probability level following the value *F*.

F-Tests and the Null Hypotheses

We next assign probability values to these *F* values; that is, we need to determine the odds that the *F*s could have occurred by chance. Prior to the collection of data we always state our null hypotheses. In this design we would have previously stated three null hypotheses that are more precise than merely that "There is no difference between the population means of our groups." These null hypotheses are:

1. There is no difference between the population means for the two conditions of being hypnotized (μ_H) and of not being hypnotized (μ_{NH}). Symbolically, this is $\mu_H = \mu_{NH}$.
2. There is no difference between the population means for the low and high degrees of hypnotic susceptibility ($\mu_{LS} = \mu_{HS}$).
3. There is no interaction between the population means for the two independent variables.[4]

---

[4] A more precise statement of this null hypothesis is: "There is no difference in the means of the four groups after the cell means have been adjusted for row and column effects." However, such a statement probably will be comprehensible to you only after further work in statistics.

TABLE 8-10 Summary of Analysis of Variance of the Learning Scores

Source of Variation	Sum of Squares	df	Mean Square	F
Among groups	(3,061.12)	(3)		
Between hypnosis	2,701.13	1	2,701.13	13.30*
Between susceptibility	288.00	1	288.00	1.41
Interaction: H × S	71.99	1	71.99	0.35
Within groups (error)	5,682.76	28	202.95	
Total	8,743.88	31		

*$P < 0.05$.

To determine the probability associated with each value of F, assume that first we have set a required level of 0.05 for each F-test. We need merely confront that level with the probability associated with each F. If that probability is 0.05 or less, we can reject the appropriate null hypothesis and conclude that the independent variable in question was effective in producing the result.[5]

Turning to the first null hypothesis, that for the hypnosis variable, our obtained F is 13.30. We have one df for the numerator and 28 df for the denominator. An F of 4.20 is required at the 0.05 level with 1 and 28 df (Table A-2 in Appendix A). Since our F of 13.30 exceeds this value, we reject the first null hypothesis and conclude that the two conditions of hypnosis led to reliably different performance. Since the mean for the hypnosis condition (-18.75) is lower than that for the nonhypnosis condition (-0.38), we can conclude that, under the conditions of this experiment, hypnosis has "a strong inhibiting effect on learning."

To test the effect of varying hypnotic susceptibility, we note that the F ratio for this source of variation is 1.41. We have 1 and 28 df available for this test. The necessary F value is, as before, 4.20. Since 1.41 does not exceed 4.20, we conclude that variation of hypnotic susceptibility does not reliably influence amount learned.

To study the interaction, refer to Figure 8-5. Note that the lines do not deviate from being parallel to any great extent which suggests that there is no reliable interaction between the variables.

To test the interaction we note that the F is 0.35. This F is considerably below 1.00. We can therefore conclude immediately that the interaction is *not reliable*. A check on this may be made by noting that we also have 1 and 28 df for this source of variation. We also know that an F of 4.20 is our criterion at the 0.05 level. Clearly 0.35 does not approach 4.20 and, hence, is not reliable. The third null hypothesis is not rejected. Incidentally, the fact that the line of the nonhypnotized condition is noticeably higher than that for the hypnotized condition is a graphic illustration of the effectiveness of the hypnosis variable.

A Briefer Example

The preceding discussion for the statistical analysis of a factorial design has been rather lengthy because of its detailed nature. But, with this background, we can now breeze through another example. This experiment was an investigation of the effect of two independent variables on the learning of concepts, the details of which need not concern us. The first question concerned the relationship between strength of word association (WA) on a concept formation task. More specifically, does varying word association (WA) from low to high strength influence the rapidity of learning a concept?

[5] Of course, we assume adequate control procedures have been exercised.

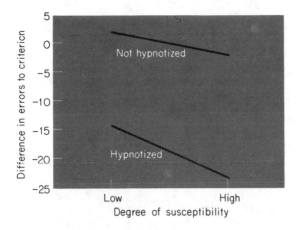

FIGURE 8-5 The actual data suggest that there is a lack of interaction between hypnotic susceptibility and degree of hypnosis.

The second question concerned an observing response (OR). Roughly, the observing response was varied by changing the location of a critical stimulus component of a complex visual field. Hence the participant's observing response was manipulated by changing or not changing the location of that critical stimulus. The OR was thus varied in two ways: (1) the critical stimulus was held constant throughout the experiment, or (2) location of the critical stimulus was systematically changed. The second question, therefore, was whether varying the observing response influenced the rapidity of learning a new concept. The third question was whether there is an interaction between the word-association variable and the observing-response variable.

A diagram of the 2 × 2 factorial design is presented in Table 8-11, along with the means of the experiment (from Table 8-12). The three null hypotheses that were tested are as follows:

1. There is no difference between the population means for the high and low word-association conditions.
2. There is no difference between the population means for the observing-response conditions.
3. There is no interaction between the population means for the word-association and observing-response variables.

TABLE 8-11 A 2 × 2 Factorial Design with Strength of Word Association and Observing Response as the Two Variables

| | Word Association Strength | |
Observing Response	Low	High
Changed	32.25	17.08
Constant	16.25	6.42

Twelve participants were randomly assigned to each condition. Table 8-12 presents, for each participant, the number of trials required to reach a criterion that demonstrated that the concept was learned.

Our first step is to compute the total SS by substituting the values in Table 8-12 in Equation 8-1.

$$\text{total } SS = 20{,}599 + 6{,}367 \\ + 11{,}709 + 1{,}405 \\ - \frac{(387 + 205 + 195 + 77)^2}{48} \\ = 24{,}528.00$$

Next we compute the among groups SS by appropriate substitutions in Equation 8-2.

TABLE 8-12   Number of Trials to Criterion[6]

	Group		
1 *Changed OR—* *Low Association*	*2* *Changed OR—* *High Association*	*3* *Constant OR—* *Low Association*	*4* *Constant OR—* *High Association*
23	12	3	33
10	3	1	2
4	32	1	2
10	18	5	1
34	12	75	1
14	10	75	4
15	17	5	5
31	28	2	12
75	59	2	4
75	4	19	10
75	6	5	2
21	4	2	1
ΣX: 387	205	195	77
ΣX^2: 20,599	6,367	11,709	1,405
$\bar{X}$: 32.25	17.08	16.25	6.42

[6]From Lachman, Meehan, and Bradley (1965).

among groups SS

$$= \frac{(387)^2}{12} + \frac{(205)^2}{12} + \frac{(195)^2}{12} + \frac{(77)^2}{12}$$
$$- \frac{(387 + 205 + 195 + 77)^2}{48} = 4,093.60$$

The within groups SS is (see Equation 8-3)

within groups $SS = 24,528.00 - 4,093.60$
$$= 20,434.40$$

Then we analyze the among groups SS into its three components: (1) between the word-association conditions, (2) between the observing-response condition, and (3) the WA × OR interaction. Considering word association first, we substitute the appropriate values in Equation 8-4 and find that

SS between word-association conditions

$$= \frac{(387 + 195)^2}{12 + 12} + \frac{(205 + 77)^2}{12 + 12}$$
$$- \frac{(387 + 205 + 195 + 77)^2}{48}$$
$$= 1,875.00$$

Substituting in Equation 8-5 to compute the SS between the two conditions of observing response:

SS between observing-response conditions

$$= \frac{(387 + 205)^2}{12 + 12} + \frac{(195 + 77)^2}{12 + 12}$$
$$- \frac{(387 + 205 + 195 + 77)^2}{48}$$
$$= 2,133.34$$

SS for the interaction component

$$= 4,093.60 - 1,875.00 - 2,133.34 = 85.26$$

The various df may now be determined:

total $(N - 1) = 48 - 1 = 47$
among groups $(r - 1) = 4 - 1 = 3$
between WA conditions $= 2 - 1 = 1$
between OR conditions $= 2 - 1 = 1$
interaction: WA × OR $= 1 \times 1 = 1$
within $(N - r) = 48 - 4 = 44$

The mean squares and the Fs have been computed and placed in the summary table (Table 8-13).

TABLE 8-13 Summary of the Analysis of Variance for the Concept Learning Experiment

Source of Variation	Sum of Squares	df	Mean Square	F
Between WA conditions	1,875.00	1	1,875.00	4.04
Between OR conditions	2,133.34	1	2,133.34	4.59
Interaction: WA × OR	85.26	1	85.26	0.18
Within groups	20,434.40	44	464.42	
Total	24,528.00	47		

Interpreting the Fs. To test the *F* for the word-association variable, note that we have 1 and 44 degrees of freedom available. Assuming a 0.05-level test, we enter Table A-2 in Appendix A and find that we must interpolate between 40 *df* and 60 *df*. The *F* values are 4.08 and 4.00, respectively. Consequently an *F* with 1 and 44 *df* must exceed 4.06 to indicate reliability. The *F* for word association is 4.04; we therefore fail to reject the first null hypothesis and conclude that variation of the word-association variable did not reliably affect rapidity of concept of learning.

We have the same number of *df* available for evaluating the effect of the observing-response variable, and, therefore, the *F* for this effect must also exceed 4.06 to be reliable. We note that it is 4.59, and we can thus reject the second null hypothesis. The empirical conclusion is that variation of the observing response reliably influences rapidity of forming a concept.

We can visually study these findings by referring to Figure 8-6. First, observe that the points for the changed observing-response conditions are higher than those for the constant observing-response conditions. Since this variable reliably influenced the dependent variable scores, maintaining a constant observing response facilitated the formation of a concept.

Second, note that the data points are lower for the high word-association condition than for the low word-association condition; although this decrease came very close to the required *F* value of 4.06, it still is not reliable.

Finally, we note that the two lines are ap-proximately parallel. The suggestion is thus that there is a lack of interaction between the independent variables, which is confirmed by the *F* value for the interaction source of variation, namely, this *F* is well below 1.0 and we can thus immediately conclude that it is not reliable.

In Conclusion. This completes our examples of the statistical analysis of factorial designs. We have discussed factorial designs generally but have illustrated only the analysis for the 2 × 2 case. More complex factorial designs are illustrated at the end of this chapter and in Chapter 12, where their great importance for generalizing your results is discussed. In Chapter 12 we also elaborate further on the importance of interactions for limiting your generalizations. For princi-

FIGURE 8-6 Data points for the concept learning experiment. Since the lines are approximately parallel, there probably is no interaction.

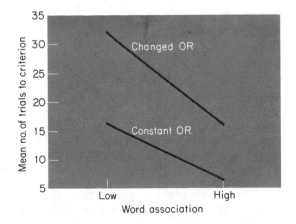

ples of the statistical analysis of more complex factorial designs, you should consult advanced statistics books or take a more advanced course. It is not likely, however, that you will get beyond the 2×2 design in your elementary work.

Selecting an Error Term

The error term, the denominator of the F ratio, has been the within-groups mean square. When you have explicitly selected the values of your independent variables, this is the correct error term to use. In contrast, if you randomly select the values of your independent variables from a large population of them, the within-groups mean square is *not* the appropriate error term. Since you will no doubt intentionally select the values of your independent variables in your elementary work, we need not go into the matter further here. You should be content with using the within-groups mean square as your error term. However, we will develop this matter a bit further in Chapter 12. There we shall see that, in using the within-groups mean square, you are employing a fixed model, rather than a random model, which has significance for the process of generalization.

Understanding which is the appropriate error term constitutes another reason for comprehending the analysis variance procedure rather than blindly relying on a computer program that somebody hands you.

THE IMPORTANCE OF INTERACTIONS

Our goal in psychology is to arrive at statements about the behavior of organisms that can be used to explain, predict, and control behavior. To accomplish these purposes we would like our statements to be as simple as possible. Behavior is anything but simple, however, and it would be surprising if our *statements* about behavior were simple. It is more reasonable to expect that complex statements must be made about complex

events. Those who talk about behavior in simple terms are likely to be wrong. This is illustrated by "commonsense" discussions of behavior. People often say such things as "she is smart; she will do well in college," or "he is handsome; he will go far in the movies." However, such matters are not that uncomplicated; there are variables other than intelligence that influence how well a person does in college, and there are variables other than appearance that influence job success. Furthermore such variables do not always act on all people in the same manner. Rather, they *interact* in such a way that people with certain characteristics behave one way, but people with the same characteristics in addition to other characteristics behave another way. Let us illustrate by speculating about how these two variables might influence a young man's success in films. Consider two values of each: handsome and not handsome, high intelligence and low intelligence. We could then collect data on a sample of four groups: handsome men with high intelligence, handsome men with low intelligence, not handsome men with high intelligence, and not handsome men with low intelligence. Suppose that our dependent variable is the frequency with which men in these four groups starred in films and that we found they ranked as follows with the first group winning the most starring roles: (1) handsome men with low intelligence, (2) not handsome men with high intelligence, (3) handsome men with high intelligence, and (4) men of low intelligence who are not handsome.

If these findings were actually obtained, the simple statement "He is handsome; he will have no trouble winning starring roles in the movies" is inaccurate. Appearance is not the whole story; intelligence is also important. We cannot say that handsome men are more likely to win starring roles any more than we can say that unintelligent men are more likely to do so. The only accurate statement is that appearance and intelligence interact. As depicted in Figure 8-7, handsome men with low intelligence were more frequently chosen than were non-

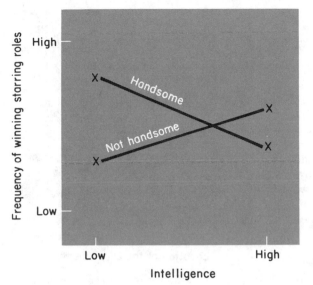

FIGURE 8-7 A possible interaction between appearance and intelligence.

handsome men with low intelligence, but nonhandsome men with high intelligence starred more frequently than did handsome men with high intelligence.

Still, we have just begun to make completely accurate statements when we talk about interactions between *two* variables. Interactions of a much higher order also occur—interactions among three, four, or any number of variables. To illustrate, not only might appearance and intelligence interact, but in addition such variables as motivation, social graces, and so on. Hence, for a really adequate understanding of behavior, we need to determine the large number of interactions that undoubtedly occur. In the final analysis, if such ever occurs in psychology, we will probably arrive at two general kinds of statements about behavior: those statements that tell us how everybody behaves (those ways in which people are similar), with no real exceptions, and those statements that tell us how people differ. The latter will probably involve statements about interactions, for, in the presence of the same stimuli, people with certain characteristics act differently than do people with other characteristics. Statements that describe the varied behavior of people will probably rest on accurate determination of

interactions. If such a complete determination of interactions ever comes about, we will be able to understand the behavior of what is called the "unique" personality.

INTERACTIONS, EXTRANEOUS VARIABLES, AND CONFLICTING RESULTS

Now let us refer the concept of interaction back to Chapter 2 where we discussed ways in which we become aware of a problem. One way is by becoming aware of contradictory findings in a series of experiments. Consider two experiments on the same problem with the same design, but with contradictory results. Why would this occur? One reason might be that a certain variable was not controlled in either experiment. Hence it might have one value in the first experiment but a different value in the second. If such an extraneous variable interacts with the independent variable(s), then the discrepant results become understandable. A new experiment could then be conducted in which that extraneous variable becomes an independent variable. As it is purposively manipulated along with the original independent variable, the nature of the interaction can be determined. In this way, not only would the apparently contradictory results be understood, but a new advance in knowledge would be made.

This situation need not be limited to the case in which the extraneous variable is uncontrolled. For instance, the first experimenter may hold the extraneous variable constant at a certain value, whereas the second experimenter may also hold it constant but at a different value. The same result would obtain as when the variable went uncontrolled: contradictory findings in the two experiments. Let us illustrate by returning to two previously discussed experiments on language suppression (p. 19). In the first experiment prior verbal stimulation produced a verbal suppression effect for the experimental group but not for the control group. The relevant extraneous variable was the location of the experimenter, and in this study the student-participants could *not* see the experimenter. In the repetition of the experiment, however, the students *could* see the experimenter, with the result that there was no suppression effect for the experimental, as compared with the control, group. The ideal solution for this problem, we said, would come by conducting a new experiment using a factorial design that incorporates experimenter location as the second variable. Hence, as shown in Table 8-14, the first variable is the original one (prior verbal stimulation), which is varied in two ways by using an experimental and a control group. The second variable—experimenter location—has two values: the student cannot see

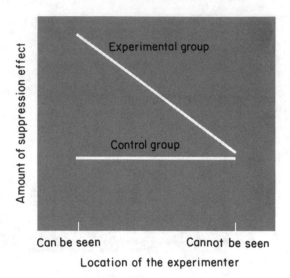

FIGURE 8-8   Illustration of an interaction between the independent variable and location of the experimenter. When the experimenter's location was systematically varied, the reason for conflicting results in two experiments became clear.

see the experimenter, and the student can see him or her.

In short, we repeat the original experiment under two conditions of the extraneous variable. A graphic illustration of the expected results is offered in Figure 8-8. We can see that the experimental group exhibits a larger suppression effect than does the control group when the student can see the experimenter. But when the student *cannot* see the experimenter, there is no reliable difference between the two groups. There is an interaction between the location of the

TABLE 8-14   A Design to Investigate Systematically the Effect of an Extraneous Variable

| Location of Experimenter | Prior Verbal Stimulation | |
	None (control group)	*Some* (experimental group)
Cannot be seen		
Can be seen		

experimenter and the variable of prior verbal stimulation. What at first looked like a contradiction is resolved by isolating an interaction between the original independent variable and an extraneous variable. The problem is solved by resorting to a factorial design.

Undoubtedly these considerations hold for a wide variety of experimental findings, for the contradictions in the psychology literature are legion. Such problems can often be resolved by shrewd applications of the factorial design.

VALUE OF THE FACTORIAL DESIGN

For years the two-group design was standard in psychological research. Statisticians and researchers in such fields as agriculture and genetics, however, were developing other kinds of designs. One of these was the factorial design, which, incidentally, grew with the development of analysis of variance. Slowly, psychologists started trying out these designs on their own problems. Some of them were found to be inappropriate, but the factorial design is one that has enjoyed success, and the extent of its success is still widening, even finding many applications in psychotherapy research. Although each type of design that we have considered is appropriate for particular situations, and although we cannot say that a certain design should *always* be used where it is feasible, the factorial design is generally superior to the other designs that we discuss. The eminent pioneer Sir Ronald Fisher elaborated this matter as follows:

We have usually no knowledge that any one factor will exert its effects independently of all others that can be varied, or that its effects are particularly simply related to variations in these other factors. On the contrary, when factors are chosen for investigation, it is not because we anticipate that the laws of nature can be expressed with any particular simplicity in terms of these variables, but because they are variables which can be controlled or measured with comparative

ease. If *the investigator, in these circumstances, confines his attention to any single factor, we may infer that he is the unfortunate victim of a doctrinaire theory as to how experimentation should proceed, or that the time, material or equipment at his disposal is too limited to allow him to give attention to more than one narrow aspect of his problem. . . .* Indeed, in a wide class of cases an experimental investigation, at the same time as it is made more comprehensive, may also be made more efficient if by more efficient we mean that more knowledge and a higher degree of precision are obtainable by the same number of observations. (Fisher, 1953, pp. 91–92; italics ours)

Following up on this matter of efficiency, first note that the amount of information obtained from a factorial design is considerably greater than that obtained from the other designs, relative to the number of participants used. For example, say that we have two problems: (1) Does variation of independent variable K affect a given dependent variable? and (2) Does variation of independent variable L affect the same dependent variable? If we investigated these two problems by the use of a two-group design, we would obtain two values for each variable; that is, K would be varied in two ways (K_1 and K_2) and similarly for L (L_1 and L_2). With 60 participants for each experiment, the design for the first problem would be

Experiment 1

Group K_1	Group K_2
30 participants	30 participants

And, similarly, for the second problem

Experiment 2

Group L_1	Group L_2
30 participants	30 participants

With a total of 120 participants we are able to evaluate the effect of the two independent variables. However, we would not be able to tell if there is an interaction between K and L if we looked at these as two separate experiments.

But what if we used a factorial design to solve our two problems? Assume that we still want 30 participants for each condition. In this case the factorial would be as in Table 8-15—four groups with 15 participants per group. But for comparing the two conditions of K, we would have 30 participants for condition K_1 and 30 participants for K_2, just as for experiment 1. And the same would hold for the second experiment: We have 30 participants for each condition of L. Here we accomplish with the 2×2 factorial design everything that we would with the two separate experiments with two groups. With those two experiments we required 120 participants to have 30 available for each condition, but with the factorial design we need only 60 participants to have the same number of participants for each condition. The factorial design is much more efficient because we use our participants simultaneously for testing both independent variables. In addition, we can evaluate the interaction between K and L—something that we could not do for the 2 two-group experiments. Although we may look at the information about the interaction as pure "gravy," we should note that some hypotheses may be constructed specifically to test for interactions. Thus it may be that the experimenter is primarily interested in the interaction, in which case the other information may be regarded as "gravy." But whatever the case, it is obvious that the factorial design yields considerably more information than do separate two-group designs and at considerably

less cost to the experimenter. Still other advantages of the factorial design are elaborated later in this book and also in more advanced courses.

TYPES OF FACTORIAL DESIGNS

Let us conclude this chapter by opening some vistas that you can pursue in your future work. For this we shall very briefly mention factorial designs with two and three independent variables presented in a number of ways.

Factorial Designs with Two Independent Variables

The 2 × 2 Factorial Design. In this design we study the effects of two independent variables, each varied in two ways. The *number* of numbers in the label indicates how many independent variables there are in the experiment. The value (size) of those numbers indicates how many ways the independent variables are varied. Since the 2×2 design has two numbers (2 and 2), we can tell immediately that there are two independent variables. Since their values are both 2, we know that each independent variable was varied in two ways. From "2×2" we can also tell how many experimental conditions (cells) there are: 2 multiplied by 2 is 4.

The 3 × 2 Factorial Design. Two independent variables are studied, one varied in three ways, while the second assumes two values. As in Table 8-16, verbalization is varied in three ways (none, little, great) and amount of information furnished (great and small) in two ways. The details of these ex-

TABLE 8-15 A 2×2 Design That Incorporates 2 Two-Group Experiments (the numbers of participants for cells, conditions, and the total number in the experiment are shown)

		K		
		K_1	K_2	
L	L_1	15	15	30
	L_2	15	15	30
		30	30	60

TABLE 8-16 A 3×2 Factorial Design

Amount of Information	Amount of Verbalization		
	None	Little	Great
Small			
Great			

periments need not concern us, as we are merely illustrating the nature of these extended designs.)

The 3 × 3 Factorial Design. To investigate two independent variables, each varied in three ways, we assign participants to nine experimental conditions. As in Table 8-17, both independent variables (intensity of punishment and duration of punishment) are varied in three ways (little, moderate, and great).

The K × L Factorial Design. In the generalized factorial design for two independent variables, *K* stands for the first independent variable and L similarly denotes the second independent variable. K and L might then assume any value. If one independent variable is varied in four ways and the other in two ways, we would have a 4 × 2 design. If one independent variable is varied in six ways and the second in two ways, we would have a 6 × 2 design. If five values are assumed by one independent variable and three by the other, we would have a 5 × 3 design, and so forth.

Factorial Designs with More Than Two Independent Variables

The 2 × 2 × 2 Factorial Design. In principle, the number of variables that can be studied is unlimited. In this, the simplest factorial for studying three independent variables varied in two ways, there are eight experimental conditions. As an illustration of a 2 × 2 × 2 factorial design, consider

Table 8-18, in which *stimulus probability* is varied from $P = 1.0$ versus $P = 0.5$. Note that half of the participants serve under each condition; for example, those in the first four cells to the left all have the same stimulus probability condition of 1.0. Similarly, those assigned to the last four cells on the right all serve under the $P = 0.5$ condition. The second independent variable—*participant's set*—is varied as either being constant or changing. Note also that half the participants serve under the constant condition and half under the changing condition. Finally, for the third independent variable—*response type*—half of the subjects were allowed to respond freely, whereas the other half were forced in a particular manner.

The K × L × M Factorial Design. In the general case for the three-independent-variable factorial design K, L, and M may assume whatever positive integer value the experimenter desires. For instance, if each independent variable assumes three values, a 3 × 3 × 3 design results. If one independent variable (*K*) is varied in two ways, the second (*L*) in three ways, and the third (M) in four ways, a 2 × 3 × 4 design results. A 5 × 3 × 3 design is diagrammed in Table 8-19 such that the independent variable (*K*) is varied in five ways, and the second and third independent variables (*L* and *M*) are each varied in three ways: that is, there are three levels of L under the condition of M_1, the same three levels under M_2, and similarly for the third value of the *M* independent variable.

TABLE 8-17   Illustration of a 3 × 3 Factorial Design

Duration of Punishment	Intensity of Punishment		
	Little	Moderate	Great
Little			
Moderate			
Great			

TABLE 8-18   Illustration of a 2 × 2 × 2 Factorial Design

Response Type	Stimulus Probability			
	1.0 Participant's Set		0.5 Participant's Set	
	Constant	Changing	Constant	Changing
Forced				
Free				

TABLE 8-19   Illustration of a K × L × M Factorial Design in Which K = 5, L = 3, and M = 3

		K_1	K_2	K_3	K_4	K_5
M_1	L_1					
	L_2					
	L_3					
M_2	L_1					
	L_2					
	L_3					
M_3	L_1					
	L_2					
	L_3					

CHAPTER SUMMARY

I. The factorial design (one in which all possible combinations of the selected values of each of the independent variables are used) is generally the most efficient and valuable design in psychological research because
   A. You can simultaneously study two or more independent variables.
   B. Possible interactions between independent variables can be assessed [an interaction is present if the dependent-variable value resulting from one independent variable is influenced by the specific value assumed by the other independent variable(s)].
   C. Use of participants is efficient, since all may be used to answer all three questions.

II. For the statistical analysis of factorial designs, an analysis of variance and the *F*-test are used: The total variance is analyzed into among- and within-group components. In a 2 × 2 design the among-groups variance is then analyzed into
   A. That between conditions for the first independent variable.
   B. That between conditions for the second independent variable.
   C. That for the interaction between the two independent variables.

Three *F*-tests are then conducted by dividing the between-groups sources of variation by within-groups (error term) to determine statistical reliability.

The within-groups means square is the appropriate error term only for a fixed model, wherein the values of the independent variables have been selected for a specific reason.

III. Interactions, which can be studied only with factorial designs, are of great importance to psychology.
   A. They help us to understand complex behavior, since responses are not determined simply by one independent variable; rather, behavior is determined by a complex of stimuli that intricately interact.
   B. They can be used systematically to explore the reasons for conflicting results in previous experiments by systematically varying a previous extraneous variable that assumed different values in the two conflicting experiments.

IV. Types of factorial designs.
   A. The *K* × *L* design indicates that there are two independent variables. For a 2 × 3 design, one variable is varied in two ways and the second in three ways.
   B. Factorial designs with three independent variables may be symbolized by *K* × *L*

$\times$ M, where the values of K, L, and M indicate the number of ways each independent variable is varied, for example, $5 \times 4 \times 4$.

V. Specific procedures for conducting an analysis of variance and an *F*-test are summarized in the following section.

SUMMARY OF AN ANALYSIS OF VARIANCE AND THE COMPUTATION OF AN *F*-TEST FOR A 2 × 2 FACTORIAL DESIGN

To check on the accuracy of a computer program that you might use, assume that the following dependent-variable values have been obtained for the four groups in a 2 × 2 factorial design.

Condition A

		A_1	A_1
		2	3
		3	4
		4	5
B_1		4	7
		5	9
		6	10
		7	13
Condition B			
		5	4
		6	6
		7	7
B_2		8	9
		8	10
		8	11
		8	14

1. The first step is to compute ΣX, ΣX^2, and n for each condition. The values have been computed for our example:

Condition A

		A_1	A_2
	B_1	$\Sigma X = 31$ $\Sigma X^2 = 155$ $n = 7$	$\Sigma X = 51$ $\Sigma X^2 = 449$ $n = 7$
Condition B			
	B_2	$\Sigma X = 50$ $\Sigma X^2 = 366$ $n = 7$	$\Sigma X = 61$ $\Sigma X^2 = 599$ $n = 7$

2. Using Equation 8-1, we next compute the total *SS*:

$$\text{total } SS = (\Sigma X_1^2 + \Sigma X_2^2 + \Sigma X_3^2 + \Sigma X_4^2)$$
$$- \frac{(\Sigma X_1 + \Sigma X_2 + \Sigma X_3 + \Sigma X_4)^2}{N}$$
$$= (155 + 449 + 336 + 599)$$
$$- \frac{(31 + 51 + 50 + 61)^2}{28} = 238.68$$

3. The overall among-*SS* is computed by substituting in Equation 8-2:

$$\text{among-groups } SS$$
$$= \frac{(\Sigma X_1)^2}{n_1} + \frac{(\Sigma X_2)^2}{n_2} + \frac{(\Sigma X_3)^2}{n_3} + \frac{(\Sigma X_4)^2}{n_4}$$
$$- \frac{(\Sigma X_1 + \Sigma X_2 + \Sigma X_3 + \Sigma X_4)^2}{N}$$
$$= \frac{(31)^2}{7} + \frac{(51)^2}{7} + \frac{(50)^2}{7} + \frac{(61)^2}{7}$$
$$- \frac{(31 + 51 + 50 + 61)^2}{28} = 67.25$$

4. The within-*SS* is determined by subtraction, Equation 8-3:

$$\text{total } SS - \text{overall among } SS = \text{within } SS$$
$$238.68 - 67.25 = 171.43$$

5. We now seek to analyze the overall among *SS* into its components, namely, the between-A *SS*, the between-B *SS*, and the A × B *SS*. The between-A *SS* may be computed with the use of Equation 8-4.

$$\text{between-A } SS$$
$$= \frac{(\Sigma X_1 + \Sigma X_3)^2}{n_1 + n_3}$$
$$+ \frac{(\Sigma X_2 + \Sigma X_4)^2}{n_2 + n_4}$$
$$- \frac{(\Sigma X_1 + \Sigma X_2 + \Sigma X_3 + \Sigma X_4)^2}{N}$$
$$= \frac{(31 + 50)^2}{7 + 7} + \frac{(51 + 61)^2}{7 + 7}$$
$$- \frac{(31 + 51 + 50 + 61)^2}{28} = 34.32$$

The between-B *SS* may be computed with the use of Equation 8-5.

between-B SS

$$= \frac{(\Sigma X_1 + \Sigma X_2)^2}{n_1 + n_2} + \frac{(\Sigma X_3 + \Sigma X_4)^2}{n_3 + n_4}$$
$$- \frac{(\Sigma X_1 + \Sigma X_2 + \Sigma X_3 + \Sigma X_4)^2}{N}$$
$$= \frac{(31 + 51)^2}{7 + 7} + \frac{(50 + 61)^2}{7 + 7}$$
$$- \frac{(31 + 51 + 50 + 61)^2}{28} = 30.04$$

The sum of squares for the interaction component (A × B) may be computed by subtraction:

(8-6)   A × B = overall among SS
$\qquad$ − between-A SS − between-B SS
$\qquad$ 67.25 − 34.32 − 30.04 = 2.89

6. Compute the several degrees of freedom. In particular, determine *df* for the total source of variance Equation 8-7, for the overall among source Equation 8-8, and the within source Equation 8-9. Following this, allocate the overall among degrees of freedom to the components of it: namely, that between A, that between B, and that for A × B.

$$\text{total } df = N - 1$$
$$= 28 - 1 = 27$$

$$\text{overall among } df = r - 1$$
$$= 4 - 1 = 3$$

$$\text{within } df = N - r$$
$$= 28 - 4 = 24$$

The components of the overall among *df* are

$$\text{between } df = r - 1$$
$$\text{between A} = 2 - 1 - 1$$
$$\text{between B} = 2 - 1 = 1$$

A × B df = (number of df for between A)
$\qquad \times$ (number of df for between B)
$\qquad = 1 \times 1 = 1$

7. Compute the various mean squares. This is accomplished by dividing the several sums of squares by the corresponding degrees of freedom. For our example, these operations, as well as the results of the preceding ones, are summarized:

Source of Variation	Sum of Squares	df	Mean Square	F
Between A	34.32	1	34.32	4.81
Between B	30.04	1	30.04	4.21
A × B	2.89	1	2.89	0.40
Within groups	171.43	24		
Total	238.68	27		

8. Compute an *F* for each "between" source of variation. In a 2 × 2 factorial design there are three-*F*-tests to run. The *F* is computed by dividing a given mean square by the within-groups mean square (assuming the case of fixed variables). These *F*s have been computed and entered in the preceding table.

9. Enter Table A-2 in Appendix A to determine the probability associated with each *F*. To do this find the column for the number of degrees of freedom associated with the numerator and the row for the number of degrees of freedom associated with the denominator. In our example they are 1 and 24, respectively. The *F* of 4.81 for between A would thus be reliable beyond the 0.05 level, and, accordingly, we would reject the null hypothesis for this condition. The *F* between B (4.21) and that for the interaction (0.40), however, are not reliable at the 0.05 level; hence, we would fail to reject the null hypotheses for these two sources of variation.

CRITICAL REVIEW FOR THE STUDENT

1. Important terms and concepts that you should be able to define:
    Interaction
    Factorial design
    Data values for a sample (statistics) versus values for a population (parameters)
    Error term for an analysis of variance
2. Specify different types of factorial designs and how they are labeled.
3. Assess the value of factorial designs relative to other experimental designs.
4. Problems
    A. An experimenter wants to evaluate the effect of a new drug on "curing" psychotic tendencies. Two independent variables are studied—the amount of the drug administered and the type of psychotic

condition. The amount of the drug administered is varied in two ways—none and 2 cc. The type of psychotic condition is also varied in two ways—schizophrenic and manic-depressive. Diagram the factorial design used.

B. In the drug experiment the psychologist used a measure of normality as the dependent variable. This measure varies between 0 and 10, in which 10 is very normal and 0 is very abnormal. Seven participants were assigned to each cell. The resulting scores for the four groups were as follows. Conduct the appropriate statistical analysis and reach a conclusion about the effect of each variable and the interaction.

Psychotic Condition

Schizophrenics		Manic-Depressives	
Received Drug	Did Not Receive Drug	Received Drug	Did Not Receive Drug
6	2	5	1
6	3	6	1
6	3	6	2
7	4	7	3
8	4	8	4
8	5	8	5
9	6	9	6

C. How would the preceding design be diagrammed if the experimenter had varied the amount of drug in three ways (zero amount, 2 cc, and 4 cc) and the type of psychotic tendency in three ways (schizophrenic, manic-depressive, and paranoid)?

D. How would you diagram the preceding design if the experimenter had varied the amount of drug in four ways (zero, 2 cc, 4 cc, and 6 cc) and the type of participant in four ways (normal, schizophrenic, manic-depressive, and paranoid)?

E. A cigarette company is interested in the effect of several conditions of smoking on steadiness. They manufacture two brands: Old Zincs and Counts. Furthermore, they make each brand with and without a filter. A psychologist conducts an experiment in which two independent variables are studied. The first is brand, which is varied in two ways (Old Zincs and Counts), and the

second is filter, which is also varied in two ways (with a filter and without a filter). A standard steadiness test is used as the dependent variable. Diagram the resulting factorial design.

F. In the smoking experiment the higher the dependent variable score, the greater was the steadiness. Assume that the results came out as follows (10 participants per cell). What conclusions did the experimenter reach?

Old Zincs		Counts	
With Filter	Without Filter	With Filter	Without Filter
7	2	2	7
7	2	3	7
8	3	3	7
8	3	3	8
9	3	3	9
9	4	4	9
10	4	4	10
10	5	5	10
11	5	5	11
11	5	6	11

G. An experiment is conducted to investigate the effect of opium and marijuana on hallucinatory activity. Both independent variables were valid in two ways. Seven participants were assigned to cells, and the amount of hallucinatory activity was scaled so that a high number indicated considerable hallucination. Assuming that adequate controls have been realized and that a 0.05 criterion level was set, what conclusions can be reached?

Smoked Opium		Did Not Smoke Opium	
Smoked Marijuana	Did Not Smoke Marijuana	Smoked Marijuana	Did Not Smoke Marijuana
7	5	6	3
7	5	5	2
7	4	5	2
6	4	4	1
6	3	4	1
5	3	4	0
4	3	3	0

chapter 9

CORRELATIONS AND EXPERIMENTAL DESIGNS

Major purpose:

To understand the concept of correlation and how it is used in nonexperimental and experimental research.

What you are going to find:

1. Statistical methods for determining the degree to which two variables are correlated and how to interpret those correlations.

2. The two-matched-groups experimental design.

3. Experimental designs for repeated treatments using groups.

What you should acquire:

The ability to conduct correlational research and experiments using a two-matched-groups design and repeated treatments for group designs.

CORRELATIONAL RESEARCH

This is a specific kind of nonexperimental research. In using nonexperimental methods, recall that we do not purposively manipulate independent variables. After discussing **correlational research** we shall consider how the concept of correlation is involved in the **two-matched-groups design** and in **repeated treatments for groups designs**.

The Meaning of Correlation

A correlation is a statement of a possible relationship between two (or more) variables, and it is exemplified by the statement that those variables are *co-related*. Any variables that are measured on an individual may be studied to see if they are correlated. For instance, we may attempt to correlate intelligence and height by measuring intelligence and height on one person, then another, and so on. We would then assess the degree of relationship between intelligence and height by computing a correlation coefficient. Note that both measures are taken on each individual being studied—it would be fruitless to correlate intelligence of one set of people with the height of another set of people. Such a correlation would obviously be zero because the two variables would be totally independent.

In psychological research, correlations are typically computed between two organismic variables such as height and intelligence, between dependent variables such as rate of learning and latency of responding, and between one dependent and one organismic variable. Correlations are also computed between repeated measures of the same dependent variable, as we discussed in assessing the reliability of a dependent variable.

Correlational research is most often conducted when it is not feasible to manipulate independent variables purposively. Examples abound in social psychology and in sociology in which it is difficult, if not impossible, to manipulate social institutions systematically. Although it would be interesting and highly informative, we simply could not use type of government as an independent variable, randomly assigning a democratic form to one country and an autocratic form to another.

Negative, Positive, and Zero Correlations.

The most refined development of correlational research came in the late nineteenth century when the famous statistician Karl Pearson showed how we can effectively quantify the relationship between two variables. The most prominent correlational statistic is thus named in his honor—the **Pearson product moment coefficient of correlation**.

Pearson's index of correlation is symbolized by r, and its precise value indicates the *degree* to which two variables are linearly related. The value that r may assume varies between $+1.0$ and -1.0. A value of $+1.0$ indicates a perfect **positive correlation**, -1.0 indicates a perfect **negative correlation**. To illustrate, say that a group of people have been administered two different intelligence tests. Both tests presumably measure the same thing so the scores should be highly correlated, as in Table 9-1.

The individual who received the highest score on test A also received the highest score on test B and so on down the list, with person 6 receiving the lowest score on both tests. A computation of r for this very small sample would yield a value of $+1.0$. The scores on the two tests are positively correlated because the person who scored highest on one test also scored highest on the other test; the one who scored second highest on one test also scored second highest on the other test and the same relationship holds for the remainder of individuals. The fact that there is no exception indicates that the correlation is perfect.[1]

If there were one or two exceptions in the ranking of test scores— such that person 1

TABLE 9-1 Fictitious Scores Received by Each Person on Two Intelligence Tests

Person Number	Score on Intelligence Test A	Score on Intelligence Test B
1	120	130
2	115	125
3	110	120
4	105	115
5	100	110
6	95	105

---

[1] Actually, another necessary characteristic for the Pearson product moment coefficient of correlation to be perfect is that the interval between successive pairs of scores on one variable must be proportional to that for corresponding pairs on the other variable. In our example, five IQ points separate each person on each test. However, this requirement is not crucial to the present discussion.

had the highest score on test A but the third highest score on test B, that person 3 ranked third on test A but first on test B, and that all other relative positions remained the same—the correlation would not be perfect (1.0) but would still be rather high (it would actually be 0.77).

To illustrate a perfect negative correlation where $r = -1.0$, we might administer two tests: one of democratic characteristics and one that measures amount of prejudice (see Table 9-2). The person who scores highest on the first test receives the lowest score on the second, with an inverse relationship holding for all participants without exception. If we had one or two exceptions in the inverse relationship, the r would be something like -0.70, indicating a negative relationship between the two variables, but one short of being perfect.

To Summarize. Given measures on two variables for each individual, *a positive correlation exists if as the value of one variable increases, the value of the other one increases also.* If there is no exception, the correlation will be high and possibly even perfect; if there are relatively few exceptions, it will be positive but not perfect. Thus, as test scores on intelligence test A increase, the scores on test B also increase. Additional examples of positive correlations would be the height and weight of a person, one's IQ and ability to learn, and one's grades in college and high school. On the other hand, *if the value of one variable decreases while that of the other variable increases, a negative (inverse) correlation exists.* No exception indicates that the negative relation is high and possibly perfect. Hence, as the extent to which people exhibit democratic characteristics increases, the amount of their prejudice decreases, which is what we would expect. We would also expect to find negative correlations between the amount of heating fuel a family uses and the outside temperature, and the weight of a person and success as a jockey.

Finally, when $r = 0$ there is a total lack of (linear) relationship between the two measures. Thus, as the value of one variable increases, the value of the other varies in a random fashion. Examples of situations in which we would expect r to be zero would be where we would correlate height of forehead with intelligence, or number of books that a person reads in a year with the length of toenails.[2]

In science we seek to find relationships between variables. And a negative relationship (correlation) *is just as important* as a positive relationship. Do not think that a negative correlation is undesirable or that it indicates a lack of relationship. To illustrate, for a fixed sample, a correlation of -0.50 indicates just as strong a relationship as a correlation of $+0.50$, and a correlation of -0.90 indicates a stronger relationship than does one of $+0.80$. Think about this point for a minute and realize that whether scores on a scale of measurement are positive or negative can be quite arbitrary. In scoring an item on a prejudice test, as in Table 9-2, we could equally count each item as a positive or as a negative point, so that we would have precisely the reverse values for prejudice in Table 9-2, turning the correlation of -1.0 into $+1.0$.

Scattergrams

A good general principle for understanding your data, whether they derive from ex-

TABLE 9-2 Fictitious Scores on Two Personality Measures

Participant Number	Score on Test of Democratic Characteristics	Score on Test of Prejudice
1	50	10
2	45	15
3	40	20
4	35	25
5	30	30
6	25	35

[2] However, it has been argued that this would actually be a positive correlation on the grounds that excessive book reading cuts into a person's toenail-cutting time. Resolution of the argument must await relevant data.

perimental or correlational research, is simply to draw a "picture" of them. Not only can you better visualize possible relationships between variables, but by actually working with the various values, trying one thing and then another, confusion can often give way to clear insights. In experimental research, for instance, it is typically helpful to plot your dependent-variable values on a graph as a function of independent-variable values. In correlational research, a diagram of a relationship is referred to as a **scattergram** or scatterplot, *which is a graph of the relationship between two measures on the same individuals*. Such diagrams can often reveal more about your data than mere statistics such as $\overline{X}$, t, or r. This is another good reason why you should not blindly enter data into a computer program. Rather, it is preferable to work with your data before you conduct your statistical tests.

Perfect Correlations (r = 1.0). The data in Table 9-1 are presented as a scattergram in Figure 9-1. The person who made the highest score on intelligence test A (120),

also made the highest score on intelligence test B (130). The values for each other person may be similarly read from the vertical axis for test A and from the horizontal axis for test B (which axis is used for which variable is arbitrary). The fact that each data point falls precisely on the straight line indicates that the relationship is perfect (r = 1.0). Furthermore, this is a positive correlation because as the value of one variable increases, the value of the second also increases; for example, the data point for the least intelligent person falls at the lower left, whereas that for the most intelligent person is at the upper right.

A scattergram plotting the data of Table 9-2 indicates a perfect negative correlation (Figure 9-2). Thus, as the value of democratic characteristics increases, the degree of prejudice decreases. Because each data point falls precisely on a straight line, this is a perfect negative correlation (r = 1.0).

Predictions. A salient characteristic of correlations is that they allow you to predict from one variable to another. For instance,

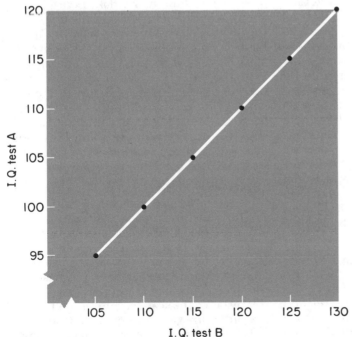

Perfect positive (+1.00)

FIGURE 9-1 A perfect positive linear correlation between two variables. As the values on the first variable (test A) increase, so do the values of the second variable. Since each data point falls on a straight line, the correlation coefficient is maximal.

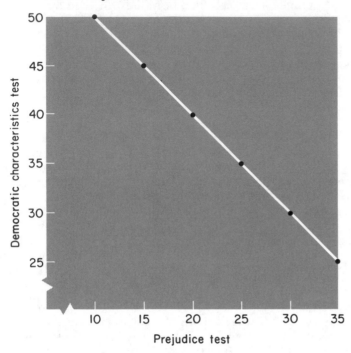

FIGURE 9-2 A perfect negative linear correlation between two variables. As the values on the first variable (democratic characteristics) decrease, values on the second variable increase.

if we knew only the democratic characteristic scores of a new sample of individuals from the same population on which the correlation was computed, we could predict the prejudice scores for individuals about whom we have no information. If the score of a new individual on the democratic test was 32, we would read over from that value on the vertical axis of Figure 9-2 and find that the corresponding value on the straight line is 28 for the measure of prejudice. However, even though the correlation is perfect, the prediction, as always in the real world, would be only probabilistic. It is unreasonable to expect that we can make *perfect* predictions of this nature, which is precisely why we need to resort to statistics.

Reliable Correlations Less Than 1.0. The scattergram for a moderately negative correlation (about − 0.70) is illustrated in Figure 9-3. (A moderately positive correlation would be similar to this, but the data points would be distributed in the direction of Fig-

ure 9-1.) Although the data points cluster about a straight line, which is the line of best fit, they deviate somewhat from it. With a high correlation like this, we can be moderately successful in predicting one variable from the other. But, as for all of our statistics, we can expect success only in the long run, that is, by considering a large number of cases. Thus, although the principles discussed in this section are valid, they really hold only for larger numbers of cases than we have used for illustrative purposes.

Zero-Order Correlations. If you consider the infinitely large number of variables in the universe, it must be that most of them are *unrelated.* A task of science is to specify those relatively few that *are* related (correlated). If we are not very astute, we might attempt to correlate height of forehead with number of airplane trips taken in a year. In this instance the scattergram would look like that in Figure 9-4. Rather than a clear relationship between these two variables, we can-

Moderate negative (−0.70)

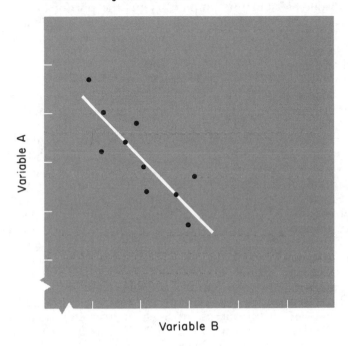

FIGURE 9-3 A moderately negative correlation occurs when the values of one variable decrease while the values of the second variable increase, with a number of deviations from the line of best fit.

Unrelated (0.00)

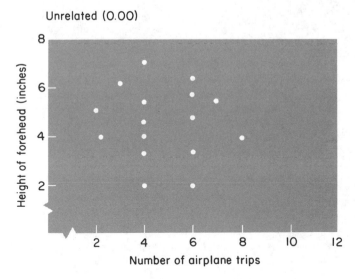

FIGURE 9-4 A fictitious array of data indicating a total lack of relationship between two variables.

not predict at all the value of one variable from the other. For instance, for a value of 4 inches for forehead height, the full range of airplane trips has been plotted. The data in Figure 9-4 clearly do not have a linear fit, and, in fact, one wit characterized the "line of best fit" for such data as a circle. To be serious, though, the line of best fit need *not* be linear, for it may be a curve.

Curvilinear Relationships

We have concentrated on *linear* relationships, as with the Pearson product moment coefficient of correlation that expresses the degree to which two variables are linearly related. By this we mean that the value of *r* indicates the extent to which the data for the two variables fit on a straight line. In science we follow a principle of **inductive simplicity** (see page 134). When applied here this means that we make inferences from one variable to another on the basis of the simplest possible relationship between them, which is a straight line or linear function. However, as Einstein reminded us, "Every-

thing should be made as simple as possible, but not simpler." Thus the portion of the world that we study is often *not* simple and often requires that we postulate more complex relationships than linear ones.

Consider, for instance, the relationship between success in life and a person's degree of tension. Would you postulate a linear relationship between these variables, such as that the less tense a person is, the more success the person experiences? Or, rather than this negative relationship, would you think that the greater the tension, the greater the success? After a little reflection, you realize that neither of these simplistic statements suffices, for some degree of tension in a person is necessary just to be alive. An individual who is not tense at all would be but a vegetable. On the other hand, an overly tense individual "chokes" and thereby fails. There is thus an optimal amount of tension for success—too little or too much causes one to be unsuccessful. Such an inverted U-shaped function is presented in Figure 9-5. A rough glance at these data suggests that a linear correlation would approximate zero—as the scores for the first variable (tension) in-

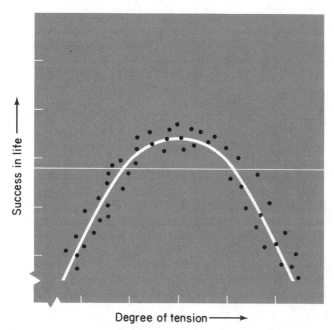

FIGURE 9-5 A curvilinear correlation computed by (η).

crease, the values for the second variable (success in life) first increase, level off, then decrease. A straight line fitted to these data could well be horizontal so that, for any value of tension, there is a wide range of values for success in life. But in contradistinction to the scattergram of Figure 9-4, in which r also equals zero, in Figure 9-5 there *is* a systematic relationship between the two variables. This systematic relationship would *not* be indicated by a linear correlation coefficient. How would we quantify such a curvilinear correlation? The answer is by use of the most generalized coefficient of correlation known as *eta* and symbolized η. The value for η, which you could easily compute by referring to a standard statistics book, would thus be high—approaching 1.0—for the data in Figure 9-5. But since in your present work it is more important to learn how to compute linear relationships, we shall now turn to those procedures. Various curvilinear functions were discussed in Chapter 7.

THE COMPUTATION OF CORRELATION COEFFICIENTS

The Pearson Product Moment Coefficient of Correlation

Equation 9-1 is convenient for computing a Pearson product moment coefficient of correlation directly from raw data.

$$(9\text{-}1) \quad r_{XY} = \frac{n\Sigma XY - (\Sigma X)(\Sigma Y)}{\sqrt{[n\Sigma X^2 - (\Sigma X)^2][n\Sigma Y^2 - (\Sigma Y)^2]}}$$

The components for Equation 9-1 are quite easy to obtain, even though the equation may look at bit forbidding at first. To illustrate the calculation procedures, let us enter the data from Table 9-2 into Table 9-3.

First, we compute the sum of the scores for the first variable, namely, $\Sigma X = 225$. Then we obtain ΣX^2 by squaring each value on the first test and summing those values so that $\Sigma X^2 = 8,875$. Similarly, we obtain the sum of the scores and the sum of the squares of the scores for the second measure. As we can see in Table 9-3, $\Sigma Y = 135$ and $\Sigma Y^2 = 3,475$. Finally, we need to obtain the sum of the cross-products (ΣXY). To do this we merely multiply each individual's score on the first test by the corresponding score on the second and add them. For example, $50 \times 10 = 500$, $45 \times 15 = 675$, and so on. Summing these cross-products in the column labeled XY, we find that $\Sigma XY = 4,625$.

Noting that $n = 6$, we make the appropriate substitution from Table 9-3 into Equation 9-1 as follows:

$$r_{XY} = \frac{6(4,625) - (225)(135)}{\sqrt{[6(8,875) - (225)^2][6(3,475) - (135)^2]}}$$

$$= \frac{27,750 - 30,375}{\sqrt{(53,250 - 50,625)(20,850 - 18,225)}}$$

TABLE 9-3 Data on Two Personality Measures from Table 9-2 to Illustrate the Calculation of r

Participant Number	Scores on Test of Democratic Characteristics		Scores on Test of Prejudice		
	X	X^2	Y	Y^2	XY
1	50	2,500	10	100	500
2	45	2,025	15	225	675
3	40	1,600	20	400	800
4	35	1,225	25	625	875
5	30	900	30	900	900
6	25	625	35	1,225	875
	$\Sigma X = 225$	$\Sigma X^2 = 8,875$	$\Sigma Y = 135$	$\Sigma Y^2 = 3,475$	$\Sigma XY = 4,625$

$$= \frac{-2,625}{\sqrt{(2,625)(2,625)}}$$

$$= \frac{-2,625}{2,625}$$

$$= -1.0$$

As we previously illustrated, the actual computation of r indicates that the data in Table 9-2 and 9-3 are illustrative of a perfect negative correlation.

Dichotomized Variables

The data that we have considered so far in this chapter have not been dichotomized. Sometimes, however, one or both of your measures are dichotomies, for example, whether a student has passed or failed, whether a person is male or female, or whether a question was answered yes or no. Specialized methods of computing correlation coefficients have been developed for such cases. Suppose, for instance, you have IQ scores on students as well as a measure of whether they passed or failed a course. In this case you could compute a biserial correlation coefficient, symbolized r_b. A variation of the biserial r is the point biserial r, symbolized r_{pbi}. Whether you use the biserial r or the point biserial r depends upon whether the dichotomized variable is for a true dichotomy or whether it is really a continuous variable that was forced into the dichotomy. The series of grades made in a course, for instance, is a continuous variable ranging from A through F, but in the foregoing example grades were forced into the dichotomy as to whether the student passed or failed. Yet another kind of correlation is the tetrachoric correlation, symbolized r_t. The tetrachoric correlation coefficient is appropriate when both variables are continuous but both are artificially forced into two categories. Finally, when both variables are really dichotomous, you can compute what is known as a *phi* coefficient.

We are not enlarging further on this topic because it is probably not a major concern to you. Nevertheless, it is valuable to recognize that correlations can be computed when the variables are for genuine or artifical dichotomies. If you have need, you should consult a good statistics book on correlations, which would tell you how to compute these simple correlation coefficients quickly.

STATISTICAL RELIABILITY OF CORRELATION COEFFICIENTS

As in the case of the t-test, there are two main factors that determine whether a correlation coefficient is statistically reliable: (1) the size of the value, and (2) the number of individuals on whom it was based (which determines the degrees of freedom). For the t-test we tested to see if the difference between the means of two groups was reliably greater than zero. The comparable question for the correlation coefficient is whether *it* is reliably greater than zero. For this purpose we can refer to Table A-3 in Appendix A.

There we read the minimal value of r required for a correlation coefficient to be significantly different from zero with a probability of 0.05 or 0.01. However, as with the t tables, we need to enter Table A-3 with the number of degrees of freedom associated with our particular correlation value. For this purpose, the equation is

$$(9\text{-}2) \qquad df = N - 2$$

Thus, if we compute a correlation between the scores of 30 individuals, $df = 30 - 2 = 28$. Entering Table A-3 with 28 df, we can see that a value of 0.361 is required for the correlation to be reliably different from zero at the probability level of 0.05. If we set the more stringent requirement of $P < 0.01$, the correlation value would have to exceed 0.463. However, the probability level associated with r does not indicate its strength. The strength of the relationship is indicated by the value of r. If that value of r has an associated probability of less than 0.05, it means only that the correlation is reliably different from zero. The logic of determining whether a correlation coefficient is statistically reliable is similar to that of the *t*-test. If you conclude that you have a statistically reliable linear correlation, you have accomplished one of the goals of research—you have succeeded in finding two of the indefinitely large number of variables in the universe that *are* related. You can now predict, probabilistically, the value of one from the other. But does this give you *causal* control over the relationship?

CORRELATION AND CAUSATION

The concept of *causality* has an exceedingly complex philosophical and scientific history. In the seventeenth century the great philosopher David Hume demolished the concept by holding that cause-and-effect relationships are merely habits of the human mind projected onto nature. Events in nature that *seem* to be causally related, Hume held, are merely co-occurrences. Today Hume would say that, although there are correlations between natural events, we cannot thereby assert that one causes the other. There is mere concomitance in nature, not causality.

We shall not solve this great philosophical problem here. Instead we will only operationally define *causality* for limited use in research. For us the term means precisely the following, and nothing more: An independent variable *causes* changes in a dependent variable when such has been demonstrated in a well-conducted experiment; that is, a **cause-effect relationship** *is established when it has been shown that an independent variable systematically influences a dependent variable with the influence of the extraneous variables controlled*. The only qualification is the one that we must make for all empirical laws, namely, that although such a cause-effect relationship may approach certainty, it is still probabilistic. Although experimentation is our most powerful research method, even it yields only probabilistic laws. Even though, for instance, we attempted to eliminate all other possible causes of changes in the dependent variable, some of these extraneous

variables may not actually have been controlled. But even if we did know with certainty that we had eliminated all of these other possible causes, we still could not assert that the independent variable is the only cause. This is because the conclusion that there is a statistically reliable difference between the means of our two groups itself is only probabilistic.

One corollary of this discussion is that the conclusions from experiments differ from the conclusions using nonexperimental methods only in terms of degree of probability. Consequently we can still infer causal relationships from nonexperimental research, but those inferences have lower degrees of probability than if they were derived from actual experiments. A causal relationship inferred on the basis of systematic observation, for instance, has a higher degree of probability than one inferred from correlational research, but both would be well below the probability deriving from experimentation. In Chapter 11 we shall see that there are a variety of quasi-experimental designs other than the method of systematic observation, and from these we can infer cause-effect relationships, but still at reduced probability levels. In spite of this deficiency, however, quasi-experimental designs and correlational research remain valuable because they are often our only methods to attack some of society's most critical problems.

Let us examine possible cause-effect relationships between two variables in greater detail. If the relationship was established in a well-controlled experiment, we can be quite confident that it is a causal relationship. But in nonexperimental research, such as with the method of systematic observation, the independent variable may well be the causal one. However, since it is necessarily confounded with other participant characteristics, we cannot unequivocally specify that *it* was the cause of the dependent variable changes.

The relationship between variables that are reliably correlated is even more uncertain. If the variables X and Y are correlated, the possible causal relationships are: first, X may cause Y; second, Y may cause X; or third, the systematic relationship between X and Y may be caused by some other variable, Z, which may be any of an indefinitely large number of variables. If the price of rice in China is positively correlated with the number of ship loadings in Stockholm, we would not say that one causes the other (although through an amazing series of intervening events, even *that* is possible). Rather, the values of both variables would probably be caused by some other variable, such as world economic conditions or by something else that we couldn't even dream about. In short, although we can predict on the basis of correlations, our inferences about causal relationships are limited, to say the least. Consider two natural happenings concerning possible causal relations.

Two Examples from Everyday Life. Observations were made in Egypt that when the price of cotton was very low, 52 percent of Moslem marriages were dissolved by divorce. In contrast, when cotton prices were high, Moslem men acquired additional wives (their religion permits them to have up to four wives at one time, and to divorce them by saying "I divorce you" three times). It was reasoned that the price of cotton influenced the divorce rate. Consequently, when husbands were affluent, they could support more wives. However, the husbands' ability to support the wives was reduced due to economic pressures of falling prices. Do you think that you could infer a causal relation between cotton prices and frequency of divorce? Or might some other variable that is reflected by cotton prices, such as general economic status throughout the country, be the causal variable?

The second study indicated that nine months after a blackout of lights in New York due to an electricity failure, the birth rate jumped remarkably. Exactly nine months after the blackout, for instance, all the delivery and labor rooms in the biggest hospitals impacted by the blackout were overcrowded. There was an increase in birth rate in those hospitals that varied between 33 and 50 percent during a 36-hour period. In contrast, two other large hospitals that were not seriously affected by the blackout reported that the birth rate was normal. Was the blackout the causal variable for increased birth rate? Or did something else that was itself correlated with the blackout produce the increase in birth rate?

Why is it so important to establish causal relationships? The answer is that we seek to control nature, and we do this by identifying the cause of an effect—we want to make systematic, intentional changes in behavior. With the power of control we can institute a cause and produce the desired change (the effect). If we want our laboratory animals to respond more vigorously, we *cause* this by increasing their drive level; if we want our children to learn more, we intentionally increase the effectiveness of their educational methods. If we want to reduce crime, to increase rate of employment, or to decrease inflation, we must institute the effective causes that can systematically change those dependent variables. The concept of causality is thus critical for improving society, as we shall see in Chapter 11.

THE TWO-MATCHED-GROUPS EXPERIMENTAL DESIGN

The Basic Logic of All Experimental Designs Is the Same. Start with groups that are essentially equal, administer the experimental treatment to one and not the other, and note the difference on the dependent variable. If the two groups start with equivalent means on the dependent variable, and if, after the administration of the experimental treatment, there is a reliable difference between those means, and if extraneous variables have been adequately controlled, then that difference on the dependent variable may be attributed to the experimental treatment. The randomized-groups designs are based on the assumption that random assignment of participants to the various conditions will result in essentially equal groups.

The matched-groups design is simply one way of helping to satisfy the assumption that the groups have essentially equal dependent variable values prior to the administration of the experimental treatment (rather than relying on chance assignment).

The Logic of a Two-Matched-Groups Design. Consider a hypothesis that holds that both reading and reciting material leads to better retention than does reading alone. Of two groups of participants, one would learn material by reading and reciting, the second only by reading. With a randomized-groups design we would assign participants to the two groups at random regardless of what we might know about them. With the matched-groups design, however, we use scores on an initial measure called the **matching variable** to help assure equivalence of groups. A matching variable, as we shall see, is just what the term implies—some objective, quantified measure that can serve to divide the participants into two equivalent groups. Intelligence test scores, such as those for 10 students presented in Table 9-4 could serve as our matching variable.

Our strategy is to form two groups that are equal in intelligence. To accomplish this we pair those who have equal scores, assigning one member of each pair to each group. They can be paired as follows: 1 and 2, 3 and 4, 5 and 6, 7 and 8, and 9 and 10. Then we randomly divide these pairmates into two groups. This assignment by randomization is necessary to prevent possible experimenter biases from interfering with the matching. For example, the experimenter may, even though unaware of such actions, assign more highly motivated students to one group in spite of each pair having the same intelligence score. By a flip of a coin we might determine that student 1 goes into the reading and reciting group; student 2 then goes into the reading group. The next coin flips might determine that student 3 goes into the reading group and student 4 into the reading and reciting group, and so on for the remaining pairs (see Table 9-5).

Note that the sums (and therefore the means) of the intelligence scores of the two groups in Table 9-5 are equal. Now assume that the two groups are subjected to their respective experimental treatments and that we obtain the retention scores for them indicated in Table 9-6 (the higher the score, the better they retain the learning material). We have placed the pairs in rank order according to their initial level of ability on the matching variable; that is, the most intelligent pair is placed first, and the least intelligent pair is placed last.

Statistical Analysis of a Two-Matched-Groups Design

The values in Table 9-6 suggest that the reading and reciting group is superior, but are they *reliably* superior? To answer this question we may apply the *t*-test, although the application will be a bit different for a matched-groups design. The equation is

$$(9\text{-}3) \qquad t = \frac{\overline{X}_1 - \overline{X}_2}{\sqrt{\dfrac{\sum D^2 - \dfrac{(\sum D)^2}{n}}{n(n-1)}}}$$

The symbols are the same as those previously used, except for *D*, which is *the difference between the dependent-variable scores for each pair of students*. To find *D* we subtract the score for the first member of a pair from the second. For example, the scores for the

TABLE 9-4 Scores of a Sample of Students on a Matching Variable

Student Number	Intelligence Test Score
1	120
2	120
3	110
4	110
5	100
6	100
7	100
8	100
9	90
10	90

TABLE 9-5   The Construction of Two Matched Groups on the Basis of Intelligence Scores

Reading Group		Reading and Reciting Group	
Student Number	Intelligence Score	Student Number	Intelligence Score
2	120	1	120
3	110	4	110
6	100	5	100
7	100	8	100
10	90	9	90
	520		520

TABLE 9-6   Dependent-Variable Scores for the Pairs of Students Ranked on the Basis of Matching Variable Scores

Initial Level of Ability	Reading Group		Reading and Reciting Group	
	Student Number	Retention Score	Student Number	Retention Score
1	2	8	1	10
2	3	6	4	9
3	6	5	5	6
4	7	2	8	6
5	10	2	9	5

first pair are 8 and 10, respectively, so that $D = 8 - 10 = -2$. Since we will later square the D scores (to obtain ΣD^2), it makes no difference which group's score is subtracted from which. We could just as easily have said: $D = 10 - 8 = 2$. The only caution is that we need to be consistent; that is, we must always subtract one group's score from the other's, or vice versa. Completion of the D calculations is shown in Table 9-7

TABLE 9-7   Computation of the Value of D for Equation 9-3

Initial Level of Ability	Reading Group	Reading and Reciting Group	D
1	8	10	-2
2	6	9	-3
3	5	6	-1
4	2	6	-4
5	2	5	-3

Equation 9-3 instructs us to perform three operations with respect to D. First, obtain ΣD, the sum of the D values; that is,

$$\Sigma D = (-2) + (-3) + (-1) + (-4) + (-3) = -13$$

Second, obtain ΣD^2, the sum of the squares of D; that is, square each value of D and sum these squares as follows:

$$\Sigma D^2 = (-2)^2 + (-3)^2 + (-1)^2 + (-4)^2 + (-3)^2$$
$$= 4 + 9 + 1 + 16 + 9 = 39$$

Third, compute $(\Sigma D)^2$, which is the square of the sum of D scores; that is,

$$(\Sigma D)^2 = (\Sigma D)(\Sigma D)$$

Recall that n is the number of participants in a group (not the *total* number in the experiment). When we match (pair) participants, we may safely assume that the number in each group is the same. In our example $n = 5$. The numerator is the difference between the (dependent-variable) means of the two groups, as with the previous application of the *t*-test. The means of the two groups are 4.6 and 7.2. Substitution of all these values in Equation 9-3 results in the following:

$$t = \frac{7.2 - 4.6}{\sqrt{\dfrac{39 - \dfrac{(-13)^2}{5}}{5(5 - 1)}}} = 5.10$$

The equation for computing the degrees of freedom for the matched *t*-test is $df = n - 1$. (Note that this is a different equation for *df* from that for the two-randomized-groups design.) Hence, for our example, *df* $= 5 - 1 = 4$. Consulting our table of *t* (p. 292), with a *t* of 5.10 and four degrees of freedom we find that our *t* is reliable at the 0.01 level ($P = < 0.01$). We thus reject our null hypothesis (that there is no difference between the population means of the two groups) and conclude that the groups differ reliably. If these were real data we would note that the mean for the reading-reciting group is higher and conclude that the hypothesis is confirmed.

Incidentally, in the case of the matched-groups design, the independence assumption for the *t*-test takes a slightly different form than that on page 116; the assumption is that the values of *D* are independent. In previous designs, each value of *X* had to be independent of each other value of *X*. In this design, however, the values of *X* are not independent—they are correlated because of our matching. But our independence assumption remains tenable because the *difference* between the values of *X* is independent.[3]

___
[3] A more precise statement of the independence assumption is that the treatment effects and the error are independent; that is, in terms of the symbols used for the fourth assumption, *I* and *E* are independent (page 116).

Selecting the Matching Variable

Recall that in matching participants we have attempted to equate our two groups with respect to their mean values on the dependent variable. In other words, we selected some initial measure of ability by which to match participants so that the two groups are essentially equal on this measure. If the matching variable is highly correlated with the dependent-variable scores, our matching has been successful, for in this event we largely equate the groups on their dependent-variable values by using the indirect measure of the matching variable. If the scores on the matching variable and the dependent variable do not correlate to a noticeable extent, however, then our matching is not successful. In short, the degree to which the matching-variable values and the dependent-variable values correlate is an indication of our success in matching.

How can we find a matching variable that correlates highly with our dependent variable? It might be possible to use the dependent variable itself. For example, we might seek to compare two methods of throwing darts at a target. What could be better as an initial measure by which to match the participants than dart throwing itself? We could have all participants throw darts for five trials and use scores on those five trials as a basis for pairing them off into two groups. Then we would compare groups on the dependent-variable measure of dart throwing after training by the two methods. If the initial measures from the first five trials of dart throwing correlate highly with the later dependent-variable measure of dart throwing, our matching would be successful. Since both the initial matching scores and the later dependent-variable measure scores are both on the task of dart throwing, the correlation between them should be high. In short, *an initial measure of the dependent-variable is the best possible criterion by which to match individuals to form two equivalent groups prior to the administration of the experimental treatment.*

However, it is not always feasible to match participants on an initial measure of the dependent variable. Suppose, for instance, that the dependent variable is a measure of rapidity in solving a problem. If practice on the problem is first given to obtain matching scores, then everyone would know the answer when it is administered later as a dependent variable. Or consider when we create an artificial situation to see how people react under stress. Using the same artificial situation to take initial measures for the purpose of matching individuals would destroy its novelty. In such cases we must find other measures that are highly correlated with dependent-variable performance. In the problem-solving example we might give the participants a different, but similar, problem to solve and match on that. Or, if our dependent variable is a list of problems to solve, we might select half of that list to use as a matching variable and use the other half as a dependent variable.

We have said that a matched-groups design should be used only if the matching and dependent variables correlate highly. To determine that a high correlation exists between these two measures, you might consult previous studies in which these or similar measures were empirically correlated. Of course, you should be as sure as possible that a similar correlation value holds for your participants with the specific techniques that you use. Or you might conduct a pilot study in which you make a number of measures on some participants, including your dependent-variable measures. Selection of the measure most highly correlated with the dependent variable would afford a fairly good criterion, if it is sufficiently high. If it is too low, you should pursue other matching possibilities or consider abandoning the matched-groups design.

One procedural disadvantage of matching occurs in many cases. When using initial trials on a learning task as a matching variable, you need to bring the participants into the laboratory to obtain the data on which to match them. Then, after computations have been made and the matched groups formed, the participants must be brought back for the administration of the indepen-

dent variable. The requirement that people be present twice in the laboratory is sometimes troublesome. It is more convenient to use measures that are already available, such as intelligence test scores or college board scores. It is also easier to administer group tests, such as intelligence or personality tests, which can be accomplished in the classroom. On the basis of such tests appropriate students can be selected and assigned to groups before they enter the laboratory.

Entering our table of t (Table A-1 in Appendix A) with a value of 2.53 and 4 df, we can see that a t of 2.776 is required to be reliable at the 0.05 level. Hence we cannot reject the null hypothesis and thus cannot assert that variation in anxiety level resulted in different performance at the difficult choice points. In fact, we can even observe that the direction of the mean is counter to that of the prediction; that is, the low-anxiety group actually made more errors than did the high-anxiety group.

Which Design to Use: Randomized Groups or Matched Groups?

Sometimes the results from a randomized-groups design seem unreasonable, and the experimenter wonders whether random assignment actually resulted in equivalent groups. An advantage of the matched-groups design is that the matching pretests assure approximate equality of the two groups prior to the start of the experiment. That equality is not helpful, however, unless it is equality as far as the dependent variable is concerned. Hence, if the matching variable is highly correlated with the dependent variable, then the equality of groups is beneficial. If not, then it is not beneficial—in fact, it can be detrimental. To understand this, note a general disadvantage of the matching design. Recall that the equation for computing degrees of freedom is $n - 1$. The equation for degrees of freedom with the randomized-groups design is $N - 2$. Therefore, when using the matched-groups design you have fewer degrees of freedom available than with the randomized-groups design, assuming equal numbers of participants in both designs. For instance, if there are seven participants in each group, $n = 7$ and $N = 14$. With the matched-groups design, we would have $7 - 1 = 6$ degrees of freedom, whereas for the randomized-groups design we would have $14 - 2 = 12$. We may also recall that the greater the number of degrees of freedom available, the smaller will be the value of t required for statistical reliability, other things being equal. For this reason the matched-groups design suffers a disadvantage compared with the randomized-groups design. Thus a given t might indicate a reliable mean difference with the randomized-groups design but not with the matched-groups design. Suppose that $t = 2.05$ with 16 participants per group, regardless of the design used. With a matched-group design we would have 15 *df* and find that a t of 2.131 is required for reliability at the 0.05 level; hence, the t is not reliable. But with the 30 *df* available with randomized groups, we need only 2.042 for reliability at the 0.05 level.

To summarize this point concerning the choice of a matched-groups or a randomized-groups design—an advantage of the former is that we help assure equality of groups if there is a positive correlation between the matching variable and the dependent variable. On the other hand, one loses degrees of freedom when using the matched-groups design; half as many degrees of freedom are available with it as with the randomized-groups design. Therefore, if the correlation is large enough to more than offset the loss of degrees of freedom, then one should use the matched-groups design.[4] If it is not, then the randomized-groups design should be

used.[5] In short, *if you are to use the matched-groups design, you should be rather sure that the correlation between your matching and your dependent variable is fairly high and positive.*

At this point a bright student might say: "Look here, you have made so much about this correlation between the matching and the dependent variable, and I understand the problem. You say to try to find some previous evidence that a high correlation exists. But maybe this correlation doesn't hold up in our own experiment. I think I've got this thing licked. Let's match our participants on what we think is a good variable and then actually compute the correlation. If we find that the correlation is not sufficiently high, then let's forget that we matched participants and simply run a t-test for a randomized-groups design. If we do this, we can't lose; either the correlation is pretty high and we offset our loss of degrees of freedom using the matched-groups design, or it is too low so we use a randomized-groups design and don't lose our degrees of freedom."

"This student," we might say, "is thinking, and that's good. But the thinking is wrong." An extended discussion of what is wrong with the thinking must be left to a course in statistics, but we can say that the error is similar to that previously referred to in setting the probability level for t as a criterion for rejecting the null hypothesis. There we said that the experimenter may set whatever level is desired, *providing it is set* before *the conduct of the experiment.* Analogously, *the experimenter may select whatever design is desired, providing it is selected* before *the experiment is conducted.* In either case *the decision must be adhered to.* If one chooses a matched-groups design, there is also a mortgage to a certain type of statistical test (e.g., the matched t-test, which has a certain probability attached to its results). If one changes the design, the

---

[4] Note that if the number of participants in a group is large (e.g., if $n = 30$), then one can afford to lose degrees of freedom by matching. That is, there is but a small difference between the value of t required for reliability at any given level with a large *df*. Hence one would not lose much by matching participants even if the correlation between the independent and dependent variables is zero. The loss of *df* consideration is therefore only an argument against the matched-groups design when n is relatively small.

[5] If you are further interested in this matter, a technical elaboration of these statements was offered in the chapter appendix of previous editions of this book. That rather labored discussion was eliminated here to help the student move along to higher-priority matters.

probability that can be assigned to the t through the use of the t table is disturbed. If you decide to use a matched-groups design, that decision must be adhered to. Perhaps the following experience might be consoling to you in case you ever find yourself in the unlikely situation described. I once used a matched-groups design for which previous research had yielded a correlation between the matching and the dependent variable of 0.72—an excellent opportunity to use a matched-groups design. However, it turned out that the correlation was -0.24 for the data collected. And, as we shall see in the next section, a negative correlation *decreases* the value of t. Consequently, not only were degrees of freedom lost, but the value of t was actually decreased.[6]

In conclusion, the matched-groups design can be quite useful in selected situations, but its disadvantages can be sizable. In the past it has been used quite frequently, perhaps because of the intuitive security it gave because it resulted in equivalent groups, but it is now less popular and more remote in the researchers' arsenal of experimental designs.

Error Variance and the Matched-Groups Design

The generalized equation for the t-test that is appropriate for both the two-independent-groups design and the two-matched-groups design is presented as Equation 9-4.

$$t = \frac{\overline{X}_1 - \overline{X}_2}{\sqrt{\dfrac{s_1^2}{n_1} + \dfrac{s_2^2}{n_2} - 2\,(r_{12})\left(\dfrac{s_1}{\sqrt{n_1}}\right)\left(\dfrac{s_2}{\sqrt{n_2}}\right)}}$$

___

[6] Another disadvantage of matching is that there is a statistical regression effect if the matching involves two different populations. The regression effect is a statistical artifact that occurs in repeated testings such that the value of the second test score regresses toward the mean of the population. This effect may suggest that a change in dependent-variable scores exists when in fact there is none.

Recall that the denominator of Equation 9-4 represents the error variance, the size of which is determined by the variances of the two groups (s_1^2 *and* s_2^2), the number of participants in each group (n_1 and n_2), and the value of the correlation r_{12}. The value of r_{12} is determined by the correlation between the matching variable and the dependent variable in the study.[7] We may note that from the variances we subtract r_{12} (and also s_1 and s_2, but these need not concern us here). Without being concerned with the technical matters here, the value of r_{12} is an indication of the size of the correlation between our matching and our dependent-variable scores. Any subtraction from the variances of the two groups will result in a smaller denominator with, as we said, an attendant increase in t. Hence, if the correlation between the matching variable and the dependent variable is large and positive, we may note that the denominator is decreased.

By way of illustration, assume that the difference between the means of the two groups is 5 and that there are nine participants in each group (n_1 and n_2 both equal 9). Further, assume that s_1 and s_2 are both 3 (hence s_1^2 *and* s_2^2 are both 9) and that r_{12} is 0.70. Substituting these values in Equation 9-4 we obtain

$$t = \frac{5}{\sqrt{\dfrac{9}{9} + \dfrac{9}{9} - 2(0.70)\left(\dfrac{3}{\sqrt{9}}\right)\left(\dfrac{3}{\sqrt{9}}\right)}}$$

$$= 6.49$$

It should now be apparent that the larger the positive value of r_{12}, the larger will be the term that is subtracted from the variances of the two groups. In an extreme case of this illustration, in which $r_{12} = 1.0$, we may note that we would subtract 2.00 from the sum of the variances (2.00); this leaves a denominator of zero, in which case t might be considered to be infinitely large. On the other hand, suppose that r_{12} is rather small, say

___

[7] A more extensive consideration of the nature of r_{12} was presented in earlier editions of this book.

0.10. In this case we would merely subtract 0.20 from 2.00, and the denominator would be only slightly reduced. Or, if $r_{12} = 0$, then zero would be subtracted from the variances, not reducing them at all. The lesson should now be clear: *The larger the value of r_{12} (and hence the larger the value of the correlation between the matching variable and the dependent variable), the larger is the value of t.*

One final consideration of the value of r_{12} is what the effect of a negative correlation would be on the value of t. Recall that a negative correlation *increases* the denominator, thus decreasing t. In this case, instead of subtracting from the variances, we would have to add to them ("a minus times a minus gives us a plus"). Furthermore, the larger the negative correlation, the larger our denominator becomes. For example, suppose that in the previous example instead of having a value of $r_{12} = 0.70$, we had $r_{12} = -0.70$. In this case we can see that our computed value of t would decrease from 6.49 to 2.72. That is,

$$t = \frac{5}{\sqrt{\dfrac{9}{9} + \dfrac{9}{9} - 2(-0.70)\left(\dfrac{3}{\sqrt{9}}\right)\left(\dfrac{3}{\sqrt{9}}\right)}}$$
$$= 2.72$$

We previously said that Equation 9-4 is a generalized equation applicable to either of the two designs that we have discussed. One might ask, however, in what way it is applicable to the randomized-groups design, for it contains a correlation term and we have not referred to any correlation when using it. It is absurd, for instance, to talk about the correlation between pairs of participants on the dependent variable when using the randomized-groups design, for by its very nature participants are not paired. The answer to this is that since participants have not been paired, the correlation between any random pairing of participants in the long run is zero. That is, if we randomly selected any participant in an experimental group, paired that value with a randomly selected participant in the control groups, and con-

tinued this procedure for all participants, we would expect the correlation between the dependent-variable values to be zero (or more precisely, the correlation would not be reliably different from zero). There simply would be no reason to expect other than a zero correlation since the participants were not paired together on more than a chance basis. When using the randomized-groups design, we assume that r_{12} of Equation 9-4 is zero, and, being zero, the term that includes r_{12} "drops out." Thus Equation 9-4 assumes the following form for the randomized-groups design:

$$(9\text{-}5) \qquad t = \frac{\overline{X}_1 - \overline{X}_2}{\sqrt{\dfrac{s_1^2}{n_1} + \dfrac{s_2^2}{n_2}}}$$

One Final Note Although we have labeled the type of design discussed in this chapter as the *matched-groups design*, we have limited our discussion to the case of two groups. The two groups may be said to be matched because we paired participants with similar scores. Since all participants were paired, the groups had to be approximately equivalent. This fact may be determined by comparing the distribution of matching values for the two groups. The best such comparison would probably be to compare the means and standard deviations of the two groups. We would expect to find that the two groups would be quite similar on these two measures.

The technique of pairing participants together is a specific design that results in matched groups. For this reason it is also called the **paired-groups design**. The two-matched-groups design (or, if you prefer, the two-paired-groups design) implies that the design could be extended to more than two groups, which it can.

EXPERIMENTAL DESIGNS FOR REPEATED TREATMENTS USING GROUPS

Between- vs. Within-Groups Designs. The two-randomized-groups design, the more-than-two-randomized-groups design, the factorial design, and the matched-groups design are all examples of **between-groups designs**. This is so because there are two or more values of the independent variable and *one* value is administered to *each* group in the experiment. We then calculate the mean dependent-variable values for each group, compute the mean difference *between* groups, and thus assess the effect of varying the independent variable. An alternative to a between-groups design is a **repeated-treatments** or **within-groups design** *in which two or more values of the independent variable are administered*, in turn, *to the same participants*. A dependent-variable value is then obtained for each participant's performance under each value of the independent variable; comparisons of these dependent-variable values under the different experimental treatments then allow assessment of the effects of varying the independent variable.

In short, for between-groups designs we compare dependent-variable values *between* groups who have been treated differently. In repeated-treatment designs, the same individuals are treated differently at different times, and we compare their scores as a function of different experimental treatments. For example, suppose that we wish to ascertain the effects of a certain drug on perceptual accuracy. For a between-groups design we would probably administer the drug to an experimental group and a placebo to a control group. A comparison between the means of the two groups on a test of perceptual accuracy would determine possible effects of the drug. But, for a repeated-treatments design, we would administer the test of perceptual accuracy to the sample people: (1) when they are under the influence of the drug, and (2) when they are in a normal condition. If the means of the same people change as they go from one condition to the other, we ascribe the change in behavior to the drug, if controls are adequate.

The Two-Repeated-Treatments Design

We already have some familiarity with the *t*-test for matched groups, so this provides us with a good basis for studying the simplest kind of repeated-treatments design. In this case a measure is obtained for each participant when performing under one experimental condition; then the same measure is taken again when the participant performs under a second experimental condition. A mean difference between each pair of measures is computed and tested to determine whether it is reliably different from zero.[8] If this difference is not reliable, then the variation of the independent variable probably did not result in behavioral changes. Otherwise, it did. For example, consider an experiment in which the hypothesis was that individuals subvocalize when they write words (just as when they read). The measure of subvocalization was chin electromyograms (EMG) in students engaged in handwriting. (*Electromyograms* are covert response measures of the electrical activity of muscles.) The students first relaxed and then either drew ovals or wrote words (in counterbalanced order). The motor task of drawing ovals is not a language task and thus served as a control condition. The question was: Are speech muscles covertly more active while writing words than during a comparable nonlanguage activity? To answer this question, amplitude of chin EMG during resting was subtracted from that during writing for each person. Then each individual's increase in chin EMG amplitude while drawing ovals was similarly measured. As shown in Table 9-8, there was an increase in amplitude of covert speech responding of 23.5 μV (μV = microvolt, which is one-millionth of a volt) during writing for student number 1; the comparable increase while drawing ovals was 12.0 μV—and so on for the other students. The question is: Is there a reliably greater increase during the writing period than during the "ovals" period? To answer this question we compute the difference in response measures; for student number 1 the difference is 11.5 μV. To conduct a statistical test, we compute the sum of

---

[8]The design popularly referred to as the *pretest-posttest* design fits this paradigm.

these differences and the sum of the squared differences, as at the bottom of Table 9-8. If the mean of these difference values is reliably greater than zero, we can assert that variation of the experimental tasks produced a change in covert speech behavior. The appropriate test is the matched *t*-test, in which $\overline{X}_D$ is the difference between the means of the two conditions.

$$(9\text{-}6) \qquad t = \frac{\overline{X}_D}{\sqrt{\dfrac{\Sigma D^2 - (\Sigma D)^2/n}{n(n-1)}}}$$

Substitution of the appropriate values from Table 9-8 results in

$$t = \frac{34.91}{\sqrt{\dfrac{28{,}578.32 - (384.00)^2/11}{11\,(11-1)}}} = 2.97$$

Also, $df = n - 1 = 11 - 1 = 10$.

Referring to Table A-1 in Appendix A, we find that a $t = 2.97$ (with 10 *df*) indicates that the mean of the differences between the two conditions is reliably different from zero; that is, $P < 0.05$ (P actually would have been less than 0.02 had we set this as our criterion). Thus the conclusion is that the students emitted a reliably larger amplitude of covert speech responding during silent handwriting than during a comparable motor task that was nonlanguage in nature (drawing ovals). The interpretation of this finding is that individuals engage in covert *language* behavior when receiving and processing language stimuli (words).[9]

Changes From A Baseline Condition. Incidentally, the question on which we focused was: Is there a greater change in the dependent variable when the participants engaged in task A than in task B? Often, as in this case, performance in the two tasks is ascertained by comparison with some standard condition, such as during a resting state. In this event another, but related, question can also be asked, namely, did performance under condition A (and B) change reliably from the standard condition? The data in Table 9-8 can also provide answers to these questions. Since the values under "Handwriting" and "Drawing Ovals" are themselves difference values, they can also be analyzed by the *t*-test. That is, a measure was obtained for each person during rest, and then when writing. The score 23.5 for student number 1 was thus obtained by subtracting the resting level from the level during writing. To determine whether there was a reliable *increase* in covert speech behavior when the students changed from resting to writing, one merely needs to compute the sum of the values under the "Handwriting" column, the mean of that value for the numerator, and the sum of the squares of these scores. Then these values can be substituted into Equation 9-6 to ascertain whether the resulting *t* value is reliable. Is it? How about the values for the "ovals" condition?

Several-Repeated-Treatments Designs

The repeated-treatments design in which two experimental treatments are adminis-

TABLE 9-8 Changes in Chin Electromyograms (μV) During Handwriting and While Drawing Ovals (from McGuigan, 1970)

Student	Handwriting	Drawing Ovals	Difference
1	23.5	12.0	11.5
2	.3	5.8	− 5.5
3	86.8	52.8	34.0
4	33.3	− 29.3	62.6
5	46.4	22.9	23.5
6	− 1.6	− 24.1	22.5
7	26.2	− 20.7	46.9
8	6.6	− 6.0	.6
9	16.9	− 13.1	30.0
10	43.6	22.6	21.0
11	143.6	6.7	136.9

$$\Sigma D = 384.00$$
$$\Sigma D^2 = 28{,}578.34$$

[9] A compatible interpretation resulted from a comparison with the different nonlanguage motor task of drawing musical clefs.

tered to the same participants can be extended indefinitely. Let us briefly illustrate one extension by considering a classic experiment in which four values of the independent variable were administered to the same group of participants. First, all participants experienced a condition (1) in which no lists of words were studied. Then, in condition (2), they studied two lists of paired adjectives; in condition (3), four lists of paired adjectives, and finally, in condition (4), six such lists. Following these four conditions, they all completely learned a different list of paired adjectives. After 25 minutes had elapsed, they were tested for recall on this different list. The dependent variable was the number of those paired adjectives that they could correctly recall. The results are presented in Figure 9-6, where it can be noted that the fewer the number of prior lists studied, the better was the recall. As you perhaps noted, this was an experiment on proactive inhibition (interference); that is, when we study something and then learn some other (related) material, the first learned material inhibits the recall of the later learned material. Put another way, ear-

lier learned material proactively interferes with the retention of later learned material, and in this experiment the greater the number of prior lists learned, the greater the amount of proactive inhibition. Regardless of the subject matter findings, the point here is that participants can be administered a number of experimental treatments by means of the repeated-treatments design.

Statistical Analysis for More Than Two Repeated Treatments

To illustrate the statistical analysis for a four-conditions repeated-treatments design consider a study of a person's efficiency of internally processing information. Each person serves under each condition of A, B, C, and D. Assume that the dependent-variable scores are those in Table 9-9. The statistical procedure to use is an analysis of variance with F-tests. For this, we first compute the total sums of squares (SS), as before. Then we analyze that total SS into three components: (1) among conditions, (2) among students, and (3) an error term (which will be the denominator of the F-tests).

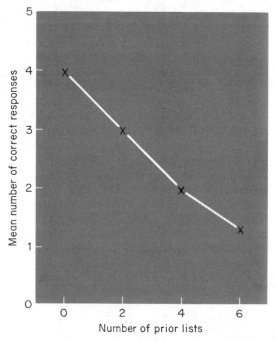

FIGURE 9-6 A repeated-treatments design in which participants learned under four different verbal list conditions. The larger the number of lists studied before learning, the greater was the amount of proactive inhibition (after Underwood, 1945).

TABLE 9-9 Assumed Dependent-Variable Values for a Repeated-Treatments Design in Which Each Person Serves Under All Four Conditions

Student	Information Processing Condition				
	A	*B*	*C*	*D*	Σ*S*
1	4	2	8	3	17
2	14	7	5	13	39
3	6	6	6	10	28
4	11	3	8	4	26
5	7	5	7	5	24
6	10	4	8	9	31
7	9	4	8	7	28
Σ*X*:	61	31	50	51	193
Σ*X*²:	599	155	366	449	

The equation for computing total sums of squares is

$$(9\text{-}7) \quad \text{total } SS = (\Sigma X_1^2 + \Sigma X_2^2 + \Sigma X_3^2 + \Sigma X_4^2$$
$$- \frac{(\Sigma X_1 + \Sigma X_2 + \Sigma X_3 + \Sigma X_4)^2}{N}$$

The only difference between this application of Equation 9-7 and Equation 8-1 is that, in a repeated-treatments design, N is the number of participants multiplied by the number of conditions. Hence, for this example, four conditions multiplied by seven students yields $N = 28$. The other values required for Equation 9-7 have been computed and entered at the bottom of Table 9-9. Substituting them, we compute the total sums of squares as follows:

$$\text{total } SS = (599 + 155 + 366 + 499)$$
$$- \frac{(61 + 31 + 50 + 51)^2}{28}$$
$$= 238.68$$

To compute the among-conditions SS we employ Equation 9-8.

$$(9\text{-}8) \quad \text{among-conditions } SS =$$
$$\frac{(\Sigma X_1)^2}{n_1} + \frac{(\Sigma X_2)^2}{n_2} + \frac{(\Sigma X_3)^2}{n_3} + \frac{(\Sigma X_4)^2}{n_4}$$

$$- \frac{(\Sigma X_1 + \Sigma X_2 + \Sigma X_3 + \Sigma X_4)^2}{N}$$

Making the appropriate substitutions from Table 9-9, we find

among-conditions $SS =$

$$\frac{(61)^2}{7} + \frac{(31)^2}{7} + \frac{(50)^2}{7} + \frac{(51)^2}{7}$$
$$- \frac{(61 + 31 + 50 + 51)^2}{28} = 67.25$$

To compute a sum of squares among students, we use Equation 9-9.

$$(9\text{-}9) \quad \text{among-students } SS =$$
$$\frac{(\Sigma S_1)^2}{K} - \frac{(\Sigma S_2)^2}{K} + \ldots + \frac{(\Sigma S_7)^2}{K}$$
$$- \frac{(\Sigma X_1 + \Sigma X_2 + \Sigma X_3 + \Sigma X_4)^2}{N}$$

Note in Table 9-9 that we have computed a sum of the dependent-variable values for each student in the column labeled "Σ*S*." For instance, the total of the scores for student 1 (Σ*S*) is 17. The quantity $(\Sigma S_1)^2/K$ is computed for each participant in the experiment. (K is the number of conditions; therefore $K = 4$.) In Equation 9-9 we have indicated that there are seven such quantities, but if you had nine participants, there would be nine such factors [i.e., $(\Sigma S_9)^2/K$]. Similarly, in the last quantity, the value Σ*X* is computed for each condition, where we have four such values; if you had three conditions (only A, B, and C) there would be only three values of Σ*X* in the last quantity of Equations 9-7, 9-8 and 9-9. Substituting these values from Table 9-9 into Equation 9-9.

among-students $SS =$

$$\frac{(17)^2}{4} + \frac{(39)^2}{4} + \frac{(28)^2}{4} + \frac{(26)^2}{4}$$
$$+ \frac{(24)^2}{4} + \frac{(31)}{4} + \frac{(28)^2}{4}$$

$$- \frac{(61 + 31 + 50 + 51)^2}{28}$$

$$= \frac{(289)}{4} + \frac{1521}{4} + \frac{784}{4} + \frac{676}{4} + \frac{576}{4}$$

$$+ \frac{961}{4} = \frac{784}{4}$$

$$- \frac{37,249}{28}$$

$$= 72.25 + 380.25 + 196.00 + 169.00$$

$$+ 144.00 + 240.25 + 196.00 - 1,330.32$$

$$= 67.43$$

The error term sum of squares is obtained by subtraction, just as was done for the previous error term labeled "within-groups":

$$(9\text{-}10) \quad \text{error } SS = \text{total } SS$$
$$- \text{among-conditions } SS$$
$$- \text{among-students } SS$$
$$= 238.68 - 67.25 - 67.43$$
$$= 104.00$$

This completes the computations of the sums of squares for a repeated-treatments design in which there are more than two treatments. The values are summarized under *SS* in Table 9-10.

The equations for computing degrees of freedom are

$$(9\text{-}11) \quad \text{total } df = N - 1 = 27$$

$$(9\text{-}12) \quad \text{among conditions} = K - 1$$
$$= 4 - 1 = 3$$

$$(9\text{-}13) \quad \text{among students} = n - 1$$
$$= 7 - 1 = 6$$

TABLE 9-10 Summary of Analysis of Variance for a Repeated-Treatments Design

Source of Variation	SS	df	MS	F
Among conditions	67.25	3	22.42	3.88*
Among students	67.43	6	11.25	1.94
Error	104.00	18	5.78	
Total	238.68	27		

*$P < 0.05$.

$$(9\text{-}14) \quad \text{error term} = (K - 1)(n - 1)$$
$$= 3 \times 6 = 18$$

Note that the equation for error term *df* is merely the product of those for the among *df*. As before you can also check yourself by adding the component sums of squares to make sure that they equal the total (238.68) in Table 9-10, and, similarly, for degrees of freedom (27). Obviously the mean square and *F* values do not sum to anything sensible.

Next we need to compute our mean squares and then conduct our *F*-tests. As before, we divide the sums of squares by the appropriate number of degrees of freedom to obtain the mean squares, for example, for among conditions 67.25/3 = 22.42, as in Table 9-10. To conduct the *F*-test for among conditions, we divide that mean square by the error term, namely, 22.42/5.78 = 3.88. Similarly, the value of *F* among students = 11.24/5.78 = 1.94. These values will tell us whether there is a reliable difference among conditions and among students, respectively. First, to test among conditions we note that the *F*-test was based on three degrees of freedom for the numerator and 18 degrees for the denominator; entering Table A-2 with these values, we find that our *F* must exceed 3.16 to indicate statistical reliability at the 0.05 level. Since our computed value of 3.88 does exceed that tabled value (as indicated by the asterisk in Table 9-10), we can conclude that variation of internal information processing conditions did reliably influence the dependent variable. To test for a reliable difference among students, we enter Table A-2 with 6 and 18 degrees of freedom to find a tabled value of 2.51 at the 0.05 level. Since our *F* ratio of 1.94 is less than that tabled value, we conclude that the among-students source of variation is not reliable—that there is no reliable difference among students on the dependent-variable measure.

This concludes our statistical analysis for a repeated-treatments design with more than two conditions. Implicitly, we have tested two null hypotheses: (1) that there is no true difference among the means of the four treatments, and (2) that there is no true difference among the means of the seven students. We thus have rejected the first null hypothesis but have failed to reject the second. The empirical conclusion is that variation of internal information processing conditions reliably affects the dependent-variable measure. However, there was no reliable difference in the performance among the participants. We may add only that if you are interested in an alternative set of null hypotheses for the independent variable, you would use a different statistical analysis. For instance, if you were interested in certain pairwise comparisons, you would not have needed to conduct an analysis of variance but could have gone directly to paired *t*-tests between those conditions, using Equation 9-6: You would have used the procedure for planned comparisons. Similarly, if you were interested in all possible pairwise comparisons, you would follow the procedure for post hoc comparisons, adjusting your nominal levels of reliability with the Bonferroni test, or some other multiple-comparison procedure.

Statistical Assumptions

For completeness, we must briefly mention the statistical assumptions for a repeated-treatments design because they are different from those for between-groups designs. If you have two groups, the assumption of independence is that the values of *D* as in Table 9-8 are independent. This is obviously not a demanding assumption because it merely means that the dependent-variable values for each participant are not dependent on (influenced by) those of other participants. For more than two treatments, however, there is an additional assumption that can be stated in several ways. While it should be studied more thoroughly in later courses, briefly, the new assumption holds that there is no reliable interaction between the row and treatment variables (here the rows are the seven subjects and the treatments are the four experimental condi-

tions). If there is a reliable interaction, this means that any covariances between pairs of treatment levels are heterogeneous (different)—that is, this design assumes that the population covariances for all pairs of treatment levels are homogeneous. To get an approximate idea of what this means, it states that the trend is approximately the same from treatment to treatment. Therefore, as you go from treatment A to treatment B, the scores are about the same; as you go from treatment B to C, they are similarly homogeneous; and likewise as you go from C to D. Statistics books provide you with methods for precisely testing whether you violated this assumption. If you did, there are corrections that can be used, such as *Box's correction*, which, very simply, is an adjustment of your degrees of freedom.[10]

Order of Participants in Repeated-Treatments Designs

This concerns the assignment of participants to the order of conditions; that is, how do you determine whether a participant number 1 experiences condition A first, B second, and so on? There are two feasible answers: You could randomly assign the order of conditions such that, for instance, for participant number 1 you randomly determine the order of A, B, C, and D, and similarly for the other students. Then you would simply align their dependent-variable values in columns such as in Table 9-10, regardless of the order in which they were experienced; or you could counterbalance order of conditions, as discussed in Chapter 4. Each procedure has advantages and disadvan-

---

[10]Assuming a fixed-effects model, a complete and more precise statement of the assumptions is: (1) that the observations in the cells are randomly selected from the population, (2) that the populations for those cells are normally distributed, (3) that the variances of those populations are homogeneous, and (4) that the row and column effects are additive—that is, the scores within each row have the same trend over conditions. If 4 is true, there is no reliable interaction between row and treatment conditions. Absence of an interaction means that the covariances between all pairs of treatment levels are equal.

tages, as we discussed in Chapter 4. Furthermore, while it is methodologically sound to randomize the order of the treatments, this random-order procedure may increase the error variance relative to that of counterbalancing.

Evaluation of Repeated-Treatments Designs

There are advantages and disadvantages of repeated-treatments and between-groups designs. Three straightforward advantages of the repeated-treatments design are as follows:

1. Uses Participants More Economically. The repeated-treatments design is far more economical of participants since there are dependent-variable values for all of them under *all* treatment conditions; for example, with two groups (two treatments) in a between-groups design there would be 20 participants in each group for a total of 40 dependent-variable values. But in a repeated-treatments design with all participants serving under both conditions you could: (1) study only 20 participants to obtain that same number of dependent-variable values (namely, 40), or (2) you could still study 40 participants but have 80 dependent values for each treatment condition.

2. Saves Laboratory Time. The repeated-treatments design is also relatively advantageous if your experimental procedure demands considerable time or energy in preparing to collect your data. For example, for psychophysiological research it takes a fair amount of time and patience to attach electrodes properly on a person; similarly, for neuropsychological research you may make a sizable investment in implanting brain electrodes in animals. By using the repeated-treatments design, you also decrease the amount of time required to administer instructions, particularly if the experiment is a complicated one. Once you make such investments in your preparation, you should collect numerous data, probably by studying your participant under a variety of conditions.

3. Reduces Error Variance. The most frequently cited advantage is that the error variance is less than with a repeated-treatments design than a comparable between-groups design. As we have seen, matching participants on an initial measure can increase the precision of your experiment. The same logic applies here. By taking two measures on the same participant, you can reduce your error variance in proportion to the extent to which the two measures are correlated. Put another way, one reason that the error variance may be large in a between-groups design is that it includes the extent to which individuals differ. But because you repeat your measures on the same participants in the within-groups design, you remove individual differences from your error variance. Hence, rather than having an independent control group, each individual serves as his or her own control.[11]

You are probably getting suspicious by now, wondering what the disadvantages are.

1. Treatment Effects May Not Be Reversible. If one treatment comes first, it may not be reasonable to present the other. For instance, if you inject RNA into an organism and need a control condition that does not receive RNA, you must use a between-groups design; that is, you could not first administer RNA, test the animals, and then take RNA out of them and retest them. The effect of administering RNA is irreversible.[12] *An* **irreversible effect** *is one in which a*

---

[11] However, although it is true that the dependent-variable values for participants will change less under repeated treatments relative to values with between-treatments designs, they still have a sizable error component; that is, individuals behave with some similarity when repeatedly tested under different conditions, but they still react differently at different times, even if they are retested under precisely the same conditions. They change with respect to paying attention, what they are thinking, amount of fidgeting, and so on, all of which contribute error to the dependent-variable measure.

[12] You might ask, "Why not test all the rats first *without* RNA and *then* inject them?" The problem is that there would be order effects such that practice would be confounded with injection; to control for order effects, you cannot counterbalance because, once again, you cannot remove the RNA.

given set of operations is performed in such a way that subsequent measurements are biased by the effects of those original operations.

2. There May Be Asymmetrical Transfer Effects. There may be problems with the order in which the experimental treatments are presented to the same participants. The purpose of counterbalancing, we have said, is to control order (practice and fatigue) effects—to distribute these extraneous variables equally over all experimental conditions, But, we pointed out, by thus controlling these variables, you might inherit problems of a different sort, namely, asymmetrical transfer effects. Hence, if you use a counterbalanced design, you should demonstrate (by appropriate statistical analysis) that there was no differential transfer among your conditions. On the other hand, if you expect ("fear" might be a better word) asymmetrical transfer effects, you can use the methodologically sound procedure of randomization of the order of the treatments. To emphasize, if you have three treatments (A, B, and C) and all participants are to receive all treatments, then you randomly determine the order of A, B, and C for each participant.

3. Repeated-Treatments and Between-Groups Designs May Yield Contradictory Results. The conditions in a repeated-treatments design may interact with each other. For example, the experience of serving under condition A may influence the dependent-variable values for participants who also serve under condition B. Let us be clear about the seriousness of this problem. If you assume that one condition does not interact with another, when in fact it does, your conclusions can be drastically distorted. For example, let us reexamine Ebbinghaus's classic forgetting curve. Recall that he memorized lists of nonsense syllables and later tested himself for recall. Implicit in Ebbinghaus's assumptions, as we look back from our present vantage point, was that his treatments did not interact to affect his independent variable. Put more simply, the assumption was that the learning of one list of nonsense

syllables did not affect the recall of another. His results indicated that most of what we learn is rapidly forgotten; for example, after one day, according to Ebbinghaus's forgetting curve, about 66 percent is forgotten. The consequence of this research, incidentally, has been sizable and long the source of discouragement to educators (and students). However, we now know that the basic assumption of Ebbinghaus's experimental design is not tenable; that is, there is considerable competition for recall among various items that have been learned. Thus, where there are no previous lists learned, little is forgotten. For example, in Figure 9-7 we can see that, when there were no previous lists learned, recall after 24 hours hovered around 80 percent. When, on the other hand, some twenty lists had been learned, the recall 24 hours later was about 10 percent.

Underwood (1957) astutely demonstrated this defect in Ebbinghaus's design, for he showed that Ebbinghaus, by learning a large number of lists, created a condition in which he *maximized* the amount of forgetting. If fewer lists had been learned previously, forgetting would not necessarily have been so great. When many lists are learned, forgetting is great, but if there have been no previous lists learned, only about 25 percent is forgotten after one day. The lesson should be clear: By using a repeated-treatments design, Ebbinghaus gave us a highly restricted set of results that were greatly overgeneralized and that led to erroneous conclusions about forgetting. Had he used a between-groups design in which each participant learned only one list, he would have concluded that the amount forgotten was relatively small, as in Figure 9-7.

To illustrate further how the two types of designs may yield contradictory conclusions, consider an experiment in which the intensity of the conditional stimulus was varied. For this purpose both designs were used. In the between-groups design, one group received a low-intensity conditional stimulus (soft tone), while a second group received a high-intensity conditional stimulus (loud

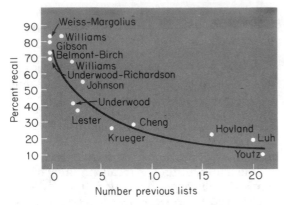

FIGURE 9-7 Illustration of conditions that interact such that the greater the number of previous lists of verbal material learned, the greater is the forgetting. If, as in a between-groups design, there were no previous lists learned, forgetting is small. However, if there had been previous lists learned as in the repeated-treatments design, forgetting is great (Underwood, 1957).

tone). For the repeated-treatments design, all participants received both values of the conditional stimulus. The question was: Did variation of the intensity of the conditional stimulus affect the strength of the conditional response? The results presented in Figure 9-8 indicate that in both experiments there was an increase in the percentage of conditional responses made to the conditional stimulus. But the slopes of the curves are dramatically different. The difference in percent of conditional responses as a function of stimulus intensity was not statistically reliable for the between-groups design ("one stimulus"), while it *was* for the within-groups design (in which the participants received "two stimuli"). In fact, the magnitude of the intensity effect is more than five times as great for the two-stimuli condition than for the one-stimulus condition. Hence the dependent-variable values were influenced by the number of conditions in which the participants served; there was an interaction between stimulus intensity and number of presentations of stimuli. Apparently the participants could compare the two stimuli and

such contrasting influenced their behavior. On the other hand, with the between-groups design the individuals could not compare the stimuli because they were presented singly, never together.

Research in other areas has also resulted in contradictory conclusions, depending on whether the researcher employed repeated-treatments or between-groups designs; for example, Pavlik and Carlton (1965) studied the effects of continuous reinforcement versus intermittent ("partial") reinforcement schedules (participants receive reinforcement on all the learning trials versus reinforcement on less than 100 percent of the trials). The usual intermittent reinforcement effects of greater resistance to extinction and higher terminal performance were found when using the between-groups design, but *not* for the within-groups design. On perhaps a more menancing dependent-variable measure, Valle (1972) found that frequency of defecation of rats was differen-

FIGURE 9-8 Percent of conditional responses during the last 60 trials depends on whether a between-groups design was used (the one-stimulus condition) versus a within-groups design (the two-stimuli condition) (after Grice and Hunter, 1964).

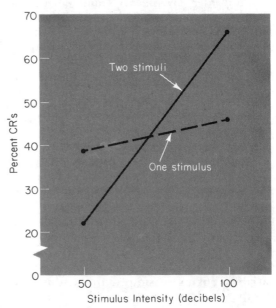

tially affected by the type of design used (repeated-treatments versus between-groups) in studying free and forced exploration.

In short, different answers may be given to the same problem depending on whether a between-groups or repeated-treatments design is used. In effect you may be studying *different phenomena* when you address the same problem.

4. There Are Controversies over Statistical Analysis. There is much disagreement as to the validity of different statistical analyses of repeated-treatments designs, such as *longitudinal designs, gains designs*, and various other designs in which repeated measures are taken on the same individual. In gains designs, improvement is sought from one testing period to another, but the amounts of these improvements are not comparable; for example, does a student who improves from an F to a C in a course manifest the same amount of gain (degree of improvement) as one who moves from a C to an A? The problem of nonindependence may also and usually does, disturb the nominal probability level of the *F*- or *t*-test. The procedure of analysis of covariance is often used wherein the dependent variable measures are adjusted for differences in pretest scores among participants, but there are great potential difficulties with the analysis of covariance. Finally, repeated-treatments designs may result in what are referred to as *unwanted range effects* which may lead to unwarranted conclusions. These matters, all beyond the present level of treatment, are merely mentioned to alert you to their importance in your future study.

A Summary Assessment

In summary, it is quite clear that there are several advantages of the repeated-treatments design over the between-groups design, and vice versa. If you do proceed with a repeated-treatments design but cannot effectively handle the control problems entailed by counter-balancing, then you can present your treatments to your participants in a random order. However, if you are not satisfied with your counterbalancing, you

probably should use a between-groups design, including the matched-groups design.

If your conditions interact to produce different dependent-variable values, then it should be clear that you would be studying different phenomena, depending on whether you use a between-groups design or a repeated-treatments design. Simply put, in a between-groups design the participants experience the condition in relative isolation. However, in a repeated-treatments design the participants experience one condition relative to another condition, which constitutes a more complex phenomenon. You simply should be clear about which phenomenon you wish to study.

The problem of how to analyze statistically various kinds of repeated-treatments designs (instances of which are variously called *pretest-posttest designs, gains designs, repeated-measures designs, longitudinal designs*, or *developmental designs*) has long constituted a major stumbling block to their proper employment. Many years ago on a very pleasant walk with Mr. Snedecor, I enjoyed listening to him consider this problem out loud. He admitted that we did not have a good solution, but that we did have to use repeated-treatments designs under some conditions. Consequently we might just as well do the best we can "for now," hoping that with continued contrasts of repeated-treatments and between-groups designs, a good solution will eventually evolve. I think we *are* making some progress in better understanding the problem.

OVERVIEW OF EXPERIMENTAL DESIGNS AND THEIR STATISTICAL TESTS

The designs in this chapter are the last experimental designs for groups to be considered in the book. In an attempt to guide you in summary fashion through the maze of group experimental designs and the statistical analyses that we have discussed, we offer you the accompanying "flow chart" (Figure 9-9) (with appreciation to Professor Ronald Webster for an earlier version).

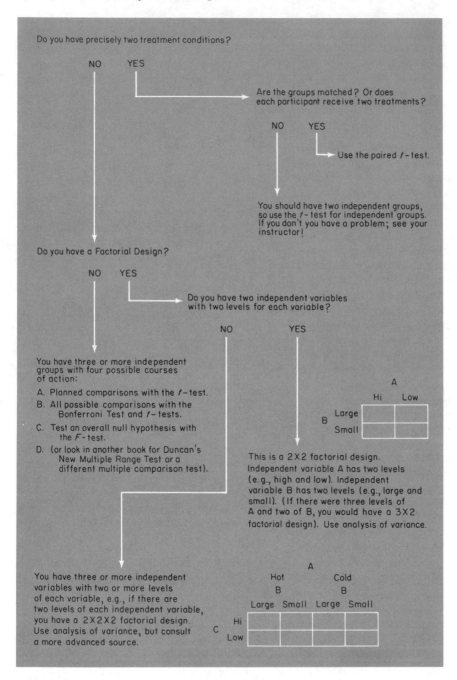

Do you have precisely two treatment conditions?

NO   YES

Are the groups matched? Or does each participant receive two treatments?

NO   YES

Use the paired *t*-test.

You should have two independent groups, so use the *t*-test for independent groups. If you don't you have a problem; see your instructor!

Do you have a Factorial Design?

NO   YES

Do you have two independent variables with two levels for each variable?

NO   YES

You have three or more independent groups with four possible courses of action:

A. Planned comparisons with the *t*-test.

B. All possible comparisons with the Bonferroni Test and *t*-tests.

C. Test an overall null hypothesis with the *F*-test.

D. (or look in another book for Duncan's New Multiple Range Test or a different multiple comparison test).

This is a 2×2 factorial design. Independent variable A has two levels (e.g., high and low). Independent variable B has two levels (e.g., large and small). (If there were three levels of A and two of B, you would have a 3×2 factorial design). Use analysis of variance.

You have three or more independent variables with two or more levels of each variable, e.g., if there are two levels of each independent variable, you have a 2×2×2 factorial design. Use analysis of variance, but consult a more advanced source.

FIGURE 9-9   A flow chart for specifying type of design and method of statistical analysis.

CHAPTER SUMMARY

I. A correlation is a relationship between variables that is important for conducting nonexperimental research and for understanding experimental research.

II. Statistical methods for determining correlations are:
   A. The Pearson product moment coefficient of correlation (r) for linear relationships.
   B. The correlation coefficient (eta, symbolized η), an index of the degree of relationship between two variables that may be linearly or curvilinearly related.

III. Linear correlation coefficients vary from $+1.$ through 0 to -1.0; the higher the absolute value of the correlation coefficient (i.e., regardless of whether it is positive or negative), the stronger the relationship between the two variables.
   A. A positive relationship indicates that as the value of one variable increases, so does the value of the other (this is a *direct* relationship).
   B. A negative relationship indicates that as the value of one variable increases, the value of the other variable decreases (this is an *inverse* relationship).
   C. A zero-order correlation coefficient indicates that the two variables are not related.

IV. A plot of data points on a graph provides a "picture" of the relationship known as the scattergram, or scatterplot.

V. The Pearson correlation coefficient is appropriate when both variables are continuous. When one or both variables are dichotomous (they are assigned one of two values, "di" referring to two), other correlation coefficients can be computed as summarized under "Dichotomized Variables."

VI. The value of r may be tested to see if it is reliably different from zero by referring to Table A-3.

VII. A cause-effect relationship is one in which an independent variable is shown systematically to affect a dependent variable in a well-controlled experiment in which the differential influences of extraneous variables are ruled out.
   A. A correlation can only suggest that:
      1. One variable may causally affect the second.
      2. The second may causally affect the first.
      3. Both are causally controlled by another variable or set of variables.

VIII. For a two-matched-groups design, participants are measured on some objective, quantified variable, and thereby paired. A member of each pair is then randomly assigned to one of two groups, and it is randomly determined which group receives which treatment.

IX. The *t*-test for paired groups can determine whether the groups reliably differ on the dependent variable.

X. If the variable on which the participants are matched and then paired into groups is not positively correlated with the dependent-variable measure, it is preferable to use a two-randomized-groups design because:
   A. You would increase error variance with the matched-groups design.
   B. You have only $n - 1$ degrees of freedom available for the matched-groups design versus $N - 2$ for the randomized-groups design.

XI. In a repeated-treatments design, the same individuals serve under different experimental conditions. By contrast, in a between-groups design, individuals serve under only one experimental condition.

XII. For a two-condition repeated-treatments design, the mean dependent-variable difference may be tested to see if it is reliably different from zero by means of the paired *t*-test.

XIII. If there are more than two repeated treatments, a special application of the analysis of variance may be used to determine whether there is a true difference among the means of the four treatment conditions' effects on the dependent variable and also whether there is a true difference among the means of the participants.

XIV. You can either randomly assign the order of the treatments for each participant or you can systematically counterbalance them.

XV. There are pluses and minuses for repeated-treatments designs.
   A. They generally require fewer participants than do between-groups designs.
   B. They are more efficient of laboratory time.

C. They may reduce error variance by using the same participant as his or her own control.
D. The treatment effects may not be reversible, invalidating the use of this design.
E. You may have trouble controlling order and interaction effects. Most seriously, a between-groups and a repeated-treatments design may give you conflicting results, which means that the problem presented to the participants may actually be different in the two designs.
F. We still are not completely satisfied with the method of statistical analysis for this type of design; it has shortcomings.

SUMMARY OF STATISTICAL COMPUTATIONS

Correlations

Assume that the following scores were obtained on two dependent-variable measures (X and Y) and that you are interested in determining whether it would suffice to record but one of them in future research:

1. First, you need to compute the following components for Equation 9-1: ΣX, ΣX^2, ΣY, ΣY^2, ΣXY, and $n = 10$.

(9-1) $\quad r_{XY} = \dfrac{n\Sigma XY - (\Sigma X)(\Sigma Y)}{\sqrt{[n\Sigma X^2 - (\Sigma X)^2][n\Sigma Y^2 - (\Sigma Y)^2]}}$

2. These values have been computed in the preceding table. We then substitute them into Equation 9-1 as follows:

$r_{XY} =$
$$\dfrac{10(120,960) - (700)(1720)}{\sqrt{[10(49,096) - (700)^2][10(299,300) - (1720)^2]}}$$

3. Performing the computations as indicated we determine that

$r_{XY} =$
$$\dfrac{1,209,600 - 1,204,000}{\sqrt{(490,960 - 490,000)(2,993,000 - 2,958,400)}}$$
$$= \dfrac{5,600}{\sqrt{(960)(34,600)}} = \dfrac{5,600}{\sqrt{(33,216,000)}}$$
$$= \dfrac{5,600}{\sqrt{5,763.33}} = 0.97$$

4. Entering Table A-3 with nine degrees of freedom ($df = N - 2$) and the correlation coefficient value of 0.97, we find that this value is reliably different from zero at the 0.01 level. Since the correlation between the two dependent variables is so high and statistically reliable, we may conclude that in future research it is sufficient to record but one of them.

Computation of t for a Two-Matched-Groups Design

Assume that two groups of participants have been matched on an initial measure as

Participant Number	Dependent Variable X	Dependent Variable Y	X^2	Y^2	XY
1	66	145	4,356	21,025	9,570
2	70	180	4,900	32,400	12,600
3	68	165	4,624	27,225	11,220
4	76	210	5,776	44,100	15,960
5	74	190	5,476	36,100	14,060
6	70	165	4,900	27,225	11,550
7	66	150	4,356	22,500	9,900
8	70	170	4,900	28,900	11,900
9	68	160	4,624	25,600	10,880
10	72	185	5,184	34,225	13,320
	$\Sigma X = 700$	$\Sigma Y = 1,720$	$\Sigma X^2 = 49,096$	$\Sigma Y^2 = 299,300$	$\Sigma XY = 120,960$

indicated, and that the following dependent-variable scores have been obtained for them.

Initial Measure	Group 1	Group 2
1	10	11
2	10	8
3	8	6
4	7	7
5	7	6
6	6	5
7	4	3

1. The equation for computing t, Equation 9-3, is

$$t = \frac{\overline{X}_1 - \overline{X}_2}{\sqrt{\dfrac{\Sigma D^2 - \dfrac{(\Sigma D)^2}{n}}{n(n-1)}}}$$

2. Compute the value of D for each pair of participants, and then the sum of D (ΣD), the sum of the squares of D (ΣD^2), the sum of D squared [$(\Sigma D)^2$], and n.

Initial Measure	Group 1	Group 2	D
1	10	11	−1
2	10	8	2
3	8	6	2
4	7	7	0
5	7	6	1
6	6	5	1
7	4	3	1

$$\Sigma D = 6$$
$$\Sigma D^2 = 12$$
$$n = 7$$

3. Determine the difference between the means. This may be done by computing the mean of the differences. Since the latter is easier, we shall do this.

$$\text{Mean of the differences} = \frac{\Sigma D}{n} = \frac{6}{7} = 0.86$$

4. Substitute the values in Equation 9-3

$$t = \frac{0.86}{\sqrt{\dfrac{12 - \dfrac{(6)^2}{7}}{7(7-1)}}}$$

5. Perform the operations as indicated and determine the value of t.

$$t = \frac{0.86}{0.40} = 2.15$$

6. Determine the number of degrees of freedom associated with the computed value of t.

$$df = n - 1 = 7 - 1 = 6$$

7. Enter the table of t with the computed values of t and df. Determine the probability associated with this value of t. In this example, $0.1 > P > 0.05$. Therefore, assuming a criterion of 0.05, the null hypothesis is not rejected.

Two Repeated Treatments Design

Assume that an industrial psychologist is called on to test the safety factor of two different automobiles. He has four drivers drive the two automobiles through a test-course in counterbalanced order, and obtains the following safety ratings for each automobile. Which automobile, if either, is safer?

Safety Ratings
(The higher the value, the more safe the automobile)

Driver Number	Bloopmobile	Dudwagen	Differences (D)
1	8	4	4
2	6	1	5
3	9	4	5
4	7	4	3

$$\Sigma D = 17$$
$$\Sigma D^2 = 75$$
$$\overline{X}_D = 4.25$$

1. The first step is to calculate the values required for the paired t-test, which are $\overline{X}_D$, ΣD^2, ΣD, and $n = 4$. They have been entered.

$$t = \frac{\overline{X}_D}{\sqrt{\dfrac{\Sigma D^2 - (\Sigma D)^2/n}{n(n - 1)}}}$$

2. Substituting into Equation 9-6 and performing the indicated operations, we find t to be

$$t = \frac{4.25}{\sqrt{\dfrac{75 - (17)^2/4}{4(4 - 1)}}} = \frac{4.25}{\sqrt{\dfrac{75 - 289/4}{4 \cdot 3}}}$$

$$= \frac{4.25}{\sqrt{\dfrac{75.000 - 72.25}{12}}} = \frac{4.25}{\sqrt{\dfrac{2.75}{12}}}$$

$$= \frac{4.25}{\sqrt{0.2292}} = \frac{4.25}{0.479} = 8.87$$

3. Entering Table A-1 with $t = 8.87$ and $df = n - 1 = 3$, we find that this value exceeds the tabled value at the 0.005 level. Consequently we conclude that the mean difference between safety factors of these two automobiles is statistically reliable, and, since the Bloopmobile had the higher mean safety factor, the psychologist concludes that it is the safer vehicle.

More Than Two Repeated Treatments

Assume that three automobiles were tested in counterbalanced order using six drivers, with the following safety ratings:

Safety Ratings

Driver Number	Bloopmobile	Dudwagen	Lemollac	Σ Drivers (D)
1	8	4	1	13
2	5	2	6	13
3	6	4	3	13
4	8	8	2	18
5	7	2	4	13
6	2	6	4	12
ΣX:	36	26	20	82
ΣX²:	242	140	82	

1. First, we compute the total sums of squares with Equation 9-7 modified merely for three repeated treatments, as follows: (N = number of participants multiplied by the number of treatments = $6 \times 3 = 18$).

$$(9\text{-}7) \quad \text{total } SS = (\Sigma X_1^2 + \Sigma X_2^2 + \Sigma X_3^2)$$
$$- \frac{(\Sigma X_1 + \Sigma X_2 + \Sigma X_3)^2}{N}$$

$$\text{total } SS = (242 + 140 + 82)$$
$$- \frac{(36 + 26 + 20)^2}{18}$$

$$= 464.00 - 373.56 = 90.44$$

2. Next we compute the among-conditions sums of squares by modifying Equation 9-8 for three repeated treatments:

$$(9\text{-}8) \quad \text{among-conditions } SS =$$
$$\frac{(\Sigma X_1)^2}{n_1} + \frac{(\Sigma X_2)^2}{n_2} + \frac{(\Sigma X_3)^2}{n_3}$$
$$- \frac{(\Sigma X_1 + \Sigma X_2 + \Sigma X_3)^2}{N}$$

Making the appropriate substitutions and performing the operations indicated we find that

$$\text{among-conditions } SS =$$
$$\frac{(36)^2}{6} - \frac{(26)^2}{6} + \frac{(20)^2}{6} - 373.56$$
$$= 216.00 + 112.67 + 66.67 - 373.56$$
$$= 21.78$$

3. Next we compute the among-drivers SS as follows:

$$(9\text{-}9) \quad \text{among-drivers } SS =$$
$$\frac{(\Sigma D_1)^2}{K} + \frac{(\Sigma D_2)^2}{K} \cdots \frac{(\Sigma D_6)^2}{K}$$
$$- \frac{(\Sigma X_1 + \Sigma X_2 + \Sigma X_3)^2}{N}$$

where K, the number of treatments, $= 3$.

$$\text{among-drivers } SS =$$
$$\frac{(13)^2}{3} + \frac{(13)^2}{3} + \frac{(13)^2}{3} + \frac{(18)^2}{3}$$

$$+ \frac{(13)^2}{3} + \frac{(12)^2}{3} - 373.56$$

$$= 56.33 + 56.33 + 56.33 + 108.00$$

$$+ 56.33 + 48.00 - 373.56$$

$$= 381.32 - 373.56 = 7.76$$

4. Then we obtain the error term sum of squares:

(9-10) error SS = total SS − among-conditions SS − among-students SS
= 90.44 − 21.78 − 7.76 = 60.90

5. Computation of the degrees of freedom is:

(9-11) total $df = N - 1 = 18 - 1 = 17$

(9-12) among conditions $- K - 1$
$= 3 - 1 = 2$

(9-13) among students $= n - 1$
$= 6 - 1 = 5$

(9-14) error term $= (K - 1)(n - 1)$
$= 2 \cdot 5 = 10$

6. To compute the two values of F for this design we divide the among-conditions mean square by the error term as follows:

$$F = \frac{10.89}{6.09} = 1.79$$

Then we divide the among-drivers mean square by the error term as follows:

$$F = \frac{1.55}{6.09} = 0.25$$

7. Summarizing these values in the following table,

Summary of Analysis of Variance
for a Repeated-Treatments Design

Source of Variation	SS	df	MS	F
Among conditions	21.78	2	10.89	1.79
Among drivers	7.76	5	1.55	0.25
Error	60.90	10	6.09	
Total	90.44	17		

8. Finally, to interpret the Fs we enter Table A-2, first with $F = 1.79$ and $df = 2$, then with $F = 0.25$, and $df = 5$. We find that the probability associated with these values is less than 0.05. The conclusion, then, is that there is no reliable difference among the means for either conditions or drivers. We thus cannot conclude that one vehicle is safer than the other by this test, nor can we conclude that one driver is safer than the other.

CRITICAL REVIEW FOR THE STUDENT

Terms You Should Understand

1. Correlation coefficient, positive correlation, negative relationship, zero-order relationship, perfect correlation, scattergram, curvilinear relationship, coefficient of correlation, η, causality and cause-effect relationships, reliable r.

2. Problem
    Suppose that you have counted the number of fidgets (X) made by five of your classmates in your research class and that also over the past two weeks you have tallied the number of minutes (Y) that they left class before it was actually terminated. These values are tabulated below. Are these two measures of classroom behavior reliably related?

Number of Fidgets and Minutes

Student Number	X	Y
1	24	29
2	19	16
3	21	17
4	18	23
5	20	18

3. What are the criteria for selecting a matching variable for a matched-groups design?

4. Why might you select a randomized-groups design over a matched-groups design, or vice versa?

5. Problems
    A. A psychologist seeks to test the hypothesis that the Western grip for holding a tennis racket is superior to the Eastern grip. Participants are matched on the basis of a physi-

cal fitness test; they are then trained in the use of these two grips, respectively, and the following scores on their tennis-playing proficiency are obtained. Assuming that controls are adequate, that a 0.05 level for rejecting the null hypothesis is set, and that a higher score indicates better performance, what can be concluded with respect to the empirical hypothesis?

Score on Dependent Variable

Rank on Matching Variables	Eastern Grip Group	Western Grip Group
1	10	2
2	5	8
3	9	3
4	5	1
5	0	3
6	8	1
7	7	0
8	9	1

B. To test the hypothesis that with higher induced anxiety, learning is better, an experimenter formed two groups of participants by matching them on an initial measure of anxiety. Next, considerable anxiety was induced into the experimental group but not into the control group. The following scores on a learning task were then obtained; the higher score indicating better learning. Assuming adequate controls were exercised and that a criterion of 0.05 was set, was the hypothesis confirmed?

Dependent Variable Scores

Rank on Matching Variable	Experimental Group	Control Group
1	8	6
2	8	7
3	7	4
4	6	5
5	5	3
6	3	1
7	1	2

C. A military psychologist wishes to evaluate a training aid that was designed to facilitate

the teaching of soldiers to read a map. Two groups of participants were formed, matching them on the basis of a visual perception test (an ability that is important in the reading of maps). A criterion of 0.02 for rejecting the null hypothesis was set, and proper controls were exercised. Assuming that a higher score, indicates better performance, did the training aid facilitate map-reading proficiency?

Rank on Matching Variable	Scores of Group That Used the Training Aid	Scores of Group That Did Not Use the Training Aid
1	30	24
2	30	28
3	28	26
4	29	30
5	26	20
6	22	19
7	25	22
8	20	19
9	18	14
10	16	12
11	15	13
12	14	10
13	14	11
14	13	13
15	10	6
16	10	7
17	9	5
18	9	9
19	10	6
20	8	3

6. Distinguish between repeated-treatments and between-groups designs. Identify examples of each category. Are these designs necessarily experimental designs, or might the method of systematic observation be used with either type?

7. Summarize some of the arguments for and against the use of repeated-treatments designs. You might include a discussion of the efficiency as far as number of participants is concerned, the relevance of the concept of error variance, the irreversibility issue, order effects, and interaction among experimental treatments.

8. If you were limited to the *t*-test, which form of it would you employ for a repeated-treatments design—the randomized or the paired *t*? (Im-

plied here is the question of *why* you would use which form.)

9. Problem

Ten participants studied four different lists of nonsense syllables that varied in their degree of meaning. The lists were presented in randomized order, and the memory percentages for each are as follows.

Dependent-Variable Memory Scores as a Function of Increasing Degree of Meaning

Participant Number	1 (Low)	2	3	4 (High)
1	90	88	100	99
2	65	75	88	82
3	42	62	95	84
4	75	70	97	97
5	68	35	92	96
6	76	76	98	92
7	65	63	67	98
8	70	71	89	94
9	72	69	94	89
10	68	70	97	97

Conduct a repeated-treatments analysis of variance and reach the appropriate conclusions.

chapter 10

EXPERIMENTAL DESIGN: SINGLE-SUBJECT ($N = 1$) RESEARCH

Major purpose:

To understand the "strategy" of studying a single participant under a repeated-treatments design with replication.

What you are going to find:

1. A criticism of group experimentation, along with the rationale for extensive study of the behavior of single organisms.

2. Definitions of critical terms in the Experimental Analysis of Behavior and other $N = 1$ research.

3. How to determine whether an independent variable is effective through graphic and statistical analysis.

4. Presentation of basic $N = 1$ designs together with discussions of their strong and weak points.

What you should acquire:

An understanding of the advantages and disadvantages of single-subject methodology, together with the ability to employ this research approach.

TWO RESEARCH STRATEGIES

The Strategy of Studying Groups. With previous experimental designs many subjects (participants) were studied for a short time. The effects of varying the independent variable were assessed by testing the difference between computed-for-groups means relative to the amount of error in the experiment. If a difference between means was sufficiently larger than experimental error, it was concluded that there was a relationship between the independent and the dependent variables. For example, the value of the numerator of the *t*-test or *F* ratio is an indication of the effects of varying the independent variable (the mean difference or the among-groups mean square); the denominator (e.g., the within-groups mean square) is the error variance. The *t*-or *F*-test yields a significant value if the numerator is sufficiently larger than the denominator. In short, the strategy has been to determine whether changes in behavior produced by the independent variable were sufficiently great to show through the "noise" (error variance) in the experiment. Such group designs, which we started to employ around the turn of the century, have now become quite sophisticated. This increased sophistication has occurred with the development of inferential statistics and sampling theory, especially as developed by R. A. Fisher (page 178).

History of Studying the Individual. Psychology, though, actually began with intensive, prolonged study of the individual. This single-participant research strategy followed from the earlier scientific paradigms employed by physiologists. Foremost was the classic research of the great French physiologist Claude Bernard in the 1830s. Bernard's strategy of concentrating on the individual was widely accepted in physiology when he won a scientific argument concerning physiological knowledge of European urine. A proposal had been advanced to collect specimens of urine from a centrally located train station and compute average values. However, Bernard convinced his colleagues, that the averages based on specimens of groups would yield but a fictitious and abstract value that would not tell anything about any individual European's urine. Fortunately, the original reason for this research has dimmed with time.

The individual approach of Gustav Fechner in 1860 had earth-shaking consequences for the development of a new science of psychology when he developed our methods of psychophysics and also formalized Weber's famous law. Even more significant for psychology was the research of Ivan Pavlov who studied the long-term conditioning history of his dogs to provide us with our contemporary principles of conditional responses. Wilhelm Wundt and other early psychologists studied mental processes under one or more sequential conditions, all within the same person. The classical experiments on memory performed by Hermann Ebbinghaus (1913) provide one final example of the successful, early use of single-subject research in psychology. This pioneer, it will be recalled, memorized several lists of nonsense syllables and then tested himself for recall at various times after learning was completed. He then calculated the percentage of each list that he had forgotten after varying periods of time. For example, he found that he had forgotten about 47 percent of one list 20 minutes after he had learned it, 66 percent of a second list after one day, 72 percent of a third list after two days, and so forth. By thus taking repeated measures on himself, Ebbinghaus was able to plot amount forgotten as a function of the passage of time since learning and thus obtained his famous forgetting curve.[1]

Nomothetic Versus Idiographic Strategies. The argument about the relative values of single-subject versus between-group

---

[1] It is fortunate, incidentally, that Ebbinghaus was not a professional psychologist. If he had been, he would have known that what he accomplished was "impossible"—psychologists of his time typically held that the "higher mental processes" (e.g., memory) were not susceptible to experimental attack.

methodologies has continued to this day. These two classic approaches to understanding behavior have been referred to as the **idiographic** (intensive long-term study of the individual) versus the **nomothetic** (determining averages of groups) strategies. Other terms reflecting these two different approaches are longitudinal (developmental) versus cross-sectional research. In between-groups, nomothetic, and cross-sectional research, group means are computed. In idiographic, (longitudinal, developmental) research, however, data points across time are usually plotted for individuals so that averages for groups are usually not computed. Let us now turn from these classic experiments conducted on single individuals using repeated-treatments designs to the single-participant design as it is often applied in contemporary psychology.

THE EXPERIMENTAL ANALYSIS OF BEHAVIOR

Group experimentation with statistical analysis has been most vigorously criticized by Professor B. F. Skinner (e.g., 1959) and researchers in his tradition (especially Murray Sidman, 1960). In its place Skinner employs single-participant research with replication, a methodology that he refers to as the **Experimental Analysis of Behavior**. Rather than studying a relatively large number of participants for a short period of time, Skinner advocated studying one participant over an extended period. Then he replicated the experiment with one or more additional participants. The overriding strategy is to reduce the error variance in the experiment.

We can conceive of experimental error as having two major components: (1) that due to individual differences among the participants, and (2) that due to ineffective control procedures. Briefly, the former is eliminated in this design, simply put, by studying only one participant at a time under all conditions of the experiment—this is the classic strategy of using the same participant as his or her own control. The "noise" is reduced by

establishing highly controlled conditions in the experimental situation.

The key is to develop very precise and effective control over the experimental environment, rather than allow extraneous variables randomly to affect the participant's behavior. With such enhanced control, the chances are increased that an independent variable can be shown to influence a dependent variable. Generalization to others is achieved by successfully replicating the experiment with several additional participants.

Skinner's pioneering research over a half century ago was with white rats, then with pigeons. Since then his methods have been used with about every conceivable species: mice, turtles, chimpanzees, fish, cats, dogs, college students, mentally retarded individuals, neurotics, psychotics, military personnel, industrial workers, and yet others. The results have been generalized to a wide variety of human situations such as the classroom, the clinic, mental hospitals, industry, and even government.

The Basic Experiment: Operant Conditioning

To illustrate the methodology, consider a white rat placed in a well-controlled environment such as an operant conditioning chamber, more popularly referred to as a *Skinner box*. In that chamber, increased control is achieved primarily through the methods of elimination of extraneous variables and of holding them constant (Chapter 4); for example, external noises are shielded out and masked through sound deadening, extraneous olfactory cues are prevented from entering, lighting intensity is held constant.

The basic experiment is to condition the white rat to press a lever when a special light appears. First, the animal is placed in the chamber for an extended period to establish a baseline level of performance. *The frequency with which an organism presses the level prior to conditioning is called the* **operant level**. The response to be learned is to press the lever only when the light is on, following which the animal receives a pellet of food. Once a stable operant level of lever pressing is established, conditioning starts. The light signal is referred to as a **discriminative stimulus**, symbolized S^D. The presence of S^D means that the occasion is appropriate for the animal to press the lever and be reinforced with the food pellet. Conditioning thus takes the form of increasing the strength of the stimulus-response connection between the special light and the lever-pressing response. More precisely, with successful conditioning the probability that the animal will respond in the presence of the discriminative stimulus (S^D) is increased. In contrast, when the light is *not* on, the occasion is *not* appropriate for making the response; that is, a response in the absence of S^D is not reinforced. The response class such as the lever pressing response is referred to as an *operant*. Responses selected as operants for animal-conditioning experiments are objectively measurable, easily performed, and not demanding so that the organism can repeatedly make them without becoming fatigued. In **operant conditioning** the organism increases the rate of operant responding beyond the *operant level*, the preexperimental or control rate of responding. In operant conditioning the operant behavior is controlled by its consequences. If those consequences are positive, they are **reinforcers** or reinforcing stimuli. Reinforcers are thus made contingent on the organism emitting the operant when the occasion is appropriate—that is, when S^D is present, but not when S^D is absent. Further-

more they may be positive or negative as in Table 10-1.

Contingencies of Responding

In Table 10-1 we may observe two stimulus operations: The stimulus may be presented or withdrawn. Similarly, the stimulus is either positive ("pleasant") or negative ("noxious"). **Positive reinforcement** is the operation of presenting a positive stimulus contingent upon a specific response (such as giving a child an ice cream cone when the child makes a constructive response, lower left-hand cell of Table 10-1). **Negative reinforcement** is the withdrawal of a negative stimulus contingent upon a specific operant (such as removing a student's bad grade when a test is made up, upper right-hand cell). In the cases of both positive and negative reinforcement, the strength of the responses increase. Positive punishment occurs when a negative stimulus is presented contingent on the occurrence of a response (such as spanking a child, upper left-hand cell). Negative punishment is the withdrawal of a positive stimulus contingent on a response (such as taking an ice cream cone away from a child, lower right-hand cell). In the cases of positive and negative punishment, the response may cease to occur.

These are the possible consequences of responding. Operant conditioning occurs when the operant is reinforced either positively or negatively. But when the response is punished, the response is usually sup-

TABLE 10-1 Possible Consequences of Presenting and Withdrawing Positive and Negative Stimuli

	Stimulus Operation	
Stimulus Quality	*Presentation*	*Withdrawal*
Negative ("Noxious")	Positive Punishment (Response Decreases)	Negative Reinforcement (Response Increases)
Positive ("Pleasant")	Positive Reinforcement (Response Increases)	Negative Punishment (Response Decreases)

pressed as long as the punishment or the threat of punishment perseveres (punishment generally does not permanently modify behavior—a response is not thereby eliminated because the response typically returns to operant level when the punishment ceases).

The Cumulative Record

To reach such conclusions about behavior, experimenters use **rate of responding** to indicate the strength of the operant—*rate* is the frequency of responding within a given time and indicates the probability that a response will be made on the appropriate occasion (when the S^D is present). Quantifying the dependent variable as a rate of responding has proven to be enormously valuable for psychology. In many laboratory and applied studies, rate of responding has provided a very sensitive index of the effectiveness of independent variables. Professor Skinner, in fact, when asked to rank the importance of his many contributions, pointed to his selection of rate of responding as the most important. This dependent-variable measure is effectively studied through the **cumulative record**.

A *cumulative record* indicates the total frequency of an operant that occurred and precisely when it occurred. The primary data of the experiment are thus contained in the cumulative record, which is established as follows. The writing pen on an ink recorder is automatically activated each time the rat presses the bar. The pen writes on a continuously moving piece of paper and is elevated one unit for each bar press, as in Figure 10-1. Imagine that the paper is moving from right to left, and each bar press moves the pen up one unit. When no response is made, the pen indicates this by continuing to move horizontally. Hence we can note that after one minute a response was made, another response was made when two minutes had elapsed, that a third response was made after two and one-half minutes, and so forth. If we wish to know the total number of re-

sponses made after any given time in the experimental situation, we merely read up to the curve from that point and over to the vertical axis. For example, we can see that after five minutes the rat had made five responses, as read off the vertical axis. Incidentally, the cumulative response curve is a summation of the total number of responses made since time zero; this means that the curve can never decrease; that is, after a response has been made, as indicated by an upward mark, that response can never be unmade, and the pen can never move down. Think about this point, if the cumulative response curve is new to you.

We have shown in Figure 10-1 only a short portion of the cumulative response curve. More realistically, the participant responds much longer, so that considerable experimental history is recorded. Eventually performance becomes quite stable—the operant-level response rate becomes rather constant. Once this steady operant level has been established, it is reasonable to extrapolate the curve indefinitely, as long as the conditions remain unchanged. At this time the experimenter introduces some unique treat-

FIGURE 10-1 A cumulative response curve shown in detail.

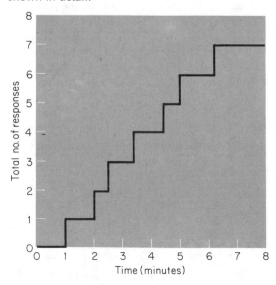

ment. The logic is quite straightforward—if the response curve changes, that change can be ascribed to the effects of the new stimulus condition. Once it has been established that the curve changes, the experimental condition can be removed and, providing there are no lasting irreversible effects, the curve should return to its previously stable rate. Additional conditions can then be presented, as the experimenter wishes.

A more extended conditioning curve for a white rat is presented in Figure 10-2. First, we can see a rather low response rate for the operant-level period wherein the lever was seldom pressed. Then operant conditioning started, whereupon we see a dramatic increase in the slope. This increase in the slope indicates a greater response rate in that the rat is making more responses per unit time—the strength of the S^D-operant connection has been noticeably increased. Finally, reinforcement was withdrawn, and extinction occurred as the curve returned to operant level. It can thus be seen that this is a repeated-treatments design in which the first treatment was no reinforcement (call it A), followed by reinforcement (B), and finally the treatment condition is returned to that of nonreinforcement (A). This type of design is labeled the *A-B-A paradigm*.

Graphic Analysis for Assessing Response Changes

In viewing Figure 10-2 how can we conclude that a change in response rate—the dependent variable—is reliable? We have answered the analogous question in group designs by means of the *t*-test and the *F*-test. Skinner and those who employ his methodology have traditionally avoided statistical analysis, relying instead on **graphic analysis** or, synonymously, visual analysis and **criterion by inspection**. The cumulative record in Figure 10-2 is thus a display of behavior that can be analyzed. From the cumulative record it can be concluded whether control of behavior is reliable; more specifically a visual graphic analysis can indicate whether changes in response rate are reliable. If the introduction of the treatment is accompanied by changes in response rate, it may be concluded that the independent variable *does* influence the dependent variable. On the other hand, if response rate does not systematically change as the independent variable is presented and withdrawn, it is concluded that the independent variable does *not* influence the dependent variable.

Graphic analysis thus is a visual process whereby changes in behavior are ascribed to sys-

FIGURE 10-2 An operant conditioning experiment employing the A-B-A withdrawal paradigm.

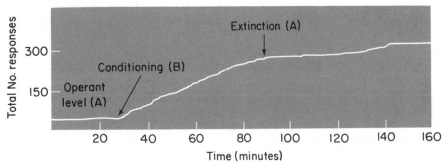

tematic changes of the independent variable; that conclusion depends on whether the behavioral changes are great enough to be observed with the naked eye. Consequently, graphic analysis is not a very sensitive method of data analysis, which is regarded as an advantage by researchers who employ this method. The reasoning is thus: If the effect of the independent variable is not sufficiently great to produce a really noticeable change in the cumulative record, the change is judged not to be a reliable one. In this way statistical analyses may be avoided. The advantage of graphic analysis over statistical analysis, these researchers believe, is that it prevents you from concluding that weak and unstable independent variables are effective. With large-scale statistical analysis, on the other hand, you may reach a conclusion that there is a reliable change, but the change may be so small that it has no practical significance. For instance, we may well find that a difference in IQ between two groups of school children is statistically reliable, but since it is only a difference of 1.2 IQ points, it would have no practical significance. The arguments are thus two-fold: Statistical analysis should not be employed, not should data obtained from groups of participants be pooled.

The important variables in the Experimental Analysis of Behavior are thus identified as those with sufficient power and generality that they can be detected through graphic analysis. They are thus more widely applicable in the sense of being practically significant when applied to everyday problems; that is, independent variables whose effects are repeatedly and generally manifested through graphic analysis can transfer readily to the real world. Learning to apply them can thus be easily learned by such would-be behavioral engineers as teachers or parents who are untrained in the Experimental Analysis of Behavior.

Graphic analysis, as we say, is the traditional method used in single-participant research, and it is still the primary method for reaching conclusions. However, effective and powerful methods of statistical analysis have come forth and are increasingly used for this purpose. The effective methods of statistical analysis with $N = 1$ designs allow you to analyze single-participant research statistically, but this is still not group research. In Appendix B to this chapter statistical analysis of $N = 1$ designs will be studied.

PARADIGMS FOR $N = 1$ EXPERIMENTAL DESIGNS

Overview. With this understanding of how conclusions are reached as to whether changes in the dependent variable are reliable, let us examine more closely the question of how we conclude that those reliable changes in the response curve are actually due to variations of the independent variable—that is, might the response changes have occurred regardless of whether schedules of reinforcement, extinction, etc. were administered as they were? A variety of paradigms have been introduced to increase the likelihood of the conclusion that any response changes actually are a function of the introduction or withdrawal of an experimental treatment. In all of them, however, the cardinal principle is that you vary only one independent variable at a time. In the A-B-A design, for example, following condition A, condition B and only condition B is instituted. One would not also add a condition C confounded with B to make an A-B-C-A design. While some researchers do introduce more than one variable at a time to attempt to study interactions between them, the procedure is fraught with numerous difficulties and is basically unsound.

In general, the success of $N = 1$ research rests on achieving a stable baseline. Considerable variability in the baseline makes it exceedingly difficult to determine whether a treatment is effective in changing response rate. Stable baselines are seldom a problem in laboratory research, but in applied settings, especially in clinical work, they often are difficult to establish. The more data points that one can obtain, the better is the estimate of the baseline to determine just

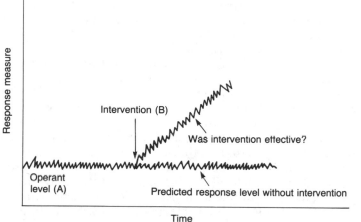

FIGURE 10-3 The logic of an A-B design. You predict that behavior would continue along the same course as for the baseline if no treatment is administered. At the point of intervention, if the response measure noticeably increases, you *may* conclude that your intervention was effective in producing that change. But the conclusion is weak.

how stable it is. In any event, three data points are minimal for plotting any trend, as we noted in Chapter 7.

Since $N = 1$ procedures require observations of behavior made repeatedly over a period of time, they form a subclass of repeated-treatments designs known as **time-series designs**. We shall also study time-series designs further in the next chapter as they are one of the two most prominent kinds of quasi-experimental designs. Much of what we have to say with regard to the following time-series designs will be directly applicable to quasi-experimental designs. Consequently, you should pay special attention here to maximize your transfer of learning to the next chapter. The most prominent of these designs in the Experimental Analysis of Behavior is the **withdrawal design**.

Withdrawal Designs.[2] As the name implies, the experimental treatment that is in-

troduced following a baseline period is then withdrawn. The treatment can be systematically presented and withdrawn in several ways. The basic logic is to establish an operant level, introduce an independent variable, note any changes in response rate, and withdraw the independent variable to see if response rate returns to operant level, as we studied in the A-B-A paradigm of Figure 10-2.

Shortcomings of the A-B Paradigm. This, the simplest of the research strategies for $N = 1$ designs, is presented only to enable you to better understand other designs; because the confounding is so atrocious it should be used only as a last resort. In the A-B design, you establish a baseline and then predict what the behavior would continue to be if no treatment was administered (Figure 10-3). Then, if your response measure departs from that prediction following intervention (B), you *might* attribute that response change to the effect of the treatment.

One problem is that you really don't know what the response measure might have been had no treatment been administered. Another problem is that you don't know whether any response change was produced because of the specific treatment intervention—it could have changed just because you did something different, precisely what you did being irrelevant. We shall later elab-

---

[2]Sometimes the withdrawal design is erroneously referred to as a reversal design. The error is in thinking that reversal refers to the removal or withdrawal of the treatment variable that is applied following the baseline period; that is, "reversing" back to baseline. Obviously, however, it is inappropriate to refer to this sequence as a reversal design since there is no reversal of conditions at all—there is merely a withdrawal of the treatment in the second A phase. This distinction will become clearer shortly when we discuss a true reversal design. The important point is that you recognize the principles involved rather than focus on inconsistently used labels.

orate on this **placebo effect** as a limitation in some of these designs.[3]

One way that you can enhance the possibility that any response change *was* induced by the introduction of a treatment is to later make a second measure of the response—somewhat after the first response measure. Then, if the response change in the second period is the same as that obtained immediately following the administration of the treatment, your belief that the treatment did influence behavior would be enhanced. That is, two measures of a change in behavior that were consistent increases the probability that the response changed and that the change was due to the treatment.

The A-B-A Paradigm. If behavior does change from A (e.g., the baseline or control period) to B (the treatment condition) and back to baseline (A) when the independent variable or treatment is withdrawn. When it does return then the likelihood that the response change is a function of the independent variable is increased. This paradigm is immensely more effective than the A-B paradigm because of the test as to whether the withdrawal of the treatment does result in a return of the response measure to baseline.

The A-B-A-B Paradigm. To increase further the likelihood of the conclusion that behavior is functionally related to the independent variable, one may introduce an A-B-A-B sequence. The experimental effect is produced twice so as to study changes from two operant-level phases. Behavior may change from the first operant level (A) to a treatment phase (B); then it may decrease during the second (A) phase when B is withdrawn. Finally, behavior may increase again with the reintroduction of the treatment (B). Consequently, the inference as to a functional relationship between the treatment

(B) and the behavioral measure is considerably strengthened over that which may result from the A-B-A paradigm.

Let us illustrate an A-B-A-B design with an experiment on a four-year-old boy who cried a great deal after he experienced minor frustrations. The question was: What is the reinforcing event that maintains this crying behavior? The experimenters hypothesized that it was the special attention from the teacher that the crying brought. The paradigm is thus the same as that for the rat in the operant chamber: When the response is made (the bar is pressed or the child cries), reinforcement occurs (food is delivered or the teacher comes to the child). After 10 days when the response rate was stabilized (A), the experimental treatment was introduced (B). For the next 10 days the teacher ignored the child's crying episodes, but she did reinforce more constructive responses (verbal and self-help behaviors) by giving the child approving attention.

It was determined that the boy cried about eight times during each school morning (as seen in Figure 10-4). The cumulative number of crying episodes was thus about 80 for the first 10 days of the experiment. At that time the teacher withdrew reinforcement for crying, whereupon it can be seen that the number of crying episodes sharply decreased. In fact, during the last 5 of these 10 days, only one crying response was recorded. During the next 10 days reinforcement was reinstated (A)—whenever the child cried, the teacher attended to the boy as she had originally done. Approximately the original rate of responding was reinstituted. Then for the last 10 days of the experiment, reinforcement for crying was again withdrawn (B) and the response rate returned to a near-zero level. Furthermore it remained there after the experiment was terminated. The experiment was replicated with another four-year-old boy, with the same general results.

Let us emphasize this last point, namely, that once it has been determined with a single participant that a treatment affects a response measure, the experiment is repli-

---

[3] The term *placebo* comes from a latin word, meaning "to please." It refers to what appears to be medication prescribed by a physician in order to please the patient. Even though it may only be a sugar pill or other inert substance, the suggestion that the patient will improve can have powerful (if only temporary) effects.

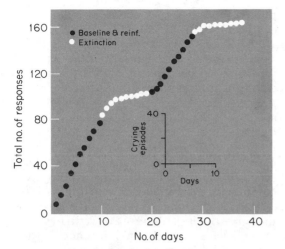

FIGURE 10-4   Cumulative record of the daily number of crying episodes. The teacher reinforced crying during the first 10 days (dark circles) and withdrew reinforcement during the second 10 days (light circles). Reinforcement was reinstituted during the third period of 10 days (dark circles) and withdrawn again during the last 10 days (after Harris, Wolf, and Baer, 1964).

cated. When under highly controlled conditions it is ascertained that other participants behave in the same way to the change in stimulus conditions, the results are generalized to the population sampled. A point we made earlier also applies here; that is, the extent to which the results can be generalized to the population of organisms depends on the extent to which that population has been sampled.

Variations of the A-B-A-B Design. We have illustrated the withdrawal design for the A-B-A paradigm through the conditioning of a white rat and for the A-B-A-B paradigm in a real-life behavior modification experiment. Although these research designs have been pioneered in the laboratory, they have found many applications outside the laboratory in behavior modification research. The interested student can find many variations of these designs in the growing behavior modification literature, such as in the *Journal of the Applied Analysis of Behavior.* For instance, another way in which the

relationship between a behavioral change and the introduction of the independent variable may be further confirmed is by introducing the experimental treatment at a random point in the experimental session rather than at a predetermined time. That is, rather than introducing the experimental treatment after 10 days, as in Figure 10-4, the day on which the schedule change is effected could be randomly determined as any day—perhaps between day 5 and day 15. Assume that the same behavioral change always occurs in several participants immediately after the introduction of the experimental treatment. In this case, because the treatment appeared randomly at different times for each participant, one could more firmly conclude that the two are functionally related.

A-B-A-B paradigm can increase the likelihood that a response change is caused by a specific treatment. *The design* to further increase that likelihood can be extended with additional withdrawals and returns to baseline conditions. For example, one can institute A-B-A-B-A or A-B-A-B-A-B-A sequences.

The basic paradigm of the A-B-A-B sequence thus is a replication design such that the repeated A-B phases are replications of the first A-B phase. One might use such an extended sequence, for instance, in the behavioral control of overeating. A participant's weight level could be established during the first A phase and changes studied during the introduction of a behavioral intervention (B). Then the participant could be taken off the control program (it is withdrawn during the second A phase), reintroduced during the second B phase, and so on. If weight is lost during each B phase but regained during subsequent A phases, one could conclude that the behavioral intervention was indeed successful. In this example, however, one might expect some generalization of the therapy so that the weight loss is eventually maintained when the treatment is withdrawn. Thus, weight reduction that is maintained during later A phases indicates that the therapy is successful. A similar example would be treatment for cigarette smoking. Eventually, one would hope that the cessation of smoking would be generalized to all phases of life and situations when the treatment was withdrawn. Thus, in a late A (treatment) phase, number of cigarettes smoked would drop to zero.

Another variation of the A-B-A-B design is with an A-B-A-C-A design to assess the effects of two different treatments (B and C) relative to baseline A. However, while you can tell with this design whether B and C affect behavior, you cannot assess their relative efficacies; that is, you cannot tell whether one treatment is more effective than the other. One proposal to determine the relative effectiveness of two treatments B and C and thus to estimate which affects behavior to the greatest extent is to employ an A-B-A-B-A-C-A design.

One shortcoming of the A-B paradigm that we mentioned also applies to the A-B-A-B paradigm to some extent. The problem is that an observed behavioral change may not be caused by your specific treatment. Rather, it could have resulted merely because *something* (anything) different was done to the participant—it need not have been that the unique treatment itself was effective. What is required is a control for the attention and activity that is present when a participant is merely in any treatment condition, regardless of what it is. One pro-

posed solution is analogous to a "placebo" condition as in an A-B-C-B design (Figure 10-5). In this variation of the A-B-A-B design, instead of withdrawing a treatment and returning to baseline in the third phase, a different treatment is administered. For instance, a reinforcer could be administered specifically contingent on a given response during phase B. Then, in phase C, reinforcers could also be administered, but according to a random, noncontingent schedule. Finally, in the fourth phase, the contingent reinforcement schedule is reinstated. Ideally, one would want the response measure during phase C to return to operant level. If it does, the inference that the behavioral change occurred due to the specific treatment that was introduced during the B phase is greatly enhanced; it was thus not merely due to noncontingent reinforcers. Such a behavioral change probably was not due merely to added attention or added activity since it did not occur during the control phase (C).

Alternating-Treatments Designs. A specific subclass of the A-B-A-B design is that in which there need be no baseline. Rather, A and B are two different treatments that are alternated randomly with a single individual—treatment A is thus withdrawn and replaced, not with a baseline, but with another treatment. The purpose for which the

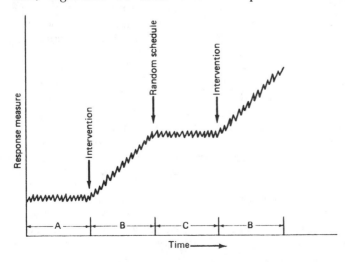

FIGURE 10-5 A control design for "placebo" effects. If behavior changes during the B phases, but returns to baseline level during the control (C) phase, the likelihood that the response measure is produced by the specific treatment is considerably enhanced.

alternating-treatments design is used is to attempt to evaluate the relative effectiveness of two (or more) treatments. For instance, an extended series of treatments might be alternated in an A-B-A-B-A-B design in which A and B are two different methods for controlling the smoking habit. Over an extended period of time, one method might end up being relatively effective, while the other would not. In practical situations, it could be seen that this kind of design, which has been increasingly used in recent years, has the advantage that treatment is used without a withdrawal and return to baseline. It is only that two different treatments are each in effect 50 percent of the time.

Another use of an alternating-treatments design would be to administer one kind of therapy to a client for one week and another kind the next week. The presentation of the two treatments would be randomized over a number of weeks. The two series of data points would be plotted separately so that all the data points for treatment A are connected, and, in a separate curve, all data points for treatment B are connected. The two curves are then compared to see which treatment was more effective.

Still, there are alternating treatments in which baselines are taken. One study was designed, in part, to consider the effect of two kinds of intervention on stereotypic hair twirling relative to a no-intervention condition. Consequently, there were three conditions: (1) no intervention, (2) positive practice, and (3) physical restraint of hair twirling. The baselines were taken before any of the three treatments were administered, and the values appear to the left of Figure 10-6. Hair twirling decreased dramatically during periods when there was physical restraint. The decrease in hair twirling was much greater, however, following positive practice.

A synonym for alternating-treatments design is "between-series designs," the logic being that one is comparing results between two separate series of data points. The basic logic of this design has also been referred to as a multiple-schedule design, multiple-element baseline design, and a simultaneous-treatment design.

With this consideration of the withdrawal design, let us briefly consider the second basic design used in the experimental analysis of behavior, known as the *reversal design*.

The Reversal Design

For this design two alternative, incompatible behaviors are selected for study. Operant levels (baselines) are then established for

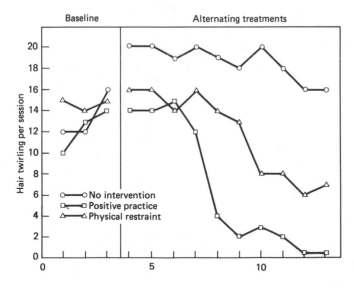

FIGURE 10-6 The use of an alternating-treatments design to evaluate different treatments for hair twirling behavior (modified from Ollendick, Shapiro, & Barrett, 1981).

both classes of behavior. Several strategies may then be used. For instance, one behavior can be subjected to a specific treatment while the other, incompatible behavior receives simultaneously another type of treatment. The effects of the two treatments are then evaluated. After sufficient data are thus accumulated, the treatment conditions are *reversed* so that the first behavior receives the treatment initially given the second behavior and the second behavior receives the treatment that was given the first behavior. There is thus literally a reversal of the treatment conditions for the two behaviors.

Consider as an example the two incompatible behaviors of talking and crying (Figure 10-7). After operant levels are established for both, each time the child talks (the first behavior) reinforcement would be administered. However, any time the child cried during that period, the crying (the second behavior) would not be reinforced (the second treatment condition). One would expect that under these conditions the rate of talking would increase while the rate of crying would not, as depicted in Figure 10-7. Once initial conclusions during phase 1 are reached with this design, the reversal is effected during the second phase. Hence in this second phase, crying would be reinforced and talking ignored.

However, as we shall shortly develop, it would be unfortunate to leave the participant in this condition (though unfortunately in everyday life many children are continuously reinforced for crying in order to bring peace and tranquility to harassed parents). In this example, one would probably want to institute a final condition in which the desired treatment is reinstated such that talking, and therefore not crying, would be reinforced.

Changing-Criterion Designs

The basic strategy of the changing-criterion design is that the effectiveness of a treatment is judged according to whether specified gradual changes in behavior occur during the period of the intervention. The criteria are actual components of the intervention and specify that behavior should change in increments to match changes in the criteria. As with almost all single-subject designs, the changing-criterion design commences with a baseline phase (A) in which records are made of a single class of behavior; following that the treatment is administered (Figure 10-8). The difference from other designs is that during the intervention there are several subphases, each with different preestablished criteria. Thus, during a learning study the first criterion may specify a very low level for administering rein-

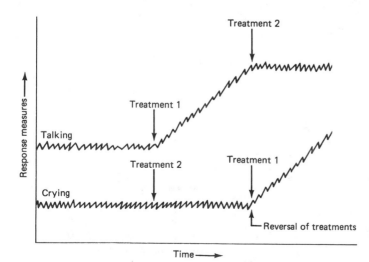

FIGURE 10-7 Illustration of a reversal design. During the first phase (treatment 1), one class of behavior (e.g., talking) would be reinforced while the incompatible, second class of behavior (treatment 2, e.g., crying) would not be reinforced. Then, following the reversal of treatments, talking would not be reinforced while crying would be reinforced. The increased response rate following treatment 1, regardless of the class of behavior to which it was applied, indicates that that treatment (positive reinforcement) was effective.

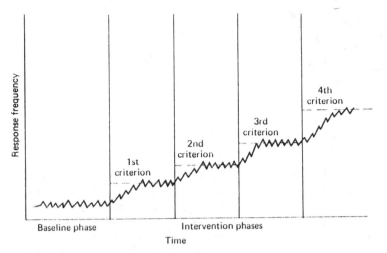

FIGURE 10-8 The changing criterion design. After establishing a stable baseline, the treatment is introduced. When the participant reaches the first criterion, indicated by the dashed line, the criterion for frequency of responding is raised. Additionally, more demanding criteria may be established according to the nature of the study.

forcers. After the learner's behavior satisfies that criterion, the next criterion would require a somewhat higher level of achievement in order to receive a reinforcer. Successively higher levels of achievement are demanded in each of the ensuing subphases for reinforcers to be administered.

An example offered by Kazdin (1982) is to increase frequency of exercise. The participant never exercises during the baseline period, but during the intervention phase a criterion is set at 10 minutes of exercise per day. If that criterion of 10 minutes of exercise per day is met or exceeded, a reinforcing consequence is earned, such as money for purchasing some desired item. When the first criterion is satisfied for several successive days, slightly more exercise, such as 20 minutes per day, is required. As performance stabilizes at the new level, the criterion is again shifted upward, being continuously increased until the desired terminal level of performance is achieved.

The changing-criterion design is an improvement over the other designs discussed in that the subphases continue to test the effectiveness of the interventions. If the treatment is actually effective, changes in behavior systematically follow the shifts in the criterion. That is, if the performance corresponds closely to the changing criteria, it is reasonable to ascribe the behavioral changes

to the intervention. On the other hand, if behavior does not systematically follow the changes in criteria over the course of the intervention phase, the treatment can be judged to be not effective.

Kazdin (1982) illustrates the changing-criterion design by using a study in which an effort was made to improve the academic performance of two disruptive elementary school boys who refused to complete assignments or who completed them at low rates. For four days, baseline observations were made of the number of mathematical problems correctly solved before recess. Then, for the intervention, the children could go to recess and play basketball if they completed 5 problems correctly. If they did not complete 5 problems, they had to remain in the room during recess until the criterion was achieved. When the first criterion was satisfied, the next criterion was increased to 6, as illustrated in Figure 10-9. Then additional criteria were gradually increased to 7, 8, 9, and 10 problems correctly solved. The data for one child, illustrated in Figure 10-9, indicate that the criteria were consistently satisfied in each subphase. During the final phase, the criterion was to solve more realistic textbook problems. As can be seen, with two exceptions, the child satisfied that criterion.

The changing-criterion design is a valu-

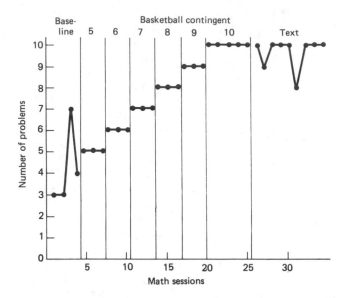

FIGURE 10-9 A record of the number of math problems correctly solved by Dennis, a "behavior disordered" boy; values are plotted during baseline, recess, and the opportunity to play basketball, which were contingent on changing levels of performance. (From Etzel, LeBlanc, and Baer, 1977.)

able one clinically since it does not require withdrawing a treatment that may be effective, nor does it require reverting behavior toward the levels achieved in baseline to show the effectiveness of an intervention. The design is valuable in any kind of learning process, such as in changing behavior clinically, and acquiring motor skills and linguistic skills; in such cases, gradual approximation (shaping) of a terminal level of desired performance is the goal. It is very difficult to change behavior drastically or to acquire new behaviors of these sorts. More realistically, we need gradually to approximate a final behavior through shaping, in which increasingly demanding levels of performance are required. For further evaluation and variations of the changing-criterion class of design, see Kazdin (1982).

This concludes our presentation of single-subject designs, though another frequently used class is presented in Appendix B at the end of this chapter that is the multiple-baseline design in which there are three subcategories: those in which several baselines are plotted across subjects, those plotted across behaviors, and those across environments. The interested student is encouraged to study these designs in greater detail.

MAINTAINING BEHAVIOR THAT IS ACQUIRED

We have been emphasizing the acquisition of responses such as increasing response rate as a function of reinforcement. However, once a new behavior is acquired, particularly if it is a desirable behavior in a practical situation, it is important to maintain that behavior even when the treatment is withdrawn. If your cumulative record indicates a stable response rate you could remove the treatment. If a decrease in response rate follows, then apparently the treatment is required to maintain behavior. Confirmation of this conclusion would follow if the treatment is reintroduced and the response rate returns to the level at which maintenance is desired. This strategy, obviously, is appropriate for any kind of behavioral measure, not just response rate. Maintenance of desired behavior is especially important in many applications, such as in behavior therapy.

FIELDS OF APPLICATION

There are two areas of psychology and related fields in which single-participant designs are especially applicable: behavior therapy and drug evaluation. Research in these fields offer us an opportunity to elaborate on some phases of single-participant methodology.

Behavior Therapy

The methodology used in the Experimental Analysis of Behavior has found special application in evaluating behavior therapies. In turn, the development of behavior therapies has led to increased sophistication in single-subject methodology. Another consequence of the application of single-subject methodology in behavior therapy is that clinicians have been guided more in the direction of objectively evaluating all kinds of therapies. The first step in objectively evaluating a therapy is to be able to specify some behavioral characteristic of a patient that might be improved. Behavior therapies must specify such relevant target behaviors so that they are a considerable advance over therapies involving nebulous phenomena such as one's ego and superego. Eysenck (1983) has summarized the results of numerous evaluations of various kinds of therapies and has concluded that behavior therapies are considerably more effective than "verbal psychotherapies." Furthermore, since we devote considerable attention to ethics in Appendix D, Eysenck raises the following question about verbal psychotherapy: "Even more important, from an ethical point of view, is the question of whether we have a right to make great claims for such practices as psychotherapy, demand exorbitant fees for performing an increasingly doubtful service, and train aspiring psychologists in the arcane and mysterious rites of this profession" (p. 319).

The operant conditioning principles that have been developed in the laboratory have been successfully applied for behavior therapy and more generally for behavior modification in education, industry, rehabilitation medicine, and the like. We have illustrated some of these designs in this chapter.

Drug Evaluations

The long-standing paradigm of a participant serving as his or her own control has been especially prominent in evaluating the effects of drugs. One common strategy has been to establish a baseline phase (A) followed by a placebo phase (A_1), then administration of an active drug (B), readministration of a placebo (A_1), and finally readministration of the active drug (B). One can, with this A-A_1-B-A_1-B strategy, assess the effect of the placebo in going from A to A_1 and the effect of the drug in going from A_1 to B in both episodes.

The assessment of the A to A_1 placebo phase tells us something about the expectation of the participant for improvement. That suggestive placebo effect due to the subject's expectations is separated out from the actual pharmacological effects of the drug. This design thus assesses two variables, the suggestion effect and the actual drug effect.

The problems in drug evaluations are often unique, and certainly numerous. For instance, there may be long-term carryover effects of the drug being evaluated so that a sequence such as the A-A_1-B-A_1-B just described would not be appropriate; this is because the effect of the active drug might carry over from the active drug phase (B) into the second placebo phase (A_1). These and other issues in drug evaluation are well discussed by Barlow and Hersen (1984).

The possible suggestive effect on a participant has sometimes been controlled with a **single-blind strategy** in which the participant is unaware of the difference between the drug and the placebo phases. That is, the participant does not know whether or not a drug is actually administered because the placebos and drugs are identical in appearance. However, sometimes it is not possible to disguise the change from the placebo to the drug condition (e.g., if a drug has an immediate dizzying effect, the participant would surely know that it is not a placebo).

In the **double-blind strategy** *neither* the patient nor the researcher knows which medication the patient is receiving at any point during the evaluation. As before, the placebos and drugs are identical in appearance. Once again, however, if the drug has some definite side effects, the researcher as well as the participant might know that it was not the placebo. For instance, shaking of the body as in muscle tremors might occur and that would be strange, to say the least, as a result of taking a sugar pill.

This gives us some insight into the applications of single-participant research in drug evaluation. The variations of the paradigms are numerous, as illustrated in Table 10-2, which is taken from Barlow and Hersen (1984). There we may note that designs 1,2, and 3 are essentially A-B designs with all of their shortcomings. Designs 4,5, and 6 are essentially A-B-A designs, while designs 7, 8, and 9 are B-A-B designs. Further variations of these 15 basic drug designs could involve the assessment of different levels of a single drug to determine effective dosage.

DIFFICULTIES ENCOUNTERED WITH SINGLE-SUBJECT METHODOLOGY

Irreversible Effects. Perhaps the most obvious limitation is that some treatments are simply not reversible. Once a surgical lesion is made, for instance, short of calling in Dr. Frankenstein, it cannot be withdrawn. Similarly, we saw in drug evaluation research that the effects of some drugs linger on into what should be a return-to-baseline phase, with some drugs like marijuana even being effective for months after initial administration. Other irreversible effects are learning phenomena such as reading and playing tennis. Once the ability is acquired, it would obviously be foolhardy to try to return the learner to baseline.

Sometimes an effect may actually be reversible, but it would be unethical, or at least practically difficult, to withdraw the treatment. In evaluating a therapy in an A-B-A design, for instance, if it appears to be effective in the B phase following baseline, the design would require removing the therapy during the final A phase. You would thus deny the patient the benefit of the therapy with a return to baseline. If you have eliminated a neurotic condition such as a phobia, you would reinstate the phobia with great trepidation to say the least. Or suppose a treatment is effective with hyperactive children. One can just imagine a teacher's reaction if the researcher attempted to reinstate the hyperactive behavior in the classroom. If the therapy is not beneficial, or even detrimental as some therapies may be, withdrawing treatment would, of course, be no problem.

TABLE 10-2 Single-Case Experimental Drug Strategies (from Barlow & Hersen, 1984, Table 6-1)

No.	Design	Type	Blind Possible
1	A-A$_1$	Quasi-experimental	None
2	A-B	Quasi-experimental	None
3	A$_1$-B	Quasi-experimental	Single or double
4	A-A$_1$-A	Experimental	None
5	A-B-A	Experimental	None
6	A$_1$-B-A$_1$	Experimental	Single or double
7	A$_1$-A-A$_1$	Experimental	Single or double
8	B-A-B	Experimental	None
9	B-A$_1$-B	Experimental	Single or double
10	A-A$_1$-A-A$_1$	Experimental	Single or double
11	A-B-A-B	Experimental	None
12	A$_1$-B-A$_1$-B	Experimental	Single or double
13	A-A$_1$-B-A$_1$-B	Experimental	Single or double
14	A-A$_1$-A-A$_1$-B-A$_1$-B	Experimental	Single or double
15	A$_1$-B-A$_1$-C-A$_1$-C	Experimental	Single or double

Note: A = no drug; A$_1$ = placebo; B = drug 1; C = drug 2.

Withdrawal and reversal designs are thus precluded when you have irreversible effects. One possible solution is to employ a multiple-baseline design (see Appendix B at the end of this chapter) in which withdrawal or reversal of treatments is not required.[4] Consequently, if the treatment affects one baseline, but does not affect the other (control) baselines, it could be concluded that the irreversible treatment is effective. Another possible solution with a beneficial therapy would be to use a B-A-B design in which the treatment is administered first, then it is withdrawn, and finally reinstated, leaving the patient with any benefit that might have resulted from the treatment. Still, the lack of an initial baseline precludes an effective evaluation of the treatment in the first B phase. It would be preferable in this case, then, to use an A-B-A-B design.

Order and Interaction Effects. In all times-series designs there can be order effects resulting in confounding. Practice on one treatment may improve performance under a later treatment, or the first treatment may lead to fatigue or sensitization for the second. Another kind of effect might lead to a limitation in generalization. For instance, if a therapy is being evaluated, it could be ineffective in the first B phase of an A-B-A-B design but effective in the second B phase. The conclusion would be that for successful application, the therapy should be presented, then withdrawn, and presented again. While this could be a novel approach, its serious advocacy would probably startle and confound both therapist and patient.

Was a Treatment Effective? Was any change in behavior a reliable one as a function of the introduction of a treatment condition? First, there may have been a change, but it may not have been large enough to allow us to conclude that it was truly a reliable modification in behavior. We will discuss this issue under graphic and statistical analysis in Appendix A at the end of this

chapter. But assuming that a reliable change in the behavior occurred, was it specifically produced by the introduction of the independent variable, or was it merely because something different was done? One solution, as we discussed when considering the control problem of the placebo effect, is to employ an A-B-C-B design. As we saw, if the behavior during the C phase resembles that during the A phase, the likelihood is increased that the change during the B phase is specifically produced by the intervention.

Baseline Problems. The designs discussed in this chapter, as well as some in the next chapter, rest on the assumption that a stable baseline has been established. If the baseline varies considerably, it is difficult to assess any reliable change in behavior following intervention.

Another baseline problem could occur with an A-B-A-B design if the second baseline is markedly different from the first. If, for instance, there is a considerable improvement in the second baseline, a definitive assessment of the effect of the intervention would be precluded. One would not know whether there was a positive transfer from the B to the second A phase, or whether there was an improvement in the response measure merely because the individual had experience in the research environment.

Some additional problems have been discussed by Barlow and Hersen (1984) in some detail under the topic of "Deteriorating Baselines." They present some possible solutions for decreasing baselines, for variable baselines, for variable-stable baselines, for increasing-decreasing baselines, and for decreasing-increasing baselines. However, these problems require more detailed analysis than would be profitable here. One example should suffice. If you are studying number of facial tics that a person emits, suppose that your baseline increases over time. Then, when a treatment is applied, suppose that there is no change in slope; rather, the response measure continues to increase at the same rate as it did during the baseline period. In that case, perhaps the

---

[4] Another solution would be the use of a changing-criterion design, as discussed earlier.

treatment was ineffective because it did not result in a change in slope. On the other hand, perhaps it *was* effective, and, had it not been introduced, the baseline slope would have decreased. If there was a decrease in the slope following intervention, one could reasonably conclude that the treatment caused a deterioration in the response measure.

Should you encounter any of these baseline problems, you could consult Barlow and Hersen (1984) for possible solutions.

Researcher Bias. Earlier in this chapter we discussed the possible bias on the part of the researcher as to when a treatment is applied or withdrawn. That is, the researcher could be responding to cues that the participant's behavior is about to change, at which time the treatment would be introduced or withdrawn. Such possible bias could be prevented when establishing the time periods for the study. For example, before data are collected, the length of the baseline and of the treatment phases would be precisely specified and rigidly adhered to. These time values could be kept from the data collector who is measuring the behavior so that the researcher would not know when the conditions had changed. Researcher bias is also a problem with regard to "seeing" the effects that one expects when they are not really there.

Practical Limitations. A single-subject design is feasible only if you have a participant who will cooperate by giving sufficient (sometimes considerable) amounts of time and will willingly be measured repeatedly. Such difficulties, seldom present with rats and pigeons, are sometimes problems with humans.

Sometimes the treatment is not one that can be administered repeatedly, or the dependent variable cannot be measured repeatedly. For instance, once certain problems are solved, there is no further dependent-variable measure to be taken.

Generalization. Some researchers have concluded that limitation of generalizability has retarded single-participant methodology more than any other factor. However, this is an excessively harsh condemnation since the problems of generalizing are essentially the same for both single-participant methodology and for group designs, as we shall take up in Chapter 12. To generalize from results on one participant, we would need to replicate a study systematically with several other participants. But more than that, ideally, we should have different researchers replicate the study, and it should also be replicated in different laboratories. If such replications confirm the original findings, one could generalize the effect of the treatments to laboratories (environments), to researchers, and to participants.

Magnitude of Effects. One shortcoming of designs in which repeated treatments are given to the same individual concerns the degree to which a treatment is effective for naive individuals, that is, for individuals who have not experienced those previous treatments. It is true that when participants have been exposed to previous conditions, we can estimate whether an intervention *is* effective. But since a change in behavior following that intervention has followed some previous treatment(s), we cannot tell *how* effective the intervention is for individuals who have *not* experienced those previous conditions. Of course, if there is no previous condition other than baseline, as in an A-B design, there is no problem. Another way to estimate the magnitude of the effect of treatment is to use a between-groups design in which a change in behavior can be evaluated relative to a control group. A "compromise" approach would be to replicate successfully a study in which there are several treatments using participants with single-subject methodology and then to conduct the between-groups experiment to assess the magnitude of the effect with a sample of untreated (naive) participants.

COMMENTS ON GROUP DESIGNS

The Issue of Averages Again. Earlier we noted a criticism of the group designs in that the conclusions gained from them rest on group means that may be misleading for individuals. Under some conditions, the means of the groups may or may not be sufficiently indicative of individual behavior. In such cases clearly we need to employ idiographic methodology.

Error Variance. One presumed advantage of studying the individual versus groups concerns the reduction of error variance. Several times we have noted that repeated-treatment designs employ the same participant as his or her own control, thus eliminating individual differences. The effect is to reduce error variance in the study, where error variance is a measure of the variance for which we cannot account. Advocates of the single-subject approach hold that a major advantage of single-subject methodology is the reduction of error variance and, it is hoped, its complete elimination. As we have emphasized, however, this goal is not unique to single-subject researchers since all scientists want to reduce error variance as much as possible. However, it is not possible to eliminate error variance *completely*. The reason for this hinges on an ongoing philosophical debate: Is there some built-in indeterminism in this world that limits us to only probabilistic scientific laws? Or is the universe really 100 percent deterministic and our inability to state scientific laws with absolute certainty due merely to insufficiently effective control procedures?

CONCLUSION

Single-participant methodology, which has been used exclusively in the Experimental Analysis of Behavior, as well as in many other areas of research, has much to recommend it. Skinner's work, and that inspired by him, has had a major influence on contemporary psychology. In addition to his contributions to pure science, this methodology has had a sizable impact in such technological areas as education (e.g., programmed learning), social control, clinical psychology (through behavior modification), and so

forth. It is likely that, should you continue to progress in psychology, you will find that you can make good use of this type of design. Particularly at this stage in the development of psychology we should encourage a variety of approaches for we have many questions that are difficult to answer. No single methodological approach can seriously claim that it will be universally successful, and we should maintain as large an arsenal as possible. Sometimes a given problem can be most effectively attacked by one kind of design, whereas another is more likely to yield to a different design.

CHAPTER SUMMARY

I. There are many applications of the paradigm in which a single participant is intensively studied under different conditions over an extended period of time. When there is more than one treatment condition, this is an instance of a repeated-treatments design.

II. The most thorough systematic application is the Experimental Analysis of Behavior in which the strategy is to reduce error variance primarily by reducing individual differences and by increasing experimental control.

A. For the Experimental Analysis of Behavior, an operant level is first established, namely, the frequency of responding per unit time (this is response *rate*) prior to introducing the experimental treatment.

B. Controlling operants: an operant is a well-defined, objectively measurable, easily performed response that is controlled by its consequences. When a positive or negative reinforcement is *contingent* on them, their rate (probability) is increased. But when a negative stimulus is presented contingent on the operant, or when a positive stimulus is withdrawn contingent on the response, punishment occurs; in this case the response is suppressed as long as the punishment or the threat of punishment persists (but the response is not permanently eliminated).

C. The dependent-variable measure is expressed in a cumulative record that indicates the total number of operants that occurred and precisely when they occurred.

D. The cumulative record is subjected to graphic analysis, a process whereby any response changes are ascribed to changes in treatments.

E. Statistical analysis of a cumulative record (or other longitudinal measures of the dependent variable) can also be conducted.

III. Types of single-participant designs with replication.

A. The withdrawal (A-B-A) paradigm is basic. For this an operant level is established (A), the independent variable is introduced (B), and then withdrawn (A). Changes in behavior can thus be systematically ascribed to the introduction and withdrawal of the independent variable.

1. The A-B-A-B paradigm is an extension of the A-B-A paradigm in which the independent variable is introduced again (and so on, e.g., A-B-A-B-A . . .).

2. Modifications may be made so that the behavior to be controlled may be represented as A and the withdrawal of the contingent stimulus as B.

3. Alternating-treatments designs are a specific subclass of the A-B-A-B design in which two treatments are alternated for a single individual.

B. For the reversal design measures taken on two incompatible behaviors. An operant level is established for both; then a treatment such as reinforcement or punishment is administered for one but not the other. At an appropriate time the treatment conditions are reversed.

C. Changing-criterion designs systematically shift the criteria for administering consequences during the intervention phase.

IV. Fields of application.

A. In behavior therapy, objectively measurable characteristics of patients are dependent variables for evaluating therapeutic treatments.

B. For drug evaluations, a variety of designs can be used to assess effectiveness.

V. Difficulties encountered with single-subject methodology.

A. Irreversible effects.

B. Order and interaction effects.

C. Questions as to whether the treatment was effective (though this question is not unique to single-subject designs).

D. Baseline problems.

E. Dependent (nonindependent) behaviors.

F. Researcher bias.

G. Length of time required for a participant.

H. Practical limitations.

I. Generalization.

J. Magnitude of effects.

VI. Appendices

A. Statistical analysis of time-series designs.

1. An autocorrelation is computed between data points for a single participant. If the correlation is low or nonexistent, one can apply a t-or F-test to assess the effect of a treatment.

2. You can compute a C statistic to determine if trends in the data series are significantly different during intervention relative to during baseline.

B. Multiple-baseline designs are those in which the treatment is successively administered to one target behavior at a time while several compatible behaviors are used as baseline control measures. Two other multiple-baseline designs are those in which several different individuals are studied in the same environment and where different participants are studied in different environments.

CRITICAL REVIEW FOR THE STUDENT

1. Discuss operant conditioning paradigms within the context of repeated-treatments designs. Would you apply a statistical test to determine whether an experimental effect with an $N = 1$ design is reliable?

2. Do you subscribe to the basic "logic" of between-groups designs, or are you more positively influenced by the logic of $N = 1$ research? Perhaps there are problems for which you think one design might be more appropriate and other problems for which the other approach is more appropriate; if so what would be the difference between those problems?

3. Basic terms from the Experimental Analysis of Behavior that you should be able to define:
   Operant level
   Operant conditioning
   Discriminitive stimulus
   Classes of reinforcement and punishment
   Cululative record
   Graphic analysis
   Withdrawal design

A-B-A paradigm
A-B-A-B paradigm
Reversal design
Changing-criterion designs

4. What position do you take on graphic analysis versus statistical analysis of time-series designs?

5. Can you apply one of the paradigms discussed in this chapter to a practical problem in your everyday life; for example, how would you help a friend to lose weight or a relative to stop smoking or help someone to drive more safely?

6. Do you generally favor an idiographic or a nomothetic approach in research?

7. Other terms you should define are
Response rate
Dependent behavior
Autocorrelation
Single-blind experiment
Double-blind experiment

Appendix A
Statistical Analysis of Time-Series Designs

We noted earlier that graphic analysis through visual inspection is the usual method for assessing the effects of treatments in single-subject research. Many idiographic researchers even look at statistical tests with disdain. However, one's confidence in the effectiveness of an intervention can be increased when graphic analysis and a statistical analysis lead to the same conclusion. When they do not, the statistical analysis apparently indicates a reliable effect that is not so apparent in the graphic analysis. Statistical analysis is more precise and accurate than merely "eyeballing" the data using the familiar "eye test." A statistically reliable finding may be obtained when the data are too noisy and chaotic to reach a positive conclusion through graphic analysis. This is particularly true for applied research in everyday life settings where control is poor.

The Assumption of Independence. The major problem is statistical analysis that we discussed in Chapter 9 on repeated treatments designs is that successive observations on the same participant are not independent. Since the single-participant design is one variation of a repeated-treatments design, it too is subject to the problem of violation of the assumption of independence of data points when considering statistical analysis of the data—each data point in the single-participant design is related to (dependent on) each preceding data point.

The essence of *dependent* data points in time-series designs, such as we have been discussing in this chapter, is that you can to some extent predict a later data point for one participant on the basis of that participant's earlier data points. The essential question is, to just what extent *can* you successfully make such predictions? The first step, then, in statistical analysis of time-series data is actually to assess the extent to which dependency exists among successive data points. If the dependency is computed to be low or nonexistent, then the advice is to proceed with a statistical analysis.

Assessing the Extent of Dependency. We compute what is known as an *autocorrelation*, which is a correlation between data points separated by different time intervals in the series. The time interval selected is referred to as a "lag." The simplest lag is called "lag 1," which is generally sufficient to reveal serial dependency in the data. An autocorrelation of lag 1 is computed by pairing the first data point with the second, the second with the third, the third with the fourth, and so on throughout the entire series of data points. For instance, in a series of 4, 5, 3, 2, 4, 1, 5, and 6, one would pair the values as follows:

4	5	(the first two are paired, i.e., 4 and 5)
5	3	(the next two are paired, etc.)
3	2	
2	4	
4	1	
1	5	
5	6	

Then one would compute a correlation coefficient between these two columns of data. If the correlation computed between such data were close to zero, you could proceed with your statistical analysis as follows.

Statistical Analysis with Low Dependency. Suppose you have an A-B design where, as usual, A is the baseline and B is the intervention. The strategy is to use all the data points during baseline as the data for one condition and the data points during the B phase for the other condition. For instance, in the foregoing series, suppose that the first four data points are from the baseline and the second four are from the treatment condition. In this case, we could compute a *t*-test between the values of 4, 5, 3, and 2 versus the treatment values of 4, 1, 5, 6. If the computed value of *t* were significant and if the mean were higher for the treatment condition, we could conclude that the response measure changed reliably after the intervention. The same general principles could be followed with other designs such as in an A-B-A design or an A-B-A-B design. In these cases you would have three and four conditions, whereupon you would follow the principles developed in Chapter 7 for multigroup designs. The difference here is that you would be reaching conclusions with regard to single participants rather than groups. Generalization to a population of participants occurs with replication. Consequently, if you found a significant effect for one participant, you would replicate your study with other individuals. If statistically reliable changes in behavior were found for all the several participants studied individually, your confidence in your conclusions about the effectiveness of your treatment would be sizable.

Other Considerations. Sizable advances have been made in statistical analysis of time-series designs, and there are a number of variations that can be applied for different problems. This is true for single-participant as well as group time-series designs. We shall discuss group time-series designs in the next chapter. Here we have discussed only the simplest possible statistical analysis, but to extend briefly your thinking in this area, we may note that analyses may consider changes in the slopes of the curves. For instance, suppose that there is an increase in slope in the baseline but a more marked increase in slope following intervention. You could ask the question as to whether the change in slope was a statistically reliable effect. Other problems occur when baselines are unstable or when the autocorrelation that you compute is in fact statistically reliable. Yet other questions arise concerning the number of data points that are required for successful analysis of time-series designs. Some authorities recommend at least 50 and preferably 100 data points (but see the following discussion of a procedure recommended by Tryon 1982). For these and other issues, you are also referred to Kratochwill (1978), to Kazdin (1982), and to Chapter 9 in Barlow and Hersen (1984).

A Simplified Time-Series Analysis. The foregoing procedure is time consuming and requires numerous data points for each experimental phase. Tryon (1982) presents a simpler computation, of the statistic C. The advantages of computing C are that it can be calculated by hand, can be used with as few as 8 data points, and helps to ascertain whether responding during the phase is stabilized.

The primary question to be answered

with the C statistic is whether or not the time series contains any trends, that is, systematic departures from random variation. First, the baseline data are evaluated to determine whether or not there is a trend. If there is no trend, the first treatment series can be combined with the baseline series of data and the ensemble can be tested. If the C statistic is significant, it is evidence that the treatment series departs from the baseline series. The conclusion is that the treatment was probably effective.

As an example, Tryon (1982) presents some data on the frequency of "talking-out" behavior in a class of 15 mentally retarded children ages 9 to 11 years. A talk-out was defined as all vocalizations that were not authorized by the teacher. Ten baseline data points were obtained, as presented in Figure 10-10. The computation indicated that C was not reliable. Thus the baseline does not have a significant trend, which is desired.

During the treatment phase, the teacher put a token in a glass jar on the teacher's desk at the end of every 5-minute period in which no talking-out behavior occurred by any class member. Each student received the number of tokens that were in the jar at the end of each period, and the tokens could be exchanged for edibles.

The computation of C confirmed the graphic analysis that there was a shift in the trend of the time series from the baseline observations to that during intervention.

Finally, the procedure of giving tokens to the group was discontinued for a two-week period. C indicated that there was no reliable trend in this period, again as desired.

The use of the C statistic is an elegant procedure and C is relatively simple to compute. If you find occasion to use this statistic, you are referred to Tryon (1982). Kazdin (1982) also discusses statistical techniques for single-subject designs.

Appendix B
Multiple-Baseline Designs

The concept of this class of design is that several baselines are simultaneously established prior to the administration of the treatment(s). We shall discuss three kinds of multiple-baseline designs: (1) the multiple-baseline design across behaviors, (2) the multiple-baseline design across subjects, and (3) the multiple-baseline design across conditions (environments).

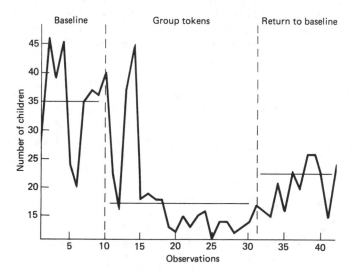

FIGURE 10-10 The total number of children participating in all incidents of unauthorized talk-outs during baseline 1, contingent presentation of group tokens, and baseline 2 phases. (From Tryon, 1982).

The Multiple-Baseline Design across Behaviors.

In this design, several compatible behaviors, that is, behaviors that occur simultaneously in the individual, are selected for study. After baselines for each class of behavior are established, a treatment is introduced for one target behavior (Figure 10-11). If that class of behavior changes while the other (control) behaviors remain stable at the baseline level, the treatment could be judged effective for that specific behavior. Then, after some time has elapsed, the same treatment is also applied to a second class of the compatible behaviors and its effects on that second target behavior are recorded. The remaining classes of behavior are, in their turn, also subjected to the treatment in this time-staggered fashion. If the treatment is effective in changing response rate following administration to each of the several classes of behaviors, there would be considerable confidence in the effectiveness of the treatment. In short, in using this design, a treatment is introduced to several behaviors with their multiple baselines of different lengths; if there is a change in each target behavior following intervention, but not in the other behaviors, it is quite likely that the change was produced by the specific treatment.

Dependent Behaviors.

The multiple-baseline designs across behaviors assume that the different responses being studied are independent. Consequently, an intervention that affects one behavior but not the others may be judged to be effective. However, if the behaviors are correlated, an intervention that affects one baseline would appear also to affect the other, correlated, behaviors, even though the treatment was not applied to those other responses. The interpretation here is difficult. On the other hand, there could be generalized effects of a treatment indicating response generalization; that is, the treatment first affected one response and subsequently affected the others through generalization. Yet another interpretation could be that the treatment had generalized effects on all behaviors; for example, the treatment could have produced widespread, general arousal of the individual. In that case, the treatment could not be said to have uniquely affected the target behavior. However, one could only determine this difficulty by taking a number of response measures simultaneously.

Multiple-Baseline Design across Subjects.

In the multiple-baseline design across behaviors, the same treatment is applied sequentially across different behaviors emitted by a single participant. Another application of the multiple-baseline design is that in which a particular treatment is applied in sequence to the same behavior of different individuals in the same environment. In this case, though, the treatment is applied to one participant after perhaps one hour, to a second after two hours, and so forth. Because

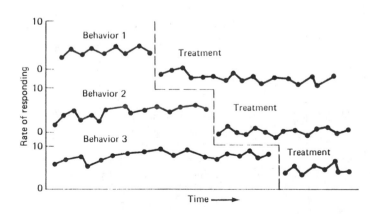

FIGURE 10-11 Illustrating a multiple-baseline design across behaviors in a single subject. A treatment is applied contingent only on behavior #1 occurring. Later, after a longer baseline, the treatment is then applied to behavior #2. Then, eventually, the treatment is applied to the third measure of behavior. If all three measures of behavior change following the intervention after multiple baselines, the treatment is judged to be effective.

of this time-staggered intervention after different baseline periods, this design is sometimes labeled a "time-lagged control design."

As an illustration of a multiple baseline across-subjects design, Singh and Millichamp (1987) used verbal and physical prompts to teach eight profoundly mentally retarded adults how to enhance their independent play. The study resulted because institutionalized mentally retarded persons fail to engage in appropriate play and leisure activities. The participants were adult females between the ages of 15 and 25 years of age, residing in an institution for mentally retarded persons.

During baseline the participants were instructed to play with toys, but if they did not they were verbally prompted to return to their seats. Two different kinds of behavior were recorded: independent play and inappropriate play. As can be seen in Figure 10-12, baselines were taken for 5, 9, 13, 17, 21, 25, 29, and 33 play periods, which were of one-hour duration each. For each of the participants (Kim through Ruby) we can notice that the baselines are typically low for both independent and inappropriate play. During intervention, both verbal and physical prompts were given: they were verbally instructed to play with one of the toys that was directly in front of them and provided physical guidance if they did not. The physical guidance consisted of placing their hands on the toys and gently guiding them in play actions. For instance, Kim had a baseline established by recording the two dependent-variable measures during each of five play periods. Then on the sixth play period Kim was prompted both verbally and physically, whereupon Kim's amount of independent play dramatically increased. Eventually, the amount of Kim's inappropriate play stabilized at a relatively low level. We can also notice that in follow-up sessions some weeks later there was long-term maintenance of Kim's independent play behavior while Kim's inappropriate play behavior remained at a very low level. Kim's behavior was typical of all other participants so that we can conclude that in all cases there was an increased

amount of independent play behavior that was maintained. The specific amount of independent play behavior during baseline had mean rates ranging from 0 to 5 percent, rising substantially during prompting and being maintained in follow-up sessions.

In another study, Dahlquist and Gil (1986) attempted to control periodontal disease, a major cause of the loss of teeth when people pass the age of 35. To help prevent periodontal disease, four children were taught to floss their teeth following different baseline periods in which two measures of percent of plaque (interproximal and facial/lingual) were measured. Figure 10-13 shows that both measures of amount of plaque (which contributes to periodontal disease) decreased during the treatment phase. Of greater importance, however, the parents were taught how to maintain the flossing behavior during a three-to four-month follow-up period in which rewards were administered contingent upon the flossing.

Multiple-Baseline Design across Conditions (Environments). In this design, a treatment is applied to different participants who are in different conditions or environments. For example, you might have three different patients in three different rooms. Different baseline periods would be established for each participant, for example, 30 minutes for one, 45 minutes for another, and 60 minutes for another. After each baseline period is concluded, the treatment, such as reinforcement, might be applied contingent on a certain kind of response being emitted. Once again, if there is a response change in all participants following the intervention, the treatment is likely to be effective.

Summary. Multiple-baseline designs may be used to evaluate the effect of independent variables across: (1) several different behaviors emitted by the same participant, (2) several different individuals in the same environment, and (3) different participants who are in different environments.

Let us emphasize the difference between the second and third variations of the multiple-baseline designs. In the multiple-base-

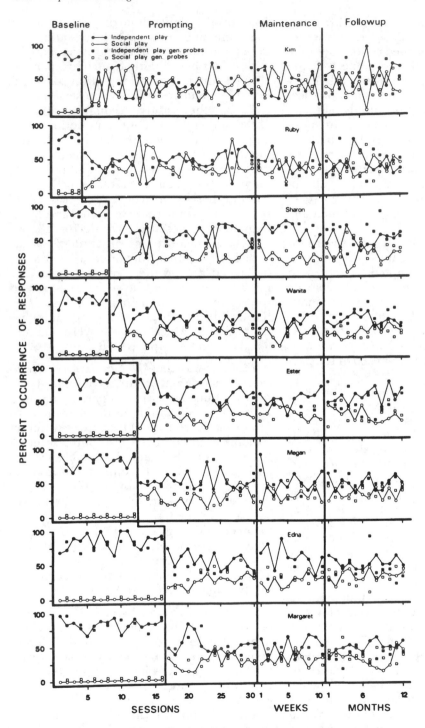

FIGURE 10-12   Illustration of the multiple-baseline-across-subjects design. The percentage of independent and inappropriate play for all subjects. Following session 65, maintenance data were collected one day a week (adapted from Singh & Millichamp, 1987).

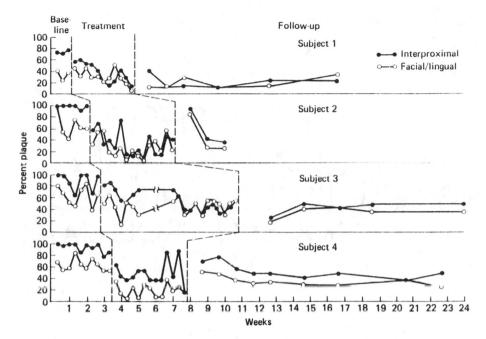

FIGURE 10-13 Illustration of a multiple-baseline design across subjects. Note that different baselines were established for each of the four subjects. The treatment was effective in reducing amount of plaque in the mouth, as also shown by follow-up data (from Dahlquist & Gil, 1986).

line design across subjects, a treatment is applied to the same class of behavior in different participants who are in the same environment. However, in the third variation, the treatment is applied to the same behavior when the participants are in different environments.

It should now be obvious that a major advantage of any kind of multiple-baseline design is that there is no need to withdraw the treatment once it has been applied (in contrast to some of the other designs that we have studied), so that it avoids the ethical problem of withdrawing a beneficial treatment to a participant in a real-life, practical situation.

chapter 11

QUASI-EXPERIMENTAL DESIGNS: SEEKING SOLUTIONS TO SOCIETY'S PROBLEMS

Major purpose:

To attempt to solve problems of everyday life through systematic research when it is not feasible to conduct an experiment.

What you are going to find:

1. The beneficial interrelationship that exists between pure and applied science (technology).
2. The two most prominent quasi-experimental designs:
   a. the method of systematic observation (nonequivalent comparison groups)
   b. interrupted time series
3. The limitations of quasi-experimental designs.

What you should acquire:

1. The ability to infer causal relationships between independent and dependent variables with varying degrees of probability, depending on the methodological soundness of the design on which the inferences are based.
2. An understanding that conditions of society can be improved through the application of causal relationships; this is accomplished by instituting an independent-variable condition and thereby achieving the desired outcome (a value of the dependent variable).

APPLIED VERSUS PURE SCIENCE

The spirit in which this book was originally written (1960) was that pure and applied psychology are not mutually exclusive and that they can facilitate each other. There should be no controversy between science and technology, or between "experimental" and "clinical" psychology. The fruits of pure science can often be applied for the solution of society's problems, just as research on technological (applied, practical) problems may provide foundations for scientific ("basic," "pure") advances. The existence of practical problems may make gaps in our scientific knowledge apparent, and technological research can demand the development of new methods and principles in science. It is, furthermore, common for a researcher to engage in both scientific and applied research at different times, or a research project may be astutely designed to yield scientific knowledge while also curing some of society's ills. The issue, then, is not whether we are to favor pure science to the exclusion of applied matters or vice versa—we can address both. One need not be an experimentalist *or* a clinician—one could be an experimental clinician. Contrary to much popular opinion, we do not have to choose up sides on such issues.

APPLYING PSYCHOLOGICAL PRINCIPLES TO IMPROVE SOCIETY

Professor B.F. Skinner, the major contemporary driving force behind single-participant research designs, is a good example of a scientist-technologist. Although Professor Skinner spent much of his life acquiring knowledge for its own sake (science), he probably spent more of it applying principles of behavior for the solution of society's problems (technology).

Historically, society has made minimal use of control conditions in attempts to solve practical problems. Skinner characterized it this way: "So far, men have designed their cultures largely by guesswork, including some very lucky hits; but we are not far from a stage of knowledge in which this can be changed" (Skinner, 1961, p. 545). The guesswork has, much to Skinner's dismay, often involved punitive techniques—the principles of the Old Testament ("An eye for an eye and a tooth for a tooth") are often applied for controlling behavior. How often do we observe parents beating their children to "get them to behave"?

Science has shown that selective reinforcement of behavior not only is more effective than punishment, but reinforcement also has none of the unfortunate consequences of punishment. In simplest form, the principle is to reinforce culturally desirable responses and not to reinforce undesirable behavior. Only under certain conditions, should undesirable behavior be punished to allow alternative, more desirable behavior to occur. In his classic *Walden Two* (1948), Skinner illustrated in detail how he would design and achieve the ideal culture. The key is to arrange effective contingencies of reinforcement to develop and maintain socially desirable responses. To accomplish this one should wisely reinforce desirable social responses and selectively withhold reinforcement or sometimes punish socially undesirable responses.

Skinner thus principally advocated the application of existing scientific knowledge to solve our practical problems. Certainly the wise and effective application of behavioral principles to such mounting problems as those of crime, drugs, auto accidents, and child-rearing abuses would be far better than mere guesswork. In conducting business at our various governmental levels, we are constantly changing policies and introducing reforms. A new president or mayor is elected with campaign promises to change this or that—to abolish welfare, to extend it, to modify the penal system, and so on. Unfortunately, however, society seldom systematically evaluates the effects of reforms, and we have little in the way of an objective basis for ascertaining whether a new policy has actually improved matters. The same can be said of many other aspects of our society, such as in our universities and colleges. We are constantly changing our education practices, the character of our curricula, our graduation requirements. The pendulum endlessly swings between extremes of decreasing and increasing course requirements for students. *The essence of this chapter is that we are often in a position to evaluate programs and policies systematically and thus gradually to develop objectively established prac-*

tices that are beneficial for society. The Declaration of Independence does not guarantee us happiness, only the opportunity to pursue it, which we can do more effectively as the result of systematic research.

Some may deny that current societal reforms are only guesswork and say that data *are* presently collected on various cultural practices. Certainly there are acres and acres of governmental records that constitute data of sorts. However, they are seldom used to improve a governmental practice by systematically relating them to independent-variable conditions under which they were gathered. Systematic research *can* replace unused data gathered under conditions of chaotically changing policies! Unfortunately, however, we often cannot conduct experiments in everyday life with proper control conditions. So we have a dilemma, for a major theme of this book is that we countenance sound, and shun shoddy, research. For instance, in Chapter 4 in the section "When to Abandon an Experiment" we suggested that if there is an important unsolvable confound you should consider abandoning your study. This statement is easy to make when we talk about acquiring knowledge for its own sake ("pure science")—it is hard to conceive of a situation in which poorly designed *scientific* research can be tolerated. But many technological issues pose another question. To solve an important problem of society, the researcher may simply not be able to conduct a well-controlled experiment properly. Consider a study of the effects of welfare programs on unemployment, or the effects of capital punishment for deterring crime. One can imagine the national furor if we attempted randomly to assign half of the present welfare population to a control condition in which their welfare checks were discontinued, or if we randomly assigned convicted murderers to experimental conditions either of death or life imprisonment. The Nazis in World War II conducted atrocious medical experiments with little regard for human life, but in a civilized society such extremes for the sake of research are simply not tolerated—the kind of research cited in Chapter 4 in which half of the "participants" were administered a potentially effective antidote to prevent death due to poisoning may have been allowable in ancient times but not today.

Since it is often not feasible to conduct research that satisfies the highest scientific standards, the question is whether certain compromises in rigorous methodology are justifiable. If the problem is sufficiently important, one that *demands* solution, it may be better to compromise research standards than not to attempt a research-based solution at all. Society is replete with examples in which some research was better than none. For instance, research that fell short of high laboratory standards effectively eliminated airplane hijackings. The quasi-experimental designs presented by Cook and Campbell (1979) have been prominently applied to solve practical problems.

QUASI-EXPERIMENTAL DESIGNS

Seeking Cause-Effect Relations. The defining feature of a quasi-experimental design is that participants are *not* randomly assigned to different conditions. The method of systematic observation is a quasi-experimental design in which participants are classified according to some characteristic, such as high versus low intelligence; the performance of the high and low groups is then compared on a dependent-variable measure. The shortcoming of such a quasi-experimental design is that the independent variable is confounded with extraneous variables so that we do not know whether any change in the dependent variable is actually due to variation of the independent variable; that is, the probability of a conclusion that the independent variable produced a given behavioral change (reduced dependence on welfare, decreased drug traffic, and so on) is lower when using a quasi-experimental design than when it results from an experiment. Although we can infer a causal relationship between an independent and dependent variable in *any* study, that inference is most probably true when it results from an experiment. In earlier chapters we recognized that we never know anything about the empirical world with certainty, but we do seek conclusions with the highest probability, consonant with reasonable effort. The best of our experiments may yield faulty conclusions, as in rejecting the null hypothesis 5 times out of 100 when it should not be rejected. Consequently the empirical probability of a causal conclusion from a well-designed experiment may be, say, only 0.92. If we *must* settle for less than a rigorous experiment, as using a good quasi-experimental design, perhaps the probability of a cause-effect relationship may drop to 0.70. Even less rigorous quasi-experimental designs may yield lower probabilities (perhaps 0.50, or 0.40). The probability of a causal conclusion from a correlational, clinic, or case history study would be yet lower (perhaps 0.25) but still may be the best information that we have. Certainly it is preferable for us to operate on the basis of low-probability (yet statistically reliable) knowledge than on no knowledge (0.00-probability relationships) whatsoever. As Campbell has developed this theme,

The general ethic, here advocated for public administrators as well as social scientists, is to use the very best method possible, aiming at "true experiments" with random control groups. But where randomized treatments are not possible, a self-critical use of quasi-experimental designs is advocated. We must do the best we can with what is available to us (Campbell, 1969, p. 411).

In short, to improve society we should accumulate as much knowledge of as high degree of probability as we can. For such a purpose we *need* quasi-experimental designs.

Cook and Campbell (1979) presented a variety of quasi-experimental designs and applied them to a number of societal problems. There are two major classes of such quasi-experimental designs: (1) *nonequivalent comparison-group designs*, and (2) *interrupted time-series designs*. To facilitate our discussion of these designs and specific variations of them, let us first summarize the notational system used by Cook and Campbell.

Notational System for Quasi-Experimental Designs

Remember that quasi-experimental designs employ groups that are already formed so that individuals are not randomly assigned to conditions. Consequently, in this chapter we are not discussing *control* groups (for they are composed of randomly assigned participants), but we are discussing *comparison* groups (those already formed and susceptible to study). This distinction between control and comparison groups is an important labeling difference because it immediately alerts the researcher to expect confounding; that is, the term *comparison group* implies confounding with an attendant reduction in the confidence that one may place in the conclusion that any change in the dependent variable could be attributed to the independent variable, the treatment condition.

Also note that many characteristics of these designs and their limitations were discussed in Chapter 10: While some of these designs are used in single-participant research, they are also applicable to group research. It is thus well for you to review Chapter 10 as a basis for proceeding with this chapter. Much of what we said there need not be repeated here.

There are two symbols for notation: X represents a treatment condition (an intervention of the independent variable into the data series), and O stands for an observation of behavior. Subscripts to O (O_1, O_2) indicate repeated observations in which data are collected—they are the dependent-variable measures. The simplest type of design is referred to as the **one-group posttest-only design** for which the paradigm is

$$\overline{\quad X \quad O \quad}$$

The notation thus tells us that one group of participants has experienced a treatment

(X), after which a dependent-variable measure (O) was taken on them. The confounding is so atrocious with this design that we present it only as a start of the notational system and for discussing the control shortcomings of quasi-experimental designs. Although the value of the independent-variable (treatment) condition *may* be related to the value of the observation (O), any causal inference is precluded. The lack of a comparison group that did not experience the treatment essentially prevents any inference that a change in the dependent-variable score is ascribable to the treatment.

The One-Group Pretest-Posttest Design

$$\overline{O_1 \quad X \quad O_2}$$

This design is an improvement on the one-group posttest-only design because it establishes a baseline prior to the intervention with the treatment. One can thus recognize that this is an A-B-A design with the virtues and limitations of that design that we discussed in Chapter 10.

You can continue to translate the symbols used for representing single-participant designs into those for quasi-experimental designs to facilitate your transfer of learning between the two. The design $\overline{X \quad O}$, in a single-participant methodology, would be labeled simply B, which once again emphasizes how little we can learn from that design. The distinction is maintained to emphasize that if an A-B-A design is used, it is for a single-participant, while if an $\overline{O_1 \quad X \quad O_2}$ label is used, it is for a group study.

The pretest (O_1) is typically a measure of the dependent variable prior to the intervention. Following this the group experiences the treatment (X), and a posttest is administered on the dependent variable (O_2). One could statistically analyze this design by computing the gain scores from O_1 to O_2 and then test the mean difference with the paired *t*-test (Chapter 9). If so, recall possible problems discussed there about gain scores.

An example of this design would be the introduction of a new curriculum or method of instruction in a school or university. As is so frequently done in education, great new "insights" are obtained by the current generation of educators as we institute the "new math," "return to the basic three Rs," revolutionize the educational process with programmed learning, and on and on. When we are somewhat more astute than merely using the posttest-only design, we take measures (O_1) on our students *prior* to intervention with the new method. Then we introduce the new method and almost universally conclude on the basis of improved scores at the end of the course (O_2) that the new method is successful in improving education. Such a conclusion *is* possibly valid, but it certainly has a low degree of probability!

Shortcomings of This Design. Perhaps the most important reason that *any* intervention seems successful is because of the suggestive placebo effect—merely doing *anything* new or different may heighten motivation, leading students to work harder; similarly there are demand characteristics wherein everybody expects the new method to produce better results, which influences both students and administrators positively in that direction. Clearly, an experiment in which there is no *control* group necessitates such confounding.

Another difficulty with this design is that something else beneficial may have happened to the students between the pretest and the posttest. Apparently, improved learning from O_1 to O_2 may have actually occurred because of other academic courses or because of events outside the educational setting.

Finally, there may be an improvement in dependent-variable scores *regardless* of the treatment intervening between the pretest and posttest. Taking the pretest may itself have been a learning experience so that the students performed better on the posttest only because of practice on the pretest. Perhaps the students matured somewhat over the semester and became a bit wiser and better educated in general leading to improved performance on the posttest, regardless of the new method. The addition of at least a comparison group improves this design somewhat, as in the following case.

Nonequivalent Comparison-Group Designs

These are probably the most commonly used of the quasi-experimental designs, an instance of which is the method of systematic observation discussed in earlier chapters. Two or more groups that have already been assembled naturally are studied, as with two fifth-grade classes in an elementary school. The participants thus have *not* been randomly assigned to the two groups, so that neither is a control group—only a comparison group.

The simplest instance of this design is that in which observations are made only after the treatment has been experienced by one of the groups.

The Posttest-Only Design with Nonequivalent Comparison Groups. Adding a comparison group to the one-group-only posttest design, we arrive at the following instance of a nonequivalent comparison-group design:

$$
\begin{array}{cc}
\underline{} \\
X & O \\
\text{-------} \\
& O \\
\underline{}
\end{array}
$$

Here one group experiences the treatment, following which a dependent-variable measure is taken on both groups. Because the groups may differ in so many respects, there is but a low probability that any dependent-variable difference between the groups can be ascribed to the treatment condition. This design, as with the one-group posttest-only design, is considered "generally uninterpretable," by which is meant the confounding precludes unambiguous conclusions about any causal relationships between the treatment and dependent-variable values.

One application of this design is where several groups receive different indepen-

dent-variable values. An example was suggested by Cook and Campbell in which nonequivalent groups of future parolees receive different lengths of counseling while still in prison. This design could be represented as follows, with the subscript indicating the treatment period in months. For instance, one group might have had 12 months of counseling so their treatment is symbolized as (X_{12}); then a second group had 9 months (X_9); a third, 6 months (X_6); another, 3 months (X_3); and finally, one group had no counseling (X_0).

$$
\begin{array}{cc}
\underline{} \\
X_{12} & O \\
\text{------} \\
X_9 & O \\
\text{------} \\
X_6 & O \\
\text{------} \\
X_3 & O \\
\text{------} \\
X_0 & O \\
\underline{}
\end{array}
$$

Assume that the dependent variable (O) is the frequency with which members of each group violated their paroles and that the length of counseling was positively related to the dependent variable scores. Thus we could conclude that the longer the counseling period, the less frequently the parolees violated their paroles. Because the length of the treatment was varied systematically, with attendant increases in the response measure, the probability was increased that the independent and dependent variables are functionally related. This design is thus a noticeable improvement on the two-group posttest-only design with nonequivalent comparison groups. However, because the participants are not assigned randomly to groups we must hasten to emphasize that interpretations other than that of causal relationships are possible. For instance, the individuals least likely to be returned to prison could have been selected to receive the longer parole period. For example, the administrators who assigned prisoners to counseling groups could have wanted the parole counseling to appear beneficial and therefore could have (intentionally or unconsciously) assigned high-probability-of-success prisoners to the longer-period counseling groups. With such confounding, even this variation of the posttest-only design with nonequivalent groups should be used solely under conditions of desperation.

The statistical analysis of these designs with two or more groups presents no unusual problems for us. We merely test for reliable differences between means with the *t*-test, as we developed in Chapter 6.

The Untreated Comparison-Group Design with Pretest and Posttest.[1] The following paradigm shows that there are two groups on which pretest measures are taken (O_1), following which one group receives the treatment (X) and both groups receive a posttest (O_2) which is a measure of the dependent variable. The researcher should, preferably, randomly determine which of the two or more groups receives the experimental treatment. Both groups are administered a pretest, which provides some information as to their "equality" prior to the administration of the experimental treatment. However, even if the two groups are shown to be equivalent with regard to the pretest, they no doubt differ in many other ways—even with identical pretest scores we have no reason to consider them as equivalent groups, e.g., if pretest scores are equal for IQ, the groups still may differ on means for emotionality scores.

$$\begin{array}{ccc} O_1 & X & O_2 \\ \hline O_1 & & O_2 \end{array}$$

Regardless of whether the groups are equivalent on the pretest, the experimental treatment is administered to one of the groups, following which both groups receive posttests on the dependent variable. The researcher should, preferably, randomly determine which of the two or more groups receives the experimental treatment.

Campbell and Stanley (1963) illustrated this design with a study that was conducted by Sanford and Hemphill at the United States Naval Academy at Annapolis. The question was whether midshipmen who took a psychology course developed greater confidence in social situations. The second-year class was chosen to take the psychology course while the third-year class constituted the comparison group. The second-year class reliably increased confidence scores on a social-situations questionnaire from 43.26 to 51.42, but the third-year class increased their scores only from 55.80 to 56.78. From these data one might conclude that taking the psychology course *did* result in greater confidence in social situations. However, although this conclusion is possible, alternative explanations are obvious. For instance, the greater gains made by the second-year class could have been due to some general sophistication process that occurs maximally in the second year and only minimally in the third year. If this were so, the sizable increase in scores for the second-year class would have occurred whether the midshipmen took the psychology course or not. This alternative conclusion is further strengthened by noting that the second-year class had substantially lower pretest scores and, although their gain score was greater, their posttest score was still not as high as the pretest score of the third-year class.[2]

One method of statistical analysis of this type of design would be that discussed in Chapter 9 on two repeated treatments. You could, for instance, evaluate gain scores for

---

[1]Cook and Campbell refer to the first three aforementioned designs as "generally *un*interpretable," whereas this design is "generally interpretable." Let us repeat only that *all* quasi-experimental designs are confounded, so that Cook and Campbell's use of "interpretable" here merely reflects that the inference of a causal independent-dependent-variable relationship is somewhat higher for this class of design than for the previous ones. No quasi-experimental designs are interpretable in the sense that experiments are interpretable.

[2]A preferable design would have been to form two groups from the second-year class and to have given the psychology course to only one (randomly chosen).

each group separately so that you could determine whether there was a reliable change in the dependent-variable measure for each of your groups. For this purpose you could employ the paired *t*-test. Finally, you may wish to determine whether any change from pre-to posttest was greater for one of the groups than for the other. For this purpose you could conduct an independent-groups *t*-test (Chapter 6) between the two groups, employing a gain score for each of the participants in the study. However, be sure to recall our discussion of problems in measuring gain (Chapter 9).

Although some extraneous variables are controlled with this design (e.g., both groups receive the pretest and the posttest), there are numerous differences in how the groups are treated during the conduct of the research. For instance, the two classes probably had two different teachers, perhaps they met at different times of the day and were influenced by different characteristics in the separate classrooms, and there are other confounds of the independent variable with extraneous variables that you, yourself, can think about.[3]

This introduces the basic principles for nonequivalent-group designs, but a number of variations have been used in some most interesting research applications. Cook and Campbell astutely discuss these variations and show how under some conditions rather reasonable inferences *can* be drawn from the results. Now, however, let us turn to the second kind of widely used quasi-experimental design, that in which extended-data series are studied. Much of our discussion of this class of design for single participants is also applicable here when we are considering groups. We should also repeat that when any design is applied in an everyday life "field" situation, much less control is possible than

when used under laboratory conditions. In general, the designs discussed in this chapter are applied in everyday life situations, whereas the designs in Chapter 10 in "The Experimental Analysis of Behavior" typically originated in the laboratory.

Interrupted Time-Series Designs

For this type of design periodic measurements are made on a group or individual in an effort to establish a baseline. Eventually, some kind of change is made during the ongoing time series of measurements, and the researcher seeks to determine whether a change in the dependent variable occurs. If so, one attempts to infer that the change in the time series (the dependent variable) was systematically related to the treatment.

Simple Interrupted Time-Series Designs. For this, the most basic time-series design, a number of observations are made during baseline (O_1, O_2, O_3, O_4, O_5, and so on), then the treatment (X) is introduced. The post-treatment series of observations (O_6, O_7, O_8, O_9, O_{10}, and so on) may then be analyzed according to whether there is a change in the level or in the slope following the introduction of treatment.

$$O_1 \quad O_2 \quad O_3 \quad O_4 \quad O_5 \quad X \quad O_6 \quad O_7 \quad O_8 \quad O_9 \quad O_{10}$$

Level and Slope Changes. In Chapter 10 we discussed ways in which an intervention may affect a series of observations. Cook and Campbell discuss two common forms of change in the data series that are similar to that discussion: (1) a change in the *level*, and (2) a change in the *slope*. To be very simplistic, assume that you have a baseline of observations that consists of values of 4, 4, 4, 4, at which point you introduce the treatment. If the values then shift upward to 6, 6, 6, 6, or downward to 2, 2, 2, 2, there is a sharp discontinuity at the point of interruption, which indicates a change in level. To indicate a similar discontinuity for a change in slope you could simply refer to Figure 10-3 as an

---

[3]Campbell (1969) cautioned about matching participants of the two groups on pretest scores, because this matching procedure results in regression artifacts, a phenomenon that is, incidentally, a shortcoming of matched-groups designs in general.

illustration; that is, once a stable operant level was established in the conditioning experiment, reinforcement started, whereupon there was a dramatic increase in the slope of the cumulative record. *Changes of either level or slope are used as bases for inferring that the treatment causally affected the dependent variable.*

An Example. Cook and Campbell illustrate this design with the classic study of the British Industrial Fatigue Research Board, which introduced experimental quantitative management science. This methodology was a substantial leap forward in the use of quasi-experimental designs. The question was, what would happen to productivity if the workday were shortened from 10 to 8 hours. To answer this question, hourly output in dozens of hours was computed each month for 17 months to establish a baseline. As we can note in Figure 11-1, the change from 10 to 8 hours in August 1919 was followed by a noticeable increase in hourly output. This upward shift in level led to the conclusion that shortening the workday from 10 to 8 hours *improved* hourly productivity.

PROBLEMS WITH THE DESIGN. Some of the reasons that this conclusion can be questioned, however, are as follows. First, perhaps the improvement would have occurred anyway, since it is obvious that there is an upward slope *before* the treatment was introduced; this upward slope could well have continued in spite of the intervention. Incidentally, an advantage of the time-series designs over other quasi-experimental designs becomes apparent here; that is, you can assess any developing slope in the baseline, prior to intervention, and take it into account, as in this example.

Second, some event other than the change in length of workday may have oc-

FIGURE 11-1 Change in hourly productivity as a result of shifting from a 10-hour to an 8-hour work day (after Farmer, 1924).

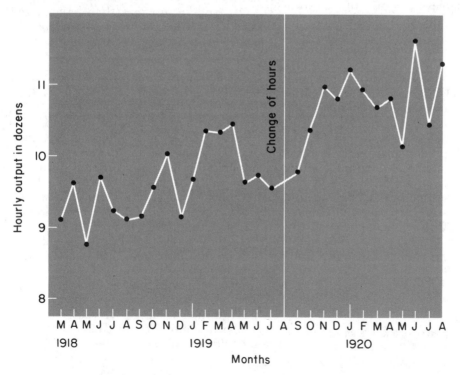

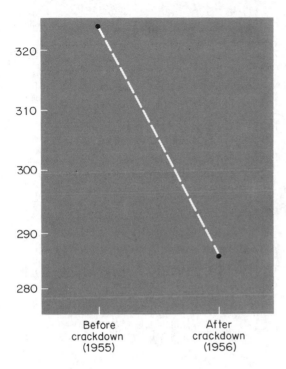

320 —

310 —

300 —

290 —

280 —

Before
crackdown
(1955)

After
crackdown
(1956)

FIGURE 11-2 Connecticut traffic fatalities (after Campbell, 1969, copyright, 1969, by the American Psychological Association; reprinted by permission).

curred. Such a confounded extraneous variable may have been responsible for the change in the dependent variable.

Third, the validity of the data may be questioned. In Figure 11-1 we can note that the baseline is based on data collected for 17 months, at which point the intervention occurred. Possibly there was a change in the way the records were kept from the baseline period to the posttreatment period; that is, special interest in the project may have led to more accurate (or even "fudged") records after intervention.

Finally, what is known as the **Hawthorne effect** may have played a role here. In the classical Hawthorne studies reported by Roethlisberger and Dickson (1939), factory workers were separated from their larger work groups and were allowed to rest systematically according to certain experimental schedules. The researchers were interested in studying the effects of rest on productivity. However, merely isolating this small group of workers could account for an increase in productivity regardless of the introduction of experimental rest periods, as with the suggestive placebo effect. Just the fact that there *was* a change and special attention was paid to the participants could account for the increased posttreatment level.

The Hawthorne effect thus means that merely by paying special attention to the participants, as in that study, you may well influence their behavior regardless of the particular treatment.

Cyclical patterns are also important to observe in time-series research, as they may account for any apparent change in the dependent variable. In Figure 11-1, for instance, we may note that August 1918 was a low month followed by an increase in level; similarly the treatment was introduced in August 1919 which was also followed by an increase in level. Introduction of a treatment at the appropriate point in a cyclical pattern is thus confounded; for example, the cyclical pattern of retail sales is such that it peaks every December and declines in January. Consequently, if you introduce a treatment

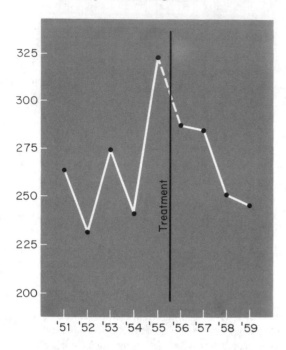

FIGURE 11-3 Connecticut traffic fatalities (same data as in Figure 11-2 presented as part of an extended time series) (after Campbell, 1969, copyright, 1969 by the American Psychological Association, reprinted by permission).

in December and use retail sales as your dependent variable, you can expect an increase regardless of your treatment. Another common cyclical pattern is that the frequency of outdoor recreation peaks in the summer and declines in the fall (except maybe in Minnesota).[4]

As another illustration of the interrupted time-series design, Campbell (1969) presented some data on the 1955 Connecticut crackdown on speeding. After record high traffic fatalities in 1955, a severe crackdown on speeding was initiated. As can be noted in Figure 11-2, a year after the crackdown, the number of fatalities decreased from 324 to 284. The conclusion the governor offered was that "With the saving of 40 lives in 1956, a reduction of 12.3% from the 1955 motor vehicle death toll, we can say that the program is definitely worthwhile" (Campbell,

1969, p. 412). However, in Figure 11-3 the data of Figure 11-2 are presented as part of an extended time series. There we may note that the baseline actually is quite unstable, which illustrates one of the difficulties in employing this design in the field situation—quite in contrast to the single-participant design of Chapter 10 in which the operant methodology calls for greater control to establish a stable baseline. With such an unstable baseline, it is difficult to evaluate the effect of a treatment, regardless of when in the time series the treatment is introduced. In Figure 11-3 the "experimental treatment" (the crackdown) was initiated at the highest point of the time series. Consequently the number of fatalities in 1956 would on the average be less than in 1955, regardless of whether the crackdown had been initiated at that point. Campbell attributes this feature to the instability of the time-series curve and refers to the reduction in fatalities from 1955 to 1956 as at least in part due to a "regression artifact":

[4]One way to solve this problem is to remove the cyclical variation from the series by expressing your dependent variable as a deviation from the expected cyclical pattern.

Regression artifacts are probably the most recurrent form of self-deception in the experimental social reform literature. It is hard to make them intuitively obvious. . . . Take any time series with variability, including one generated of pure error. Move along it as in a time dimension. Pick a point that is the "highest so far." Look then at the next point. On the average this next point will be lower, or nearer the general trend. (Campbell, 1969, p. 414)

In short, we could expect the time series to have decreased after the high point regardless of any treatment effect.

Another reason that we cannot firmly reach a conclusion about a causal relationship in this study is that death rates in the U.S. were already going down year after year, relative to miles driven or population of automobiles, regardless of the crackdown. Consequently other variables may have operated to produce the decrease after 1955, and these were thus confounded with the independent variable. To illustrate further how one may attempt to reason with the use of the interrupted time-series design (and with quasi-experimental designs more generally), we may note that Campbell did argue against this latter interpretation. He pointed out that in Figure 11-3 the general slope prior to the crackdown is an increasing one, whereas it is a decreasing slope thereafter. If the national trend toward a reduction in fatalities had been present in Connecticut prior to 1955, one would have expected a decreasing slope prior to the crackdown. This reasoning does help somewhat to increase the likelihood of the conclusion that the crackdown was beneficial.

The interrupted time-series design would typically be used when no control group is possible and where the total governmental unit has received the experimental treatment (that which is designed as the social reform). Because of the serious confounding with this design, Campbell argued for the inclusion of comparison groups wherever possible, even though they may be poor substitutes for control groups. The next design is an effort to improve on the interrupted time-series design by adding a comparison series of data measurements from a similar institution, group, or individual not undergoing the experimental change.

Interrupted Time Series with a Nonequivalent No-Treatment Comparison-Group Time Series. This design is basically that of the nonequivalent comparison-group design with the exception that multiple time-series measures of the dependent variable are taken. The paradigm for this design is as follows:

O_1	O_2	O_3	O_4	O_5	X	O_6	O_7	O_8	O_9	O_{10}
O_1	O_2	O_3	O_4	O_5		O_6	O_7	O_8	O_9	O_{10}

For instance, the time-series data for Connecticut in Figure 11-3 might be compared with similar data from some neighboring state such as Massachusetts. If the decreasing slope of the curve of Figure 11-3 after the crackdown is in contrast to values for Massachusetts, the conclusion that the reduction in traffic fatalities was produced by the crackdown would gain strength. With this design, then, any possible dependent-variable change may be evaluated relative to a baseline value (as in the preceding design) and also relative to a change or lack of change in a comparison series for another governmental unit. One further method of increasing the likelihood of a valid conclusion is to introduce the experimental treatment randomly at some point in the series, a strategy we noted in Chapter 10.

Problems with the Design. Cook and Campbell present some other shortcomings of interrupted time-series designs. Some of these are as follows:

1. Many treatments are not implemented rapidly, but they slowly diffuse through a population so that any change in the posttreatment observations may be so gradual as to be indiscernible.

2. Many effects are not instantaneous but have unpredictable time delays which may differ

among populations and from moment to moment.

3. Many data series are longer than those considered here but are shorter than the 50 or so observations usually recommended for statistical analyses. The statistical analysis of time-series designs is rather complex and will not be elaborated here. Rather, you are referred to our discussion of this topic in Chapter 10, and you can also consult Cook and Campbell (1979) and Kratochwill (1978) on this topic.

4. Many archivists are difficult to locate and may be reluctant to release data. Released data may involve time intervals that are longer than one would like, and some data may be missing or look suspicious.

A number of variations of these basic time-series have been used and can be studied further in Cook and Campbell (1979).

CONCLUSION

These examples illustrate for us the nature of quasi-experimental designs. Some of the difficulties in carrying out experiments in everyday life are obvious, but the shortcomings of the quasi-experimental designs make it clear that experiments are to be preferred if at all possible. As we previously discussed, laboratory experiments are justified as analytic methods for teasing out causal relationships. If you wish to test such a causal relationship for *external validity* (to see if the laboratory conclusion is valid for the "real world"), the laboratory experiment can be replicated in the field. Or one can start to solve a problem directly with field experimentation. In either case, in conducting a field experiment you should recognize the possibility that it may fail in some way. Field experimentation typically is expensive in that you are manipulating social institutions, so that it is advisable also to plan the experiment as a possible quasi-experiment. If you start to conduct a field experiment, you should have a fallback quasi-experimental design in mind in order to salvage what data you can. As Cook and Campbell conclude, "Designing a randomized experiment

should never preclude the simultaneous design of fallback quasi-experiments which will use the same data base as the randomized experiment" (1979, p. 386).

Our study of quasi-experimental designs may be profitable in learning how to solve some technological problems. We also should better understand their limitations in terms of confounding and restrictions on our ability to generalize conclusions. It can also provide us with an opportunity to appreciate experimentation better, for by recognizing the shortcomings of quasi-experimental designs, we might thereby improve our ability to plan and conduct well-designed experiments.

CHAPTER SUMMARY

I. To solve society's problems, we need to call on the products of basic scientific research (knowledge gained for its own sake) as well as on technological, applied research (knowledge gained from research directed toward the solution of a practical problem).

II. The soundest knowledge comes from experimentation, regardless of whether it is within the realm of science or technology. Unfortunately, however, sometimes it is not feasible to intervene into the ongoing working of societal institutions to the extent required to conduct an experiment. In this case, at least some knowledge can be gained by conducting a quasi-experiment.

III. A quasi-experimental design is one that resembles an experiment, the defining deviation being that participants are not randomly assigned to different conditions and in general the treatments are not randomly determined for groups.

IV. Causal relationships may be inferred between an independent and dependent variable in any study, but they have a relatively low probability of being true when they derive from nonexperimental research. Causal relationships are valuable to us because they provide us with the knowledge of how to manipulate our world systematically.

V. Types of designs
   A. The simplest is the one-group posttest-only design, which is essentially useless.

$$X \qquad O$$

B. If independent-variable measures are taken both before and after the intervention (still lacking a comparison group), the design is improved, but the inference is still weak: that a change in the dependent variable was due to the intervention, the independent variable.

$$O_1 \qquad X \qquad O_2$$

C. Nonequivalent comparison-group designs are like those of the method of systematic observation.
   1. In the posttest-only with a nonequivalent comparison-group design, one group receives the treatment, and dependent-variable measures are taken on both groups.

$$X \qquad O$$
$$ \qquad O$$

   2. For the untreated comparison-group design with pretest and posttest, the addition of a comparison group increases the likelihood that any change in the dependent variable is due to the independent variable.

$$O_1 \qquad X \qquad O_2$$
$$O_1 \qquad \qquad O_2$$

D. Interrupted time-series designs
   1. Simple interrupted time-series designs. Repeated measures are made on the dependent variable. The independent variable is then introduced at some point in the time series, preferably after a stable baseline has been established. An inductive inference can be made that a change in the dependent variable following the intervention is due to the independent variable. The basis for such an influence may be a change in

level (the data series shifts upward or downward with a sharp discontinuity) or in slope (the rate of change is modified).

$$O_1 \quad O_2 \quad O_3 \quad O_4 \quad O_5 \quad X \quad O_6 \quad O_7 \quad O_8 \quad O_9 \quad O_{10}$$

   2. Interrupted time series with a nonequivalent, no-treatment comparison-group time series.

$$O_1 \quad O_2 \quad O_3 \quad O_4 \quad O_5 \quad X \quad O_6 \quad O_7 \quad O_8 \quad O_9 \quad O_{10}$$
$$O_1 \quad O_2 \quad O_3 \quad O_4 \quad O_5 \qquad O_6 \quad O_7 \quad O_8 \quad O_9 \quad O_{10}$$

E. Effects of a dependent variable
   1. A change in dependent variable is usually noted when the measure changes in level or in slope.
   2. Effects may also be continuous (they persist well after the intervention) or discontinuous (they decay, indicating a temporary effect).
   3. Effects may also be instantaneous or delayed.
   4. The characterizations are not unique for time-series designs, but they can be ascertained only if repeated observations are made after an intervention.

CRITICAL REVIEW FOR THE STUDENT

1. Distinguish between applied and pure science. Must a scientist always be one or the other?
2. If you are a clinical psychologist, does this mean that you cannot also be an experimental psychologist?
3. Can a public administrator, well educated in everyday wisdom of life, adequately solve our problems if merely given the power to do so? Or must governmental authorities rely on systematic technological research over the long run to make real progress?
4. If you were given complete power over the penal systems or the welfare systems in this country what would you do? Would you attempt to change the systems? If so, precisely how would you proceed?

5. Distinguish between experimental and quasi-experimental designs.

6. Confounding is always present in a quasi-experimental design. True or false? Why?

7. No doubt you would want to review and summarize well for yourself the various types of quasi-experimental designs presented, including especially the method of systematic observation discussed in previous chapters.

8. Consider some instances in which you would advocate the use of naturalistic observation.

9. How would *you* attempt to solve what you regard as some of society's most pressing problems? To help you get started, here is how one student (a police lieutenant) answered this question.

"I would like to develop a more effective deterrent to drunk driving. The following is my hypothesis: A radical response will significantly reduce incidents of recidivism among drivers arrested for D.U.I. (driving under the influence, or 'drunk driving').

"My study would involve a 12-month time frame and the 26 law enforcement agencies in the region. Beginning at 0001 on 1 January and running through 2400 on 31 December, every individual arrested for D.U.I. would be assigned a number, in numerical sequence.

"Every odd-numbered individual, while being transported to court the morning after his or her arrest would have the opportunity to witness his or her automobile (which was impounded at the time of his or her arrest) being reduced to a small cube of metal at the local wrecking yard.

"Those with even numbers would not have their vehicles so modified and would continue to be processed through the court system in the traditional manner.

"At the conclusion of the 12-month study, odd-numbered arrestees would have their criminal records compared with those of the even-numbered arrestees. I strongly suspect that seeing one's VW or Rolls Royce crushed (without financial compensation) would somehow influence an individual's decision not to drive after consuming alcohol, let alone while under the influence of alcohol. In any event it would be interesting" [to which we all would have to concur].

Appendix
Possible Effects of the Treatment

Continuous versus Discontinuous Effects. We have discussed dependent-variable changes in level and slope. Another way of characterizing effects concerns whether the effects persist over time or whether they decay. A *continuous* effect is one that persists for a considerable time after the intervention with treatment. Continuous effects may be indicated by either a shift in the level or a change in the slope. On the other hand, a *discontinuous* effect is one that decays—it does not persist over time so that the change in the posttreatment series of observations is temporary and the response curve returns to the preintervention baseline value.

Immediate versus Delayed Effects. Another dimension for characterizing effects is whether they are *instantaneous* or *delayed*. If there is a change in the level or slope of the curves shortly after introducing the treatment, the effect is obviously instantaneous. On the other hand, it may be some time before the treatment influences the series of observations, in which case it becomes more difficult to relate that change to the treatment—maybe other events could have intervened between the introduction of the treatment and the change in the response curve. Such delayed effects have recently become more important to society as we have increased our awareness of environmental degradation. Many citizens argue against environmental controls because they can see no effects of pollution (they are *not* instantaneous), but if controls are withheld for a few years detrimental effects could be established (cancer, for one, is an effect delayed for many years).

Using All Three Measures. To conclude this note on effects, the results of interrupted time-series research can be assessed simultaneously along all three of these dimensions. Thus a researcher can study a time series to determine whether the treatment seemed to influence: (1) the level or slope; (2) the duration, whether it was continuous or discontinuous; and (3) its latency, whether it was immediate or delayed. Most positive conclusions for this design have immediate and continuous changes in level.

chapter 12

GENERALIZATION, EXPLANATION, AND PREDICTION IN PSYCHOLOGY

Major purpose:

To provide a broad perspective of science within which you may incorporate a specific experiment that contributes to our storehouse of knowledge.

What you are going to find:

1. A discussion of the critical processes of scientific reasoning as they are reconstructed through the inductive schema.

2. Specification of the methods by which we test hypotheses; for this, we make inductive and deductive inferences from evidence reports to and from hypotheses.

3. Procedures for determining whether you should restrict your empirical generalization; to do this you test for an interaction between an independent variable and one of secondary interest.

What you should acquire:

The ability to generalize, explain, and predict on the basis of your findings. As a consequence you can employ these and related processes to understand and better control the world in which we live and to have foresight about it.

We have now covered most of the phases of the scientific method as developed in Chapter 1. In these final phases of research we turn to the following questions: (1) How and what does the experimenter **generalize**? (2) How do we **explain** our results? and (3) How do we **predict** other situations?

To approach these questions, recall our distinctions between applied science (technology) and basic (pure) science: In applied science, attempts are made to solve limited problems, whereas in basic science, efforts are to arrive at general principles. The answer that the applied scientist obtains is usually applicable only under the specific conditions of the experiment. The basic scientist's results, however, are likely to be more widely applicable. For example, an applied psychologist might study why soft drink sales in Atlanta, Georgia, were below normal for the month of December. The basic scientist, on the other hand, would study the general relationship between temperature and consumption of liquids. Perhaps sales declined because Atlanta was unseasonably cold then. The basic scientist, however, might reach the more general conclusion that the amount of liquid consumed by humans depends on the air temperature—the lower the temperature, the less they consume. Thus the finding of the general relationship would solve the specific problem in Atlanta, as well as be applicable to a wide variety of additional phenomena. Such a general statement, then, can be used to explain more specific statements, to predict new situations, and also to facilitate inductive inferences to yet more general statements. To enlarge on these matters, let us obtain an overview of these important characteristics of science by studying the **inductive schema**, developed by Professor Hans Reichenbach.

THE INDUCTIVE SCHEMA

"Dr. Watson, Sherlock Holmes," said Stamford introducing us.

"How are you?" he said cordially, gripping my hand with a strength for which I should hardly have given him credit. "You have been in Afghanistan, I perceive."

"How on earth did you know that?" I asked in astonishment . . . "You were told, no doubt."

"Nothing of the sort. I knew you came from Afghanistan. From long habit the train of thoughts ran so swiftly through my mind that I arrived at the conclusion without being conscious of intermediate steps. There were such steps, however. The train of reasoning ran, 'Here is a gentleman of a medical type, but with the air of a military man. Clearly an army doctor, then. He has just come from the tropics, for his face is dark, and that is not the natural tint of his skin, for his wrists are fair. He has undergone hardship and sickness, as his haggard face says clearly. His left arm has been injured. He holds it in a stiff and unnatural manner. Where in the tropics could an English army doctor have seen so much hardship and had his arm wounded? Clearly in Afghanistan.' The whole train of thought did not occupy a second. I then remarked that you came from Afghanistan, and you were astonished" (Doyle, 1938, pp. 6, 14).[1]

This, their first meeting, is but a simple demonstration of Holmes's ability to reach conclusions that confound and amaze Watson. Holmes's reasoning is reconstructed in Figure 12-1. The observational information available to Holmes is at the bottom. On the basis of these data Holmes inferred certain intermediate conclusions. For example, he observed that Watson's face was dark, but that his wrists were fair, which immediately led to the conclusion that Watson's skin was not naturally dark. He must therefore have recently been exposed to considerable sun (which was certainly not in London); Watson had probably "just come from the tropics." From these several intermediate conclusions it was then possible for Holmes to induce the final conclusion, that Watson had just recently been in Afghanistan. You should trace through each step of Holmes's reasoning process in the inductive schema and perhaps even construct such a schema for yourself from other amazing processes of Holmes's reasoning.

---

[1] Reprinted by permission of the Estate of Sir Arthur Conan Doyle.

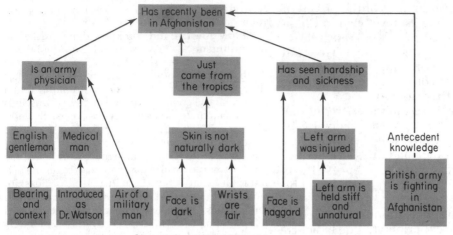

Observational information

¹Reprinted by permission of the Estate of Sir Arthur Conan Doyle.

FIGURE 12-1   An inductive schema based on Sherlock Holmes's first meeting with Dr. Watson.

Scientific Reasoning. The most magnificent scientific advances have been in the most sophisticated science, physics. Unfortunately it will be a very long time before we can so extensively illustrate such scientific reasoning in psychology. Consider the inductive schema in Figure 12-2. In the bottom row are some of the evidence reports from which more general statements were made. For instance, Galileo conducted some experiments in which he rolled balls down inclined planes. He measured two variables, the time that the bodies were in motion and the distance covered at the end of various periods of time. The resulting data led to the generalization known as the law of falling bodies from which the distance traveled could be specifically predicted from the amount of time that the bodies were in motion.²

---

²More precisely, the law of falling bodies is that $S = \frac{1}{2} gt^2$ in which S is the distance the body falls, g the gravitational constant, and t the time that it is in motion. History is somewhat unclear about whether Galileo conducted similar experiments in other situations, but it is said that he also dropped various objects off the Leaning Tower of Pisa and obtained similar measurements.

Copernicus was dissatisfied with the Ptolemaic theory that the sun rotated around the earth and on the basis of extensive observations and considerable reasoning advanced the heliocentric (Copernican) theory of planetary motion—that the planets rotate around the sun. Kepler based his laws on his own meticulous observations, the observations of others, and on Copernicus' theory. The statement of his three laws of planetary orbits (among which was the statement that the earth's orbit is an ellipse) was a considerable advance in our knowledge.

There has always been interest in the height of the tides at various localities, and it is natural that precise recordings of this phenomenon would have been made at various times during the day. Concomitant observations were made of the location of the moon, leading to the relationship known as the *tides-moon law,* namely, that high tides occur only on the regions of the earth nearest to, and farthest from, the moon. As the moon moves about the earth, the location of high tides shifts accordingly.

Using these relationships, Newton was able to formulate his magnificant law of

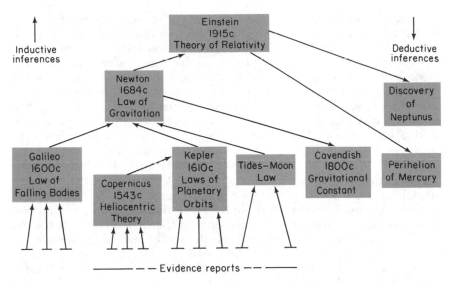

FIGURE 12-2 An inductive schema which partially represents the development of physics (after Reichenbach).

gravitation.[3] Briefly this law states that the force of attraction between two bodies varies inversely with the square of the distance between them. As an example of a prediction from a general law (the first downward arrow of Figure 12-2) the gravitational constant was predicted from Newton's law, determined by Cavendish.

The crowning achievement in this evolution was Einstein's statement of his general theory of relativity. Another example of a prediction is from the theory of relativity concerning the perihelion of Mercury. Newton's equations had failed to account for a slight discrepancy in Mercury's perihelion, a discrepancy that was precisely accounted for by Einstein's theory. Furthermore, that research on the movement of Mercury's perihelion was associated with the discovery of the planet Neptunus by Leverrier.

This brief discussion is, of course, inadequate for a proper understanding of the evolution of this portion of physics. Each

step in the story constitutes an exciting tale that you might wish to follow up in detail. And where does the story go from here? A problem that has plagued physicists and philosophers is how to reconcile the area of physics depicted in Figure 12-2 with a similar area known as *quantum mechanics*. To this end physicists such as Einstein and Schrödinger attempted to develop a "unified field" theory to encompass Einstein's theory of relativity as well as the principles of quantum mechanics. Arriving at such high-level general principles is even more difficult than the evolution depicted in Figure 12-2, which may well be our greatest intellectual achievement.

With this inductive schema we can now enlarge on several characteristics of science. Since inferences are at the very heart of the scientific process, let us first consider the two possible kinds.

Inductive and Deductive Inferences

Inductive (Probability) Inferences. In Figure 12-2, observe that inductive inferences are represented when arrows point up, deductive inferences by arrows that point

---

[3] He was asked how he was able to see so far, how he was able to gain such magnificent insight? Newton replied, because he stood on the shoulders of giants (those lower in the inductive schema).

down. Recall that inductive inferences are liable to error. In Figure 12-1, for instance, Watson was introduced as "*Dr.* Watson"; on the basis of this information Holmes concluded that Watson was a medical man. Is this necessarily the case? Obviously not, for he may have been some other kind of doctor, such as a doctor of philosophy. Similarly, consider the observational information, "left hand held stiff and unnatural," on the basis of which Holmes concluded that "the left arm was injured." This conclusion does not necessarily follow, since there could be other reasons for the condition (Watson might have been organically deformed at birth or simply wore a poorly fitting coat. In fact, was it necessarily the case that Watson had just come from Afghanistan? The story may well have gone something like this: Holmes: "You have been in Afghanistan, I perceive." Watson: "Certainly not. I have not been out of London for forty years. Are you out of your mind?"

In a similar vein we may note that Galileo's law was advanced as a general law, asserting that *any* falling body *anywhere at any time* obeyed it. Is this necessarily true? Obviously not, for perhaps a stone falling off Mount Everest or a hat falling off a man's head in New York may fall according to a different law than that offered for a set of balls rolling down an inclined plane in Italy many years ago. (We would assume that Galileo's limiting conditions such as that concerning the resistance of air would not be ignored.)

And so it is with the other statements in Figure 12-2. Each conclusion may be in error. *As long as you make inductive inferences, the conclusion will only have a certain probability of being true.* Yet **inductive inferences** are necessary for generalization. Since a generalization says something about phenomena not yet observed, it *must* be susceptible to error. To help further develop our broad perspective of how experimentation fits within the scientific method, we will enlarge on these important concepts of induction and deduction.

Let us start with a set of statements that constitutes our evidence reports, which we denote by A. These statements contain information on the basis of which we can reach another statement, B. Now when we proceed from A to B we make an **inference**—that is, *a conclusion reached on the basis of certain preceding statements*—it is a process of reasoning whereby we start with A and arrive at B. In both inductive and deductive inferences, our belief in the truth of B is based on the assumption that A is true. The essential difference is the degree of confidence that we have in believing that B is true. In induction the inference is that if A is true, B follows with some degree of probability; however, in deduction if A is true, B is *necessarily* true.

Suppose that statement A is "Every morning that I have arisen, I have seen the sun rise." On the basis of this statement we may infer the statement B: "The sun will always rise each morning." Now does B necessarily follow from A? It *does not*, for although you may have repeatedly observed the rise of the sun in the past, it does not follow that it will *always* rise in the future. Statement B is not *necessarily* true on the basis of A. Although it may seem unlikely to you now, it is entirely possible that one day, regardless of what you have observed in the past, the sun will not rise. Statement B is only probable (is probably true) on the basis of A. Inductive inferences with a certain degree of probability are thus synonymously called *probability inferences*.

Probability inferences may be precisely specified, rather than having probabilities described as "high," "medium," or "low." Conventionally, the probability of an inductive inference may be expressed by any number from zero to one. Thus the probability (P) of the inference from A to B may be 0.40, or 0.65. Furthermore, the closer P is to 1.0, the higher is the probability that the inference will result in a true conclusion (again, assuming that A is true). The closer P is to 0.0, the lower is the probability that the inference will result in a true conclusion. Thus, if the probability that B follows A is

0.99, it is rather certain that B is true.[4] The inference that "the sun will always rise each morning" has a *very* high probability indeed. On the other hand, the inference from "a person has red hair" (A) to "that person is very temperamental" (B) would have a very low probability. Incidentally, a probability value is not properly expressed as a percentage. Thus, rather than saying the probability of rain is 70%, one should say $P = 0.70$.

In Short. The degree-of-probability value expresses the degree of our belief that an inference is true—the closer the value is to 1.0, the more likely it is that the inference results in a true conclusion.

Deductive Logic. Note in Figure 12-2 that Galileo's and Kepler's laws were generalized by Newton's. *It follows that they may be deduced from them.* In this case it may be said, "If Newton's laws are true (A), then it is necessarily the case that Galileo's (B) is true, and also that Kepler's (B) are true." Similarly, on the basis of Newton's laws, the gravitational constant was deduced and empirically verified by Cavendish. This **deductive inference** takes the form: "If Newton's laws are true, then the gravitational constant is such and such." Similarly, if Einstein's theory is true, then the previous discrepancy in the perihelion of Mercury is accounted for.

A deductive inference is thus made when the truth of one statement is necessary, based on another one or set of statements, that is, statement A *necessarily* implies B. Valid deductive inferences follow specific rules of deductive logic. For example, we might inductively infer that "all anxious people bite their nails" and, further, that "John Jones is anxious." We may therefore deductively infer that "John Jones bites his nails." In this example, if the first two statements are true (they are called *premises*), the final statement (the *condition*) is necessarily true.

However, note that a deductive inference does not guarantee that the conclusion is

true. The deductive inference, for example, does not say that Galileo's law is true. It *does* say that *if* Newton's laws are true, Galileo's law is true. One may well ask, at this point, how we determine that Newton's laws are true. Or, more generally, how do we determine that the premises of a deductive inference are true. The answer is with inductive logic. For example, empirical investigation indicates that Newton's laws have a *very* high degree of probability, so high that they *are* true (in an approximate sense, of course).

Concatenation

As we move up the inductive schema, statements become increasingly general, whereupon there is a certain increase in the probability of the statement being true. This increase is the result of two factors. First, since the more general statement rests on more numerous and more varied evidence, it usually has been confirmed to a greater degree than has a less general statement. For example, there is a certain addition to the probability of Newton's law of gravitation that is not present for Galileo's law of falling bodies, since the former is based on inductions from more numerous data of wider scope. Put another way, a theory that is supported by varied evidence reports is more probable than is one supported by a narrow spectrum of data. Second, the more general statement is *concatenated* with other general statements. By **concatenation** we mean that the statements are "chained together" with other statements and are thus consistent with those other statements. For example, Galileo's law of falling bodies is not concatenated with other statements, and Newton's law is. The fact that Newton's law is linked with other statements gives it an increment of probability that cannot be said of Galileo's. We may say that the probability of the whole system in Figure 12-2 being true is greater than the sum of the probabilities of each statement taken separately. It is the compatibility of the whole system and the

---

[4] Recall that inductive (probability) inferences may be symbolized as here that A $\underset{P}{\psi}$ B.

support gained from the concatenation that provide the added likelihood.

It also follows that, when each individual generalization in the system is confirmed, the entire system gains increased credence. For instance, if Einstein's theory were based entirely on his own observations and those that it stimulated, its probability would be much lower than it actually is, considering that it is also based on all the lower generalizations in Figure 12-2. Or, suppose that a new and extensive test determined that Galileo's law was false. This would mean the complete "disconfirmation" of Galileo's law, but it would only slightly reduce the probability of Einstein's theory since there is a wide variety of additional confirming data for the latter.

Generalization

Galileo conducted a number of specific experiments. Each experiment resulted in a statement that there was a relationship between the distance traveled by balls rolling down an inclined plane and the time that they were in motion. From these specific statements he then advanced to a more general statement: The relationship between distance and time obtained for the bodies in motion was true for *all* falling bodies, at all locations, and at all times.

Copernicus observed the position of the planets relative to the sun. After making a number of specific observations, he was willing to generalize to positions of the planets that he had not observed. The observations that he made fitted the heliocentric theory that the planets revolved around the sun. He then made the statement that the heliocentric theory held for positions of the planets that he had not observed. And so it is for Kepler's laws and for the tides-moon law. In each case a number of specific statements based on observation (evidence reports) were made. Then from these specific statements came a more general statement. It is this process of proceeding from a set of specific statements to a more general statement that is referred to as **generalization**. The

general statement, then, includes, not only the specific statements that led to it, but also a wide variety of other phenomena that have not been observed.

This process of increasing generalization continues as we read up the inductive schema. Thus Newton's law of gravitation is more general than any of those that are lower in the schema. We may say that it generalizes Galileo's, Copernicus', Kepler's, and the tides-moon laws. Newton's law is more general in the sense that it includes these more specific laws and that it makes statements about phenomena other than the ones on which it was based. In turn, Einstein formulated principles that were more general than Newton's, principles that included Newton's and therefore all of those lower in the schema. Since the precise methods by which we generalize in psychology are of such great importance to research, the topic will be covered in detail later in the chapter. But for now let us illustrate the next phase in the scientific method, that of explaining our findings.

Explanation

Nonscientific Concepts. **Explanation**, as used in science, is sometimes difficult to understand, probably because of the commonsense use of the term to which we are exposed. One of the commonsense "meanings" of the term concerns familiarity. Suppose that you learn about a scientific phenomenon that is new to you. You want it explained; you want to know "why" it is so. This desire on your part is a psychological phenomenon, a motive. When somebody can relate the scientific phenomenon to something that is already familiar to you, your psychological motive is satisfied. You feel as if you understand the phenomenon because of its association with knowledge that is familiar to you. A metaphor is frequently used for this purpose. At a very elementary level, for example, it might be said that the splitting of an atom is like shooting an incendiary bullet into a bag of gunpowder.

Scientific Explanation. However, any satisfaction of your motive to relate a new phenomenon to a familiar phenomenon is far from an explanation of it. *Explanation is the systematic placing of a statement within the context of a more general statement.* If we are able to show that a specific statement belongs within the category of a more general statement, the specific statement has been explained. To establish this relationship we must show that the specific statement may be logically deduced from the more general statement. For instance, to explain the statement that "John Jones is anxious" we must logically deduce it from a more general statement, for example, "If it is true that 'all men who bite their fingernails are anxious,' and if it is true that 'John Jones is a man who bites his fingernails,' then it is true that 'John Jones is anxious.'" We have logically deduced that specific statement from the more general statement. By so deductively inferring this conclusion, we have explained why John Jones is anxious (on the assumption that the more general statement is true).

Referring to Figure 12-2 we can see that Kepler's laws are more general than is the Copernican theory. And since the latter is included in the former, it may be logically deduced from it—Kepler's laws explain the Copernican theory. In turn, Newton's law, being more general than Galileo's, Kepler's, and the tides-moon laws, explains these more specific laws; they may all be logically deduced from Newton's law. And, finally, all of the lower generalizations may be deduced from Einstein's theory, and we may therefore say that Einstein's theory explains all of the lower generalizations. We shall now consider this important process in greater detail.

Antecedent Conditions and General Laws. When a mercury thermometer is rapidly immersed in hot water, there is a temporary drop of the mercury column, after which the column rises swiftly. *Why* does this occur? That is, how might we explain it? Since the increase in temperature affects at first only the glass tube of the thermometer, the tube expands and thus provides a larger space for the mercury inside. To fill this larger space the mercury level drops, but as soon as the increase in heat is conducted through the glass tube and reaches the mercury, the mercury also expands. Since mercury expands more than does glass (i.e., the coefficient of expansion of mercury is greater than that of glass), the level of the mercury rises.

Now this account, as Hempel and Oppenheim (1948) pointed out in a classic paper, consists of two kinds of statements: (1) statements about *antecedent* conditions that exist before the phenomenon to be explained occurs, for example, the fact that the thermometer consists of a glass tube that is partly filled with mercury, that it is immersed in hot water, and so on; and (2) statements of general laws, an example of which would be about thermal conductivity of glass. Logically deducing a statement about the phenomenon to be explained from the general laws in conjunction with the statements of the antecedent conditions constitutes an explanation of the phenomenon. We determine that a given phenomenon can be subsumed under a general law by deducing (deductively inferring) the former from the latter. The schema for accomplishing an explanation is as follows:

$$\text{Deductive inference:} \begin{cases} \text{Statement of the general} \\ \quad \text{law(s)} \\ \text{Statement of the antecedent} \\ \quad \text{condition(s)} \end{cases}$$
→ Description of the phenomenon to be explained

Thus the phenomenon to be explained (the immediate drop of the mercury level, followed by its swift rise) may be logically deduced according to this schema. As a final brief illustration of the nature of explanation, consider an analogy using the familiar syllogism explaining Socrates' death. The syllogism contains the two kinds of statements that we require for an explanation. First, the general law is that "All men are mortal." Second, the antecedent condition is that "Socrates is a man." From these statements we can deductively infer that Socrates is mortal.

Deductive inference:
{
General law: All men are mortal.
Antecedent condition: Socrates is a man.
}
→Phenomenon to be explained (i.e., Why did Socrates die?): Socrates is mortal.

Explanation in Psychology. With this understanding of the general nature of explanation, let us now ask where the procedure enters the work of the experimental psychologist. Assume that a researcher wishes to test the hypothesis that the higher the anxiety, the better is the performance on a relatively simple task. To vary anxiety in two ways, the researcher selects two groups of participants such that one group is composed of individuals who have considerable anxiety, a second group of those with little anxiety. The evidence report states that the high-anxiety group performed better than did the low-anxiety group. The evidence report is thus positive, and, since it is in accord with the hypothesis, the hypothesis is confirmed. The investigation is completed, the problem is solved. But is it really? Although this may be said of the limited problem for which the study was conducted, there is still a nagging question—why is the hypothesis "true"? How might it be explained? To answer this question, we must refer to a principle that is more general than that hypothesis. Consider a principle that states that performance is determined by the amount learned multiplied by the drive-level present.

Anxiety is defined as a specific drive so that the high-anxiety group exhibits a strong drive factor and the low-anxiety group exhibits a weak drive factor. To simplify matters, assume that both groups learned the task equally well, thus causing the learning factor to be the same for both groups. Clearly, then, the performance of the high-drive (high-anxiety) group should be superior to that of the low-drive group, according to this more general principle. The principle is quite general in that it ostensibly covers all drives in addition to including a consideration of the learning factor. Following our previous schema, then, we have the following situation:

Deductive inference:
{
General law: The higher the drive, the better the performance.
Antecedent conditions: Participants had two levels of drive, they performed a simple task, anxiety is a drive, etc.
}
→Phenomenon to be explained: High-anxiety participants performed a simple task better than did low-anxiety participants.

Since it would be possible logically to deduce the hypothesis (stated as "the phenomenon to be explained") from the general principle together with the necessary antecedent conditions, we may say that the hypothesis is explained.

There is an ever-continuing search for a higher-level explanation for our statements, as in Figure 12-2. Here we have shown how a relatively specific hypothesis about anxiety and performance can be explained by a more general principle about: (1) drives in general, and (2) a learning factor (which we ignored because it was not relevant to the present discussion). The next question, obviously, is how to explain this general principle. But, since our immediate purpose is accomplished, we shall leave this question to the next generation of budding psychologists.

To emphasize that the logical deduction is made on the assumption that the general principle and the statement of the antecedent conditions were actually true, a more cautious statement about our explanation would be this: Assuming that (1) the general law is true and (2) the antecedent conditions obtained, then the phenomenon of interest is explained. But how can we be sure that the general principle is, indeed, true? We can never be *absolutely* sure, for it must always assume a probability value. It might someday turn out that the general principle used to explain a particular phenomenon was actually false. In this case what we accepted as a "true" explanation was in reality no explanation at all. Unfortunately, we can do nothing more with this situation—our explanations must always be of a tentative sort. As Professor Herbert Feigl has put it, "*Scientific truths are held only until further notice.*" We must, therefore, always realize that we explain a phenomenon on the assumption that the general principle used in the explanation is true. If the probability of the general principle is high, then we are rather safe. We can, however, never be absolutely secure, which is merely another indication that we have but a "probabilistic universe" in which to live. The sooner we learn to accept this fact (in the present context, the sooner we learn to accept the probabilistic nature of our explanations), the better adjusted to reality we will be.

One final thought on the topic of explanation. We have indicated that an explanation is accomplished by logical deduction. But how frequently do psychologists actually explain their phenomena in such a formal manner? How frequently do they actually cite a general law, state their antecedent conditions, and deductively infer their phenomena from them? The answer, clearly, is that this is done very infrequently. Almost never will you find such a formal process being used in the actual report of scientific investigations. Rather, much more informal methods of reasoning are substituted. One need not set out on a scientific career armed with books of logical formulas. However, familiarity with the basic logical processes can prevent you from making invalid inferences. Furthermore, while you need not rigidly follow the procedures that we have set down, you *could* explain a finding in a formal logical manner if you wished. These considerations should enhance your prespective of where

psychological experimentation fits into the broad scientific enterprise. Thus, rather than merely putting one research foot in front of the other, you can now better understand what you are trying to accomplish and how best to get there. Let us, then turn to the final phase of the scientific method—that of predicting to novel situations.

Prediction

Definition. To predict, we apply a generalization to a situation that has not yet been studied. The generalization states that all of something has a certain characteristic. When we extend the generalization to the new situation, we expect that the new situation has the characteristics specified in the generalization. In its simplest form this is what a prediction is, and we have illustrated three predictions in Figure 12-2: the gravitational constant, the perihelion of Mercury, and the discovery of Neptunus. Whether the prediction is confirmed, of course, is quite important for the generalization. For if it is, the probability of the generalization is considerably increased. If it is not, however (assuming that the evidence report is true and the deduction is valid), then either the probability of the generalization is decreased, or the generalization must be restricted so that it does not apply to the phenomena with which the prediction was concerned.

A Psychological Illustration. Consider a hypothesis about the behavior of schoolchildren in the fourth grade. Say that it was tested on those children and found to be probably true. The experimenter may generalize it to all schoolchildren. From such a generalized hypothesis it is possible to derive specific statements concerning any given school grade. For example, the experimenter could deductively infer that the hypothesis is applicable to the behavior of schoolchildren in the fifth grade, thus predicting to as-yet-unobserved children.

The Processes of Predicting and Explaining are Precisely the Same. Everything we have said about explanation is applicable to prediction. The only difference is that a prediction is made *before* the phenomenon is observed, whereas explanation occurs *after* the phenomenon has been recorded. In explanation, then, we start with the phenomenon and logically deduce it from a general law and the attendant antecedent conditions. In prediction, on the other hand, we start with the general law and antecedent conditions and derive our logical consequences; that is, from the general law we infer that a certain phenomenon should occur. We then conduct an experiment, and, if the phenomenon does occur, our prediction is successful resulting in an increase in the probability of the general law.

Boundary Conditions. Earlier in this chapter we discussed inductive (probability) inferences in our formulation of general laws and how those inferences may be in error. In making predictions on the basis of past observations, we must recognize that there are certain limits that should not be exceeded. Weber's law, for instance, can tell us something very valuable about human ability to discriminate between different amounts of weight. However, it obviously does not apply when the weight is so great that a person cannot lift it (e.g., a weight of 1 ton) or, at the other extreme, when the weight is so infinitesimal that we are not even aware of it, such as in lifting atoms. Consequently, in stating a law, boundary conditions (the limits of applicability of a statement) should be precisely specified. Take a very simple series of observations, for instance, such as the observation of a dozen white pigeons in a park. The process of induction by enumeration might lead you to infer that the next pigeon you come upon would also be white, or perhaps that indeed all pigeons in the park are white. Such inferences are sound, but we must be careful of making an induction by enumeration without specifying reasonable boundary conditions. In this instance, a boundary condition is that the conclusion applies only to this particular park—other parks may have only dark pigeons. To make the point vividly, let

us briefly describe some conclusions from the respectable scientific journal entitled the *Journal of Irreproducible Results.*

One prediction made was that if everyone keeps stacking *National Geographics* in garages and attics instead of throwing them away, the weight of the magazines will soon sink the continent 100 feet and we will all be inundated by the oceans. The article is entitled "*National Geographic,* the Doomsday Machine." The scientist pointed out that more than 6.8 million issues of *National Geographic,* each weighing 2 pounds, are sent to subscribers monthly and that not one copy has been thrown away since publication began almost 95 years ago. The scientist inferred that soon the geologic substructure of the country can no longer support the load so that rock formations will compress, then become plastic, and begin to flow. Great faults will appear and the continent will sink and be inundated by the seas. A further prediction from the studies was that the increases in earthquake activity in California was triggered by the population growth in the state which led to the subsequent increase in *National Geographic* subscriptions. Recognizing the urgency of the situation, the scientist called for congressional action or presidential edict to halt the publication of the *National Geographic.*

In true scientific fashion, the article was criticized by another scientist in the *Journal* with the title "*National Geographic*: Doomsday Machine or Benefactor? A Vindication." In a complex table of data the criticizing scientist concluded that while the prediction was correct, the timetable calling for an immediate catastrophe was off so that the continent will not sink for another 25 billion years.

Yet another scientist in a third article criticized the second article, calling it a whitewash of the impending catastrophe. Two critical miscalculations were made: the assumption that the circulation of the *National Geographic* would not increase in the future and that the magazine would be evenly distributed over the 48 continental United States. Consequently, since more than half of the U.S. population lives in the one-quarter of land mass along the Eastern Seaboard and because the West Coast population is increasing, the truth is that only the two coasts will sink while the central portion of the United States will actually rise. Rather than occurring in 25 billion years, it would occur much sooner, in 3 million years.

In a different study, it was predicted that if the number of microscope specimen slides submitted to one St. Louis hospital lab continues to increase at its current rate, St. Louis will be buried under 3 feet of glass by the year 2224. In an article "The Glass and Spleen Explosions," the data base was that the number of slides at the lab has been doubling every 9.49 years. The same hospital with the slide problem will also, by the year 2224, be handling 8.3 billion spleen biopsies a year.

In another article entitled "A New Contribution to Beach Erosion and Its Consequences," the scientist extrapolated measurements of sand made on several departing beachgoers. If beachgoers keep returning home with as much sand clinging to them as they do now, 80 percent of the country's coastline will disappear in 10 years.

Another extrapolation has been that if the population of the world increases at its present rate, not long into the next century everyone will have but one square foot of ground (there will be standing room only for elephants). Furthermore, with the projected increase of scientific publications everyone will be standing on top of three feet of journals.

These predictions all have sound data bases. What is wrong with them is that boundary conditions have been ignored. In each case, there obviously are limits to the growth curves that should be imposed.

With this understanding of how inferential processes are employed in generalization, explanation, and prediction, we will now examine more closely the ways in which they are used to test hypotheses. For this purpose let us return to the foundation from which these inferences are made—that constructed on the basis of experimental results.

FORMING THE EVIDENCE REPORT

Definition. Recall that an evidence report (or, synonymously, *observational sentence, protocol sentence, concept by inspection*) is a summary statement of the results of an empirical investigation; it is a sentence that precisely summarizes what was found. In addition, the evidence report states that the antecedent conditions of the hypothesis were realized. It therefore consists of two parts: a statement that the antecedent conditions of the hypothesis held and a statement that the consequent conditions were found to be either true or false. The general form for stating the evidence report is thus that of a conjunction. The hypothesis is "If a, then b," in which a denotes the antecedent conditions of the hypothesis and b the consequent conditions. Hence the possible evidence reports are "a and b," or "a and not b," in which the consequent conditions are found to be (probably) true or false, respectively. The former is a positive evidence report; the latter, a negative one.

Illustration. Let a stand for "an industrial work group is in great inner conflict" and b for "that work group has a lowered production level." If in our research an industrial work group was in great inner conflict, we may assert that the antecedent conditions of our hypothesis were realized. To determine whether the consequent conditions of the hypothesis are true or false, we need a control group as a basis of comparison. For without such a basis, "lower production level" in our example does not mean anything—it must be lower than something. If the finding is that that work group had a lower production level than a control group, the consequent conditions are true. Therefore the evidence report is "An industrial work group was in great inner conflict *and* that work group had a lowered production level." That the hypothesis implicitly assumes the existence of a control group is made explicit by stating the hypothesis as follows: "If an industrial work group is in great inner conflict, then that work group will have a lower production level *than that of a group that is not in inner conflict.*" If the statistical analysis indicates that the production level is reliably lower, the consequent conditions are probably true. But if the group with inner conflict has a reliably higher production level, or if there is no reliable difference between the two levels, the consequent conditions are probably false. The evidence report would then be: "An industrial work group was in great inner conflict and that work group did not have a lowered production level."

With this format for forming the evidence report, we shall now consider the nature of the inferences made from it to the hypothesis.

DIRECT VERSUS INDIRECT STATEMENTS

Science deals with two kinds of statements: direct and indirect. *A* **direct statement** *is one that refers to limited phenomena that are immediately observable*—that is, phenomena that can be observed directly with the senses, such as "that bird is red." With auxiliary apparatus such as microscopes, telescopes, and electrodes, the scope of the senses may be extended to form such direct statements as "there is an amoeba," "there is a sunspot," or "that is a covert response," respectively. The procedure for testing a direct statement is straightforward: Compare it with a relevant evidence report. If they agree, the direct statement is true; otherwise, it is false. To test the direct statement "that door is open," we observe the door. If the evidence report states that it is open, our observation agrees with the direct statement, and we conclude that the statement is true. If we observe the door to be closed, we conclude that the direct statement is false.

An **indirect statement** is one that cannot be directly tested. Such statements usually deal with phenomena that cannot be directly observed (logical constructs such as electricity or habits) or that are so numerous or extended in time that it is impossible to view

them all. A universal hypothesis is of this type—"All men are anxious." It is certainly impossible to observe all men (living, dead, and as yet unborn) to see if the statement is true. The universal hypothesis is the type in which scientists are most interested, since it is an attempt to say something about variables for all time, in all places.[5]

Testing Indirect Statements. Since indirect statements cannot be directly tested, deductive inferences must be used to reduce them to direct statements. Consider an indirect statement S. By drawing deductive inferences from S we may arrive at certain logical consequences, which we shall denote $s_1, s_2,$ and so forth (Figure 12-3). Now among the statements $s_1, s_2,$ and so on, some direct ones may be tested by comparing them with appropriate evidence reports. If *these directly testable consequences of the indirect statement S are found to be true, we may deductively infer that the indirect statement itself is probably true; that is, although we cannot directly test an indirect statement, we can derive deductive inferences from such a statement and directly test them.* If such directly testable statements turn out to be true, we may inductively infer that the indirect statement is probably true. But if the consequences of S turn out to be false, we must infer that the indirect statement is also false. *In short, indirect statements that have true consequences are themselves probably true, but indirect statements that have false consequences are themselves false.*

To illustrate, consider the universal hypothesis "All men are anxious." Assume we know that "John Jones is a man" and "Harry Smith is a man." From these statements (premises) we can deductively infer that "John Jones is anxious" and "Harry Smith is anxious." Since the universal hypothesis is an indirect statement, *it* cannot be directly tested. However, the deductive inferences derived from this indirect statement *are* directly testable. We need only to determine

---

[5] Don't get too universal, though, as one student did who defined a universal statement as a "relationship between *all* variables for all time and for all places."

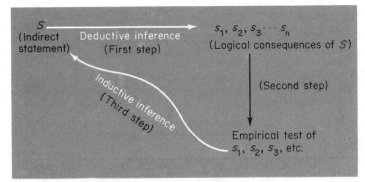

FIGURE 12-3 The procedure for testing indirect statements. (1) Deductive inferences result in consequences s_1, s_2, and so on, of general statements (S) that are empirically testable. (2) Those directed statements are confirmed in empirical tests. (3) Those confirmed consequences form the basis for an inductive inference that the indirect sentence is probably true.

the truth or falsity of these direct statements. If we perform suitable empirical operations and thereby conclude that the several direct statements are true, we may now conclude, by way of an *inductive inference*, that the indirect statement is confirmed.

Since this indirect statement makes assertions about an infinite number of instances, it is impossible to test all of its logically possible consequences; for example, we cannot test the hypothesis for all men. Furthermore, it is impossible to make a deductive inference from the direct statements back to the indirect statement; rather, we must be satisfied with an inductive inference. We know that an inductive inference is liable to error; its probability must be less than 1.0. Consequently, as long as we seek to test indirect statements, we must be satisfied with a probability estimate of their truth. We will never know absolutely that they are true. We can never know for sure that anything is absolutely true—our "truths" are held only until further notice.

CONFIRMATION VERSUS VERIFICATION

Our goal as scientists is to determine whether a given universal statement is true or false. To accomplish this goal we reason thusly: *If* the hypothesis is true, *then* the direct statements that are the result of deductive inferences are also true. If we find that the evidence reports are in accord with the

logical consequences (the direct statements), we conclude that the logical consequences are true. If the logical consequences are true, we inductively infer that the hypothesis itself is probably true (Figure 12-3).

Note that we have been cautious and limited in our statements about concluding that a universal hypothesis is false. Under certain circumstances, it is possible to conclude that a universal hypothesis is strictly false (not merely improbable or probably false) on the assumption that the evidence report is reliable. More generally (i.e., with regard to any type of hypothesis), it can be shown that under certain circumstances it is possible strictly to determine that a hypothesis is true or false, rather than probable or improbable, but always on the assumption that the evidence report is true. We will here distinguish between the processes of **verification** and **confirmation**. *By verification we mean a process of determining that a hypothesis is strictly true or strictly false; confirmation is a process of determining whether a hypothesis is probable or improbable.* This ties in with the distinction between inductive and deductive inferences. Under certain conditions, it is possible to make a deductive inference from the consequence of a hypothesis (which has been determined to be true or false) back to that hypothesis. Thus, where it is possible to make such a deductive inference, we are able to engage in the process of verification. Where we must be restricted to inductive inferences, the process of confirmation is used. To enlarge on this matter, let us now turn to a consideration of the ways in which the various types of hypotheses are tested.

INFERENCES FROM THE EVIDENCE REPORT TO THE HYPOTHESIS

Universal Hypotheses

Testing Confirmation with a Positive Evidence Report. Recall that the universal hypothesis "If *a*, then *b*" specifies that all things referred to have a certain characteristic, that we are referring to *all a*'s and *all b*'s. For example, if *a* stands for "rats are reinforced at the end of their maze runs" and *b* for "those rats will learn to run that maze with no errors," we are talking about all rats and all mazes. To test this hypothesis, we proceed as follows:

Universal hypothesis: If *a*, then *b*.
Evidence report: *a* and *b*

Inductive inference

Conclusion: "If *a*, then *b*" is probably true.

For instance, let us form two groups of rats; group E is reinforced at the end of each maze run, but group C is not. Assume that after 50 trials group E is able to run the maze with reliably fewer errors than does group C; in fact they make no errors. Since the antecedent conditions of the hypothesis are realized and the data are in accord with the consequent condition, the evidence report is positive. The inferences involved in the test of this hypothesis are as follows:

Universal hypothesis: If rats are reinforced at the end of their maze runs, then those rats will learn to run that maze with no errors.
Positive evidence report: A (specific) group of rats was reinforced at the end

of their maze runs, and those rats learned to run the maze with no errors.
Conclusion: The hypothesis is probably true.

These specific steps in testing a hypothesis should give you insight into the various inferences that must be made for this purpose. In your actual work, however, you need not specify each step, for that would become cumbersome. Rather, you should simply rely on the brief rules that we present for testing each type of hypothesis. *The rule for testing a universal hypothesis with a positive evidence report is that, since the evidence report agrees with the hypothesis, that hypothesis is confirmed* (but not verified).

Verification with Negative Results. To test a universal hypothesis when the evidence report is negative, we can apply the procedure of verification. This is possible because the rules of deductive logic tell us that a deductive inference may be made from a negative evidence report to a universal hypothesis. The procedure is as follows:

Universal hypothesis: If *a*, then *b*.
Evidence report: *a* and not *b*

Deductive inference

Conclusion: "If *a*, then *b*" is false.

For example,

Universal hypothesis: If rats are reinforced at the end of their maze runs, then those rats will learn to run that maze with no errors.
Negative evidence report: A group of rats was reinforced at the end of their maze runs, and those rats did not learn to run that maze without any errors.
Conclusion: The hypothesis is false.

In Summary. *We can determine that a universal hypothesis is (strictly) false (through verification) if the evidence report is negative. But if the evidence report is positive, we cannot determine that the hypothesis is (strictly) true; rather, we can say only that it is probable (through confirmation).* A universal hypothesis thus is *unilaterally verifiable*—that is, it can be determined that it is strictly false through verification in accordance with the rules of deductive logic. But, since the universal hypothesis cannot be deductively verified in the case of a positive evidence report, it can only be confirmed. The hypothesis is thus unilaterally verifiable because it can be strictly falsified with a negative evidence report, but it cannot be strictly determined that it is true. Unilateral verification is a strict inference that goes only in one direction

Existential Hypotheses

Verification with a Positive Evidence Report. The extistential hypothesis asserts that there is at least one thing that has a certain characteristic. Our example, stated as a positive existential hypothesis, would be: "There is a (at least one) rat that, if it is reinforced at the end of its maze runs, will learn to run that maze with no errors." The existential hypothesis is tested by observing a series of appropriate events in search of a single positive instance. If a single positive case *is* observed, that is sufficient to determine that the hypothesis is strictly true through the process of verification. For the positive evidence report, then, the paradigm is

Existential hypothesis:	There is an *a* such that if *a*, then *b*.
Positive evidence report:	*a* and *b*

Deductive inference

Conclusion:	Therefore, the hypothesis is (strictly) true.

To illustrate by means of our previous example,

Existential hypothesis:	There is a rat that, if it is reinforced at the end of its maze runs, will learn to run that maze with no errors.
Positive evidence report:	A group of rats was reinforced at the end of their maze runs, and at least one of those rats learned to run that maze with no errors.
Conclusion:	The hypothesis is (strictly) true.

Confirmation with Negative Results. On the other hand, if we keep observing events in search of the characteristic specified by the hypothesis and never come upon one, we can start to believe that the hypothesis is false. But we cannot be sure because if we continue our observations, we may yet come upon a positive instance, and a single positive instance, as we saw, is sufficient to verify that the hypothesis is true. However, our patience is not infinite—once we have made a reasonable number of observations and failed to find a single positive instance, we get to the point where we decide to formulate a negative evidence report. From this negative evidence report we can inductively infer that the hypothesis is probably not true. Thus existential hypotheses can also be unilaterally verified—we can determine that one is strictly true through verification, but we can only inductively infer that it is probably false. The inference for the case of a negative evidence report is then:

Existential

hypothesis: There is an *a* such that if *a*, then *b*.

Negative evidence

report: *a* and not *b*

|

Inductive inference

|

Conclusion: Therefore, the hypothesis is not confirmed.

And, for the example, it is

Existential hypothesis: There is a rat that, if it is reinforced at the end of its maze runs, will learn to run that maze with no errors.

Negative evidence report: A group of rats was reinforced at the end of their maze runs, and none of those rats learned to run that maze with no errors.

Conclusion: The hypothesis is not confirmed.

Our Philosophical Strategy. Let us pause for a moment and reflect on this matter of confirmation, of how we test hypotheses. We have emphasized that our approach throughout the book is a practical one from the point of view of the operating researcher. Philosophical arguments, by which we mean arguments in the philosophy of science, have been vigorously waged for centuries, they are waged today, and no doubt they will continue as long as there are philosophers. In science and in the philosophy of science, fads come and fads go, but the basic problems of how to test hypotheses remain with us. In an erudite and insightful book, Glymore (1980) reviews the principal kinds of strategies that have been employed for testing hypotheses. No strategy that has ever been used or is used today solves all the problems involved. As he says, "All of these strategies have their difficulties, but some

have more of them than others" (p. 13). The strategy that Glymore prefers is the one that we use throughout this book. The essence of this method, developed so explicitly by the great philosophers Rudolph Carnap and Hans Reichenbach, is that "hypotheses are confirmed by deducing them or positive instances of them from [evidence reports]" (p. 12). The essential idea is that confirmation is by instances; theoretical (general, indirect) sentences are confirmed by obtaining instances of them from evidence reports.

"The historical importance of this idea is hard to overestimate. It formed . . . the major positivist application of the idea of analytic truth, and it was the major idea behind Reichenbach's vastly influential analyses of physical theories" (p. 48).

The importance of this discussion by Glymore for us is that the strategies that we have followed here and throughout the book remain as the pillars of our practical day-to-day scientific research. As Glymore concludes, "*The strategies that earlier empiricists used remain at the center of various contemporary methodological systems, and insofar as they do the difficulties that beset empiricist approaches to confirmation are difficulties of contemporary systems as well*" (p. 13, italics added).

Recognizing that the goal of science is to reach sound general statements about nature, and with the perspective gained throughout this book for the importance of this task, it is fitting that we conclude our discussion of the phases of the scientific method by detailing the specific procedures by which we do generalize our findings. We must also consider how we determine the limitations of our generalizations.

THE MECHANICS OF GENERALIZATION

Consider a scientific experiment with 20 people. The interest is obviously not in these 20 people in and for themselves; rather, they are studied because they are typical of a larger group. Whatever the researcher finds out about them is assumed to be true for the larger group. In short, the wish is to *generalize* from the sample of 20 individuals to the larger group, the *population*. A researcher defines a population of participants about which to make statements. It is usually quite large, such as all students in the university, all dogs of a certain species, or perhaps even all humans. Since it is not feasible to study all members of such large populations, the experimenter randomly selects a sample therefrom that is *representative* of the population. Consequently, what is probably true for the sample is also probably true for the population; a generalization is made from the sample to the entire population from which they came.[6]

Representative Samples

The *most important* requirement for generalizing from a sample is to obtain a **representative sample** of the population. The technique that we have studied for obtaining representativeness is randomization; if the sample has been randomly drawn from the population, it is reasonable to assume that it is representative of the population. *Only if the sample is representative of the population can you generalize from it to the population.* We are emphasizing this point for two reasons: because of its great importance in generalizing to populations, and because of our desire to state a generalization. We want to generalize from what we have said about populations or organisms to a wide variety of other populations. When you conduct an experiment, you actually have a *number* of populations,

---

[6] Even though this statement offers the general idea, it is not quite accurate. If we were to follow this procedure, we would determine that the mean of a sample is, say, 10.32 and generalize to the population, inferring that its mean is also 10.32. Strictly speaking this procedure is not reasonable, for it could be shown that the probability of such an inference is 0.00. A more suitable procedure is known as *confidence interval estimation*, whereby one infers that the mean of the population is "close to" that for the sample, that it falls within a certain interval that can be computed. Hence, the more appropriate inference might be that, on the basis of a sample mean of 10.32, the population mean is between 10.10 and 10.54.

in addition to a population of people, dogs, and so on, to which you might generalize.

To illustrate, suppose you are conducting an experiment on knowledge of results. You have two groups of people: one that receives knowledge of results, and one (control) group that doesn't. We have here *several* populations: (1) people, (2) experimenters, (3) tasks, (4) stimulus conditions, and so on. To generalize to the population of people, we randomly select a sample therefrom and randomly assign them to the two groups. The finding—the knowledge-of-results group performs better than does the control group—is asserted to be true for the entire population of people sampled.

Representative Experimenters

But what about the experimenter? We have controlled this variable, presumably, by having a single experimenter collect data from all the participants. If so, can we say that the knowledge-of-results group will always be superior to the control group *regardless of who is the experimenter*? In short, can we generalize from the results obtained by our single experimenter to all experimenters? This question is difficult to answer. Let us imagine a population of experimenters, made up of all psychologists who conduct experiments. Strictly speaking, then, we should take a random sample from that population of experimenters and have each member of our sample conduct a separate experiment. Suppose that our population includes 500 psychologists from which we randomly select a sample of 10 experimenters. Assume with a sample of 100 participants, we would then randomly assign the participants to two groups of 50 each. Finally, we would randomly assign 5 participants in each of the two groups to each experimenter. In effect, we thus repeat the experiment 10 times, with each experimenter collecting data from 5 participants in each group. We have now not only controlled the experimenter variable by balancing, but we have also sampled from a population of experiments. Assume that the results come out approximately the same for each experimenter—that the performance of the knowledge-of-results participants is about equally superior to their corresponding controls for all 10 experimenters. In this case we generalize as follows: For the population of experimenters sampled and for the population of participants sampled, providing knowledge of results *under the conditions of this experiment* leads to superior performance (relative to the performance of the control group).

Representative Tasks

By "under the conditions of this experiment" we mean two things: with the specific task used, and under the specific stimulus conditions that were present. Concerning the first, our question is this: Since we found that the knowledge-of-results group was superior to the control group on one given task, would that group also be superior in learning other tasks? Of course, the answer is that we do not know from this experiment. Consider a population of *all* the tasks that humans could learn, such as drawing lines, learning Morse code, hitting a golf ball, assembling parts of a radio, and so forth. To make a statement about the effectiveness of knowledge of results for *all* tasks, we must also obtain a representative sample from *that* population. By selecting one particular task, we held the task variable constant so that we cannot generalize back to the larger population of tasks. The proper procedure to generalize to all tasks would be to select randomly a number of tasks from that population. We would then replicate the experiment for each of those tasks. If we find that on each task the knowledge-of-results group is superior to the control group, then we can generalize that conclusion to all tasks.

Representative Stimuli

Now what about the various stimulus conditions that were present for our participants? For one, suppose that visual knowledge of results was withheld by blind-folding them. But there are different techniques for "blindfolding" people. One experimenter might use a large handkerchief, another might use opaque glasses, and so on. Would the knowledge-of-results condition be superior regardless of the technique of blindfolding? What about other stimulus conditions? Would the specific temperature be relevant? How about background noise level? And so on—one can conceive of a number of stimulus populations. Strictly speaking, if an experimenter wishes to generalize to all populations of stimuli present, random samples should be drawn from those populations. Take temperature as an example. If one wishes to generalize results to all reasonable values of this variable, then a number of temperatures should be randomly selected. The experiment would then be replicated for each temperature value studied. If the same results are obtained regardless of the temperature value, one can generalize those findings to the population of temperatures sampled. Only by systematically sampling the various stimulus populations can the experimenter, strictly speaking, generalize results to those populations.

APPLYING FACTORIAL DESIGNS

At this point it might appear that the successful conduct of psychological experimentation is hopelessly complicated. One of the most discouraging features of psychological research is the difficulty encountered in confirming the results of previous experiments. When one experimenter (Jones) finds that variable A affects variable B, all too frequently another experimenter (Smith) achieves different results. Perhaps the differences in findings occurred because some conditions were held constant at one value by Jones and at a different value by Smith. For example, Jones may have held the experimenter variable constant and implicitly generalized to a population of experimenters. Strictly speaking, that should not have been done, for Jones did not randomly sample from a population of experimenters. Jones's generalization may have been in error, and those results obtained are thus valid only for experimenters like Jones. If so, different results would be expected with a different experimenter.

Psychological research (or *any* research for that matter) frequently becomes discouraging. After all, if you knew what the results would be, there would be little point (or joy) in going through the motion. The toughest nut to crack yields the tastiest meat. Psychologists, however, are accepting the challenge and are now systematically studying extraneous variables more thoroughly than in the past to account for conflicting results. This is one of the reasons that factorial designs are being more widely used, for they are wonderful devices for sampling a number of populations simultaneously. To illustrate, suppose that we wish to generalize our results to populations of people, experimenters, tasks, and temperature conditions. We could conduct several experiments here, but it is more efficient and productive of knowledge to conduct one experiment using four independent variables varied as follows: (1) knowledge of results varied two ways (knowledge and no knowledge), (2) experimenters varied in six ways, (3) tasks varied

TABLE 12-1 A 6 × 5 × 4 × 2 Factorial Design for Studying the Effect of Knowledge of Results When Randomly Sampling from Populations of Experimenters, Tasks, Temperatures, and People

		Knowledge of Results						No Knowledge of Results					
		1	*2*	*3*	*4*	*5*	*6*	*1*	*2*	*3*	*4*	*5*	*6*
Temperature 4	Task *E*												
	D												
	C												
	B												
	A												
Temperature 3	Task *E*												
	D												
	C												
	B												
	A												
Temperature 2	Task *E*												
	D												
	C												
	B												
	A												
Temperature 1	Task *E*												
	D												
	C												
	B												
	A												

in five ways, and (4) temperature varied in four ways. Assume that we have chosen the values of the last three variables at random. The resulting $6 \times 5 \times 4 \times 2$ factorial design is presented in Table 12-1.

What if we find a significant difference for the knowledge of results variable, but no significant interactions? In this case we could rather safely generalize about knowledge of results to our experimenter population, to our task population, to our temperature population, and also, of course, to our population of humans—providing, that is, that we use the appropriate model.

Models and the Choice of a Correct Error Term

Recall our discussion from Chapter 8 on the factorial design in which we said that the experimenter usually selects the values of the independent variable for some specific reason. As in the case of knowledge of results versus no knowledge of results, one does not randomly select values of such independent variables from the population of possible values. This, thus, is a **fixed model**. In contrast, for a **random model** we define a population and then randomly select values from that population. The relevance of this distinction is that only for the case of the random model can you safely generalize to the population. If you select the values of your variables in a nonrandom (fixed) fashion, any conclusions must be restricted to those values. Let us illustrate by considering the temperature variable again. Suppose that we are particularly interested in three specific values of this variable: 60 degrees, 70 degrees, and 80 degrees Fahrenheit. Now, whatever our results, they will be limited to those particular temperature values. On the other hand, if we are interested in generalizing to all temperatures between 40 and 105, we could write each number between 40 and 105 on a piece of paper, place all these numbers in a hat, and draw several values from the hat. Then, whatever the experimental results we obtain, we can safely generalize back to that population of values,

for we have randomly selected our values from it.[7]

If we selected the values of our variables for specific reasons and not by randomization, we have used a *fixed model*. With a fixed model we have said that within-groups means square is the appropriate error term to use for the denominator of the *F*-test. But if the values of the independent variables have been randomly selected from a population, a *random model* is used, in which case you can generalize to that population. Finally, if the value of one independent variable is randomly selected but the values of the others are fixed, a *mixed model* is used. Different error terms for the *F*-test are required for random and mixed models. Let us briefly expand on these three cases.

The Case of a Fixed Model. If, in a 2×2 design, the values of the two independent variables were selected for some particular reason, we have a fixed model. The two values of each independent variable thus were not chosen in a random manner—we are interested in method A of teaching (a specific method) versus method B, for example. Or we choose to study 10 hours of training versus 20 hours. Similarly we decide to give 50 versus 100 golf trials, selecting these particular values for a special reason. For this case of a fixed model, the within-groups mean square is the correct error term for all *F*-tests being run. If we refer to our two independent variables as *K* and *L*, and the interaction as $K \times L$, mean squares between the two conditions of *K*, between the two conditions of *L*, and for $K \times L$ all should be divided by the within-groups mean square. As we said, this is the case most frequently encountered in psychological research.

The Case of a Random Model. Consider how we arrive at the two values of the two independent variables: number of trials and

---

[7] Assuming, of course, that we select a sufficient number of values to study. Just as with sampling from a population of people, the larger the number of values selected, the more likely it is that the sample is representative of the population.

IQ of participants. For this, we would specify all possible reasonable numbers of trials and all possible reasonable IQs, then select two values of each at random. We might consider as reasonable possible values of the first independent variable—numbers of trials—those from 6 to 300. We could then place these 295 numbers in a hat and draw 2 from them. The resulting numbers would be the values that we would assign to our independent variable. The same process could be followed with regard to the IQ variable.

The procedure for testing the between-groups mean squares for the case in which both independent variables are random variables is as follows: *Test the interaction mean square by dividing it by the within-groups mean square. Then test the other mean squares by dividing them by the interaction mean square.* That is, test the $K \times L$ mean square by dividing it by the mean square within groups. Then test the mean square between the two conditions of K by dividing it by the $K \times L$ mean square, and also test the mean square between L by dividing it by the $K \times L$ mean square. We might remark that designs in which values of both variables are selected randomly are relatively rare in psychological research.

The Case of a Mixed Model. This is a less uncommon case than that for a random model, but it still does not occur as frequently as the case of a fixed model. The case of a mixed model occurs when values of one independent variable are fixed and the other are random. The procedure for testing the three mean squares for this case is as follows: *Divide the within-groups mean square into the interaction mean square; divide the interaction mean square into the mean square for the fixed independent variable; and divide the within mean square into the mean square for the random independent variable.*

These are the three cases that are most likely to be encountered in your research, although there are a number of variations that can occur. The importance of these rules is that with a random or mixed model, the statistical analysis allows you to generalize to the population sampled if you use the correct error term as the denominator of your *F*-test. A detailed explanation of *why* these are the correct error term was presented in the earlier editions of this book, or they can be obtained from contemporary statistics books. If you are using a computer analysis, you must make sure that the program employs the proper error term. If the program does not ask you which model you are using, you could make a serious error, which is another argument for also conducting a statistical analysis by hand.

With this background let us now look at the other side of the coin, namely, how do we know when to restrict our generalizations?

THE LIMITATION OF GENERALIZATIONS

Ascertaining the Reason for Conflicting Results

How widely is it reasonable to generalize? Let's say that we are interested in whether method A or method B of learning leads to superior performance. Assume that one experimenter tested these methods on a sample of college students and found method A to be superior. Unhesitatingly, a generalization of the results was made to all college students. Another experimenter replicates the experiment, and finds that method B is superior. We wish to resolve the contradiction. After studying the two experiments we may find that the first experimenter was in a women's college, whereas the second was in a men's college. A possible reason for the different results is now apparent. The first experimenter generalized to a population of male and female students without randomly sampling from the former (as also did the second, but without sampling females). To determine whether we have correctly ascertained the reason for the conflicting results we design a 2×2 factorial experiment in which our first variable is methods of learning, varied in two ways, and our second is gender, varied, of course, in two ways. We randomly draw a sample of males and females from a college population. Assume that our results come out with the mean values and that the higher the score, the better is the performance (Table 12-2).

By graphing these results we can see an interaction between gender and methods such that females are superior with method A and males are superior with method B (Figure 12-4). We have thus confirmed the results of the first experiment in that method A is superior for females; similarly we have confirmed the results of the second experiment since we found that method B is superior for males. We have therefore established the reason for conflicting results. But we cannot make a simple statement about the superiority of a method that generally applies to everybody; the discovery of this interaction limits the extent to which a simple generalization can be offered.

Using Stratification to Generalize. We see, then, that experiments can be explicitly designed to determine whether some characteristic of our participants interacts with our independent variable, as in this case of a gender × methods interaction. For this, you could systematically sample a population and incorporate a number of different values into a factorial design. For instance, if you are interested in whether intelligence interacts with your independent variable, you might classify your participants as high IQ, medium IQ, or low IQ (this is called *stratification*). In this case you can generalize to your participant population as far as IQ is concerned if there is no IQ × methods interaction. Furthermore, and this is a somewhat more advanced point, you can reduce your error variance by using this type of design—that is, when you stratify participants

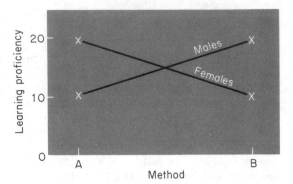

FIGURE 12-4   An interaction between methods of learning and gender that explains conflicting results.

into levels (the vertical rows of the factorial), you compute the variation in the dependent variable due to levels (here, three levels of IQ) as we did for rows in the repeated-treatments design of Chapter 10, then this variation due to levels of IQ is "automatically" taken out of the error term, resulting in an increase in the precision of the experiment. In short, you can stratify your participants by repeating your experiment at different levels of homogeneous participants, thus decreasing your error variance while also establishing the extent to which you can generalize. As another example, to determine if intelligence interacts with your independent variable, you could classify your participants as high IQ, medium IQ, or low IQ (this is called stratification). If there is no IQ × methods interaction, you can generalize to your participant population as far as IQ is concerned.[8]

_____

[8] A somewhat more advanced point is that you can reduce your error variance by using this type of design—that is, when you stratify participants into levels (the vertical rows of the factorial), you compute the variation in the dependent variable due to levels (here, three levels of IQ) as we did for rows in the repeated-treatments design of Chapter 9; then this variation due to levels of IQ is "automatically" taken out of the error term, resulting in an increase in the precision of the experiment. In short, you can stratify your participants by repeating your experiment at different levels of homogeneous participants, thus decreasing your error variance while also establishing the extent to which you can generalize.

TABLE 12-2   A 2 × 2 Factorial Design to Resolve Contradictory Results

Gender	Methods	
	A	B
Males	10	20
Females	20	12

Testing for Interactions between Variables of Primary and Secondary Interest. We will now consider the matter of limiting our generalizations in a broader fashion. Our purpose is to make general statements, but we would also like them to be as simple (parsimonious) as possible (see page 43). Unfortunately, though, nature does not always oblige us, and, to make general statements, we often must complicate them in order to describe accurately events that we study. This means that we can expect to find a number of interactions between our experimental treatments, so we should explicitly design our experiments to discover them. The alternative of failing to look for interactions amounts to blinding ourselves to truth; the consequence is that we arrive at simplistic statements that are erroneous and we fail to confirm results of previous experimentation.

In general, then, the experimenter should systematically study variables that might interact with the variables of primary interest. It is often very easy to construct experimental designs to study such interactions. In the previous example one can conveniently analyze the results as a function of gender or other participant characteristics such as anxiety. When more than one experimenter collects data in a given experiment (and this happens in about half of published experiments), it is "a natural" to analyze the results as a function of experimenters to see if this variable interacts with that of primary interest. Similar variables that may be built into a factorial design for this purpose might be environmental temperature, type of task, nature of equipment used (e.g., apparatus X versus apparatus Y), and so forth.

Let us now examine more closely the possible outcomes for the variable of secondary interest. Assume that we vary the independent variable of primary interest in two ways using an experimental and a control group. The variable of secondary interest may be varied in several ways, but for the moment let us vary it in only two ways. For instance, let us say that two experimenters collect data in a two-randomized-groups design so that

TABLE 12-3 A Two-Groups Design in Which the Data Are Analyzed as a Function of Two Experimenters

	Independent Variable	
Experimenter	*Experimental*	*Control*
1		
2		

we can analyze the data as a 2 × 2 factorial design (see Table 12-3). There are three possible outcomes, cases I, II, and III.

Case I. Generalization to an Ineffective Secondary Variable. This case occurs when experimenters 1 and 2 obtain essentially the same results as in Figure 12-5. The lines are parallel, indicating that the variable of secondary interest does not influence the dependent variable measure—it does *not* interact with our variable of primary interest. In this case a difference between our experimental and control groups can be general-

FIGURE 12-5 Population values for case I showing no interaction between a variable of secondary interest (e.g., experimenters) and the primary independent variable. Variation of the variable of secondary interest does *not* differentially affect the dependent-variable values.

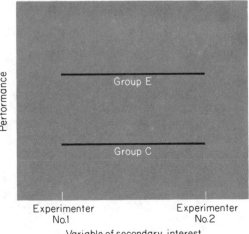

ized with regard to the variable of secondary interest. There is one remaining point, however: We could not possibly have known this unless we had designed and analyzed our experiment to find it out.

An empirical illustration of case I involving two methods of learning and three data collectors is presented in Figure 12-6. Hence we have some reason for generalizing the methods results to a population of experimenters, although, of course, a larger sample of this population would be preferred.

Case II. Generalization to an Effective Secondary Variable. The second general possibility is that variation of the variable of secondary interest *does* affect the dependent variable. However, it affects all participants in the same way, regardless of the experimental condition to which those participants were assigned. In Figure 12-7 for example, participants assigned to experimenter 1 (or temperature A, or task X) perform at a

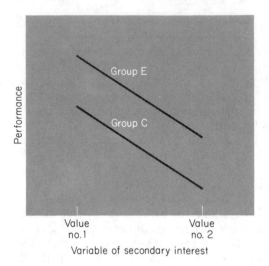

FIGURE 12-7 Population values for case II showing no interaction between variables of the primary and secondary interest. But the variable of secondary interest does influence the dependent-variable values.

FIGURE 12-6 Sample values illustrating case I using three experimenters and two methods (knowledge of results). The lack of a reliable interaction between experimenters and methods allows us to generalize to a population of experimenters (from McGuigan, Hutchens, Eason, and Reynolds, 1964).

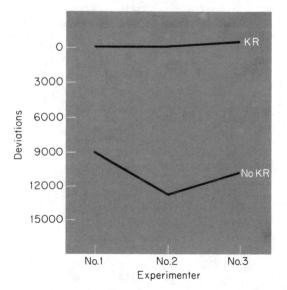

higher level on the average than do those assigned value number 2. The experimental group in either case is equally superior to the control group for both experimenters, or what have you. For empirical example, in Figure 12-8 there is a significant difference between experimenters, but lack of an interaction between experimenters and methods. Thus, in case II we can reach the same conclusion for the variable of primary interest, regardless of which experimenter conducted the experiment, and can generalize the results with regard to methods to that population of experimenters. There is no interaction to limit our generalization. As an adjunct, however, we note that behavior *is* influenced by this secondary variable—information that may be valuable for further experimentation.

Case III. An Interaction Limits Generalization to the Secondary Variable. In cases I and II we have justification for generalizing to the population of the secondary variable to the extent to which that population has been sampled. In case III, however, we must deal with an interaction. To take an extreme ex-

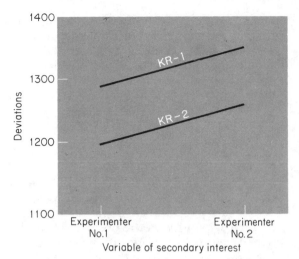

FIGURE 12-8 Sample values illustrating case II. The results are for two methods of presenting knowledge of results by two experimenters (from McGuigan, 1959).

ample, suppose that the control group is superior to the experimental group for one experimenter but that the reverse is the case for the second experimenter (Figure 12-9). In this event the extent to which we can generalize to a population is sharply restricted, particularly since we probably don't know the precise ways in which the two experimenters differ. To understate the matter, the discovery of an interaction of this sort

FIGURE 12-9 Population values for case III showing one possible interaction between a variable of secondary interest (here experimenters) and the primary independent variable.

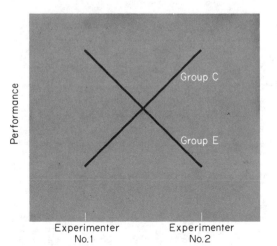

tells us to proceed with caution. To understand this more concretely, let us examine two interesting studies in which interactions with experimenters have been established.

The first was a verbal conditioning study using the response class of hostile words emitted in sentences. Whenever the participant unknowingly used a hostile word in a sentence, the experimenter subtly reinforced that response by saying "good." Two groups were used, a different experimenter for each group. The two experimenters differed in gender, height, weight, age, appearance, and personality:

The first . . . was . . . an attractive, soft-spoken, reserved young lady . . . 5′½″ in height, and 90 pounds in weight. The . . . second . . . was very masculine, 6′5″ tall, 220 pounds in weight, and had many of the unrestrained personality characteristics which might be expected of a former marine captain—perhaps more important than their actual age difference of about 12 years was the difference in their age appearance: The young lady could have passed for a high school sophomore while the male experimenter was often mistaken for a faculty member. (Binder, McConnell, & Sjoholm, 1957, p. 309)

The results are presented in Figure 12-10. Note that since the number of hostile words emitted by both groups increases as the number of trials increases, the participants of both experiments were successfully conditioned. During the first two blocks of

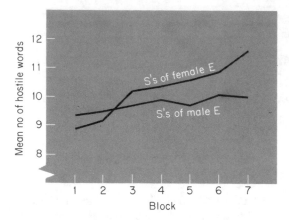

FIGURE 12-10   Learning curves for two groups treated the same, but with different experimenters. The steeper slope for the participants of the female experimenter illustrates an interaction between experimenters and stage of learning (after Binder et al., 1957).

learning trials, however, the participants of the female experimenter were inferior to those of the male experimenter. On succeeding blocks the reverse is the case, and the two curves intersect. In short, there is an interaction between experimenters and learning trials such that the slope of the learning curve for the female experimenter is steeper than that for the male experimenter. If we therefore wish to offer a generalization about the characteristics of the learning curve, it must be tempered by considering the nature of the experimenter. Exactly why this difference occurred is not clear, but we may speculate with the authors that the female experimenter provided a less threatening environment, and the participants consequently were less inhibited in the tendency to increase their frequency of usage of hostile words. Presumably some reverse effect was present early in learning.

In the second example of case III, a group of people were selected who scored high on the hysteria scale of the Minnesota Multiphase Personality Inventory and a second who scored high on the psychasthenic scale. The participants were then given one of two sets when they entered the experi-

mental situation: For the positive set, the participant was told that the experimenter was a "warm, friendly person, and you should get along very well"; for the negative set, the participant was told that the experimenter may "irritate him a bit, that he's not very friendly, in fact kind of cold." The experimenter was the same person in both cases!

The participants were then conditioned to emit a class of pronouns that was reinforced by saying "good." The results indicated a reliable difference between positive and negative sets for the experimenter such that participants with the positive set conditioned better than those with a negative set. Furthermore, and this is the point of present interest, there was a significant interaction between set for the experimenter and personality of the participant (whether the individual was a hysteric or a psychasthenic). To illustrate this interaction we have plotted the terminal conditioning scores under these four conditions in Figure 12-11. We can thus see that the hysterics who were given a positive set had higher scores than those given a

FIGURE 12-11   An interaction between set for the experimenter and personality characteristic of participants. The effect of set depends on whether people are hysterics or psychasthenics (after Spires, 1960).

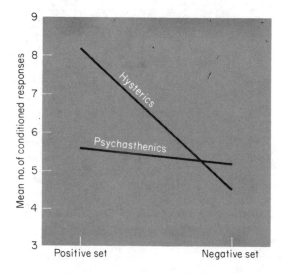

negative set. There is, though, little difference between the two groups of psychasthenics.

This type of research is especially valuable to us because of its analytic nature; it suggests, for instance, that we can generalize conditioning results with regard to this particular experimenter characteristic for one kind of person but not for another kind. Continuous and sustained analyses of the various secondary variables in an experimental situation can eventually allow us to advance our generalizations so that we can have great confidence in them.

Summary for Limiting Generalizations

Having now specified these three cases, let us summarize where we stand.

First, if you have not sampled from a population of some variable, you should, strictly speaking, not generalize to that population. If, for instance, there is but one data collector for your experiment the best that you can do is to attempt to hold his or her influence on the participants constant. If, however, you have previous knowledge that no interaction has been found between your independent variable and the populations for other variables to which you wish to generalize, then your generalization to those populations will probably be justified.

Second, if you have systematically varied some variable of secondary interest to you, then you should investigate the possibility that an interaction exists between it and your variable of primary interest. If, for instance, more than one data collector has been used, you should: (1) specify techniques for controlling this variable, (2) analyze and report your data as a function of experimenters, and (3) test for interactions between experimenters and treatments. Should your analysis indicate that the experiment is an instance of cases I and II, the results are generalizable to a population to the extent to which that population has been sampled.[9]

We grant that completely satisfactory sampling of secondary variables can seldom occur, but at least some sampling is better than none. And it is beneficial to *know* and be able to *state* that, within those limitations, the results appear to be instances of cases I or II.

Third, if you find that your data are an instance of case III, then you cannot offer a simple generalization for them. If your variable of secondary interest is operationally defined, then your generalization can be quite precise, if a bit complicated. On the other hand, if you cannot adequately specify the ways in which values of your secondary variable differ (as in the case of different data collectors), the extent to which you can generalize is sharply limited. You can say, for instance, only that method A will be superior to method B when experimenters similar to Jones are used, but that the reverse is the case when experimenters are similar to Smith. This knowledge is valuable, but only in a negative sense since probably only their spouses might suspect what the different relevant characteristics are; an interaction of this kind tells us to proceed with considerable caution (cf. McGuigan, 1963).

An Elementary Strategy. This may all sound rather demanding, and it *is* for reaching an advanced understanding in our science. However, rather than conclude this topic on such a note, let us return to the most typical situation that you are likely to face in your elementary work, namely, that specified in the first point mentioned.

If you have no knowledge about interactions between your independent variable and the populations to which you wish to generalize, then it is possible tentatively to offer your generalization. Other experimenters may then repeat your experiment in their own laboratories. This implies that the various extraneous variables will assume different values from those that occurred in your experiment (either as the result of intentional control or because they were allowed to vary randomly). If in the repetitions of your experiment your results are

---

[9]We are assuming that a random model is used (see page 280).

confirmed, it is likely that the populations to which you have generalized do not interact with your independent variable. On the other hand, if repetitions of your experiment by others, with differences in tasks, stimulus conditions, and other factors do not confirm your findings, then there is probably at least one interaction that needs to be discovered. At this point thorough and piecemeal analysis of the differences between your experiment and the repetitions of it needs to be done to discover the interactions. Such an analysis might assume the form of a factorial design such as that diagrammed in Table 12-2 and illustrated by Figure 12-4.

Standardized versus Nonstandardized Experimentation. This last point leads us to consider an interesting proposal. Some experimenters have suggested that we should use a highly standardized experimental situation for studying particular types of behavior. All experimenters who are studying a given type of behavior should use the same values of a number of extraneous variables—lighting, temperature, noise, and so forth. In this way we can exercise better control and be more likely to confirm each other's findings. The Skinner box is a good example of an attempt to introduce standardized values of extraneous variables into an experiment because the lighting is controlled (the box is opaque), the noise level is controlled (it is sound deadened), and a variety of other external stimuli are prevented from entering into the experimental space. On the other hand, under such highly standardized conditions the extent to which we can generalize our findings is sharply limited. If we continue to proceed in our present direction with extraneous variables assuming different values in different experiments, then, when experimental findings are confirmed, we can be rather sure that interactions do not exist. When findings are not confirmed, we suspect that we have interactions present that limit our generalizations, and hence we should initiate experimentation in order to discover them. Re-

gardless of your opinion on these two positions—that in favor of standardization or that opposed—the matter is probably only academic. It is unlikely that much in the way of standardization will occur in the foreseeable future. In fact, within recent years there has been a movement quite in the opposite direction, one which holds that laboratory experiments conducted under highly controlled conditions lack **external validity**. By *external validity* is meant the extent to which laboratory results can be generalized to the "real world." The argument is that since they are conducted under highly "artificial" conditions wherein the numerous extraneous variables of the natural environment are prevented from differentially influencing the dependent variable, laboratory conclusions cannot be transferred outside the laboratory.

Earlier in the book we dealt with this type of argument, which was advanced well before the recent assertion that ecological studies are more important than laboratory experiments. The very point of bringing a "real-world event" into the laboratory is to determine which variables do control it, a feat that usually cannot be accomplished with extraneous variables randomly affecting behavior. Only when the event is dissected under suitable controls we can increase our understanding of its natural occurrence. Finally, there is nothing wrong with conducting a field experiment, which is a true experiment conducted in a natural setting. The major shortcoming of field experiments is that they have inflated error variances. This issue is very complicated, however, and the interested student should refer to the astute answers given to criticisms of laboratory experiments by Berkowitz and Donnerstein (1982).

A LOOK TO THE FUTURE

This concludes our presentation. You have finished a book on research methods, but the topic itself is endless. Among those who have studied this book, some will go on to become talented researchers; we hope that those who do will themselves discover some new and interesting characteristics of behavior. For all, we hope that an increased appreciation for sound psychological knowledge was gained. An enlightened citizenry certainly needs to discriminate between sound and spurious practices.

CHAPTER SUMMARY

I. *Generalized* statements that derive from scientific research can be used to *explain* and *predict* (as well as to control).

II. Inferences, which are processes by which we reach a conclusion on the basis of relevant preceding statements, may be of two kinds:
   A. Deductive inferences, wherein the conclusion is necessarily true if the statements on which it is based are true.
   B. Inductive inferences, wherein the conclusion follows from the antecedent statements with only a degree of probability.

III. The inductive schema is a concatenated chain of statements that represents reasoning processes based on inductive and deductive inferences. Concatenation means that the statements are chained together to form a compatible system; this interlocking system increases the probability of any given statement over that taken in isolation. When used to reconstruct a scientific enterprise, the schema can illustrate the following basic scientific reasoning procedures:
   A. Generalization—the process of inductively inferring a more general statement from one or more specific statements.
   B. Deduction—placing a specific statement within a context of the more general statement (deductively inferring it), thereby explaining the specific statement.
   C. Prediction—deductively inferring a consequence from a generalization such that the consequence has to do with as-yet-unobserved phenomena.

IV. The foundation for inferences is the evidence report, which is a summary statement of empirical findings. It is a direct statement referring to limited phenomena that are immediately observable.

V. However, generalizations are indirect statements insofar as they refer to phenomena which cannot reasonably be directly observed. To test an indirect, generalized statement, we need to infer deductively logical consequences from it that *can* be directly tested. Then we may inductively infer that the generalized statement is probably true or false depending on the truth or falsity of the direct statement derived therefrom (see Figure 12-3).

VI. Depending on the way the empirical hypothesis is formed, and on the truth or falsity of the evidence report obtained to test the hypothesis, we may make several kinds of inferences. If the inference from the evidence report to the hypothesis is inductive, the hypothesis has a certain degree of probability (confirmation). If the inference is deductive, the hypothesis is inferred to be strictly true or strictly false (verification).
   A. Universal hypotheses:
      1. May be confirmed as probably true through an inductive inference, if the evidence report is positive.
      2. May be deductively inferred to be false if the evidence report is negative.
   B. Existential hypotheses:
      1. May be deductively inferred to be true if the evidence report is positive.
      2. May be inductively inferred to be probably false if the evidence report is negative.

VII. In experimentation one can generalize from the evidence report to the hypothesis to the extent to which populations have been sampled.
   A. If the sample of participants is representative of the population studied, you may generalize from that sample to that population.
   B. Similar statements may be made for other populations with which the experiment is concerned, for example, experimenters, tasks, stimulus conditions.
   C. The factorial design is an excellent method for allowing such generalizations to be made. However, such generalizations are restricted if you have employed a fixed model. In a fixed model you have selected specific values of your independent variable, in which

case you can reach a conclusion only about those specific values.

1. For a fixed model, you use the within-groups mean square for your error term for all *F*-tests in your analysis of variance.
2. For a random model, you randomly select values of your independent variables and may thus generalize to those independent-variable dimensions.
3. For a mixed model, you employ a random model for one independent variable but a fixed model for the other.
4. In the case of random or mixed models (which you are unlikely to use at this elementary level), you should consult page 000 for the correct error term for your analysis of variance.

VIII. To determine whether your generalization along one independent-variable dimension should be limited, you need to test for interactions between your independent variables. There are three cases:
   A. For case I, there is no interaction, and the variable of secondary interest does not affect the variable of primary interest. In this case you can generalize for your two independent variables to the extent to which you have sampled them.
   B. For case II, the variable of secondary interest does affect the primary independent variable, but there is no interaction. In this case you may generalize to your independent variable.
   C. For case III, there is an interaction between your two independent variables so that the generalization is restrictive—you must state the specific nature of the interaction in your conclusion.

CRITICAL REVIEW FOR THE STUDENT

1. To help yourself better understand the nature of the inductive schema, you might construct a schema from one of Sherlock Holmes's other stories.
2. Review basic definitions such as generalization, prediction, and explanation.
3. Did Sherlock Holmes misuse the word "deduction"? Do you notice the word being misused in your newspaper and other aspects of everyday life?

4. Perhaps you would also want to consider developing an inductive schema for some area of scientific inquiry that is especially interesting for you. For instance, you might develop one for a given theory of vision, for the "big bang" theory of the origin of the universe, or for a theory of how life developed. In so doing, you would then emphasize the basic terms of explanation, generalization, and prediction in a new context.
5. You might outline for yourself the basic procedures by which universal and existential hypotheses are subjected to empirical tests. Basic here, of course, is the use of inductive and deductive inferences.
6. Summarize the procedures by which we generalize from a sample to a population. Consider how you assure that you have a representative sample.
7. Does the sample from which you generalize have to be restricted to organisms? What other populations exist in an experiment from which you should obtain random samples?
8. Review Table 12-1. You might consider an experiment that you have conducted or would like to conduct and diagram a similar factorial design for your experiment in order to generalize to various populations.
9. Specify the ways in which interactions limit the extent to which you can advance your generalization.
10. Define the three cases relevant to the advancing of generalizations. Can you find instances of these three cases in the scientific literature? You might look for them when you read over the journals in your library. In experiments in which you are involved, how might you explain your findings, and how might you make predictions to new situations?
1. You probably will want to make sure that you can define the basic terms used throughout the book, and especially in this chapter. Perhaps the glossary at the end of the book will also be useful for your review. Some basic terms that you should not forget are: evidence report, various kinds of hypotheses, the difference between inductive and deductive inferences, direct versus indirect statements, confirmation versus verification, and the conditional relationship (the "if . . . then . . ." proposition).

appendix A
STATISTICAL TABLES

TABLE A-1 The Distribution of t for One- and Two-Tailed Tests

	Proportion in One Tail												
df / P	0.45	0.40	0.35	0.30	0.25	0.20	0.15	0.10	0.05	0.025	0.01	0.005	0.0005
(two tails)	0.9	0.8	0.7	0.6	0.5	0.4	0.3	0.2	0.1	0.05	0.02	0.01	0.001
1	0.158	0.325	0.510	0.727	1.000	1.376	1.963	3.078	6.314	12.706	31.821	63.657	636.619
2	0.142	0.289	0.445	0.617	0.816	1.061	1.386	1.886	2.920	4.303	6.995	9.925	31.598
3	0.137	0.277	0.424	0.584	0.765	0.978	1.250	1.638	2.353	3.182	4.541	5.841	12.924
4	0.134	0.271	0.414	0.589	0.741	0.941	1.190	1.533	2.132	2.776	3.747	4.604	8.610
5	0.132	0.267	0.408	0.559	0.727	0.920	1.156	1.476	2.015	2.571	3.365	4.032	6.869
6	0.131	0.265	0.404	0.553	0.718	0.906	1.134	1.440	1.943	2.447	3.143	3.707	5.959
7	0.130	0.263	0.402	0.549	0.711	0.896	1.119	1.415	1.895	2.365	2.998	3.499	5.408
8	0.130	2.262	0.399	0.546	0.706	0.889	1.108	1.397	1.860	2.306	2.896	3.355	5.041
9	0.129	0.261	0.398	0.543	0.703	0.883	1.100	1.383	1.833	2.262	2.821	3.250	4.781
10	0.129	0.260	0.397	0.542	0.700	0.879	1.093	1.372	1.812	2.228	2.764	3.169	4.587
11	0.129	0.260	0.396	0.540	0.697	0.876	1.088	1.363	1.796	2.201	2.718	3.106	4.437
12	0.128	0.259	0.395	0.539	0.695	0.873	1.083	1.356	1.782	2.179	2.681	3.055	4.318
13	0.128	0.259	0.394	0.538	0.694	0.870	1.079	1.350	1.771	2.160	2.650	3.012	4.221
14	0.128	0.258	0.393	0.537	0.692	0.868	1.076	1.345	1.761	2.145	2.624	2.977	4.140
15	0.128	0.258	0.393	0.536	0.691	0.866	1.074	1.341	1.753	2.131	2.602	2.947	4.073
16	0.128	0.258	0.392	0.535	0.690	0.865	1.071	1.337	1.746	2.120	2.583	2.921	4.015
17	0.128	0.257	0.392	0.534	0.689	0.863	1.069	1.333	1.740	2.110	2.567	2.898	3.965
18	0.127	0.257	0.392	0.534	0.688	0.862	1.067	1.330	1.734	2.101	2.552	2.878	3.922
19	0.127	0.257	0.391	0.533	0.688	0.861	1.066	1.328	1.729	2.093	2.539	2.861	3.883
20	0.127	0.257	0.391	0.533	0.687	0.860	1.064	1.325	1.725	2.086	2.528	2.845	3.850
21	0.127	0.257	0.391	0.532	0.686	0.859	1.063	1.323	1.721	2.080	2.518	2.831	3.819
22	0.127	0.256	0.390	0.532	0.686	0.858	1.061	1.321	1.717	2.074	2.508	2.819	3.792
23	0.127	0.256	0.390	0.532	0.685	0.858	1.060	1.319	1.714	2.069	2.500	2.807	3.767
24	0.127	0.256	0.390	0.531	0.685	0.857	1.059	1.318	1.711	2.064	2.492	2.797	3.745
25	0.127	0.256	0.390	0.531	0.684	0.856	1.058	1.316	1.708	2.060	2.485	2.787	3.725
26	0.127	0.256	0.390	0.531	0.684	0.856	1.058	1.315	1.706	2.056	2.479	2.779	3.707
27	0.127	0.256	0.389	0.531	0.684	0.855	1.057	1.314	1.703	2.052	2.473	2.771	3.690
28	0.127	0.256	0.389	0.530	0.683	0.855	1.056	1.313	1.701	2.048	2.467	2.763	3.674
29	0.127	0.256	0.389	0.530	0.683	0.854	1.055	1.311	1.699	2.045	2.462	2.756	3.659
30	0.127	0.256	0.389	0.530	0.683	0.854	1.055	1.310	1.697	2.042	2.457	2.750	3.646
∞	0.12566	0.25335	0.38532	0.52440	0.67449	0.84162	1.03643	1.28155	1.64485	1.95996	2.32634	2.57582	3.291

Table A–1 is reprinted from Table IV of Fisher: *Statistical Methods for Research Workers*, 1949, published by Oliver and Boyd Ltd., Edinburgh, by permission of the author and publishers.

TABLE A-2 Table of F

df ASSOCIATED WITH DENOMINATOR	P	df ASSOCIATED WITH NUMERATOR									
		1	2	3	4	5	6	8	12	24	∞
1	0.01	4052	4999	5403	5625	5764	5859	5981	6106	6234	6366
	0.05	161.45	199.50	215.71	224.58	230.16	233.99	238.88	243.91	249.05	254.32
	0.10	39.86	49.50	53.59	55.83	57.24	58.20	59.44	60.70	62.00	63.33
	0.20	9.47	12.00	13.06	13.73	14.01	14.26	14.59	14.90	15.24	15.58
2	0.01	98.49	99.00	99.17	99.25	99.33	99.33	99.36	99.42	99.46	99.50
	0.05	18.51	19.00	19.16	19.25	19.30	19.33	19.37	19.41	19.45	19.50
	0.10	8.53	9.00	9.16	9.24	9.29	9.33	9.37	9.41	9.45	9.49
	0.20	3.56	4.00	4.16	4.24	4.28	4.32	4.36	4.40	4.44	4.48
3	0.01	34.12	30.81	29.46	28.71	28.24	27.91	27.49	27.05	26.60	26.12
	0.05	10.13	9.55	9.28	9.12	9.01	8.94	8.84	8.74	8.64	8.53
	0.10	5.54	5.46	5.39	5.34	5.31	5.28	5.25	5.22	5.18	5.13
	0.20	2.68	2.89	2.94	2.96	2.97	2.97	2.98	2.98	2.98	2.98
4	0.01	21.20	18.00	16.69	15.98	15.52	15.21	14.80	14.37	13.93	13.46
	0.05	7.71	6.94	6.59	6.39	6.26	6.16	6.04	5.91	5.77	5.63
	0.10	4.54	4.32	4.19	4.11	4.05	4.01	3.95	3.90	3.83	3.76
	0.20	2.35	2.47	2.48	2.48	2.48	2.47	2.47	2.46	2.44	2.43
5	0.01	16.26	13.27	12.06	11.39	10.97	10.67	10.29	9.89	9.47	9.02
	0.05	6.61	5.79	5.41	5.19	5.05	4.95	4.82	4.68	4.53	4.36
	0.10	4.06	3.78	3.62	3.52	3.45	3.40	3.34	3.27	3.19	3.10
	0.20	2.18	2.26	2.25	2.24	2.23	2.22	2.20	2.18	2.16	2.13
6	0.01	13.74	10.92	9.78	9.15	8.75	8.47	8.10	7.72	7.31	6.88
	0.05	5.99	5.14	4.76	4.53	4.39	4.28	4.15	4.00	3.84	3.67
	0.10	3.78	3.46	3.29	3.18	3.11	3.05	2.98	2.90	2.82	2.72
	0.20	2.07	2.13	2.11	2.09	2.08	2.06	2.04	2.02	1.99	1.95

TABLE A-2 *Continued*

df Associated with Denominator	P	\multicolumn{10}{c}{df Associated with Numerator}

df Associated with Denominator	P	1	2	3	4	5	6	8	12	24	∞
7	0.01	12.25	9.55	8.45	7.85	7.46	7.19	6.84	6.47	6.07	5.65
	0.05	5.59	4.74	4.35	4.12	3.97	3.87	3.73	3.57	3.41	3.23
	0.10	3.59	3.26	3.07	2.96	2.88	2.83	2.75	2.67	2.58	2.47
	0.20	2.00	2.04	2.02	1.99	1.97	1.96	1.93	1.91	1.87	1.83
8	0.01	11.26	8.65	7.59	7.01	6.63	6.37	6.03	5.67	5.28	4.86
	0.05	5.32	4.46	4.07	3.84	3.69	3.58	3.44	3.28	3.12	2.93
	0.10	3.46	3.11	2.92	2.81	2.73	2.67	2.59	2.50	2.40	2.29
	0.20	1.95	1.98	1.95	1.92	1.90	1.88	1.86	1.83	1.79	1.74
9	0.01	10.56	8.02	6.99	6.42	6.06	5.80	5.47	5.11	4.73	4.31
	0.05	5.12	4.26	3.86	3.63	3.48	3.37	3.23	3.07	2.90	2.71
	0.10	3.36	3.01	2.81	2.69	2.61	2.55	2.47	2.38	2.28	2.16
	0.20	1.91	1.94	1.90	1.87	1.85	1.83	1.80	1.76	1.72	1.67
10	0.01	10.04	7.56	6.55	5.99	5.64	5.39	5.06	4.71	4.33	3.91
	0.05	4.96	4.10	3.71	3.48	3.33	3.22	3.07	2.91	2.74	2.54
	0.10	3.28	2.92	2.73	2.61	2.52	2.46	2.38	2.28	2.18	2.06
	0.20	1.88	1.90	1.86	1.83	1.80	1.78	1.75	1.72	1.67	1.62
11	0.01	9.65	7.20	6.22	5.67	5.32	5.07	4.74	4.40	4.02	3.60
	0.05	4.84	3.98	3.59	3.36	3.20	3.09	2.95	2.79	2.61	2.40
	0.10	3.23	2.86	2.66	2.54	2.45	2.39	2.30	2.21	2.10	1.97
	0.20	1.86	1.87	1.83	1.80	1.77	1.75	1.72	1.68	1.63	1.57
12	0.01	9.33	6.93	5.95	5.41	5.06	4.82	4.50	4.16	3.78	3.36
	0.05	4.75	3.88	3.49	3.26	3.11	3.00	2.85	2.69	2.50	2.30
	0.10	3.18	2.81	2.61	2.48	2.39	2.33	2.24	2.15	2.04	1.90
	0.20	1.84	1.85	1.80	1.77	1.74	1.72	1.69	1.65	1.60	1.54
13	0.01	9.07	6.70	5.74	5.20	4.86	4.62	4.30	3.96	3.59	3.16
	0.05	4.67	3.80	3.41	3.18	3.02	2.92	2.77	2.60	2.42	2.21
	0.10	3.14	2.76	2.56	2.43	2.35	2.28	2.20	2.10	1.98	1.85
	0.20	1.82	1.88	1.78	1.75	1.72	1.69	1.66	1.62	1.57	1.51

14	0.01	8.86	6.51	5.56	5.08	4.69	4.46	4.14	3.80	3.43	3.00
	0.05	4.60	3.74	3.34	3.11	2.96	2.85	2.70	2.53	2.35	2.13
	0.10	3.10	2.73	2.52	2.39	2.31	2.24	2.15	2.05	1.94	1.80
	0.20	1.81	1.81	1.76	1.78	1.70	1.67	1.64	1.60	1.55	1.48
15	0.01	8.68	6.36	5.42	4.89	4.56	4.32	4.00	3.67	3.29	2.87
	0.05	4.54	3.68	3.29	3.06	2.90	2.79	2.64	2.48	2.29	2.07
	0.10	3.07	2.70	2.49	2.36	2.27	2.21	2.12	2.02	1.90	1.76
	0.20	1.80	1.79	1.75	1.71	1.68	1.66	1.62	1.58	1.53	1.46
16	0.01	8.53	6.23	5.29	4.77	4.44	4.20	3.89	3.55	3.18	2.75
	0.05	4.49	3.63	3.24	3.01	2.85	2.74	2.59	2.42	2.24	2.01
	0.10	3.05	2.67	2.46	2.33	2.24	2.18	2.09	1.99	1.87	1.72
	0.20	1.79	1.78	1.74	1.70	1.67	1.64	1.61	1.56	1.51	1.43
17	0.01	8.40	6.11	5.18	4.67	4.34	4.10	3.79	3.45	3.08	2.65
	0.05	4.45	3.59	3.20	2.96	2.81	2.70	2.55	2.38	2.19	1.96
	0.10	3.03	2.64	2.44	2.31	2.22	2.15	2.06	1.96	1.84	1.69
	0.20	1.78	1.77	1.72	1.68	1.65	1.63	1.59	1.55	1.49	1.42
18	0.01	8.28	6.01	5.09	4.58	4.25	4.01	3.71	3.37	3.00	2.57
	0.05	4.41	3.55	3.16	2.93	2.77	2.66	2.51	2.34	2.15	1.92
	0.10	3.01	2.62	2.42	2.29	2.20	2.13	2.04	1.93	1.81	1.66
	0.20	1.77	1.76	1.71	1.67	1.64	1.62	1.58	1.53	1.48	1.40
19	0.01	8.18	5.93	5.01	4.50	4.17	3.94	3.63	3.30	2.92	2.49
	0.05	4.38	3.52	3.13	2.90	2.74	2.63	2.48	2.31	2.11	1.88
	0.10	2.99	2.61	2.40	2.27	2.18	2.11	2.02	1.91	1.79	1.63
	0.20	1.76	1.75	1.70	1.66	1.63	1.61	1.57	1.52	1.46	1.39
20	0.01	8.10	5.85	4.94	4.43	4.10	3.87	3.56	3.23	2.86	2.42
	0.05	4.35	3.49	3.10	2.87	2.71	2.60	2.45	2.28	2.08	1.84
	0.10	2.97	2.59	2.38	2.25	2.16	2.09	2.00	1.89	1.77	1.61
	0.20	1.76	1.75	1.70	1.65	1.62	1.60	1.56	1.51	1.45	1.37

TABLE A-2 *Continued*

df Associated with Denominator	P	df Associated with Numerator									
		1	2	3	4	5	6	8	12	24	∞
21	0.01	8.02	5.78	4.87	4.37	4.04	3.81	3.51	3.17	2.80	2.36
	0.05	4.32	3.47	3.07	2.84	2.68	2.57	2.42	2.25	2.05	1.81
	0.10	2.96	2.57	2.36	2.23	2.14	2.08	1.98	1.88	1.75	1.59
	0.20	1.75	1.74	1.69	1.65	1.61	1.59	1.55	1.50	1.44	1.36
22	0.01	7.94	5.72	4.82	4.31	3.99	3.76	3.45	3.12	2.75	2.31
	0.05	4.30	3.44	3.05	2.82	2.66	2.55	2.40	2.23	2.03	1.78
	0.10	2.95	2.56	2.35	2.22	2.13	2.06	1.97	1.86	1.73	1.57
	0.20	1.75	1.73	1.68	1.64	1.61	1.58	1.54	1.49	1.43	1.35
23	0.01	7.88	5.66	4.76	4.26	3.94	3.71	3.41	3.07	2.70	2.26
	0.05	4.28	3.42	3.03	2.80	2.64	2.53	2.38	2.20	2.00	1.76
	0.10	2.94	2.55	2.34	2.21	2.11	2.05	1.95	1.84	1.72	1.55
	0.20	1.74	1.73	1.68	1.63	1.60	1.57	1.53	1.49	1.42	1.34
24	0.01	7.82	5.61	4.72	4.22	3.90	3.67	3.36	3.03	2.66	2.21
	0.05	4.26	3.40	3.01	2.78	2.62	2.51	2.36	2.18	1.98	1.73
	0.10	2.93	2.54	2.33	2.19	2.10	2.04	1.94	1.83	1.70	1.53
	0.20	1.74	1.72	1.67	1.63	1.59	1.57	1.53	1.48	1.42	1.33
25	0.01	7.77	5.57	4.68	4.18	3.86	3.63	3.32	2.99	2.62	2.17
	0.05	4.24	3.38	2.99	2.76	2.60	2.49	2.34	2.16	1.96	1.71
	0.10	2.92	2.53	2.32	2.18	2.09	2.02	1.93	1.82	1.69	1.52
	0.20	1.73	1.72	1.66	1.62	1.59	1.56	1.52	1.47	1.41	1.32
26	0.01	7.72	5.53	4.64	4.14	3.82	3.59	3.29	2.96	2.58	2.13
	0.05	4.22	3.37	2.98	2.74	2.59	2.47	2.32	2.15	1.95	1.69
	0.10	2.91	2.52	2.31	2.17	2.08	2.01	1.92	1.81	1.68	1.50
	0.20	1.73	1.71	1.66	1.62	1.58	1.56	1.52	1.47	1.40	1.31
27	0.01	7.68	5.49	4.60	4.11	3.78	3.56	3.26	2.93	2.55	2.10
	0.05	4.21	3.35	2.96	2.73	2.57	2.46	2.30	2.13	1.93	1.67
	0.10	2.90	2.51	2.30	2.17	2.07	2.00	1.91	1.80	1.67	1.49
	0.20	1.73	1.71	1.66	1.61	1.58	1.55	1.51	1.46	1.40	1.30
28	0.01	7.64	5.45	4.57	4.07	3.75	3.53	3.23	2.90	2.52	2.06
	0.05	4.20	3.34	2.95	2.71	2.56	2.44	2.29	2.12	1.91	1.65
	0.10	2.89	2.50	2.29	2.16	2.06	2.00	1.90	1.79	1.66	1.48
	0.20	1.72	1.71	1.65	1.61	1.57	1.55	1.51	1.46	1.39	1.30

df	α										
29	0.01	7.60	5.42	4.54	4.04	3.73	3.50	3.20	2.87	2.49	2.03
	0.05	4.18	3.33	2.93	2.70	2.54	2.43	2.28	2.10	1.90	1.64
	0.10	2.89	2.50	2.28	2.15	2.06	1.99	1.89	1.78	1.65	1.47
	0.20	1.72	1.70	1.65	1.60	1.57	1.54	1.50	1.45	1.39	1.29
30	0.01	7.56	5.39	4.51	4.02	3.70	3.47	3.17	2.84	2.47	2.01
	0.05	4.17	3.32	2.92	2.69	2.53	2.42	2.27	2.09	1.89	1.62
	0.10	2.88	2.49	2.28	2.14	2.05	1.98	1.88	1.77	1.64	1.46
	0.20	1.72	1.70	1.64	1.60	1.57	1.54	1.50	1.45	1.38	1.28
40	0.01	7.31	5.18	4.31	3.83	3.51	3.29	2.99	2.66	2.29	1.80
	0.05	4.08	3.23	2.84	2.61	2.45	2.34	2.18	2.00	1.79	1.51
	0.10	2.84	2.44	2.23	2.09	2.00	1.93	1.83	1.71	1.57	1.38
	0.20	1.70	1.68	1.62	1.57	1.54	1.51	1.47	1.41	1.34	1.24
60	0.01	7.08	4.98	4.13	3.65	3.34	3.12	2.82	2.50	2.12	1.60
	0.05	4.00	3.15	2.76	2.52	2.37	2.25	2.10	1.92	1.70	1.39
	0.10	2.79	2.39	2.18	2.04	1.95	1.87	1.77	1.66	1.51	1.29
	0.20	1.68	1.65	1.59	1.55	1.51	1.48	1.44	1.38	1.31	1.18
120	0.01	6.85	4.79	3.95	3.48	3.17	2.96	2.66	2.34	1.95	1.38
	0.05	3.92	3.07	2.68	2.45	2.29	2.17	2.02	1.83	1.61	1.25
	0.10	2.75	2.35	2.13	1.99	1.90	1.82	.72	1.60	1.45	1.19
	0.20	1.66	1.63	1.57	1.52	1.48	1.45	1.41	1.35	1.27	1.12
8	0.01	6.64	4.60	3.78	3.32	3.02	2.80	2.51	2.18	1.79	1.00
	0.05	3.84	2.99	2.60	2.37	2.21	2.09	1.94	1.75	1.52	1.00
	0.10	2.71	2.30	2.08	1.94	1.85	1.77	1.67	1.55	1.38	1.00
	0.20	1.64	1.61	1.55	1.50	1.46	1.43	1.38	1.32	1.23	1.00

Table A–2 is abridged from Table V of Fisher and Yates. *Statistical Tables of Biological, Agricultural, and Medical Research*, 1949 published by Oliver and Boyd Ltd., Edinburgh, by permission of the author and publishers.

TABLE A-3   Values of *r* at the 0.05 and the 0.01 Levels of Reliability*

Degrees of Freedom (N − 2)	0.05	0.01	Degrees of Freedom	0.05	0.01
1	0.997	1.000	24	0.388	0.496
2	0.950	0.990	25	0.381	0.487
3	0.878	0.959	26	0.374	0.478
4	0.811	0.917	27	0.367	0.470
5	0.754	0.874	28	0.361	0.463
6	0.707	0.834	29	0.355	0.456
7	0.666	0.798	30	0.349	0.449
8	0.632	0.765	35	0.325	0.418
9	0.602	0.735	40	0.304	0.393
10	0.576	0.708	45	0.288	0.372
11	0.553	0.684	50	0.273	0.354
12	0.532	0.661	60	0.250	0.325
13	0.514	0.641	70	0.232	0.302
14	0.497	0.623	80	0.217	0.283
15	0.482	0.606	90	0.205	0.267
16	0.468	0.590	100	0.195	0.254
17	0.456	0.575	125	0.174	0.228
18	0.444	0.561	150	0.159	0.208
19	0.433	0.549	200	0.138	0.181
20	0.423	0.537	300	0.113	0.148
21	0.413	0.526	400	0.098	0.128
22	0.404	0.515	500	0.088	0.115
23	0.396	0.505	1000	0.062	0.081

Table A-3 is abridge from Table V.A. of Fisher: *Statistical Methods for Research Workers*, Oliver and Boyd Ltd., Edinburgh, 1949, by permission of the authors and publishers. Additional entries were taken from Snedecor, *Statistical Methods*, Iowa State College Press, Ames, Iowa, 1956, by permission of the author and publisher.

*The probabilities given are for a two-tailed test of reliability, that is, with the sign of *r* ignored.

appendix B

WRITING UP YOUR EXPERIMENT

Major purpose:

To help you acquire the ability to communicate your research goals, methods and findings effectively.

What you are going to find:

1. A step-by-step, detailed exposition of phases in the write-up of your research reports.
2. Some informal advice on how to improve the sophistication of your writing and how to avoid a number of common ineffective expressions and errors in exposition.

What you should acquire:

The ability to communicate in writing all aspects of your research sufficiently well that someone else could repeat your study solely on the basis of your report. They should also be able incisively to compare their new results and interpretations with yours.

GETTING YOURSELF PREPARED

After the data are collected, the researcher statistically analyzes and interprets them with one of the methods presented in Chapters 6 through 11, reaches an appropriate conclusion, and then writes up the study. The same general format for writing up an experiment should be used whether it is to be published in a scientific journal or it is a research course assignment. This increases the transfer of learning to the actual conduct of research as professional psychologists, which is a major goal of this book: to help students acquire important professional behaviors with a minimum of "busy work."

The following is an outline that can be used for writing up an experiment or other research. There are also a number of suggestions that should help to eliminate certain errors that students frequently make and several other suggestions that should lead to a closer approximation to scientific writing.

First, we should be aware that learning to write up research manuscripts is a difficult (although eventually rewarding) endeavor. It is often frustrating for the student as well as for the professor who reads the student's write-up. Consequently we want to concentrate especially on this section so that the end product is profitable for all.

The general goal of the research report is to communicate scientific or technological information. If the researcher conducts an experiment but never reports it to the scientific world, the work might as well not have been undertaken. The same can be said if an article is not understandable. The scientific report is the heart of science. We seek to learn to write well-organized reports that communicate clearly, are accurate, and are easily understandable by the reader. How does one reach such a goal? The answer is the same as it is for achieving a high degree of proficiency for any difficult task—by practice and more practice.

Before starting your writing, you should study a model journal, one to which you would plan submitting your experiment for publication. For instance, you might select the *Journal of Experimental Psychology: General*, available in your library. Look over several recent issues of the journal, reading sample articles in detail. Note precisely how the authors have communicated each step of the experimental method. In your literature survey you have already noticed how authors dealt with some factors that *you* will have to consider in your write-up.

The *main principle* to follow in writing up an experiment is that the report must include every relevant aspect of the experiment; *someone else should be able to repeat your experiment solely on the basis of your report.* If this is impossible, the report is inadequate. On the other hand, you should not become excessively involved in details. Those aspects of an experiment which the experimenter judges to be *irrelevant* should not be included in the report. In general, then, the report should include every important aspect of the experiment but should also be as concise as possible, for scientific writing is economical writing.

The writer should also strive for clarity of expression. If an idea can be expressed simply and clearly, it should not be expressed complexly and ambiguously; "big" words, technical jargon, and "high-flown" phrases should be avoided wherever possible (and don't invent words, for example, "irregardless").

As psychologists, we adhere to certain standard conventions. The conventions and related matters about writing up an experiment may be found in the *Publication Manual of the American Psychological Association.*[1]

The *Publication Manual* offers some excellent suggestions about how to write effectively, how to present your ideas with an economy and smoothness of expression, how to avoid ambiguity in your sentences, and how to increase readability generally. Precision in the use of words is also emphasized. You can do well to study the manual in some detail.

The close relationship between the write-up and the outline of the experimental plan of Chapter 5 should be noted. Frequent reference should be made to that outline in the following discussion, for you have already accomplished much of the write-up there.

OVERVIEW OF THE COMPONENTS OF A MANUSCRIPT

The following are the elements that you would include should you submit your article for publication in a journal. Arrange the pages of the manuscript as follows and num-

---

[1]The *Publication Manual* can often be obtained in your local bookstore, from a friendly professor, or by writing to Publication Sales, American Psychological Assn., 1200 17th St. NW, Washington, D.C. 20036.

ber all pages, except the figures, consecutively.

- Title page with title, author's name and affiliation, and running head (separate page, numbered page 1)
- Abstract (separate page, numbered page 2)
- Text (start on a new page, numbered page 3)
- References (start on a new page)
- Appendixes (start on a new page)
- Author identification notes (start on a new page)
- Footnotes (start on a new page)
- Tables (place each on a separate page)
- Figure captions (start on a new page)
- Figures (place each on a separate page)

This would not be the way that your report would be printed, but it is the way that copy editors and printers handle manuscripts submitted for publication. It is good practice for you to follow these procedures. In addition, for your class research you should include your raw data and your statistical analysis in an appendix. This allows your instructor to review your procedures and possibly offer you suggestions. It also prepares you for including your raw data in a thesis or dissertation should you work for an advanced degree. ("Raw data" is a term that implies that the data have not been statistically treated.)

PAGES OF A MANUSCRIPT: TITLE PAGE

The first page is the title page. It contains three elements: title, author(s) with the affiliation, and a running head, as illustrated in the sample of a report on page 310. The title should be short and indicative of the exact topic of the experiment. If you are studying the interaction of drive level and amount of reinforcement, include in the title a statement of the variables of drive and reinforcement. *Every* topic included in the report need not be specified in the title. Abbreviations should not be used in the title. The

recommended maximum length of the title is 12 to 15 words, and it needs to be unique—it should distinguish your study from all other investigations. Introductory phrases such as "A study of . . ." or "An investigation of . . ." should be avoided, since it is understood that you are studying something. A good title would be "The Interaction of Drive and Reinforcement in the Acquisition of a Motor Skill."

The title is typed in upper-case and lower-case letters centered on the page. Then the short title, typed at the upper right of the page, could be "Drive and Reinforcement." The running head is an abbreviated title which is printed at the top of the pages of a published article to identify the article for readers. It is short, less than 50 characters, and is typed in all capital letters at the bottom of the title page. A running head could read "Drive and Reinforcement in Motor Learning"; type the page number directly underneath.

Author's Name and Institutional Affiliation

One double-spaced line below the title you should type your name and your college or university centered under your name. If there are more than two authors of the report, type their names one right after the other on the same line, separated by commas. Do not specify the psychology department within the institution. Sometimes an entire class collaborates on an experiment, in which case they are multiple authors. If so, it is best to use only your name rather than listing all of them, including the professor.

ABSTRACT PAGE

The abstract is on the second page of your article. You should write it after you have completed the rest of your paper. The abstract, typed on a separate sheet of paper, includes the short title and page number at the upper right. The abstract summarizes the article and quickly gives the reader the essence of your research. In 100 to 150 words, state your problem, method (here include number, type, age, and gender of participants; research design; apparatus), results (including statistical significance levels), and conclusions and implications. Results and inferences drawn from the results are the most important part of the abstract. Do not cite references in the abstract.

You should also add key words at the bottom of your abstract. These key words are useful in computer searches. They help another researcher to identify specifically the research of direct interest, out of a mass of articles that would otherwise be retrieved. For instance, the word "anxiety" by itself would retrieve thousands of articles, but if the words "drive" and "reinforcement" are added, only the most relevant articles can be retrieved.

TEXT PAGES

Begin the text on page 3, typing the short title and the number 3 at the upper right-hand corner of the page. Type the title of the paper centered at the top of the page and then type the text under it. All sections of the text follow each other without a break. For instance, do not start the "Method" or the "Results" sections on new pages. Every page of the manuscript, except those for figures, has the short title and the page number typed in the upper-right hand corner.

Introduction

(But don't label it "Introduction.") You have already developed a basis for the introductory section of your report in the literature survey portion of your research plan. In the introduction, you should develop your problem logically, citing the most relevant studies. A summary statement of the problem should then be made, preferably as a question. The results of the literature survey should lead smoothly into the statement of the problem. For instance, if you are study-

ing the effects of alcohol on performance of a cancellation task (e.g., striking out all letter E's in a series of letters), you should summarize the results of previous experiments that show detrimental effects of alcohol on various kinds of performance. Then indicate that there is no previous work on the effects of alcohol on the cancellation task and that the purpose of your experiment was to extend the previous findings to that task. Accordingly, the problem is, "Does the consumption of alcohol detrimentally affect performance on a cancellation task?" The steps leading up to the statement of the hypothesis should also be logically presented, but the hypothesis itself should be stated in one sentence, preferably in the "If . . ., then . . ." form. The statement of the hypothesis and the definition of the variables may help your reader to understand what it is you intended to do, what you expected your results to be, and why you expected them. Why you expected them entails the development of a theory, if you have one.

Many features of your write-up are arbitrary, such as where you define your variables—they may be precisely defined in the introduction or in the method section of the study.

Method

The main function of this section is to tell your reader precisely *how* the research was conducted. Put another way, this section serves to specify the methods of gathering data that are relevant to the hypothesis, data that will serve to test the hypothesis. It is here that the main decisions need to be made on which matters of procedure are relevant and which are irrelevant. If you specify every detail that is necessary for someone else to repeat the experiment, but no more, the write-up is successful. To illustrate, assume that you conduct a study in which you conditioned your dog to stay out of the street. You would tell the reader that, say, a dog biscuit was used for reinforcement. You would then specify the precise nature of the dog biscuit, precisely when it was administered contingent on what specific behavior of the dog, and precisely how you measured your dependent variable. You don't have to relate that the color of the curb in your street was white cement, or that the name of your street was Snoopy Avenue, since variables such as these would not influence performance. It would be strange indeed if dogs conditioned differently depending upon the name of the street.

Although the subsections under "Method" are not rigid and may be modified to fit any given experiment, in general, the following information should be found, and usually in the following order:

Participants (or Subjects). The population should be specified in detail, as well as the method of drawing the sample studied. In specifying the population, include such details as sex, age, general geographic location, type of institution from whence they came, etc. If any participants from the sample had to be "discarded" (students didn't show up for their appointments or couldn't perform the experimental task), this information should be included, for the sample may not be random because of these factors. The total number of participants and the number assigned to each experimental condition should be stated. State that the treatment of participants (human or animal) was in accordance with the ethical standards of the American Psychological Association. (See Appendix D for our discussion of ethics in research.)

Apparatus. All relevant aspects of the apparatus should be included. Where a standard type of apparatus is used (e.g., the Ralph Gerbrands tachistoscope), only its name need be stated. Otherwise, the apparatus has to be described in sufficient detail (including a model number) for another experimenter to obtain or construct it. It is a good practice for the student to include a diagram of the apparatus in the write-up, although in professional journals this is only done if the apparatus is complex and novel.

Design. The type of design used should be included in a section after the apparatus

has been described. The method of assigning participants to groups and labels to groups are both indicated (e.g., group E may be the experimental group and group C the control group, and so on). The variables contained in the hypothesis need to be (operationally) defined if they have not been defined in the introduction; it is also desirable (at least for your practice) to indicate which are the independent and the dependent variables. The techniques of exercising experimental control may be included here. For example, if there was a particularly knotty variable that needed to be controlled, the techniques used for this purpose may be discussed. Relevant here are any unusual compromises in your experimental manipulation, randomization procedures, counterbalancing, or other control procedures.

Procedure. Just how you collected the data should be specified in detail. You must include or summarize instructions to the participants (if they are human), the maintenance schedule and the way in which the participants were "adapted" to the experiment (if they are not humans), how the independent variable was administered, and how the dependent variable was recorded.

Results

The heart of the results section, of course, is the presentation of the data relevant to the test of the hypothesis. These data are summarized as a precise sentence (the evidence report). If the data are in accord with the hypothesis, then the hypothesis is confirmed. If they are not of the nature predicted by the hypothesis, then the hypothesis is disconfirmed.

This section is one of the most difficult for students to learn to write up. Even after the instructor has given individual comments to students on two or three research reports in a course, many students still have difficulty in effectively presenting results. Consequently, your *special* attention to this section is recommended.

The purpose of this section is to provide sufficient information for the reader to understand how you reached a conclusion. This includes the systematic presentation of data and the reasoning from the data to the conclusions. The reader is thereby given the opportunity to determine whether the conclusions were justified, and whether those conclusions were properly related to the empirical hypothesis.

As we shall shortly develop, for the typical between-groups study, start by reporting means, explaining them in detail, and *then* present the results of the statistical analysis. Do not, however, interpret the findings in this section. The data are interpreted and discussed in the "Discussion" section.

To emphasize the importance of your attention to the "Results" section, consider some common student errors or shortcomings. For instance, a student might propel the reader directly into a conclusion without even referring to data in a table, much less explaining how those data were obtained. Or some students merely include a table of means with the disarming conclusion that "There were no reliable differences." One valuable learning technique is for each student in a course to select an article from a good journal and report on the major methodological steps taken by the published author. In their brief presentations the students can pay special attention to the major components of the results section for presenting, analyzing, and reaching conclusions. Such learning experiences, incidentally, do not always have a favorable outcome for the journal articles selected, providing us with the opportunity to learn that even published articles can be sizably improved. Other dividends from this teaching procedure is to help the student to become familiar with the journals in our field, to acquire the habit of visiting the library and at least skimming the current journals as they come in, to build up one's storehouse of knowledge about current research, and so on. The serious student who gets the "journal habit" early will benefit in many ways, including the discovery of especially interesting articles about topics that they wish to pursue (research?) in greater detail.

Constructing Tables. A *summary* of the data on which the evidence report is based is typically accomplished with a table, but figures are also advantageous. Whether *tables* or *figures* or both are used depends on the type of data and the ingenuity and motivation of the writer. Both are used to summarize and organize data. They are not used for presenting all the data.

A *table* consists of numbers that summarize the main findings of the experiment. It should present these numbers systematically, precisely, and economically. A *figure*, on the other hand, is a graph, chart, photograph, or like material. It is particularly appropriate for certain kinds of data, such as showing the progress of learning. Information should, however, be presented only once; that is, the same data should not be presented in a table and a figure or in the written text.

In constructing a table, one should first determine the main points to be made apparent. Decide the most economical way to make these points meaningfully. Since the main point of the experiment is to determine whether certain relationships exist between specific variables, the table should show whether these relationships were found. To illustrate the format of a table, consider a study of the effects of a psychological stressor on cigarette smoking. Starting with the notion that stressful stimuli increase cigarette smoking, Pomerleau and Pomerleau (1987) induced two levels of anxiety in their participants: (1) high anxiety was induced by having the participants perform mental arithmetic with competitive pressure, and (2) under the low-anxiety condition no competitive pressure was applied while performing mental arithmetic. While the study involved many aspects of the consequences of smoking, we shall focus only on the possible effects of smoking on mental arithmetic performance as a function of anxiety condition. We may observe in Table 1 that the mean score (number of correct subtractions) before smoking for the high-anxiety condition was 38.3 and that this value changed only slightly following smoking.

Similarly, there was little change in the mean number of correct subtractions due to smoking for the low-anxiety condition. A statistical analysis confirmed that the effects of smoking did not produce a statistically significant change in mental arithmetic performance. On the other hand, performance was reliably better during the low-anxiety condition than during the high-anxiety condition, independent of whether the task was performed before or after smoking: $F (\frac{1}{8}) = 19.29$, $P < 0.01$, two-tailed.

The important point for us is to observe the format of the table. It is important to observe the precise format used, for some students ignore such necessary details. First, note every aspect of the table and exactly how all of its components are formatted. For instance, the title of the table is very informative. We can see at a glance the possible relationships between the variables, we know immediately how many participants there were, and so forth. The previously stated requirements of a good table are satisfied.

By studying Table 1 and other tables throughout this book, as well as those in journal articles in your library, you can acquire the ability to present your data efficiently and systematically. In some cases you will want to include the numbers of participants in your groups; you will often want to use means for your dependent variable and include some measure of variability, such as standard deviations. If you use abbreviations to conserve space, explain them in a note or caption to the table (same for figures). Also, don't make your reader refer to the text to understand the table or figure—tables and figures should be self-contained.

More than one table can be presented, and they may be used for purposes other than presenting data. For example, the design of the experiment may be made more apparent by presenting the separate steps in tabular form (this use of tables is particularly recommended for a student paper, as it helps to "pull the experiment together").

Constructing Figures. The same general principles stated for the construction of tables hold for figures. A figure typically illustrates a relationship between the independent and the dependent variables. The vertical axis (sometimes erroneously, as you can see in a dictionary, called the *ordinate*) is for plotting the dependent-variable scores; the horizontal axis (which is *not* synonymous with *abscissa*) can be used to show the levels, values, or time (days, hours). In a learning study, for example, it may present learning data as a function of time[3] or number of trials.

Another common format is the bar graph or histogram, as represented in Figure 1 for the smoking study. There we may study the volume of smoke inhaled (total puff volume) as a function of anxiety condition. The total puff volume under the low-anxiety condition can be seen to be approximately 500 (arbitrary units), while under the high-anxiety condition, it rose to approximately 600 arbitrary units. The total puff volume in the high-anxiety condition was significantly higher than in the low-anxiety condition: $t (9) = 2.82$, $P < 0.01$. Once again, we can see that a point is immediately made by referring to Figure 1, that is, that the dependent-variable value changed as a function of anxiety condition. Then, we presented the results of the statistical analysis. You should study the format for Figure 1 and the format of other figures throughout the book and in your journals.

TABLE 1 Anxiety and Mental Arithmetic Performance[2]

Mean Mental Arithmetic Performance Scores ($N = 10$) (Number of Correct Subtractions)		
Anxiety Conditions	Smoking	
	Pre	*Post*
High	38.3	38.1
Low	45.4	46.3

[2]From Pomerleau & Pomerleau (1987).

---

[3]Time, often studied in psychology, has been explicitly defined as "nature's way of keeping everything from happening at once."

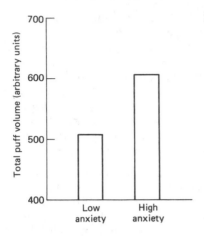

FIGURE 1 Mean total puff volume for high- and low-anxiety conditions: $N = 10$ (from Pomerleau & Pomerleau, 1987).

Some Elaborations on the Results Section. The order of presenting data in tables and in figures relative to statistical analyses is important. A table of means, or a figure in which means are plotted, demonstrates your major experimental effects. Your statistical analysis indicates whether your means are reliably different from each other. Hence the statistical analysis comes *after* the means are presented unless a table includes both.

The source of the numbers presented in your tables and figures must be *precisely* identified and explained. Often a reader spends considerable time puzzling over the question of just what the numbers mean—although they may seem clear to the author, the write-up may have missed a step. For instance, rather than saying that the "means for performance are given in Table 1," one could be more precise and say that "the mean mental arithmetic performance scores (number of correct subtractions) are presented in Table 1 as a function of anxiety condition before and after smoking." Or, in another case, rather than merely referring to "the number of responses" one should say, "The median number of responses during the 15-minute extinction period." This information may be presented in the text, in the table heading, or in the figure caption.

For student write-ups it is a good idea to state the null hypothesis as it applies to your experiment and also the reliability level that you have adopted. Then from your table of means and your statistical tests, indicate in detail whether you have rejected your null hypothesis. For example, "The null hypothesis was: There is no difference between the population means of the experimental and control groups on the dependent variable." You may have found that your t-test yielded a value of 2.20, which, with 16 degrees of freedom, was reliable beyond the 0.05 level. If so, you would then state this information as follows: "$t(16) = 2.20, P < 0.05$"; that is, you specify that you used the t-test with the number of degrees of freedom within the parentheses, that you obtained the computed value indicated, and that this value was or was not reliable at the selected probability level (here, 0.05). You may then continue: "It is therefore possible to reject the null hypothesis." You then form your evidence report which asserts that the antecedent conditions of your hypothesis held and that the consequent conditions were either found to be the case or not. For instance, you might state, "In summary, as anxiety level of the students was systematically increased, speed of learning also increased. Since this finding is in accord with the empirical hypothesis, we may conclude that that hypothesis is confirmed." Of course, if you used the empirical hypothesis to predict that the null hypothesis would be rejected, but it was not, then it may be concluded that the empirical hypothesis was not confirmed.

Having made a point about the null hypothesis, let us immediately point out that the null hypothesis is not mentioned in journal articles. Rather, what we have made explicit here is, for professional experimenters, implicitly understood. Perhaps your understanding of the null hypothesis can be enhanced should your write-up specifically include the steps mentioned here, and, once this process is clear to you, it can be dropped from later reports.

The steps in computing the statistical tests (the actual calculations) should not be included under "Results." In student write-ups, however, we have said that it is advisable to include the raw data and the steps in the computation of the statistical test in a special appendix so that your instructor can correct any errors.

Don't forget that each table and each figure goes on a separate page and is included at the end of your report. All figure captions go on a separate page, but table headings go at the top of the table. The author indicates where tables and figures should be located in the text as follows:

```
---------------------------
    Insert Table 1 about here
---------------------------
```

The preceding information should be sufficient to get you started, but you are strongly advised to continue your study of techniques for constructing figures and tables. To do this, consult the elementary statistics books that are available in your library and concentrate on figures and tables in psychological journals.

Discussion

The main functions of this section are to *interpret the results of the investigation* and to *relate those results to other studies*. The interpretation is an attempt to explain the results, perhaps with some existing theory. If the hypothesis was derived from a general theory, then the confirmation of the hypothesis serves to strengthen that theory. The findings, in turn, are explained by that hypothesis in conjunction with the larger theory. If the findings are contrary to the hypothesis, then some new explanation is required so that you may advance a new, different hypothesis. Or perhaps the faulty hypothesis can be modified to make it consistent with the results so that a "patched-up" hypothesis is advanced for future test.

In relating the results to other studies, the literature survey may again be brought to bear. By considering the present results along with previous ones, new insights may be obtained. They may provide the one missing piece that allows the solution of a puzzle.

New hypotheses may also be advanced about any unusual deviation in the results. For instance, one may wonder why there is a sudden rise in the terminal portion of a learning curve. Is this a reliable rise? If it is, why did it occur? In short, what additional problems were uncovered that suggest fruitful lines for further investigation? Like the three princes of Serendip (Chapter 3), you might find something more valuable than that which you originally sought.

If there are limitations in your experiment, this is the place to discuss them, for example, what variables might have been inadequately controlled? (Not controlling a crucial extraneous variable means you wouldn't want to publish your report.) How would one modify the experiment if it were to be repeated?

Here also consider the extent to which the results may be generalized. To what populations may you safely extend them? How might the generalizations be limited by uncontrolled variables, and so on?

Negative results occur when a hypothesis predicts something, but the results are contrary to that prediction. It also means that the null hypothesis was not rejected. Some experimenters, strangely, feel "guilty" or "embarrassed" when they have obtained negative results. Whatever the reason, you should not make long (or even short) "alibis" for them. Brief speculation about why they were obtained is sufficient.

Negative results constitute a serious problem for our science because they are seldom published in our journals. One then wonders how biased might the results be that *are* published. To illustrate, if you conduct 100 experiments to test a hypothesis that is false, five of those tests will erroneously confirm the hypothesis ("by chance"). It is alarming that many of our published experiments have, in this way, merely capitalized on chance. One answer is to publish only experiments that have been confirmed in replications. Another is to develop a *Journal of Negative Results*. The problem that we face is well illustrated by Hudson in his 1968 book *A Case of Need*:

There's a desert prison, see, with an old prisoner, resigned to his life, and a young one just arrived. The young one talks constantly of escape, and, after a few months, he makes a break. He's gone a week, and then he's brought back by the guards. He's half dead, crazy with hunger and thirst. He describes how awful it was to the old prisoner. The endless stretches of sand, no oasis, no signs of life anywhere. The old prisoner listens for a while, then says, "Yep. I know. I tried to escape myself 20 years ago." The young prisoner says, "You did? Why didn't you tell me, all those months I was planning my escape? Why didn't you let me know it was impossible." And the old prisoner shrugs, and says, "So who publishes negative results?" (p. 90)

To summarize, you should *start the discussion section with a brief summary of the important results, followed by a clear statement of whether they supported or failed to support the hypothesis.* Then you should *relate them to other findings and theories.* Be guided by such questions as: What have I contributed? How has my study helped to solve my problem? What conclusions and implications follow from my study? Your readers have a right to clear, unambiguous, and direct answers to these questions.

To illustrate further how you can be flexible in the sections of your write-up, if the discussion is brief, you can combine it with the results section, entitling it "Results and Discussion" or "Results and Conclusions."

Actually it may sometimes help a reader to interpret a finding immediately after it is presented, particularly if there are a number of them in a complex experiment. That is, a reader may get lost in a discussion section when trying to refer a given interpretation back to one of several findings previously presented under "Results."

REFERENCE PAGES

The main function of the reference section is to document (provide authority for) statements that you have made in your write-up. Scientists simply cannot say, "Everybody knows that. . . ." They must refer to "the proof." Proper references enable the reader to locate the source easily in the library. Throughout the write-up references to pertinent studies should be made by citing the last name [of the author(s)] and the year of publication, and enclosing these in parentheses, as follows: "A relevant study on the changes in brain waveform shape when one is making a motor response was conducted by Imashioya, Dollins, and Kakigi (1987)." Another type of citation is: "In a recent review of research findings, in this area, well over 80 percent of the studies cited found that relaxation was effective for alleviating migraine headaches" (Jones, 1988). All quotations cited must include the author's name and the page number of the journal from whence the quotation came.

All references should then be listed alphabetically at the end of the paper. *Double-check* their accuracy, and be sure that all references cited in the text appear in the reference list, and vice versa. The form and order of items for journal references is as follows: last name, initials, year of publication of the study, title of the study, the (nonabbreviated) name of the journal (underlined to indicate that it should be italicized), volume number (also underlined to indicate that it should be italicized), and page numbers. Do not include the issue number of the journal. Hence the first reference cited would be included in the "Reference" section of your write-up *precisely as follows:*

References

Imashioya, H., Dollins, A.B., & Kakigi, S. (1987). Motor response information influence on CNV shape and resolution time. The Pavlovian Journal of Biological Science, 22, 1–6.

It is very important to double-check *every* item (number, comma, and so on).[4] Instances of errors in typing references, just as in miscopying quotations or numerals repre-senting data, display shoddy scholarship. The essence of our science is the production of scholarly works of the highest quality. After you have checked a reference, quotation, or other item, it is a good practice to write lightly in pencil that the reference, and so on, has been checked, and use your initials to indicate for future reference that it was you who did it.

An Example

The following is a sample of a write up of research when she was a student, Vija Lusebrink (1984). It illustrates some of the important points in this chapter.

---

[4] Refer for details of the format for different sources (books, journals, technical reports) in journals or in the publication manual of the American Psychological Association (1983).

Top page (Abstract):

[handwritten: ← Start on new page; 100-150 words] 2

[handwritten: No indentation page]

[handwritten: 65]

Abstract

[handwritten: Double space throughout paper]

A neuromuscular model of information processing was investigated by electrically recording eye movements (electro-oculograms), covert lip and preferred arm reponses (electromyograms). This model predicts that the lips are uniquely activated when processing words beginning with bilabial sounds like "p" or "b," as is the right arm to words like "pencil" that require its use. Twelve adult female participants selected for their high imagery rating were asked to form images to three orally presented linguistic stimuli: the letter "p," the words "pencil," and "pasture," and to a control stimulus "go blank." The following findings were significant beyond the .05 level; increased covert lip responding to the letter "p," increased vertical eye activity to "p," and increased vertical eye activity and right arm responding to "pencil." Since peripheral response components of neuromuscular circuits occured during the imagery process, the results support a neuromuscular model of information processing. Key words: imagery, psychophysiology, cognitive processes, electromyography, electro-oculography, information processing.

Bottom page (Title page):

[handwritten: Running title ½" each page of text]

[handwritten: ← Page # title] 1

Psychophysiology of Imagery

[handwritten: Short, unique title; less than 16 words ↗]

Psychophysiological Components of Imagery

Vija B. Lusebrink

University of Louisville

[handwritten: ← Do not staple or use a cover (paper clip is fine)]

Running head: PSYCHOPHYSIOLOGY OF IMAGERY

[handwritten: maximum of 50 spaces ← All capitals]

circuits (McGuigan, 1978). According to this model, the meaning of a linguistic stimulus involves internal linguistic coding which is generated by the covert interaction of the speech musculature with brain processes. The eyes are also uniquely active during linguistic and non-linguistic imagery. During non-linguistic imagery such as imagining acts of movement, neuromuscular circuits are uniquely activated throughout the body.

The purpose of this study was to test specific predictions made by this model. First, it was predicted that covert responses of the lips would be made when imagining orally presented bilabial stimuli, such as words that begin with "p" or "b." The model also predicts that covert preferred are responses would be made when imagining a word that would normally require activity of the preferred are, and that the eyes would also be uniquely activated. The interpretation is that the increased covert lip responding that occurs during the imagining of "p" reflects the presence of a phonetic linguistic code and that the increased preferred are responding that occurs to imagining the word "pencil," an object associated with the activity of writing, indicates the presence of a referent code, possibly accompanied by an allographic code. Unique covert eye responding should also accompany these images. Finally, imagining to the word

Repeat title but not author

Start text on a new page

Indent→

Psychophysiological Components of Imagery

The focus of this paper is to determine some of the psychophysiological events that generate imagery. Studies have shown that during imagery, various covert psychophysiological events occur in the body. For example, McGuigan (1978) extensively summarized data implicating eye movements, electroencephalographic activity, and covert muscle responding while subjects engaged in a wide variety of cognitive activities.

Jacobson (1930) was the first to present psychophysiological data indicating that there is an isomorphism between the perception of external visual stimuli and internal visual stimuli. In a series of studies, Jacobson found that there was an increase in covert electromyographic activity and the target body locations related to different imagined activities, e.g., the eyes move in the vertical dimension when one imagines looking at the Eiffel Tower, and the preferred are is covertly active when imagining lighting a cigarette.

A neuromuscular model of information processing is the most effective in explaining how such covert responses occur at about the same time. More specifically it proposes that during cognitive acts such as perception, imagery, thought and dreams, complex covert processes interact by means of central-peripheral

502 differential amplifiers, and monitored by Tektronix Model 5103N Cathode Ray Oscilloscope.

The signals were recorded on a magnetic tape using an eight channel Hewlett Packard Sanborn 3907 Frequency Modulated Recorder. Five of the channels were used for the electrophysiological signals, two channels were used to convert the data samples to digital values; the sample rate was 1,000 samples per sec.

Procedure

Each subject was seated in a shielded room. Before the experiment led the subject through practice runs forming imagery to the noun "apple" and "go blank". The subject used a foot pedal to signal the presence of imagery. After the electrodes had been attached to the subject and checked for low resistance, the subject was instructed to close eyes and was relaxed. The subject's state of relaxation was monitored on an oscilloscope in the recording room by the principal investigator, who signalled to the subject's room via a small red light when the subject's electromyographic signals had reached a low stable baseline. The stimuli were presented orally to the subject one at a time in random order from a list of six repetitions of four stimuli. Each presentation was marked with the presentor depressing a foot pedal and the onset of imagery by the subject depressing a foot pedal. A period of relaxation followed each

---

"pasture" represents an image accompanied by minimal muscular responding, since that imagery should be extremely serene, and could involve more brain than muscle processing.

Subjects

The subjects were 12 right-handed females, ages 22-40, who scored in the upper half of the visual imagery category on the Betts Questionaire of Mental Imagery Vividness (QMIV) Scale (Sheehan, 1967) and Marks' (1973) Vividness of Visual Imagery Questionaire (VVIQ). The mean rating for the subjects on the Betts QMIV Imagery Scale was 2.02, S.D.=.675; the range of their scores on this 7-point scale was 1.00 to 3.20. Their mean rating for Marks VVIQ was 2.09, S.D.=.350, with a range on a 5 point scale of 1.00 to 2.69.

Apparatus

Bipolar Grass E5GH electrodes were used to record the electrical signals from the subject. The electrodes were placed on the outer canthi of both eyes for the horizontal eye movement recordings, and above and below the right eye for vertical eye movements. The electromyograms were recorded from the right arm, and upper and lower lips and the electroencephalograms were recorded from the right occipital area (McGuigan, 1979). A single ground electrode was attached on top of the right hand. The signals from the subject were amplified by Tektronix Model

calculated for each .125 second interval from the digitized data. A mean value of these intervals was obtained separately for the baseline and the response periods for each presentation of the stimuli. The percent of alpha activity present was determined by a system discriminating only this frequency range, with the final means values obtained as above.

Differences between the response and baseline measures were tested using Student's t test for each stimulus separately for the different measures.

Results

The rectified mean differences between baseline and response values of the horizontal and vertical eye movement activities, covert lip and right arm activities, and the percentage of alpha activity present at the right occipital cortex are presented in Table 1. For example, the rectified mean horizontal eye movement amplitude in response to "go blank"; the decrease of $7.25\mu v$ was significant $[t_{(11)} = 3.63, p<.05]$

Insert Table 1 about here

The mean vertical eye movement amplitude in response to the letter Q shows an increase of $9.627\ \mu v$ $[t_{(11)} = 2.87, p<.05]$, and in response to "pencil," an increase of $9.148\ \mu v$ $[t_{(11)} = 4.45, p<.05]$. Similarly, the covert lip activity shows a

stimulus and response period.

Stimuli

The nouns "pencil" and "pasture" are both high imagery words. "Pencil" has an imagery (I) rating of 146.57 and a concreteness (C) rating of 7.70 (Paivio, Yuille & Madigan, 1968). "Pasture" is presumed to have a similar rating as "prairie," 146.47, C=6.80. In addition to the high imagery ratings, the three stimuli were selected so as to control for the following dimensions: (a) their simple meaning, (b) absence of negative emotional valence, and (c) absence of high activity level. All the above dimensions have been found in previous studies to influence psychophysiological variables. The stimulus "go blank" was included as a control measure. It was expected that the instructions to go blank would result in relatively low eye, lip and arm activity, but a high percentage of alpha waves.

Data Quantification Design and Design

The response period was defined as .750 sec. following the stimulus onset. The .250 sec. prior to the subject's overt response was not included because a pilot study had indicated that these intervals seemed to reflect a general arousal. A corresponding interval prior to the presentation of the stimulus was used in each instance as a baseline.

The rectified mean amplitudes of the EOG and EMG were

significant increase over the baseline in response to the letter "p" $[t (11) = 2.71, p<.05]$, and covert right arm activity in response to "pencil" $[t (11) = 2.05, p<.05]$. The percentage of the occipital alpha activity present shows a significant decrease in response to "pasture" $[t (11) = 2.47, p<.05]$.

Discussion

The three types of imagery stimuli and the control stimulus "go blank" were differentiated by the covert eye movements, lip and right arm responding. In particular, horizontal eye movement significantly decreased only to "go blank", vertical eye movement significantly increased only for "p" and "pencil," covert lip activity increased significantly for "p", and covert right arm responding significantly increased only for "pencil." Finally, percentage alpha activity significantly decreased only for "pasture." Thus, imagery is formed differentially in response to the three stimuli. The covert responses are uniquely patterned and are not due to arousal or some other aspect of the treatment. Rather, they display a specific relationship between the independent variables and a response parameter, as in Jacobson's (1930) early research.

McGuigan's (1978) neuromuscular model of information processing is supported as follows. First, the differential covert lip activity is consonant with the generation of a phonetic code. The fact that there is no significant increase

from baseline to responding in lip movement for "pencil" and "pasture" indicates that the phonetic code is more dominant with imaging "p" than with the images of "pencil" and "pasture." The presence of a referent code is indicated by the differential horizontal and vertical eye movements. The vertical eye movement activity is significantly increased over the baseline during images of "p" and "pencil," indicating the scanning eye movements of the upright shapes of the letter "p" and "pencil." In describing the image present with "pencil," several subjects indicated its diagonal placement in the visual field. The presence of the referent code is also indicated in the increase in covert arm activity over the baseline concomitant with the images of "pencil"; a linguistic allographic code could be functioning here too.

A central processing component further differentiates reactions to "pasture" from those of "p" and "pencil" in that the alpha activity component of "pasture" is significantly decreased as compared to baseline. This could possibly indicate the presence of a central processing activity involving visual components with only a marginally increased eye movement activity.

Table 1

Mean Differences Between Baseline and Covert Response

Values of Six Presentations of each Stimulus (N = 12)

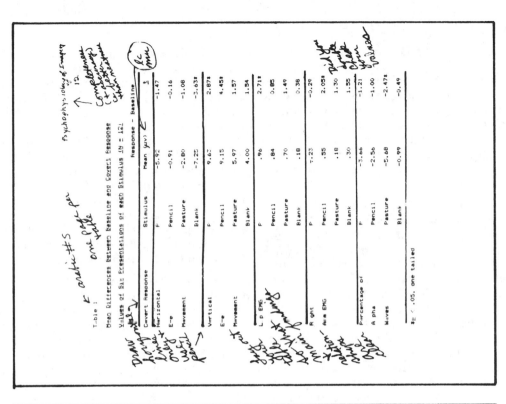

Covert Response	Stimulus	Mean μv (Response − Baseline)	t
Horizontal Eye Movement	F	−5.92	−1.47
	Pencil	−0.91	−0.16
	Posture	−2.80	−1.08
	Blank	−7.25	−3.63‡
Vertical Eye Movement	F	9.67	2.87‡
	Pencil	9.15	4.45‡
	Posture	5.97	1.57
	Blank	4.00	1.54
Lip EMG	F	.96	2.71‡
	Pencil	.84	0.85
	Posture	.70	1.49
	Blank	.18	0.36
Right Arm EMG	F	7.23	−0.29
	Pencil	.55	2.05‡
	Posture	.18	1.30
	Blank	.30	1.55
Percentage of Alpha Waves	F	−3.66	−1.21
	Pencil	−2.56	−1.00
	Posture	−5.68	−2.47‡
	Blank	−0.99	−0.49

‡ $p < .05$, one tailed

References

Jacobson, E. (1930). Electrical measurements of neuromuscular states during mental activities i. imagination of movement involving skeletal muscle. American Journal of Physiology, 91, 567-608.

Marks, D. F. (1973). Visual imagery differences in the recall of pictures. British Journal of Psychology, 64, 17-24.

McGuigan, F. J. (1978). Cognitive psychophysiology: Principles of covert behavior. Hillsdale, N.J.: Lawrence Erlbaum Associates.

McGuigan, F. J. (1979). Psychophysiological measurement of covert behavior: A guide for the laboratory. Hillsdale, N.J.: Lawrence Erlbaum Associates.

Sheehan, P. W. (1967). Visual imagery and the organizational properties of perceived stimuli. British Journal of Psychology, 58, 257-262.

SOME "DO'S" AND "DON'TS"

Finally, here are a few additional suggestions that might help improve your reports. Some items appear every year with new students, many of them minor, but if you learn properly now, you can increase your efficiency of writing up articles in the future. Many conventions facilitate communication in scientific writing.

Study Journals. The first thing to do, and this is of *great importance*, is to consult several recent psychological journals. You might start with the *Journal of Experimental Psychology: General*, although there are many other good journals in your library. Select several published articles and study them thoroughly, particularly as to format—for example, study the figures, tables, sections and subsections, and their labels; note, for example, just what words and symbols are underlined. Try to note examples of the suggestions that we have offered and particularly try to perceive the overall continuity of the articles. But be prepared for the fact that you will probably not be able to understand every point in each article. Even if there are large sections that you do not understand, do not worry too much, for this understanding will come with further learning. By the time you finish this book you will be able to understand most professional articles. Of course, some articles are extremely difficult to understand even for specialists in the field. This is usually due to the poor quality of the write-ups.

Cite An Authority. In their own write-ups, some students make assertions such as, *"It is a proven fact* that left-handed people are steadier with their right hands than right-handed people are with their left hands," or *"Everyone knows that* sex education for children is good." Perhaps the main benefit to be derived from a course in research methods is a healthy hostility toward such statements. Before making such a statement you should have the data to back it up—you should cite a relevant reference. It is poor writing to use such trite phrases as "It is a proven fact that

. . ." or "Everyone knows that. . . ." Such phrases probably really mean that the writer lacks data or hasn't bothered to look up a relevant reference. If you lack data but still want to express one of these ideas use the introductory section and state them more tentatively—for example, "It is possible that left-handed people are steadier with their right hands than right-handed people are with their left hands," or "A related question to ask is whether left-handed people. . . ." The point is that if you want to assert that something is true, cite the data (a reference) to back it up; mere opinions asserted in a positive fashion are insufficient.

Mean What You Say. Sometimes authors have a tendency to "overpresent" their research. One anonymous cynic offered a translation of some phrases found in technical writings and what they "really" might mean. You might ponder these when thinking about writing up a study: "Of great theoretical and practical importance . . ." ("It was interesting to me"); "While it has not been possible to provide definite answers to these questions . . ." (The experiment was goofed up, but I figured I could at least get a paper out of it"); "Data on three of the participants were chosen for detailed study . . ." ("The results on the others didn't make any sense and were ignored"); "The experimental dosage for the animals was unintentionally contaminated during the experiment . . ." ("accidentally dropped on the floor"); "The experimental dosage for the animals was handled with extreme care during the experiment . . ." ("not dropped on the floor"); "Typical results are illustrated . . ." ("The best findings are shown"); "This conclusion is correct within an order of magnitude . . ." ("It's wrong").

Avoid Personal References. Another point about writing up reports is that personal references should be kept to a minimum.[5] For instance, a student may write

---

[5] Although the standard convention in scientific writing is to avoid personal references, there are those who hold that such a practice should not be sustained. The

such things as "I believe that the results would have turned out differently, if I had . . ." or "It is my opinion that. . . ." Strictly speaking, your audience doesn't care too much about your emotional experiences, what you believe, feel, think; they are much more interested in what data you obtained and what conclusions you can draw from those data. Rather than stating your beliefs and feelings, then, you should say something like "the data indicate that. . . ." Similarly, don't adopt an introspective tone in your report. Many decisions in designing your study must be made, but don't make your reader agonize with you. For instance, don't say: "This researcher had to decide whether it was better for the children to be studied in the morning or in the afternoon. After much thought, this researcher decided to. . . ." Just say: "The children were studied from 3 P.M. to 4 P.M."

Avoid Harsh or Emotionally Loaded Phrases. Scientific writing should be divorced from emotional stimulation as much as possible. An example of bad writing would be: "Some psychologists believe that a few people have extrasensory perception, *while others claim it to be nonsense.*" Also, do not include evaluative adjectives in reports, such as "One interesting result was . . ." or "These disappointing findings suggest that. . . ."

Avoid Misspellings. This occurs all too frequently in student reports. You should *take the trouble to read your report over* after it is written and *rewrite if necessary*. If you are not sure how to spell a word, look it up in the dictionary. Unfortunately, far too few students have acquired the "dictionary

habit," a habit which is the mark of an educated person.

Use Words Properly. What is it that makes some engineers and scientists such lousy writers? One observer answered that it is due to "an unhealthy state of mind," identified by two "diseases." Disease 1 (quadraphobia) is characterized by an overwhelming thirst for a well-established, say-nothing phraseology, such as "I could care less." Disease 2, statumania, is an inordinate quest for status or an overpowering desire to impress. A major symptom of statumania is the misuse of words—"If it's big, it's gotta be good." An engineering executive of considerable stature, engaged in a project leading to the lunar rock hunt, wrote as follows (mutilated words in italics): "I am not the *pacific cogniss engineer on the titanium spear*; it's not even within my *preview*. And I want to *appraise* you right now of the fact that I'm *diabolically* opposed to the belief that the physical properties of titanium might be a *significant contributing* factor. But I'll be happy to *commencerate* with you about the problem. I'll even let you set the *tenure* of the discussion." The same quote, with word corrections italicized, follows: "I am not the *specific cognizant* engineer on the titanium *sphere*; it's not even within my *purview*. And I want to *apprise* you right now of the fact that I'm *diametrically* opposed to the belief that the physical properties of titanium might be a *significant contributing* factor. But I'll be happy to *commiserate* (wrong usage) with you about the problem. I'll even let you set the *tenor* of the discussion" (White, 1971, p. 25). *If you aren't sure that you have the right word, either look it up in the dictionary or use ones with which you are confident!*

Use Abbreviations and Acronyms Wisely. If you use them, explain them. And don't overuse them so that your reader gets lost in a maze of abstractions. In an entertaining article entitled "Water Beds and Sexual Satisfaction: Wike's Law of Low Odd Primes (WLLOP)," Wike (1973) illustrated this danger: "The true scientist is motivated by the quest for fame, immortality, and

---

following quotation from an article entitled "Why Are Medical Journals So Dull?" states the case for this view: "avoiding 'I' by impersonality and circumlocution leads to dullness and I would rather be thought conceited than dull. Articles are written to interest the reader, not to make him admire the author. Overconscientious anonymity can be overdone, as in the article by two authors which had a footnote.[1] "Since this article was written, unfortunately one of us has died" (Asher, 1958, p. 502)

money (FIM) [he] ... labored quasi-diligently for over two decades in that murky swamp (MS) called research, seeking a suitable principle, hypothesis, or phenomenon to [call his own]. Recently, in a flight from the MS Wike's Law of Low Odd Primes (WLLOP) [came through as] a superb mnemonic device (MD). Regarding MD, note that WLLOP spelled backwards is POLLW.... WLLOP asserts simply: *If the number of experimental treatments is a low odd prime number, then the experimental design is unbalanced and partially confounded*" (pp. 192–93). Wike concluded, "The increasing use of abbreviated names (ANs) in the psychological literature must be regarded as a genuine breakthrough. By peppering a paper with a large number of ANs, the skilled technical writer can often approach and sometimes even achieve a nirvana-like state of total incomprehensibility in his readers" (p. 192).

A few final matters are

1. Don't list minor pieces of "apparatus" such as a pencil (unless it is particularly important, as in a stylus maze).

2. The word "data" is plural; "datum" is singular. Thus it is incorrect to say "that data" or "this data." Rather, say, "those data" or "these data." Similarly, "criterion" is singular and "criteria" is plural, just as "phenomenon" is singular and "phenomena" is plural. Thus, say, "This criterion may be substituted for *those* criteria." You wouldn't be proud of yourself by saying, "This apples" or "Those apple." And certainly, don't say "a stimuli."

3. There is a difference between a probability value (e.g., $P = 0.05$) and a percentage value (e.g., 5 percent). Although a percentage can be changed into a probability and vice versa, one would not say that "The probability was 5 percent" or "The percent was 0.05" if 5 percent is really meant.

4. When reporting the results of a statistical analysis, never say, "The data are (or are not) reliable." Data are not reliable in the technical sense. Rather, the results of your statistical analysis may indicate that there is a reliable difference between your means.

5. When you quote from an article, put quotation marks around the quote and cite the author, year, and a page reference. *Then check the quotation for accuracy*, down to the commas.

6. Students may systematically collaborate during the data collection phase, but they should independently write up their articles and conduct their statistical analyses by themselves. Ask a fellow student to criticize your first draft so that a later draft can be improved. If a peer doesn't understand what you have written, your professor probably won't either.

7. Make a distinction between "negative results" and "no results." Students sometimes say that they "didn't get any results," which communicates to an amazed listener that although they invited participants into the laboratory, for some strange reason no data were collected.

8. If at all possible, type your report. Studies have shown that students who type get higher grades. Perhaps instructors have a "better unconscious mental set" in reading typed papers. In typing, remember to set your typewriter or computer on *double space* and leave it there for the *entire* report, including references and tables.

appendix C

THE USE OF COMPUTERS IN RESEARCH

COMPUTERS IN HISTORICAL PERSPECTIVE

The magnificent contributions of the modern computer to so many areas of our endeavor can only be properly understood when we view human striving throughout history to construct "calculating" machines. The first aid for calculation, of course, was our 10 fingers. Numerous other primitive counting systems were used such as that of the sheepherder who placed a stone in a pile for each sheep that went into the fields. By removing a stone as each sheep returned, the sheepherder could determine how many were lost to the wolves. Somewhat later, as quantitative thinking developed, a formal instrument, the abacus, was created as an aid to making rapid, accurate calculations.

Logic machines, which solve problems in formal logic such as the inferences we made in Chapter 12, have been basic to the modern computer. The first logic machine was a mechanical device developed in the thirteenth century by Ramon Lull, a Spanish theologian and visionary. By merely randomly rotating components of the machine, words and treatises could be produced so that even an ignorant person could write books on any subject.

Many logic devices have been developed, but the first definitely recorded machine devoted to calculation was constructed in 1642 by the famous mathematician Pascal.[1] In 1671 the famous philosopher Leibniz, influenced by Lull's work, at the age of 19 invented a versatile machine that could count, add, subtract, multiply, and divide.[2]

---

[1] Pascal's device was a system of wheels and ratchets that could automatically carry tens in order to add mechanically.

[2] As a philosopher, Leibniz foresaw the germ of a universal algebra by which all knowledge could some day be brought within a single deductive system. Leibniz suggested that two philosophers could settle any argument with the system merely by saying "let's calcu-

The first really effective calculating machine was invented by C. Babbage (1792–1871). His "analytical engine" was capable of tabulating the values of any function and printing the results.[3] Successive computers were developed that could carry out complex calculations in an instant, but they lacked memories that would allow them to deal with large blocks of data. There were also chronic problems of lack of reliability since the early solid-state devices generated heat and were very sensitive to variations in power supplies.

MODERN COMPUTERS

Computers today differ from their predecessors in that they have effective memories. This advance was first made possible by the electronic vacuum tube that could accept and store numbers for future automatic calculations. Modern computers with memories are classified as either *special-purpose* (dedicated) or *general-purpose computers*). A special-purpose computer performs specific and limited operations such as those done by your pocket calculator or those per-

formed in a car that tell you the number of miles you have driven, your rate of gasoline consumption, your average speed, and so on. It is the general-purpose computer that is of special value to us in research.

In the framework of history, the concept of a general-purpose machine was known as a universal turing machine, so named after the mathematician Alan Turing who helped break the German secret code during World War II. Turing showed that if a machine could be constructed to carry out certain basic mathematical operations, it could perform *any* kind of mathematical operation. The general-purpose computer with appropriate programming can thus, in principle, solve any problem that is solvable.

Tremendous progress has been made in recent decades in increasing computers' complexity, amount of memory, and speed of computation and in decreasing their size. There is no limit to the amount of memory. The limit for the speed of computation is that of the speed of light, which now has been reached on "supercomputers." This limitation exists because it takes time for electrons to travel from location to location within and between microchips. Even electrons moving at the speed of light require a certain amount of time to carry out computations. The future use of computers, indeed, seems to have little in the way of limits.

With regard to size, computers are classified as mainframe computers, which are the largest; as minicomputers, which are somewhat smaller; and as microcomputers, which can sit on your lap. Mainframe and minicomputers are used in large research laboratories, and in government and business, where high rates and amounts of information processing are required. The reason that today's computers are relatively small is that the large electronic vacuum tubes that filled entire rooms were replaced by transistors. Later, transistors were transformed into integrated electronic circuits on miniscale microchips. A microchip is a tiny square of silicon and metal that contains integrated circuits and the like that perform the same functions as transistors, but in

---

late." However, Leibniz's main contribution to computing machines was his insightful recognition of the advantages of a binary or base 2 system over a base 10 system. In a binary scale we can represent any integer with a series of 0's and 1's. Thus the integer 1 is represented as 1, 2 as 10, 3 as 11, 4 as 100, 5 as 101, and so on. The binary notation for 2,456 is 100,110,011,000. In the base 10 scale, integers are more complexly represented in terms of 10's. The use of the more complex base 10 scale was probably due to the accident that we use the 10 digits on our hands to count.

Leibniz's insight that we can express any integer in 0's and 1's also influenced his philosophy. He inferred, in his metaphysical fashion, that God had created the universe (1) out of nothing (0). This is a remarkable confusion for a mathematician of the stature of Leibniz. Like today's football announcers, he erroneously equated "nothing" with zero." Zero is something—it is a very important number, and thus it is not "nothing." (A similar confusion is using the letter O for zero just because they look alike—it's like saying that the Bears beat the Lions 47 to A; though this practice is acceptable in everyday life where precision is not so important.)

[3] However, after incurring considerable expense the British government, Babbage's project was abandoned, and it was placed in the Kensington Museum.

amazingly small formats. The microchip contains series of on/off switches that signify a 0 when the switch is off and a 1 when the switch is on. These two modes of switch operation establish a binary system of arithmetic in which the computer's calculations are done (see Footnote 2).

MICROCOMPUTERS

As progress has been made in electronics, the expense of microcomputers has decreased to such a level that they are commonplace in our homes. More to the point for us, the amazing increase in power and the attendant decrease in cost have made microcomputers readily available on university campuses. Most behavioral data analysis can be accomplished with the microcomputer. For that reason we shall concentrate on it. With the development of the high-speed electronic digital computer, research projects that handle a fantastic number of data and carry out an amazing number of calculations allow us to conduct research projects that we could only dream of years ago. Furthermore, the computer can do a lot of tedious work that would be error prone for a human—complex analyses can be carried out with accuracy, efficiency, and speed.

A computer is a machine that consists of a large number of electronic circuits. It will (1) receive information, (2) process that information, and (3) output that information. The basic building blocks of the microcomputer are the **central processing unit** (CPU), which is the computer's "brain;" the **memory** that we use to store programs and data; the **keyboard and screen** (cathode ray tube, CRT) through which we communicate with the system; a mass storage device which typically consists of **disks** on which we store programs and data; the **printer**, which provides the printout of materials; and communication facilities which we can use to communicate from our computer to others. The great strength of the microcomputer is that it can perform simple sequential calculations, mul-

tiply, add, divide, and subtract extremely rapidly. Since these calculations are done in binary arithmetic using zeros and ones, everything that goes into the computer must be translated into zeros and ones. While this translation is already done for the typical user, it is well for us at least to be aware of the process as it was originally developed by Leibniz. While the keyboard and the disk are the typical input devices used in microcomputers, other computer input devices include punched cards, disk storage, analog-digital converters, modems from telephone lines, and magnetic tape; voice input systems may also be used for handicapped individuals. But mainly we use a keyboard to feed information into the central processing unit (CPU).

Excluding the peripheral units, the microcomputer itself consists of a main memory and a CPU. The CPU in microcomputers is a microprocessor that processes information, while the main memory is where information is stored. Both components are manufactured in the form of silicon chips.

Information is stored in the main memory in the form of binary digits called bits [which is a contraction of "binary digit" (bi + t)]. A bit of information is a single on or off signal. That is, a bit can take on the value of 0 or 1. Bits are combined together to form a unit known as a byte. A byte is a set of locations in the memory that can store a particular piece of information coded as many on-off values in a unique location. The computer can then access the location to retrieve the information. Thus you could store a datum on one subject in one location in memory, that for another in a second location, that for another in a third location, and so forth. Then the computer could be instructed to sum those values, to square them, to compute their mean value, or whatever.

The size of memory is indicated by an approximation of how many bytes there are. Thus a microcomputer that has 64K of memory has 65,536 bytes. Most modern microcomputers have much larger memories.

Information is stored on mass storage devices called hard disks for main memory that are built into or attached to the computer and on floppy (and other) disks. Floppy disks are soft, less expensive versions of hard disks that store data magnetically. When the machine is turned off, information stored in main memory is erased, lost! Thus we use auxiliary storage systems like disks to retain information outside of the computer. Later we can enter information from disks back into the main memory and continue to process that information.

The function of a computer is to compute, which means to perform arithmetic and logical operations. These are carried out by the CPU. A display unit is typically connected to a CRT so that we can observe the information that we have entered into the CPU. The computer, under guidance of a specific program, provides your answers directly on the CRT and may present questions to guide you as you proceed. For instance, it may ask you how many numbers you wish to enter, to identify the program you wish to use, and so on.

A printer is a peripheral unit which provides hard copy so that you can retain a physical record of the computation performed by the computer.

SOFTWARE—INSTRUCTING THE COMPUTER

Computer technology can be divided into two main categories: hardware and software. The mechanical and electronic components of a computer constitute the computer's hardware—it is the machine itself. Software refers to the instructions that we give to the machine to program it to carry out our computations. It includes all the procedures that we instruct the computer to use. We typically enter programs into a microcomputer from disk storage devices.

We often give instructions to computers by using standardized packaged programs, such as to analyze data statistically by conducting a *t*-test. In these programs the instructions have already been worked out

and, it is hoped, well tested. It's like driving into a fast-food restaurant: we are given a menu, we select an order, and we instruct the computer that we want a "hamburger." The software does the rest.

The most frequently used packaged programs in psychology are those for statistical analysis. We enter the data that we want the computer to analyze and instruct it on the data manipulations. For instance, we tell the computer how many cases there are, what the variables are, how many values the variables can assume, and so on. The program tells you how to create a file of information, how to save this file, how to retrieve the file, how to edit the file to make corrections, and how to remove the file from memory.

There are many user-friendly programs for statistical analysis that are applicable for just about any computer, be it an IBM compatible, Apple, etc. The most widely used statistical packages are SPSS (Statistical Package for the Social Sciences), Minitab, BMDP (BioMedical Computer Programs), SAS (Statistical Analysis System), Statement SIZT, and Statmarks. Minitab is probably the simplest to use. A programmed package called Tadpole has an amazing capacity for behavioral analysis.[4]

As marvelous as packaged programs sound, you must know what you are doing with them. You must understand the princi-

---

[4]Tadpole data files can contain up to 9999 records, each with up to 60 fields and each field can contain a real number with up to six significant figures. Statistical tests available in Tadpole are means, standard errors, skewness, kurtosis, minimum and maximum values plus range, median, frequency analysis including bar diagrams, Student's *t*-test for paired and unpaired data, linear regression and correlation, multiple linear regression, ANOVA one-and two-way analysis for equal and unequal groups, contingency tables, chi-square, Fisher's exact test, McNemar's test for the significance of change, one sample chi-square test, Mann-Whitney U test, Wilcoxon signed-ranks matched-pairs test, Spearman's rank correlation test, Kendall's rank correlation coefficient, Kendall's coefficient of concordance, Kruskal-Wallis one-way analysis of variance, Friedman's two-way analysis of variance by ranks, and Mantel-Haenzel survivorship (Logrank) test.

ples of the statistical methods that you are using. You cannot blindly rely on a packaged program to do everything for you. Many, many times a user will get an answer with little idea of what it means, or what to do with it. We shall develop this point further before long, especially when we emphasize that you must understand in detail the nature of your data. Otherwise, as the saying goes, "garbage in, garbage out."

USING STATISTICAL PACKAGES

The manual for statistical packages provides instructions on the capabilities of the package and how to conduct your analysis. Such manuals typically illustrate program use in a step-by-step fashion.

The first step is to enter the statistical package into the computer. Then you use your computer's specific command sequence to access the package, whereupon you follow the rules and procedures of the particular package to perform your statistical analysis. When the analysis is completed, the package will provide a command for you to exit from the program. At this point the computer is free to be used for other purposes.

The program will ask about the variables with which you need to deal. You will have to input your data in the form of columns such that each column corresponds to a particular variable; for example, one column might be for the values of your experimental group, with another for the control group. At this point you will command the computer to accomplish the data analysis that you wish. For example, you may use a packaged program for descriptive statistics to compute a mean, median, mode, variance, and standard deviation of your data. You can usually also instruct the computer to provide a frequency distribution (a frequency polygon or histogram) or graph relationships between variables, or you can compute correlations between any pair of variables, conduct *t*-tests, analyses of variance, chi-squares, various nonparametric tests, and so on.

DEVELOPING YOUR OWN PROGRAM

To be more flexible, we can construct our own instructions using a computer language. There are numerous languages available in which to write programs that are entered into the computer as software. The most popular have been FORTRAN (Formula Translation) and BASIC. However, Pascal has become the standard for advanced programmers. BASIC is often available but is rarely used for serious programming as it is typically slow and unstructured; it has, however, been popular in the past because of its simple, condensed forms of English commands. One writes a program in BASIC, or Pascal, for instance, and types it into the computer's memory by means of a keyboard; for example, you tell the computer to "go to, read, and then print the outcome." The advantage of writing your own program is that the computer can do precisely what you want. On the other hand, learning to program and to debug the program is time consuming. Most researchers rely on packaged programs with their drawbacks, as we shall later discuss.

THE COMPUTER IN RESEARCH

During the literature search, the computer can be very valuable because it can access information stored in remotely located data bases. We can, for instance, search a data base containing information from *Psychological Abstracts* to obtain references relevant to our work. By combining key words, we can select the most relevant references. For instance, if we ask for a printout of references containing the key word "schizophrenia," we would probably have to wait until tomorrow for the printer to stop. But if we combined that key word with "brainwaves," our printout length would be much more reasonable and relevant. After printing out the references the computer will usually ask you if you want abstracts of any of the articles. You can request those that are most relevant to your work.

Controlling aspects of an experiment such as the presentation of stimuli by means of slides can be easily and efficiently carried out by programming into your computer controls that advance the slide projector.

You can program your computer to control one or more functions of an experiment; for example, it can control the presentation at specific intervals of stimuli by means of slides; while advancing the slide projector it can also simultaneously control other functions in the laboratory such as randomizing conditions in blocks of trials, so that stimuli can be presented in certain predetermined orders without the programmer having to change conditions manually.

The computer is extremely helpful if there are a number of repetitive operations that must be performed so that the opportunity for human error is great; for example, it can repetitively record the time when a response is made and store it on a floppy disk.

Finally, the results can be written and edited with a word processor.

We cannot overemphasize, though, that the computer programs used should be carefully tested and validated. Otherwise, bugs (errors) in a program could cause stimuli to be administered at incorrect times, response times to be recorded incorrectly, or response values from different participants to be mixed up.

There are many applications of computers in psychology other than those we have discussed. For instance, massive quantities of naturalistic observational data have been collected, reduced, and analyzed. A listing of topics from a meeting on the use of computers in psychology illustrates the widespread use that will no doubt grow and continue:

Computer networks for data gathering and analysis—the sharing of information among microcomputers with mainframe networks over long distances.

Computer analysis of physiological events—including cardiac activity and electro-oculographic changes.

The computer as a research tool—computer-administered surveys; an automated laboratory.

Computer-generated speech perception and production of synthetic speech.

Human-computer interaction—aids for writing, learning to program, and so on.

The computer in operant conditioning systems—amplitude measures of operant responding.

Clinical assessment of biofeedback data—including EEG and EKG.

Supercomputing in psychology—cognitive modeling and artificial intelligence.

Teaching applications of microcomputers—instructional programs in psychology.

Networking systems.

In Summary. You may search the literature, control aspects of an experiment, record dependent-variable data, store data, analyze the results statistically, and prepare your manuscript (including plotting figures). Shrewd planning of your research is important. In developing your research plan, you specify the particular statistical analyses (tests) that will relate to your hypotheses, along with the levels of probability for rejecting the null hypothesis. However, computer analyses are often "too easy" so that the researcher also conducts additional statistical analyses: By merely selecting other options from the menu and pushing a button, the user can generate a realm of additional analyses. Not only are there excessive analyses, but there may be a violation of the stated level of probability, as discussed in Chapter 6.

In Conclusion. The computer does what we tell it to do and we should make sure that what we tell it is correct. But its use may remove us from our data, much to our detriment. To illustrate further the importance of keeping close contact with your data, consider the following examples.

THE GREAT VALUE OF COMPUTERS

In psychology and in education, nonresearch uses include computer-assisted instruction for tutorial sessions, and rote learning. The field of artificial intelligence is a vast additional means of using computers. Computers have also been used widely in assessment. Computer-assisted assessment has facilitated the acquisition of clinical data and decisions based upon those data; for example, computers present, score, and interpret psychometric instruments such as the MMPI. To emphasize the variety and quantity of applications in psychology you should read *Behavior Research Methods, Instruments, and Computers*, which can also effectively guide you to articles that may facilitate your own work. See, for instance, the December 1987 issue that contains about 3,500 articles devoted to over 150 different topics in psychology.

The computer is certainly with us and its functions and contributions no doubt will continue to expand in many aspects of our lives. Networking, the ability of computers to communicate with each other, certainly is expanding, e.g., a common application is for a small microcomputer to communicate with a mainframe computer that might be located elsewhere in the world. There are even computer networks that allow individuals to communicate with each other around the world by means of satellites.

While much of the computer's use is in conducting statistical analyses, it is also very useful for nonnumerical operations such as in word processors. A word processor is merely a computer program that allows the computer to accept verbal material, to read it into memory, to retrieve it, edit the material, and print it out. Programs are even used in word processors and typewriters to detect spelling and grammatical errors and function as thesauruses.

COMPUTER SIMULATION

Some laboratories have been developed for teaching purposes, using computer simulation of experiments. Students do not collect "real" data, but fictitious values have been packaged into a program as if the data collection were original. Often the data result from a random number generator. Students can then efficiently, if unrealistically, continue to conduct their research. Another application is one that simulates the role of a psycho-therapist. The computer reacts to a patient's remarks, thus imitating therapeutic processes. The patient enters statements into the computer, which is programmed to respond appropriately as would a human therapist.

Some individuals, particularly those not knowledgeable about behavioral research, have advocated the use of computers to simulate the behavior of both animals and humans. Their advocacy of computer simulation has been especially strong in the fields of medicine, physiology, and physiological psychology. While computer simulation has some value, such a strategy is sterile in the long run, for a computer only knows what we tell it. The data that we input have been gained from direct study of behavior; no new knowledge can be generated by the computer beyond what we have already learned and entered into it. What the computer *can* do is perform logical operations so that stored knowledge can be presented in new configurations.

PITFALLS AND LIMITATIONS

Computer Paralysis of the Laboratory. Yet there are difficulties in using a computer. When applied for the conduct of experiments, Coren (1986) warns against laboratories suffering "computer paralysis." This is "a technologically induced disease that occurs when researchers have not been inoculated against some of the inevitable problems that attend the transition to a computerized laboratory" (p. 637). For instance, the computer need not take over the entire laboratory, as in one laboratory cited by Coren. That system was so thorough that even a voucher crediting the volunteer student with an hour's participation was automatically dispensed when the student was finished. Computerization was so complete that the experimenter was not in the laboratory.

"The *beauty* of this system is that the experimenter never has to be physically present or actually see a subject. The *problem* with this system is that the experimenter is not physically present and never sees the subjects" (Coren, p. 640). For example, in one study the data indicated that a subject had a visual color deficiency on days 1, 2, and 4, but not on day 3. On inquiry, the subject honestly admitted that on day 3 a friend of his had taken his place and later that day he had filled in for his friend. He explained that "After all, we were both on day 3, so it shouldn't make any difference." Then, in a statement that cast doubt on the validity of the whole year's enterprise he added, "A lot of us do this when the sessions are at inconvenient times."

In computerizing a laboratory one must realize that, while there are numerous advantages in saving time, facilitating data collection, transforming and reducing your data, and quantifying and conducting statistical analyses, the costs are often great in terms of initial effort to achieve the system that you seek. The costs include programming, debugging, interfacing, and, of great importance, verification "by hand" that the computer is accurately carrying out the tasks that you set it. For instance, if it is going to compute a number of correlations for you, you should compute one by yourself to check the computer. The initial expenditure of effort and money could be sizable. Computer analysis also involves the time required to learn to use the computer. Estimates of that time are from one year to forever. After that, a number of things still may go wrong; for example, programs should be updated, electronics parts and interfaces may break down. Such problems may be quite subtle so that finding and repairing them (troubleshooting) can be expensive in both time and money.

In conclusion, one often expects too much from computerization, leading the researcher to computerize aspects of the laboratory that are not beneficial and to collect too much unneeded data. The most flexible and easily programmed piece of equipment in the laboratory is the human researcher. Coren advises that we should "give the computer the task of making repetitive computations and of monitoring, but it should not take over the full functioning of the laboratory." Such caution will help you avoid the perils of computer paralysis in its many manifestations.

The Shotgun Disaster. We caution against another pitfall, "a shotgun" approach to research. It is so easy to collect and analyze data with a computer that you may have too much irrelevant data and excessive analyses. In one experiment cited by Coren, the "trial number, reaction time, stimulus presented, response selected, correct versus incorrect flag, markers indicating hand and eye used, interstimulus interval, interval between response and next stimulus presentation, and two other variables that have now slipped my mind but which pertained to the warning signal were recorded for each trial. Given that there were over 2,000 trials per subject, this represented a massive body of data" (p. 641). Even though the experimenters purchased extra memory for their microcomputer, they ultimately decided that there were too many data to deal with in any meaningful, conceptual fashion. Consequently, they stripped the data down to what they should have collected in the first place. The researcher can thus plunge into a statistical analysis without having sufficiently thought about the variables and their implications. Pages of statistics that result from a shotgun approach instead of a direct approach are not only unfortunate, they can be mind-boggling. One student who asked for all possible partial correlations from an 18×18 data matrix couldn't even carry the printout that resulted, much less comprehend it.

Don't Lose Track of Your Raw Data. The most serious problem in laboratory research is that the researcher may lose close contact with the raw data. As we saw, computers usually provide a lot of information that you don't want and may overload you. Also, you may get into trouble by misapplying a packaged program. Perhaps the analysis of variance program that you enter uses one error term whereas your application requires a different error term; for example, you may have a random model whereas the programmer selected the error term for a fixed model (Chapter 12).

A packaged program contains sets of programs that can be used with a relatively limited amount of knowledge of programming. But, to repeat, they must be used with great care, and it is important to be sure that any program you use has been checked for accuracy and adequate documentation. "Until you are fairly sure of the adequacy of a program, use it with circumspection and care—or not at all" Kerlinger (1986, p. 636) points out. The researcher should ask the question, "Does this program do what I want and need it to do? Yet it is highly likely that this question is rarely asked and virtually never answered" (Kerlinger, 1986, p. 636). While developing your own program may be unpalatable, one has to understand the basic statistics before a packaged program can be used intelligently. Some are so constructed that the user leaves important choices to the program itself. To make sure that they are accurate, one needs meticulously to compare the results from them with hand-scored results before a program can be relied on. One should carry out some routine trial-by-trial checking of the computer, looking for errors. It is also useful to have sets of previously analyzed and verified data to use to test a new procedure.

The Law of the Hammer Revisited. Recall that one runs the danger of conducting certain research merely because appropriate instrumentation is available. Etzioni (1975) pointed out the danger that the computer can set the direction of research, preempting the need for reflection and thought. Faculties and students need to recognize this danger because studies and analyses are increasingly conducted only because the computer makes them so easy.

EXAMINING THE NUMBERS THAT CONSTITUTE YOUR DATA

If one just blindly plugs numbers into a computer, obtains a final value of a statistical test without actually studying the numbers themselves, many problems can result. It is critical for researchers to work through their data, studying them from several points of view, and determining whether results are reasonable and have satisfied the assumptions underlying statistical analyses. Consider the following values:

Dependent-Variable Values for Two Groups

Group A	Group B
0.0213	0.0123
0.0214	0.0124
0.0215	0.0125
$\Sigma X_1 = 0.0642$	$\Sigma X_2 = 0.0372$
$X_1 = 0.0214$	$X_2 = 0.0124$
$\overline{X}_1 - \overline{X}_2 = 0.0214 - 0.0124 = 0.009$	

The mean difference of only 0.009 seems rather small. Now consider a second set of values:

Dependent-Variable Values for Two Other Groups

Group A	Group B
21.3	12.3
21.4	12.4
21.5	12.8
$\Sigma X = 64.2$	$\Sigma X = 37.2$
$X_1 = 21.4$	$X_2 = 12.4$

Here the mean difference of $21.4 - 12.4 = 9.0$ appears quite a bit larger. But obviously the values are relatively the same in both experiments. The only difference is a matter of decimal places. Without carefully studying and working with these data, one might believe that in the first case there was but a minor difference between the two groups, whereas in the second the difference is rather substantial. Yet the matter is more serious than that. Consider the computation of the standard deviation and the number of decimal places to retain for group A. We compute the standard deviation of 1:21.3, 21.4, 21.5 as follows: $\Sigma X = 64.20$, $\Sigma X^2 = 1,373.90$, $s^2 = 0.01$, $s = 0.10$.

We have used five decimal places but no more.

Now consider the data for Group A in the first experiment calculated to the indicated number of decimal places:

Number of Decimal Places

	Five	*Six*	*Seven*	*Eight*
ΣX_1	0.0642	0.0642	0.0642	0.0642
ΣX^2_2	0.00137	0.001374	0.0013739	0.00137390
s^2	0.00000	0.000000	0.0000000	0.00000001
s	0.00000	0.000000	0.0000000	0.0001

By carrying out calculations to five, six, or seven decimal places, the variance (s^2) remains at zero as does the standard deviation (s). It is not until you carry out your calculation to eight data places that you obtain a value of s^2 and of s that is nonzero. In working with the standard deviation, one should carry computations out to twice the number of decimal places as in the original data.

The moral, thus, is that calculators and computers have capacities for a fixed maximum number of decimal places, some even carry out to only two decimal places. One can make massive errors in such cases.

Suppose, to be liberal, that a computer is based on a maximum of 10 decimal places. If the data being used have more than 5 decimal places, there will be approximations of the foregoing type, resulting in errors, for example, the data of 0.000213, 0.000214, and 0.000215 resulting in $\Sigma X = 0.0642$, $\Sigma X^2 = 0.0000001374$, and $s = 0.0000000000$.

Since all machines have finite capacity, one must know the number of decimal places to which they are accurate and keep track of the number of decimal places in your data. If the machine is sufficiently limited, you need to apply some sort of transformation to your data. For example, for the last set of data one could multiply each number by 100,000 thus obtaining the following values: 2.13, 2.14, and 2.15. Now if you calculate the mean and standard deviation of the transformed data, you could then divide these two statistics by 100,000 and find that $\overline{X} = 0.000214$ and $s = 0.000001$.

Again the lesson here is that in computing an accurate standard deviation, twice as many decimal places must be used as inthe data. Investigators who deal with much more complicated computations, such as matrix inversion (which is common toall multiple regression problems), must follow not only this rule but others that may be violated if they don't stay close to their data.

appendix D

ETHICAL PRINCIPLES IN THE CONDUCT OF PSYCHOLOGICAL RESEARCH

RESEARCH WITH HUMAN PARTICIPANTS

Background Ethical Violations. Two studies in recent U.S. history have especially angered the public. The first, known as the *Tuskegee Study*, began in 1932 with a U.S. Public Health Service experiment on 399 black, poor, semiliterate individuals who had syphilis. One purpose was to study the effects of syphilis on untreated black males; to encourage participation, the afflicted were led to believe that they were being treated when in fact they were not. Symptoms of syphilis were periodically recorded, and autopsies were performed after each death. Forty years later the public became aware of this research, which was still in progress. The research was clearly unethical, for one reason because treatment was still being withheld from the survivors as late as in 1972, even though they could have been ef-

fectively treated with penicillin since the 1940s.

The second set of studies (in the 1960s and 1970s) was conducted by the social psychologist Milgram, who advertised for participants in a "learning" experiment. Those who volunteered were told that some would be teachers who would teach lists of words to the others, the learners. The teachers were told to administer increasingly severe shocks every time the learners made an error. In fact, however, the purpose of the experiment was *not* to study learning but to study obedience to authority. Furthermore *all* volunteers were actually "teachers"; that is, all participants were told that they were teachers, and in fact there were no learners. Consequently, everybody thought that they were administering electric shocks to the learners, who did not exist. Furthermore, there were actually no shocks at all. Nevertheless, the teachers were duped into believing that learners were complaining of pain when shocked. When instructed to increase the severity of the shocks some balked. Teachers who balked were told that the experiment required them to proceed. Those who remained reluctant were *ordered* to proceed, whereupon an amazingly large number of them did continue the sham "shocking" of learners. They even continued shocking the learners beyond the point where the learners "requested" to be released from the experiment. Public anger over this experiment centered on the deception that might have caused psychological discomfort and harm to the participants. More than that, some people overgeneralized and thought that many such psychological experiments were being conducted.

Both the Tuskegee and the Milgram research were instrumental in bringing about legal restrictions on unethical research. Federal regulation of medical, behavioral and social science research followed. Professional organizations, such as the American Physiological Society, have become quite active in "policing" themselves, even though unethical research by scientists has been minimal.

For instance, a conference held on the topic of scientific misconduct and fraud concluded that both were rare. The Public Health Services for Scientific Integrity examined 118 reported cases; 27 of those required full investigations, and 18 involved misconduct. Three involved behavioral scientists. Similarly, each year the National Science Foundation has found only 2 to 3 cases of misconduct that were serious enough to result in agency sanctions. Only four behavioral scientists have been cited for scientific misconduct in recent years. They were Steven Breuning of the University of Pittsberg who was convicted in 1988 of fabricating scientific data about drug tests on retarded children. He agreed not to work as a researcher for at least 10 years. Arnold Rincover, formerly at the University of North Carolina, Greensboro, was cited for plagiarism and falsification of data. Lonnie Mitchell of Coppon State College and Jerusa

Wilson were cited for plagiarism and inadequate supervision of a grant application.

More generally in science, David Baltimore, president of Rockefeller University was accused by an assistant of using falsified and manufactured data supplied by a colleague in an influential paper and refused to investigate warnings that the material was flawed. A cardiologist who turned out 137 papers at the University of California, San Diego, within a short period was found to have falsified data. A final example was John Darsee in 1981, a Harvard Medical cardiologist, who apparently forged data.

Considering the extremely large number of scientific researches conducted each year, these numbers are extremely small. Nevertheless, it is important that scientists and students learn to adhere to standard practices that avoid scientific integrity transgressions, such as the in following summary from that conference (as reported in the *APA Monitor*, December 1991, p. 11.)

- Data fabrication
- Data falsification ("cooking" or altering data)
- Plagiarism
- Unethical treatment of animal or human subjects
- Undisclosed conflicts of interest
- Violation of privileged material
- Irresponsible authorship credit (honorary authorship or exclusion of major contributor)
- Failure to retain primary data
- Inadequate supervision of research products
- Sloppy recording of data
- Data dredging
- Undisclosed repetition of unsatisfactory experiments
- Selective reporting of findings
- Failure to publish
- Unwillingness to share data or research materials
- Inappropriate statistical tests and procedures
- Insufficient or misleading reporting
- Redundant publication
- Fragmentary publication ("salami science")
- Inappropriate citation

- Intentional submission of "sloppy manuscripts"

In 1973 the American Psychological Association published ethical guidelines for psychologists. After critical review for some years by psychologists themselves, we now have a relatively stable and widely accepted set of principles as published in the *American Psychologist* in March 1990. We shall briefly review the major ethical principles for human research, after which we shall consider principles for the care and use of animals. Finally, we shall comment on those principles.

General Ethical Principle. The essence is that the psychologist should decide whether his or her research is potentially valuable for psychological science and human welfare. If the decision is definitively in the affirmative, the psychologist must maintain respect and concern for the dignity and welfare of the participants while conducting the research.

The Participant in Psychology at Minimal Risk. The first major consideration for implementing this general principle is the decision as to whether the participant will be a "subject at risk" or a "subject at minimal risk" according to recognized standards. If there is the possibility of serious risk for the participant, the possible outcome of the research should indeed be of considerable value before proceeding. If the researcher does continue, major steps must be taken to prevent harm to the participant. Should one, for instance, seek to determine behavioral effects of a drug with potentially serious side effects, medical and legal guidance should be sought. Since such "subject-at-risk" research is neither conducted in psychological research methods courses nor by the very large majority of research psychologists, we will concentrate on research in which the subject (participant) is "at minimal risk." A number of subprinciples have been specified by the American Psychological Association as guidelines to implement our general ethical principle for conducting research.

The Researcher's Ethical Evaluation

First, the researcher carefully assesses the ethical acceptability of the research. If there is any question here, the researcher should seek ethical advice from colleagues or, if necessary, from the relevant university committee or professional association. A study of the rate of learning words by children would clearly constitute minimal risk research in which the researcher should proceed. However, the researcher who conducted the study in which students were falsely told that their husbands had been seriously injured in an automobile accident should not have proceeded. The researcher failed to observe stringent safeguards to protect the rights of human participants.

Responsibility

It is the major investigator who is responsible for all aspects of the research, including the ethical treatment of participants by all who are collaborating in the project.

Informed Consent from Participants

Informed consent is not required in minimal-risk research. Still, it is a good idea for the investigator in all research to establish a clear and fair agreement with research participants prior to their participation. That agreement should clarify the obligations and responsibilities of each. All relevant aspects of the research are explained to the participant. Many researchers use a standard form, signed by the participant, that indicates that they understand all aspects of the research and are willing participants.

Deception May Be Necessary

In some studies, if participants are given an accurate description of what the research is about, the research would be pointless—its validity would be destroyed. If the researcher believes that deception is justified by the prospective value of the research, and if alternative procedures are not available, then the participant must be provided with a thorough explanation as soon as possible. Usually this is accomplished in the debriefing stage, as the participant is dismissed.

Debriefing

Once the data from the participant are collected, the nature of the research is carefully explained and attempts to remove any misconceptions are made. It is good practice to review the data with participants who are students and to use the debriefing session as a learning experience so that the student participant can become more sophisticated about research. Showing a student around the laboratory and explaining the apparatus is also advised. The debriefing phase is especially important for the researchers, too, in that they can better understand "where the participants are coming from." A good opening question is, "What do you think this experiment was all about?" The things that participants tell the researcher can often make idiosyncratic results understandable. They also provide good leads for new hypotheses to be tested. The interesting, unusual, and typically irrelevant hypotheses developed by participants could make a most interesting book.[1]

Freedom from Coercion

It should be made clear that the participant is free to decline to participate in or to withdraw from the research at any time. Subtle forms of coercion should be avoided, such as the participant feeling a special obligation to please a professor.

---

[1] For instance, in a study involving covert conditioning of a response in the thumb, so small as to be invisible to the naked eye, one subject thought he had learned how to produce the response and receive a monetary reward. Though the response was in no sense voluntary, he "professed to have discovered an effective response sequence, which consisted of subtle rowing movements with both hands, infinitesimal wriggles of both ankles, a slight displacement of the jaw to the left, breathing out—and then waiting" (Hefferline, Keenan, & Harford, 1958, p. 209, in McGuigan, 1966).

Protection of Participants

If there are any risks at all, be they physical or mental discomfort, harm, or danger, the researcher must inform the participant of those risks. The researcher should realize that participation in any research may produce at least some degree of stress. Thus, the participant should be carefully assured of his or her safety.

Confidentiality

Any information obtained about the participant must be kept confidential, unless the participant agrees otherwise. The researcher should recognize the possibility that others may have access to information about the participant. If so, the participant should agree to this or some other steps should be taken such as coding sensitive data.

ETHICAL PRINCIPLES FOR ANIMAL RESEARCH

The monumental contributions of research on animals to science and to the advancement of human welfare are so well documented elsewhere, e.g., A. Miller (1985), that they need not be repeated here. Our concern is that ethical principles be adhered to. Again, the number of cases in which there have been scientific transgressions in animal research are relatively few, but we want to maintain that excellent record.

The major principle in the care and use of animals is that: "An investigator of animal behavior strives to advance understanding of basic behavioral principles and/or to contribute to the improvement of human health and welfare. In seeking these ends, the investigator ensures the welfare of animals and treats them humanely. Laws and regulations notwithstanding, an animal's immediate protection depends upon the scientist's own conscience" (p. 395, *American Psychologist*, March, 1990, "Ethical Principles of Psychologists").

The first thing a researcher should do in planning to use animals is to do his or her homework. More specifically, this means that they should study the "Ethical Principles of Psychologists," many of which are directly applicable to the use of animals; focus should be on principle 10, concerning the care and use of animals. Second, they should become familiar with federal, state, provincial, and local laws and regulations, including especially the National Institutes of Health *Guide for the Care and Use of Laboratory Animals*.[2] Another, very readable and effective source is *The Biomedical Investigator's Handbook for Researchers Using Animal Models* (1987) (Washington, D.C.: Foundation for Biomedical Research, 1987). Finally, they should study university or college regulations.

Guidelines available from the American Psychological Association (or from other scientific organizations such as the American Physiological Society) should be made known to all personnel involved in the research and conspicuously posted wherever animals are maintained and used.

In assessing the research, the possibility of increasing knowledge about behavior, including benefit for health or welfare of humans and animals, should be sufficient to outweigh any harm or distress to the animals. Humane consideration for the well-being of the animals should thus always be kept uppermost in mind. If the animal is likely to be subjected to distress or pain, the experimental procedures specified in the guidelines of the American Psychological Association should be carefully followed, especially for surgical procedures. For surgery, one should distinguish between anesthetics and muscle relaxants. Muscle relaxants may be used to immobilize the animal, just as they are for human surgery, to allow delicate and precise surgical procedures to be carried out. However, surgical procedures should also include effective anesthetization. It has actually occurred in human surgical procedures that patients were immobilized by muscle relaxants but not sufficiently anesthetized. Consequently, they experienced pain but were incapable of expressing that distress to the surgeon.

The supervisor of a research project should closely monitor all aspects of the study, including the health, comfort, and humane treatment of the animals. The supervisor should also maintain records of the acquisition, use, and disposition of the animals. A veterinarian should be available for consultation and should inspect the facilities at least twice a year. All these procedures should be reviewed by a local institutional animal care and use committee.

Concerning disposition of animals when they are no longer required, efforts should be made to distribute them to colleagues who might be able to use them. However, euthanasia may be the only alternative, either as a requirement of the research or because it constitutes the most humane form of disposition of an animal at the conclusion of research. By definition, euthanasia should be accomplished in as humane a manner as possible, including under anesthesia. No animal should be discarded until its death is verified, and it should be disposed of in a manner that is legal and consistent with health, environmental, and aesthetic concerns.

EVALUATION OF OUR ETHICAL PRINCIPLES

The purpose of conducting psychological research is the noble one of advancing scientific and technological knowledge. The psychologist, as a scientist and as a technologist, is vigorously dedicated to these purposes. Participants, be they animal or human, are critical collaborators in research projects. To repeat, all involved should be treated with respect, dignity, and the utmost concern for their welfare. However, some outlandish violations have been committed which led to the ethical guidelines first published by the

---

[2]*Guide for the Care and Use of Laboratory Animals*, NIH Publication No. 85-23, Revised 1985, Office of Science and Health Reports, DRR/NIH, Bethesda, MD 20205.

American Psychological Association in 1973. For instance, some students were falsely informed that their test scores indicated they were not intelligent enough to be in college; other students were required to participate in research projects to be admitted to a low-cost rooming house. When such violations have occurred, they were dealt with vigorously, even by expulsion of the violator from the American Psychological Association and from local associations as well.

As previously noted, ethical violations during the conduct of psychological research have been extremely rare, occurring more frequently in clinical practice and in other lines of professional endeavor. They have been so infrequent, in fact, that one could argue that stated guidelines and principles are really unnecessary—any scientist who needs such detailed guidance should not have been allowed to become a scientist in the first place. The argument against the establishment of ethical principles has been that it has had a deleterious effect on research. Following the 1973 set of principles, excessively restrictive procedures were promulgated so that even minimal-risk research sometimes became difficult to conduct. These excessive restrictions on research became apparent over the years, as did the fact that violations of our ethical principles were few indeed. The erroneous assumption had been that *all experimenters are guilty until proven innocent.* One researcher, arguing thusly, amusingly (but realistically) held that the most flagrant abuse of human participants is one for which our principles of research ethics offered no real cure. He thought that there were few studies in which human participants have suffered, but in many studies

. . . the time and energy of human subjects have been wasted . . . when 80% of the papers submitted to leading journals are rejected—usually because of poor conceptualization, faulty methodology, or the triviality of the hypotheses—it is apparent that a lot of human effort is being squandered. Of course, mistakes occur in the best of families, and even the most astute researcher is going to run off a few duds. But I think the evidence suggests that some of the people who are doing psychological research ought to be doing something else instead. By changing their occupational specialty, they might save themselves a lot of headaches and disappointments, simplify the task of journal editors, and, most importantly, avoid imposing on the precious time of the subjects who serve in their experiments. If psychological research has a bad name, it is probably not because we injure a lot of subjects but because we involve subjects in trivial, ill-conceived, or clumsily executed studies. What I am proposing is that every potential researcher be allotted a quota of studies during which he must demonstrate that he is not wasting his own and his subjects' time. Those who exhaust the allotted quota without producing anything worth while should have their hunting licenses withdrawn. Such a system might make all of us a little more careful about bestowing the PhD mantle on candidates of doubtful research competence and ingenuity. Perhaps I can call [this principle] the compulsory withdrawal of hunting licenses. (Steiner, 1972, p. 768)

Regulations can restrict creativity and freedom for scientific inquiry, so that a researcher may play it safe and resort to studies that have but limited value. To be creative in research, some kind of risk is required. Furthermore, following and administering the regulations can be costly and time consuming—the energies involved by both the researcher and the regulator could be better used to advance research itself.

Animal research has some special characteristics that deserve comment. In spite of the fact that researchers have adhered to humane principles in the conduct of research with animals and that relevant professions have carefully policed themselves, periodically in history there have emerged national movements to attempt to stymie laboratory research with animals. Propaganda appealing to emotions has been widespread, and organized raids on respectable scientific laboratories have been conducted. Not only have these raids been illegal, but the destruction and graffiti left on the walls can only be described as acts of lunacy. Such disoriented raiders obviously do not understand the great benefit for society of scientific research. As Miller (1985) has summarized, the use of animals for scientific research has considerably advanced our knowledge about various species as well as having benefited mankind in numerous ways. Perhaps such raiders confuse the use of animals for scientific research with some treatments of animals by nonscientists. For instance, the slaughtering of baby seals, the torturing of animals in satanic rituals, the use of animals for testing cosmetics, and the slaughter of animals for other purposes could hardly be condoned by any humane person.

Still, the issues involved in scientific research are sometimes very delicate and complex. Scientists have conducted numerous symposia to study some of the cases that pose difficult ethical dilemmas. Sensitive areas are toxicity testing, chronic pain research, use of long-term restraint devices, and the use of conscious paralyzed animals. To illustrate by briefly elaborating on the issue of pain, if we are to understand how to control it, it must in some sense be produced. Just how do you get relevant information about the elimination or prevention of pain without producing the phenomenon either in humans or animals? If we are to continue making advances in the reduction of the tremendous amount of pain suffered by humans, as well as by animals, we obviously cannot just stop our research efforts. But we must continue them in as wise fashion as possible.

The topic of ethics for research, like any consideration of ethical principles, is exceedingly complex and the subject of considerable scholarly and practical controversy. For one thing, ethics are relative to a given culture or subculture so that what is considered right or wrong may vary considerably throughout the world and at different periods in history. By our current standards, the atrocious medical experiments conducted by the Nazis before and during World War II were among the most flagrant ethical violations in our history. Nevertheless, they were condoned and vigorously supported within the Nazi frame of reference. In addition, what is right or wrong depends in part on who is doing the perceiving. What we can, in general, agree on is that in contemporary science, principles such as those we have advanced here are widely adhered to. Society can feel secure that science itself is safeguarding the rights, welfare, and dignity of participants used in research.

appendix E

ANSWERS TO PROBLEMS

In the event that your answers to the computed values of the statistical tests approximate, but do not precisely equal, those following, you should first consider the "number of places" used in the different computations to understand discrepancies.

CHAPTER 4

1. The confounding in this study is especially atrocious. The participants in the two groups undoubtedly differ in a large number of respects other than type of method. For instance, there may be differences in intelligence, opportunity to study, and socioeconomic level, as well as differences in reading proficiency prior to learning by either method, and certainly there were different teachers. The proper approach would be to assign participants randomly from the same class in a given school to two groups and then to determine randomly which group is taught by each method, both groups being taught by the same instructor.

2. The characteristics of the individual tanks and targets are confounded with the independent variable. It may be that one tank gun is more accurate than the other and that one set of targets is easier to hit than the other. To control these variables one might have all participants fire from the same tank at the same targets, or have half of the participants from each group could fire from each tank onto each set of targets. Firing the machine gun itself gave that group extra practice, too—another confound.

3. Undoubtedly these classes differ in a number of respects, among which is age at which they are toilet trained. The dependent variable results may thus be due to some other difference between the groups such as amount of social

stimulation or amount of money spent on family needs. The obvious, but difficult, way to conduct this experiment to establish a causal relation would be to select a group of children randomly, randomly assign them to two groups, and then randomly determine the age at which each group is toilet trained.

4. The control group should also be operated on except that the hypothalamus should not be impaired. Some structure other than the hypothalamus that may be responsible for the "missing" behavior could have been disturbed during the operation, or perhaps just the trauma of the operation itself affected behavior.

5. There may be other reasons for not reporting an emotionally loaded word than that it is not perceived. For instance, *sex* may actually be perceived, but the participant may wait until being absolutely sure that that is the word, possibly saving the person from a "social blunder." In addition, the frequency with which the loaded and neutral words are used in everyday life undoubtedly differs, thus affecting the threshold for recognition of the words. A better approach would be to start with a number of words that are emotionally neutral (or with nonsense syllables), and make some of them emotionally loaded (such as associating a noxious stimulus with them). The loaded and neutral words should be equated for frequency of use.

6. One should not accept this conclusion, because there is no control for the effects of suggestion. The control group should have experienced some treatment similar to that of the experimental group, such as having a different pattern of needles inserted beneath the skin. Studies that have controlled for the effects of suggestion have indicated no such differences between acupuncture and placebo groups. Other scientific studies have independently confirmed that merely suggesting that pain will be reduced through experimental techniques is sufficient to lead patients to report decreased pain. Finally, it would have been stronger to show that the experimental group was superior to the control group.

7. This research does not allow us to draw any conclusions because of its faulty methodology in a number of respects. The two groups of students probably differed before the research was started. Not randomly assigning students to the two classes, but allowing them to be selected on the basis of class hours, produces a confound. The instructor's belief in the relative efficacy of the methods may have influenced performance of students in the two classes. Hence the students being taught by the pass-fail method may have out-performed what would have been normal for them. The most serious methodological criticism is that failure to find a difference between groups does not allow one to conclude that the two methods are equally effective. There are an infinite number of possible reasons why two conditions in any study may *not* differ significantly, only one of which is that the (population) means on the dependent-variable scores of the two groups are equal. (As we shall see later, failure to reject the null hypothesis is not equivalent to accepting the null hypothesis.) A much more likely reason for failing to find a reliable difference between groups is that there is excessive experimental error in the conduct of the research; typically this is due to poor control methodology. Finally, casual observation of a difference in "classroom atmosphere" hardly provides the kind of information on which an educational curriculum should be based. Regardless, as an extension of this kind of conclusion, one could probably predict that a course in which there were no grades at all would result in *total* freedom from "grade-oriented tensions."

CHAPTER 6

2-A. With 26 *df*, a *t* of 2.14 is reliable beyond the 0.05 level. Hence the null hypothesis may be rejected.

2-B. With 30 *df*, a *t* of 2.20 is reliable beyond the 0.05 level. Since this was the criterion set for rejecting the null hypothesis, and since the direction of the means is that specified by the empirical hypothesis, it may be concluded that the empirical hypothesis was confirmed—that the independent variable influenced the dependent variable.

2-C. With 13 *df*, the computed *t* of 4.30 is reliable beyond the 0.01 level. Since the group that received the tranquilizer had the lesser mean psychotic tendency, it may be concluded that the drug produces the advertised effect.

2-D. The computed *t* of 0.51 is not reliable. Since the experimenter could not reject the null hypothesis, the empirical hypothesis was not confirmed.

2-E. The suspicion is not confirmed—the computed t is 0.10.

CHAPTER 7

3-A.

Summary Table for an Analysis of Variance among Majors

Source of Variation	Sum of Squares	df	Mean Square	F
Among groups	55.17	2	27.58	7.81
Within groups	31.75	9	3.53	
Total	86.93	11		

With 2 and 9 degrees of freedom we find that our computed F (7.81) exceeds the required value of 4.26 at the 0.05 level. Consequently we reject the overall null hypothesis and conclude that there is a reliable difference among majors.

3-B.   groups 1 versus 2: $t = 0.70$
groups 2 versus 3: $t = 8.14*$
groups 3 versus 4: $t = 25.08*$
groups 4 versus 5: $t = 0.75$
*$P < 0.05$

Since the criterion for testing the null hypothesis was unspecified, it is assumed to be $P = 0.05$. Only the differences between groups 2 and 3 and between 3 and 4 are reliable. We note that the means for the five groups are as follows: $\bar{X}1 = 1.10$, $\bar{X}2 = 1.50$, $\bar{X}3 = 7.20$, $\bar{X}4 = 23.50$, and $\bar{X}5 = 23.90$. There seems to be a rather dramatic increase in proficiency between trials 30 and 70, with a leveling off with 70 trials of practice. Since the difference between the means of 7.20 versus 23.50 is reliable, and since the mean difference between groups 4 and 5 is not reliable, 70 training trials seems like an appropriate number to recommend based on the data of this experiment.

3-C.   groups A versus B: $t = 7.52*$
groups A versus C: $t = 5.87*$
groups B versus C: $t = 11.65*$
*$P < 0.05$

We can see that each t would have been reliable beyond the 0.05 level, but since we are making all possible comparisons we will further employ the Bonferroni test. Consequently, the adjusted criterion for testing each partial null hypothesis is 0.017. By consulting the t table we can see that each t has a probability associated with it beyond the 0.017 level. Consequently, we can reject each null hypothesis and conclude that each group is reliably different from each other group. We further note that the group means are as follows: for method A, $\bar{X} = 15.05$; for method B, $\bar{X} = 24.30$; and for the normal method, $\bar{X} = 8.45$. Since method B resulted in reliably higher scores than did either of the other methods, that method is to be preferred.

CHAPTER 8

4-A.

Type of Psychosis	Amount of Drug Administered		
	None	2 cc	4 cc
Paranoid			
Manic-depressive			
Schizophrenic			

4-B.

Analysis of Variance

Source of Variation	Sum of Squares	df	Mean Square	F
Overall among	(275.88)	(3)		
Between brands	0.03	1	0.03	0.02
Between filters	0.23	1	0.23	0.12
B × F	275.62	1	275.62	144.30
Within groups	68.90	36	1.91	
Total	344.78	39		

Since the F for "between drugs" is reliable, variation of this independent variable is effective. The mean score for the participants who received drugs is higher than that for those who did not receive drugs. Hence we may conclude that administration of the drug led to an increase in normality. The lack of reliable *F*s for the "between psychoses" and interaction sources of variation indicates that there is no difference in normality as a function of type of psychosis, nor is there an interaction between the variables.

4-C.

	Amount of Drug Administered		
Type of Psychosis	*None*	*2 cc*	*4 cc*
Paranoid			
Manic depressive			
Schizophrenic			

4-D.

	Amount of Drug Administered			
Type of Participant	*None*	*2 cc*	*4 cc*	*6 cc*
Paranoid				
Manic-depressive				
Schizophrenic				
Normal				

4-E.

	Type of Brand	
Filter	*Old Zincs*	*Counts*
Without filter		
With filter		

4-F.

Analysis of Variance

Source of Variation	*Sum of Squares*	*df*	*Mean Square*	*F*
Overall among	(275.88)	(3)		
Between brands	0.03	1	0.03	0.02
Between filters	0.23	1	0.23	0.12
B × F	275.62	1	275.62	144.30
Within groups	68.90	36	1.91	
Total	344.78	39		

Since neither variation of brands nor filters resulted in reliable differences, we may conclude that variation of these variables, considered by themselves, did not affect steadiness. However, the interaction was reliable. From this we may conclude that whether brand affects steadiness depends on whether a filter was used—that smoking Old Zincs with a filter leads to greater steadiness than does smoking Counts with a filter, but that smoking Counts without a filter leads to greater steadiness than does smoking Old Zincs without a filter. It would appear that putting a filter on Counts decreases steadiness, but putting a filter on Old Zincs increases steadiness. In fact, Counts without a filter led to about the same amount of steadiness as Old Zincs with a filter, as a diagram of the interaction would show. But we don't recommend that you smoke either brand.

4-G.

Analysis of Variance

Source of Variation	*Sum of Squares*	*df*	*Mean Square*	*F*
Overall among	(80.68)	(3)	26.89	
Between opium	30.04	1	30.04	27.81
Between marijuana	48.89	1	48.89	45.27
O × M	1.75	1	1.75	1.62
Within groups	26.00	24	1.08	
Total	106.68	27		

Since the *F*s for "between opium" and "between marijuana" are both reliable, we can conclude that smoking both of them led to hallucinatory activity and that there is no interaction between these two variables since this latter source of variation is not reliable.

CHAPTER 9

2. The computed value of $r = 0.60$ with $df = 3$ is not statistically different from zero at the 0.05 level. From Table A-3 you can see that the required value would have been $r = 0.811$.

5-A. With 7 df, the computed t of 2.58 is reliable at the 0.05 level. Hence, the null hypothesis may be rejected. However, the participants who used the Eastern Grip had a higher mean score, from which we can conclude that the empirical hypothesis is not confirmed.

5-B. The computed t of 2.97 with 6 df is reliable beyond the 0.05 level. Since the experimental group had the higher mean score, the empirical hypothesis is confirmed.

5-C. With 19 df, the computed t of 6.93 is reliable beyond the 0.02 level. Since the group that used the training aid had the higher mean score, we may conclude that the training aid facilitated map-reading proficiency.

CHAPTER 11

9.

Summary of Analysis of Variance of the Memory Scores

Source of Variation	SS	df	MS	F
Among conditions	5,653.88	3	1,884.63	22.20
Among participants	1,821.63	9	202.40	2.38
Error	2,291.87	27	84.88	
Total	9,767.38	39		

Entering the table of t with 3 and 27 degrees of freedom for the among conditions and F = 22.20, we find that this source of variation is reliable. We may thus conclude that degree of meaningfulness of the nonsense syllables influenced the memory scores. With 9 and 27 degrees of freedom, we also find that the F of 2.38 for among participants is reliable at the 0.05 level, thus leading us to conlude that there is a reliable difference among participants.

GLOSSARY OF TERMS, STATISTICAL SYMBOLS, AND STATISTICAL EQUATIONS

Accidental universality: A relationship in which there is *no* element of necessity between the antecedent and consequent conditions, that is, a noncausal relationship (see Nomic Universality and Causality) (p. 38).

Additivity (statistical assumption): In using parametric statistics, one assumes that the treatment and error effects in an experiment are additive (p. 203).

Analysis of covariance: A technique used to control an extraneous variable statistically (p. 102).

Analysis of variance. A method of analyzing into components the total variance present in an experiment. By computing ratios between those components (with the F test), various empirical questions can be answered, such as whether two or more groups in an experiment differ reliably (p. 142).

Analytic statement: A statement that is always true (it cannot be false), but is empirically empty (p. 35).

A Posteriori comparisons: See Post Hoc Comparisons.

A Priori comparisons: See Planned Comparisons.

Asymmetrical transfer: When, in a repeated-treatments design, there is differential transfer such that the transfer from one condition to a second is different from the second to the first, as in counterbalancing (p. 67).

Balancing: A technique of controlling extraneous variables by assuring that they affect members of each group equally, e.g., the experimental group is affected equally with the control group (p. 63).

Behavior: A pattern of responses usually organized to accomplish some goal (p. 48).

Between-groups designs: Experimental designs in which there are two or more independent groups of participants such that each group receives a different amount of the independent variable. Contrasted with repeated-treatment designs (p. 197).

Bonferroni test: A procedure for adjusting the stated criterion for rejecting the null hypothesis to a more realistic criterion when the desire is to make more than the legitimate number of pairwise comparisons in a multigroup experiment. To conduct a Bonferroni test the stated probability level (e.g., 0.05) is divided by the number of possible comparisons (e.g., 3) and the resulting value (e.g., 0.017) is employed as the criterion for rejecting the null hypothesis (p. 141).

Causality: A process wherein the cause of an event may be instituted to produce that event, the effect. A cause-effect relationship is specified when an independent variable has systematically influenced a dependent variable in a well-conducted experiment (p. 189).

Cause-effect relationship: See Causality.

Cell: A "box" in a factorial design in which an experimental condition is represented (p. 155).

Central tendency, measure of: A statistical measure of a representative value of all measures in a distribution. Includes the mean, median, and mode (p. 104).

Chance: A concept that indicates that an event occurs with unspecified antecedents. In a completely deterministic world, chance would be an expression of our ignorance. To the extent to which there is a lack of order (chaos) in the world, events have no determinable antecedents (p. 4).

Circularity, vicious: Fallacious reasoning that occurs when an answer is based on a question and the question is based on the answer, with no appeal to outside, independent information (p. 29).

Clinical method: A method, also known as the *case history method* or *life history method*, in which an attempt is made to help an individual solve personal problems or to collect information about an individual's history. The probability of an evidence report resulting from this method is extremely low (p. 78).

Comparison group: See Control Group.

Concatenation: The characteristic of an interlocked, compatible system that adds an increment in probability to each component proposition within the system (p. 265).

Confirmation: The process of subjecting a statement (hypothesis, theory, law, and so on) to empirical test. The consequences may be that the probability of the statement is decreased (disconfirmed, not supported) or increased (confirmed, supported). Distinguished from *replication* in that replication refers to the repe-

tition of the methods of a scientific study (p. 273).

Confirmatory experiments: Those in which an explicit hypothesis is confirmed and subjected to test; contrasted with exploratory experiments (p. 83).

Confounding: The presence of an extraneous variable, systematically related to the independent variable, such that it might differentially affect the dependent variable values of the groups in the investigation (p. 57).

Constancy of conditions: A technique of control of extraneous variables by keeping them at the same value for all conditions throughout the experiment (p. 62).

Continuous variable: A variable that may change by any amount and thus may assume any fraction of a value—it may be represented by any point along a line (p. 6).

Contradictory statement: One that always assumes a truth value of false (p. 35).

Control, experimental: Techniques employed to insure that variation of a dependent variable is related to systematic manipulation of the independent variable and not to extraneous variables (p. 55).

Control group(s): The group(s) that receive some normal or standard or zero treatment condition. A primary function is to establish a standard against which the experimental treatment administered to the experimental group(s) may be evaluated. It is important to contrast *control group* with *comparison group*, in that the former identifies a component of an experiment versus a group of participants used in one of the nonexperimental methods (Chapters 4, 5 and 6) (p. 6).

Control of the independent variable: Systematic variation of the independent variable in a known and well-specified manner (pp. 56, 58).

Correlation: A measure of the extent to which two variables are related, most commonly measured by the Pearson product moment coefficient of correlation (r). The greater the absolute value of r, the stronger is the (linear) relationship between the two variables (p. 181).

Counterbalancing: A technique for controlling progressive effects in an experiment such that each condition is presented to each participant an equal number of times, and each condition must occur an equal number of times at each practice session. In complete counterbalancing all possible orders of the variables must be presented, as distinguished from incomplete counterbalancing (pp. 66, 223).

Crucial experiment: One in which all possible hypotheses are simultaneously tested so that the *true* one can be ascertained (pp. 83).

Cumulative record: A display of the total number of responses during an experimental period as a function of time. Changes in response rate may be ascertained from a cumulative record; if systematically related to the introduction or withdrawal of an experimental treatment they may be inferred to have been produced by those changes (p. 220).

Deductive inference: An inference that conforms to the rules of deductive (versus inductive) logic; consequently the conclusion is necessarily true, based on the premises (pp. 263, 267).

Degree of probability: A probability somewhere between 0 (absolutely false) and 1 (absolutely true) (p. 21).

Degrees of freedom: A value required in ascertaining the computed probability of the results of a statistical test (such as the *t*-test). There are different equations for each statistical test. Literally, the term specifies the number of independent observations that are possible for a source of variation minus the number of independent parameters that were used in estimating that variation computation (p. 128).

Dependent variable: Some well-defined aspect of behavior (a response) that is measured in a study. The value that it assumes is hypothesized to be dependent on the value assumed by the independent variable and thus is expected to be a change in behavior systematically related to the independent variable. The dependent variable is also dependent on extraneous variables, thus requiring control procedures (pp. 6, 48).

Design, experimental: A specific plan used in assigning participants to conditions, as in a two-group design (Chapter 6) or a factorial design (Chapter 8). The plan is for systematically varying independent variables and noting consequent changes in dependent variables. This definition distinguishes the design from the method of statistical analysis. *Experimental design* has also been used to include all of the steps of the experimental plan (pp. 89, 207).

Determinism: The assumption that events are lawful so that we can establish relationships between and among variables that are lasting or permanent. Although we cannot assert that the universe is completely deterministic, the assumption of determinism is necessary (though not sufficient) to obtain knowledge (p. 4).

Differential transfer: See Asymmetrical Transfer.

Direct statement: A sentence (proposition) that refers to a limited set of phenomena that are immediately observable (p. 272).

Disconfirmed: See Confirmation.

Discontinuous or discrete variable: A variable that can only assume numerical values that differ by clearly defined steps with no intermediate values possible, as in 1, 2, and so on, but not 1.67 (p. 6).

Discriminative stimulus (S^D): The presence of S^D sets the occasion for a specific behavior to occur (p. 219).

Double-blind experiment: A procedure in which the data collector is not informed of the nature of the hypothesis or in which experimental condition the participant is serving. The purpose is to eliminate experimenter effects on the dependent variable (pp. 73, 231).

Elimination: A technique for controlling extraneous variables by removing them from the experimental situation (p. 62).

Empiricism (empirical): The study of observable events in nature in an effort to solve problems. Empiricism is necessary for the formulation of a testable statement such as an empirical hypothesis or empirical law. Contrasted with Nativism (p. 3).

Environment: The sum total of stimuli that may affect an organism's receptors. The stimuli may be in the *external* environment, such as lights that excite the eye, or in the *internal* environment, e.g., muscle contractions that excite muscle spindle receptors for the kinesthetic modality. We assume that every receptor excitation results in some behavioral change, even though that change may be extremely slight, as in covert responses (p. 6).

Error variance: The error in an experiment, defined as the denominator of the *t* or the *F* ratios. See Experimental Error (pp. 196, 204, 235).

Evidence report: The summarized results of an empirical study that are used in the confirmation process for a hypothesis (pp. 92, 271).

Existential hypothesis: A statement that asserts that a relationship holds for at least one case (pp. 39, 275).

Experimental analysis of behavior: An approach to the study of behavior developed by B. F. Skinner for the broad purpose of predicting and controlling behavior. Single-participant research with replication is the basic methodology (pp. 218, 220).

Experimental error: The sum of all uncontrolled sources of variation that affect a dependent-variable measure. It is the denominator of statistical tests such as the *t*-test and the *F*-test (pp. 196, 204, 235).

Experimental group(s): The set(s) of individuals who receive the experimental treatment(s) (p. 5).

Experimental plan: The development of steps of an experiment necessary for the conduct of a study (p. 84).

Experimental treatment(s): The set of special conditions whose effect on behavior is to be evaluated. The term *treatment* is broader than is defined here for psychology and probably derives from the early development of experimental designs and statistics in the field of agriculture, where plots of ground were literally "treated" with different combinations of plant-nurturing substances (p. 7).

Experimentation: The application of the experimental method in which there is purposive manipulation of the independent variable (p. 80).

Explanation: The process of deducing a specific statement from a more general statement, thus explaining the specific statement (pp. 1, 19, 266).

Exploratory experiments: Contrasted with confirmatory experiments in that there is little knowledge about a given problem so that vague, poorly formed hypotheses are the only statements that can be used to guide the study (p. 83).

External validity: An index of the degree to which laboratory results can be generalized to behavior in the natural environment outside of the laboratory (p. 256).

Extraneous variable control: The regulation of the extraneous variables in a study (pp. 8, 56, 87).

Extraneous variables: Variables in an experimental or nonexperimental study that may operate freely to influence the dependent variables. Such variables need to be controlled or otherwise seriously considered in order not to invalidate the study (p. 60).

F-Test (F statistic): A ratio between two variances. In the analysis of variance it is used to determine whether an experimental effect is statistically significant (most frequently, whether there is a reliable difference among the means of several groups) (p. 147).

Factorial design: An experimental design in which all possible combinations of the selected values of each independent variable are used. This is a *complete* factorial design. One can thus determine the possible influence of two or more independent variables and ascertain possible interactions among them (pp. 19, 154).

Fixed effects model: A factorial design in which all values of the independent variables about which inferences are to be made are specified in the design (p. 280).

Frequency definition of probability: See Probability, Frequency Definition of.

Frequency distribution: A distribution of scores in which numerical value is usually plotted on the horizontal axis and the number (frequency) of individuals obtaining each score is indicated on the vertical axis. Many natural phenemona have a Gaussian (bell-shaped) distribution. (p. 350).

Fundamental definition: A general definition that encompasses specific definitions of a concept (p. 53).

General implication: A logical proposition of the form "If . . . , then . . .". If certain conditions hold, then certain other conditions should also hold (Chapter 3) (p. 36).

Generalization: An inductive inference from a specific set of data to a broader class of potential observations. We inductively infer that what is found to be true for a random sample is probably true for the universe for which the random sample is representative. Generalizations conform to the calculus of probability (pp. 10, 91, 93, 234, 266).

Graphic analysis: A visual process whereby changes in behavior are ascribed to systematic changes of the independent variable. The conclusion depends on whether behavioral changes are sufficiently large that they are readily observable with the naked eye (p. 221).

Hawthorne effect: An influence on behavior that occurs merely because of special attention paid to the participants, as in a research study. See Placebo effect (p. 253).

Homogeneity of variance: Statistical assumption of equal variances (p. 203).

Hypothesis: A testable statement of a potential relationship between variables that is advanced as a potential solution to a problem (p. 35).

Idiographic strategies: Intensive long-term study of the individual. Often used in developmental and longitudinal research (p. 217).

Impasse problem: A problem that is solvable, adequately phrased, and important, but an accumulation of experiments on the problem show contradictory results with no reason for such discrepancies (p. 30).

Independence (statistical assumption): The primary statistical assumption for a parametric analysis, namely, that each dependent-variable value statistically analyzed must be independent of each other dependent-variable value. Also critical for nonparametric statistics (p. 203).

Independent variable: An aspect of the environment that is empirically investigated for the purpose of determining whether it influences behavior (pp. 6, 48).

Independent variable, control of: The variation of the independent variable in a known and specified manner, which is the defining characteristic of an experiment. The lack of such purposive manipulation is characteristic of the method of systematic observation and other quasi-experimental designs (p. 58).

Indirect statement: A sentence (proposition) that cannot be directly tested but must be reduced to a set of direct statements for confirmation (p. 272).

Inductive schema: A concatenated representation of scientific reasoning processes, including inductive and deductive inferences, scientific generalizations, concatenation, explanation, and prediction (p. 261).

Inductive simplicity: The inference that the simplest relationship provides the preferred prediction (p. 134, 186).

Inference inductive: An inference that is less than certain ($P < 1.0$) and conforms to the calculus of probability. *Probability inference* is a synonym (p. 263).

Informed consent: A written agreement on record stating that the participant engaged in the research willingly and with knowledge about what was to happen (p. 92).

Interaction: There is an interaction between two or more independent variables if dependent-variable values obtained under levels of one independent variable behave differently under different levels of the other independent variable. Dependent-variable values related to one independent variable in a factorial design thus depend on, or vary systematically with, the values of another independent variable in that design (p. 157).

Intersubjective reliability: See Objectivity.

Irreversible effect: A set of operations is performed in such a way that subsequent measurements are permanently influenced by the effects of those original operations (pp. 204, 232).

Knowledge: A statement or collection of statements of relationships among variables that have been empirically confirmed. The statements may be strictly empirical ones or they may be theoretical (based on empirical findings) with varying amounts of systematic interrelations) (see Concatenation). The statements have been empirically confirmed with a reasonably high degree of probability (Chapter 10).

Latency: The time between the onset of a stimulus to the start of a response (p. 49).

Law: A statement of an empirical relationship between or among variables (preferably, between independent and dependent variables) that has a high degree of probability (pp. 55, 267).

Logical construct: A variable that is hypothesized to help account for unobserved events intervening between stimuli and responses (as used in psychology). Logical constructs may be of two varieties: (1) hypothetical constructs, and (2) intervening variables. The distinction is that hypothetical constructs have reality status whereas intervening variables are convenient fictions (p. 267).

Matched-groups design (paired-groups design): Efforts are made to have groups with essentially equal dependent-variable values before administration of experimental treatment by using a matching variable to increase equivalence (p. 190).

Matching variable: An objective, quantified measure to help assure equivalence of groups before treatment (p. 193).

Materialism: Traditionally, a monistic position of the mind-body problem in which it is asserted that there are only physicalistic events in the universe. Materialism is a necessary assumption for solving any problem and constitutes a foundation of science (p. 4).

Mean: The arithmetic average (see Statistical equations on p. 350) (p. 104).

Meaning: A statement has meaning (is meaningful) if it is testable. Otherwise, it is meaningless or untestable (see Metaphysics and Testable) (p. 22).

Mechanism: A classic position opposed to vitalism which asserts a mechanical model for understanding behavior. Organisms thus behave according to the principles of physics (p. 4).

Median: That value above which are 50 percent of the scores in a distribution and below which are 50 percent of the scores (p. 112).

Metaphysics: Disciplines, especially those of classical philosophy and religion, that pose some (not all) questions that are empirically unsolvable. The word *questions* is thus misused here and could better be replaced by *pseudoquestions* or *pseudoproblems* (p. 22).

Method of systematic observation: A nonexperimental method of the quasi-experimental variety in which events as they naturally occur are systematically studied (pp. 58, 81).

Mixed model: A factorial design in which some independent-variable values are fixed whereas others are random samples from the larger population of possible independent-variable values (p. 280).

Mode: The most frequently occurring value in a distribution (p. 112).

Morgan's canon: The principle advanced by C. Lloyd Morgan stating that animal activity should be interpreted in terms of processes which are lower in the scale of psychological evolution and development in preference to higher psychological processes, if that is possible (p. 42).

Multigroups design: A study in which there are more than two independent groups (p. 130).

Nativism: The philosophical position that knowledge is inborn, based on the doctrine of innate ideas. (Contrast with Empiricism.)

Naturalistic observation: Empirical inquiry in which there is no intervention with the phenomena being studied. Rather, there is only systematic gathering of data on behavior as it naturally occurs; consequently there is no effort to control extraneous variables (pp. 78, 254).

Nomic universality: A statement that expresses some element of necessity between the antecedent and consequent conditions, as distinguished from accidental universality (p. 38).

Nomothetic strategies: Efforts to study behavior by determining averages of groups of individuals. Typically used in cross-sectional research (p. 217).

Nonparametric statistics: Statistics for testing null hypotheses that do not require satisfying the standard assumptions for parametric statistics as specified on p. 203.

Normality (statistical assumption): The assumption that population distributions dealt within an empirical study are normal (p. 203).

Null hypothesis: A statement specifying characteristics of parameters (versus sample values) that are statistically evaluated. In this book the only form of a null hypothesis has been specifying that differences between parametric means are zero (pp. 106, 142, 149, 165).

Null hypothesis, overall (omnibus or complete): A statement that there is no difference among the means of several groups, i.e., that all population means are equal (contrast with Partial Null Hypothesis) (p. 142).

Objectivity: A necessary characteristic of scientific observations wherein a number of observers can agree that a given event with specified characteristics has occurred. It is the demand that knowledge be based on reliable, repeatable observations. The formal statement of objectivity is in a principle of intersubjective reliability (p. 4).

Occam's razor: The principle advanced by William of Occam that entities should not be multiplied without necessity. An instance of the principle of parsimony (p. 42).

One-group posttest-only design: A study in which one group of participants experiences a treatment, after which a dependent-variable measure is taken on them (p. 247).

One-tailed test: An application of the *t* or other test in which a hypothesis specifies the direction of group means. Consequently, only one tail of the *t* distribution is used, increasing the chances of rejecting a null hypothesis (See Two-Tailed Test) (p. 110).

Operant: A response class that can be objectively measured, consisting of responses with which the organism operates on the environment to produce such consequences as reinforcing stimuli (p. 219).

Operant conditioning: Conditioning in which an organism increases rate of responding beyond the operant level because the behavior is contingent on its consequences (p. 218).

Operant level: The frequency per unit of time (and therefore rate) with which a response is made prior to intervention with an experimental treatment. A synonym is baseline (p. 219).

Operational definition: One that indicates that a certain phenomenon exists by specifying the precise methods by which the phenomenon is measured (p. 24).

Operationism: A scientific movement the major assumption of which is that the adequate definition of variables is critical for progress. Those variables should be operationally defined (p. 26).

Order effects: The effects on behavior of presenting two or more experimental treatments to the same participant. Such order effects would not occur with the use of a between-groups design in which each participant receives only one treatment. See also Counterbalancing. (pp. 66, 223).

Paired-groups design: See Matched-Groups Design.

Pairwise comparisons, all possible: Making all possible comparisons between the separate groups taken two at a time (p. 141).

Pairwise comparisons, limited: Making comparisons only between certain pairs of groups to avoid inflating the computed value of P (p. 139).

Parameter: A measure ascertained from all possible observations in a population or universe, e.g., a population mean (μ) is distinguished from a sample mean $\overline{X}$ (p. 107).

Parsimony: The principle that the simplest explanation should be preferred to more complex explanations (pp. 42, 283).

Partial null hypothesis: A null hypothesis that states that there is no difference between any pair of group means on the dependent variable in a multigroup experiment (p. 149).

Participants (subjects): Those who collaborate in an experiment for the purpose of allowing their behavior to be studied (pp. 5, 303).

Pearson product moment coefficient of correlation: Karl Pearson's index of correlation is symbolized by r, and its value indicates the degree to which two variables are linearly related. The value of r varies between $+1.0$ (positive correlation) and -1.0 (negative correlation) (pp. 181, 187).

Pilot experiment: The initial stages of experimentation in which a small number of participants are studied in order to test and modify the experimental procedures (p. 83).

Placebo effect: Improvement in performance regardless of the nature of the treatment that occurred because of the suggestion that participating in a research study implies that something positive should happen to the participant. A placebo condition controls for suggestive effects due to heightened motivation and demand characteristics, since all participants can expect beneficial results (See Hawthorne Effect).

Planned (A Priori) Comparisons: Those between-group comparisons on a dependent-variable measure that are specified prior to observing the data. They are explicit tests of the empirical hypothesis (p. 138).

Population (or universe): All possible observations made according to specified rules (pp. 89, 106).

Post Hoc (A Posteriori) Comparisons: Those comparisons between groups that are made on the dependent-variable measure after the data have been studied (p. 138).

Potentially attainable: An achievement that may or may not come within the powers of people at some future time, but which is not possessed at the present (p. 22).

Potentially testable: A hypothesis that may or may not be testable, a concept that rests on the definition of "potentially attainable" (p. 23).

Prediction: To infer inductively the nature of an unobserved event on the basis of prior knowledge. *Postdiction* employs precisely the same inductive processes as prediction. The distinction is that in prediction the event has not yet occurred; when one postdicts, the event has already occurred but has not been systematically observed. One might thus predict some characteristics of the world in 1999, but postdict that Caesar visited Ireland (pp. 11, 269).

Presently attainable: This interpretation of "possible" states that the achievement is within our power at the present time (p. 22).

Presently testable: A hypothesis that satisfies the definition of "presently attainable" and thus may be assigned a degree of probability (p. 22).

Probability: As used in this context, the empirically determined likelihood that an event did or will occur. We may empirically determine the degree of probability for a statement as varying between 0.0 and 1.0 such that no empirical statement may have a probability of 0.0 (false) or 1.0 (true) (pp. 21, 38, 140).

Probability, frequency definition of: The ratio of number of success to all observed instances. With repeated unbiased observations, the series will eventually converge to a true value. For example, in unbiased coin flipping, one would determine that 50 percent of the instances were successes, which, when divided by 100 percent of the observations, would in the long run, yield the true probability of $P = 0.50$. This concept is fundamental to science (p. 21).

Probability inferences: See Inferences, Inductive.

Probability theory of testability (meaning): A proposition is testable if, and only if, it is possible to determine a degree of probability for it (p. 21).

Problems: Questions that initiate scientific inquiries. Hypotheses that are empirically testable are posed as solutions to problems. *Problems* are to be distinguished from *pseudo problems* ("unsolvable problems") that may appear to be real questions but, on further examination, are seen to be impossible to attack through empirical means (pp. 5, 16).

Pseudohypotheses: Statements that appear to be testable hypotheses but in fact are untestable (p. 24).

Pseudoproblem: See Problems.

Pseudostatements: See Pseudohypotheses.

Purposive Manipulation: Systematic control of an independent variable in an experiment. Contrasted with selection of independent variable values. See Independent Variable, Control of. (p. 59).

Quasi-experimental design: A design that resembles that of an experiment, but participants are not randomly assigned to treatments, nor are the treatments randomly determined for the groups. Consequently they are always confounded (p. 244).

Random effects model: A factorial design model in which the independent-variable values represent a random sample from the population of possible independent-variable values (p. 280).

Randomization: A process by which each member of a universe has an equal probability of being selected, as in a table of random numbers (pp. 5, 69, 90, 100).

Random sample: A sample (in psychology usually of participants) that is selected from a population such that all possible individuals have equal probabilities of being selected (p. 89).

Range: The highest measure in a distribution minus the lowest measure. A measure of variability (p. 114).

Rate of responding: The frequency of responding for a given period of time (p. 51).

Reinforcer: A stimulus that, when it is contingent on a response, increases the response rate. This is positive reinforcement. Negative reinforcement is the withdrawal of a noxious stimulus, which similarly increases response rate (p. 219).

Reliable difference: See Significant.

Reliability: The extent to which the same observations are obtained in repeated studies (pp. 4, 9, 51, 102, 188).

Repeated-treatments designs (within-groups designs): Experimental designs in which participants receive two or more values on the independent variable. Contrasted with between-groups designs (p. 197).

Replication: The conduct of an additional study in which the method of the first (usually an experiment) is precisely repeated. The term is sometimes used to indicate that the results of the second experiment confirmed the first, although this is a confusion of confirmation and replication (repeating). In confirming, one repeats *and* obtains the same findings. Similar, but different, uses occur in statistics (pp. 14, 278).

Representative sample: A sample that has certain characteristics in the same proportion as for the population from which it was drawn. A random sample from a population may be assumed to be representative of the population (p. 277).

Response: The contraction of muscle (skeletal, smooth, or cardiac) or the secretion of glands that constitute the components of behavior (p. 48).

Sample: A subset of observations from a population (p. 89).

Scattergram (scatterplot): A graph of the relationship between two measures on the same individuals to visually illustrate the data points on which a coefficient of correlation is based (p. 182).

Science: The application of the scientific method to solve problems. (For other definitions, see pp. 1–3.)

Science (applied, technological, practical): The activity of solving problems of immediate need in everyday life. Many of these problems can be solved by the application of the fruits of pure science whereas others require the conduct of empirical research "in the field" (p. 244).

Science (pure, basic): The conduct of systematic inquiries only for the sake of knowledge itself, without regard to the solution of practical problems. Our universities are the primary agents for the search for knowledge for its own sake, and for the retention of that knowledge for society (p. 244).

Scientific method: A serial process by which the sciences obtain answers to their questions (pp. 5, 11).

Serendipity: The finding of something unexpected that is more valuable than the original purpose of the research (p. 43).

Significant: Used in statistics to indicate reliability. We say a statistical test such as the *t*-test may be statistically significant (reliable) when the null hypothesis is rejected, thus indicating that the phenomenon being studied is a reliable one (p. 10).

Single-blind strategy: Participants are unaware of the nature of the experimental condition, such as being ignorant of a drug versus a placebo phase (p. 216).

Solvable problem: A problem that poses a question that can be answered with the use of our normal capacities (pp. 3, 20).

Standard deviation: A measure of variability of a frequency distribution. See "Glossary of Statistical Equations" on p. 350.

Statistic: A value that is computed from observations of a sample from a population, e.g., a sample mean is X (p. 107).

Statistical test: Used to tell whether an event is reliable, rather than simply due to random fluctuations (chance), e.g., the difference between two groups in a single experiment (p. 9).

Stimuli: Energies of the environment (the surroundings in which we live) that affect responses (aspects of behavior) (p. 6).

Stratification: A process by which participants are classified along a dimension for the purpose of ascertaining whether some measure of behavior is systematically related to that dimension (p. 282).

Subjects: See Participants.

Sum of squares: Valves computed between groups, within groups, and total as in components of an analysis of variance (p. 104).

Synthetic statement: One that may be *either* true or false, or more precisely, has a probability varying between 0.0 and 1.0 (p. 35).

Technology: See Science (Applied).

Testable: A statement that may be directly (or indirectly, as with theories) subjected to empirical confirmation. A testable statement is one for which a determinable degree of probability may be assigned to it, in accordance with the probability theory of testability (p. 22).

Theory: A statement of a relationship between two or more variables. The term carries the connotation that it is usually more general than laws and due to concatenation with other statements, has a higher degree of possibility. Theory may also include logical constructs which themselves have not been directly observed, in which case they are indirect statements (p. 267).

Time-series designs: A subclass of repeated-treatments designs. They are quasi-experimental designs in observations of behavior, etc., and are made over a period of time (p. 237).

Truth value: The characteristic of a statement's being true or false (p. 35).

Two-independent-groups design: A study in which participants are in only one of two groups (p. 99).

Two-randomized-groups design: The random assignment of participants to two independent groups (p. 99).

Two-tailed test: Application of a statistical test such as the *t*-test in which the empirical hypothesis does not specify a direction of group means. Consequently, both tails of the *t* distribution are used (See One-Tailed Test) (p. 110).

Unilateral verifiability: The characteristic of a hypothesis as being verifiable as false but not as true or vice versa (p. 275).

Universal hypothesis: A statement that asserts that a given relationship holds for all variables contained herein, for all time and at all places (pp. 39, 274).

Unsolvable problem: A statement that appears to be a problem but is a pseudo-question and thus is unanswerable. Such pseudo-problems often concern supernatural phenomena or questions about ultimate causes (pp. 3, 20).

Validity: The characteristic that a psychological test or, in experimentation, a dependent variable, measures what it purports to measure. A valid dependent-variable measure is essential for the conduct of an experiment (p. 50).

Variability, measure of: An index of how values of a distribution are "spread out," indicating the nature of the distribution. Variability measures also tell us about the range of scores in the group (p. 112).

Variable: Anything that can change in value and thus assume different numerical values (p. 6).

Variance: The standard deviation multiplied by itself. When used in the analysis of variance, it is an effort to specify the components of the total variability of dependent-variable measures in a research study (p. 112).

Verification: A process of determining that a hypothesis is strictly true or false, as contrasted with confirmation (pp. 29, 273).

Vicious circularity: See Circularity, Vicious.

Withdrawal design: An $N = 1$ design in which the experimental treatment is introduced following a baseline period and then withdrawn to determine whether response rate returns to operant level (p. 223).

GLOSSARY OF STATISTICAL SYMBOLS

df	Degrees of freedom
η (eta)	The correlation coefficient (general-

ized for curvilinear or linear correlation)

F	The *F*-test, a ratio between two variances
MS	Mean square
μ (mu)	Mean of a population
n	Number of participants in a group
N	Total number of participants in a research study
P	Probability, as in the computed probability of a statistical test such as the *t*-test
$\ni_p$	Probability inference to the degree *p*
r	Pearson product moment coefficient of (linear) correlation
r_S	Spearman rank coefficient of (linear) correlation
s	Standard deviation of a sample
s^2	Variance of a sample
σ	Standard deviation of a population
Σ	Summation sign instructing you to add values to the right of it
SS	Sum of squares
t	Student's *t*-test
$\overline{X}$	Mean of a sample

GLOSSARY OF STATISTICAL EQUATIONS
(enumerated as identified in the text)

I. To summarize a frequency distribution (Chapter 6):

The mean (6-1),

$$\overline{X} = \frac{\Sigma X}{n}$$

Standard deviation (6-4),

$$s = \sqrt{\frac{n\Sigma X^2 - (\Sigma X)^2}{n(n - 1)}}$$

Standard deviation computed from sum of squares (6-5),

$$s = \sqrt{\frac{SS}{n - 1}}$$

Variance,

$$s^2 = s \times s$$

II. To determine whether the sample means of two independent groups reliably differ (Chapter 6):

Student's t (6-2),

$$t = \frac{\overline{X}_1 - \overline{X}_2}{\sqrt{\left[\frac{SS_1 + SS_2}{(n_1 - 1) + (n_2 - 1)}\right]\left(\frac{1}{n_1} + \frac{1}{n_2}\right)}}$$

The degrees of freedom,

$$df = N - 2$$
$$df = n_1 + n_2 - 2$$

III. To test an overall null hypothesis for the case of more than two randomized groups (Chapter 7):

The sums of squares are computed as follows:

Total sums of squares (7-2),

$$\text{total } SS = (\Sigma X_1^2 + \Sigma X_2^2 + \cdots + \Sigma X_r^2)$$
$$- \frac{(\Sigma X_1 + \Sigma X_2 + \Sigma X_3 + \cdots + \Sigma X_r)^2}{N}$$

Among sums of squares (7-3),

among $SS =$

$$\frac{(\Sigma X_1)^2}{n_1} + \frac{(\Sigma X_2)^2}{n_2} + \frac{(\Sigma X_3)^2}{n_3} + \cdots + \frac{(\Sigma X_r)^2}{n_r}$$
$$- \frac{(\Sigma X_1 + \Sigma X_2 + \Sigma X_3 + \cdots + \Sigma X_r)^2}{N}$$

Within sums of squares (7-4),

Within $SS = $ total $SS - $ among SS

To compute the degrees of freedom:

Total df (7-7),

total $df = N - 1$

Among df (7-8),

among $df = r - 1$

Within df (7-9),

within $df = N - r$

To conduct the appropriate F-test:

$$F = \frac{\text{mean square among groups}}{\text{mean square within groups}}$$

IV. To make all possible pairwise comparisons in a multigroup experiment (Chapter 7).

The Bonferroni test: Divide the stated probability (e.g., 0.05) by the number of possible comparisons (C_p) and use the adjusted probability value as the criterion for testing each pairwise comparison.

The number of possible pairwise comparisons in a multigroup experiment is

C_p (7-1),
$$C_p = \frac{r(r - 1)}{2}$$

V. To analyze a 2 × 2 factorial design:

Compute the sums of squares:

total SS (8-1),

$$\text{Total } Ss = (\Sigma X_1^2 + \Sigma X_2^2 + \Sigma X_3^2 + \Sigma X_4^2$$
$$- \frac{(\Sigma X_1 + \Sigma X_2 + \Sigma X_3 + \Sigma X_4)^2}{N}$$

Among SS (8-2)

among $SS =$

$$\frac{(\Sigma X_1)^2}{n_1} + \frac{(\Sigma X_2)^2}{n_2} + \frac{(\Sigma X_3)^2}{n_3} + \frac{(\Sigma X_4)^2}{n_4}$$
$$- \frac{(\Sigma X_1 + \Sigma X_2 + \Sigma X_3 + \Sigma X_4)^2}{N}$$

Within SS (8-3),

within $SS = $ total $SS - $ overall among SS

Between-A SS (8-4),

between-A SS

$$= \frac{(\Sigma X_1 + \Sigma X_2)^2}{n_1 + n_2} + \frac{(\Sigma X_3 + \Sigma X_4)^2}{n_3 + n_4}$$
$$- \frac{(\Sigma X_1 + \Sigma X_2 + \Sigma X_3 + \Sigma X_4)^2}{N}$$

A × B SS (8-6),

A × B SS = overall among SS

− between-A SS − between-B SS

To compute the degrees of freedom,

total $df = N - 1$

overall among $df = r - 1$

within $df = N - r$

The components of the overall among df are

between $df = r - 1$

between A = 2 − 1 = 1

between B = 2 − 1 = 1

A × B df = (number of df for between-A)

× (number of df for between-B)

VI. To compute a Pearson product moment coefficient of correlation:

r_{XY} (9-1),

$$r_{XY} = \frac{n\Sigma XY - (\Sigma X)(\Sigma Y)}{\sqrt{[n\Sigma X^2 - (\Sigma X)^2][n\Sigma Y^2 - (\Sigma Y)^2]}}$$

(9-2) $df = N - 2$

VIII. To compute a paired t-test:

t (9-3),

$$t = \frac{\overline{X}_1 - \overline{X}_2}{\sqrt{\dfrac{\Sigma D^2 - \dfrac{(\Sigma D)^2}{n}}{n(n - 1)}}}$$

IX. A generalized equation for the t-test:

t (9-4),

$$t = \frac{\overline{X}_1 - \overline{X}_2}{\sqrt{\dfrac{s_1^2}{n_1} + \dfrac{s_2^2}{n_2} - 2\,(r_{12})\left(\dfrac{s_1}{\sqrt{n_1}}\right)\left(\dfrac{s_2}{\sqrt{n_2}}\right)}}$$

X. To determine whether there is a reliable difference between two repeated treatments:

t (9-6),

$$t = \frac{\overline{X}_D}{\sqrt{\dfrac{\Sigma D^2 - \dfrac{(\Sigma D)^2}{n}}{n(n - 1)}}}$$

XI. To test for a reliable difference among more than two repeated treatments (e.g., four conditions):

First compute the sums of squares as follows:

Total SS (9-7),

total $SS = (\Sigma X_1^2 + \Sigma X_2^2 + \Sigma X_3^2 + \Sigma X_4^2)$
$$- \frac{(\Sigma X_1 + \Sigma X_2 + \Sigma X_3 + \Sigma X_4)^2}{N}$$

among-conditions SS (9-8),

among-conditions $SS =$

$$\frac{(\Sigma X_1)^2}{n_1} + \frac{(\Sigma X_2)^2}{n_2} + \frac{(X_3)^2}{n_3} + \frac{(\Sigma X_4)^2}{n_4}$$
$$- \frac{(\Sigma X_1 + \Sigma X_2 + \Sigma X_3 + \Sigma X_4)}{N}$$

Among-participants SS (9-9),

among-participants SS

$$= \frac{(\Sigma S_1)^2}{K} + \frac{(\Sigma S_2)^2}{K} + \cdots \frac{(\Sigma S_n)^2}{K}$$
$$- \frac{(\Sigma X_1 + \Sigma X_2 + \Sigma X_3 + \Sigma X_4)^2}{N}$$

Error SS (9-10),

error SS = total SS − among-conditions SS

− among-participants SS

The equations for computing degrees of freedom are:

Total *df* (11-6),

$$\text{total } df = N - 1$$

Among conditions (11-7),

$$\text{among conditions} = K - 1$$

Among participants (11-8),

$$\text{among participants} = n - 1$$

The *F*-tests are made as follows:

$$\text{among conditions} = \frac{\text{mean square among conditions}}{\text{error}}$$

$$\text{among participants} = \frac{\text{mean square among participants}}{\text{error}}$$

REFERENCES

AMERICAN PSYCHOLOGICAL ASSOCIATION. (1990). Ethical principles of psychologists. *American Psychologist, 45*, 390–395

AMERICAN PSYCHOLOGICAL ASSOCIATION. (1983). *Publication manual.* Washington, D.C.: American Psychological Association.

ASHER, R. (1958). Why are medical journals so dull? *British Medical Journal, 2*, 502.

BABICH, F. R., JACOBSON, A. L., BUBASH, SUZANNE, & JACOBSON, ANN. (1965). Transfer of a response to naive rats by injection of ribonucleic acid extracted from trained rats. *Science, 149*, 656–657.

BACHRACH, A. J. (1965). *Psychological research: An introduction* (2nd ed.). New York: Random House.

BARBER, T. X. (1976). *Pitfalls in human research: Ten pivotal points.* New York: Pergamon.

BARLOW, DAVID, H., & HERSEN, MICHEL. (1984). *Single case experimental designs.* New York: Pergamon.

BERKOWITZ, L., & DONNERSTEIN, E. (1982). External validity is more than skin deep. *American Psychologist, 37*, 245–257.

BERRY, D. S., & McARTHUR, L. Z. (1986). Perceiving character in faces: The impact of age-related craniofacial changes on social perception. *Psychological Bulletin, 100*, 3–18.

BERSH, P. J. (1951). The influence of two variables upon the establishment of a secondary reinforcer for operant responses. *Journal of Experimental Psychology, 41*, 62–73.

BINDER, A., McCONNELL, D., & SJOHOLM, N. A. (1957). Verbal conditioning as a function of experimenter characteristics. *Journal of Abnormal and Social Psychology, 55*, 309–314.

CAMPBELL, D. T. (1969). Reforms as experiments. *American Psychologist, 24*, 409–429.

CAMPBELL, D. T., & STANLEY, J. C. (1963). Experimental and quasi-experimental designs for research. *Handbook of research on teaching.* Skokie, Ill.: Rand McNally.

CANNON, W. B. (1945). *The way of an investigation.* New York: W. W. Norton.

CONANT, J. B. (1951). *On understanding science: An historical approach.* New York: New American Library.

COOK, T. D., & CAMPBELL, D. T. (1979). *Quasi-*

experimentation: Design and analysis issues for field settings. Skokie, Ill.: Rand McNally.

COREN, S. (1986). Computerizing the perception laboratory: Surviving the transition. *Behavior Research Methods, Instruments, & Computers, 18*, 637–643.

DAHLQUIST, L. M., & GIL, K. M. (1986). Using parents to maintain improved dental flossing skills in children. *Journal of Applied Behavior Analysis, 19*, 255–260.

DAVIS, W. B. (1983). *The effect of the degree of perceptual salience and perceptual difficulty on covert oral responses.* Unpublished doctoral dissertation, University of Louisville, Louisville, Kentucky.

DOYLE, A. C. (1938). *Sherlock Holmes.* Garden City, N.Y.: Garden City Press.

DUBS, H. H. (1930). *Rational induction.* Chicago: University of Chicago Press.

EBBINGHAUS, E. (1913). *Memory: [A contribution to experimental psychology]* (H. A. Ruger & C. E. Busserius, trans.). New York: Columbia University Press.

ETZEL, B. C., LeBLANC, J. M., & BAER, D. M. (1977). *New developments in behavioral research: Theory, method and applications.* Hillside, N.J.: Lawrence Erlbaum.

ETZIONI, A. (1975). Effects of small computers on scientists. *Science, 189*, 347.

EYSENCK, H. J. (1983). Special review [review of M. L. Smith, G. V. Glass, & T. I. Miller, *The benefits of psychotherapy*]. *Behaviour Research and Therapy, 21*, 315–320.

FARMER, E. (1924). *A comparison of different shift systems in the glass trade* (Report 24, Medical Research Council, Industrial Fatigue Research Board). London: Her Majesty's Stationery Office.

FISHER, A. E. (1964). Chemical stimulation of the brain. *Psychobiology.* San Francisco: W. H. Freeman. Copyright © 1964 by Scientific American. All rights reserved.

FISHER, R. A. (1953). *The design of experiments* (6th ed.). New York: Hafner Press.

FISHER, R. A. (1949). *Statistical methods for research workers.* Edinburgh: Oliver and Boyd Ltd.

FISHER, R. A., & Yates, (1948). *Statistical tables for biological, agricultural and medical research.* (3rd Ed.) Edinburgh: Oliver and Boyd Ltd.

GELLER, E. S., RUSS, N. W., & ALTOMARI, M. G. (1986). Naturalistic observations of beer drinking among college students. *Journal of Applied Behavior Analysis, 19*, 391–396.

GLYMORE, C. (1980). *Theory and Evidence.* Princeton, N.J.: Princeton University Press.

GRICE, G. R., & HUNTER, J. J. (1964). Stimulus intensity effects depend upon the type of experimental design. *Psychological Review, 71*, 247–256.

"Guide for the Care and Use of Laboratory Animals," NIH Publication No. 85-23, Revised 1985, Office of Science and Health Reports, DRR/NIH, Bethesda, Md. 20205.

HARRIS, F. R., WOLF, M. M., & BAER, D. M. (1964). Effects of adult social reinforcement on child behavior. *Young Children, 20*, 8–17.

HEIDBREDER, E. (1933). *Seven psychologies.* Englewood Cliffs, N.J.: Prentice-Hall.

HEFFERLINE, R. F., KEENAN, B., & HARFORD, R. A. (1958). Escape and avoidance conditioning in human subjects without their observation of response. In F. J. McGuigan (ed.), 1966, *Thinking: Studies of covert language processes.* New York: Appleton-Century-Crofts, p. 209.

HEMPEL, C. G., & OPPENHEIM, P. (1948). The logic of explanation. *Philosophy of Science, 15*, 135–175.

HERNÁNDEZ-PEÓN, R., SCHERRER, H., & JOUVET, M. (1956). Modification of electric activity in cochlear nucleus during "attention" in unanesthetized cats. *Science, 123*, 331–332.

HOLLAND, B. S. & LOPENHAUER, M.D. (1988). Improved Bonferoni-type multiple testing procedures. *Psychological Bulletin, 104*, 145–149.

IMASHIOYA, H., DOLLINS, A. B., & KAKIGI, S. (1987). Motor response information influence on CNV shape and resolution time. *The Pavlovian Journal of Biological Science, 22*, 1–6.

JACOBSON, A. L., FRIED, C., & HOROWITZ, S. D. (1966). Planarians and memory. *Nature, 209*, 599–601.

JENKINS, J. G., & DALLENBACH, K. M. (1924). Oblivescence during sleep and waking. *American Journal of Psychology, 35*, 605–612.

JONES, F. P. (1964). Experimental method in antiquity. *American Psychologist, 19*, 419–420.

KAZDIN, A. (1982). *Single-case research designs.* New York: Oxford.

KERLINGER, F. N. (1986). *Foundations of behavioral research.* New York: Holt, Rinehart & Winston.

KRATOCHWILL, T. R. (1978). *Single subject research: Strategies for evaluating change.* New York: Academic Press.

LACHMAN, R., MEEHAN, J. T., & BRADLEY, ROSALEE. (1965). Observing response and word association in concept shifts: Two-choice and four-choice selective learning. *Journal of Psychology, 59,* 349–357.

LUSEBRINK, V. B. (1984). Visual imagery: Its psychophysiological components and levels of information processing. Unpublished doctoral dissertation, University of Louisville, Kentucky.

McGUIGAN, F. J. (1970). Covert oral behavior as a function of quality of handwriting. *The American Journal of Psychology, 83,* 337–88.

McGUIGAN, F. J. (1978). *Cognitive psychophysiology: Principles of covert behavior.* Englewood Cliffs, N.J.: Prentice-Hall.

McGUIGAN, F. J. (1956). Confirmation of theories in psychology. *Psychological Review, 63,* 98–104.

McGUIGAN, F. J. (1959). The effect of precision, delay and schedule of knowledge of results on performance. *Journal of Experimental Psychology, 58,* 79–84.

McGUIGAN, F. J. (1963). The experimenter: A neglected stimulus object. *Psychological Bulletin, 60,* 421–428.

McGUIGAN, F. J. (1993). *Biological Psychology—A Cybernetic Science.* Englewood Cliffs, N.J.: Prentice-Hall.

McGUIGAN, F. J., HUTCHENS, C., EASON, N., & REYNOLDS, T. (1964). The retroactive inference of motor activity with knowledge of results. *Journal of General Psychology, 70,* 270–281.

MILLER, N. E. (1985). The value of behavioral research on animals. *American Psychologist, 40,* 423–440.

MORGAN, C. L. (1906). *An introduction to a comparative psychology* (2nd ed.). London: Walter Scott.

OLLENDICK, T. H., SHAPIRO, E. S., & BARRETT, R. P. (1981). Reducing stereotypic behaviors: An analysis of treatment procedures utilizing an alternating treatments design. *Behavior Therapy, 12,* 570–577.

PAGE, I. H. (1957). Serotonin. *Scientific American, 197,* 52–56.

PAVLIK, W. B., & CARLTON, P. L. (1965). A reversed partial-reinforcement effect. *Journal of Experimental Psychology, 70,* 417–423.

POMERLEAU, C. S., & POMERLEAU, O. P. (1987). The effects of a psychological stressor on cigarette smoking and subsequent behavioral and physiological responses. *Psychophysiology, 24,* 278–285.

PORTER, P. B. (1973). A highly significant comment. *American Psychologist, 28,* 189–190.

ROETHLISBERGER, F. S., & DICKSON, W. J. (1939). *Management and the worker.* Cambridge, Mass.: Harvard University Press.

RYAN, T. A. (1980). Comment on "protecting the overall rate of type I errors for pairwise comparisons with an omnibus test statistic." *Psychological Bulletin, 88,* 354–355.

SIDMAN, M. (1960). *Tactics of scientific research.* New York: Basic Books.

SINGH, N. N., & MILLICHAMP, C. J. (1987). Independent and social play among profoundly mentally retarded adults: Training, maintenance, generalization, and long-term follow-up. *Journal of Applied Behavior Analysis, 20,* 23–34.

SKINNER, B. F. (1948). *Walden two.* New York: Macmillan.

SKINNER, B. F. (1959). *Cumulative record* (3rd ed.). Englewood Cliffs, N.J.: Prentice-Hall.

SKINNER, B. F. (1961). The design of cultures. *Daedalus,* 534–46.

SNEDECOR, G. W. (1956). *Statistical Methods.* (5th Ed.) Ames, Iowa: Iowa State College Press.

SPIRES, A. M. (1960). *Subject-experimenter interaction in verbal conditioning.* Unpublished doctoral dissertation, New York University.

STEINER, I. D. (1972). The evils of research: Or what my mother didn't tell me about the sins of academia. *American Psychologist, 27,* 766–768.

TAYLOR, J. A. (1953). A personality scale of manifest anxiety. *Journal of Abnormal & Social Psychology, 48,* 285–290.

The biomedical investigator's handbook for researchers using animal models. (1987). Washington, D.C.: Foundation for Biomedical Research.

TRYON, W. W. (1982). A simplified time-series analysis for evaluating treatment interventions. *Journal of Applied Behavior Analysis, 15,* 423–429.

UNDERWOOD, B. J. (1945). The effect of successive interpolations on retroactive and proactive inhibition. *Psychological Monographs, 38,* 29–38.

UNDERWOOD, B. J. (1957). Interference and forgetting. *Psychological Review, 64,* 49–60.

VALLE, F. P. (1972). Free and forced exploration in rats as a function of between vs. within-*S*s design. *Psychonomic Science, 29,* 11–13.

WHITE, L. A. (1971). Why engineers can't write. *Research Development, 22,* 24–26.

WHITE, M. A., & DUKER, J. (1971). Some unprinciples of psychological research. *American Psychologist, 26,* 397–399.

WIKE, E. L. (1973). Water beds and sexual satisfaction: Wike's law of low odd primes (WLLOP). *Psychological Reports, 33,* 192–194.

INDEX